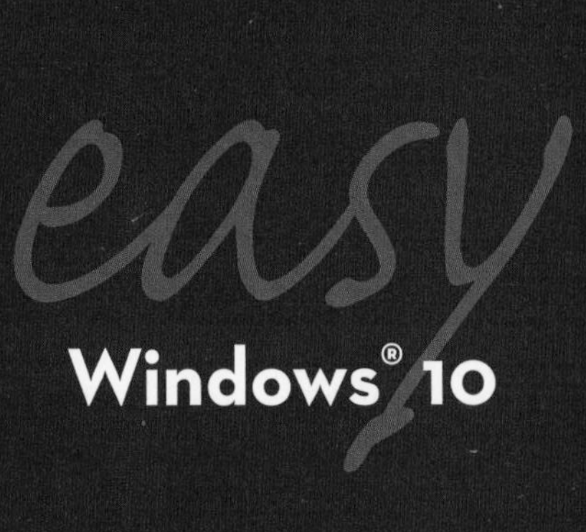

Mark Edward Soper

que®

800 East 96th Street
Indianapolis, Indiana 46240

ONLINE CONTENT
Additional tasks are available to you at www.quepublishing.com/title/9780789754530. Click the Downloads tab to access the links to download the PDF file.

CONTENTS

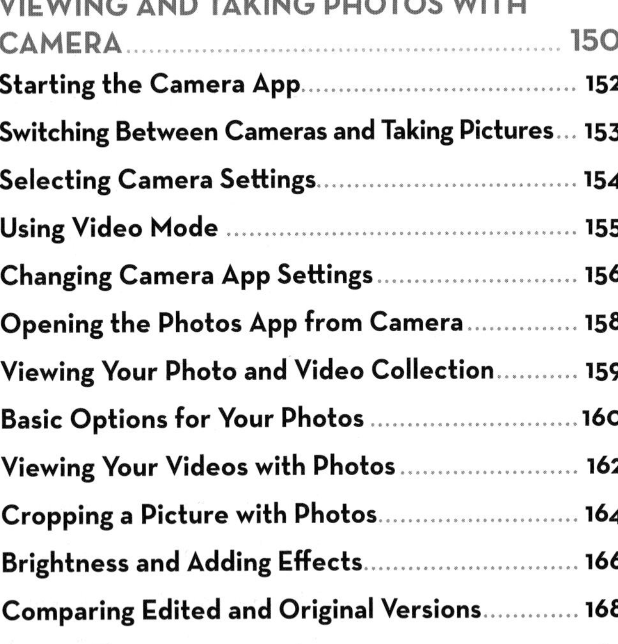

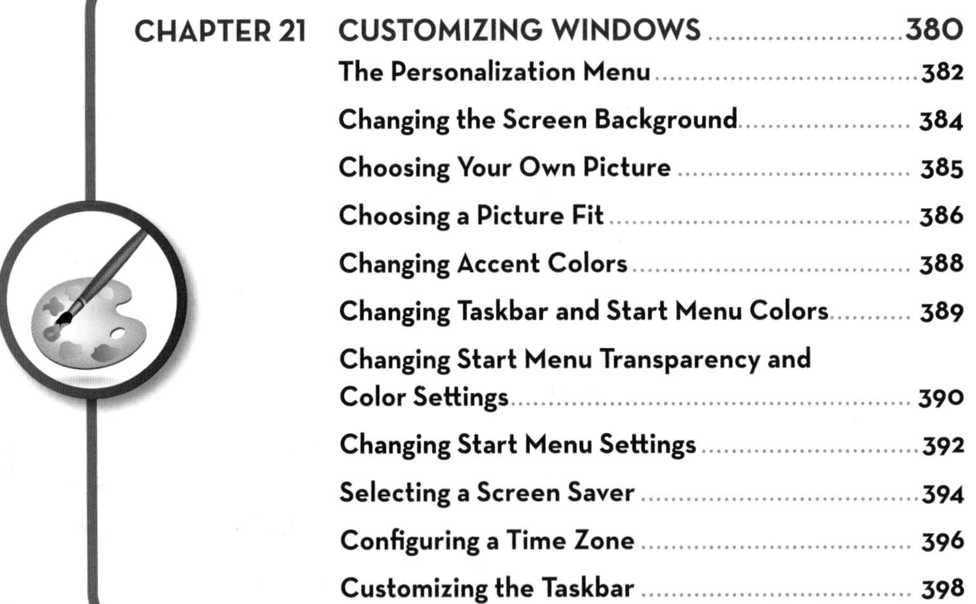

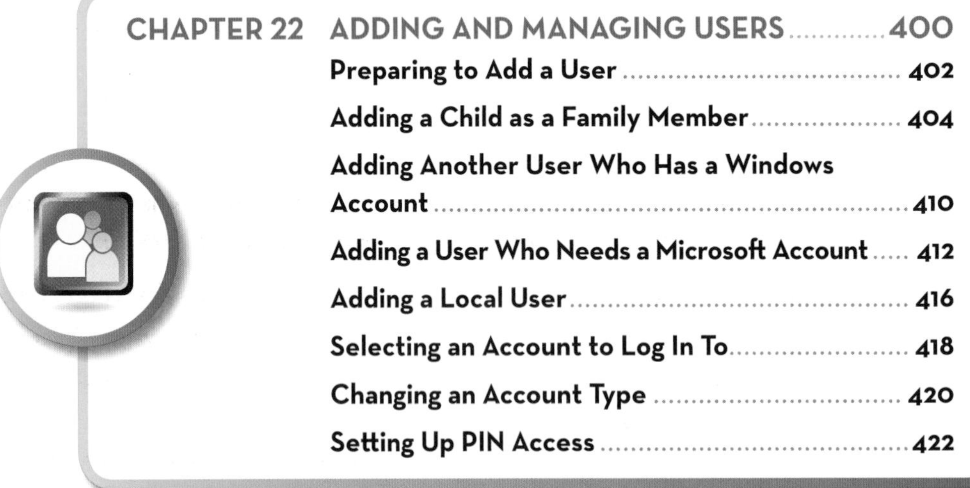

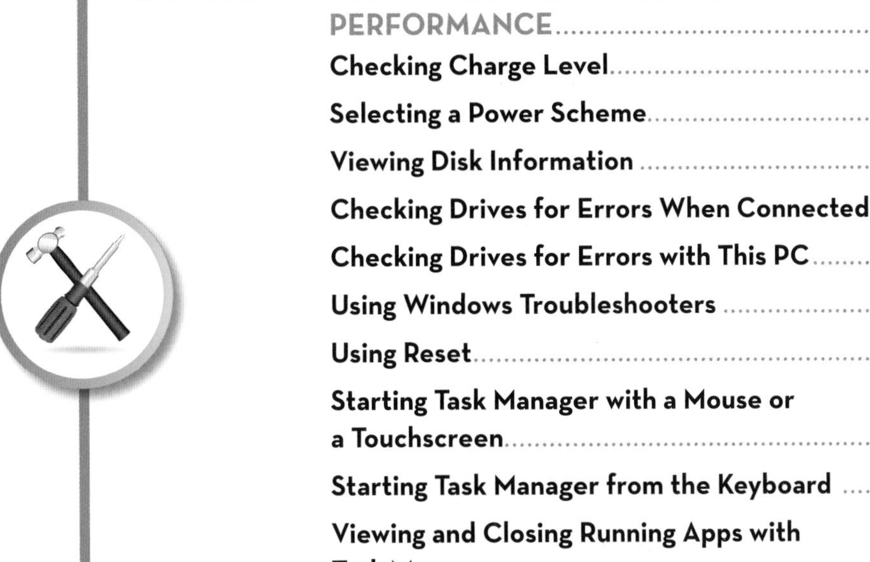

ONLINE CONTENT

Additional tasks are available to you at www.quepublishing.com/title/9780789754530. Click the Downloads tab to access the links to download the PDF file.

EASY WINDOWS® 10

ISBN-13: 978-0-7897-5453-0
ISBN-10: 0-7897-5453-3

Library of Congress Control Number: 2015938405

Printed in the United States of America

First Printing: August 2015

TRADEMARKS

All terms mentioned in this book that are known to be trademarks or service marks have been appropriately capitalized. Que Publishing cannot attest to the accuracy of this information. Use of a term in this book should not be regarded as affecting the validity of any trademark or service mark.

Windows is a registered trademark of Microsoft Corp.

WARNING AND DISCLAIMER

Every effort has been made to make this book as complete and as accurate as possible, but no warranty or fitness is implied. The information provided is on an "as is" basis. The author and the publisher shall have neither liability nor responsibility to any person or entity with respect to any loss or damages arising from the information contained in this book.

SPECIAL SALES

For information about buying this title in bulk quantities, or for special sales opportunities (which may include electronic versions; custom cover designs; and content particular to your business, training goals, marketing focus, or branding interests), please contact our corporate sales department at corpsales@pearsoned.com or (800) 382-3419.

For government sales inquiries, please contact governmentsales@pearsoned.com.

For questions about sales outside the U.S., please contact international@pearsoned.com.

Editor-in-Chief
Greg Wiegand

Acquisitions Editor
Michelle Newcomb

Development Editor
Charlotte Kughen

Managing Editor
Sandra Schroeder

Senior Project Editor
Tonya Simpson

Copy Editor
Bart Reed

Indexer
Erika Millen

Proofreader
Debbie Williams

Technical Editor
Vince Averello

Editorial Assistant
Cindy Teeters

Cover Designer
Mark Shirar

Compositor
Trina Wurst

ABOUT THE AUTHOR

Mark Edward Soper has been using Microsoft Windows since version 1.0, and since 1992 he has taught thousands of computer troubleshooting and network students across the country how to use Windows as part of their work and everyday lives. Mark is the author of *Easy Windows 8.1*, *Easy Windows 8*, *Easy Microsoft Windows 7*, *Teach Yourself Windows 7 in 10 Minutes*, and *Using Microsoft Windows Live*. Mark also has contributed to Que's *Special Edition Using* series on Windows Me, Windows XP, and Windows Vista, as well as *Easy Windows Vista* and *Windows 7 In Depth*. He has also written two books about Windows Vista: *Maximum PC Microsoft Windows Vista Exposed* and *Unleashing Microsoft Windows Vista Media Center*.

When he's not teaching, learning, or writing about Microsoft Windows, Mark stays busy with many other technology-related activities. He was written three books on computer troubleshooting, including *The PC and Gadget Help Desk*. He is a longtime contributor to *Upgrading and Repairing PCs*, working on the 11th through 18th, 20th, and subsequent editions. Mark has co-authored *Upgrading and Repairing Networks*, Fifth Edition, written several books on CompTIA A+ Certification (including two titles covering the 2012 exams), an occasional column on certification for Computerworld.com, and has written two books about digital photography: *Easy Digital Cameras* and *The Shot Doctor: The Amateur's Guide to Taking Great Digital Photos*. Mark also has become a video content provider for Que Publishing and InformIT and has posted many blog entries and articles at InformIT.com, MaximumPC.com, and other websites. He has also taught digital photography, digital imaging, and Microsoft Office for Ivy Tech Corporate College's southwest Indiana campus in Evansville, Indiana, and Windows and Microsoft Office for the University of Southern Indiana's continuing education department.

DEDICATION

For Moses. Welcome to the family!

ACKNOWLEDGMENTS

The author of a book might be the most visible presence, but like an actor, there are plenty of people behind the scenes who make the work possible and provide the encouragement needed to create a useful and enjoyable experience. Thank you for reading this book. Here are some of the people who helped make it possible.

My wife, Cheryl, is a modern-day Proverbs 31 woman. Her encouragement has helped me every moment since we first met. We celebrate 39 years of marriage this year, and more than that as a team. She is truly a gift from God.

I first saw Microsoft Windows back when it was a home for a simple paint program and a simple word-processing program that needed MS-DOS to work. Windows has come a long way, and here are some of the people who gave me the opportunity to learn about it.

Thanks go to Jim Peck and Mayer Rubin, for whom I taught thousands of students how to troubleshoot systems running Windows 3.1, 95, and 98; magazine editors Edie Rockwood and Ron Kobler, for assigning me to dig deeper into Windows; Ed Bott, who provided my first opportunity to contribute to a major Windows book; Scott Mueller, who asked me to help with *Upgrading and Repairing Windows*; Ivy Tech Corporate College and the University of Southern Indiana, for teaching opportunities; Bob Cowart and Brian Knittel for helping continue my real-world Windows education. And, of course, the Microsoft family.

Thanks also to my family, both for their encouragement over the years and for the opportunity to explain various Windows features and fix things that go wrong. Even though some of them have joined the "dark side" (they have Macs), we still get along, and thanks to Microsoft's determination to "play nicely with others," we can share photos, chat, and enjoy each other's presence from across the room or across the country.

I also want to thank the editorial and design team that Que put together for this book: Many thanks to Michelle Newcomb for bringing me back for another *Easy* series book, and thanks to Todd Brakke, Charlotte Kughen, Vince Averello, Tonya Simpson, and Bart Reed for overseeing their respective parts of the publishing process. Thanks also to Cindy Teeters for keeping track of invoices and making sure payments were timely. I also want to thank Sherry Kinkoph Gunter for her work on the lifestyle and social connections chapters and Mike Miller for performing author reviews on several chapters.

WE WANT TO HEAR FROM YOU!

As the reader of this book, *you* are our most important critic and commentator. We value your opinion and want to know what we're doing right, what we could do better, what areas you'd like to see us publish in, and any other words of wisdom you're willing to pass our way.

We welcome your comments. You can email or write to let us know what you did or didn't like about this book—as well as what we can do to make our books better.

Please note that we cannot help you with technical problems related to the topic of this book.

When you write, please be sure to include this book's title and author as well as your name and email address. We will carefully review your comments and share them with the author and editors who worked on the book.

Email: feedback@quepublishing.com

Mail: Que Publishing
ATTN: Reader Feedback
800 East 96th Street
Indianapolis, IN 46240 USA

READER SERVICES

Visit our website and register this book at quepublishing.com/register for convenient access to any updates, downloads, or errata that might be available for this book.

INTRODUCTION

WHY THIS BOOK WAS WRITTEN

Que Publishing's *Easy* series is famous for providing accurate, simple, step-by-step instructions for popular software and operating systems. Windows 10 has a big job to do: provide an operating system that works as well with a keyboard and mouse as with a touchscreen. To make Windows 10 work for you, *Easy Windows 10* is here to help you understand and use it. Whether you're a veteran Windows user or new to Windows and computers, there's a lot to learn, and we're here to help.

Easy Windows 10 gives you a painless and enjoyable way to discover Windows' essential features. We spent months with Windows 10 to discover its new and improved features and learn the best ways to show you what it does, and you get the benefit: an easy-to-read visual guide that gets you familiar with the latest Microsoft product in a hurry.

Your time is valuable, so we've concentrated our efforts on features you're likely to use every day. Our objective: to help you use Windows to make your computing life better, more productive, and even more fun.

HOW TO READ *EASY WINDOWS 10*

So, what's the best way to read this book?

You have a few options, based on what you know about computers and Windows. Try one of these:

- Start at Chapter 1, "What's New and Improved in Windows 10," and work your way through.
- Go straight to the chapters that look the most interesting.
- Hit the table of contents or the index and go directly to the sections that tell you stuff you don't know already.

Any of these methods will work—and to help you get a better feel for what's inside, here's a closer look at what's in each chapter.

BEYOND THE TABLE OF CONTENTS—WHAT'S INSIDE

Chapter 1, "What's New and Improved in Windows 10," provides a quick overview of the most important, new and improved features in Windows 10. If you're reading this book mainly to brush up on what's new and different, start here and follow the references to the chapters with more information.

Chapter 2, "Upgrading to Windows 10," is designed for users of Windows 7 or Windows 8.1 who are upgrading to Windows 10. This chapter covers the process and helps you make the best choices along the way.

Chapter 3, "Logging In, Starting Up, and Shutting Down Windows 10 with a Touchscreen," shows you how to log in to Windows 10, how to use the touch keyboard or handwriting interface, how to use shortcut keys, how to work with a touchscreen, how to lock and unlock your computer, and how to shut it down or put it into sleep mode.

Chapter 4, "Logging In to Windows 10 and Customizing the Start Menu," helps you understand how to use the Start menu and customize it.

Chapter 5, "Using Cortana Search," provides step-by-step instructions on how to enable and use the new Cortana search technology in Windows 10.

Chapter 6, "Running Apps," shows you how to search for, run, share from, and close desktop and Modern UI apps.

Chapter 7, "Web Browsing with Microsoft Edge," introduces you to Windows 10's new web browser and its exciting new features, including Web Notes and the Pen tool.

Chapter 8, "Playing and Creating Music and Audio," shows you how to manage and add to your digital music collection and create audio recordings using Groove Music and Voice Recorder.

Chapter 9, "Enjoying Videos," shows you how to manage and add to your digital video, TV, and movie collection using Video.

Chapter 10, "Viewing and Taking Photos with Camera," is your guide to the Camera and Photos apps. Whether you use your tablet's built-in webcam and backward-facing camera or a digital camera, you'll learn how to view and edit your pictures.

Chapter 11, "Connecting with Friends," shows you how to use the People, Facebook, Mail, Calendar, and Notifications apps in Windows 10, and Skype for Desktop app available from the Store, to stay in touch with friends and family.

Chapter 12, "News and Information," introduces you to key features in the new and improved News, Weather, and Maps apps.

Chapter 13, "Tracking Money and Sports News," is your guide to using the new and improved Money and Sports apps.

Chapter 14, "Storing and Finding Your Files," helps you manage files, folders, and drives, burn data discs, copy/move files safely, and use OneDrive cloud storage.

Chapter 15, "Discovering and Using Windows 10's Tools and Accessories," helps you use built-in apps such as Alarms & Clock, Calculator, Snipping Tool, and Notepad.

Chapter 16, "Using the Windows Store," takes you on a tour of the preferred way to get free and commercial apps for your device. Learn how to search for apps, download free apps, buy new apps, and uninstall apps.

Chapter 17, "Gaming," shows you how to build a gaming library from the Windows Store and connect to your Xbox One so you can stream games to your Windows device and record your best gaming moments.

Chapter 18, "Printing and Scanning," shows you how to use your printer, scanner, or multifunction device to print and scan documents and photos.

Chapter 19, "Managing Windows 10," helps you master Windows 10's Settings menu so you can add an additional display, manage devices, and much more.

Chapter 20, "Networking Your Home with HomeGroup," shows you how to connect to wireless networks and use the HomeGroup feature to set up and manage a network with Windows 7, Windows 8.1, and Windows 10 computers.

Chapter 21, "Customizing Windows," helps you make Windows look the way you want by tweaking the Start menu, desktop background, screen saver, time zone, and taskbar. It also teaches you about basic Ease of Access features.

Chapter 22, "Adding and Managing Users," introduces you to different ways to set up a Windows login for users, how to add additional users, and how to create Child accounts for use with Microsoft Family parental controls.

Chapter 23, "Protecting Your System," shows you how to keep Windows 10 updated, protect your files with backups, use Notifications, and check for spyware and viruses.

Chapter 24, "System Maintenance and Performance," helps you improve system speed and battery life, solve disk errors, schedule tasks, learn more about what Windows is doing with Task Manager, and learn to use Reset and Troubleshooters to solve problems that can prevent your system from running properly.

Baffled by PC and Windows terminology? Check out the Glossary!

Also be sure to check out additional tasks available online at www.quepublishing.com/register.

Enjoy!

WHAT'S NEW AND IMPROVED IN WINDOWS 10

Windows 10 unifies the touch and mouse/keyboard Windows interfaces, making it easy to work with whatever combination suits you best. Windows 10 also features easier management and more powerful searching. In this chapter, you learn about these and other new and improved features.

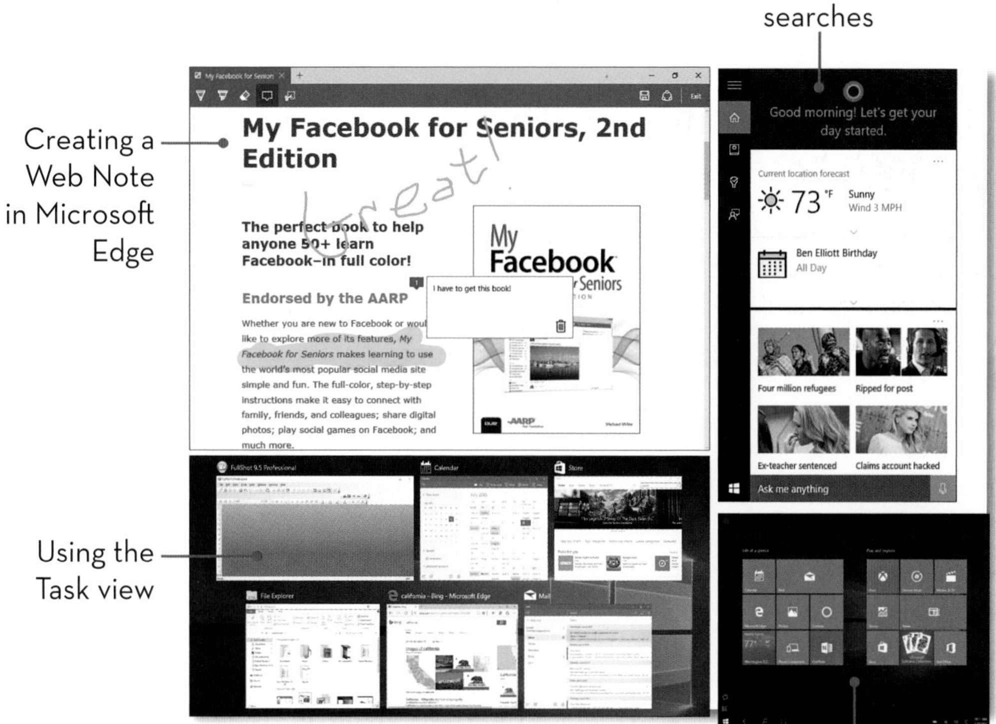
Cortana's automatic searches
Creating a Web Note in Microsoft Edge
Using the Task view
Tablet Mode Start menu
My Facebook for Seniors, 2nd Edition
The perfect book to help anyone 50+ learn Facebook–in full color!
Endorsed by the AARP
I have to get this book!
Good morning! Let's get your day started.
Current location forecast
73 °F
Sunny
Wind 3 MPH
Ben Elliott Birthday
All Day
Four million refugees
Ripped for post
Ex-teacher sentenced
Claims account hacked
Ask me anything

TABLET MODE

Whether you use a tablet, a touchscreen computer with a mouse, or a non-touchscreen computer with a mouse, Windows 10's new Tablet Mode helps you use Windows the way you prefer.

Start

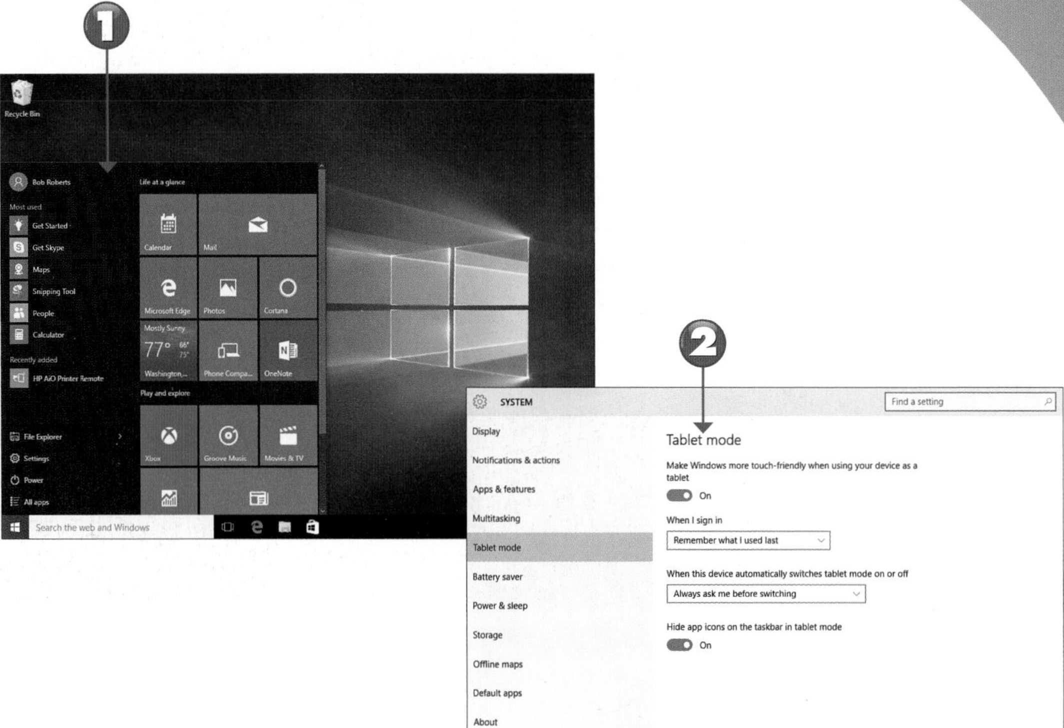

1. The Start menu in normal (desktop) mode.
2. Configuring Tablet Mode in Settings.

Continued

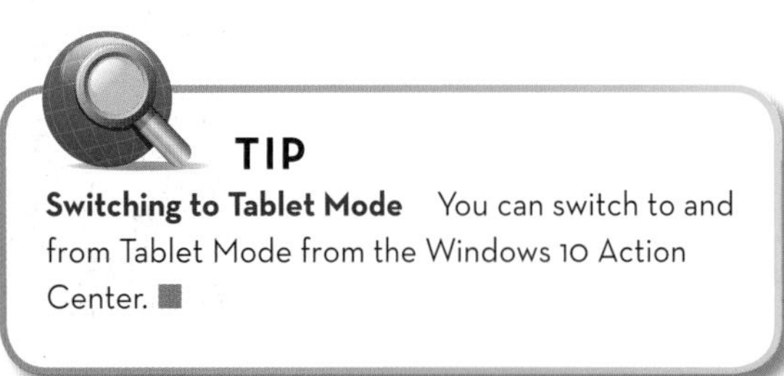

TIP

Switching to Tablet Mode You can switch to and from Tablet Mode from the Windows 10 Action Center. ■

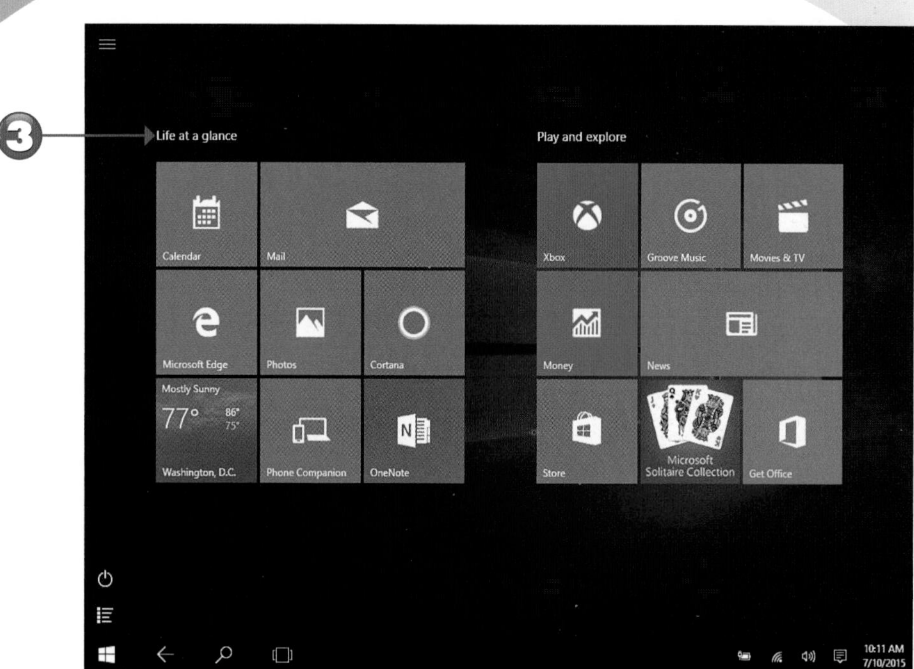

3 The Start menu in Tablet Mode.

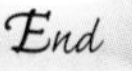

VOICE AND TEXT SEARCH WITH CORTANA

Windows 10 adds a powerful new way to search, a virtual personal assistant called Cortana. You can query Cortana with your keyboard, or talk to Cortana to have it bring up the information you need.

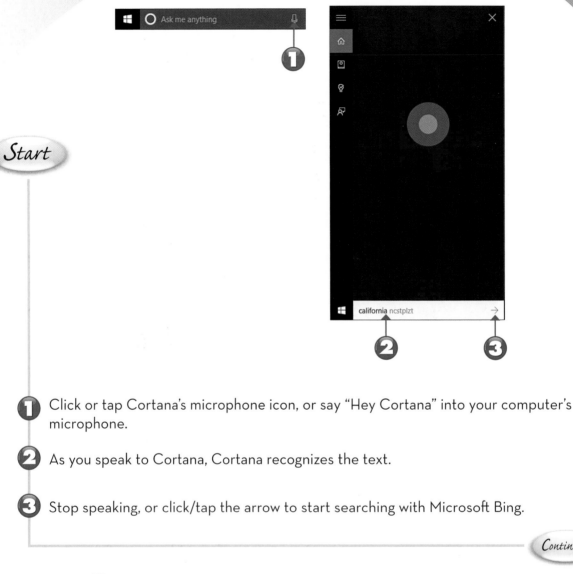

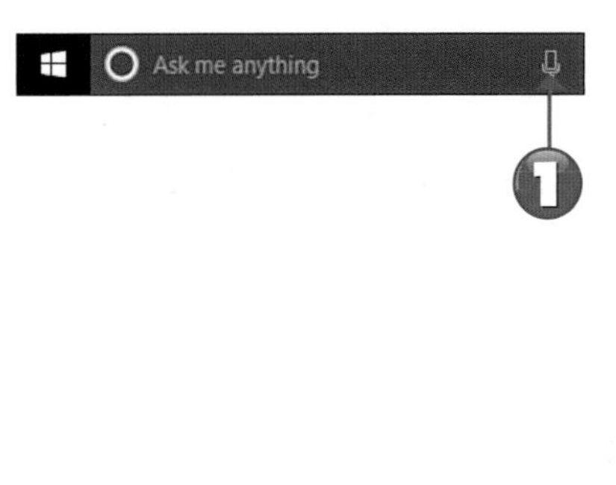

Start

1. Click or tap Cortana's microphone icon, or say "Hey Cortana" into your computer's microphone.
2. As you speak to Cortana, Cortana recognizes the text.
3. Stop speaking, or click/tap the arrow to start searching with Microsoft Bing.

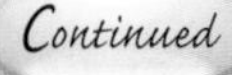

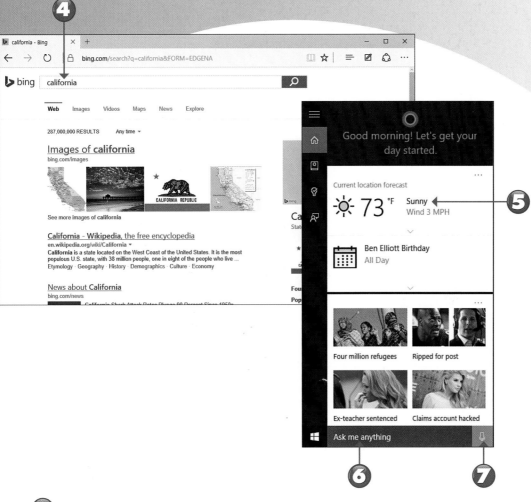

4. Bing search results are displayed in the new Microsoft Edge browser.

5. If you don't type or speak a search, Cortana offers news and weather of the day.

6. Click or tap the search window to type search terms.

7. Click or tap Cortana's microphone to search by voice at any time.

End

TOUCHSCREEN-OPTIMIZED MENUS

When you use your touchscreen, even if you're not in Tablet Mode, Windows 10 optimizes some menus to make them easier to use with a touchscreen. For example, check out the taskbar properties menu.

Start

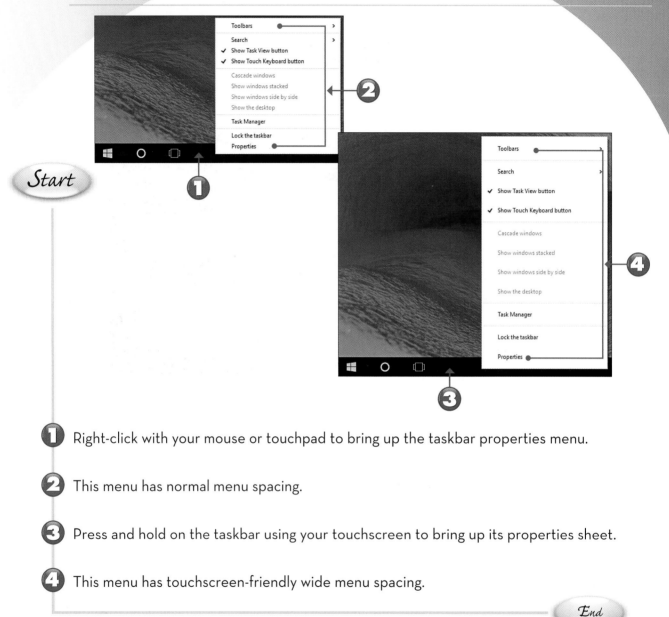

1. Right-click with your mouse or touchpad to bring up the taskbar properties menu.
2. This menu has normal menu spacing.
3. Press and hold on the taskbar using your touchscreen to bring up its properties sheet.
4. This menu has touchscreen-friendly wide menu spacing.

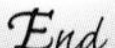

EASY APP (TASK) SWITCHING WITH TASK VIEW

Windows 10 still includes classic app switching using Alt+Tab, but adds a new way to switch between active apps: the Task View button.

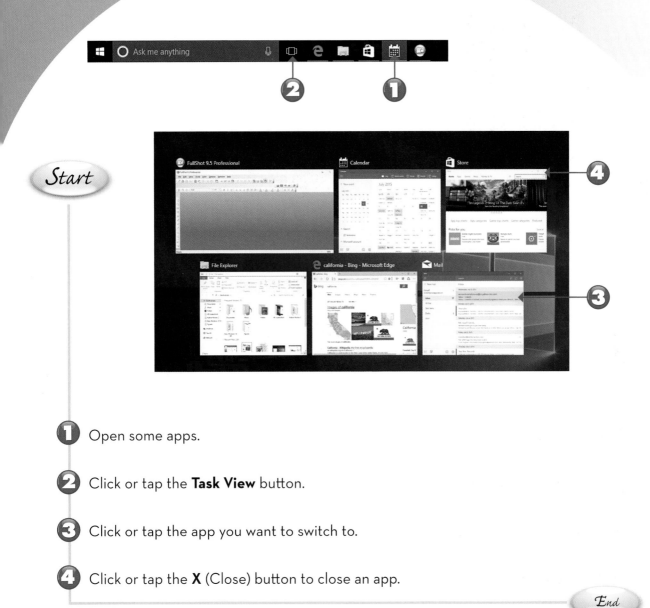

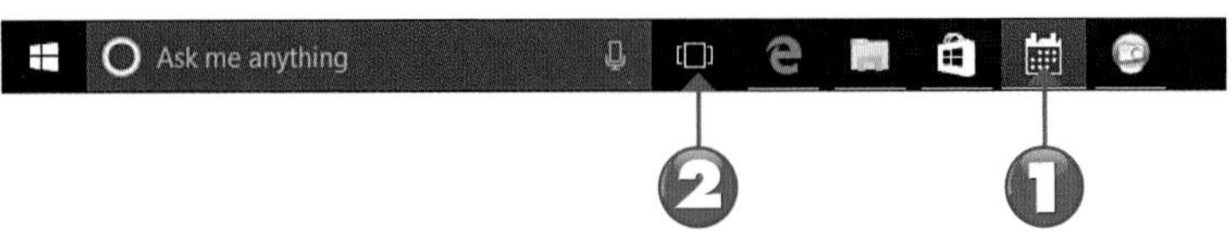

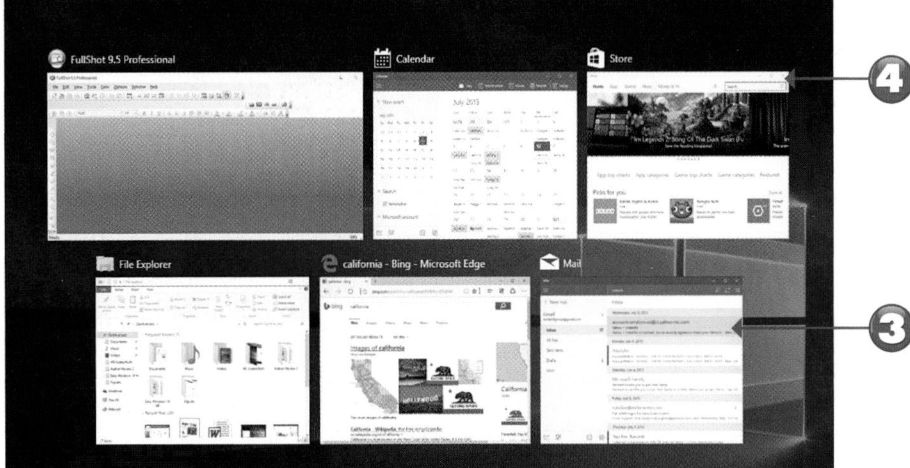

1. Open some apps.
2. Click or tap the **Task View** button.
3. Click or tap the app you want to switch to.
4. Click or tap the **X** (Close) button to close an app.

End

MICROSOFT EDGE WEB BROWSER

Windows 10 includes a brand-new web browser, Microsoft Edge. It's not only faster and easier to configure than Internet Explorer, it also includes the powerful new Web Notes feature.

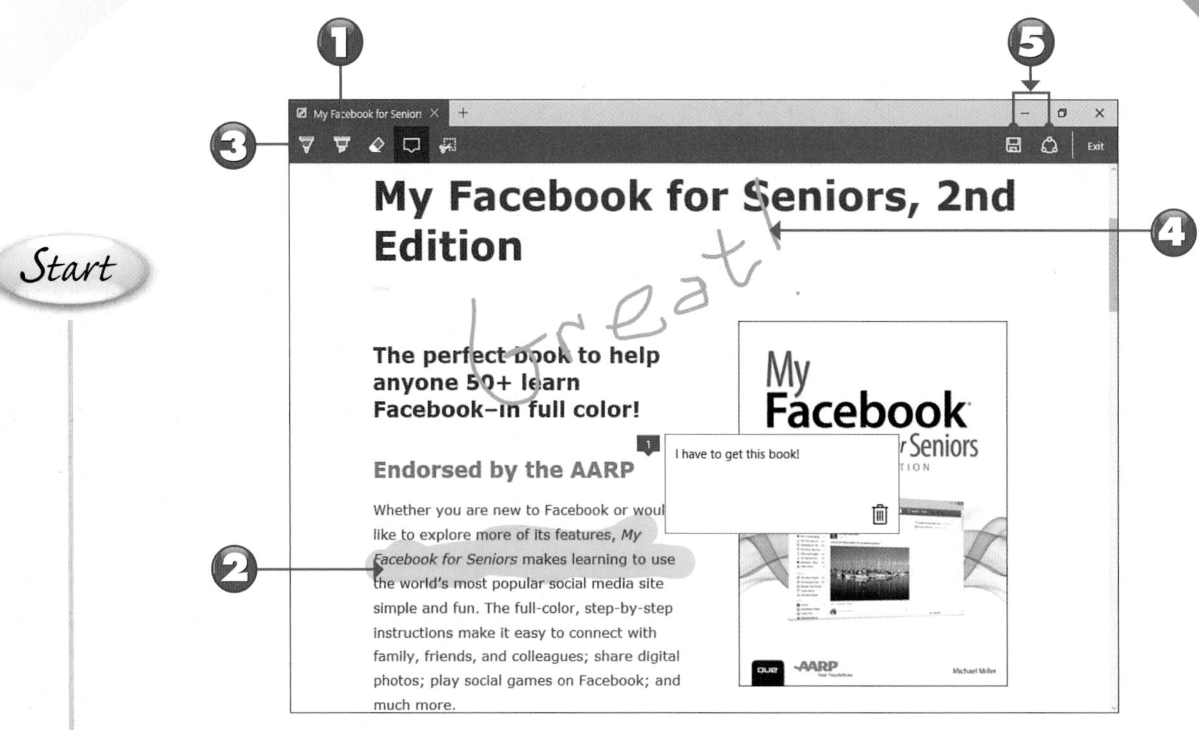

Start

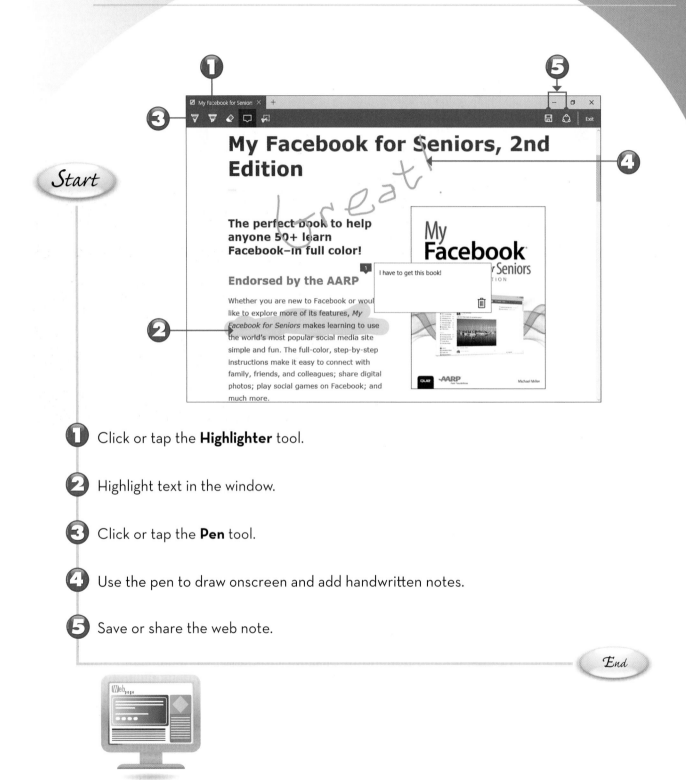

1. Click or tap the **Highlighter** tool.
2. Highlight text in the window.
3. Click or tap the **Pen** tool.
4. Use the pen to draw onscreen and add handwritten notes.
5. Save or share the web note.

End

IMPROVED CAMERA AND PHOTO APPS

Windows 10 has improved its Camera app for taking pictures to keep pace with the improved cameras found in many tablets and laptops, and it completely redid its Photo app to help you make your favorite photos even better.

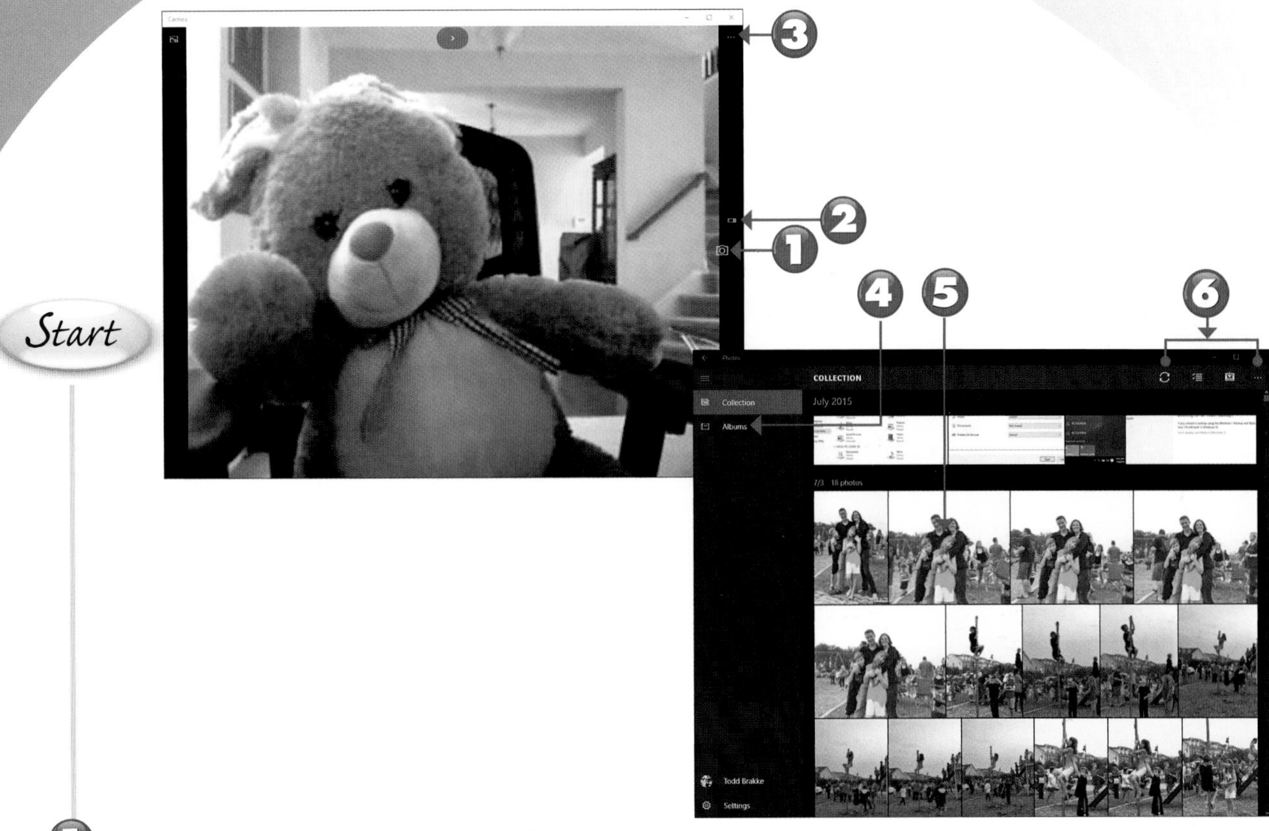

Start

1. Click or tap **Camera** to take a still photo.
2. Click or tap **Video** to enter video recording mode.
3. Click or tap the menu button to adjust settings.
4. Store and organize photos in Collections and Albums.
5. Click or tap a picture to see or edit it.
6. Use the tools at the top to work with your photos.

End

NEW XBOX ONE GAMING SUPPORT

Have an Xbox One? Windows 10 can stream live gameplay from your Xbox One and capture footage so you can relive your greatest victory. You also can stay in touch with your fellow gamers and play some Xbox One games on your Windows 10 device.

Start

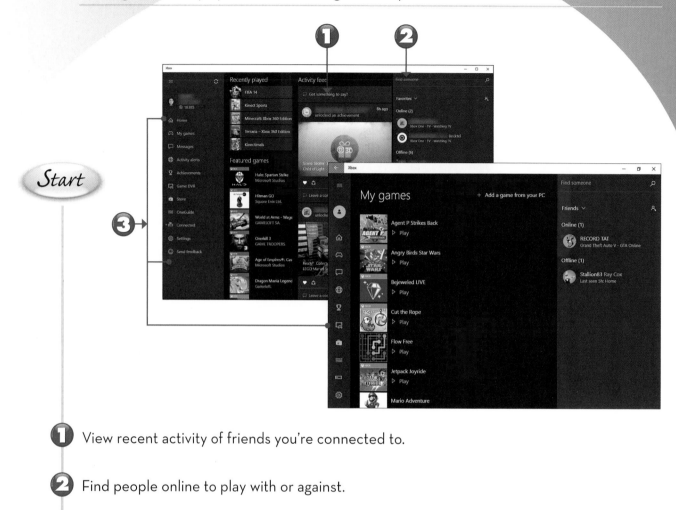

1. View recent activity of friends you're connected to.
2. Find people online to play with or against.
3. Use these tools to access Xbox features, such as choosing games to play, recording live gameplay and/or messaging friends.

EASIER MANAGEMENT WITH SETTINGS

Windows 10's Settings tool is more powerful than its predecessors but just as easy to use. Settings puts you in charge of the networking, appearance, and many more features of your Windows 10 device.

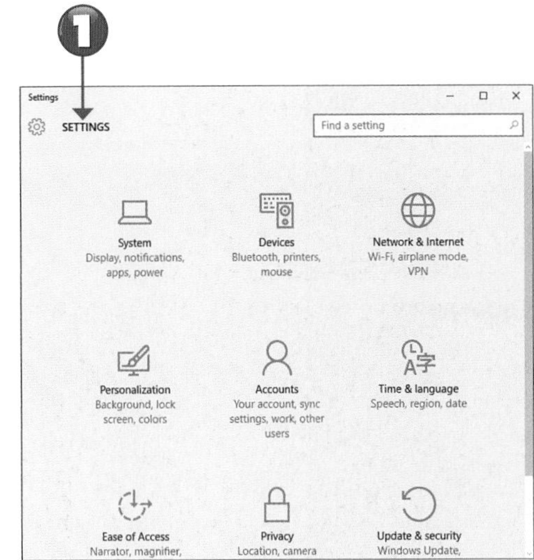

Start

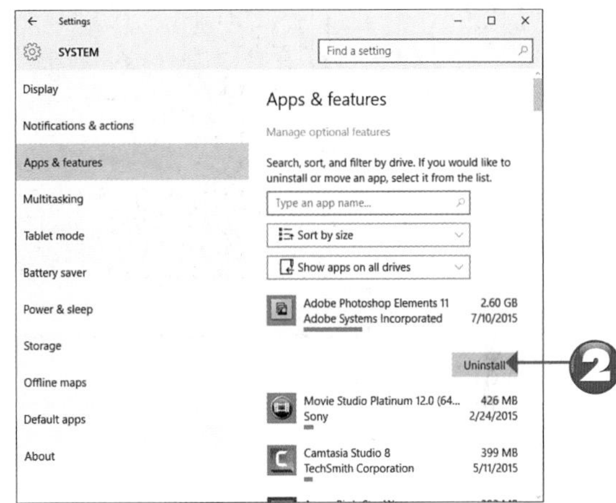

1. Use Settings to view and personalize your Windows 10 device.
2. Preparing to uninstall an app.

End

NEW NOTIFICATION AND QUICK ACTIONS

Windows 10 makes it easier than ever to see notifications and to make changes to your system settings with the Action Center (Notification) pane.

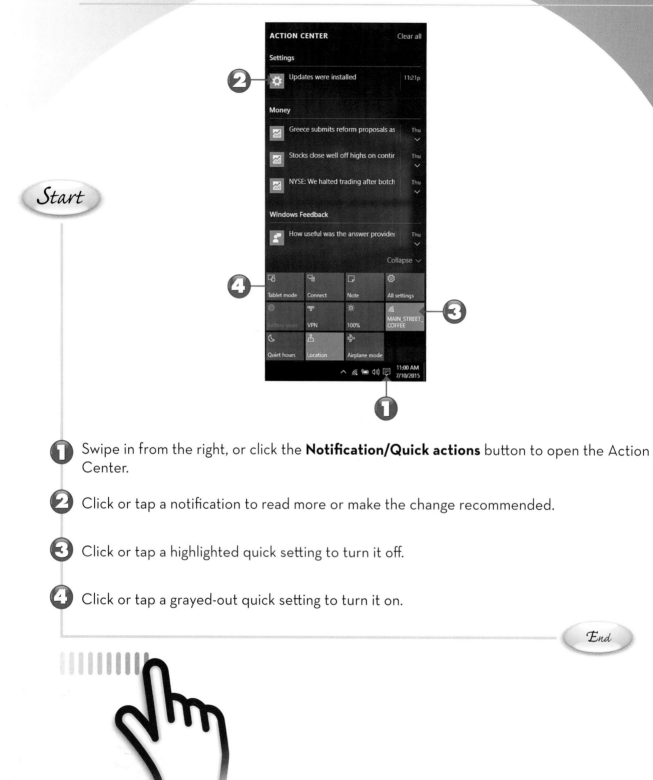

Start

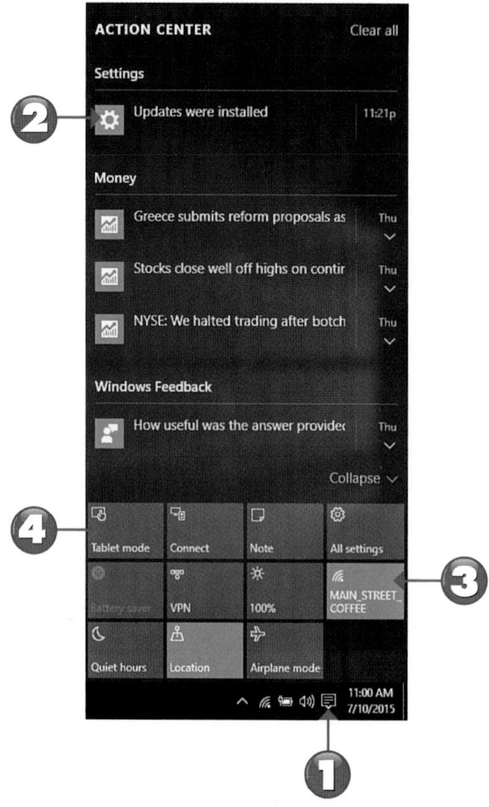

1. Swipe in from the right, or click the **Notification/Quick actions** button to open the Action Center.
2. Click or tap a notification to read more or make the change recommended.
3. Click or tap a highlighted quick setting to turn it off.
4. Click or tap a grayed-out quick setting to turn it on.

End

NEW BATTERY SAVER FEATURE

If you use a tablet or a laptop, keeping a close eye on battery life is easier than ever with the new Battery Saver feature.

Start

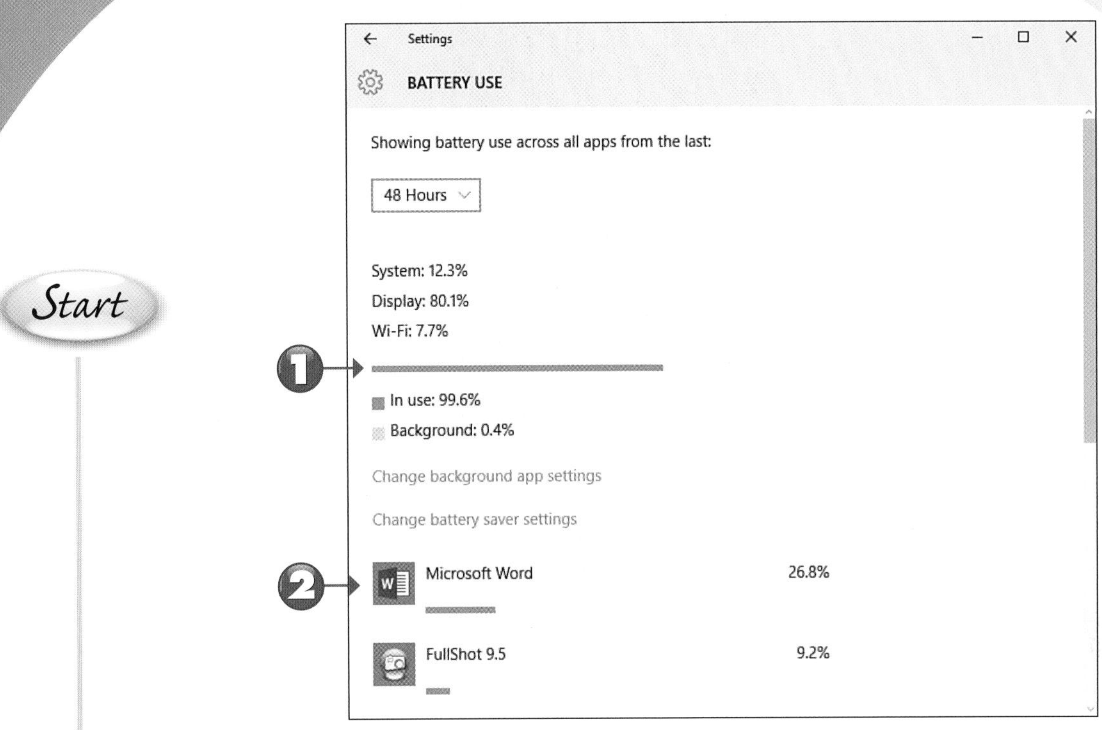

1. View your overall battery usage in Battery Saver.
2. See which apps are consuming the most battery.

End

UPGRADING TO WINDOWS 10

Whether you use Windows 7 or Windows 8.1, you can upgrade your system to Windows 10 through Windows Update, which makes the process easy. Do it within the first year, and the update is free.

And if "easy" and "free" aren't enough for you, how about "keep your apps and your information"? Windows 10 lets you bring your classic Win32 apps and your modern Windows 8.1 apps along into the brave, new world of Windows 10. There are just a few steps for you to perform, and Microsoft does the rest. Here's how to reserve your copy and upgrade to it.

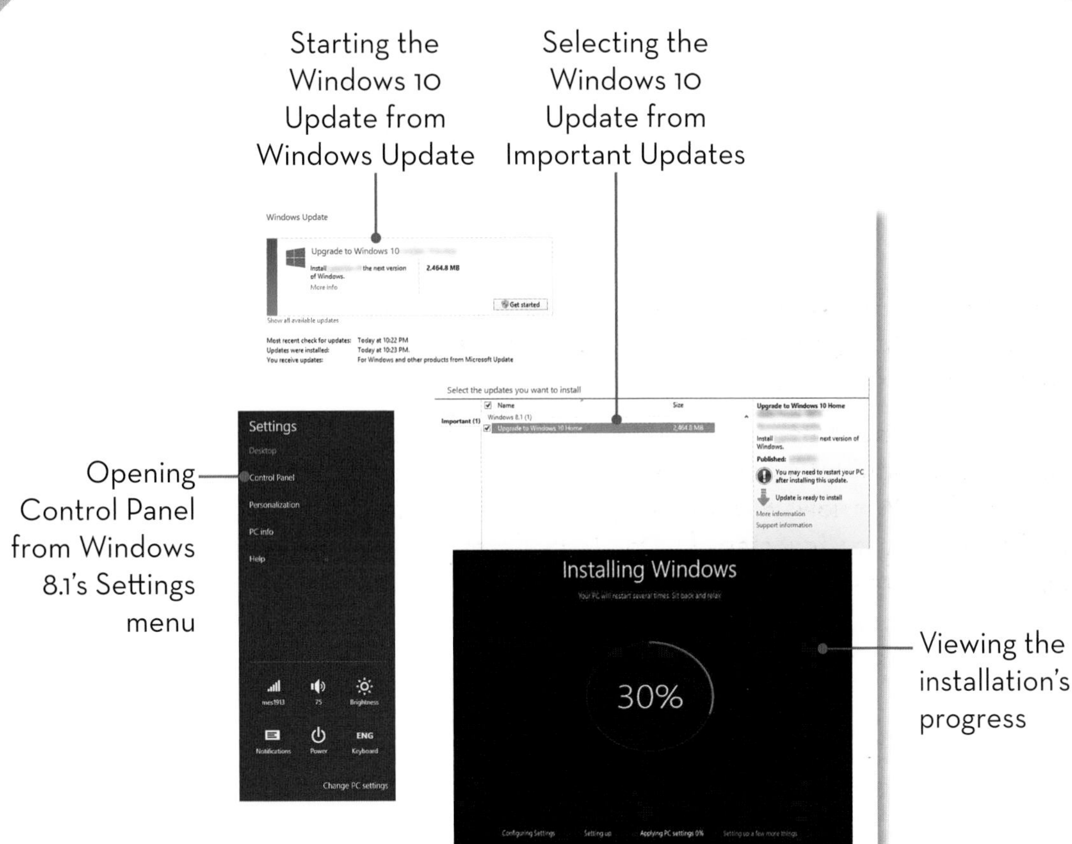
Starting the Windows 10 Update from Windows Update
Selecting the Windows 10 Update from Important Updates
Opening Control Panel from Windows 8.1's Settings menu
Viewing the installation's progress
Windows Update
Upgrade to Windows 10
Settings
Control Panel
Personalization
PC info
Help
Change PC settings
Installing Windows
30%

OPENING WINDOWS UPDATE IN WINDOWS 7

The first step to upgrading to Windows 10 is to open Windows Update from Control Panel. Here's how the process works in Windows 7.

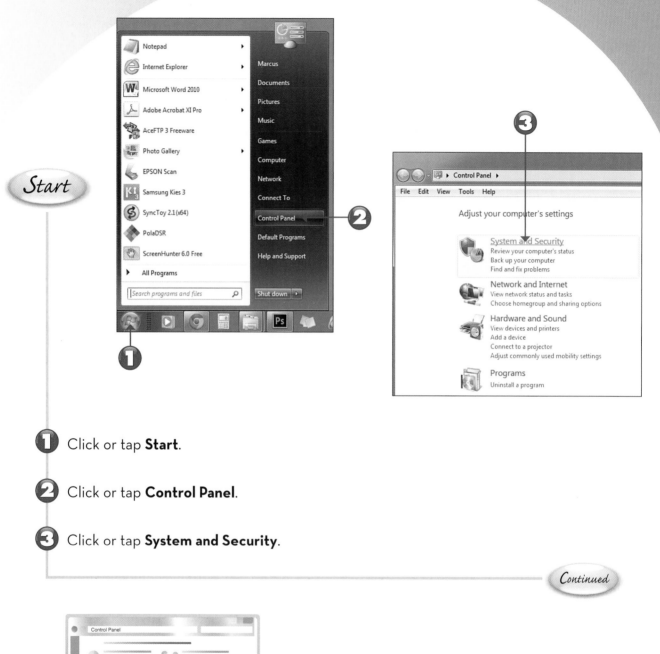

Start

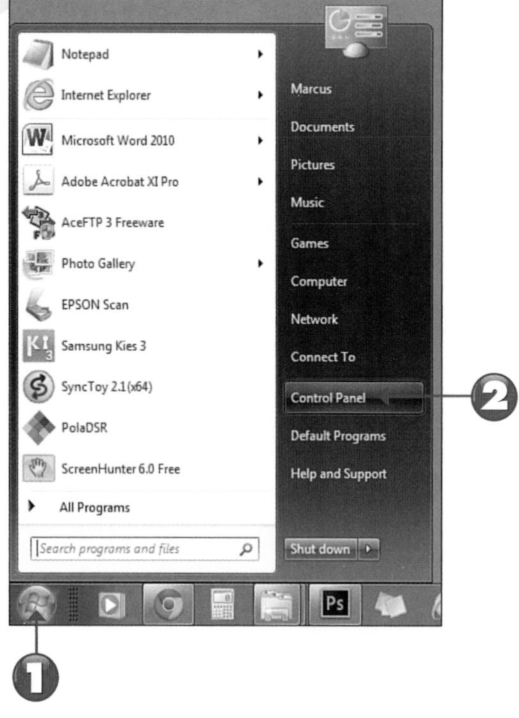

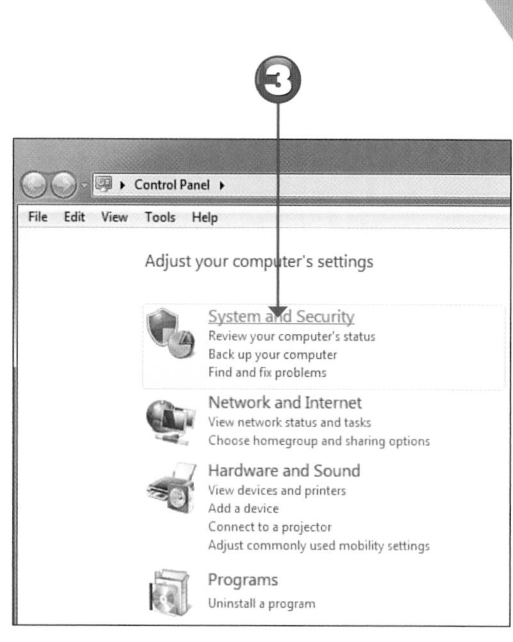

1. Click or tap **Start**.
2. Click or tap **Control Panel**.
3. Click or tap **System and Security**.

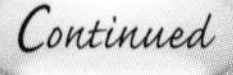

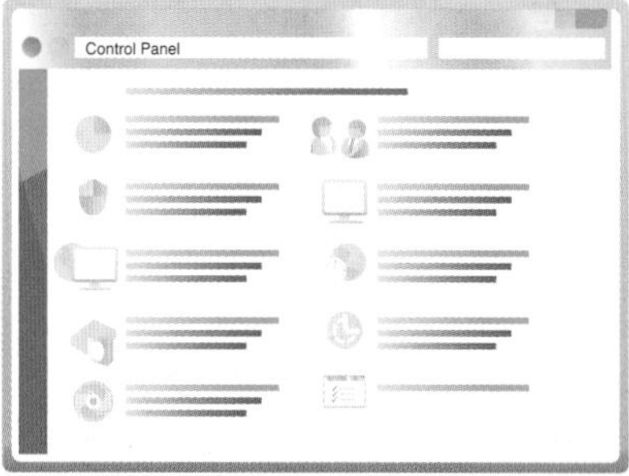

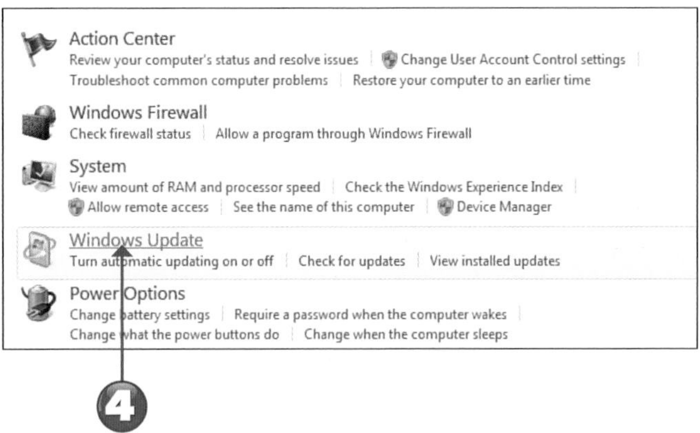

4. Click or tap **Windows Update**.

End

TIP

Opening Windows Update in Icons View If Control Panel is configured to show individual items rather than the Category view shown in step 3, click or tap **Windows Update**.

OPENING WINDOWS UPDATE IN WINDOWS 8.1

The first step to upgrading to Windows 10 is to open Windows Update from Control Panel. Here's how the process works in Windows 8.1.

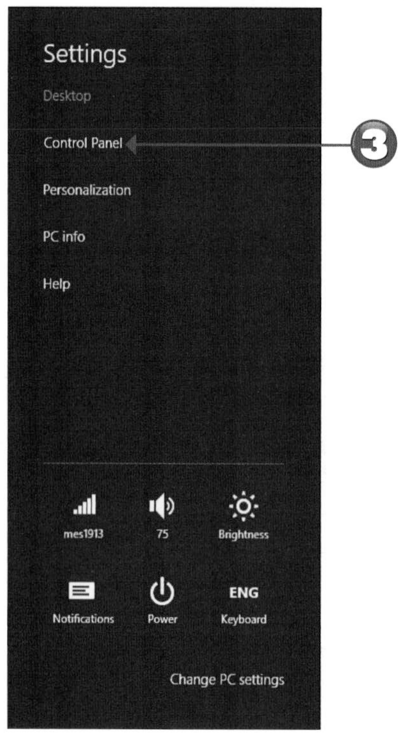

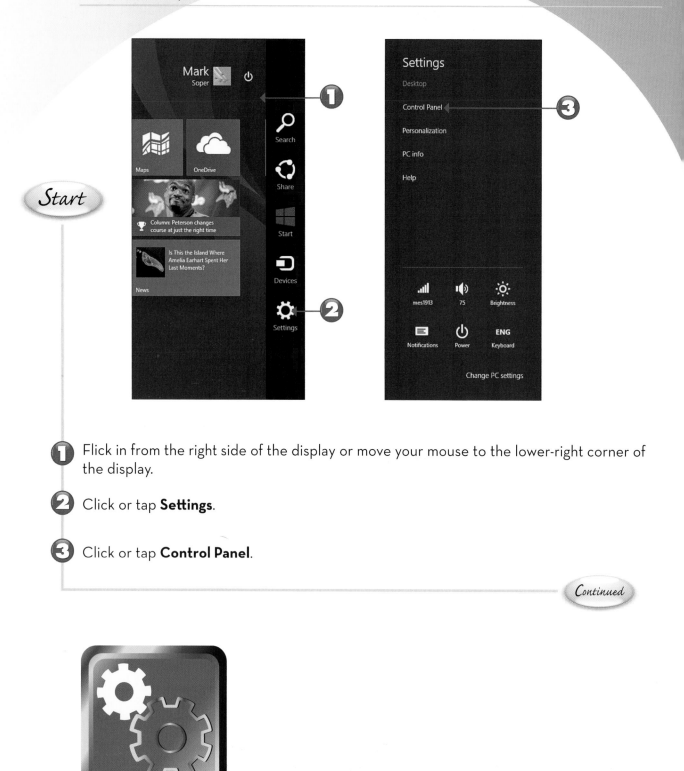

Start

1. Flick in from the right side of the display or move your mouse to the lower-right corner of the display.
2. Click or tap **Settings**.
3. Click or tap **Control Panel**.

Continued

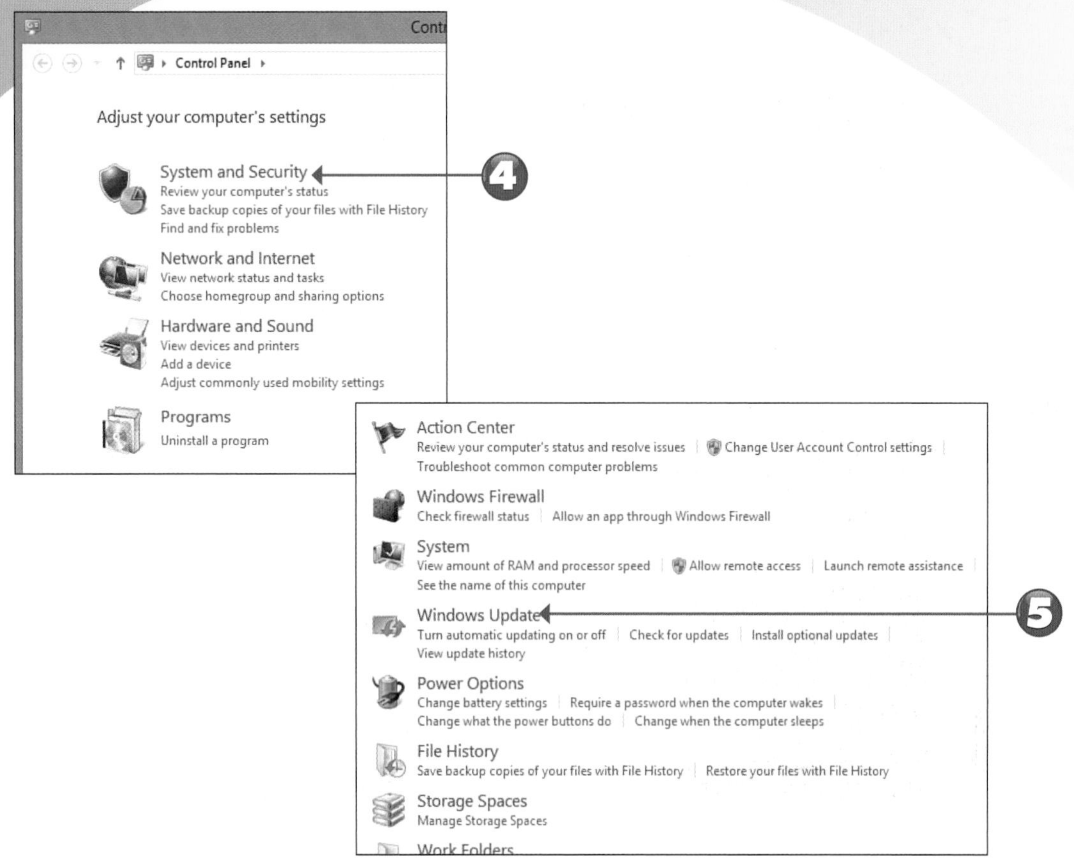

4. Click or tap **System and Security**.

5. Click or tap **Windows Update**.

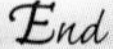

TIP

Opening Control Panel from the Keyboard To go to Control Panel from the keyboard, press the Windows key+X, and then select **Control Panel** from the pop-up menu.

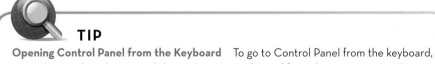

STARTING THE INSTALLATION

After you open Windows Update, just a couple of steps are needed to start the installation process. Here's what to do with either Windows 7 or Windows 8.1.

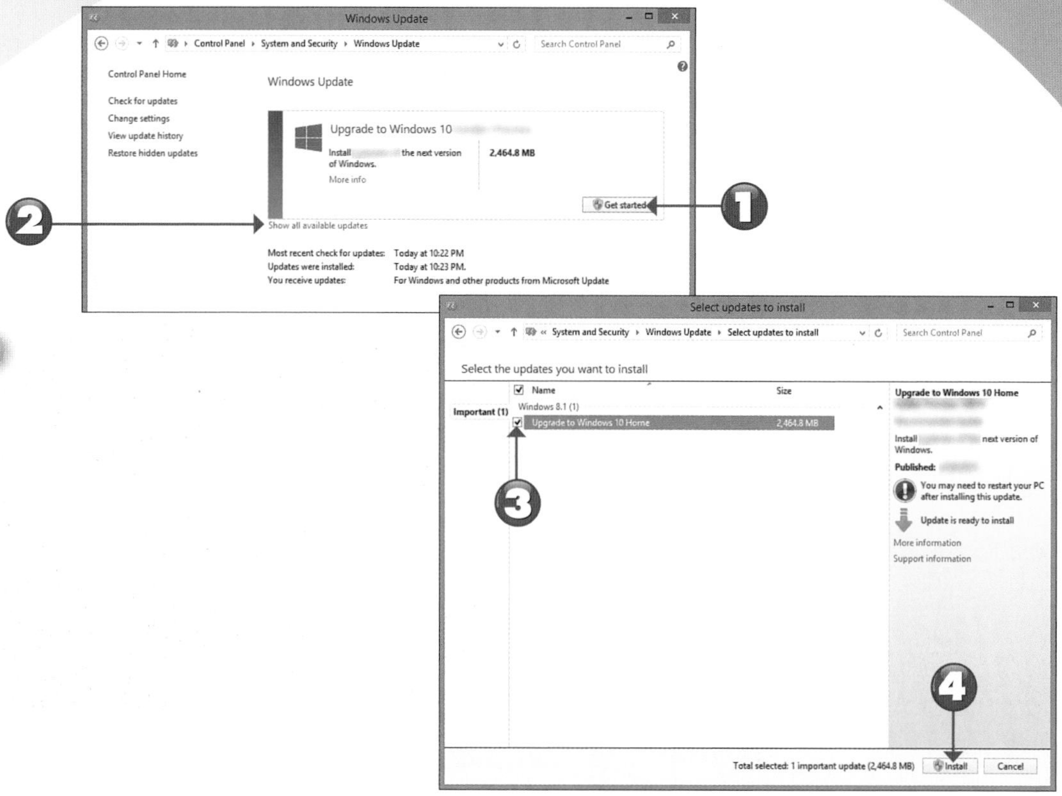

Start

1. If Windows Update displays the Windows 10 upgrade, click or tap **Get started**.
2. If the Windows 10 upgrade is not displayed, click or tap **Show all available updates**.
3. Click or tap the empty check box next to the upgrade listing to select it.
4. Click or tap **Install**.

Continued

NOTE

Operating System Updates You Need Before Moving to Windows 10 If Windows 10 is not offered through Windows Update, check the following: Make sure you are using Windows 7 Service Pack 1 (SP1) or Windows 8.1. If you are running Windows 8, use the Windows Store to upgrade to Windows 8.1, and run Windows Update to install the updates your system needs. To determine which version of Windows you are using, view System properties in Control Panel or PC Info.

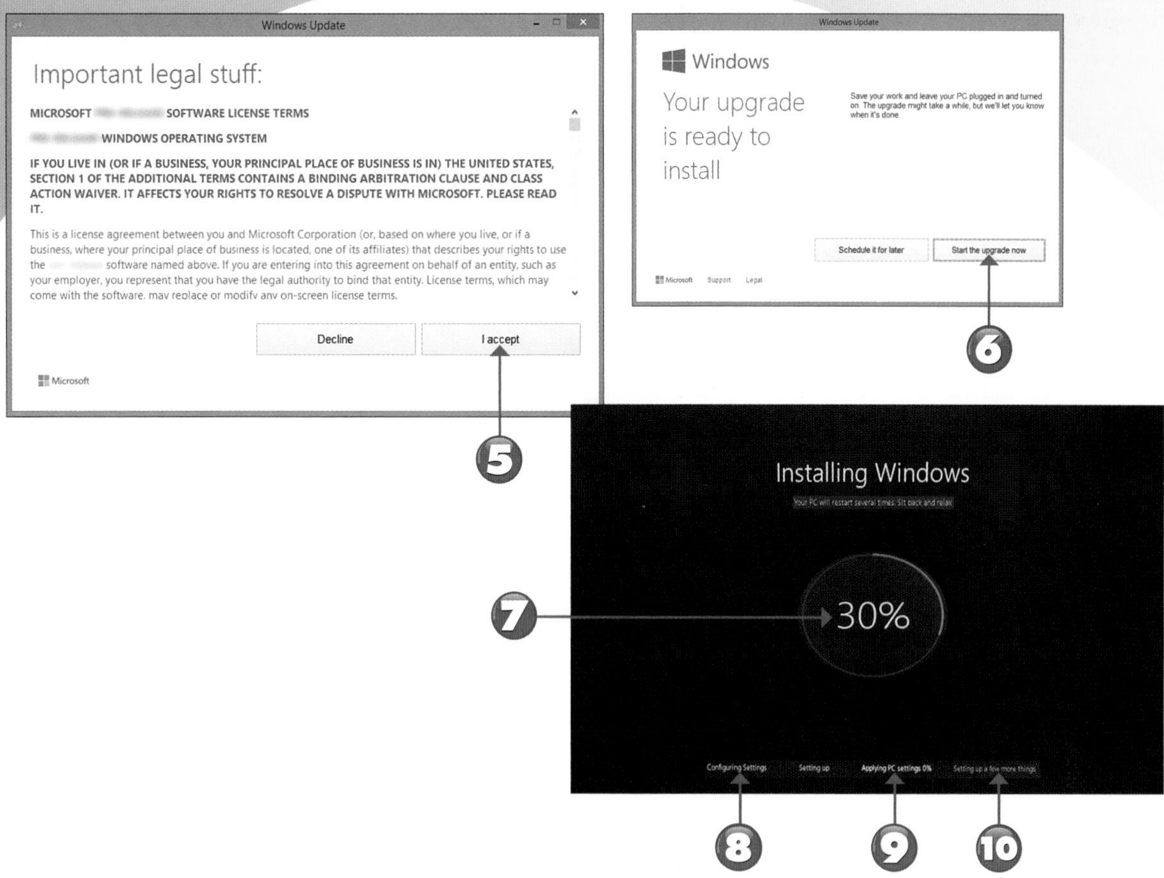

5 Review the agreement, then click or tap **I accept**.

6 Click or tap **Start the upgrade now**.

7 During the process, an overall installation percentage is displayed.

8 Completed steps are shown in bright text.

9 The current step is shown with its percentage of completion.

10 Steps to be completed are shown in normal text.

End

FINISHING UP AND LAUNCHING WINDOWS 10

Windows does most of the work during the installation process and restarts your computer a few times. However, near the end of the installation process, you are prompted to answer a few questions.

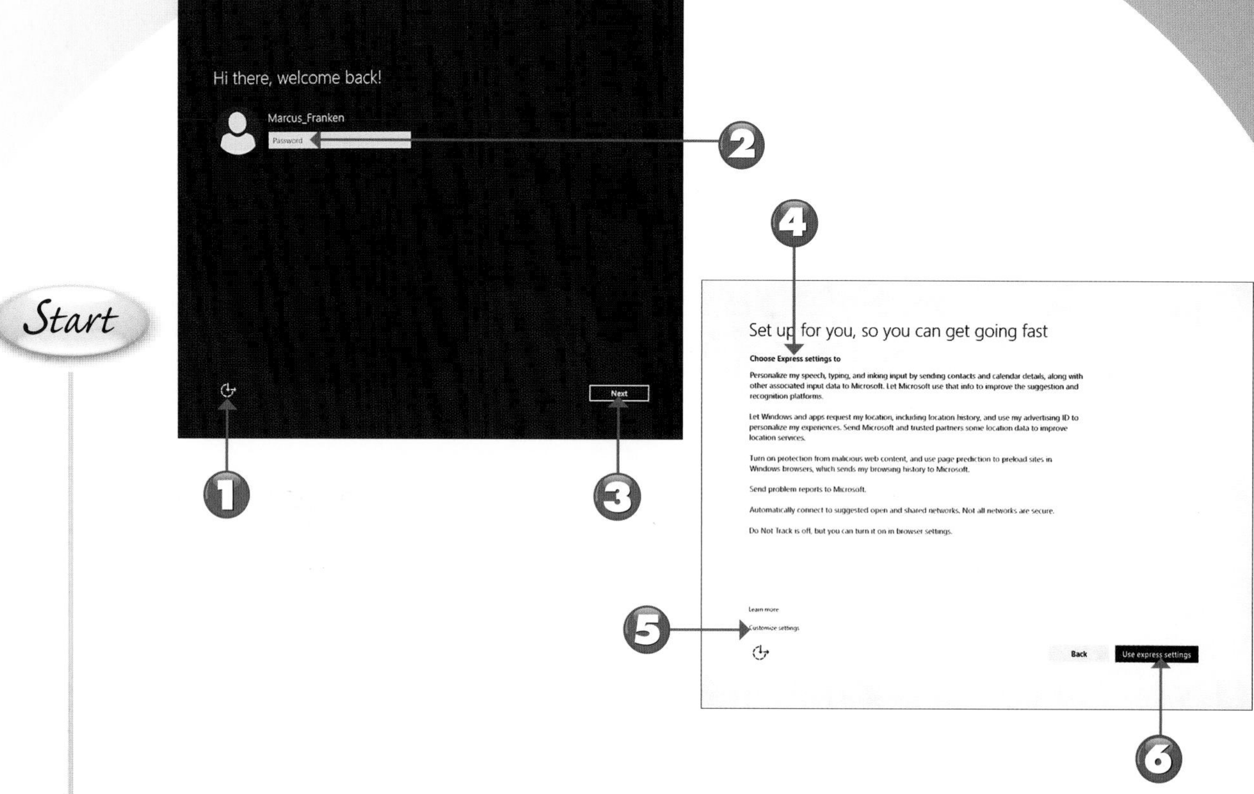

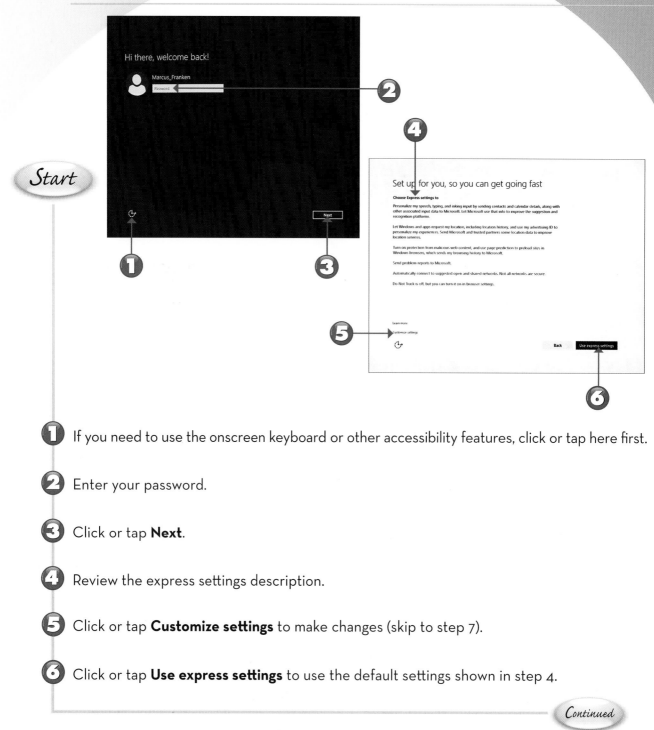

1. If you need to use the onscreen keyboard or other accessibility features, click or tap here first.
2. Enter your password.
3. Click or tap **Next**.
4. Review the express settings description.
5. Click or tap **Customize settings** to make changes (skip to step 7).
6. Click or tap **Use express settings** to use the default settings shown in step 4.

Continued

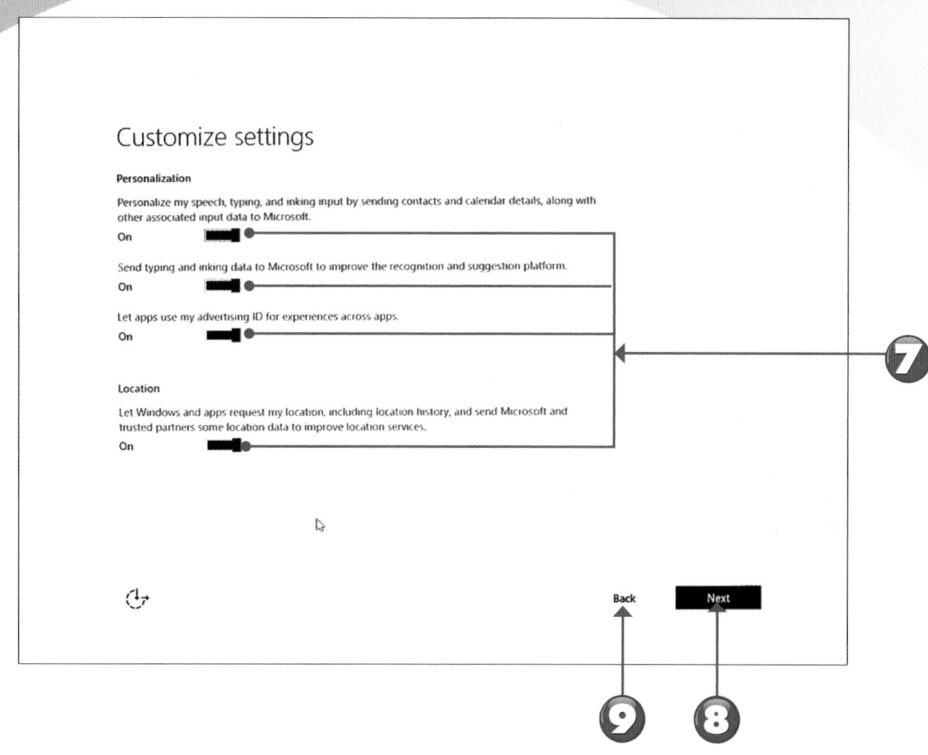

7. Click or press and drag to Off (left) to turn off any feature you don't want to use.

8. Click or tap **Next** to accept changes.

9. Click or tap **Back** to return to the previous screen.

End

NOTE

What's Next? The next dialog box you see is the Windows 10 Lock screen. To learn how to log in to Windows 10, see Chapter 3, "Logging In, Starting Up, and Shutting Down Windows 10 with a Touchscreen," or Chapter 4, "Logging In to Windows 10 and Customizing the Start Menu."

LOGGING IN, STARTING UP, AND SHUTTING DOWN WINDOWS 10 WITH A TOUCHSCREEN

Whether you're upgrading from Windows 7, switching to a new PC after running older versions of Windows, or upgrading from Windows 8/8.1, Windows 10 is designed to work the way you're accustomed to working. In this chapter, you find out how to use a touchscreen (such as those found on tablets, convertible 2-in-1 devices, or some all-in-one desktops) to log in to Windows, move around the Windows menus, and lock, sleep, or shut down your system. If you use a mouse and keyboard, skip ahead to Chapter 4, "Logging In To Windows 10 and Customizing the Start Menu."

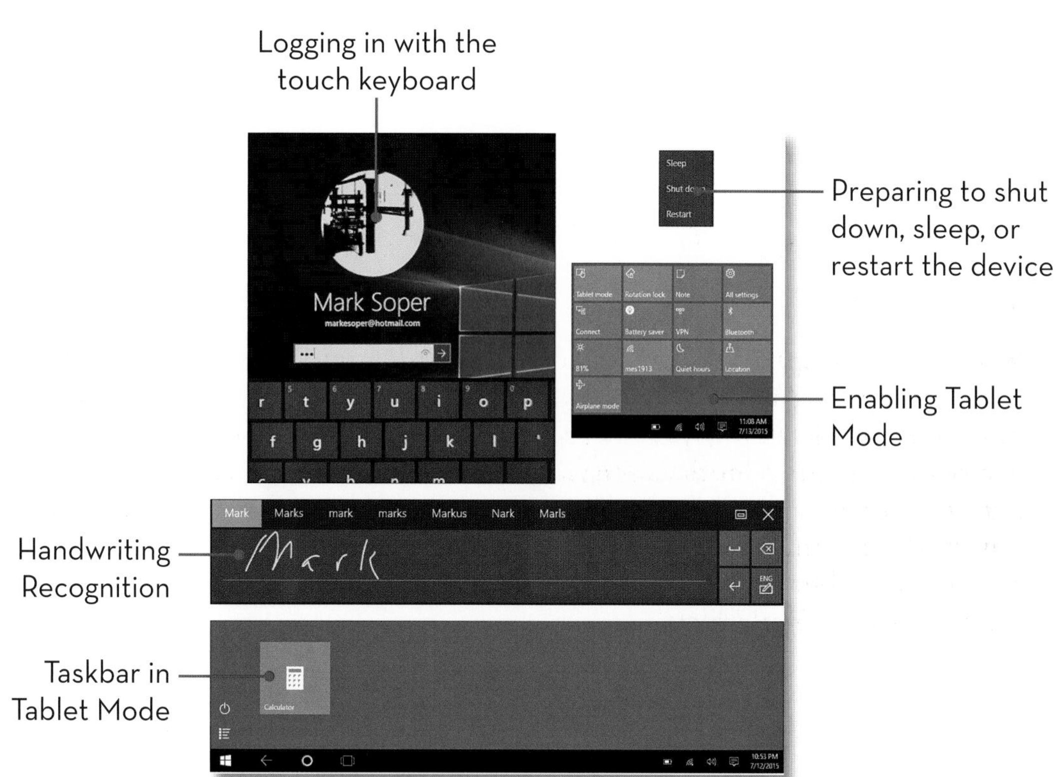

Logging in with the touch keyboard
Preparing to shut down, sleep, or restart the device
Enabling Tablet Mode
Handwriting Recognition
Taskbar in Tablet Mode
Mark Soper
Sleep
Restart
Mark
Marks
mark
marks
Markus
Nark
Marls

LOGGING IN TO WINDOWS 10 WITH A TOUCHSCREEN

To log in to Windows 10, you must know the username and password (if any) set up for your account. If you installed Windows 10 yourself, be sure to make note of this information when you are prompted to provide it during the installation process. You also log in to Windows 10 when you are waking up the computer from sleep, unlocking it, or restarting it.

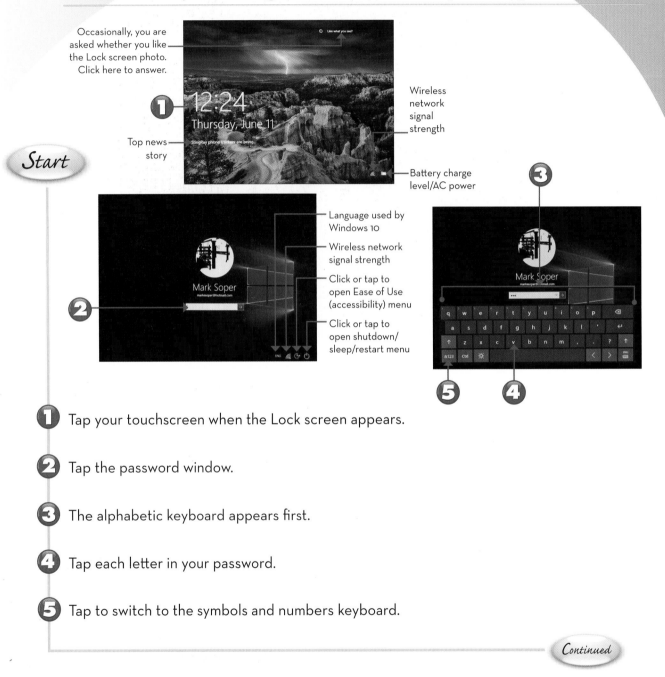

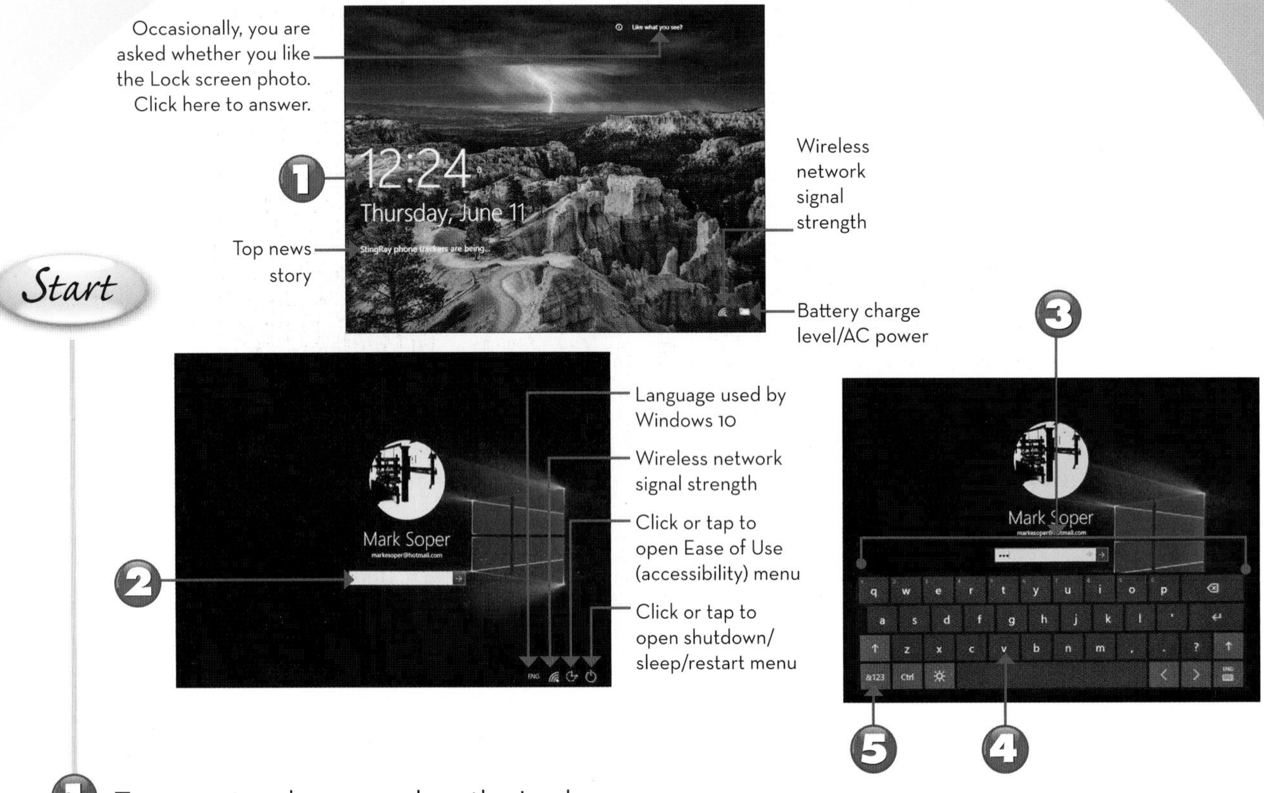

1. Tap your touchscreen when the Lock screen appears.
2. Tap the password window.
3. The alphabetic keyboard appears first.
4. Tap each letter in your password.
5. Tap to switch to the symbols and numbers keyboard.

Continued

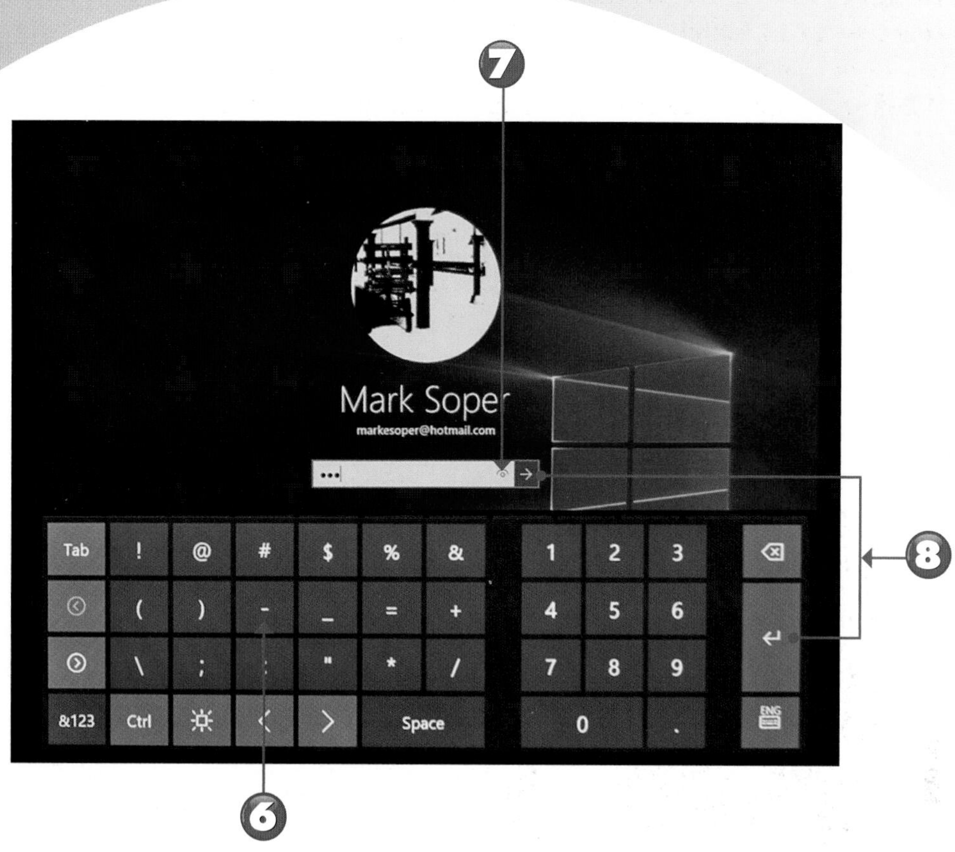

6 Tap symbols and numbers in your password.

7 To see your password as you enter it, tap the eye symbol (visible after you enter at least one character of your password).

8 Tap to start Windows.

End

NOTE

Touch Keyboards and Handwriting Recognition The touch keyboard works with any app that uses the keyboard and is also used to start Windows 10's handwriting recognition feature. See "Using Handwriting Recognition," p. 36, this chapter, for details.

NOTE

Logins for Multiple Users If you have more than one user set up on your computer, there are additional steps to follow. See the section "Selecting an Account to Log In To," in Chapter 22, "Adding and Managing Users," for details.

THE START AND ALL APPS MENUS IN TABLET MODE

Devices that do not have a physical keyboard (or have the keyboard detached) typically start Windows 10 in Tablet Mode. In this lesson, you learn the major features of Tablet Mode.

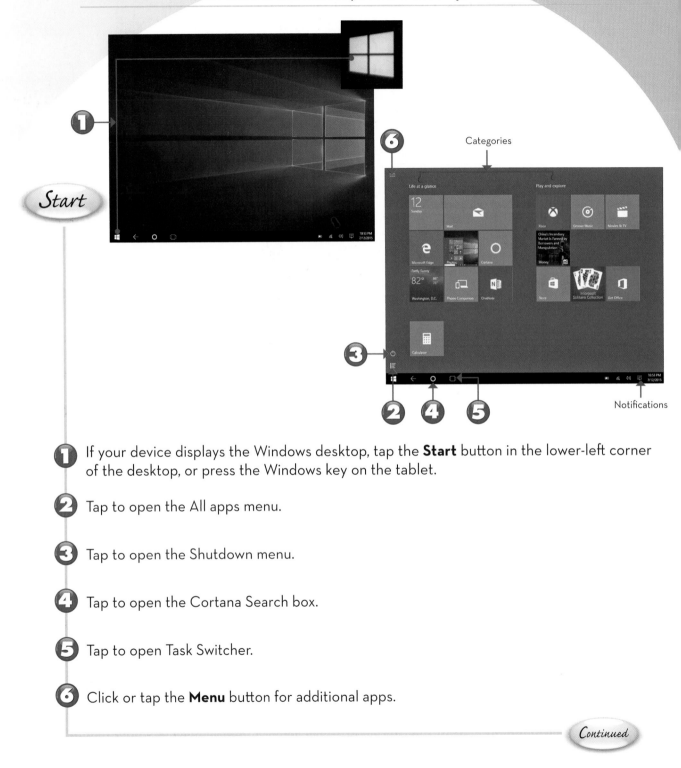

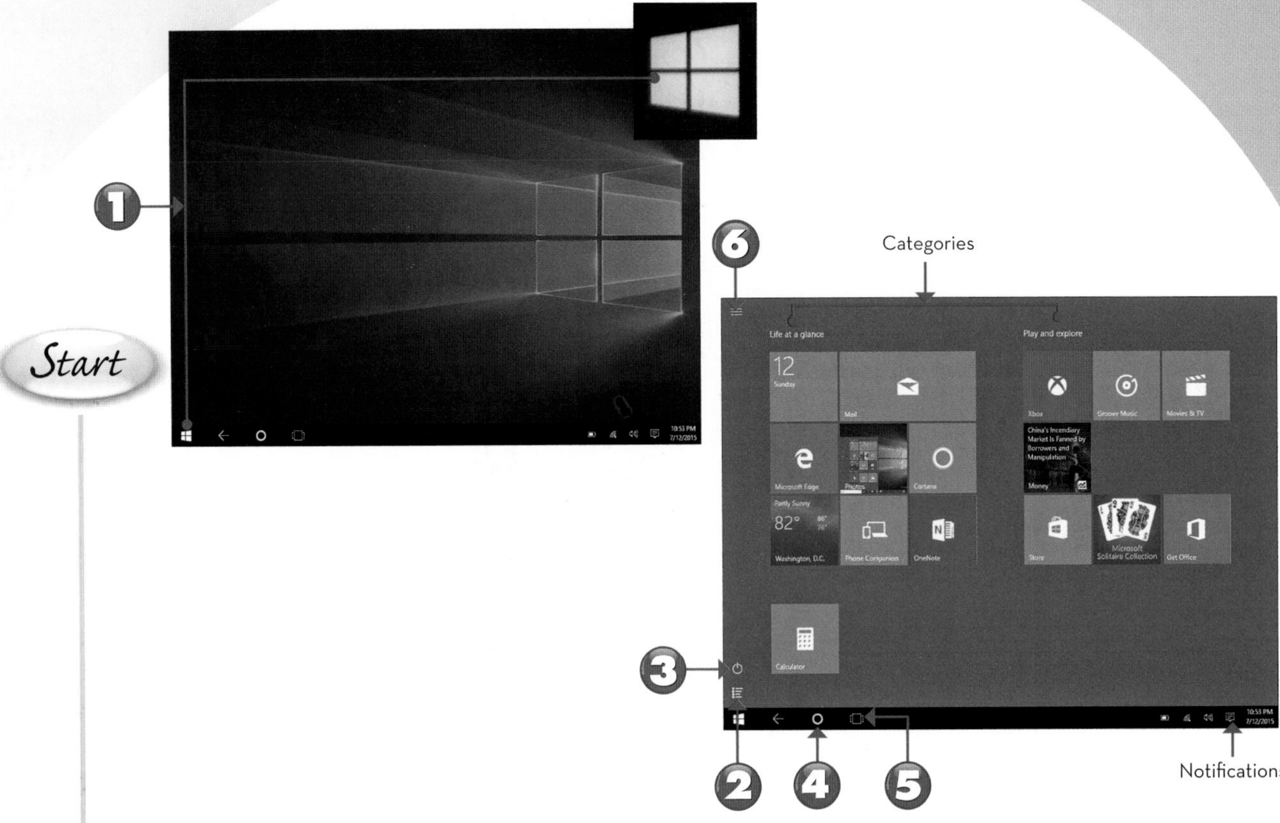

Start

1. If your device displays the Windows desktop, tap the **Start** button in the lower-left corner of the desktop, or press the Windows key on the tablet.
2. Tap to open the All apps menu.
3. Tap to open the Shutdown menu.
4. Tap to open the Cortana Search box.
5. Tap to open Task Switcher.
6. Click or tap the **Menu** button for additional apps.

Continued

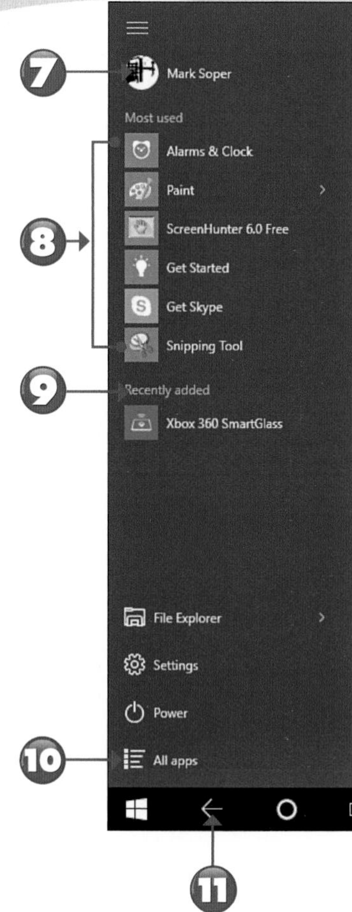

7. Click or tap to change account settings, log out, or lock the system.
8. This is a list of your most-used apps.
9. Recently added shows apps you've recently installed.
10. Click or tap to see all installed apps.
11. Click or tap to return to the previous pane.

End

ENABLING TABLET MODE

As you have seen in the previous lessons, Tablet Mode is designed to be touch-friendly. If you use a convertible or two-in-one (tablet plus laptop) device, Tablet Mode might not be configured to start automatically. If Tablet Mode did not start automatically when you started Windows, you can start it from the Notifications menu. Here's how.

Start

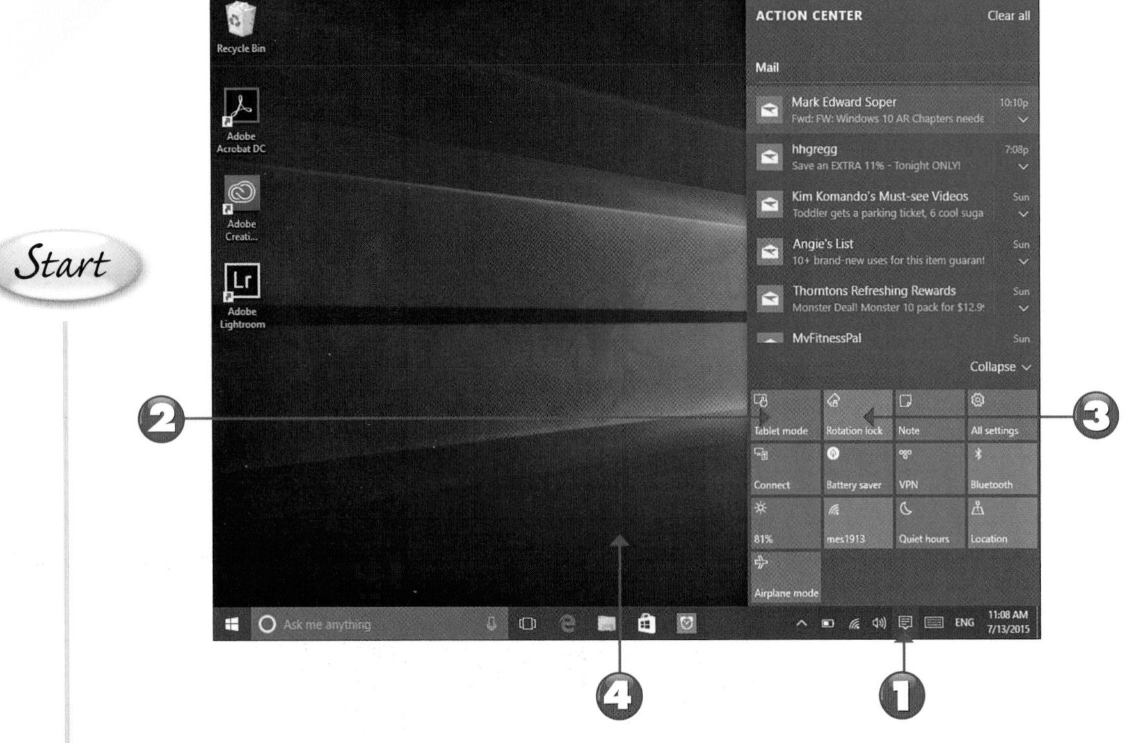

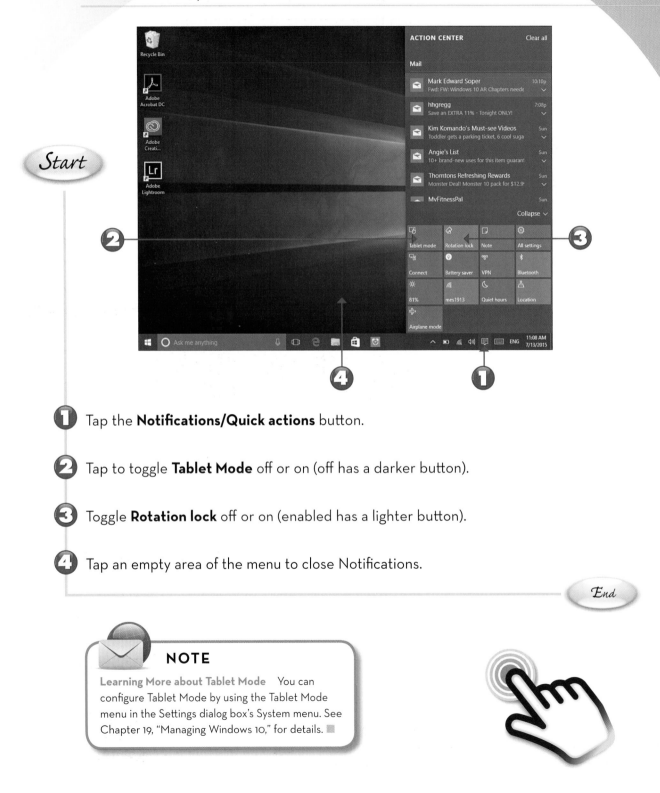

1. Tap the **Notifications/Quick actions** button.
2. Tap to toggle **Tablet Mode** off or on (off has a darker button).
3. Toggle **Rotation lock** off or on (enabled has a lighter button).
4. Tap an empty area of the menu to close Notifications.

End

NOTE

Learning More about Tablet Mode You can configure Tablet Mode by using the Tablet Mode menu in the Settings dialog box's System menu. See Chapter 19, "Managing Windows 10," for details.

STARTING AND CLOSING A UNIVERSAL OR MODERN UI APP

Modern UI apps and Universal apps (which work on any Windows device, including Windows Mobile) are optimized for touchscreens. Although they are started the same way in either regular or Tablet Mode, Tablet Mode uses a different way to close them. In this example, I start and close Calculator, which I have pinned to the Start menu.

Start

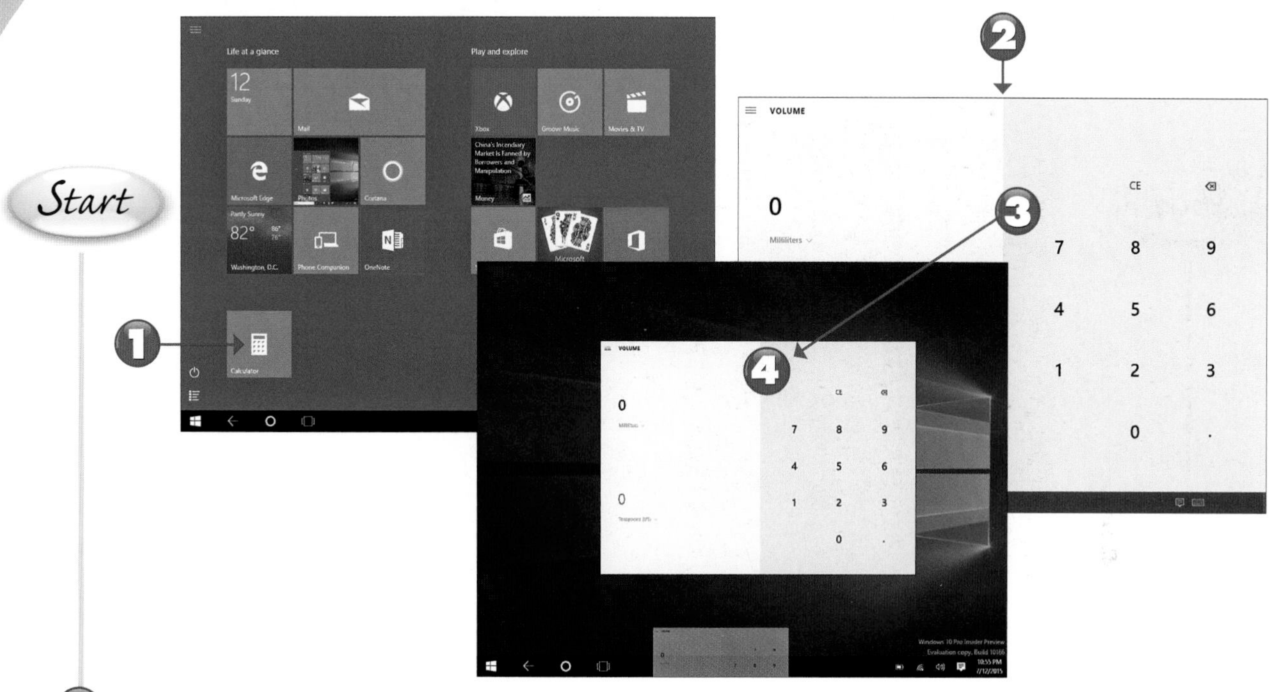

1. Tap a Modern UI or Universal app.
2. When you are finished using the app, press and hold the top edge of the screen.
3. Drag the app downward.
4. Continue to drag the app window down until it disappears. The Tablet Mode Start menu appears immediately afterward.

End

NOTE

Pinning Files and Apps To learn more about pinning files and apps to the Start menu or the taskbar, see Chapter 6, "Running Apps."

LOCKING YOUR PC

If you have a password on your account, you can lock your PC when you leave it and unlock it when you return. On laptop and desktop computers, you typically lock your system with the Windows key+L combination. However, you can also lock it with a touchscreen. Here's how.

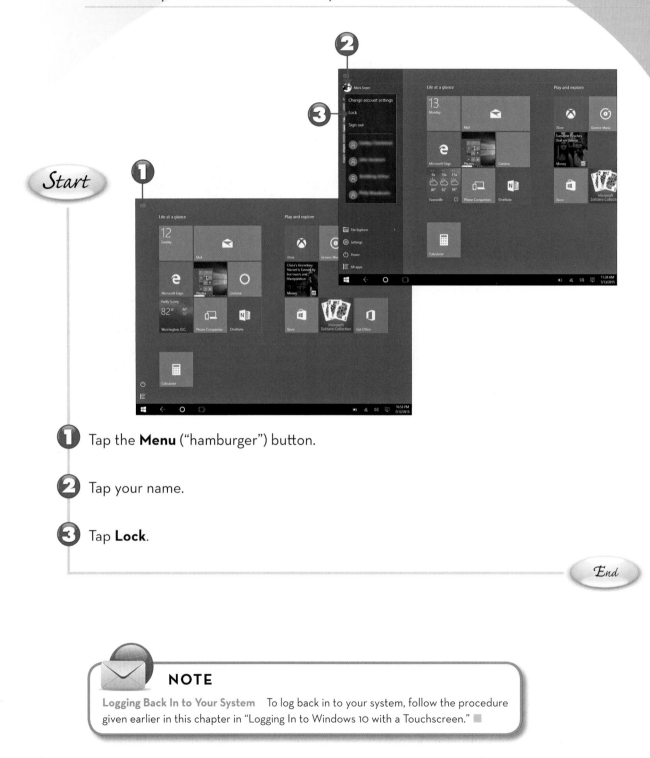

Start

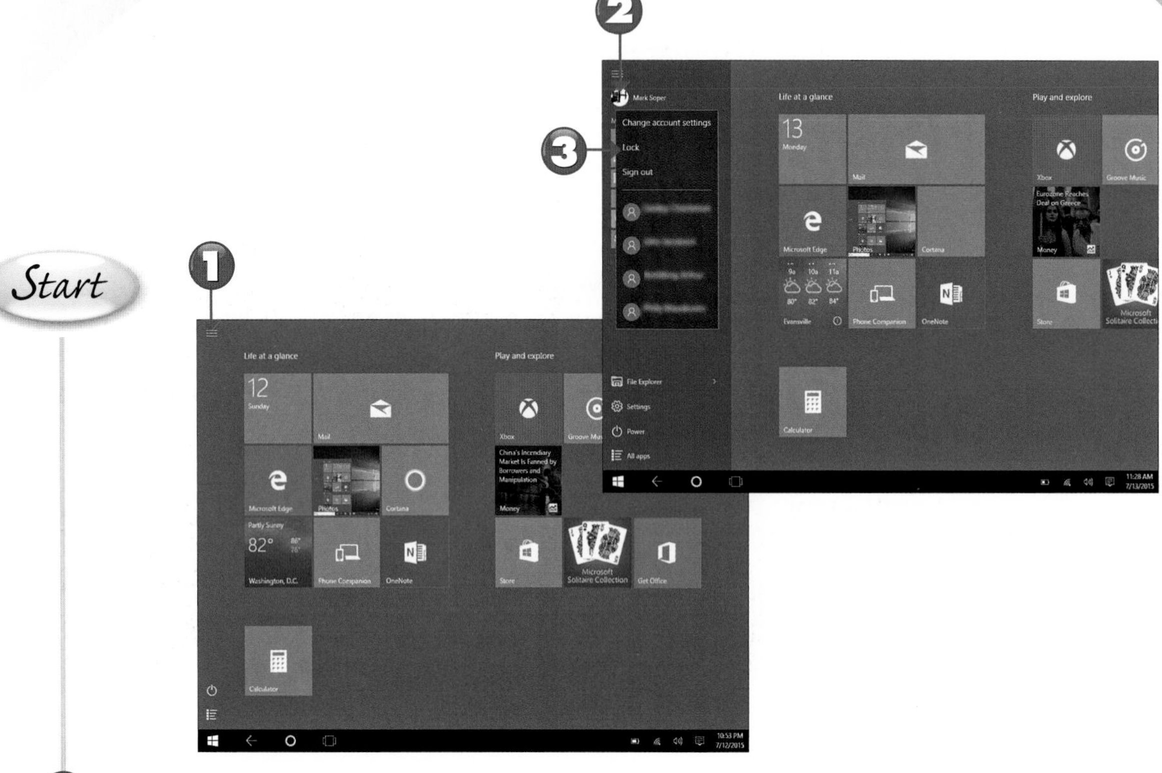

1. Tap the **Menu** ("hamburger") button.
2. Tap your name.
3. Tap **Lock**.

End

NOTE

Logging Back In to Your System To log back in to your system, follow the procedure given earlier in this chapter in "Logging In to Windows 10 with a Touchscreen."

CHOOSING SLEEP, SHUT DOWN, OR RESTART

When it's time to put away the computer, Windows 10 makes it easy. Want to go back to work (or play) right where you left off? Choose Sleep. Want to "put away" your PC and start fresh next time? Choose Shut Down. In this lesson, you learn how to perform these tasks using the Start menu's Power button. These same tasks can also be performed from the login screen shown earlier in this chapter.

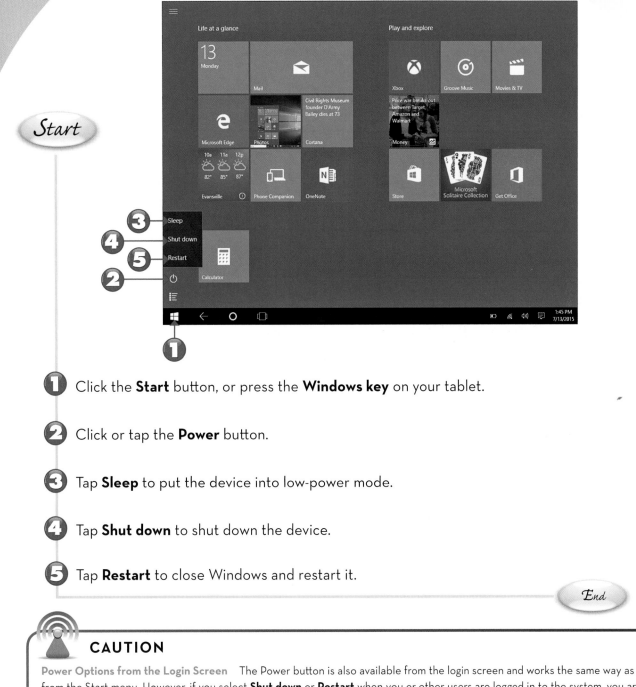

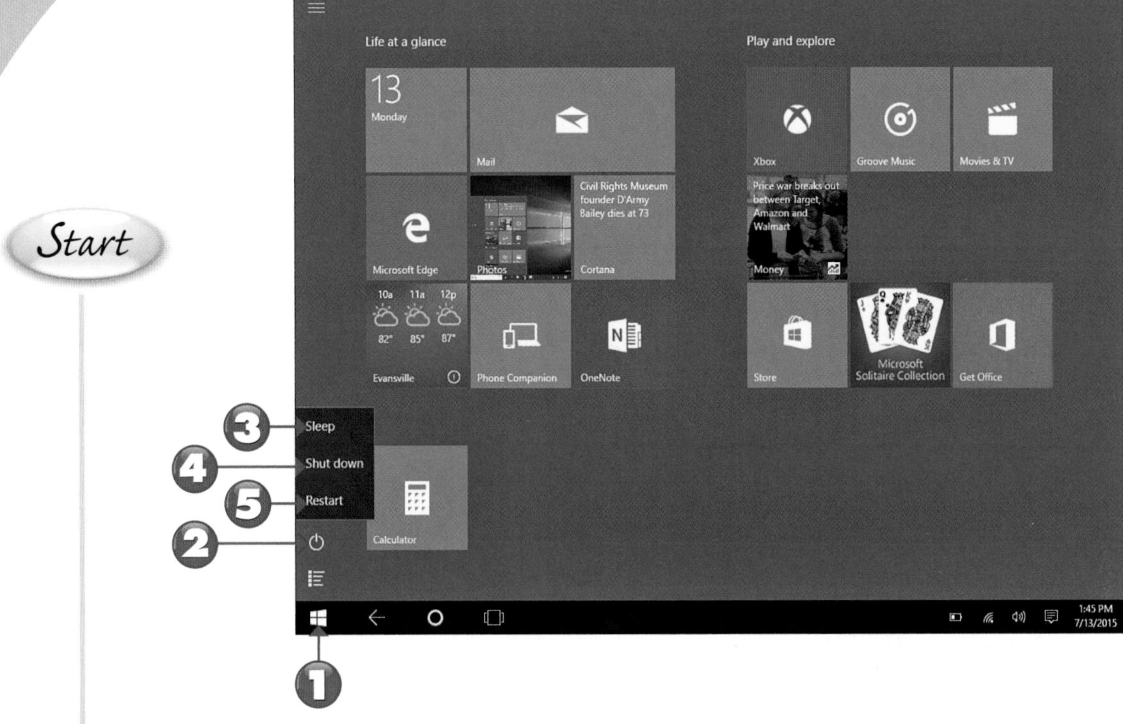

1. Click the **Start** button, or press the **Windows key** on your tablet.
2. Click or tap the **Power** button.
3. Tap **Sleep** to put the device into low-power mode.
4. Tap **Shut down** to shut down the device.
5. Tap **Restart** to close Windows and restart it.

End

CAUTION

Power Options from the Login Screen The Power button is also available from the login screen and works the same way as from the Start menu. However, if you select **Shut down** or **Restart** when you or other users are logged in to the system, you are warned that shutting down or restarting can cause data loss. Be sure that any logged-in users have saved their work and closed their apps before you shut down or restart Windows.

USING HANDWRITING RECOGNITION

On tablets and laptops with touchscreens, the touch keyboard can also be used for text input using handwriting recognition. And if you have a touchpad with a stylus, you can also use this feature. Here's how to switch to and use handwriting recognition from the touch keyboard, using WordPad as the app in this example.

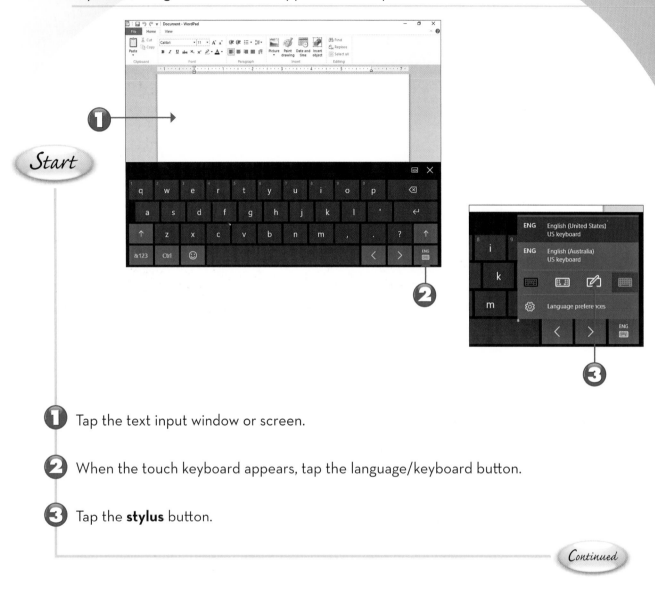

Start

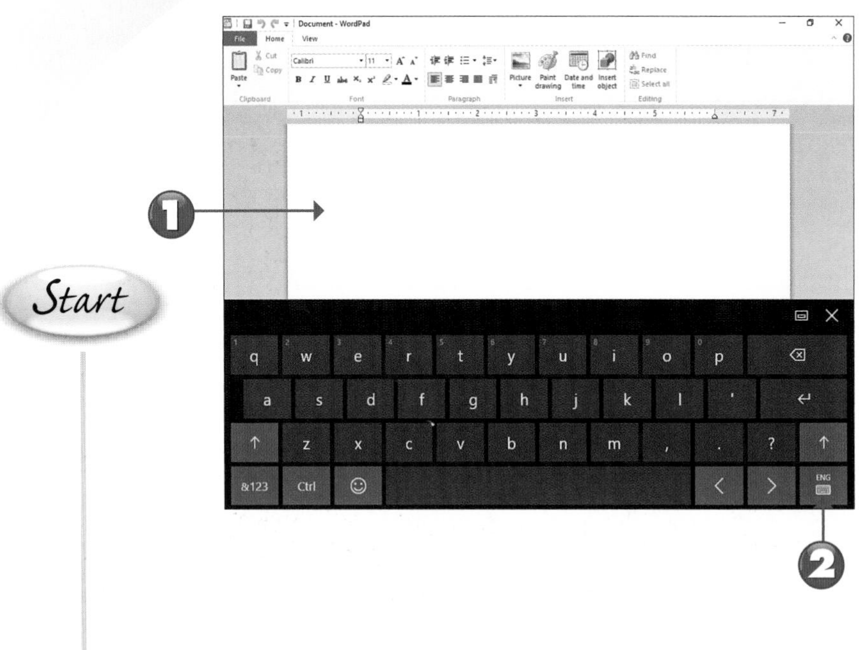

1. Tap the text input window or screen.
2. When the touch keyboard appears, tap the language/keyboard button.
3. Tap the **stylus** button.

Continued

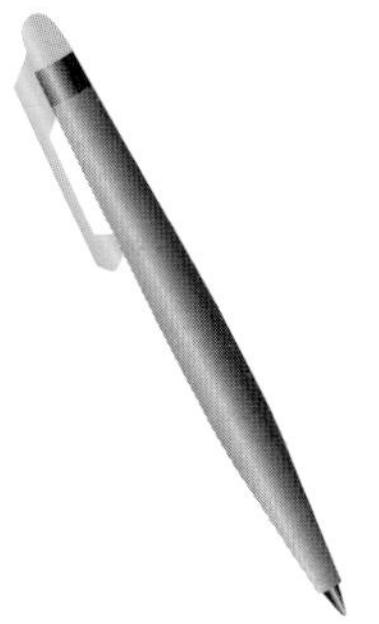

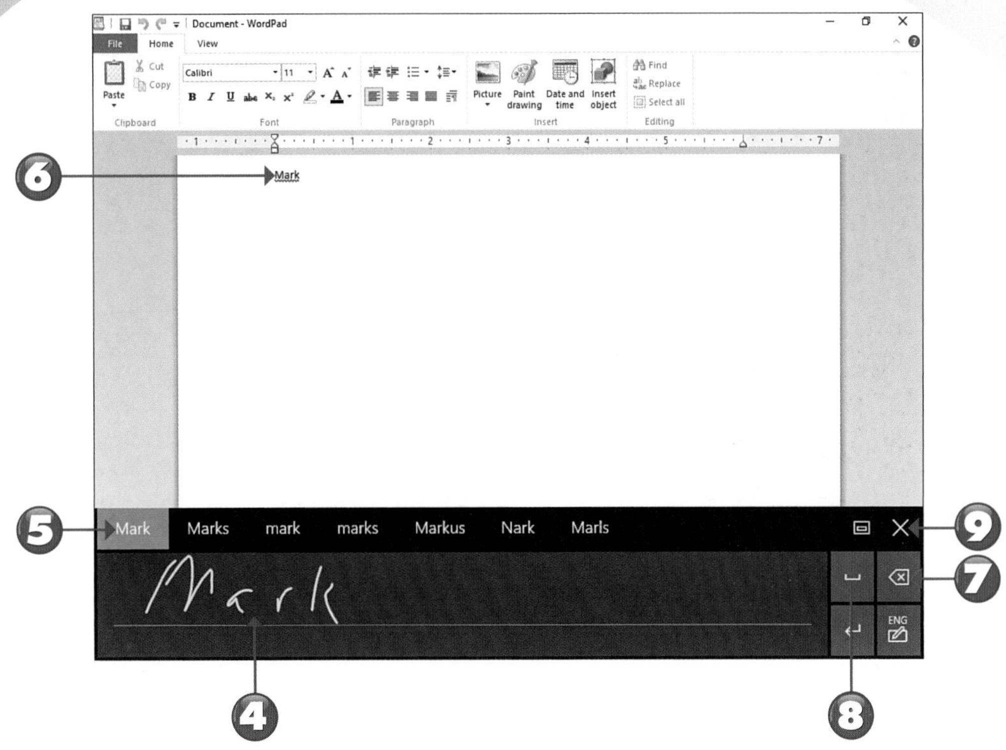

4. Print the text you want to insert with your finger or stylus.
5. If your printing is misrecognized, tap the correct word from the list (if present).
6. The text is automatically inserted into your text input area as it is recognized.
7. Tap the backspace button to remove any erroneous printing.
8. Tap the spacebar button to add a space.
9. Tap to close the keyboard when finished.

End

LOGGING IN TO WINDOWS 10 AND CUSTOMIZING THE START MENU

This chapter shows you how to log in to Windows 10 and navigate the standard Windows desktop and Start menu with a mouse and keyboard. Whether you use a mouse/keyboard or touchscreen, you find out how to customize the Start menu's contents.

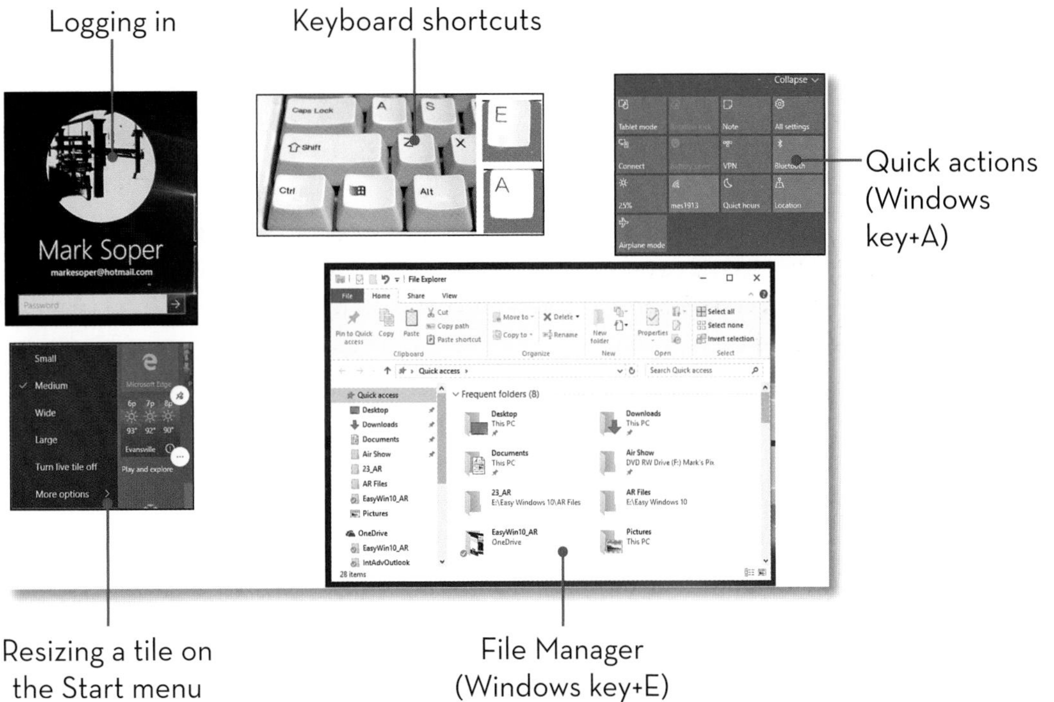

Logging in
Keyboard shortcuts
Quick actions (Windows key+A)
Mark Soper
markesoper@hotmail.com
Resizing a tile on the Start menu
File Manager (Windows key+E)

LOGGING IN TO WINDOWS 10

To log in to Windows 10, you must know the password (if any) to the account you want to log in to. If you installed Windows 10 yourself, be sure to make note of this information when you are prompted to provide it during the installation process. You also log in to Windows 10 when you are waking up the computer from sleep, unlocking it, or restarting it.

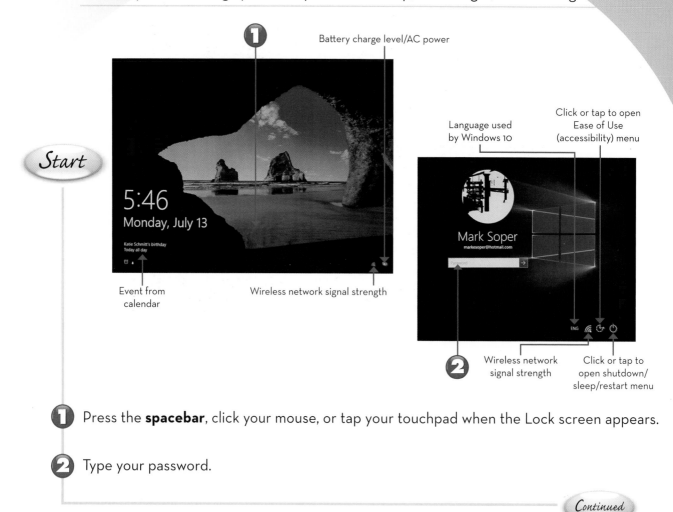

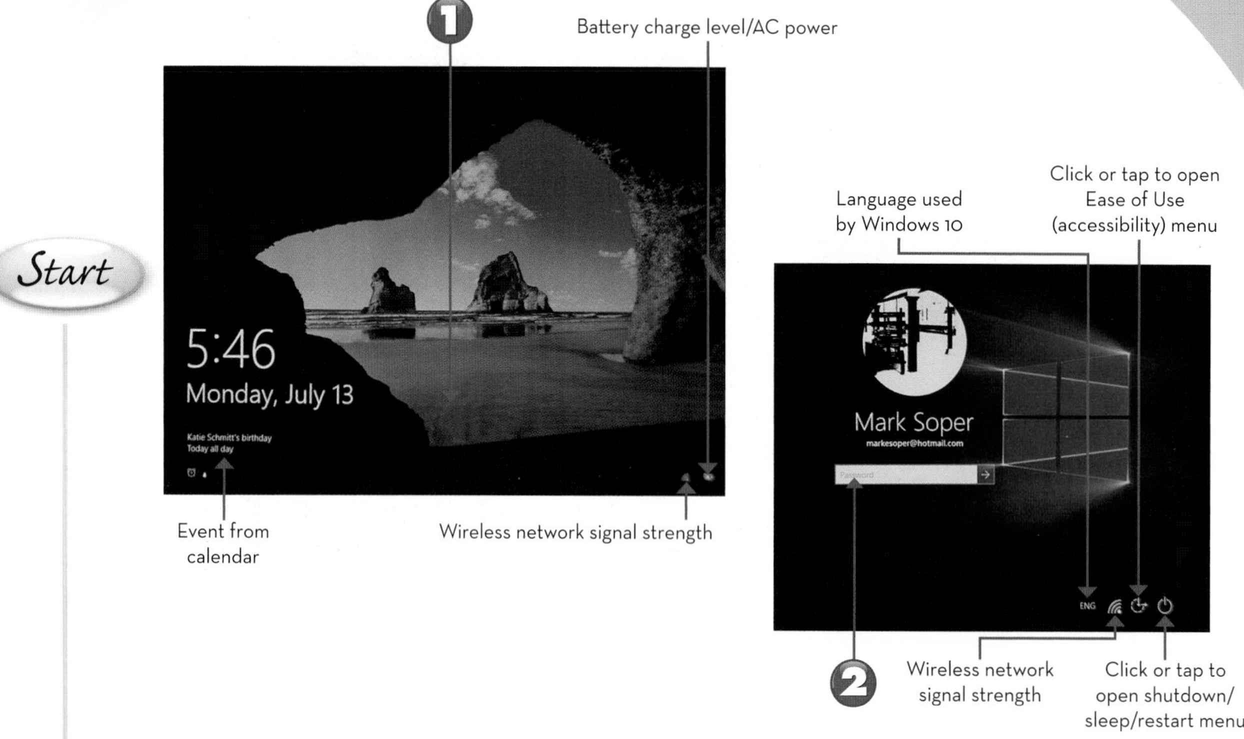

1. Press the **spacebar**, click your mouse, or tap your touchpad when the Lock screen appears.

2. Type your password.

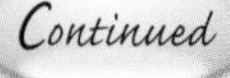

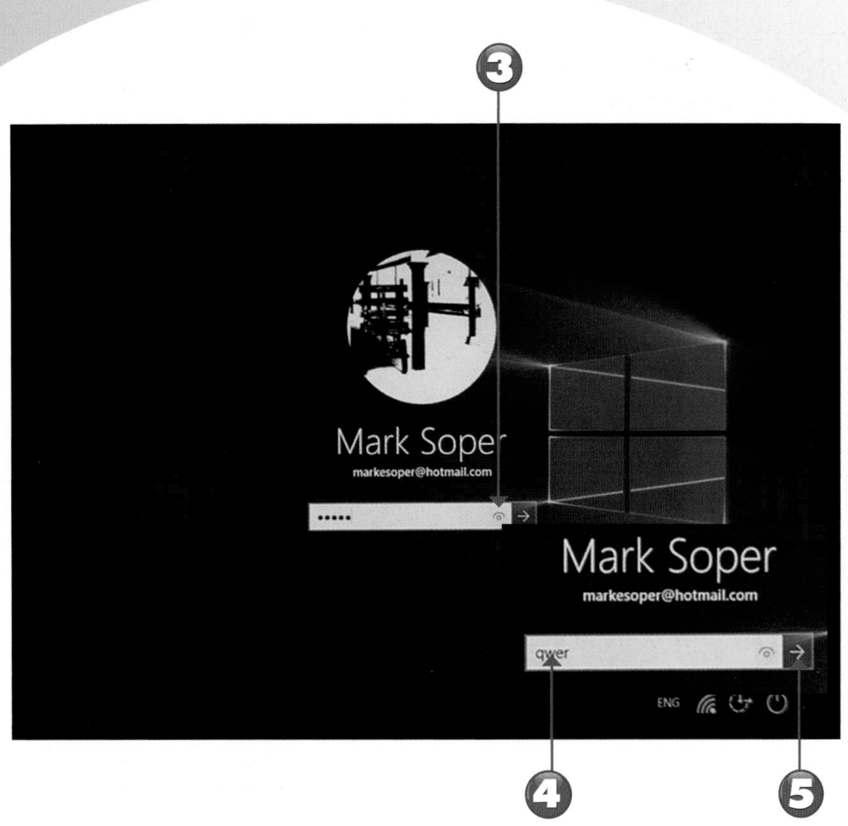

3. To see your password as you enter it, click or press and hold the eye icon (you must type at least one character to see this icon).

4. Password characters visible when you click or press the eye icon.

5. Press **Enter** or click the arrow. The Windows desktop appears.

End

NOTE

Logins for Multiple Users If you have more than one user set up on your computer, there are additional steps to follow. See the section "Selecting an Account to Log In To," in Chapter 22, "Adding and Managing Users," for details.

OPENING AND USING THE START MENU

Laptop and desktop computers running Windows 10 typically display the Windows desktop after login. In this exercise, you learn how to open the Start menu. You use the left button on your mouse, the lower-left corner of your device's integrated touchpad, or the Windows key on the keyboard or tablet.

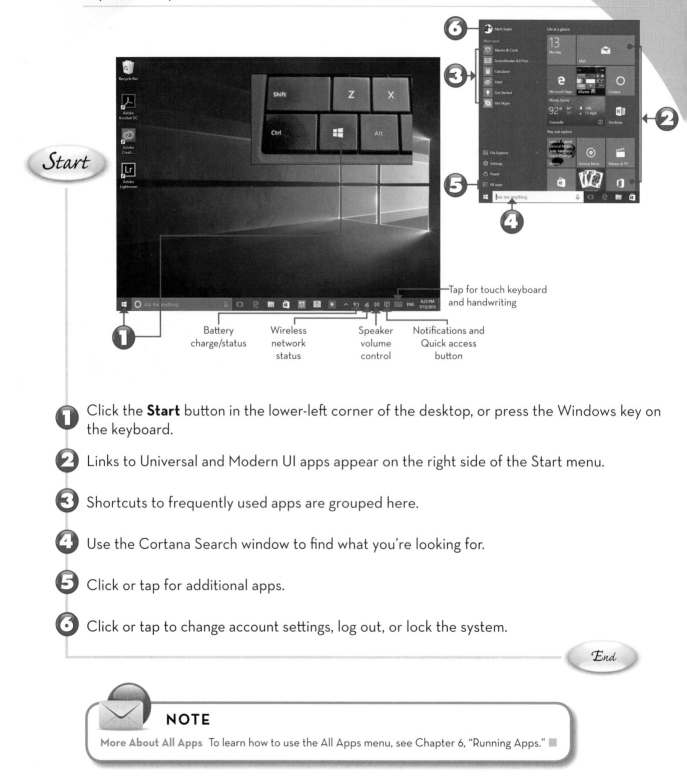

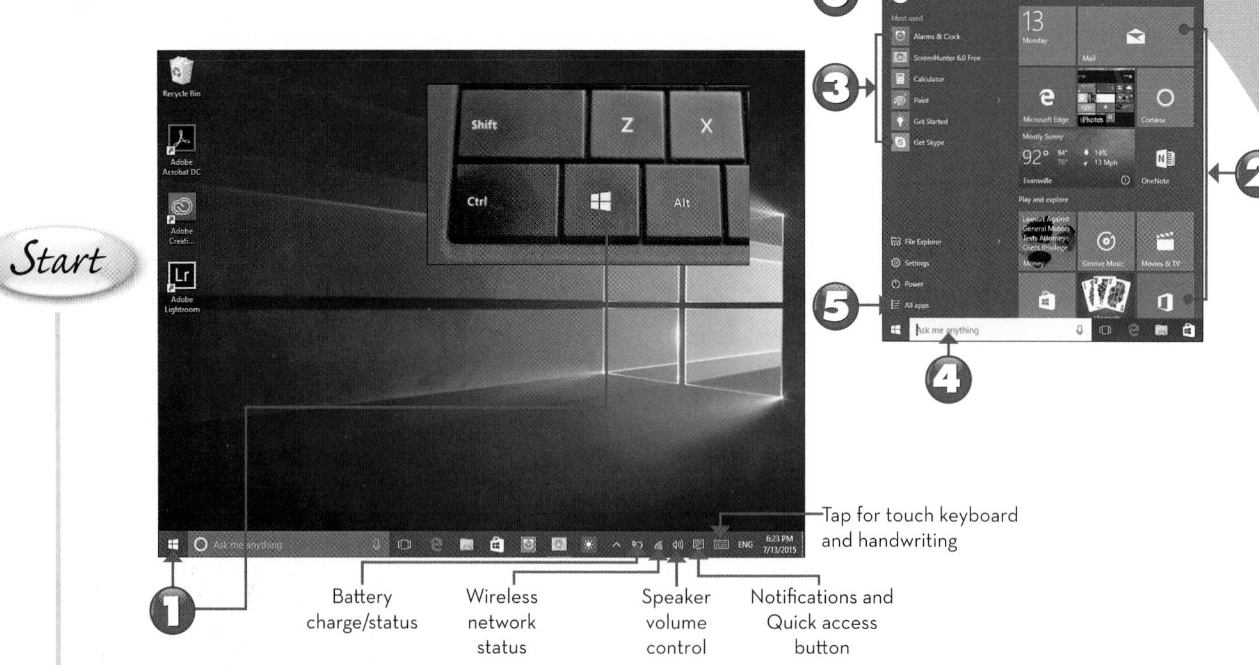

1. Click the **Start** button in the lower-left corner of the desktop, or press the Windows key on the keyboard.
2. Links to Universal and Modern UI apps appear on the right side of the Start menu.
3. Shortcuts to frequently used apps are grouped here.
4. Use the Cortana Search window to find what you're looking for.
5. Click or tap for additional apps.
6. Click or tap to change account settings, log out, or lock the system.

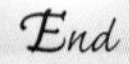

NOTE

More About All Apps To learn how to use the All Apps menu, see Chapter 6, "Running Apps."

USING KEYBOARD SHORTCUTS

Windows 10 offers new keyboard shortcuts. This lesson illustrates a few of the shortcuts that use the Windows key.

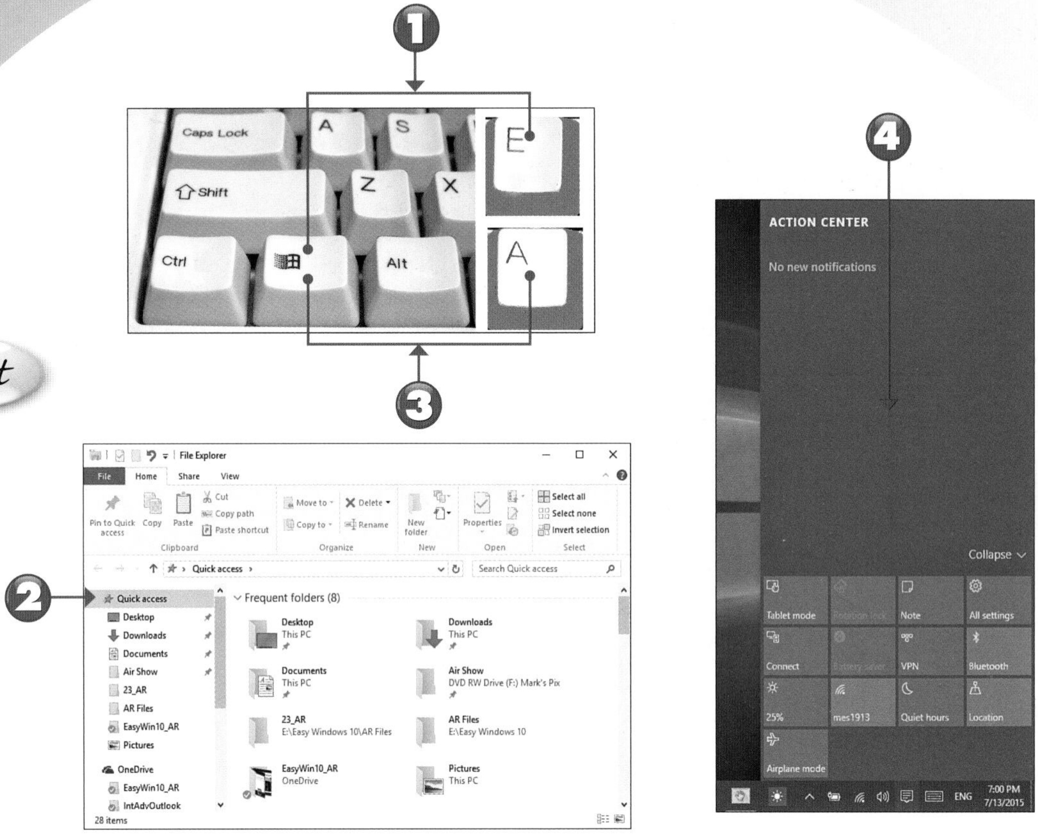

Start

1. Press **Windows key+E**.
2. The Quick access view of File Explorer opens on the Windows desktop.
3. Press **Windows key+A**.
4. The Notifications pane (Action Center and Quick actions) is displayed at the right of the Windows desktop.

End

NOTE

More Keyboard Shortcuts Some keyboard shortcuts used in Windows 7 and 8.1 also work in Windows 10. For Microsoft's official list of keyboard shortcuts for Windows and apps, go to http://windows.microsoft.com/en-us/windows/keyboard-shortcuts and select the version of Windows you use. For a discussion of Windows 10-specific keyboard shortcuts, go to http://blogs.technet.com/b/sebastianklenk/archive/2015/05/28/windows-10-keyboard-shortcuts-at-a-glance.aspx.

RESIZING TILES ON THE START MENU

You can change the size of app tiles on the Start menu to help make it easier to use, smaller, or larger. In the example shown here, the Weather app is resized, showing how it can display more or less information as its size changes.

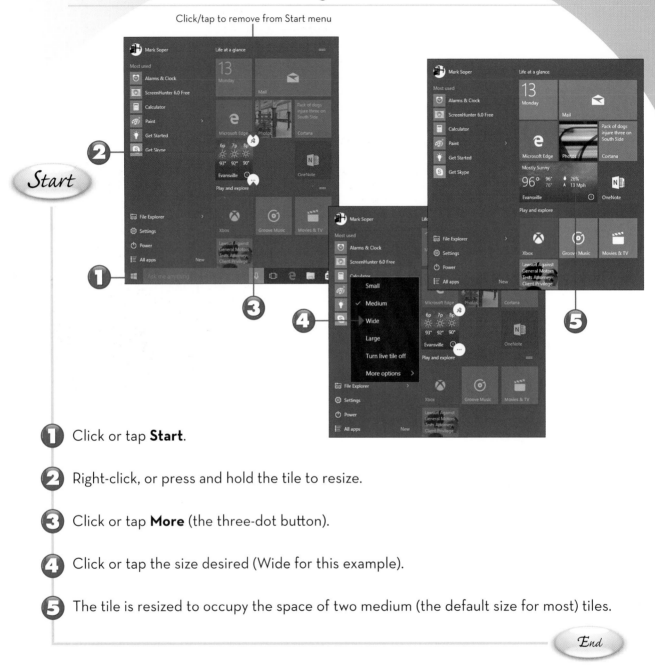

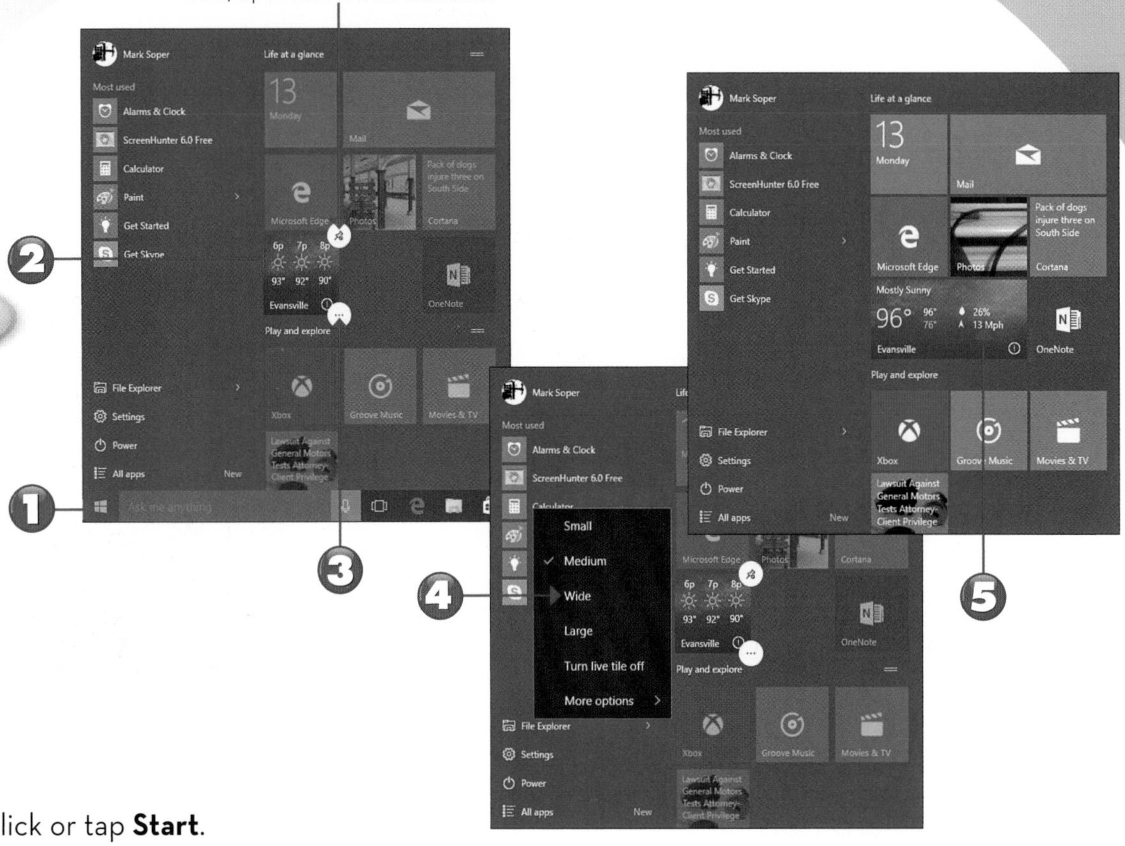

Click/tap to remove from Start menu

Start

1. Click or tap **Start**.
2. Right-click, or press and hold the tile to resize.
3. Click or tap **More** (the three-dot button).
4. Click or tap the size desired (Wide for this example).
5. The tile is resized to occupy the space of two medium (the default size for most) tiles.

End

TIP

Other Options If you click or tap Large (step 4), the tile occupies the space of four medium tiles. To turn off live updates (tiles such as Weather, Photos, Calendar, and others), click or tap **Turn live tile off**. To add a tile to the taskbar, click or tap **More options** and click or tap **Pin to taskbar**.

CHANGING TILE POSITIONS ON THE START MENU

Moving a tile to a new location is a simple drag-and-drop process, as this tutorial demonstrates.

Start

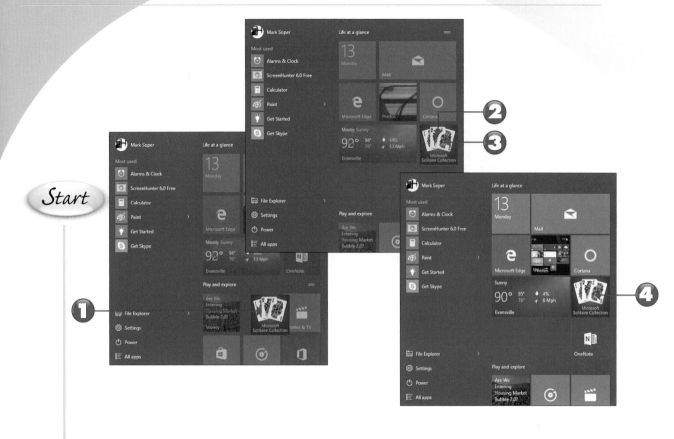

1. Click and hold or press and hold the tile to move it.

2. Drag it to the new location.

3. Release the tile when it is in the correct position.

4. The next time Start is opened, the tile is in its new position.

End

REMOVING AN APP FROM THE START MENU

You can remove an app from the Most used list on the left side of the Start menu or from the right side of the Start menu. You can still run an app from All Apps, so use these methods for apps you don't use frequently.

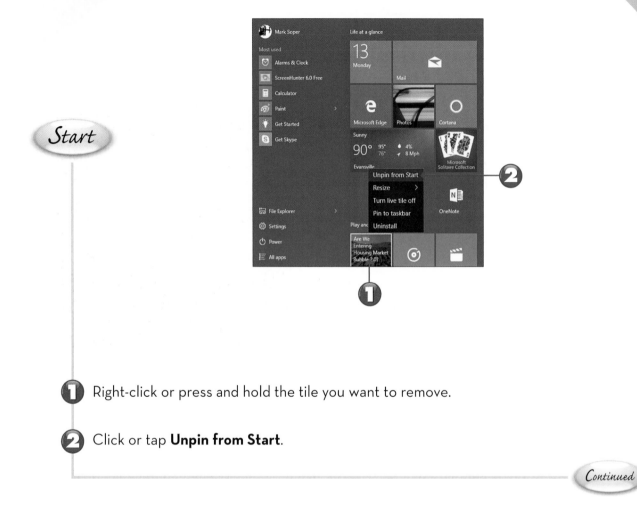

1. Right-click or press and hold the tile you want to remove.
2. Click or tap **Unpin from Start**.

Continued

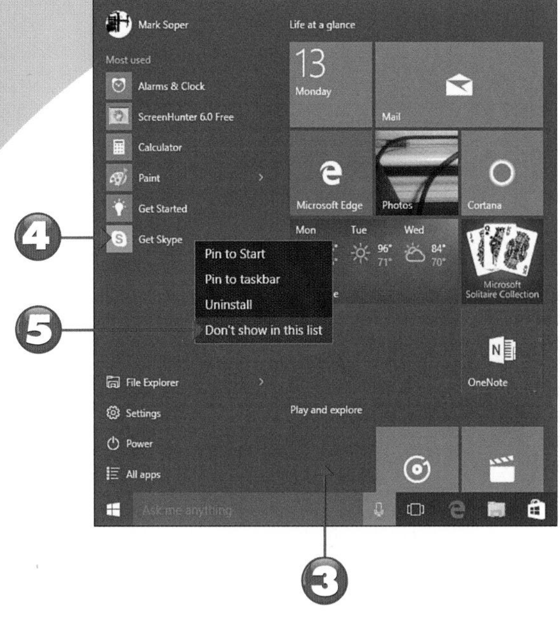

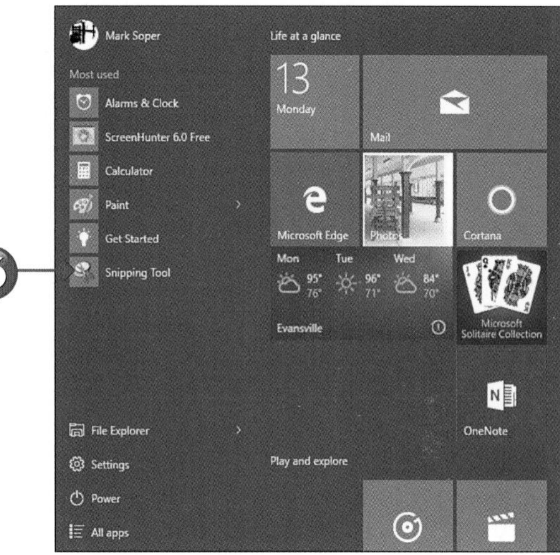

3. The tile is removed from the Start menu.
4. Right-click or press and hold an app you want to remove from the Most used list.
5. Click or tap **Don't show in this list**.
6. Another most-used app takes the place of the one you removed in step 5.

End

TIP

Other Options If you don't want to use the app anymore, choose **Uninstall** in steps 2 or 5. If you use an app frequently, you might prefer to put its shortcut on the taskbar. Choose **Pin to Taskbar** in steps 2 or 5.

LOCKING YOUR SYSTEM

You can lock your system by clicking your name/icon at the top of the Start menu (for details, see Chapter 3, "Logging In, Starting Up, and Shutting Down Windows 10 with a Touchscreen"). However, it's easier to use the keyboard, as shown in this lesson.

Start

1 Press the **Windows key+L** key on your keyboard.

2 The Lock screen appears.

End

NOTE

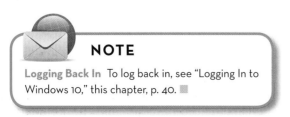

Logging Back In To log back in, see "Logging In to Windows 10," this chapter, p. 40.

CHOOSING SLEEP, SHUT DOWN, OR RESTART

When it's time to put away the computer, Windows 10 makes it easy. Want to go back to work (or play) right where you left off? Choose Sleep. Want to start from scratch the next time you start up Windows, or need to put away your PC for more than a few hours? Choose Shut Down. Need to restart the computer? Choose Restart. In this lesson, you learn how to perform these tasks using the Start menu's Power button. These same tasks can also be performed from the login screen shown earlier in this chapter.

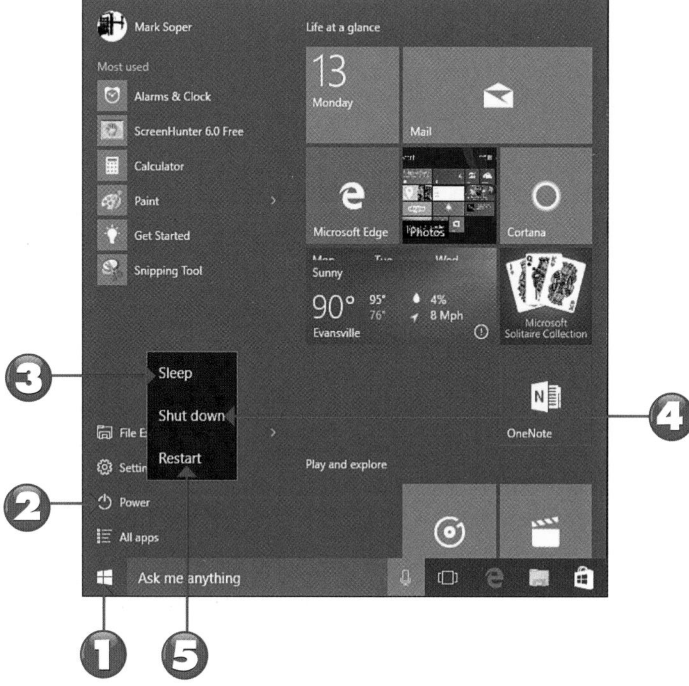

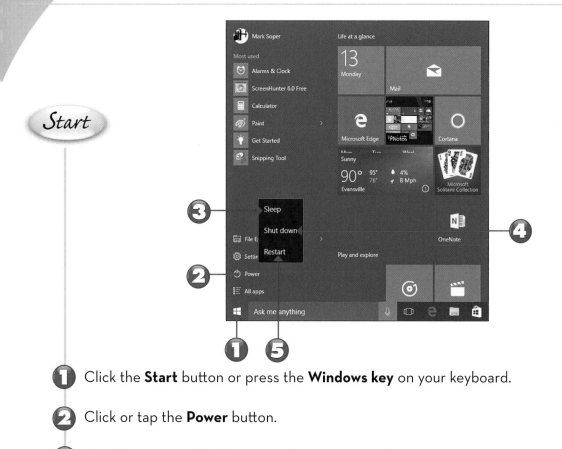

1. Click the **Start** button or press the **Windows key** on your keyboard.
2. Click or tap the **Power** button.
3. Tap **Sleep** to put the device into low-power mode.
4. Tap **Shut down** to shut down the device.
5. Tap **Restart** to close Windows and restart it.

End

CAUTION

Power Options from the Login Screen The Power button is also available from the login screen and works the same way as from the Start menu. However, if you select **Shut down** or **Restart** when you or other users are logged in to the system, you are warned that shutting down or restarting can cause data loss. Be sure that any logged-in users have saved their work and closed their apps before you shut down or restart Windows.

USING CORTANA SEARCH

Windows 10's Search includes a powerful new feature called Cortana. Cortana provides voice-activated search of both the Web and your device, can send you reminders, and works hard to discover what you like so you get better search results. However, you can also disable Cortana and use Search without it. Either way, this chapter shows you how to get the most from the enhanced search tools in Windows 10.

Configuring Cortana's speech recognition
Customized search results from Cortana
Cortana provides a local digest of news, weather, and events
Cortana's Notebook helps you customize Cortana searches
Setting up a reminder
A local content search
"Peter talks to his computer. He prefers it to typing, and particularly prefers it to pen and paper."
Movies near Evansville, IN
Notebook
Remind you about this?
Replace watch battery
Today
4:00 PM
photos

ENABLING CORTANA

The first time you click the Search box, Cortana offers to help you find information and organize your life. Here's how to get Cortana started.

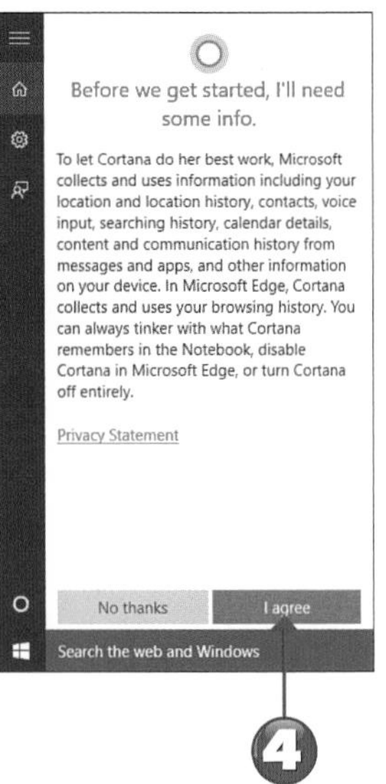

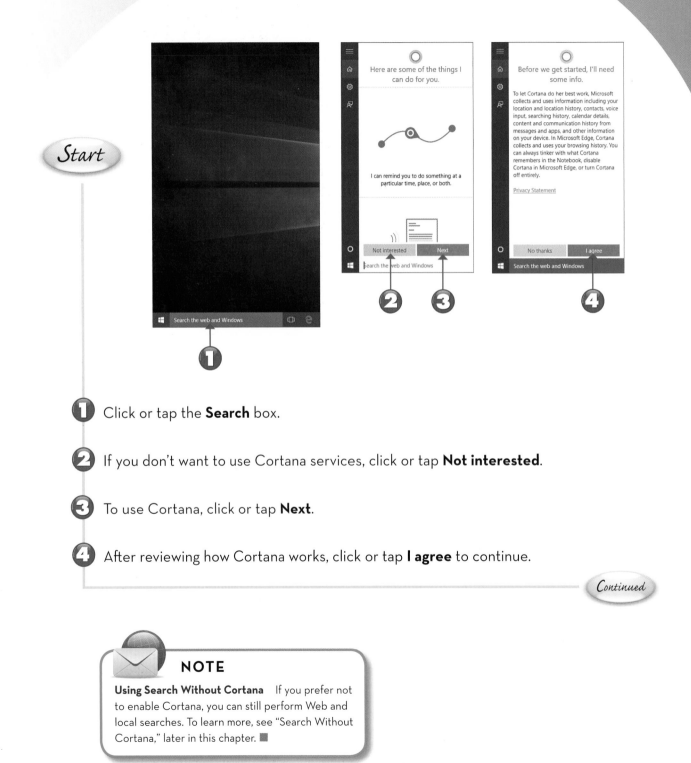

1. Click or tap the **Search** box.
2. If you don't want to use Cortana services, click or tap **Not interested**.
3. To use Cortana, click or tap **Next**.
4. After reviewing how Cortana works, click or tap **I agree** to continue.

Continued

NOTE

Using Search Without Cortana If you prefer not to enable Cortana, you can still perform Web and local searches. To learn more, see "Search Without Cortana," later in this chapter. ■

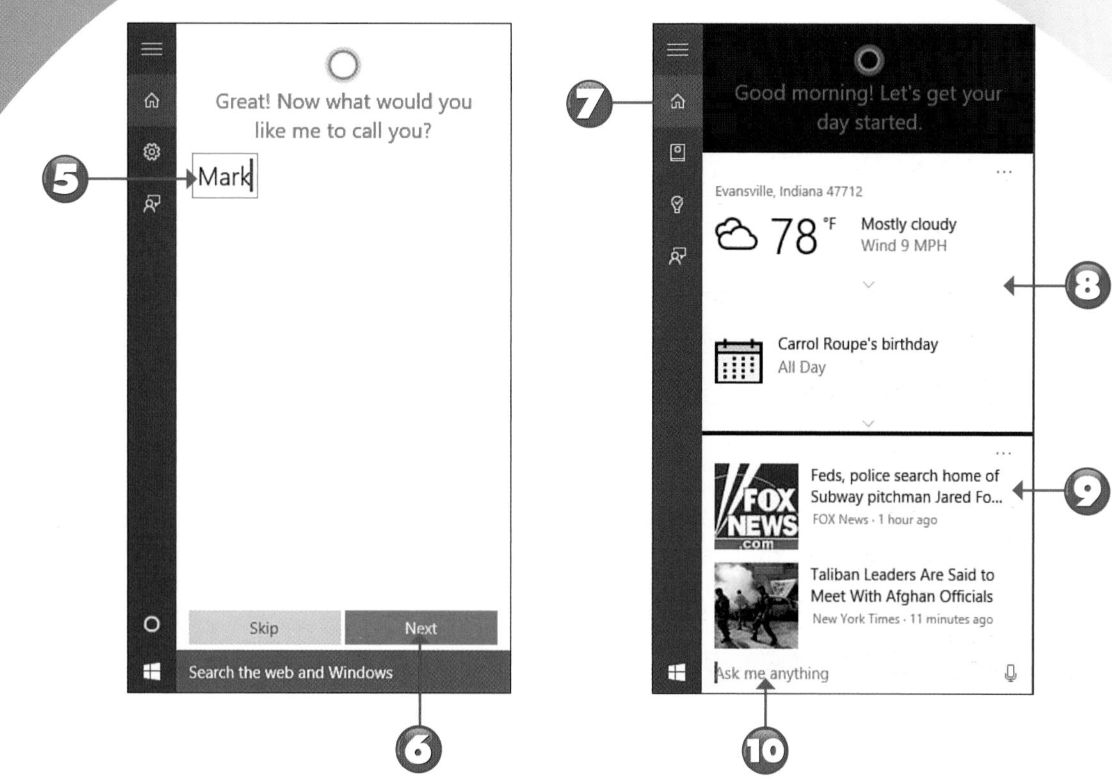

5. Enter your preferred name or nickname.

6. Click or tap **Next**.

7. Cortana opens its Home tab.

8. Local and personal calendar information appears at the top of the pane.

9. Selected news sources appear at the bottom of the pane.

10. Click or tap to search your system or the Web.

End

CONFIGURING CORTANA VOICE SEARCH

You can type or talk to Cortana—setting up Cortana for voice interaction doesn't take long. Here's how to do it.

Start

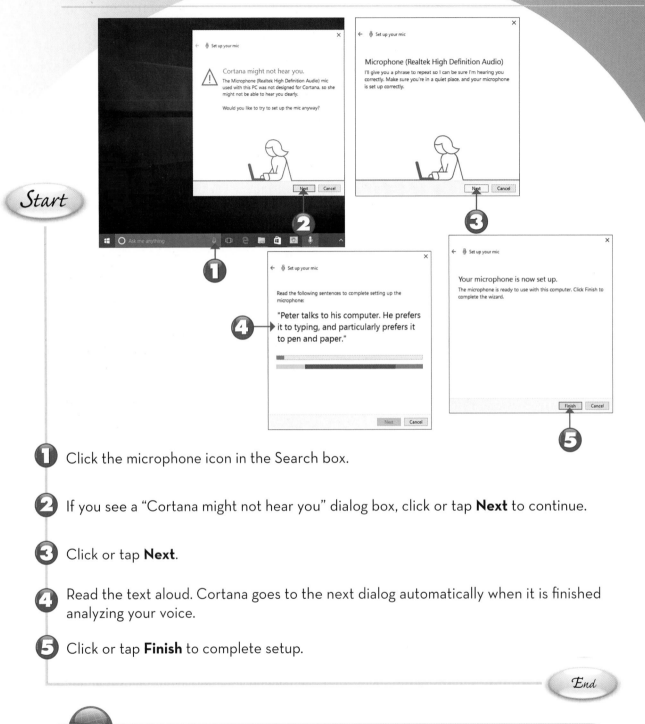

1. Click the microphone icon in the Search box.

2. If you see a "Cortana might not hear you" dialog box, click or tap **Next** to continue.

3. Click or tap **Next**.

4. Read the text aloud. Cortana goes to the next dialog automatically when it is finished analyzing your voice.

5. Click or tap **Finish** to complete setup.

End

NOTE

Troubleshooting Cortana Voice Setup If Cortana cannot detect your speech in step 4, make sure your built-in microphone is enabled and not muted, or that your plug-in microphone is plugged in and not muted. ■

SEARCHING WITH CORTANA

Cortana enables you to search by typing or by using your voice. Here's how to search by voice.

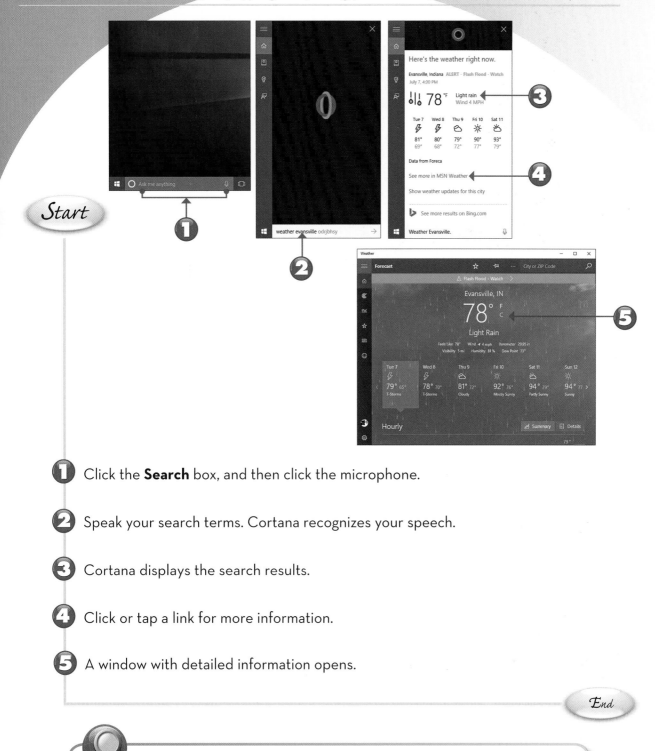

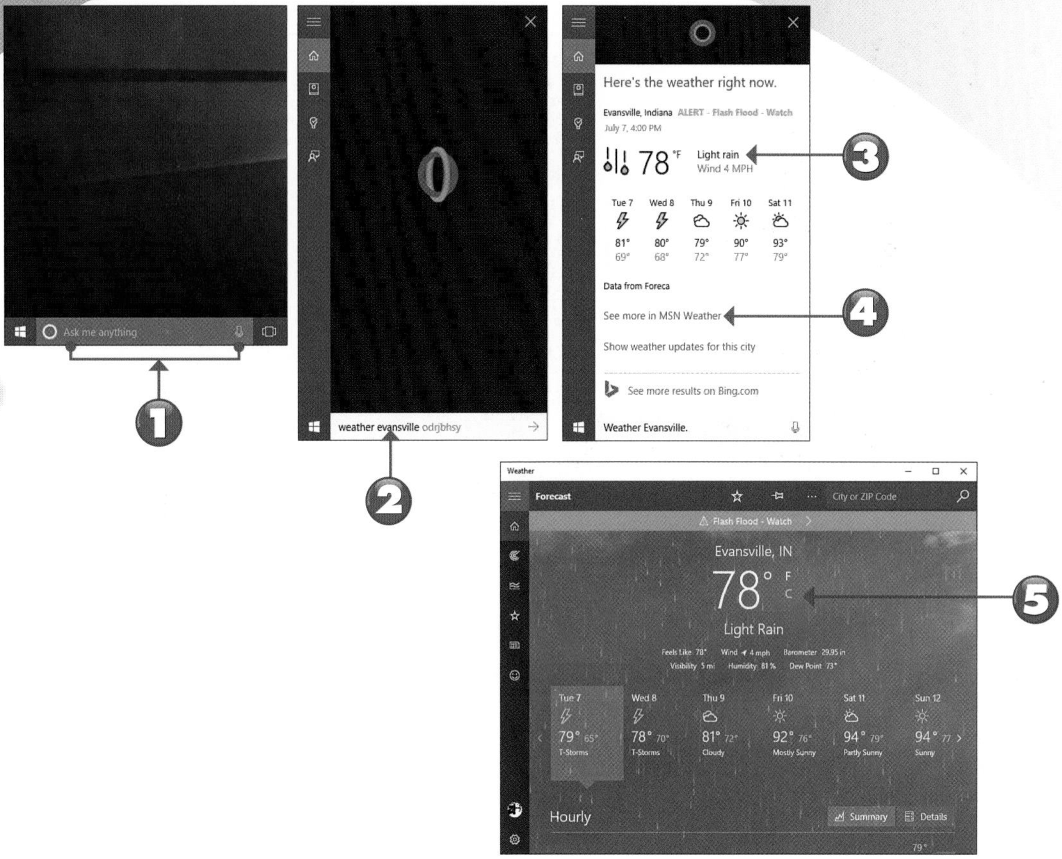

Start

1. Click the **Search** box, and then click the microphone.
2. Speak your search terms. Cortana recognizes your speech.
3. Cortana displays the search results.
4. Click or tap a link for more information.
5. A window with detailed information opens.

End

TIP

Opening Apps with Cortana After you set up Cortana voice support, you can use it to open apps. For example, click in the Search window and say "Open File Explorer." Cortana opens the app for you. ■

DISCOVERING CORTANA FEATURES

Cortana includes many features you can use to improve search results. Here's an overview.

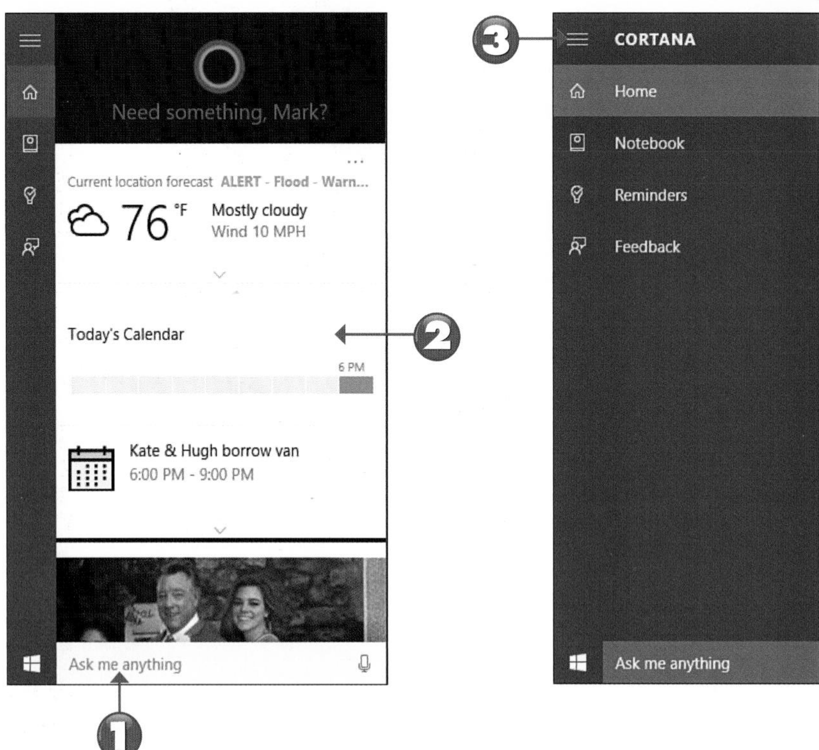

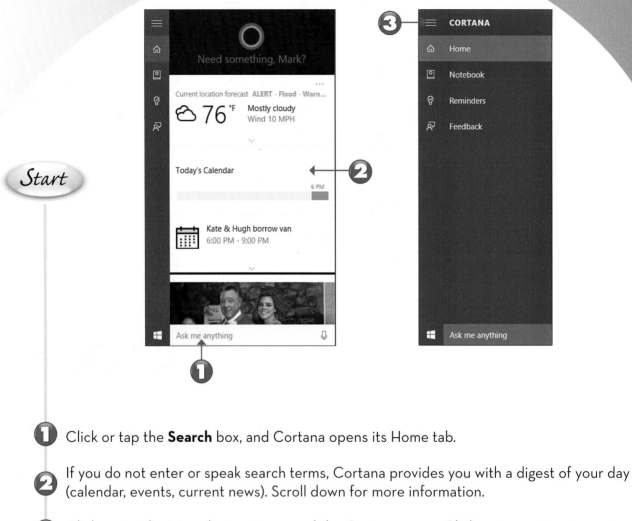

Start

1. Click or tap the **Search** box, and Cortana opens its Home tab.
2. If you do not enter or speak search terms, Cortana provides you with a digest of your day (calendar, events, current news). Scroll down for more information.
3. Click or tap the **Menu** button to expand the Cortana menu. Click or tap an item to go to that menu.

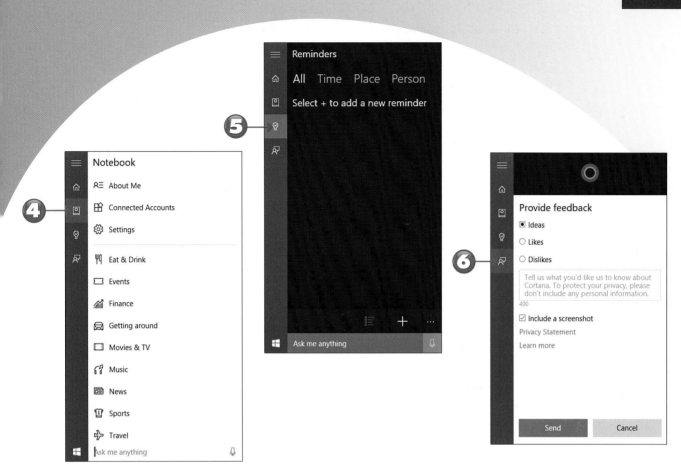

4. Click or tap the **Notebook** button if you want to provide Cortana with more information about your preferences.

5. Click or tap the **Reminders** button if you want Cortana to remind you of a particular time, place, or person.

6. Click or tap the **Feedback** button if you want to suggest improvements.

End

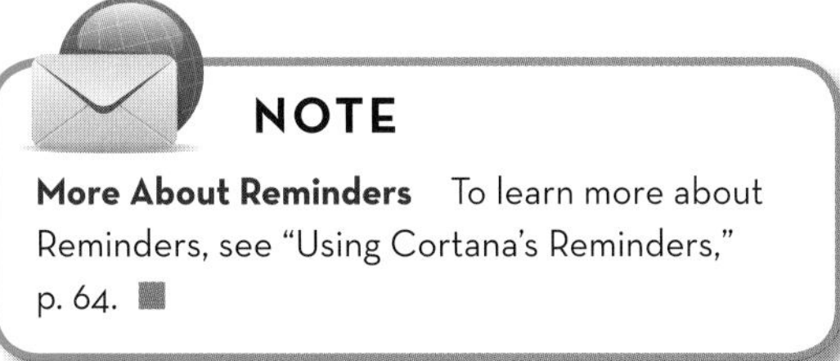

NOTE

More About Reminders To learn more about Reminders, see "Using Cortana's Reminders," p. 64. ■

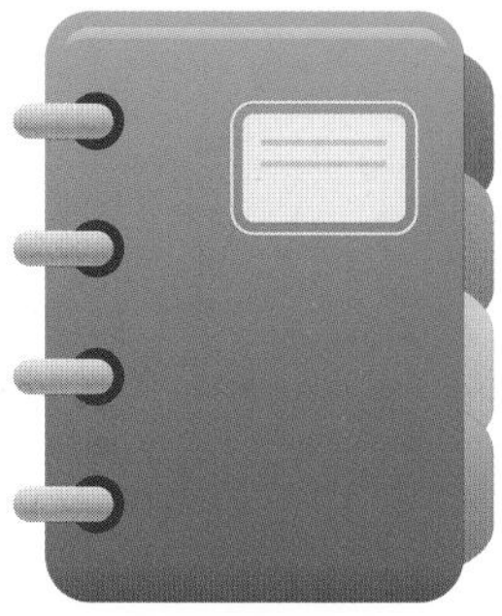

SEARCHING FOR FILES, APPS, AND SETTINGS

When you search (with or without Cortana running), your device is searched for matching files, apps, and settings before the Web is searched. Here's a typical example.

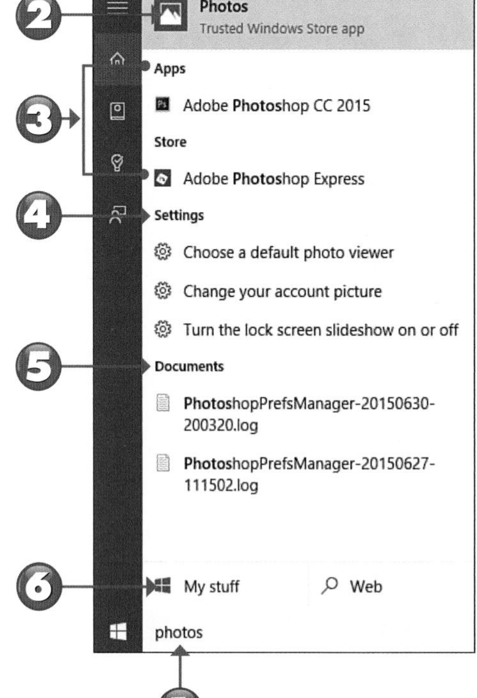

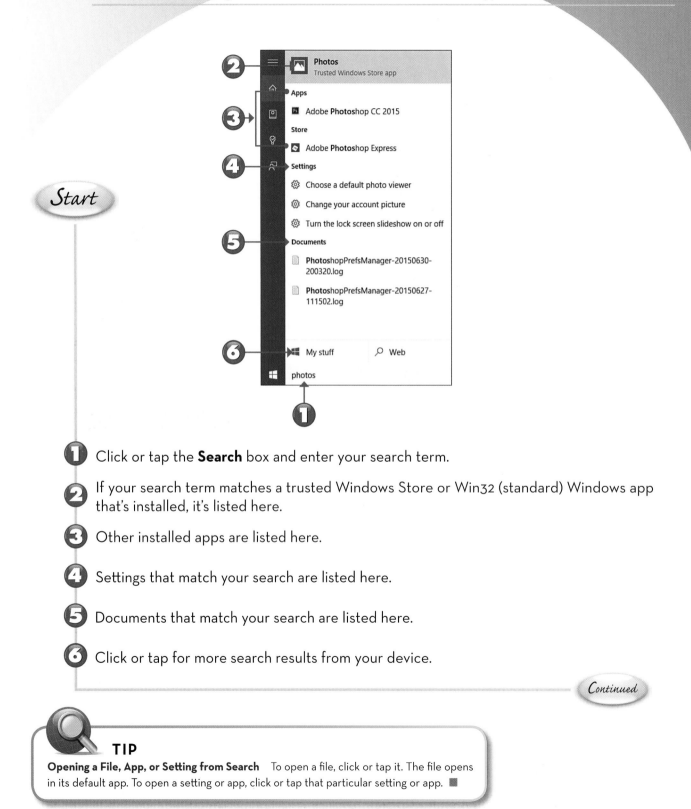

Start

1. Click or tap the **Search** box and enter your search term.
2. If your search term matches a trusted Windows Store or Win32 (standard) Windows app that's installed, it's listed here.
3. Other installed apps are listed here.
4. Settings that match your search are listed here.
5. Documents that match your search are listed here.
6. Click or tap for more search results from your device.

Continued

TIP

Opening a File, App, or Setting from Search To open a file, click or tap it. The file opens in its default app. To open a setting or app, click or tap that particular setting or app. ■

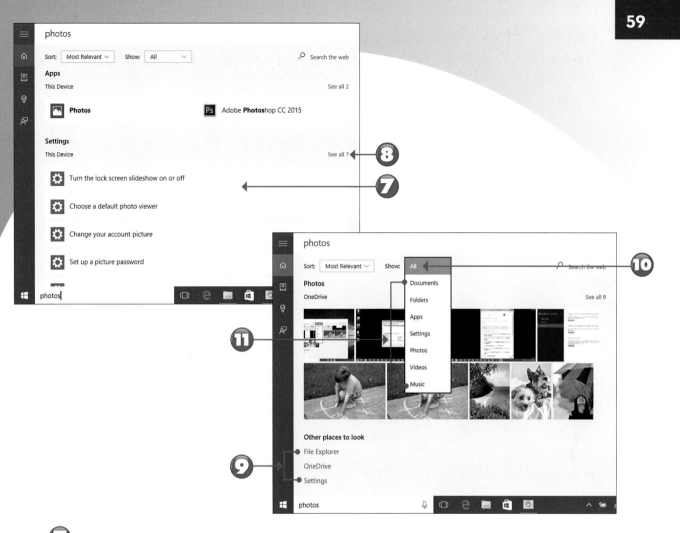

7. Scroll down to see all matches in all categories.

8. To see all matches in a particular category, click or tap **See all**.

9. Click or tap a location for more matches.

10. Click or tap **All** if you want to jump to a particular category.

11. Click or tap the category to jump to.

End

TIP

Sorting Options The default sort is Most Relevant. To change sort options, open the **Sort** menu.

IMPROVING WEB SEARCHES WITH CORTANA

You can start a web search with Cortana in two ways: directly from the Cortana Search window or by clicking the **Search the web** link visible in the previous lesson. In this lesson, you learn how your search terms affect your results.

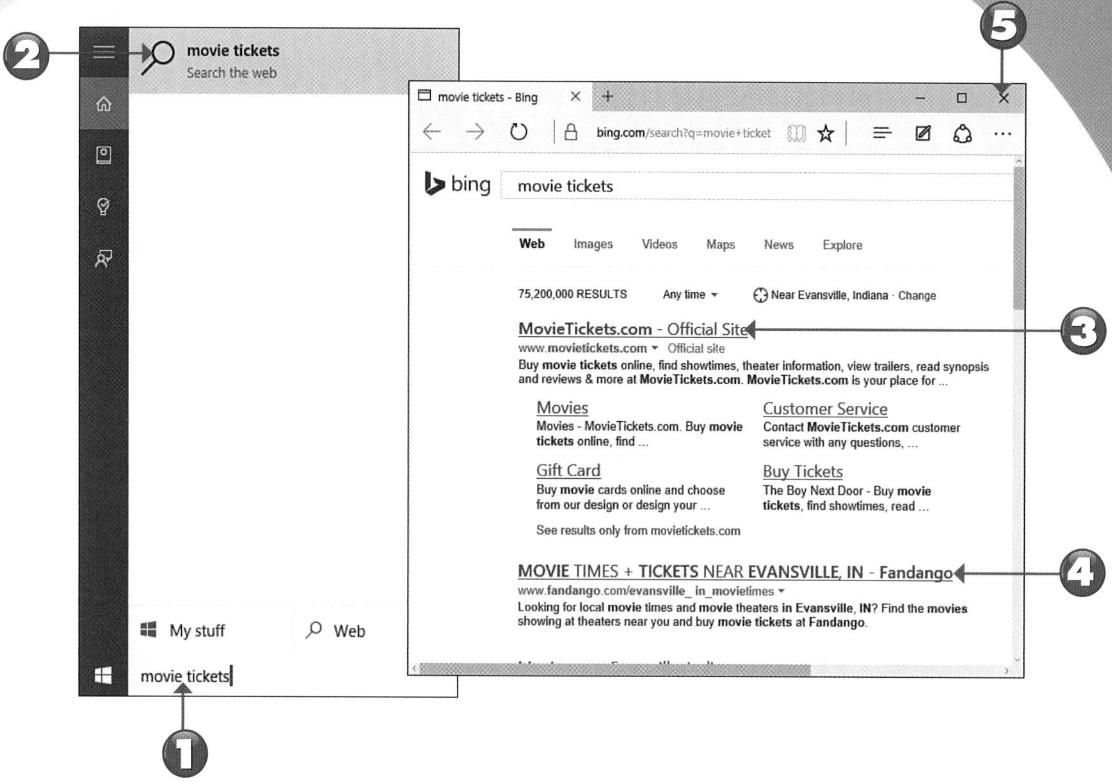

Start

1. Click or tap the **Search** box and enter your search terms.
2. If there are no matches on your device, click or tap the link for a web search.
3. If your search term finds a matching website, it is displayed first.
4. Cortana knows your location, so your results are also localized.
5. Click or tap to close the browser.

Continued

TIP

Cortana Learns from Your Searches When you do a web search with Cortana, be sure to click a link that best matches what you want. The more often you do this, the better Cortana gets at determining what you want to see. ■

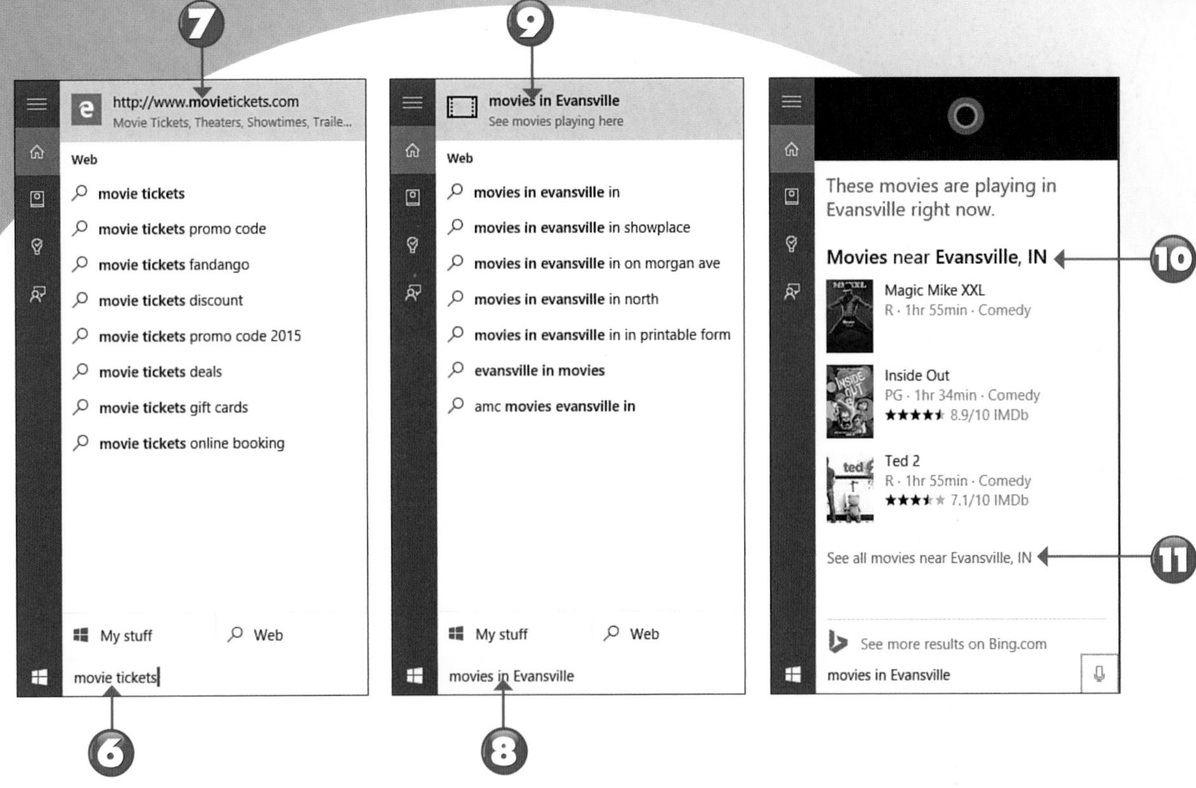

6. Enter the same search as in step 1.
7. The website found in the previous search is now listed first, followed by related searches. Click or tap one to open it.
8. Enter a localized search (for example, "movies in *city*").
9. Click or tap the link to see matches in your city.
10. Cortana displays matches in your city.
11. Click or tap the link for additional matches.

End

TEACHING CORTANA TO RECOGNIZE YOUR VOICE

As you learned in the previous lesson, Cortana learns from the searches you perform. You can make voice searches easier by using Cortana's Notebook feature to turn on "Hey, Cortana." Here's how

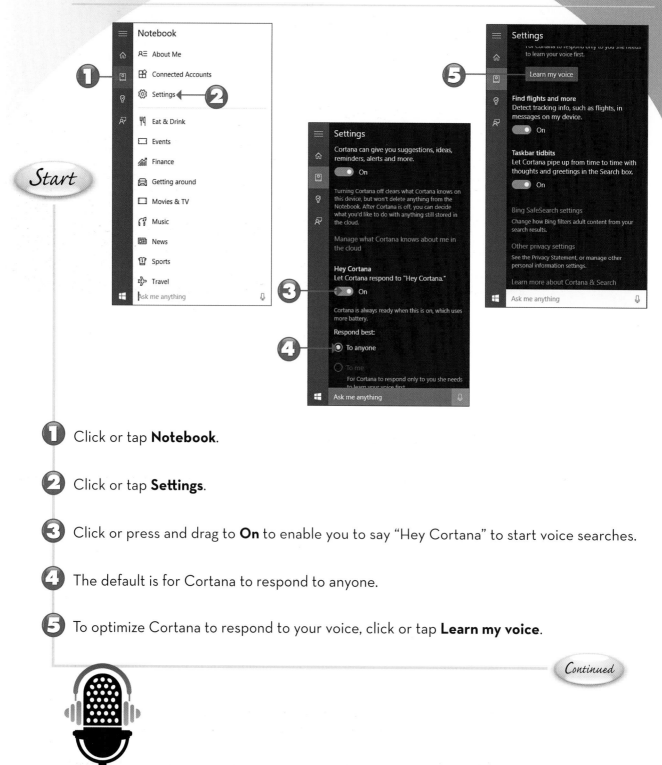

Start

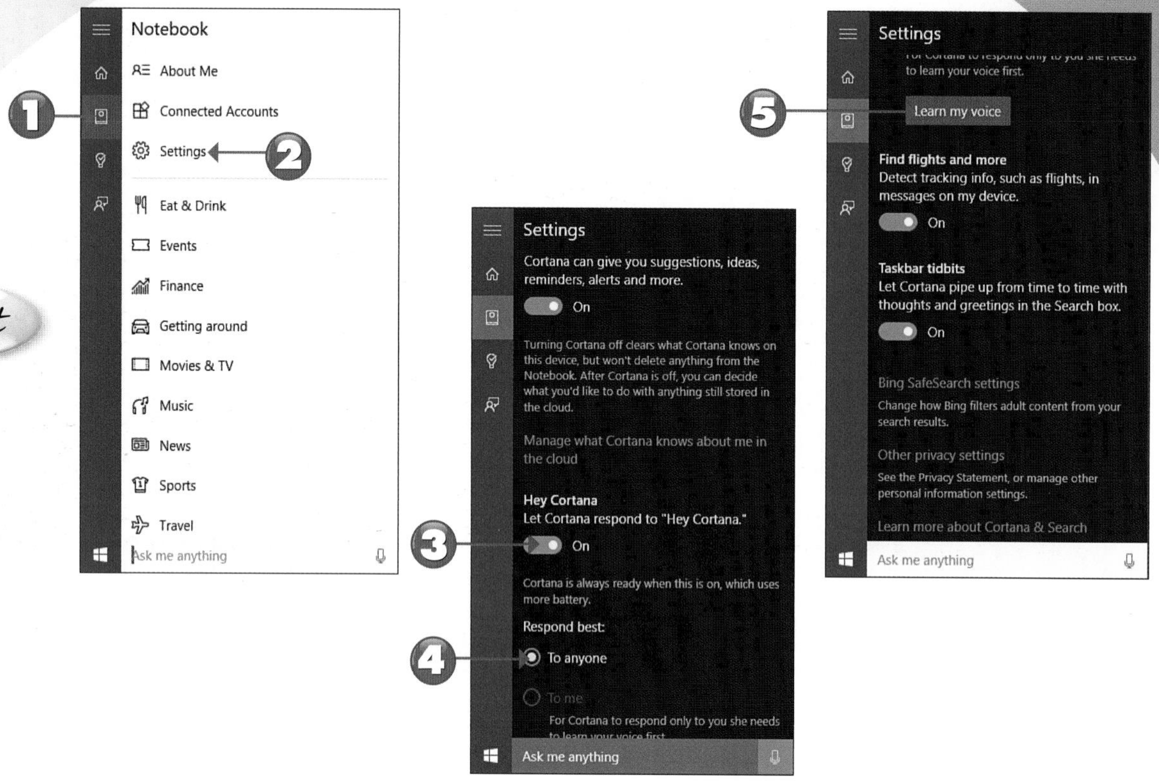

1. Click or tap **Notebook**.
2. Click or tap **Settings**.
3. Click or press and drag to **On** to enable you to say "Hey Cortana" to start voice searches.
4. The default is for Cortana to respond to anyone.
5. To optimize Cortana to respond to your voice, click or tap **Learn my voice**.

Continued

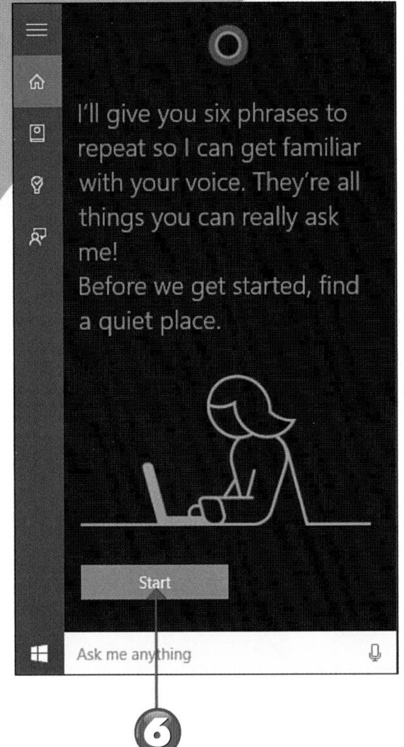

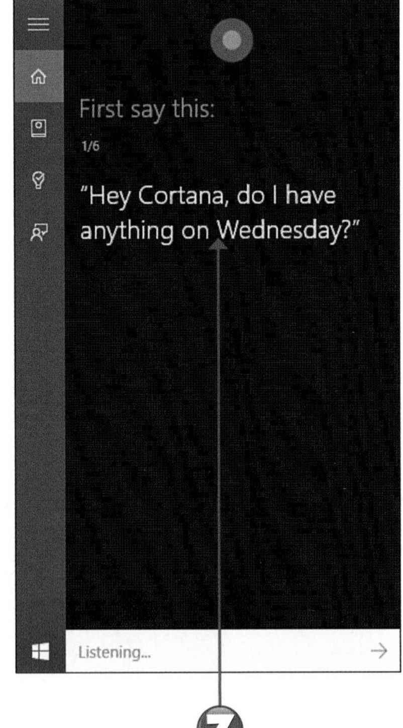

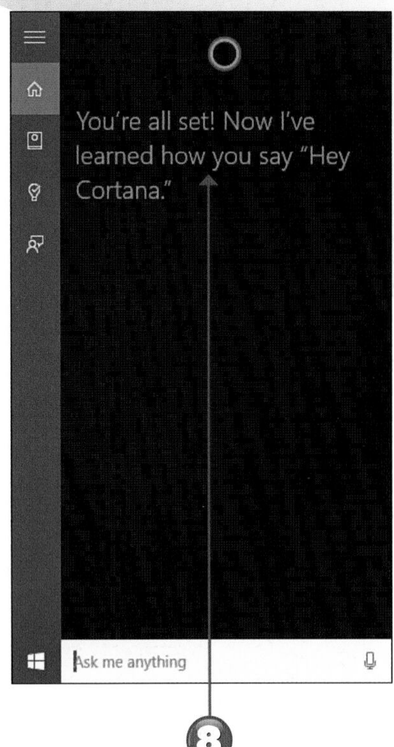

6. Read the instructions, then click or tap **Start**.
7. Speak each phrase Cortana displays. Cortana displays the next one after it recognizes the current phrase.
8. When you see this, Cortana has learned your voice. You can start a search by saying, "Hey Cortana," followed by your search or command.

End

TIP

Use Notebook to Improve Cortana's Results To improve Cortana's search results, click or tap a topic listed in Notebook (see step 2). Turn off or turn on items (recommendations, events, activities) as desired, and then click or tap **Save**. ■

USING CORTANA'S REMINDERS

You can also use Cortana to remind you about something or someone. Here's how.

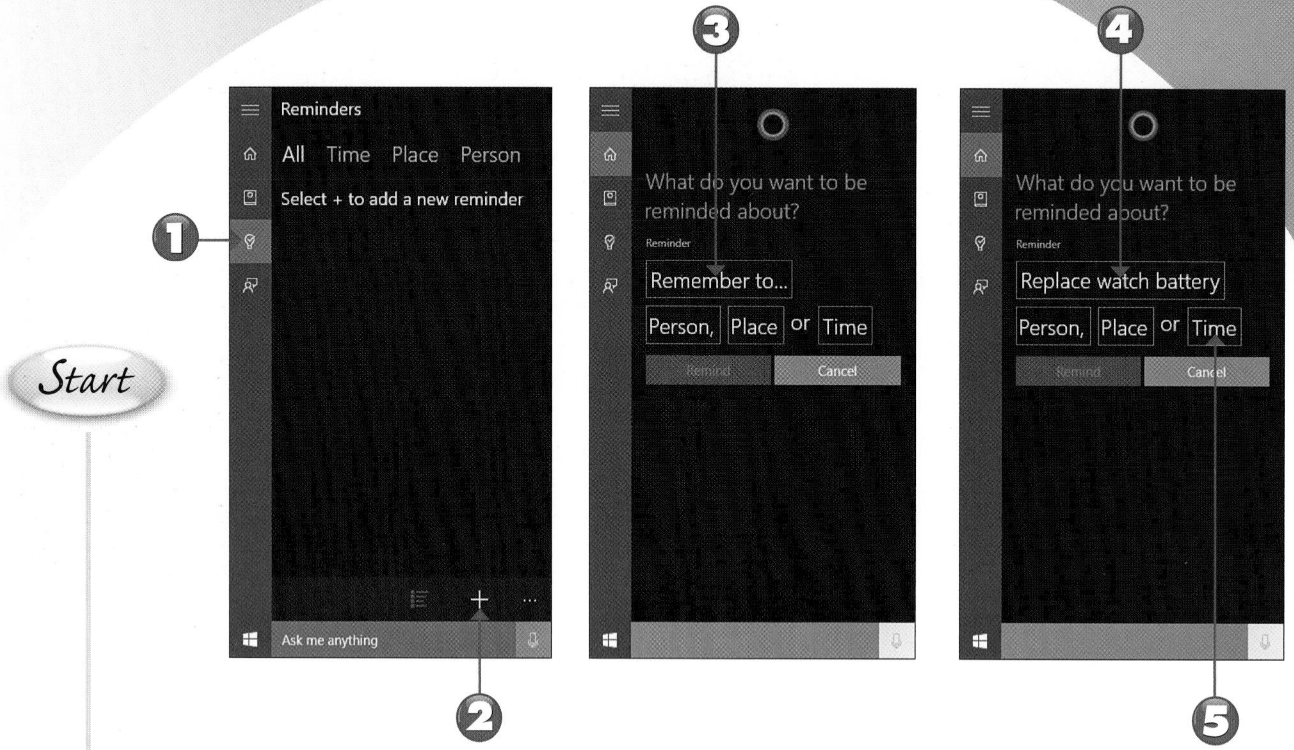

Start

1. Click or tap **Reminders**.
2. Click or tap the plus (+) sign to add a new reminder.
3. Click or tap **Remember to**.
4. Enter what you want to be reminded about.
5. Click or tap **Time** to select when you want to be reminded.

Continued

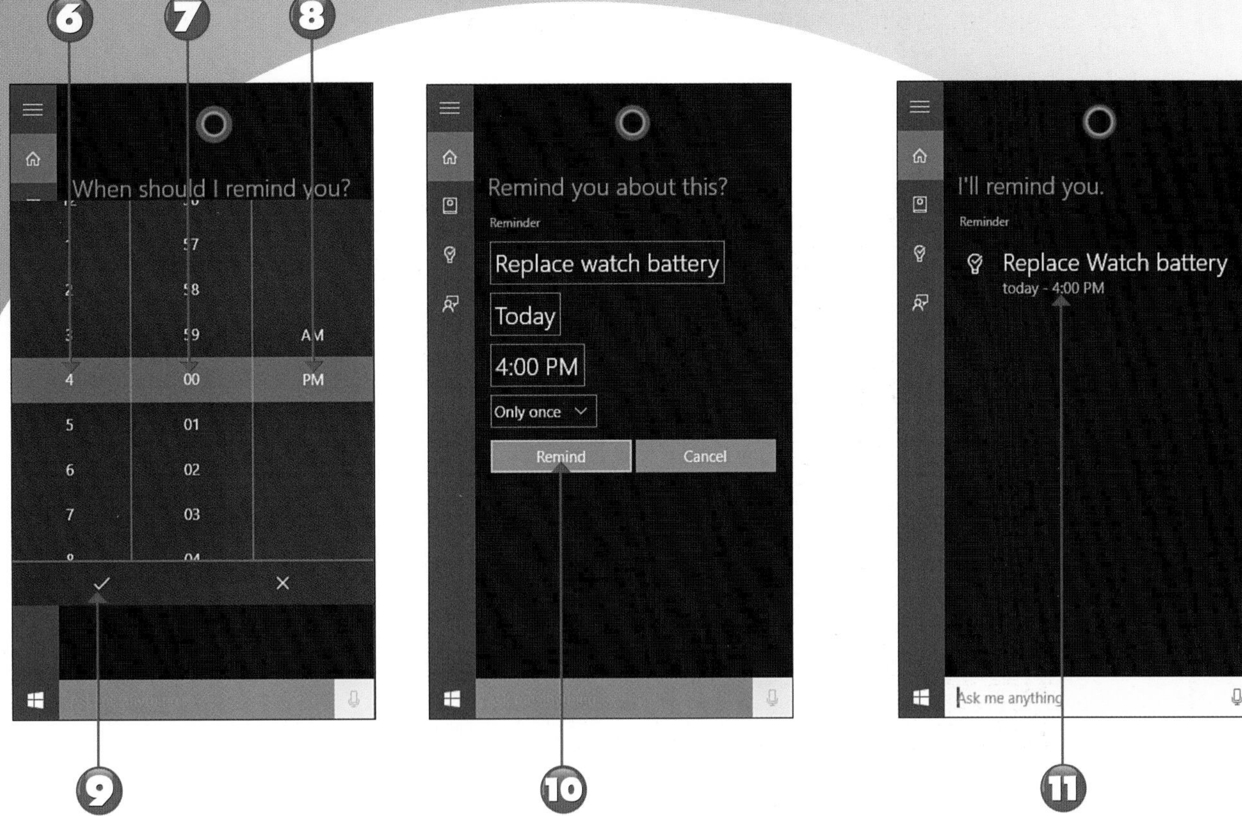

6. Scroll to select the hour.
7. Scroll to select the minute.
8. Select AM or PM.
9. Click or tap the check box to complete.
10. Click or tap **Remind** to complete the reminder.
11. Cortana reminds you at the time specified.

End

VIEWING A REMINDER

When you set a reminder, Cortana uses the Notification center to display it. Here's a typical example of how the reminder appears when it is triggered.

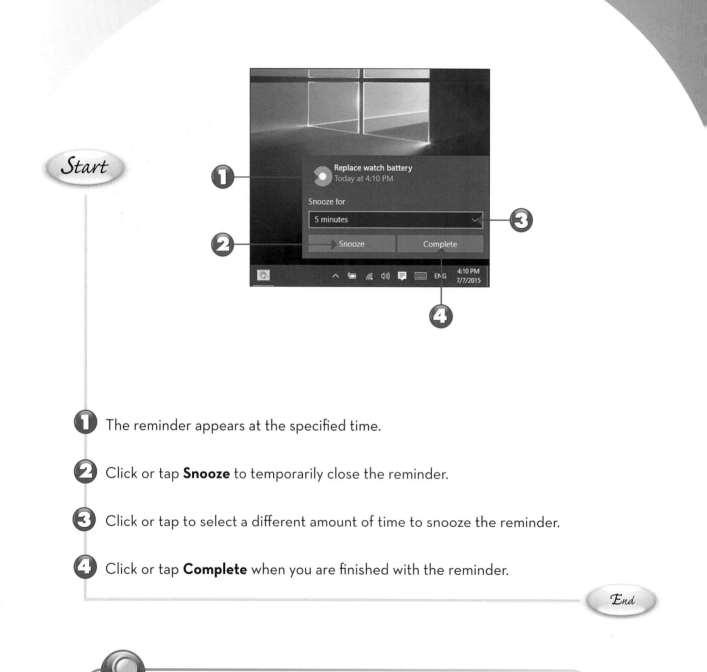

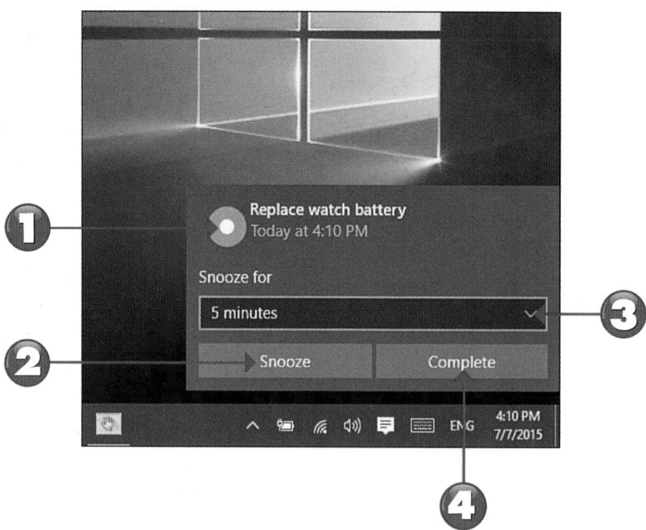

1. The reminder appears at the specified time.
2. Click or tap **Snooze** to temporarily close the reminder.
3. Click or tap to select a different amount of time to snooze the reminder.
4. Click or tap **Complete** when you are finished with the reminder.

End

TIP

Reviewing Reminders Before They Are Triggered To see upcoming reminders, click or tap the **Notifications/Quick Actions** icon in the taskbar. If you click or tap the **Search** box, reminders for that day are listed along with other news and information if you don't perform a search.

TURNING OFF CORTANA

If you prefer not to use Cortana, you can avoid ever starting it by clicking or tapping **Not interested** when Cortana offers to set itself up. However, you can also turn off Cortana after you start using it. Here's how.

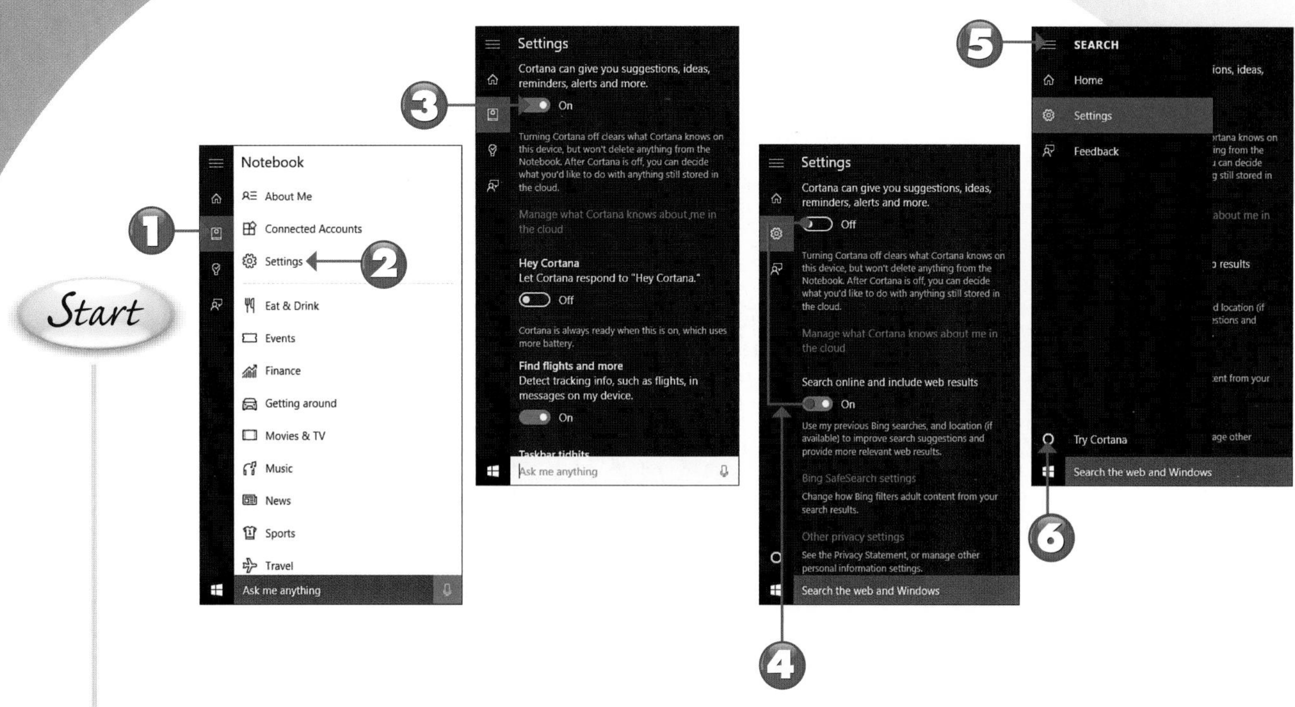

1. Click or tap **Notebook**.

2. Click or tap **Settings**.

3. Click or press and drag to **Off** to turn off Cortana.

4. Cortana is turned off, but you can still search online and include Web results.

5. Click or tap to see available menu items.

6. If you want to use Cortana again, click or tap **Try Cortana**.

End

CAUTION

Cortana Might Be Off, but the Cloud Still Remembers To remove stored Cortana and other Microsoft search information, click or tap **Manage what Cortana knows about me in the cloud**. Use the two **Clear** buttons on this page to remove this information.

SEARCH WITHOUT CORTANA

If you disable Cortana but retain Search's capability to search the Web as well as your device, Search works a little differently, as you learn in this lesson.

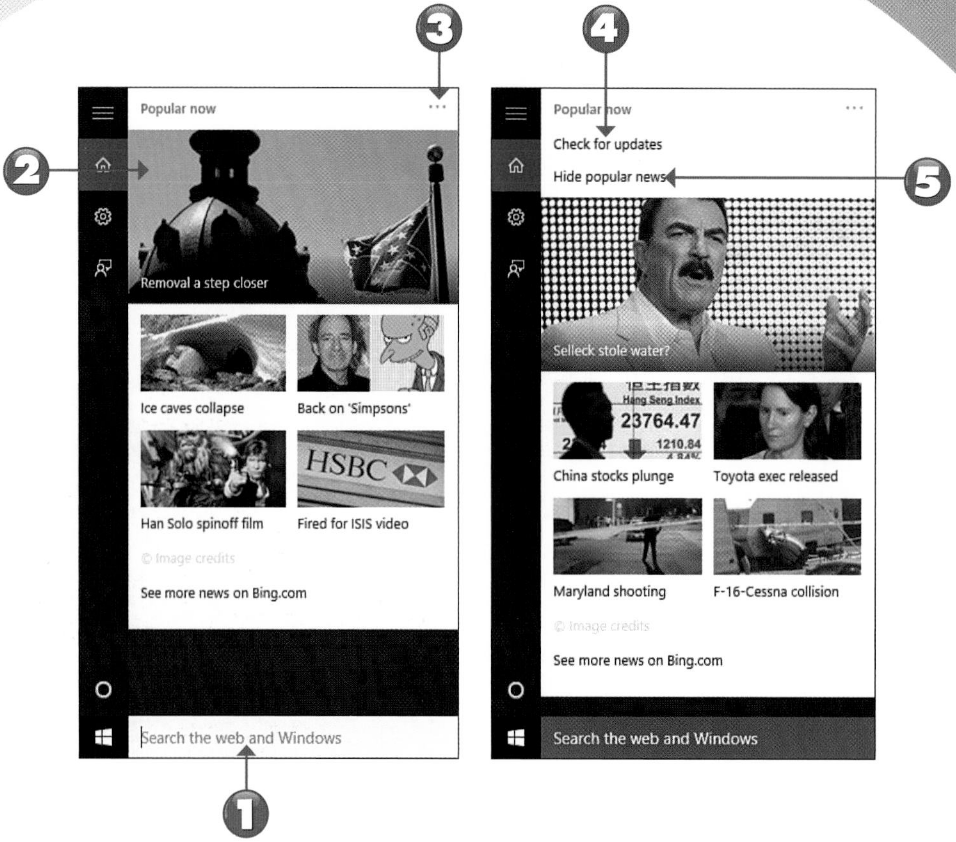

Start

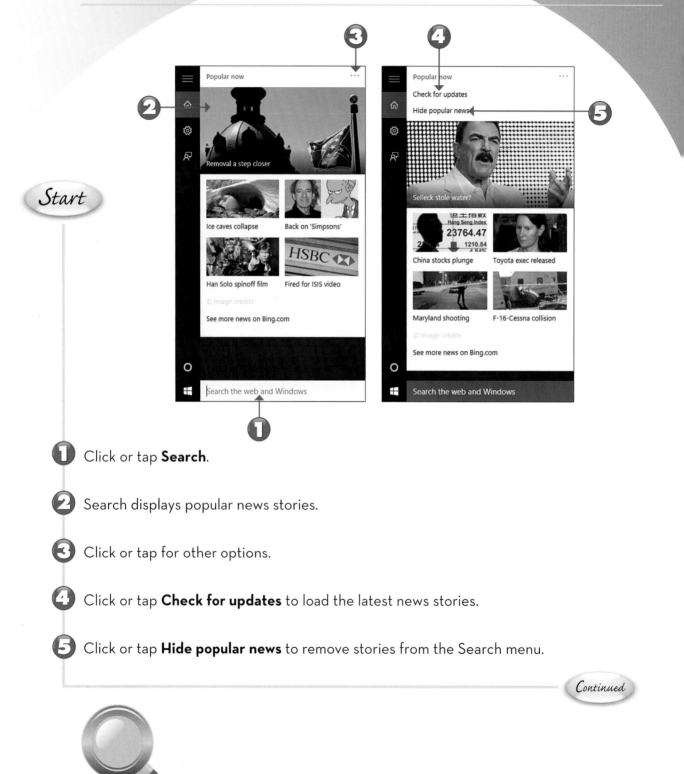

1. Click or tap **Search**.
2. Search displays popular news stories.
3. Click or tap for other options.
4. Click or tap **Check for updates** to load the latest news stories.
5. Click or tap **Hide popular news** to remove stories from the Search menu.

Continued

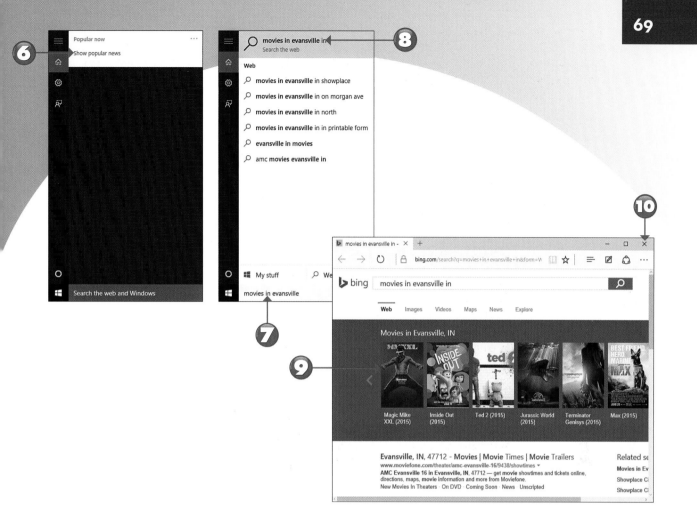

6. Click or tap **Show popular news** to restore the latest news stories to the Search menu.
7. Click or tap and enter search text.
8. If there are no local matches, the leading Web search is listed at the top of the Search dialog.
9. Online search matches are displayed.
10. Click or tap to close the browser.

End

NOTE

Local Search the Same, With or Without Cortana You work with local search results (files, apps, settings found on your device) the same way whether Cortana is enabled or not. For details, see "Searching for Files, Apps, and Settings," p. 58. ■

RUNNING APPS

Windows 10 includes both desktop apps (the same types of apps found in Windows 8.1 and earlier versions that run from the Windows desktop) and Universal apps, which are optimized for touchscreens. Both types of apps are run from the Start menu. This chapter shows you how to locate the app you want, how to switch between running apps, how to run apps in full-screen or windowed modes, how to adjust the window size, how to select the active app, and how to close an app when you're finished.

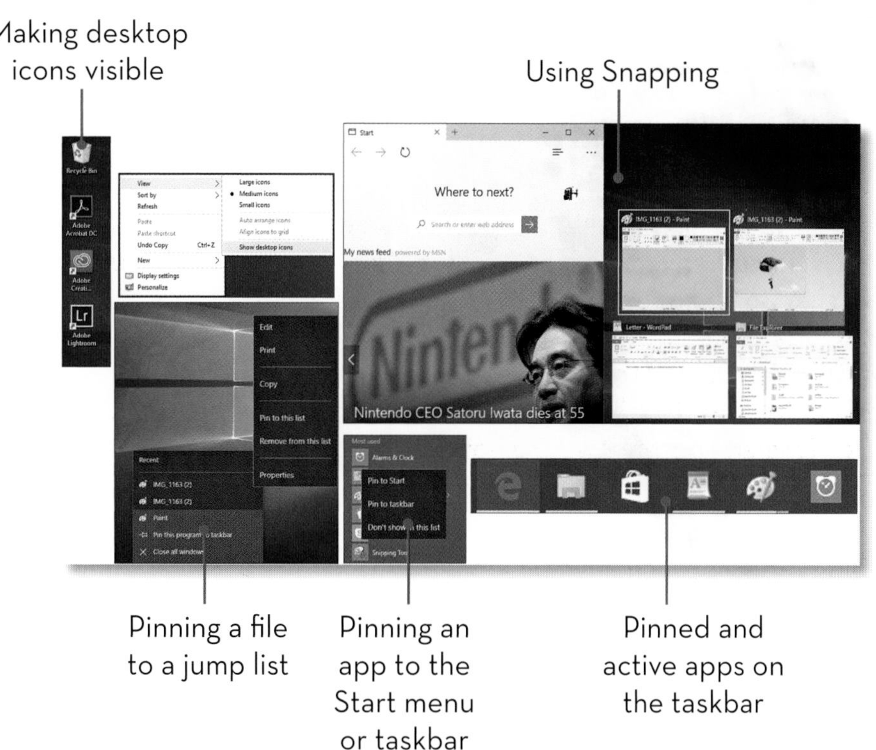

Making desktop icons visible
Using Snapping
Where to next?
Nintendo CEO Satoru Iwata dies at 55
Pinning a file to a jump list
Pinning an app to the Start menu or taskbar
Pinned and active apps on the taskbar

OPENING AND CLOSING THE ALL APPS MENU

The Start menu includes an automatically generated list called Most Used. You can also find many Universal apps on the right side of the menu. If you can't find the app you want in these locations, open the All Apps menu. Here's how.

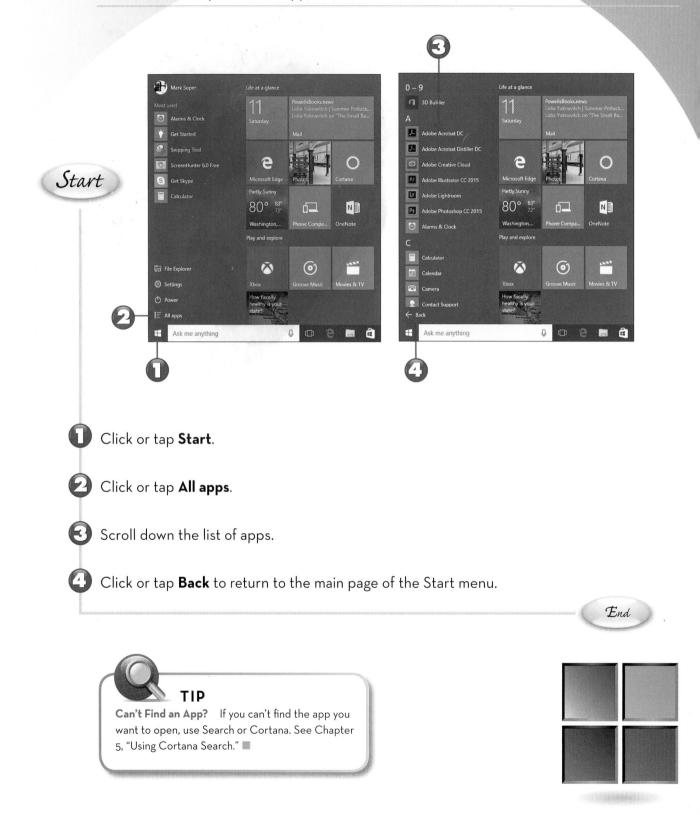

1. Click or tap **Start**.
2. Click or tap **All apps**.
3. Scroll down the list of apps.
4. Click or tap **Back** to return to the main page of the Start menu.

End

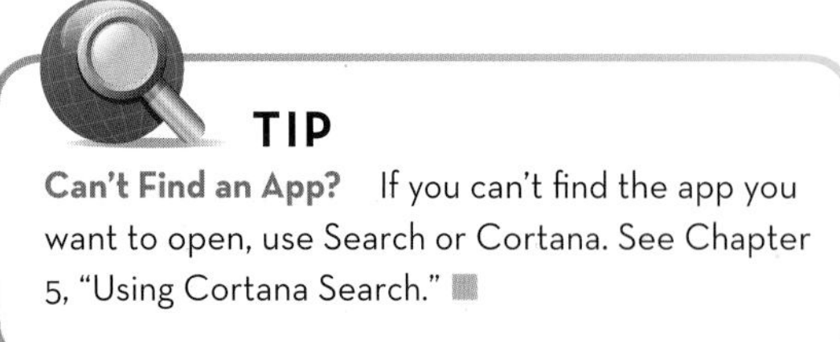

TIP

Can't Find an App? If you can't find the app you want to open, use Search or Cortana. See Chapter 5, "Using Cortana Search."

STARTING AN APP FROM THE START MENU

Starting an app from the Start menu is simple. Here's how.

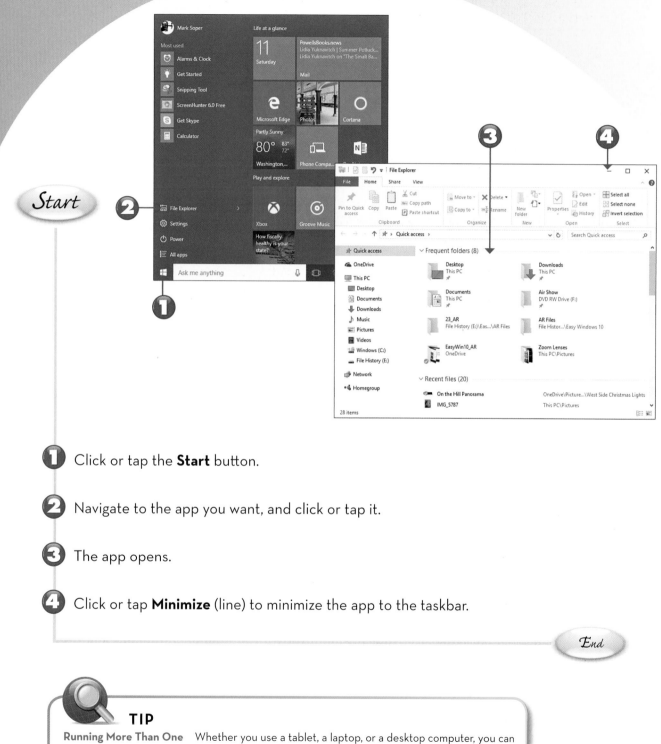

1. Click or tap the **Start** button.
2. Navigate to the app you want, and click or tap it.
3. The app opens.
4. Click or tap **Minimize** (line) to minimize the app to the taskbar.

TIP

Running More Than One Whether you use a tablet, a laptop, or a desktop computer, you can run several apps at the same time. Just repeat the steps in this task to open other apps.

OPENING AN APP FROM ALL APPS

The All Apps menu is where most Windows 10 apps and all apps you install are located. Here's how to start an app from that menu (in this example, the Paint app).

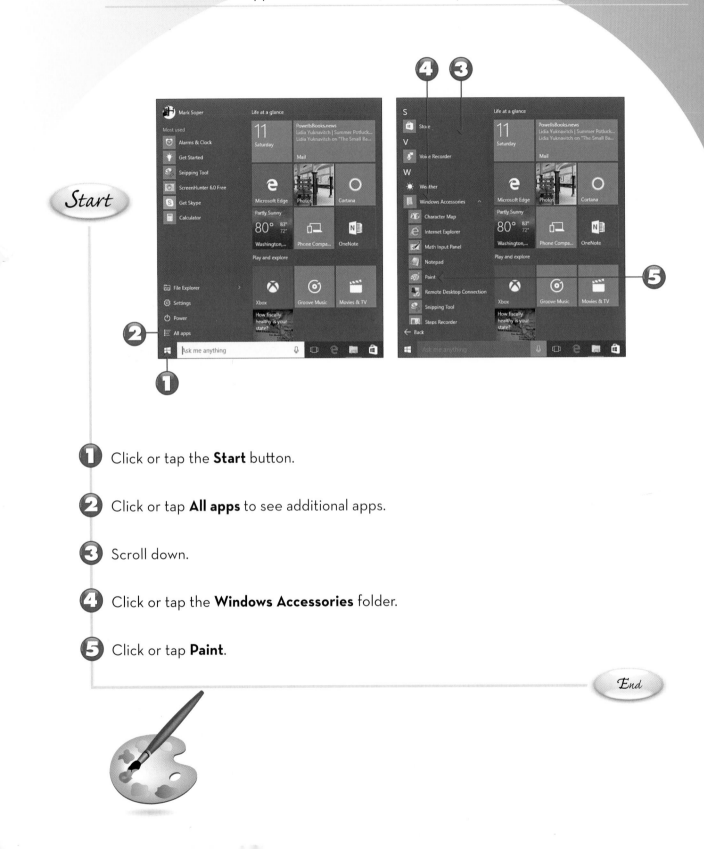

1. Click or tap the **Start** button.
2. Click or tap **All apps** to see additional apps.
3. Scroll down.
4. Click or tap the **Windows Accessories** folder.
5. Click or tap **Paint**.

End

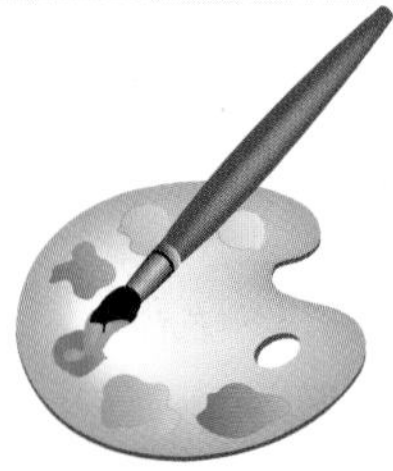

OPENING A FILE FROM WITHIN AN APP

The Paint app is a typical example of a traditional desktop app (also called a Win32 app), which is how Microsoft refers to apps that work the same way as in Windows 7 and earlier versions. The File menu works in a similar fashion in other desktop apps in Windows, such as WordPad and Notepad. This exercise explains how to open a file after starting an app.

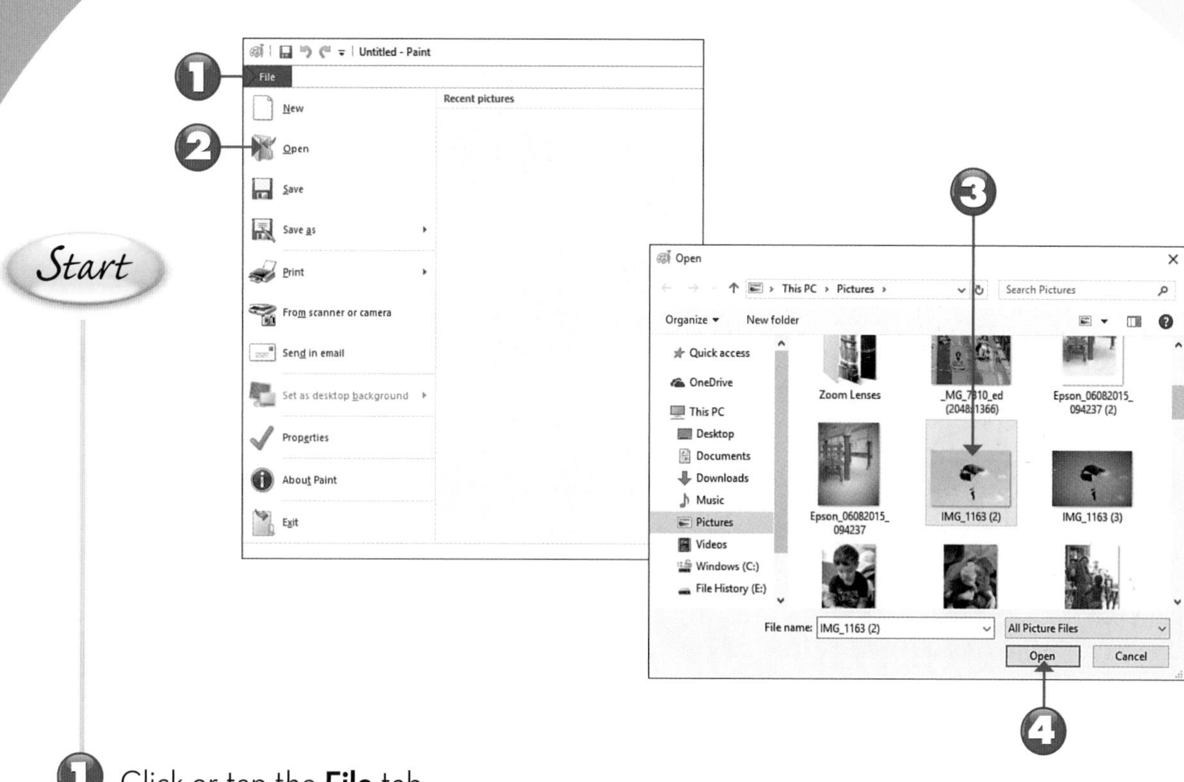

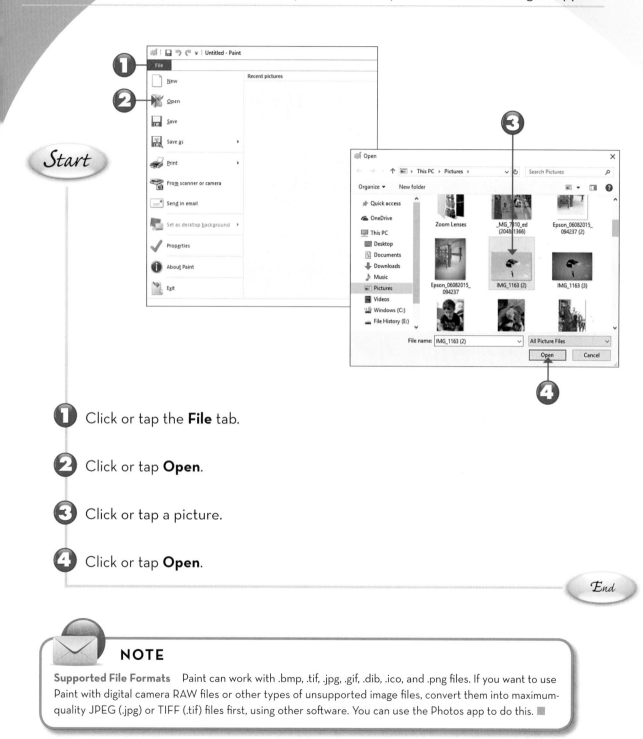

1. Click or tap the **File** tab.
2. Click or tap **Open**.
3. Click or tap a picture.
4. Click or tap **Open**.

End

NOTE

Supported File Formats Paint can work with .bmp, .tif, .jpg, .gif, .dib, .ico, and .png files. If you want to use Paint with digital camera RAW files or other types of unsupported image files, convert them into maximum-quality JPEG (.jpg) or TIFF (.tif) files first, using other software. You can use the Photos app to do this. ■

MAXIMIZING AN APP WINDOW

Some apps start in full-screen view (maximized), whereas others start in a window. If you prefer to have an app use the entire screen, you can maximize it. Here's how.

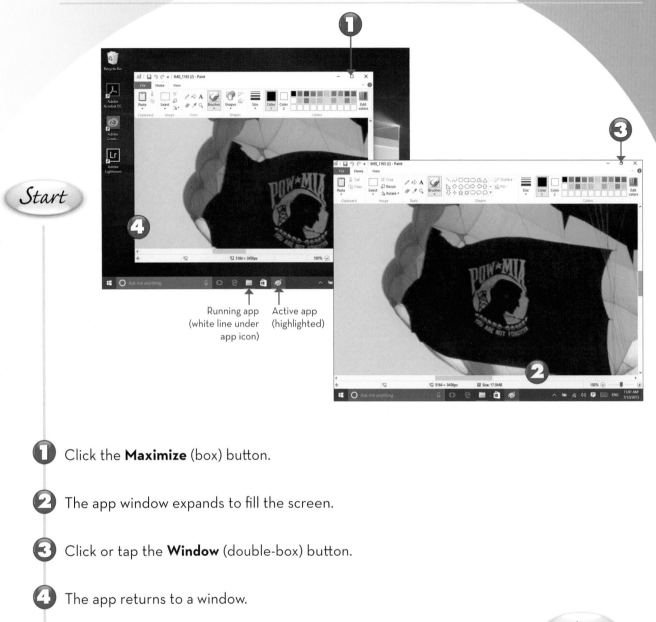

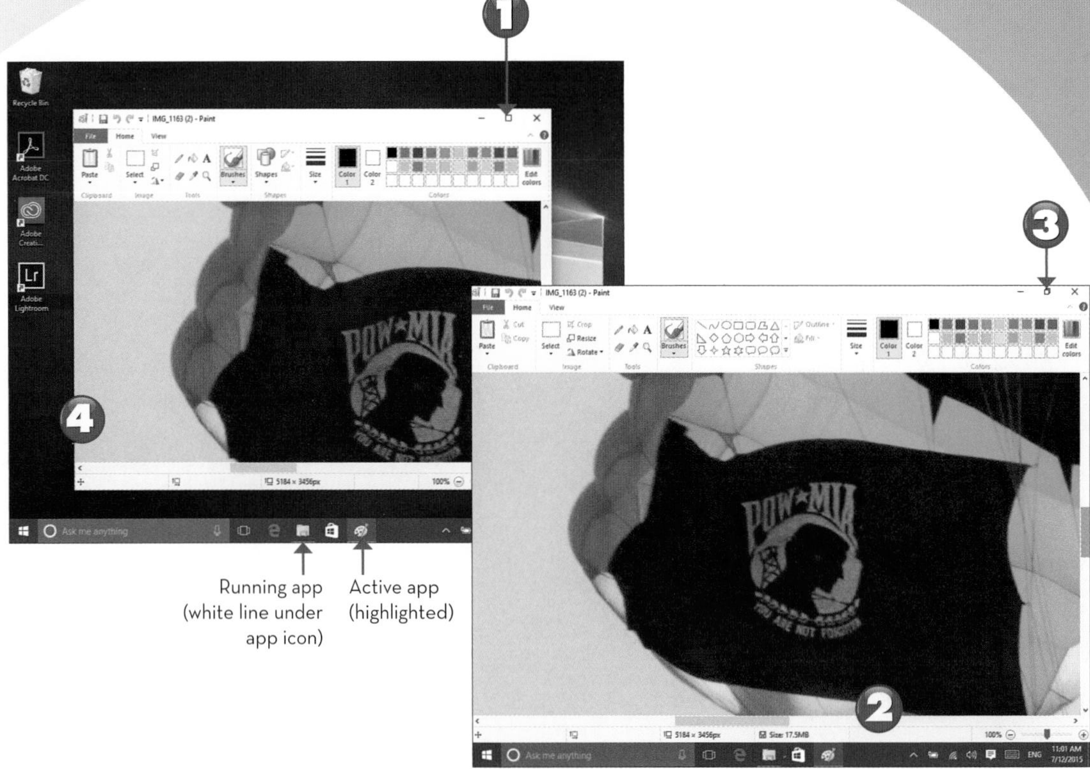

Start

1. Click the **Maximize** (box) button.
2. The app window expands to fill the screen.
3. Click or tap the **Window** (double-box) button.
4. The app returns to a window.

STARTING AN APP FROM SEARCH

As an alternative to scrolling through the Start menu for an app you use occasionally, you can search for the app. This example demonstrates how to search for Windows 10's simple word processing program, WordPad.

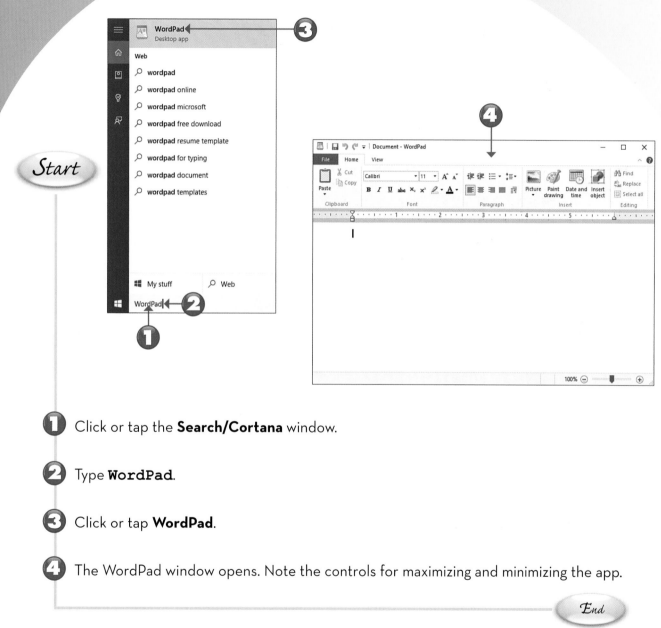

1. Click or tap the **Search/Cortana** window.
2. Type **WordPad**.
3. Click or tap **WordPad**.
4. The WordPad window opens. Note the controls for maximizing and minimizing the app.

SWITCHING BETWEEN APPS WITH THE TASKBAR

Windows 10 can run two or more apps at the same time. In this lesson, you learn how to switch between apps by using the taskbar.

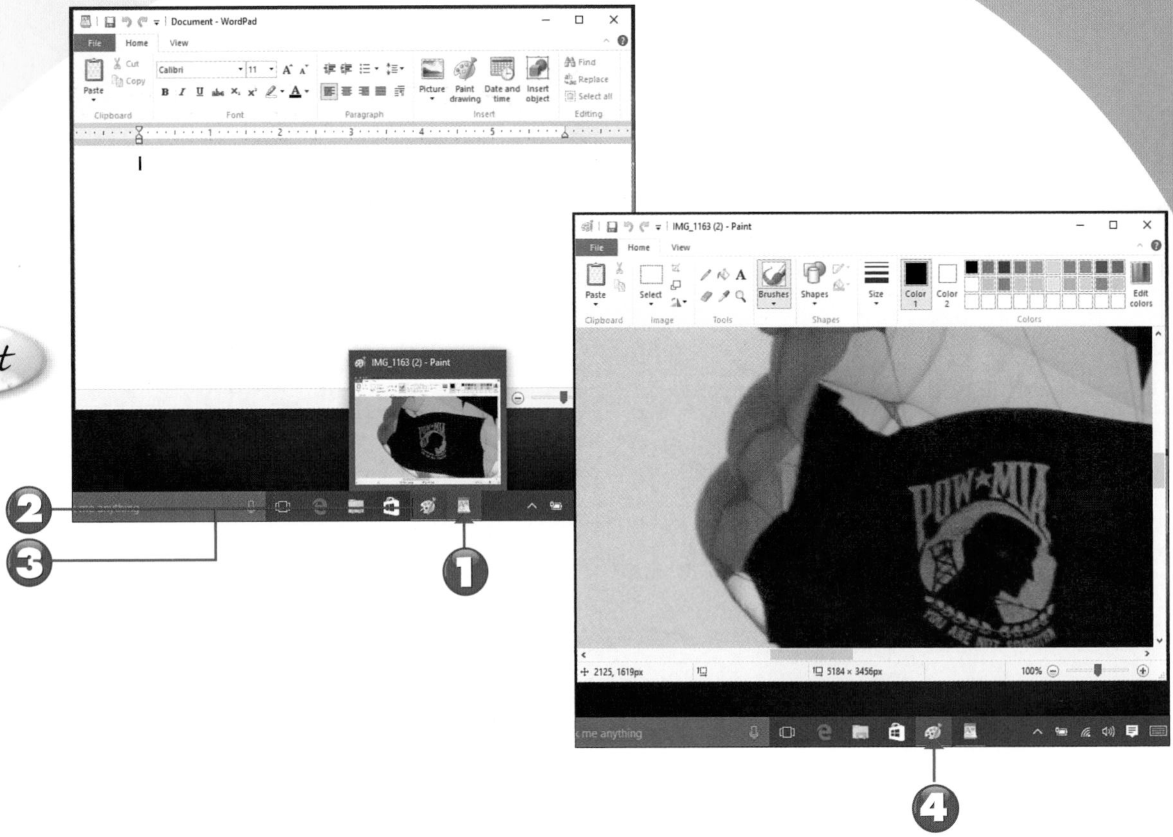

Start

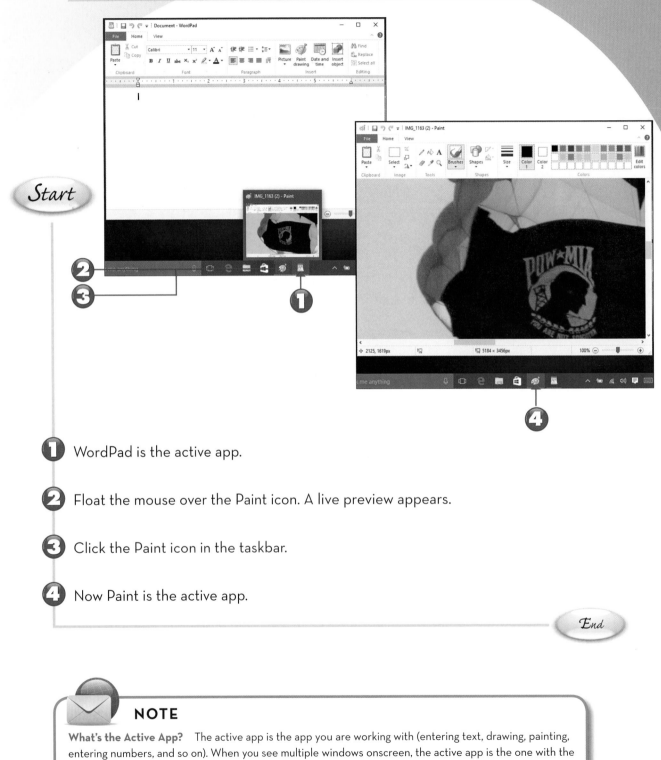

1. WordPad is the active app.
2. Float the mouse over the Paint icon. A live preview appears.
3. Click the Paint icon in the taskbar.
4. Now Paint is the active app.

End

NOTE

What's the Active App? The active app is the app you are working with (entering text, drawing, painting, entering numbers, and so on). When you see multiple windows onscreen, the active app is the one with the highlighted taskbar icon (compare WordPad in step 1 to Paint in step 4).

SWITCHING BETWEEN APPS WITH A TOUCHSCREEN

If you use a touchscreen device, you can swipe in from the left to switch between apps. Here's how to use this feature.

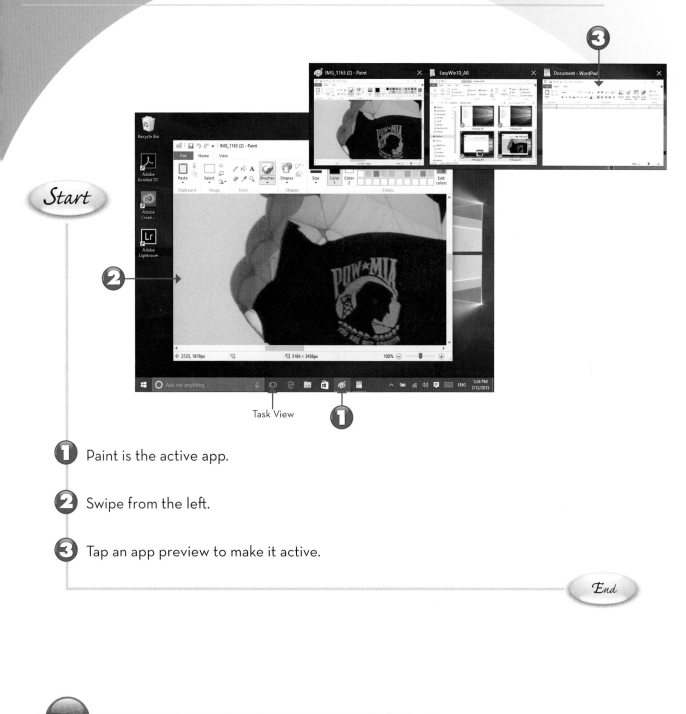

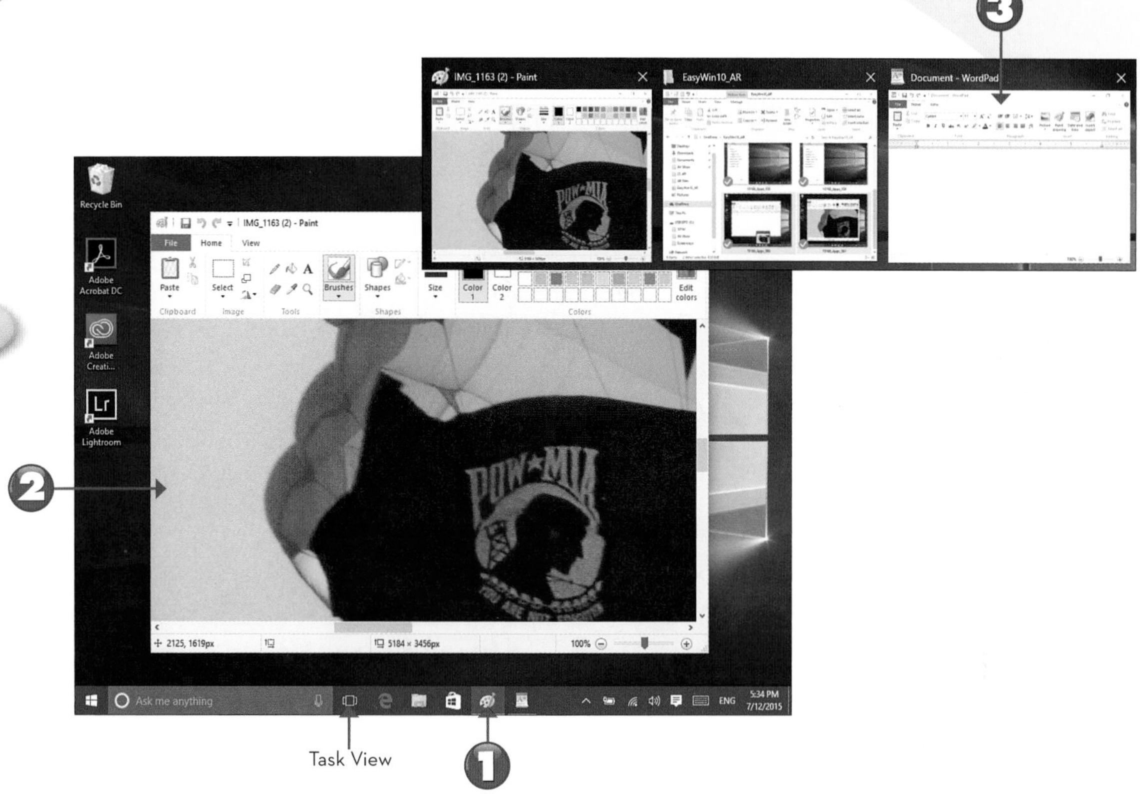

1. Paint is the active app.
2. Swipe from the left.
3. Tap an app preview to make it active.

NOTE

Using the Task View Button Instead of swiping, you can click or tap the **Task View** button (see step 2 in the previous task) to display active apps to choose from.

SWITCHING BETWEEN APPS WITH THE KEYBOARD

If you'd rather use the keyboard to switch between apps, you can do it with Windows 10. Here's how.

Start

1. Press **Alt+Tab** on the keyboard.
2. Repeat step 1 until the app you want is highlighted.
3. Release the keys to make this app active.

End

NOTE

Windows+Tab and Arrow Keys You can also use **Windows+Tab** to see currently open apps. Use the left- and right-arrow keys to highlight the app you want to use. ■

RESIZING AN APP

When you run an app in a window, the normal window size might not be what you want. If you use a mouse on a laptop or desktop PC that does not have a touchscreen, use this method to resize the window of a desktop app.

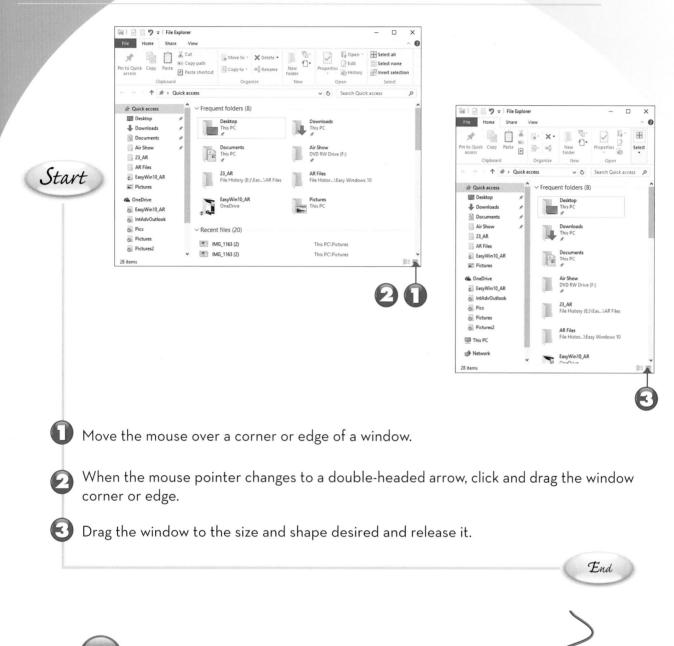

Start

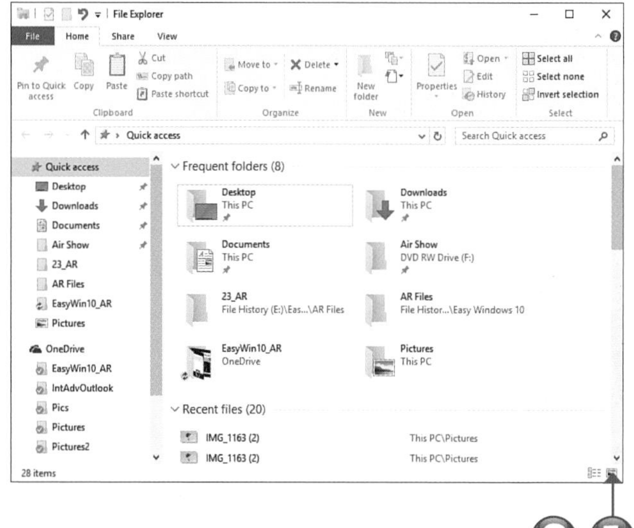

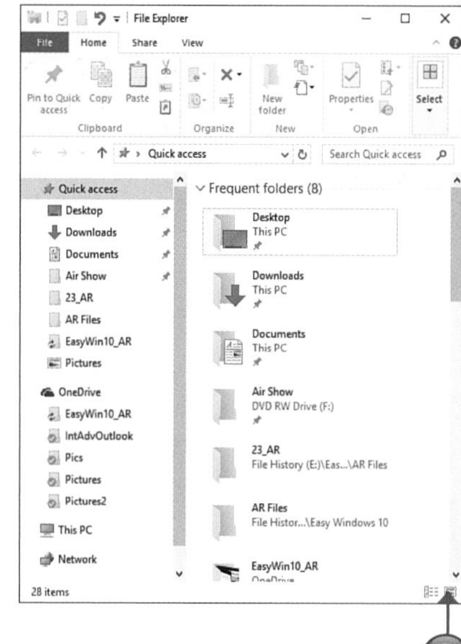

1. Move the mouse over a corner or edge of a window.
2. When the mouse pointer changes to a double-headed arrow, click and drag the window corner or edge.
3. Drag the window to the size and shape desired and release it.

End

NOTE

Note To resize a window using touch controls, instead touch and hold on the corner of a window and drag it to the position you want.

SAVING YOUR FILE

After you change a file, or if you want to save a file as a different type, you must save the new file. This lesson explains how to save a file with a new name. If you are changing an existing file, this keeps the original version intact.

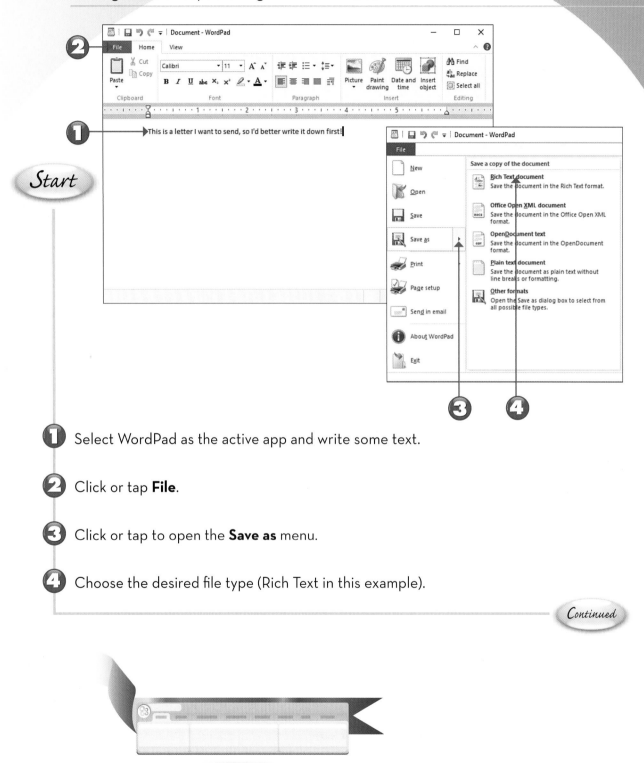

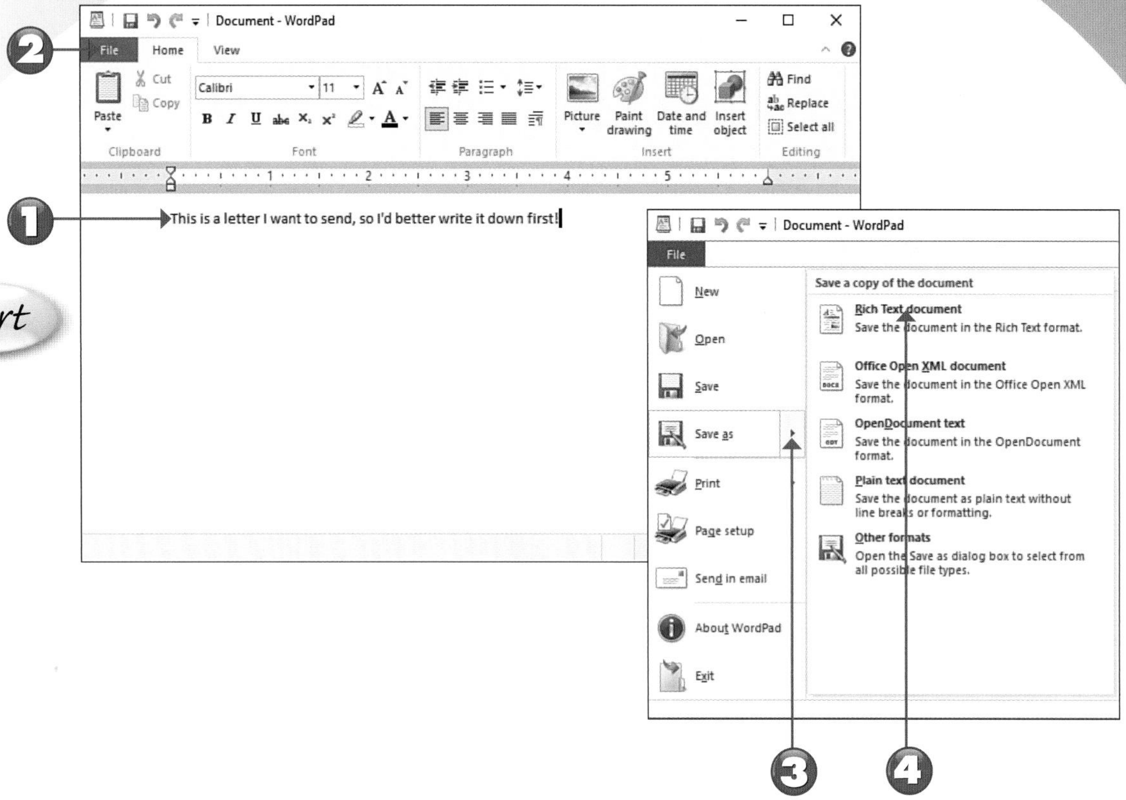

1. Select WordPad as the active app and write some text.
2. Click or tap **File**.
3. Click or tap to open the **Save as** menu.
4. Choose the desired file type (Rich Text in this example).

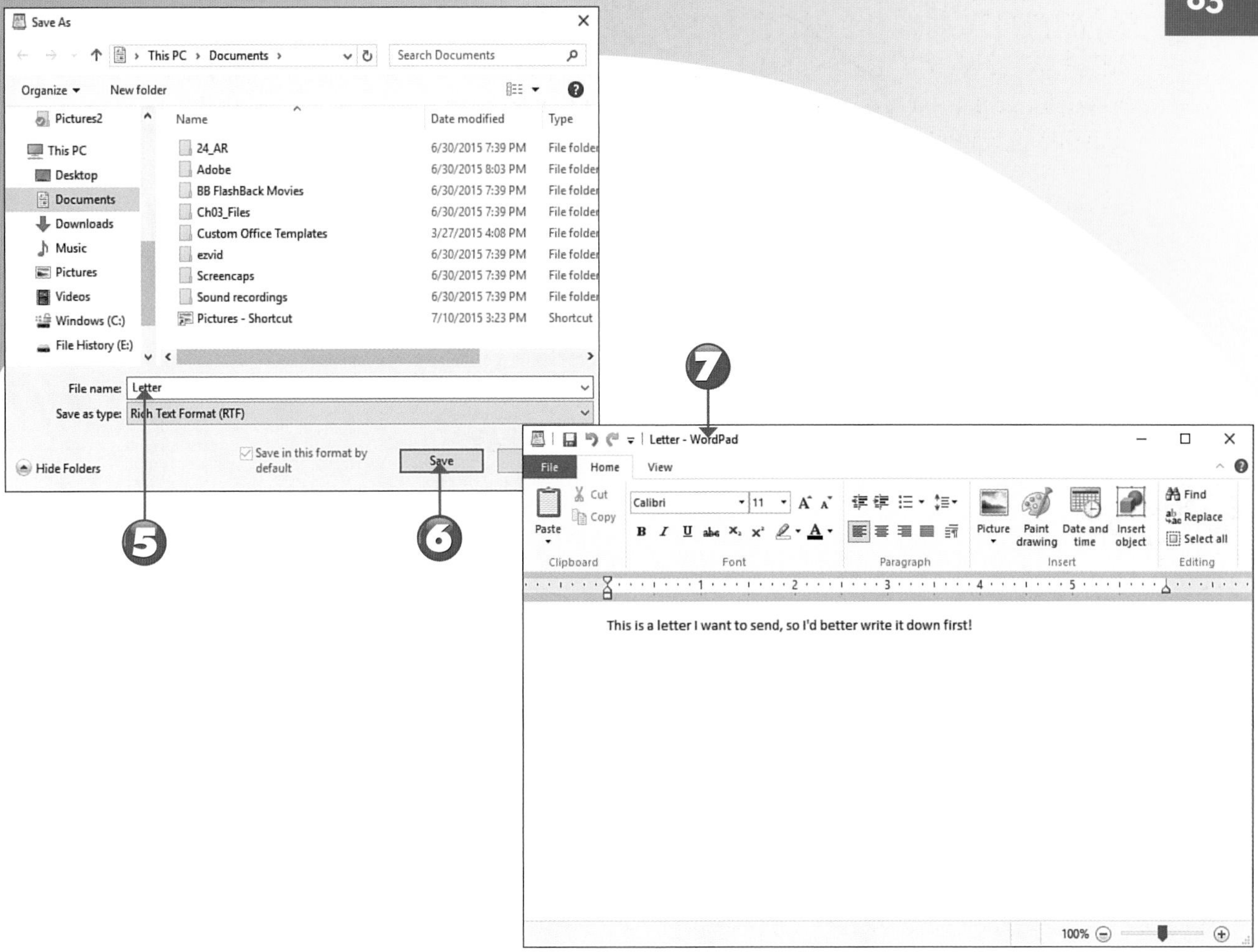

5. Enter a new name.

6. Click or tap **Save** to save the edited document.

7. The app window shows the new file name.

End

NOTE

Save As Versus Save If you use Save (step 3), you replace your original version with the changed version.

MAKING THE DESKTOP VISIBLE

Many apps offer to create a desktop icon (shortcut) during installation. If you prefer to open apps from the desktop, you might need an easy way to make open windows and maximized apps "disappear" without closing them so you can click or tap a desktop icon. Windows 10 makes it easy.

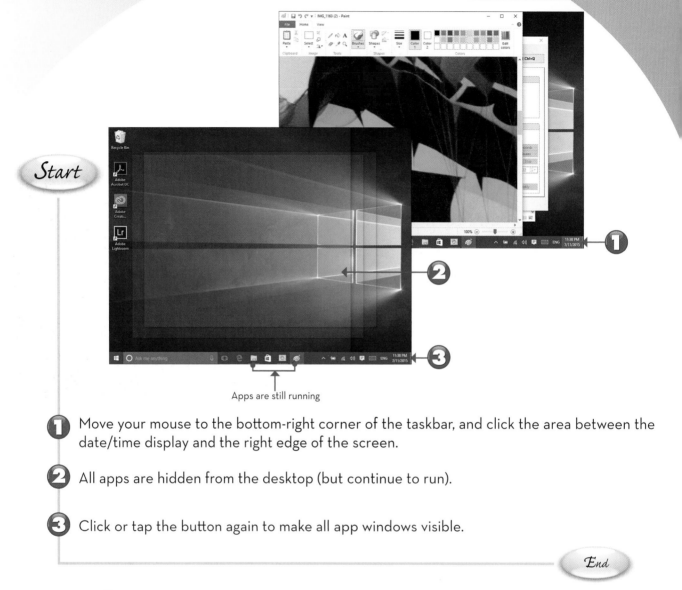

Start

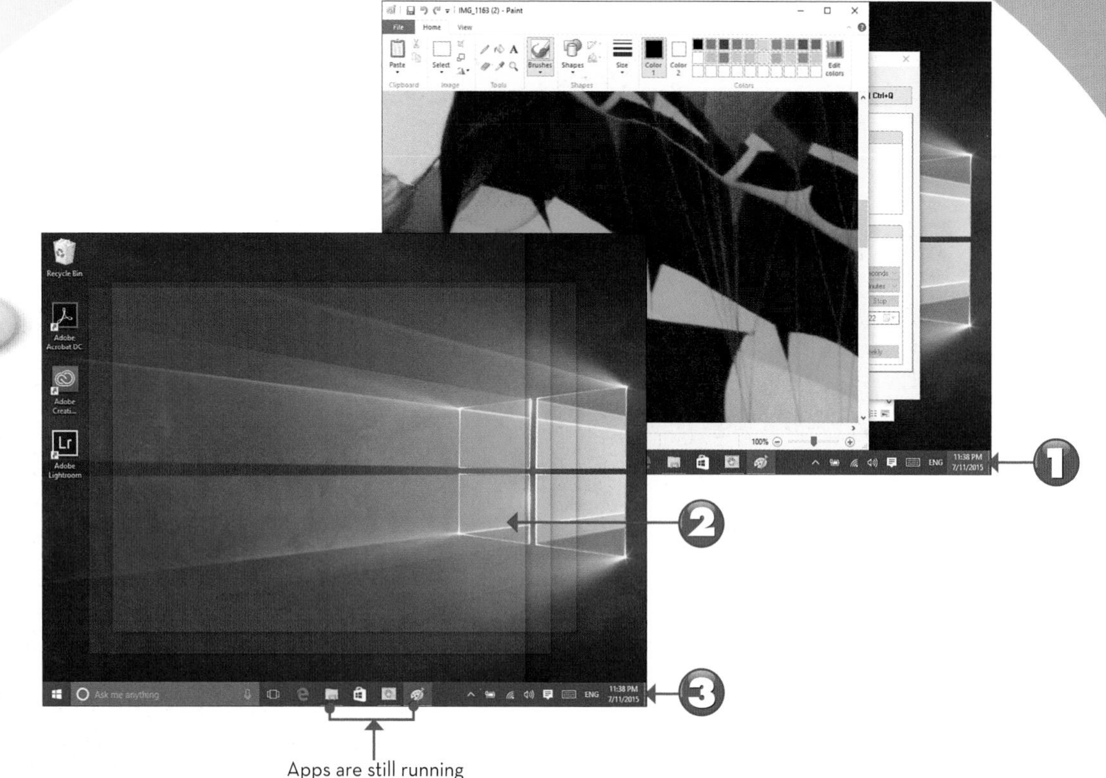

1. Move your mouse to the bottom-right corner of the taskbar, and click the area between the date/time display and the right edge of the screen.
2. All apps are hidden from the desktop (but continue to run).
3. Click or tap the button again to make all app windows visible.

End

USING DESKTOP SHORTCUTS

Most Windows desktops include shortcuts (icons) for some installed apps. If these shortcuts are not visible, here's how to make them visible and use them to open apps.

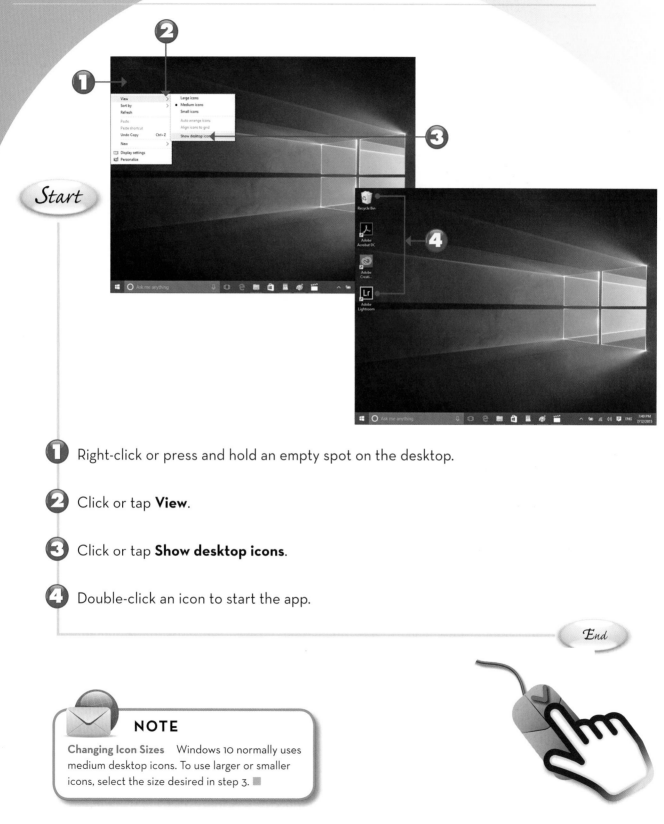

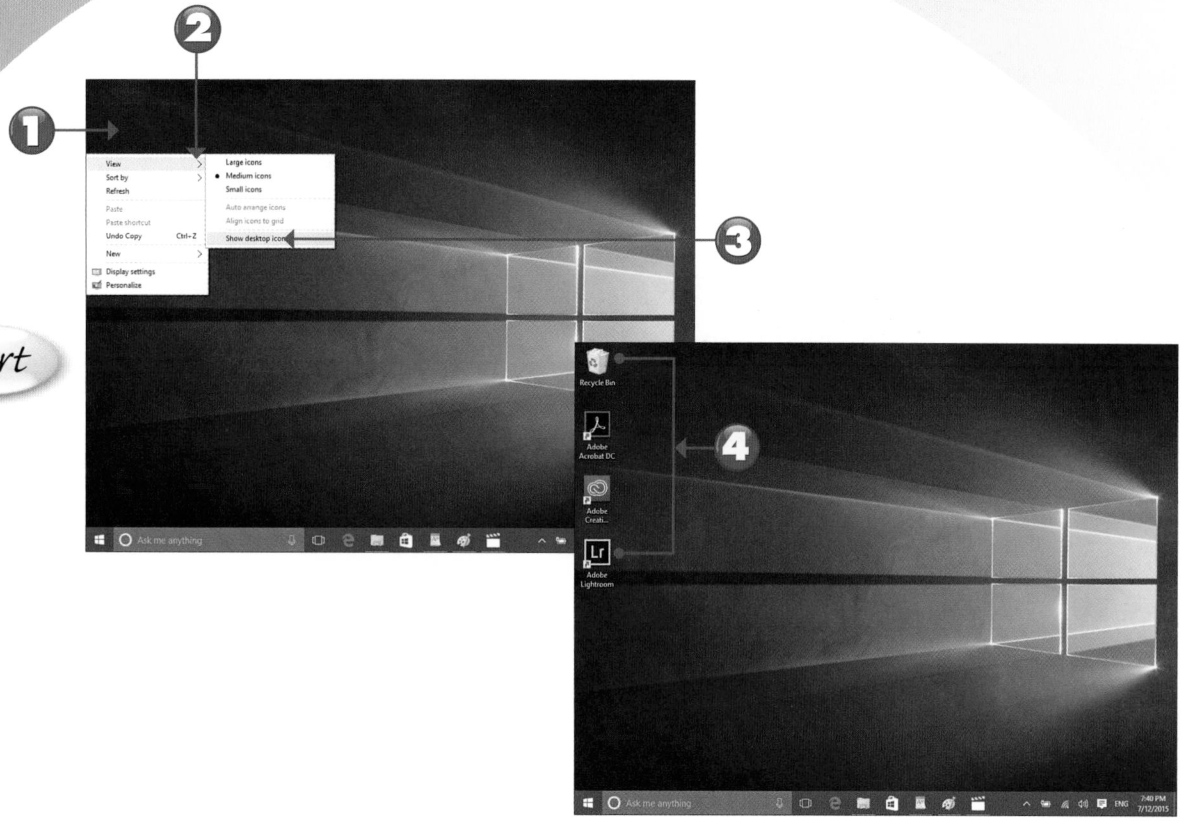

Start

1. Right-click or press and hold an empty spot on the desktop.
2. Click or tap **View**.
3. Click or tap **Show desktop icons**.
4. Double-click an icon to start the app.

End

NOTE

Changing Icon Sizes Windows 10 normally uses medium desktop icons. To use larger or smaller icons, select the size desired in step 3.

ADDING AN APP TO THE TASKBAR

The Windows taskbar is a great place to start an app. Here's how to add your favorite app to the taskbar. With this example, you pin the Alarms & Clock app to the taskbar.

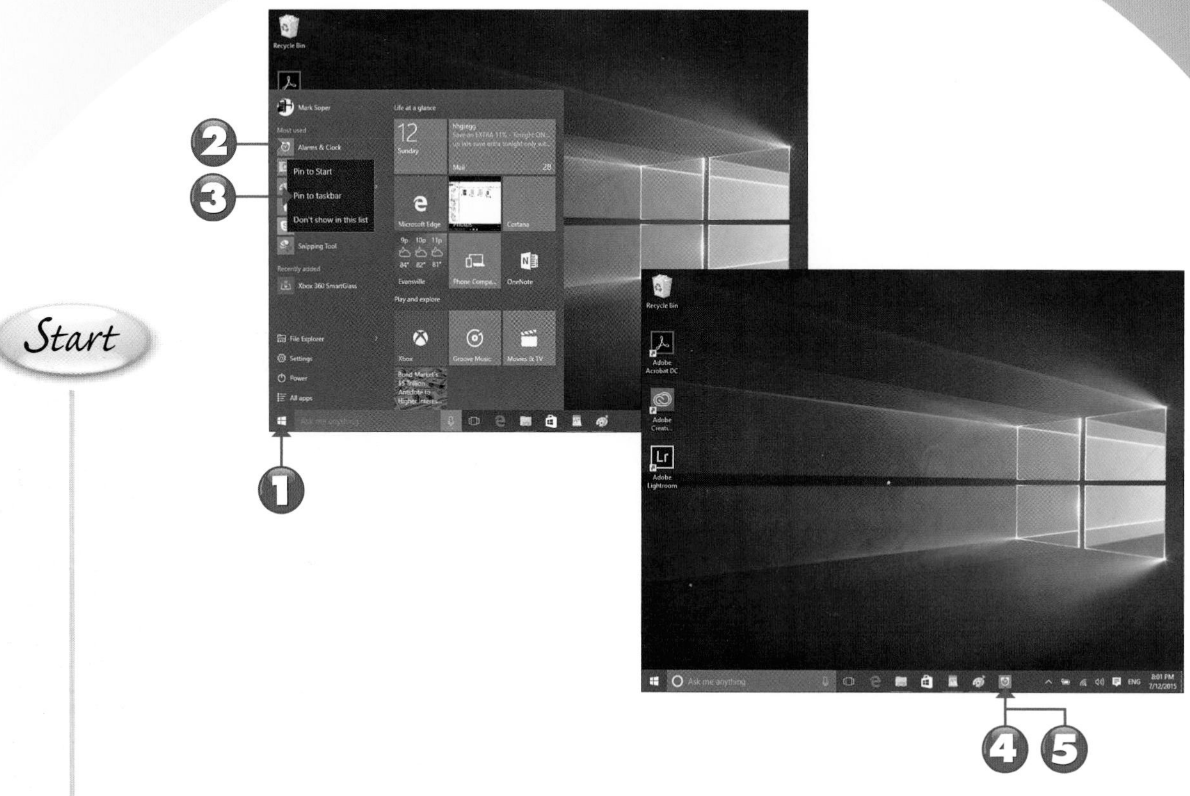

1. Click or tap **Start**.
2. Right-click or press and hold the Alarms & Clock app's icon.
3. Click or tap **Pin to taskbar**.
4. The app is added to the taskbar.
5. To start the app, click or tap the icon on the taskbar.

End

TIP

Pinning a Running App to the Taskbar To pin an app that is already running to the taskbar, right-click or press and hold the app's icon and select **Pin this program to taskbar**. See "Working with Taskbar Jump Lists" for an illustration.

WORKING WITH TASKBAR JUMP LISTS

Most icons on the taskbar also include a jump list, including recent files or common actions. Here's how to use the jump list for easier access to files you want to use again and again and to open your app with your favorite files.

Start

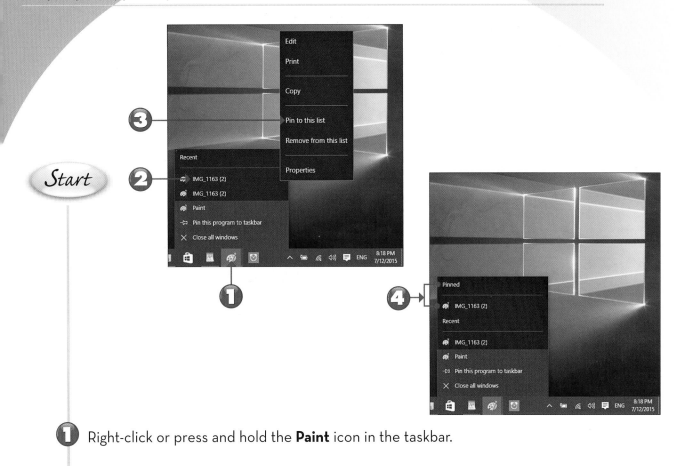

1. Right-click or press and hold the **Paint** icon in the taskbar.
2. Right-click or press and hold one of the listed files.
3. Click or tap **Pin to this list**.
4. The file will be listed as a pinned file next time you open Paint.

End

TIP

Opening and Unpinning a File You can open any file on the jump list. More recently opened files replace older files on the jump list. To remove a file from the jump list, right-click or press and hold the file, and then click or tap **Remove from this list.**

Pin files you want to use frequently, because pinned files stay on the list until you remove them. To unpin a file, right-click or press and hold the file, and then click or tap **Unpin from this list**.

SNAPPING AND CLOSING AN APP WINDOW

You can change the position and size of the active app window right from the keyboard by using a Windows feature called *snapping*. This example uses the Microsoft Edge browser app included in Windows 10.

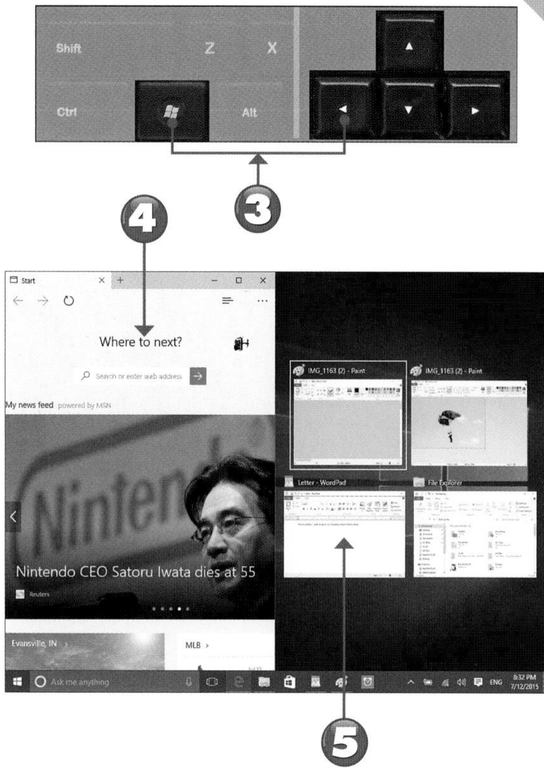

Start

1. Click or tap **Start**.
2. Click or tap **Microsoft Edge** to open it in a window.
3. Press **Windows key+left arrow**.
4. The active app (Microsoft Edge) snaps to the left edge of the current display.
5. To snap an open app into the other half of the desktop, click or tap it.

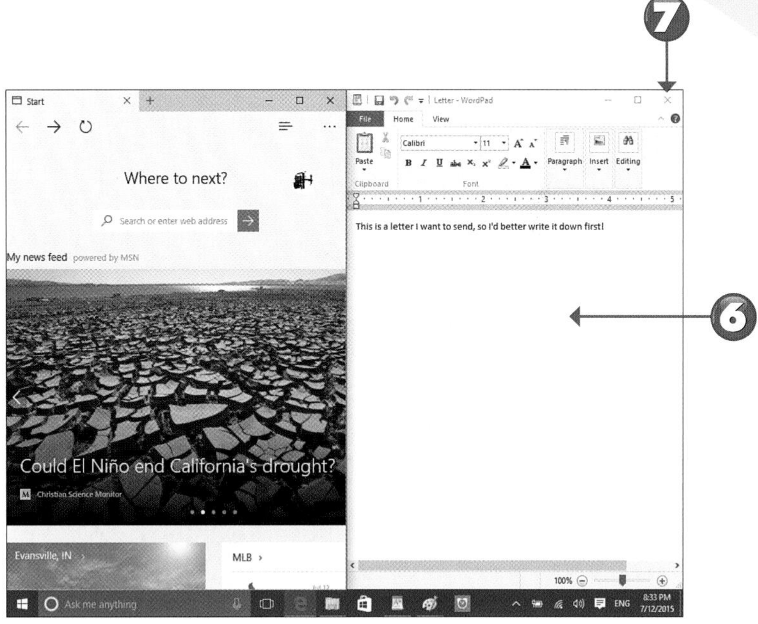

6. The selected app snaps into the right half of the desktop.

7. Click or tap to close the app.

End

NOTE

It Works Both Ways You can instead snap an app to the right of the screen first by using the Windows key+right arrow.

TIP

More Snapping Tips Press **Windows key+up arrow** to maximize the active app. If you drag a program window to the top of the screen it snaps to full screen. Press **Windows key+down arrow** to minimize the active app. To remove the other app windows from the left or right side of the desktop, press the **Esc** (Escape) key on the keyboard.

WEB BROWSING WITH MICROSOFT EDGE

Windows 10 uses the new Microsoft Edge as its default browser. Edge is a brand-new browser that's faster and easier to use than the older Internet Explorer browser—and more compatible with today's state-of-the-art websites, too. Designed for both touch and mouse/keyboard users, Edge has many new features and new takes on familiar functions. In this chapter, you learn how to use Microsoft Edge for all your web browsing.

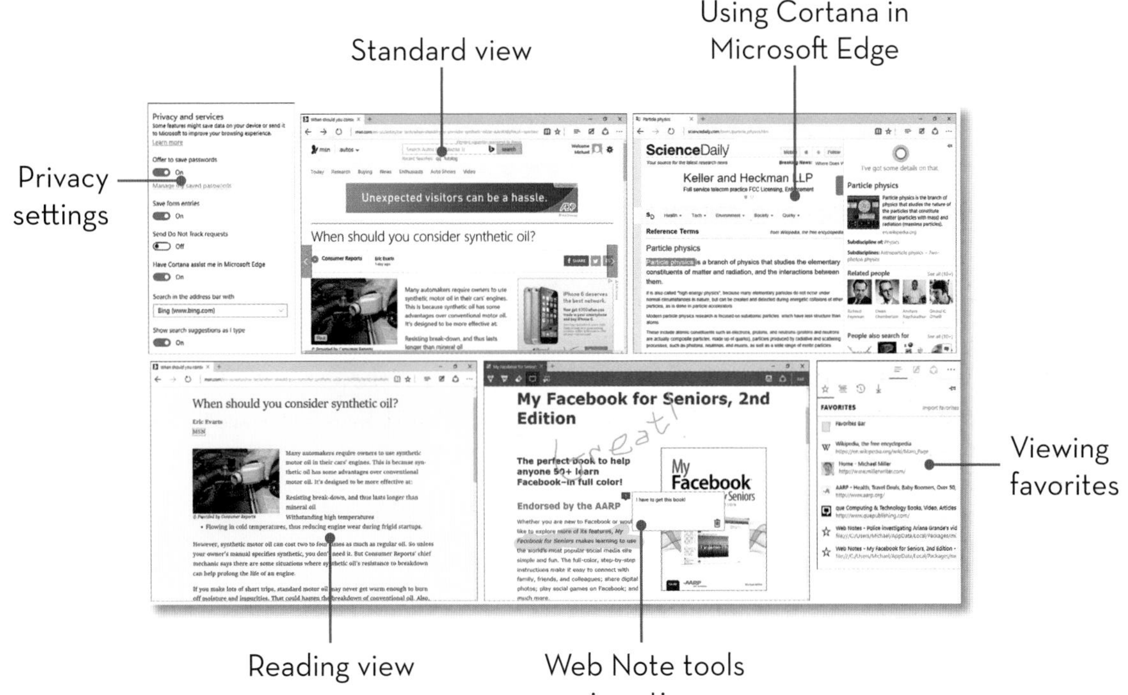

Standard view
Using Cortana in Microsoft Edge
Privacy settings
Viewing favorites
Reading view
Web Note tools in action
Privacy and services
Unexpected visitors can be a hassle.
When should you consider synthetic oil?
ScienceDaily
Keller and Heckman LLP
Particle physics
When should you consider synthetic oil?
My Facebook for Seniors, 2nd Edition
FAVORITES

STARTING MICROSOFT EDGE

Microsoft Edge might be on your system's taskbar. If not, you can launch it from the Start menu. Here's how.

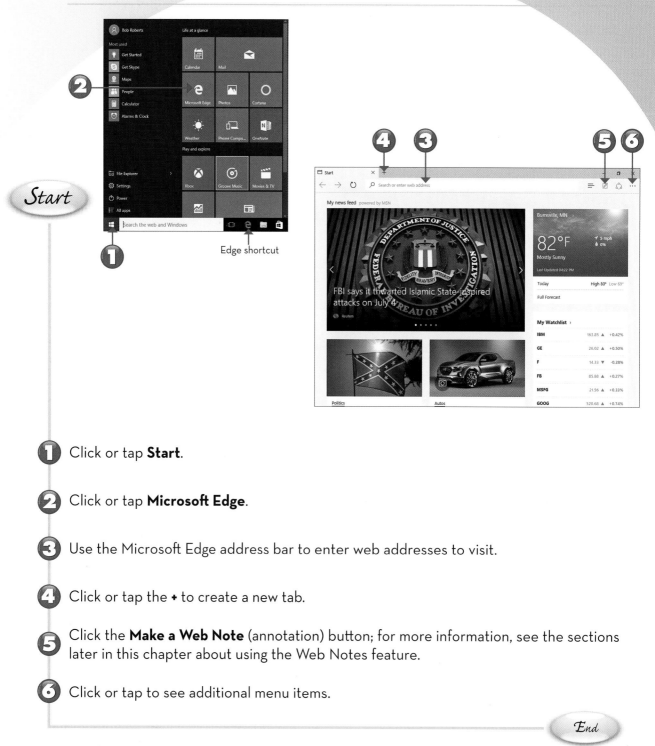

Start

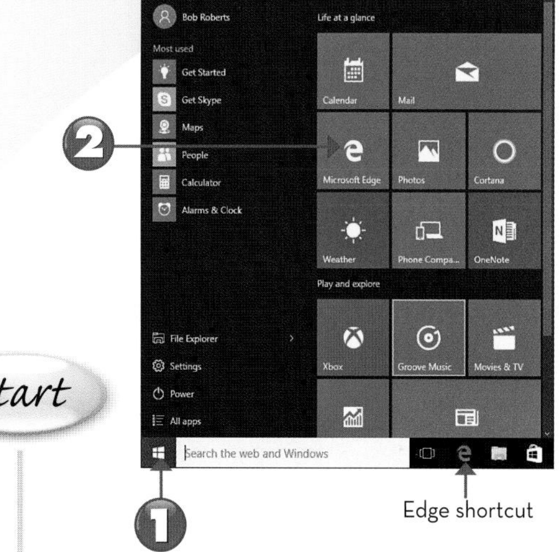

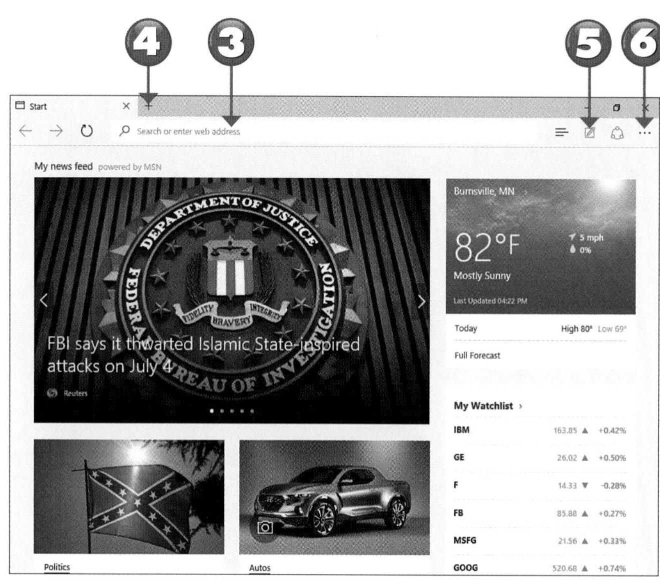

1. Click or tap **Start**.
2. Click or tap **Microsoft Edge**.
3. Use the Microsoft Edge address bar to enter web addresses to visit.
4. Click or tap the **+** to create a new tab.
5. Click the **Make a Web Note** (annotation) button; for more information, see the sections later in this chapter about using the Web Notes feature.
6. Click or tap to see additional menu items.

End

ENTERING A WEBSITE ADDRESS (URL)

Microsoft Edge displays more than just the address (URL) when you enter a URL you've previously visited. This feature makes it easier to go back to an address you've previously visited, even if you have visited several pages in the same domain.

Start

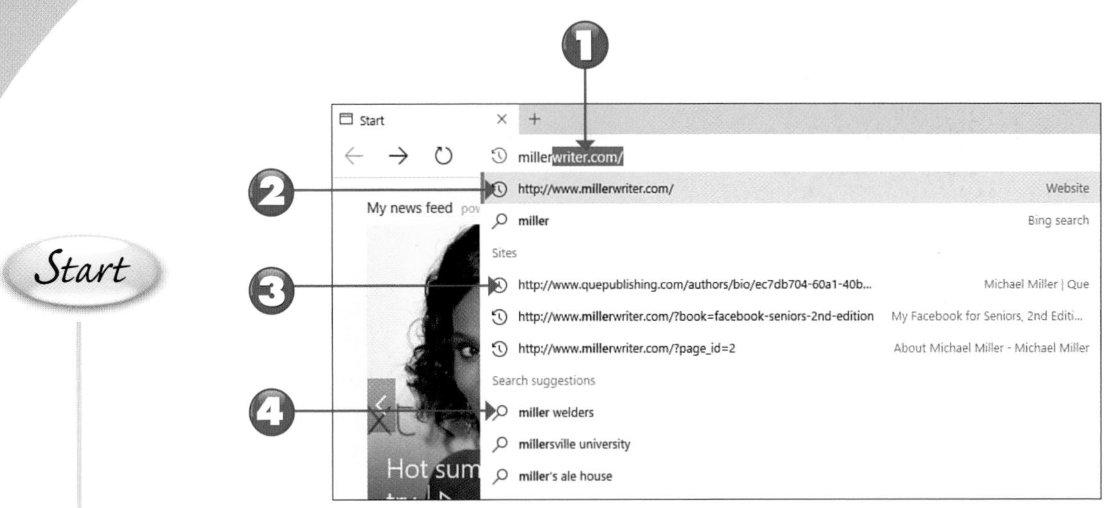

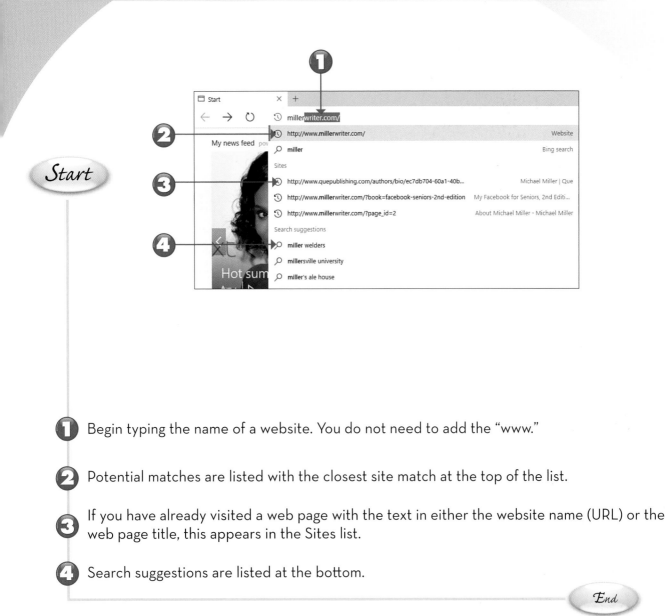

1. Begin typing the name of a website. You do not need to add the "www."
2. Potential matches are listed with the closest site match at the top of the list.
3. If you have already visited a web page with the text in either the website name (URL) or the web page title, this appears in the Sites list.
4. Search suggestions are listed at the bottom.

End

TIP

Selecting a Website or Search Use your mouse, touchpad, or touchscreen to select the website or search to open. You can also use the down arrow to highlight the page you want to load and then press Enter.

WORKING WITH TABS

Microsoft Edge includes tabbed browsing. In this tutorial, you learn how to open and work with new tabs in Microsoft Edge.

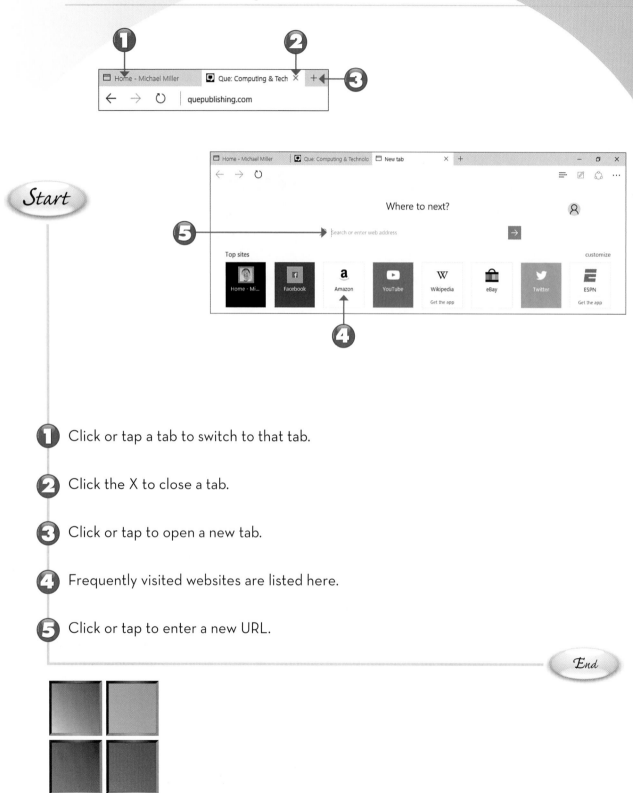

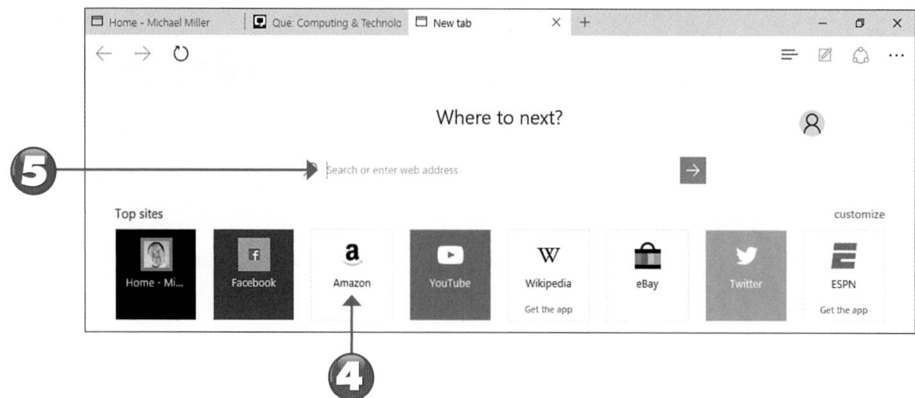

1. Click or tap a tab to switch to that tab.
2. Click the X to close a tab.
3. Click or tap to open a new tab.
4. Frequently visited websites are listed here.
5. Click or tap to enter a new URL.

End

SETTING YOUR HOME PAGE

You can change your Microsoft Edge home page whenever you want. Edge provides you with several options. Here's how to open Edge (or a new tab) with a list of your most recent pages.

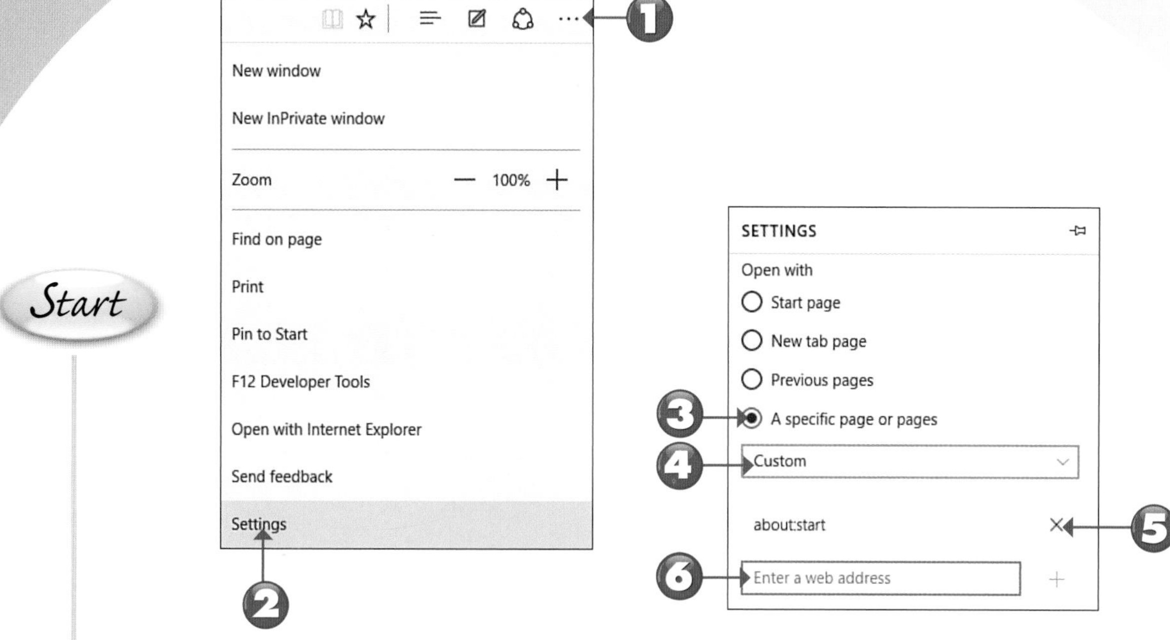

Start

1. Open the **More actions** menu.
2. Click or tap **Settings**.
3. Scroll to the Open with section, and click or tap **A specific page or pages**.
4. Click or tap to open the web page options menu, and then select **Custom**.
5. Click the X next to **about:start** to remove the default Start page.
6. Enter the URL of the page you want as your home page into the **Enter a web address** box.

End

NOTE

Default Start Page The default Start page (about:start) displays a list of your most recent pages ("top sites"). This page also displays when you open a new tab. The list changes over time to reflect your page-viewing habits.

OPENING A LINK

Because Microsoft Edge supports tabbed browsing, you can open a link to another website in one of three ways: as a replacement for the current page, as a new tab in the same window, or in a new window. When you click or tap on a link, the link could open in the same window or in a new window. To specifically open the link in a new tab or window, use the method shown in this tutorial.

1. Right-click, or press and hold the link to display the options menu.
2. Click or tap **Open in new tab**.
3. Click or tap the new tab.
4. Right-click, or press and hold a link.
5. Select **Open in new window**.

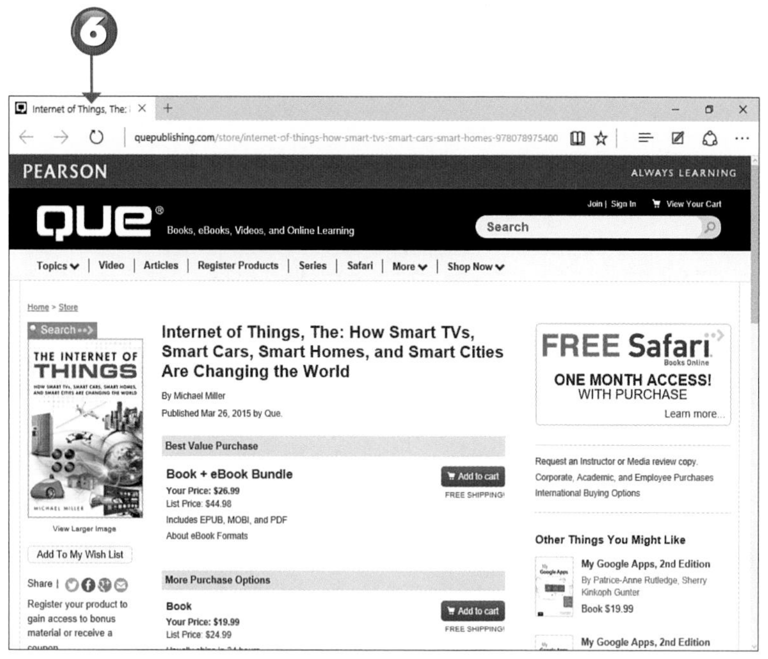

6 A new window opens to display the link.

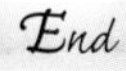

USING CORTANA IN MICROSOFT EDGE

Cortana is the powerful new search and information technology included in Windows 10. You can use Cortana within Microsoft Edge to get more information about a link or highlighted text. Here's an example of how Cortana can help you learn more about what you see in a web page.

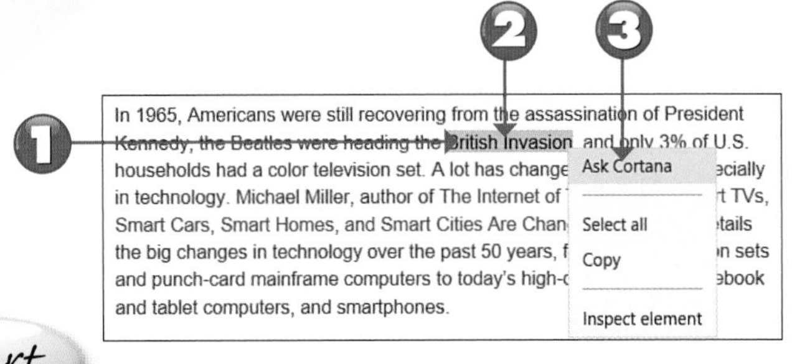

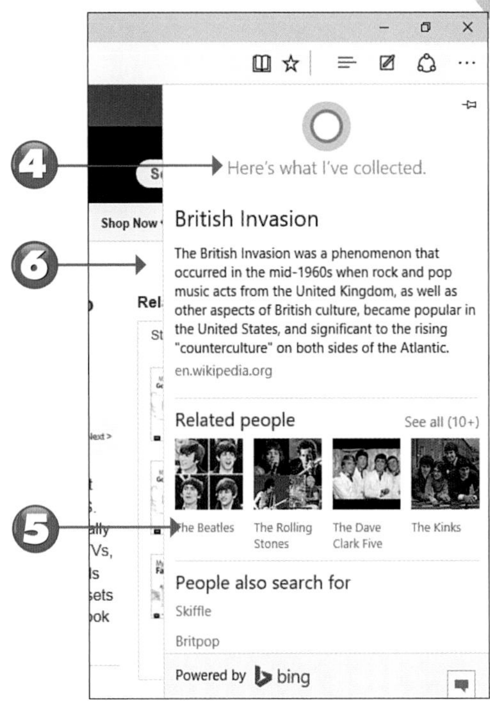

Start

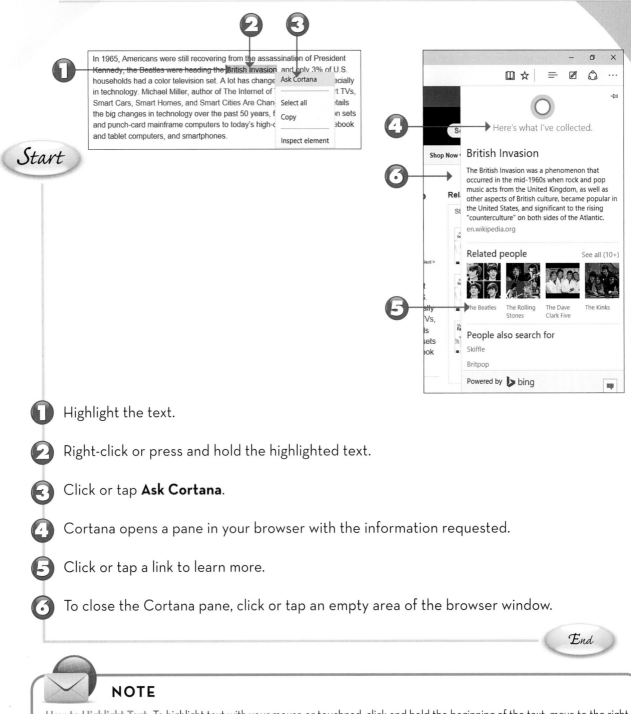

1. Highlight the text.
2. Right-click or press and hold the highlighted text.
3. Click or tap **Ask Cortana**.
4. Cortana opens a pane in your browser with the information requested.
5. Click or tap a link to learn more.
6. To close the Cortana pane, click or tap an empty area of the browser window.

NOTE

How to Highlight Text To highlight text with your mouse or touchpad, click and hold the beginning of the text, move to the right until the text is highlighted, and then release. To highlight text with your touchscreen, press and hold a word in the text until a highlight appears. Press and drag one of the circle markers at each end of the word until all of the text desired is highlighted.

COPYING AND PASTING A LINK

The same right-click menu you use for opening links or accessing Cortana can also be used to copy links that can be pasted into other apps. Here's how to use this feature with Windows 10's built-in text editor, Notepad. You can also use this technique with Microsoft Word and other word-processing programs.

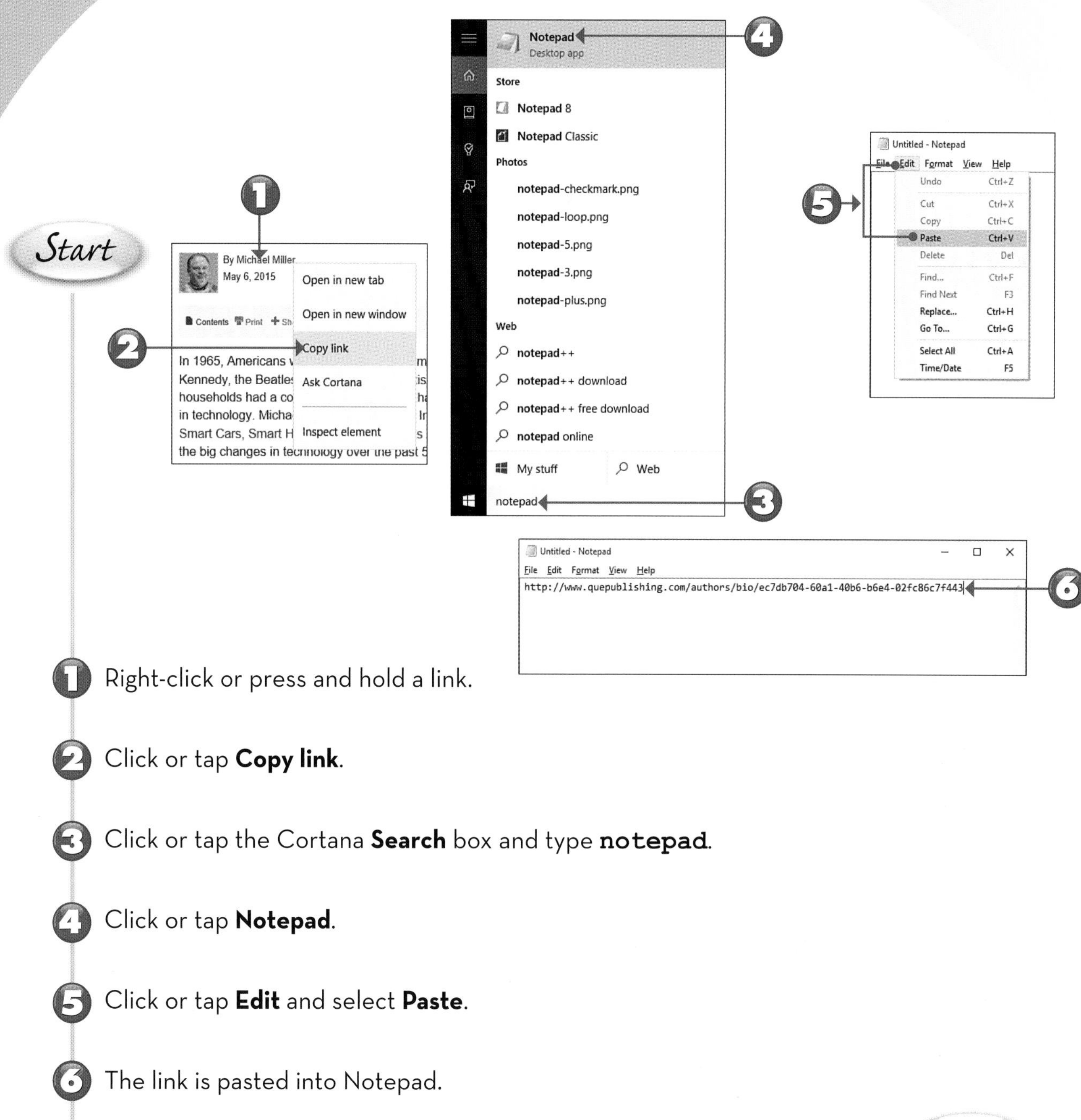

1. Right-click or press and hold a link.
2. Click or tap **Copy link**.
3. Click or tap the Cortana **Search** box and type **`notepad`**.
4. Click or tap **Notepad**.
5. Click or tap **Edit** and select **Paste**.
6. The link is pasted into Notepad.

End

USING ZOOM

Zoom enables you to increase or decrease the size of text and graphics on a web page. By increasing the size, you make pages easier to read, and by reducing the size, you enable page viewing without horizontal scrolling.

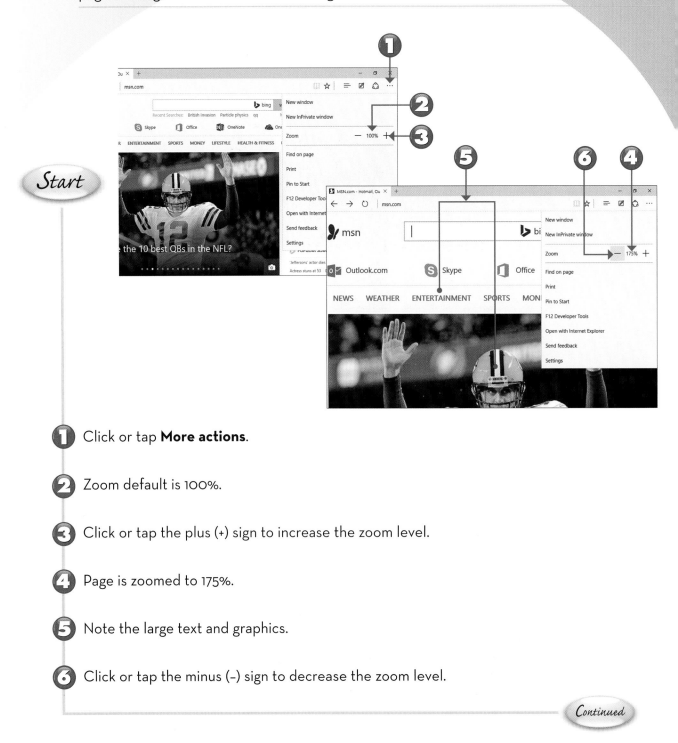

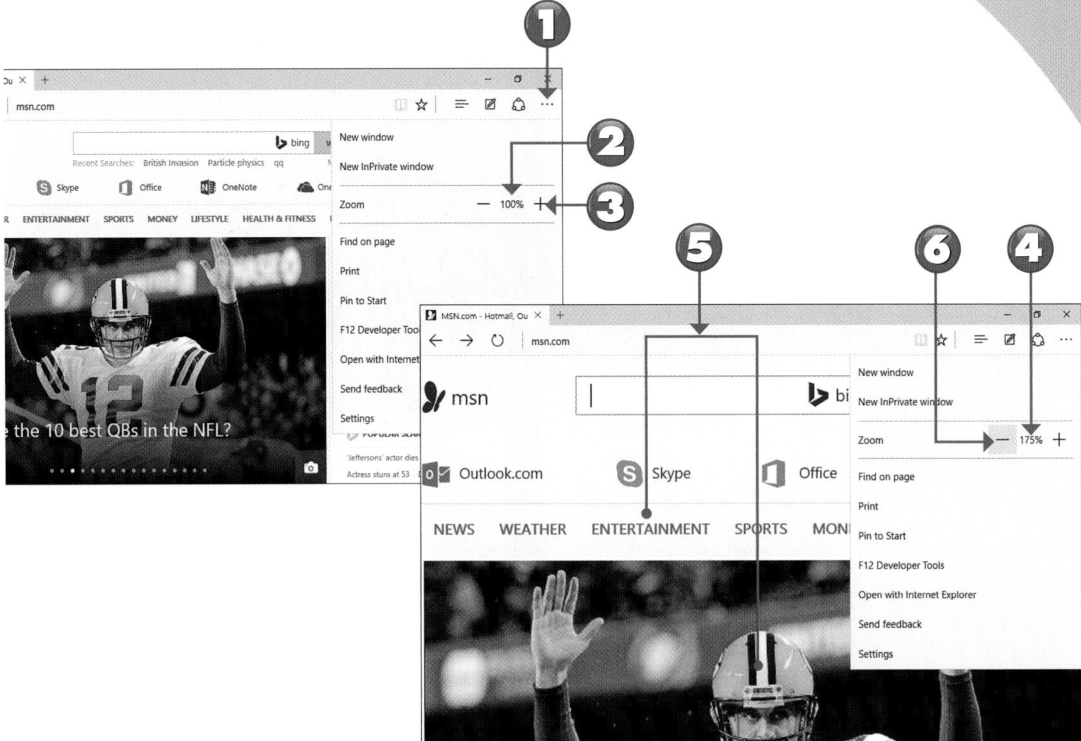

1. Click or tap **More actions**.
2. Zoom default is 100%.
3. Click or tap the plus (+) sign to increase the zoom level.
4. Page is zoomed to 175%.
5. Note the large text and graphics.
6. Click or tap the minus (-) sign to decrease the zoom level.

Continued

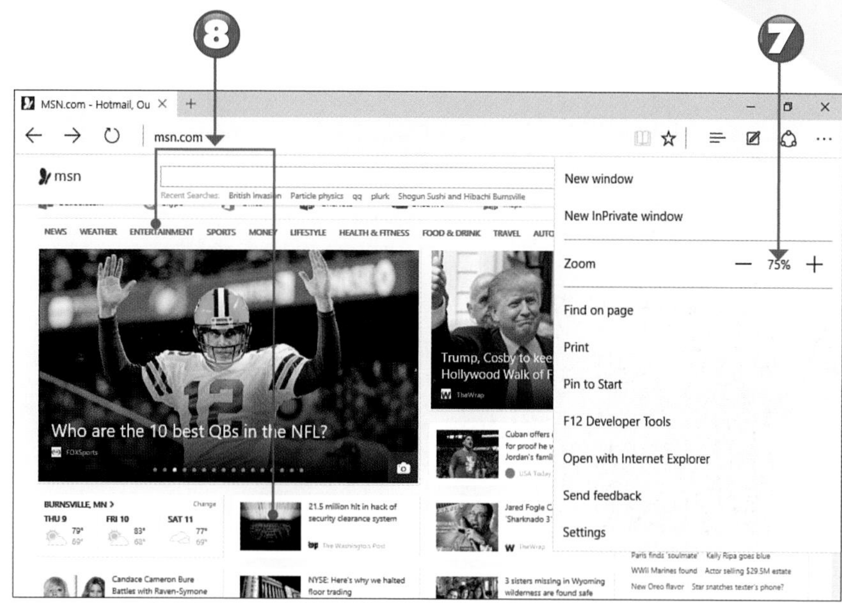

7 Page zoomed to 75%.

8 More of the page is visible, but the text is smaller.

End

NOTE

When to Zoom The 175% view shown in step 4 makes the text and pictures on a web page easier to see, but you must scroll left and right as well as up and down to see the entire page. Use zoom settings smaller than 100% if you want to see more of the page without scrolling. These settings do not affect how the page prints.

USING READING VIEW

You can read a lot of terrific articles in your browser, but most commercial sites litter articles with ads and other visual distractions. The Reading view in Microsoft Edge shows you only the main contents of the current URL without the clutter. Here's how to use it.

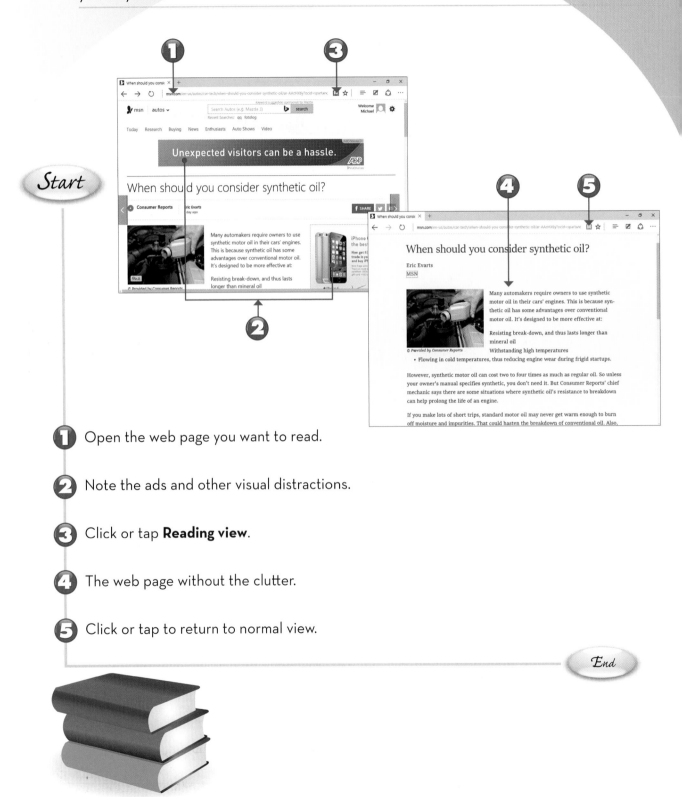

Start

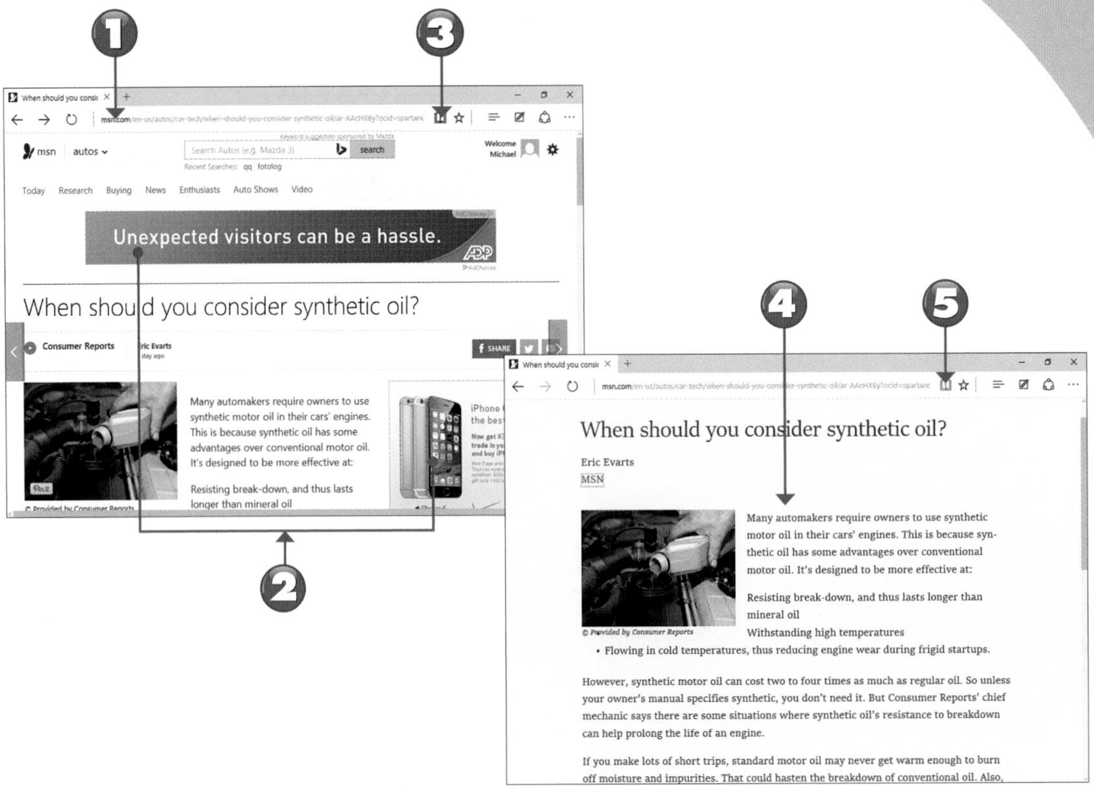

1. Open the web page you want to read.
2. Note the ads and other visual distractions.
3. Click or tap **Reading view**.
4. The web page without the clutter.
5. Click or tap to return to normal view.

End

PRINTING OR CREATING A PDF OF A WEB PAGE

Microsoft Edge enables you to preview and print web pages that give you what you need on paper. I recommend you switch to Reading view first (see the preceding exercise, "Using Reading View," for details) and then print your page as shown in this exercise.

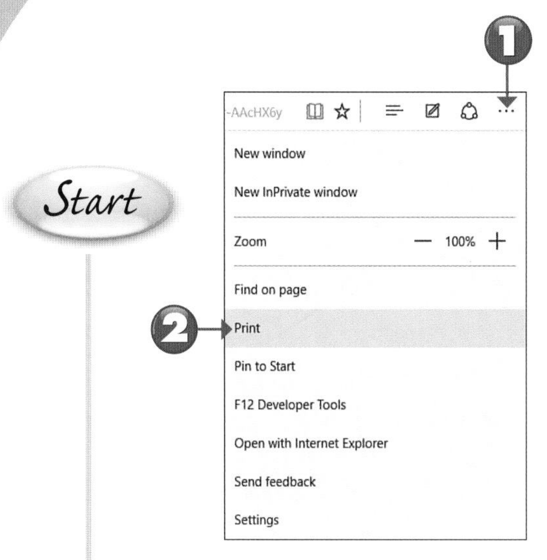

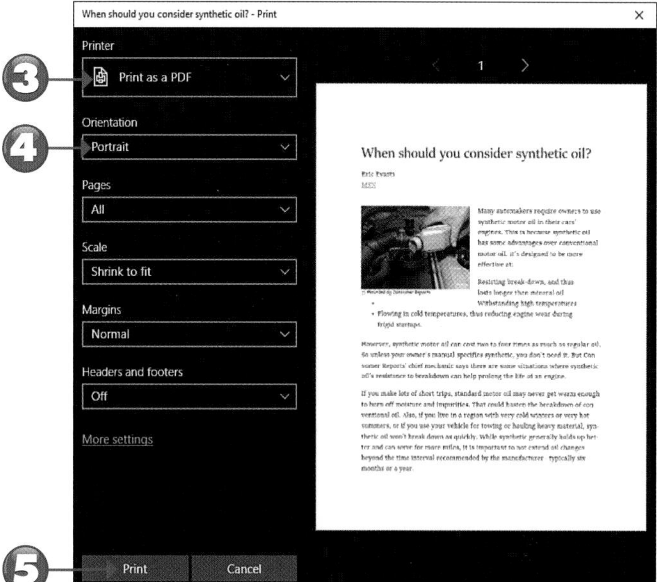

1. Click or tap **More actions**.
2. Click or tap **Print**.
3. Click or tap if you need to change printers. (To create a PDF file, select **Print as a PDF**.)
4. Click or tap to change page orientation.
5. Click or tap to print the page.

End

NOTE

Changing Paper Size, Type, and Other Settings The default paper size is usually letter or A4. To change paper size, paper type (plain paper, photo paper, and so on), and other settings, click or tap the respective control.

SWITCHING TO INTERNET EXPLORER VIEW

Microsoft Edge is designed to render pages better and more quickly than Internet Explorer (IE), which is still included in Windows 10. However, some older web pages might work better in IE. It's easy to switch between browsers if a website recommends it, as you learn in this exercise. The website used in this example is zone.msn.com.

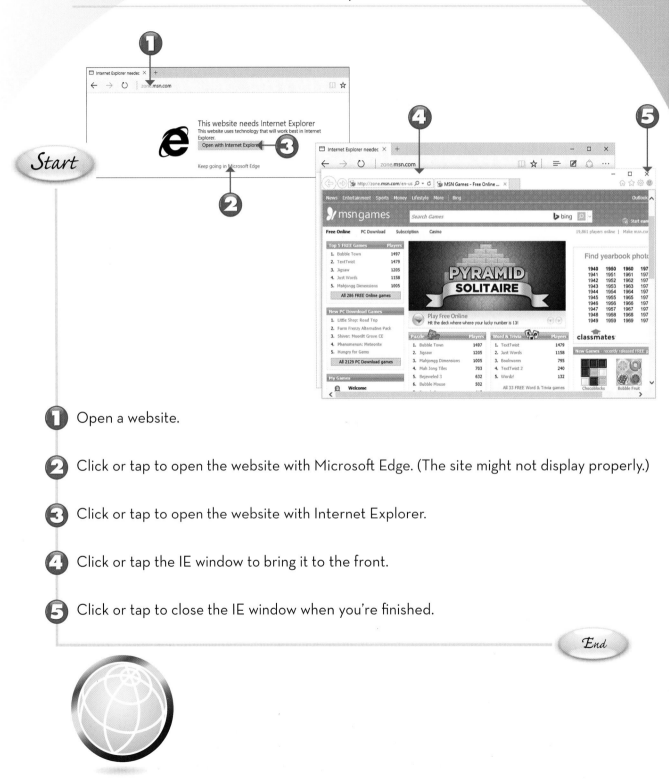

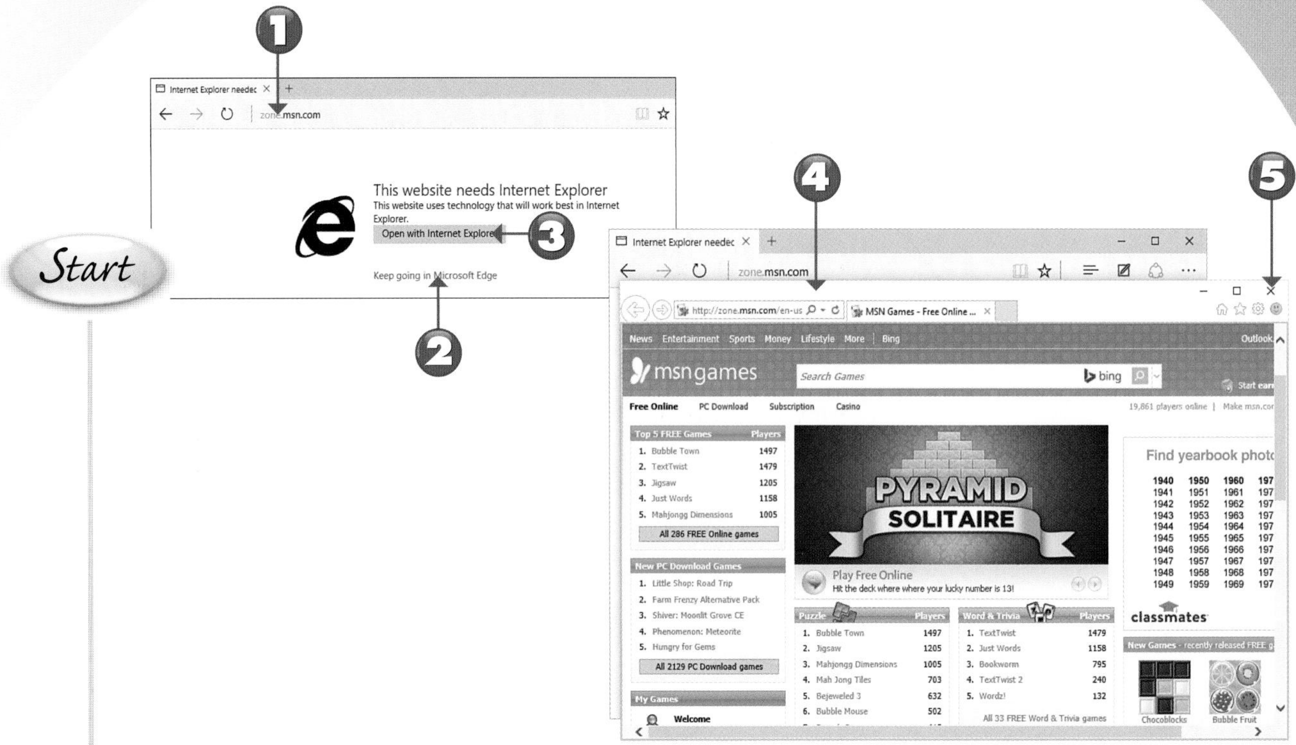

Start

1. Open a website.
2. Click or tap to open the website with Microsoft Edge. (The site might not display properly.)
3. Click or tap to open the website with Internet Explorer.
4. Click or tap the IE window to bring it to the front.
5. Click or tap to close the IE window when you're finished.

End

ADDING A WEB PAGE AS A FAVORITE

When you make a web page a favorite (also known as bookmarking a page), you can go to it quickly whenever you want. Here's how to do it using Microsoft Edge.

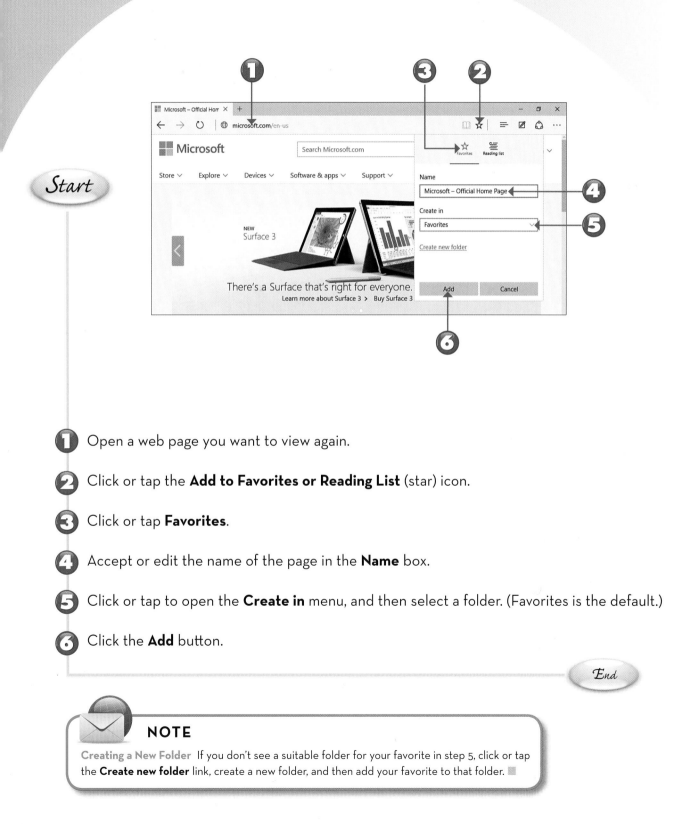

Start

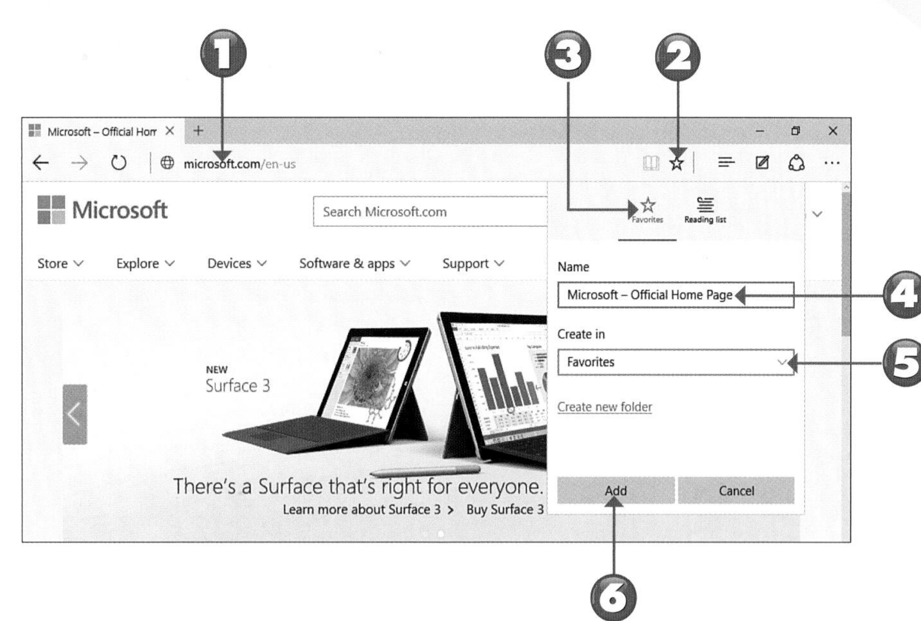

1. Open a web page you want to view again.
2. Click or tap the **Add to Favorites or Reading List** (star) icon.
3. Click or tap **Favorites**.
4. Accept or edit the name of the page in the **Name** box.
5. Click or tap to open the **Create in** menu, and then select a folder. (Favorites is the default.)
6. Click the **Add** button.

NOTE

Creating a New Folder If you don't see a suitable folder for your favorite in step 5, click or tap the **Create new folder** link, create a new folder, and then add your favorite to that folder.

ADDING A WEB PAGE TO THE READING LIST

If you want to read a web page at your leisure, use the Reading List feature built in to Microsoft Edge. Here's how.

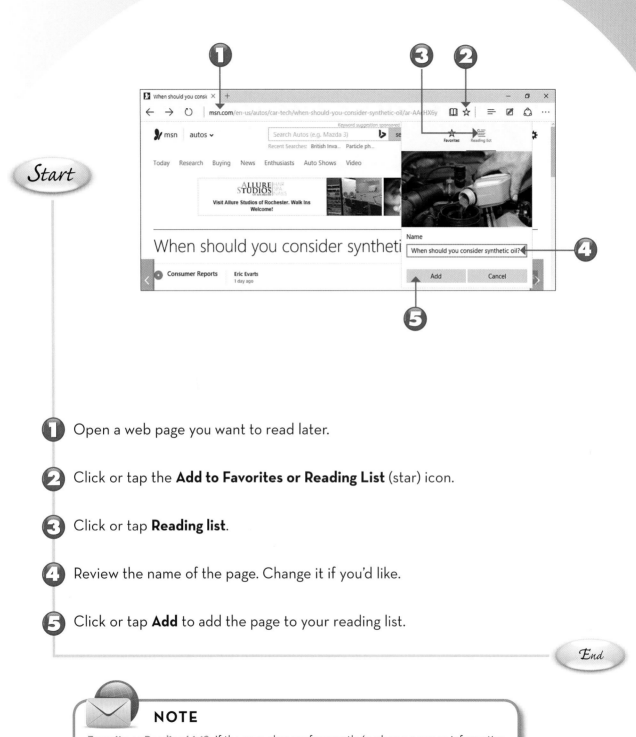

Start

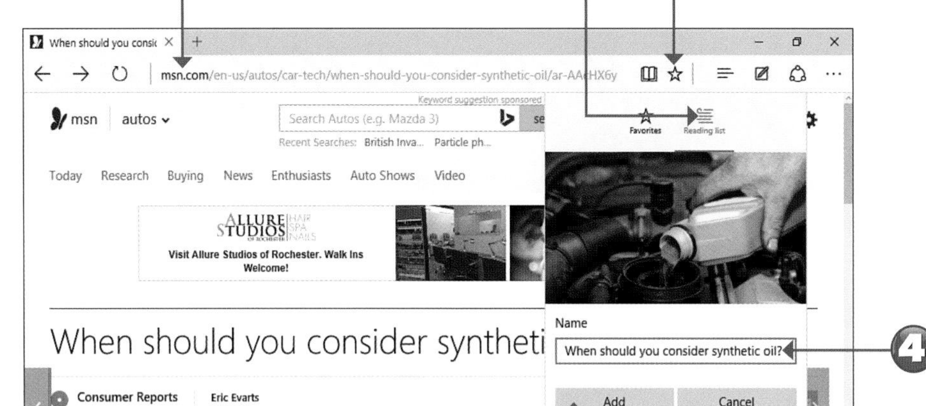

1. Open a web page you want to read later.
2. Click or tap the **Add to Favorites or Reading List** (star) icon.
3. Click or tap **Reading list**.
4. Review the name of the page. Change it if you'd like.
5. Click or tap **Add** to add the page to your reading list.

End

NOTE

Favorite or Reading List? If the page changes frequently (such as a news or information page), add it as a favorite. If the page is an article or essay, add it to your reading list.

VIEWING AND OPENING FAVORITES

You can reopen a favorite in just a couple clicks or taps, as you learn in this exercise.

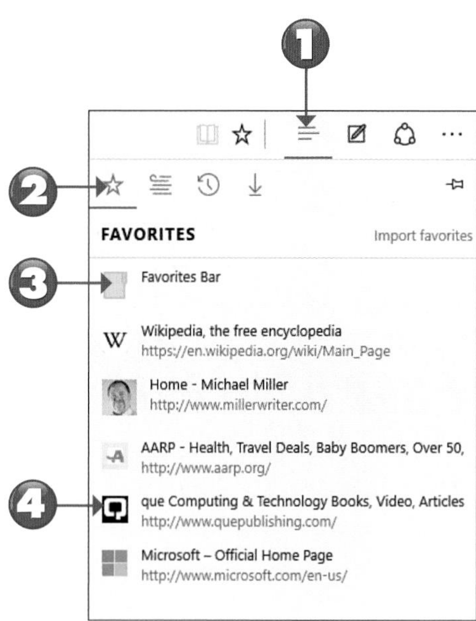

1. Click or tap the **Hub** icon.
2. Click or tap the **Favorites** (star) icon.
3. Click or tap a folder to view the website links it contains.
4. Click or tap a favorite to open it.

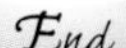

USING READING LIST

Microsoft Edge provides fast access to the web pages on your reading list. In this exercise, you learn how this feature works.

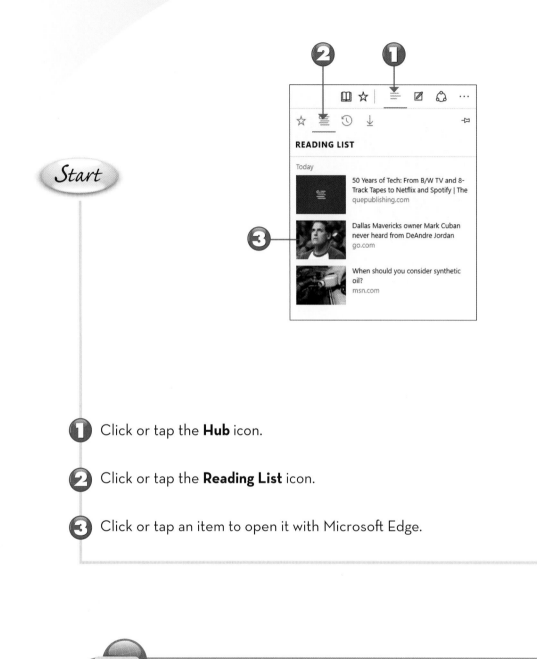

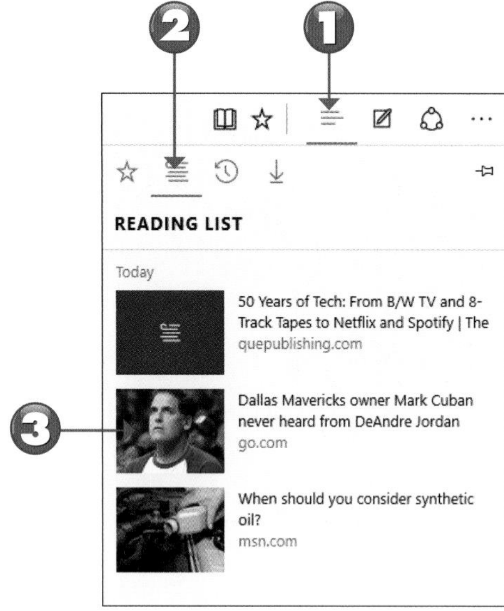

1. Click or tap the **Hub** icon.
2. Click or tap the **Reading List** icon.
3. Click or tap an item to open it with Microsoft Edge.

End

NOTE

Reading List Entries Can Become Outdated The Reading List feature stores the URL of each web page you add to it and opens the page when you click its entry. If the website is offline or the URL is no longer valid, you will not be able to view the page. If you want a permanent copy of the page, create a PDF as described in "Printing or Creating a PDF of a Web Page," p. 103.

USING DOWNLOADS

Microsoft Edge makes it easy to see what you've downloaded and to get to your downloads. Here's how to use this feature.

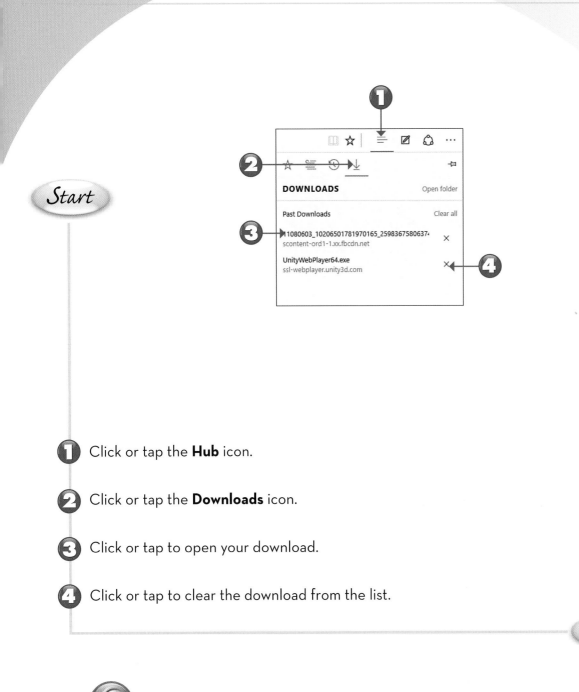

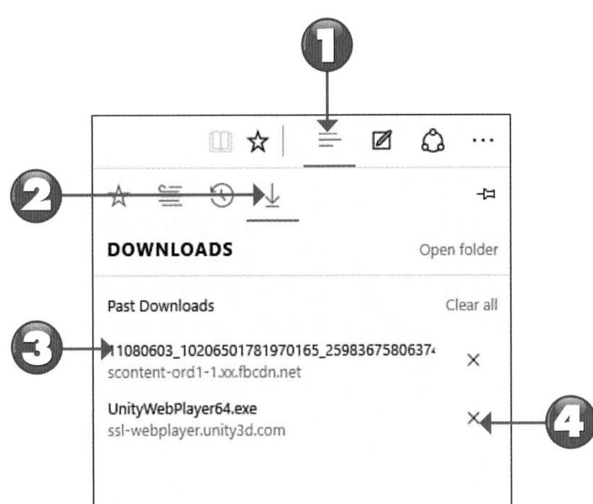

Start

1. Click or tap the **Hub** icon.
2. Click or tap the **Downloads** icon.
3. Click or tap to open your download.
4. Click or tap to clear the download from the list.

End

TIP

Downloads Not Listed Aren't Gone Clearing the Downloads list with **Clear all** or removing an individual download from the list (step 4) does not remove the downloaded files from your device. If you want to remove a downloaded file, click the **Open folder** link to open the Downloads folder in File Explorer, and then delete it there.

USING THE WEB NOTES PEN TOOL

Microsoft Edge's Web Notes feature makes it easy to grab a web page, annotate it, and share it with other users. In this exercise, you learn how to use the Pen tool.

Web Notes toolbar

Start

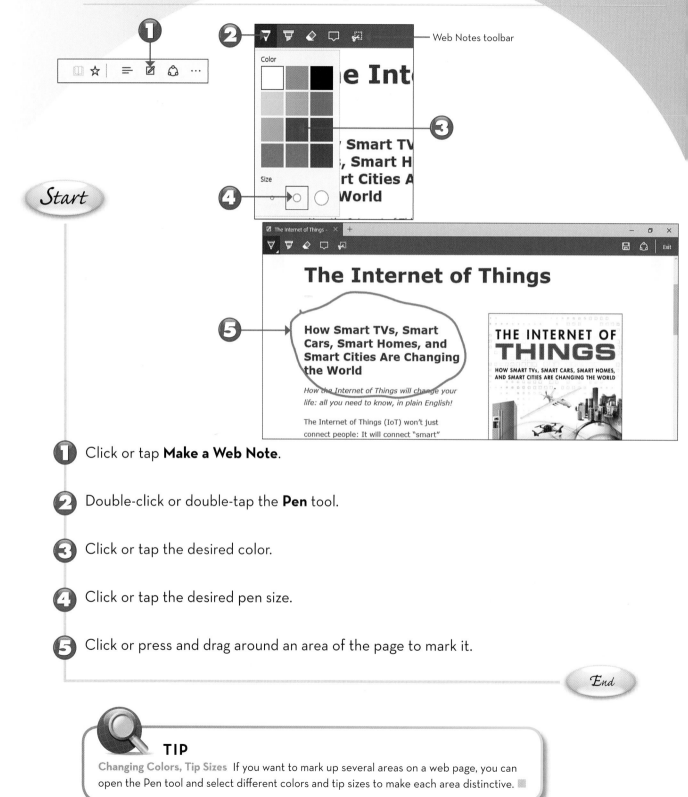

1. Click or tap **Make a Web Note**.
2. Double-click or double-tap the **Pen** tool.
3. Click or tap the desired color.
4. Click or tap the desired pen size.
5. Click or press and drag around an area of the page to mark it.

TIP

Changing Colors, Tip Sizes If you want to mark up several areas on a web page, you can open the Pen tool and select different colors and tip sizes to make each area distinctive.

USING THE WEB NOTES TEXT TOOL

In this exercise, you learn how to use the Web Notes Text tool to add notes to your web page.

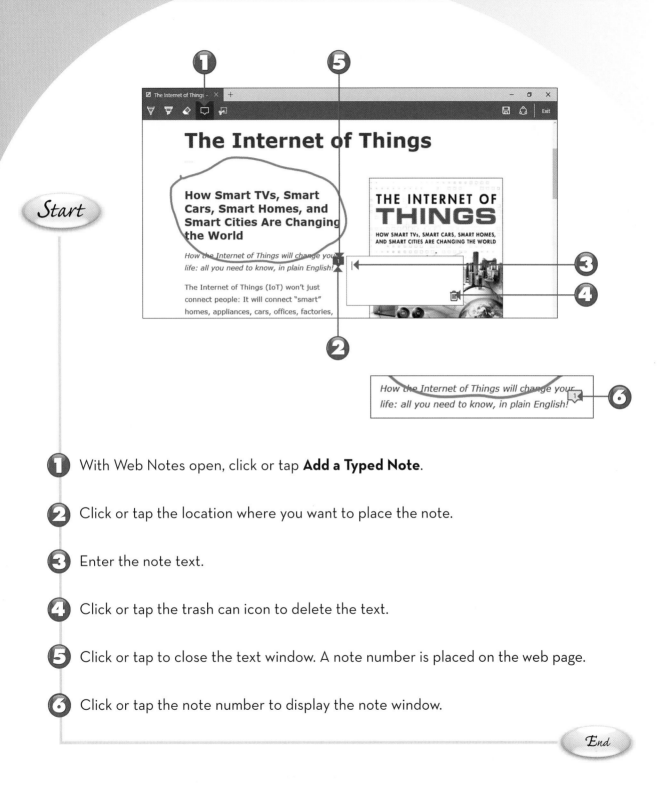

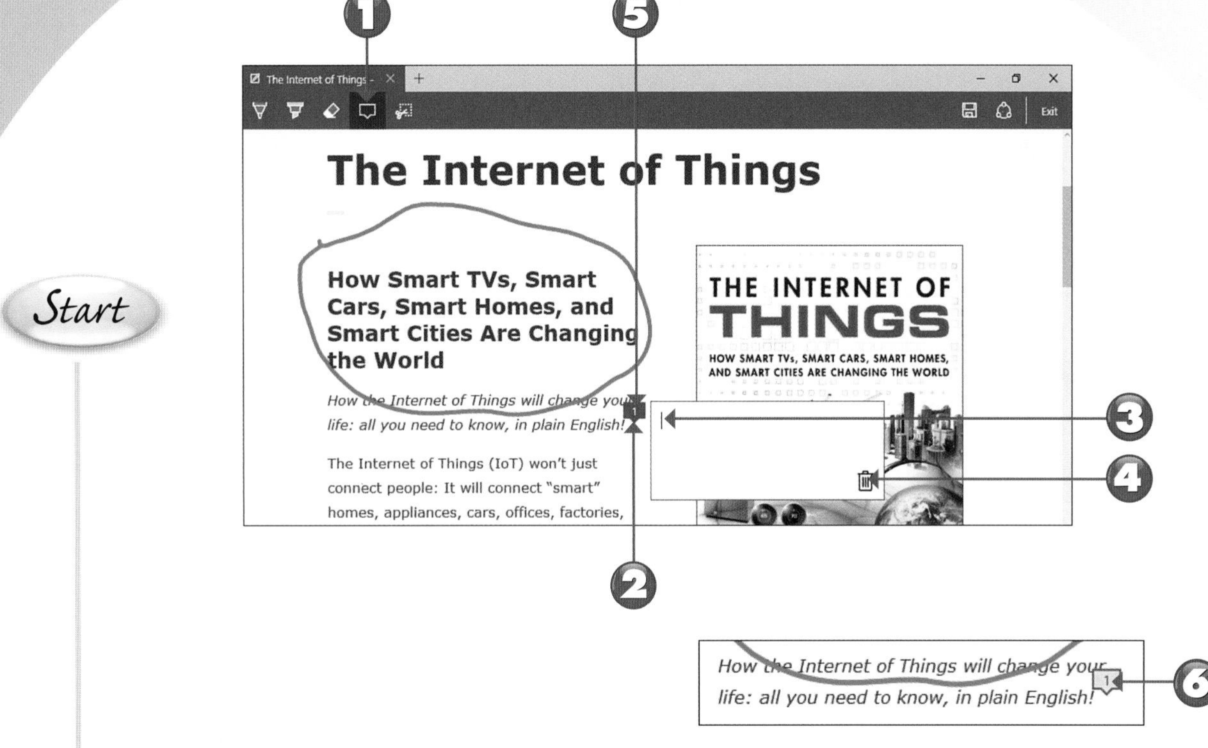

1. With Web Notes open, click or tap **Add a Typed Note**.
2. Click or tap the location where you want to place the note.
3. Enter the note text.
4. Click or tap the trash can icon to delete the text.
5. Click or tap to close the text window. A note number is placed on the web page.
6. Click or tap the note number to display the note window.

End

USING THE WEB NOTES HIGHLIGHTER TOOL

In this exercise, you learn how to use the Web Notes Highlighter tool to highlight text in a web page.

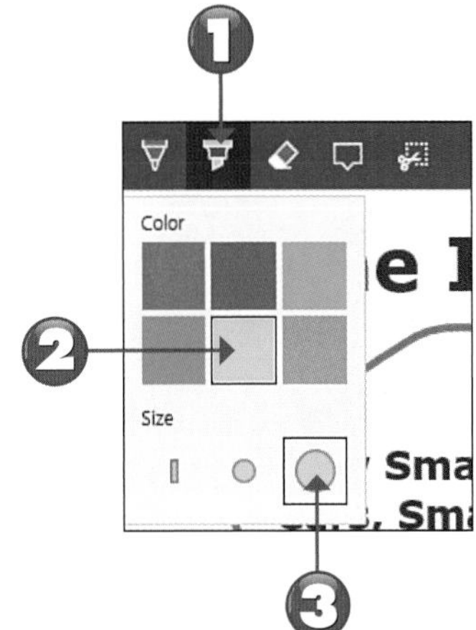

Start

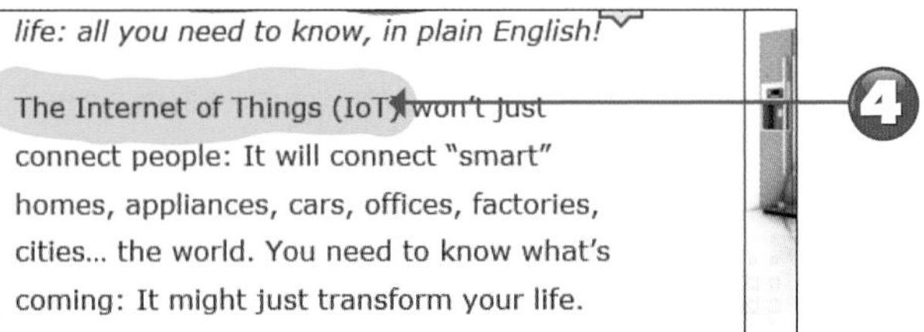

1. With Web Notes open, double-click or double-tap **Highlighter**.
2. Click or tap the desired color.
3. Click or tap the desired pen size.
4. Click or press and drag across text to highlight it.

End

TIP

Changing Colors, Tip Style If you want to highlight several areas on a web page, you can open the Highlighter tool and select different colors and tip styles to make each highlight distinctive.

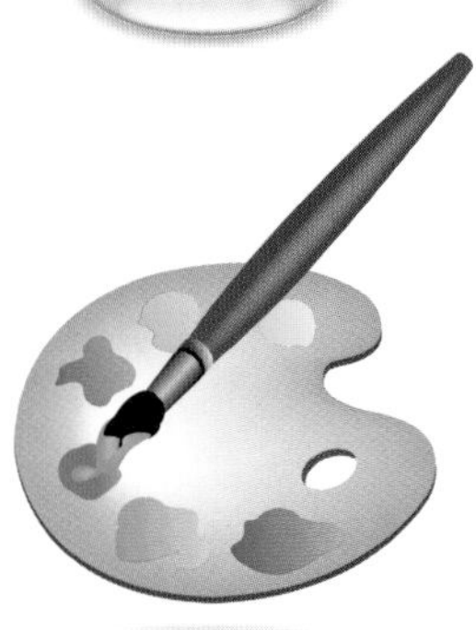

USING THE WEB NOTES CLIP TOOL

You can also use Web Notes to select a section of a web page and paste it into a document or graphics program. This example uses the Windows 10 WordPad word processor, but you could also use Paint or a commercial app such as Adobe Photoshop or Microsoft Word.

Start

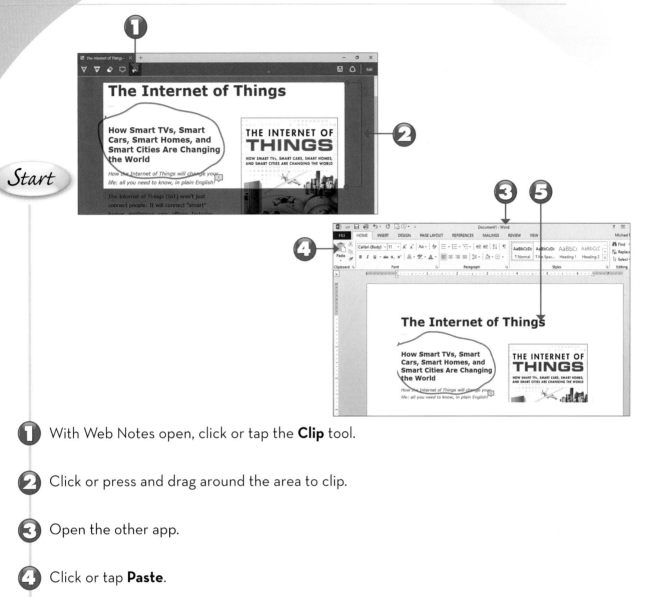

1. With Web Notes open, click or tap the **Clip** tool.
2. Click or press and drag around the area to clip.
3. Open the other app.
4. Click or tap **Paste**.
5. The clipped area is pasted into the other app.

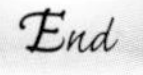

SAVING A WEB NOTE

There are two ways to make web notes available after you create them: saving them and sharing them. In this exercise, you learn how to save a web note.

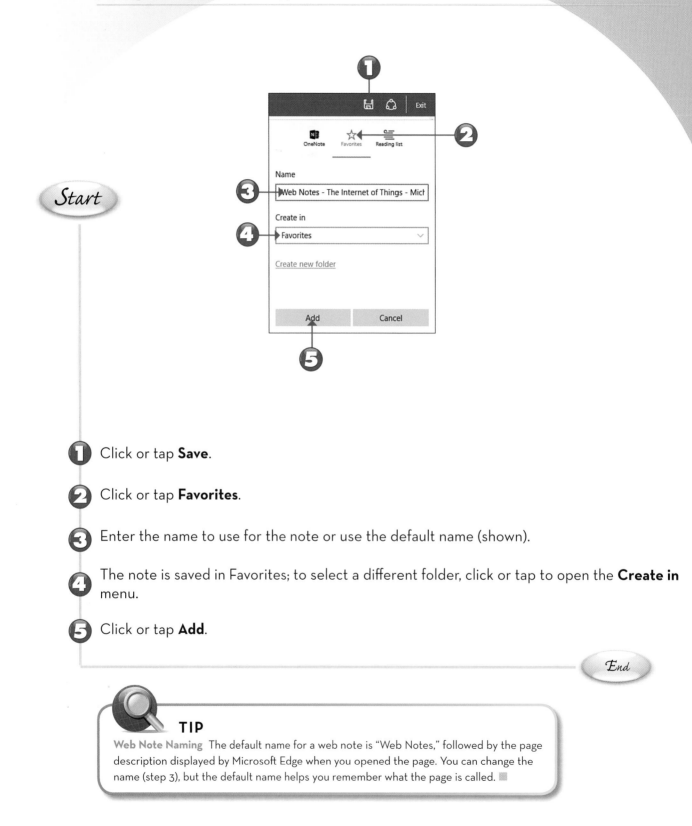

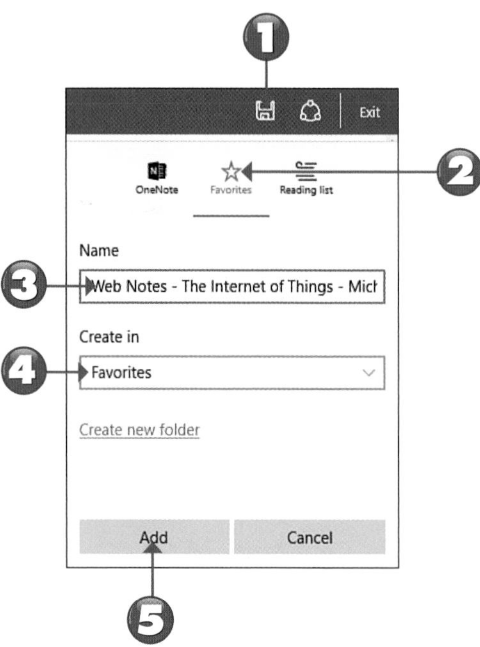

1. Click or tap **Save**.
2. Click or tap **Favorites**.
3. Enter the name to use for the note or use the default name (shown).
4. The note is saved in Favorites; to select a different folder, click or tap to open the **Create in** menu.
5. Click or tap **Add**.

End

TIP

Web Note Naming The default name for a web note is "Web Notes," followed by the page description displayed by Microsoft Edge when you opened the page. You can change the name (step 3), but the default name helps you remember what the page is called.

SHARING A WEB NOTE

There are two ways to make web notes available after you create them: saving them and sharing them. In this exercise, you learn how to share a web note with other users.

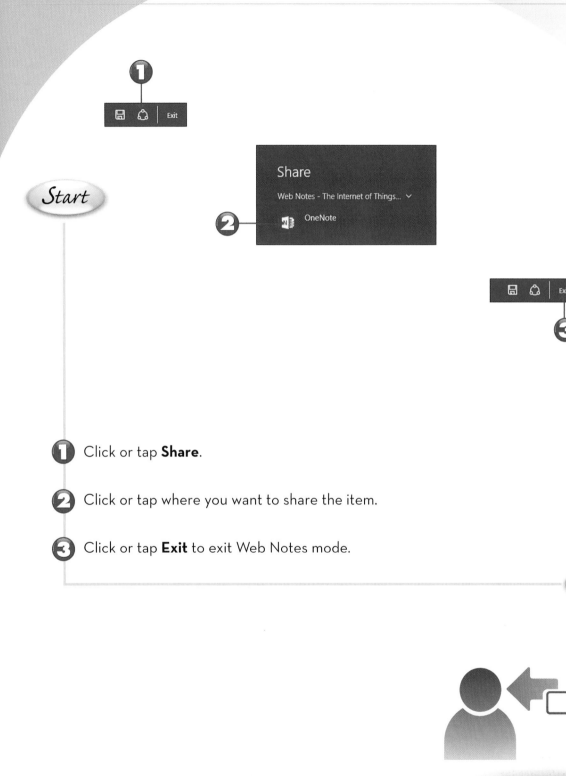

Start

1. Click or tap **Share**.
2. Click or tap where you want to share the item.
3. Click or tap **Exit** to exit Web Notes mode.

End

READING VIEW SETTINGS

Earlier in this chapter, you learned how to use Edge's new Reading view. Now, let's take a closer look at how to personalize your Reading view settings.

Start

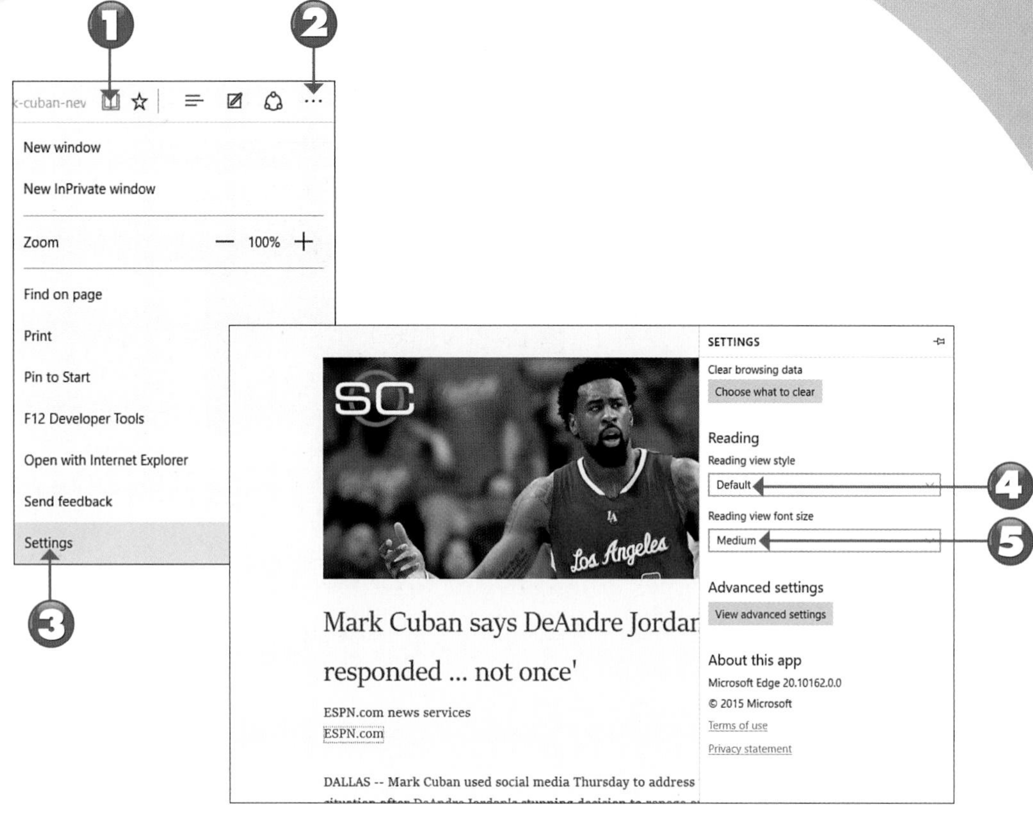

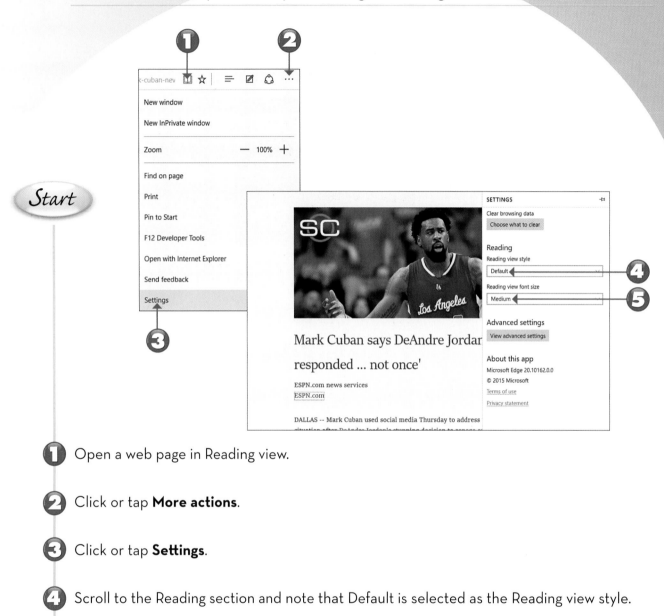

1. Open a web page in Reading view.
2. Click or tap **More actions**.
3. Click or tap **Settings**.
4. Scroll to the Reading section and note that Default is selected as the Reading view style.
5. Medium is the default font size in Reading view.

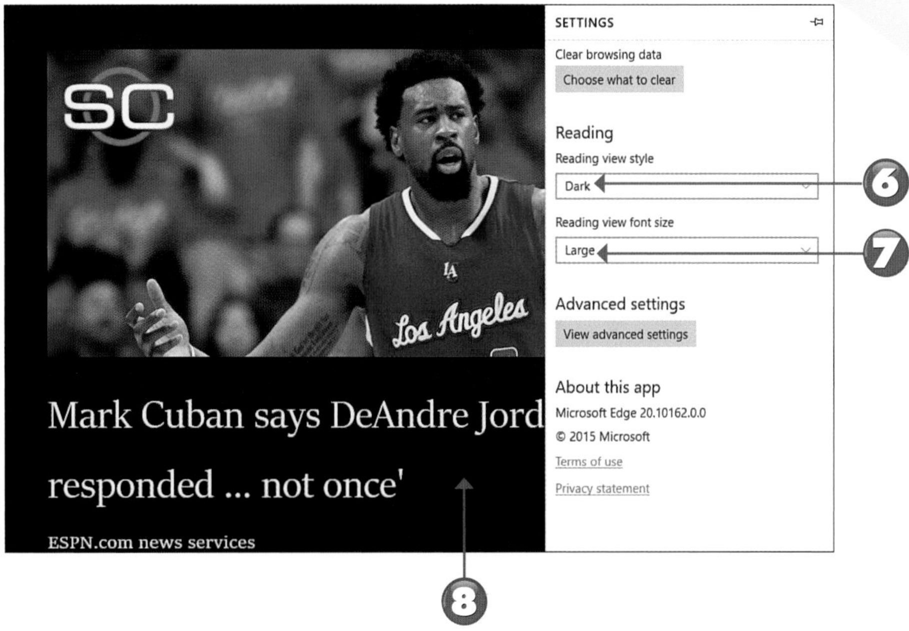

6. Click or tap to select **Dark** as the Reading view style.

7. Click or tap to select **Large** as the Reading view font size.

8. Click or tap outside the menu to close **Settings**.

End

NOTE

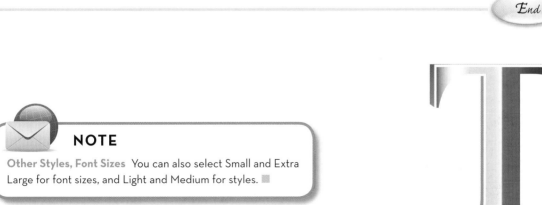

Other Styles, Font Sizes You can also select Small and Extra Large for font sizes, and Light and Medium for styles.

SETTING PRIVACY, SERVICES, AND PLATFORM CONTROLS

The Settings menu also enables you to configure privacy settings, protect your browser, and make it more efficient in page handling. Here are the options you can configure.

Start

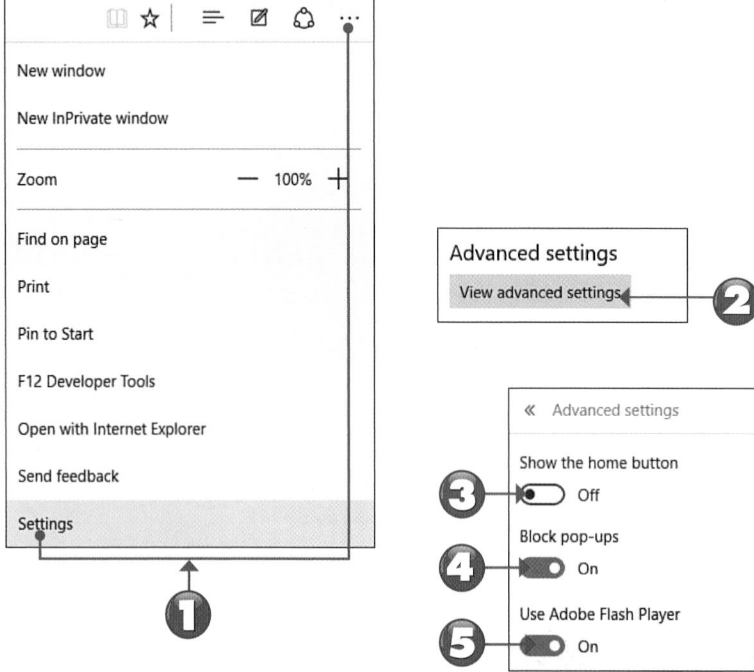

1. Click or tap **More actions** and select **Settings** to open the Settings panel.
2. Scroll to the bottom of the Settings panel and click **View advanced settings**.
3. To display a Home button next to the Address box, click or press and drag to **On**.
4. Pop-ups are blocked by default; to permit them, click or press and drag to **Off**.
5. The Adobe Flash Player should be turned on (enabled) unless it causes problems.

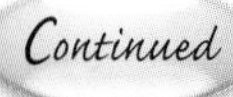

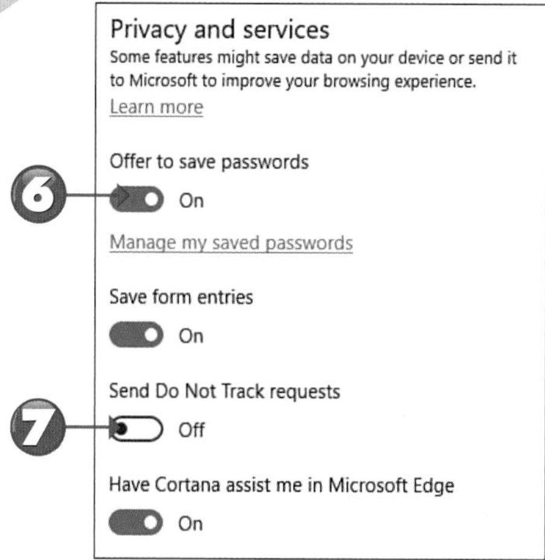

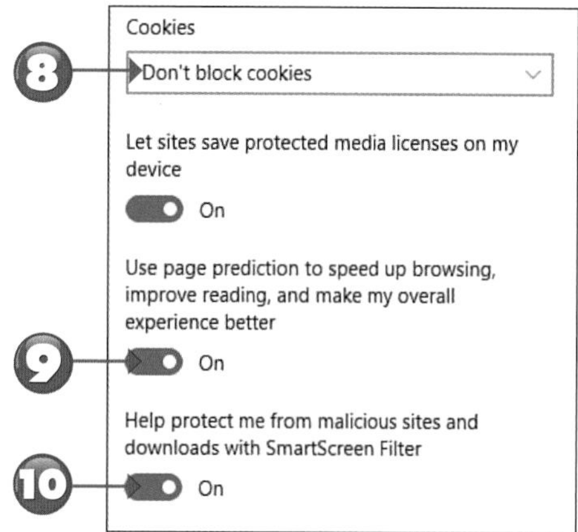

6. In the Privacy and Services section, if you do not want Edge to save passwords you enter, click or press and drag the Offer to Save Passwords control to **Off**.
7. To send Do Not Track requests to websites, click or press and drag to **On**.
8. Open the Cookies menu if you want to block third-party cookies or all cookies.
9. Page prediction preloads pages to speed up browsing; leave this enabled.
10. SmartScreen Filter helps protect your browser from malicious sites; leave this enabled.

NOTE

What the Privacy Settings Do If you block third-party cookies (step 8), you reduce the number of ads you see based on your recent search history. If you block all cookies (step 8), many e-commerce and e-banking websites won't work properly. If you turn on Do Not Track (step 7), you are requesting that websites and web apps do not track your activity. This setting also reduces the number of ads you see based on your recent search history. However, some websites disregard Do Not Track requests, so this setting is not a substitute for browser cookie management.

PLAYING AND CREATING MUSIC AND AUDIO

Windows 10 makes it easy to enjoy and build your audio collection with Groove Music and also provides easy voice recording and editing with Voice Recorder. This chapter shows you how to use the most important features of both apps.

Displaying the albums in your music collection

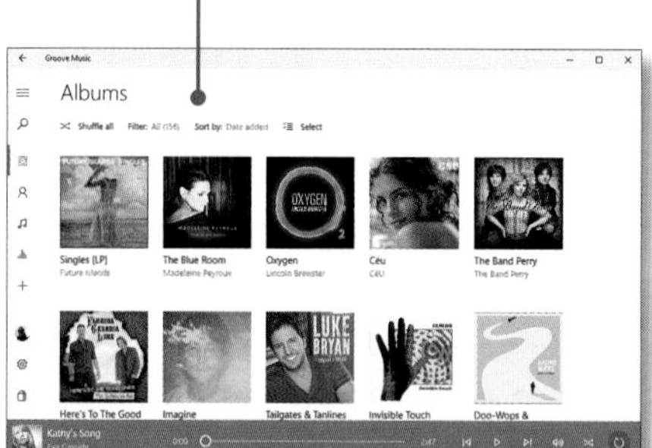

Displaying all albums by an artist

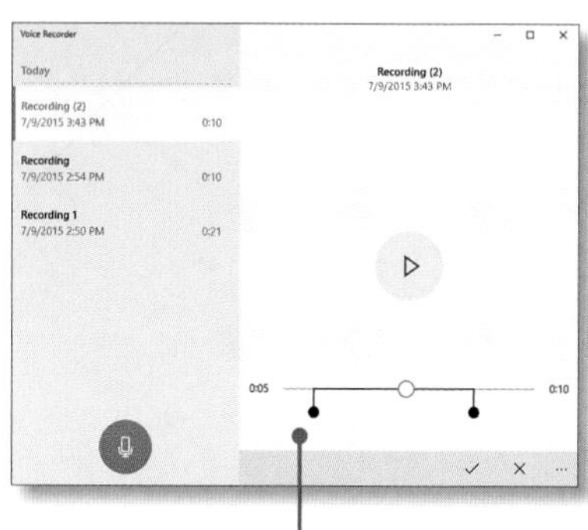

Editing a recording with Voice Recorder

STARTING THE GROOVE MUSIC APP

The Groove Music app in Windows 10 acts as a one-stop shop for your computer music needs, whether you want to listen to files on your computer or purchase more music online. First, let's learn how to start the Groove Music app and see its major features.

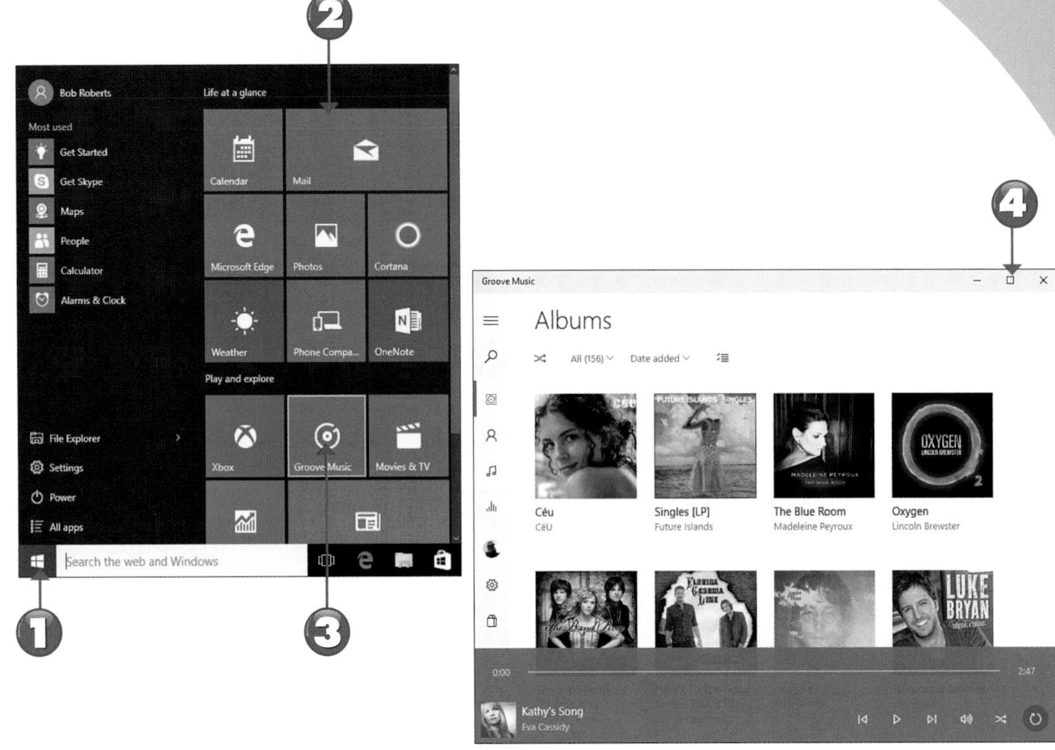

1. Click or tap **Start**.
2. Scroll down the right pane of the Start menu.
3. Click or tap **Groove Music**.
4. If Groove Music is running in a small window, click the **Maximize** button to display it full screen.

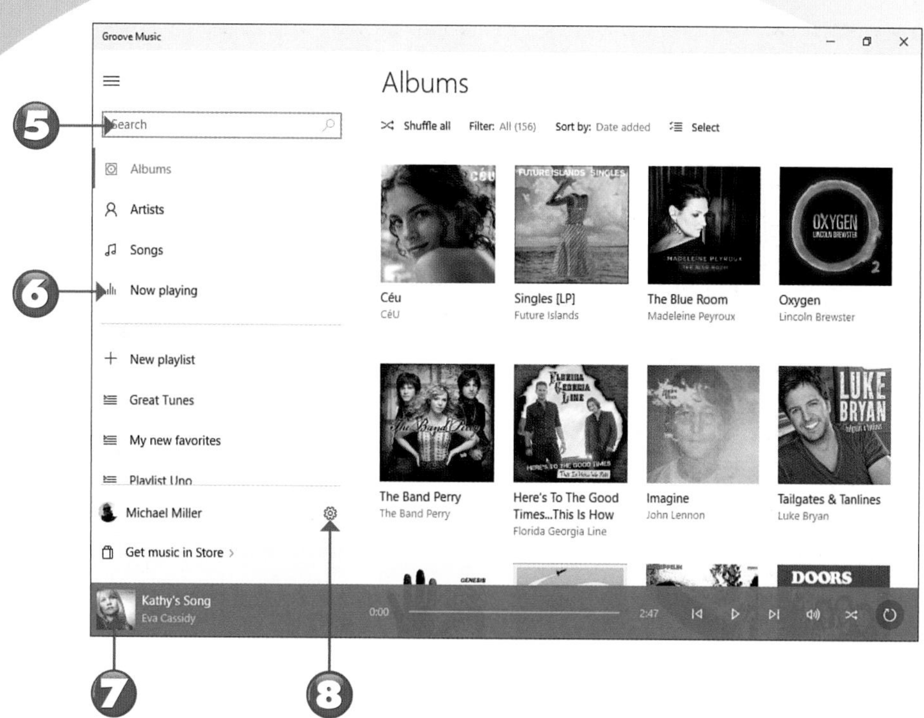

5. Click or tap to search for music.
6. Click or tap to see what's playing.
7. Currently playing track.
8. Click or tap to configure Groove Music settings.

End

VIEWING OPTIONS FOR YOUR MUSIC COLLECTION

The Music app makes it easy to see the types of music in your collection and where it's located. Here's how to use these features.

Start

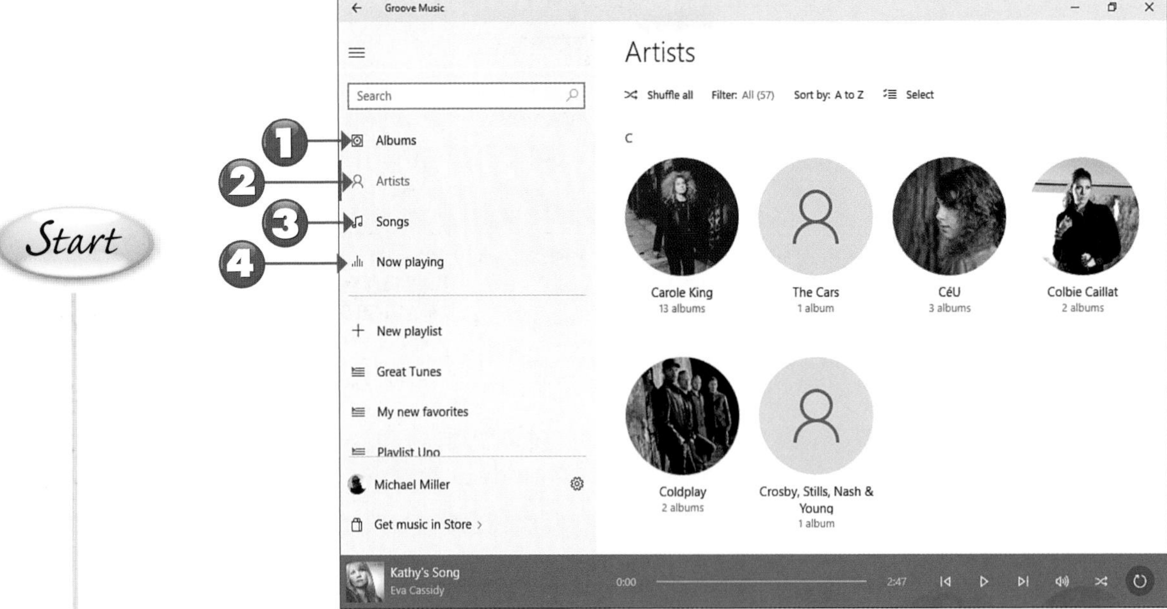

1. Click or tap to view your music by album.
2. Click or tap to view your music by artist.
3. Click or tap to view your music by song.
4. Click or tap to view the currently playing track.

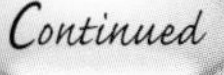

5. Click or tap to filter music—select **All**, **Available offline**, **Streaming**, **Only on this device**, or **On OneDrive**.

6. Click or tap to sort music—by **Date added**, **A to Z**, **Release year**, **Genre**, or **Artist**.

End

PLAYING YOUR MUSIC COLLECTION

By default, Groove Music displays your music collection by album. Here's how to play an album.

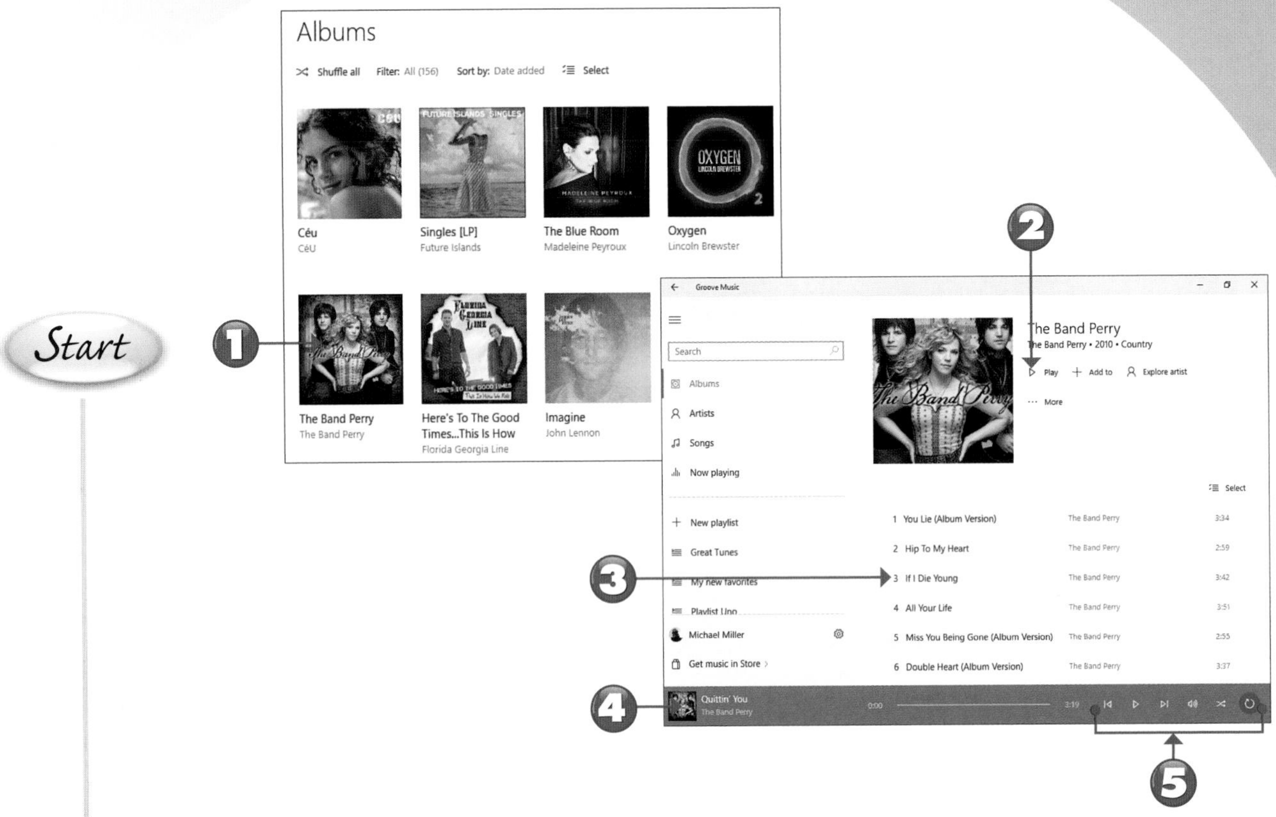

Start

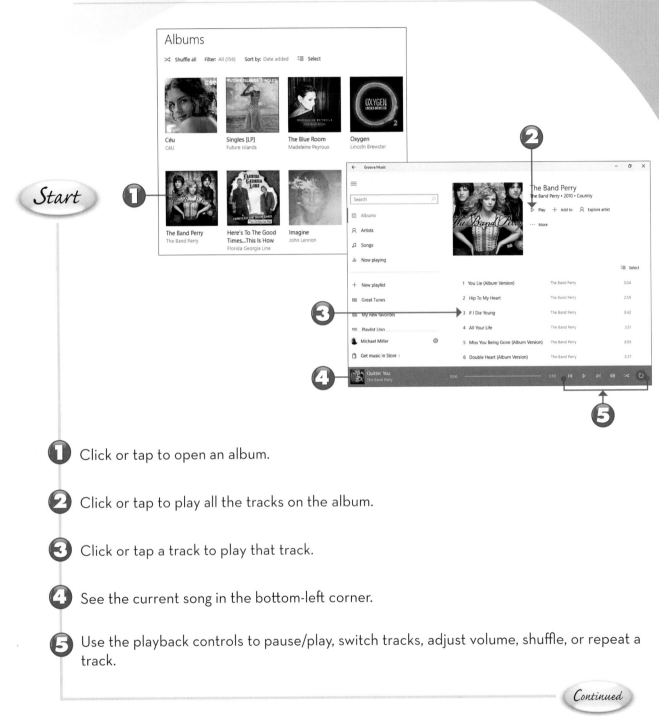

1. Click or tap to open an album.

2. Click or tap to play all the tracks on the album.

3. Click or tap a track to play that track.

4. See the current song in the bottom-left corner.

5. Use the playback controls to pause/play, switch tracks, adjust volume, shuffle, or repeat a track.

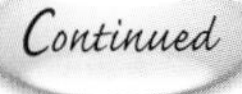

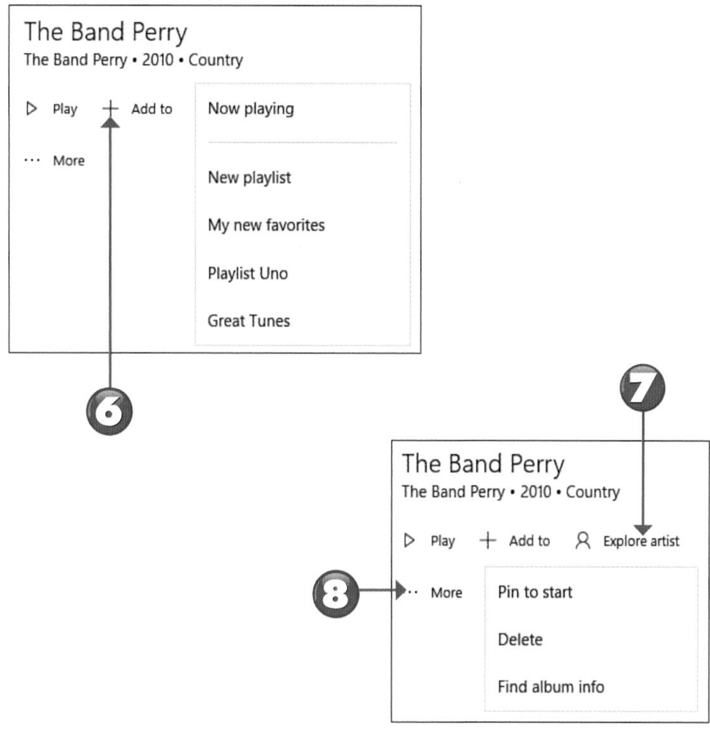

6. Click or tap to add the album to the Now playing list, an existing playlist, or a new playlist.

7. Click or tap to display more information about the artist.

8. Click or tap to pin the album to the Start menu, delete the album, or find album information.

End

SEARCHING FOR YOUR FAVORITE MUSIC

When you have a large music library, it might be difficult to browse through all your albums and tracks. Instead, you can search your entire music library from the Groove Music app. Here's how.

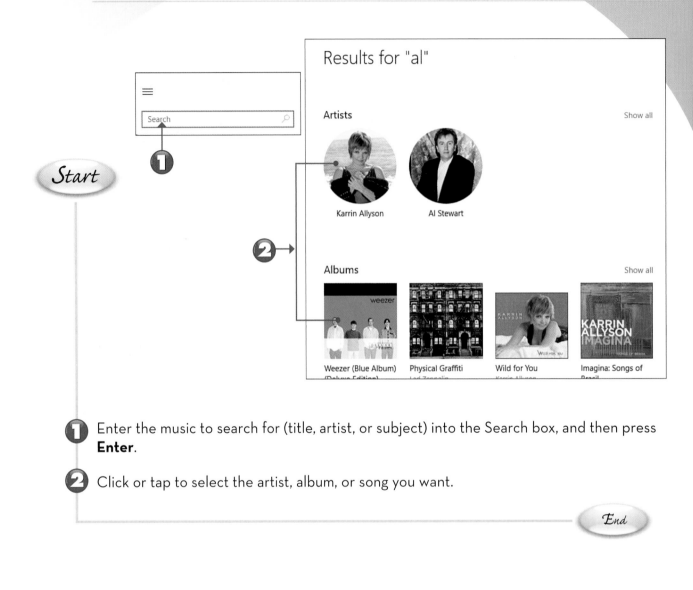

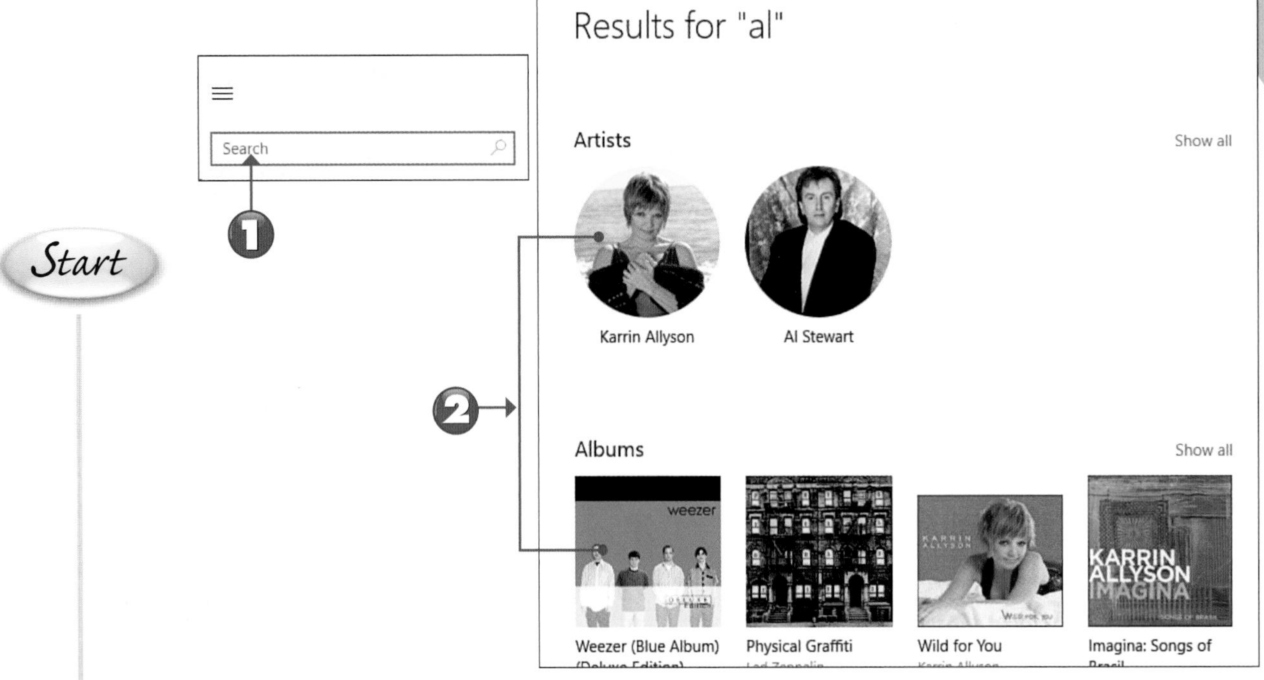

1. Enter the music to search for (title, artist, or subject) into the Search box, and then press **Enter**.
2. Click or tap to select the artist, album, or song you want.

End

NOTE

Groove Music Service Through the Groove Music app, Microsoft also offers the Groove Music streaming audio service. The Groove Music service offers more than 40 million tracks, ad-free, for listening on your Windows computer or mobile device. To sign up for the Groove Music service (a free trial is available), click the **Settings** button in the Groove Music app and click **Get a Groove Music Pass**.

CREATING A PLAYLIST

You can create a playlist from any selected tracks in your music collection. Here's how.

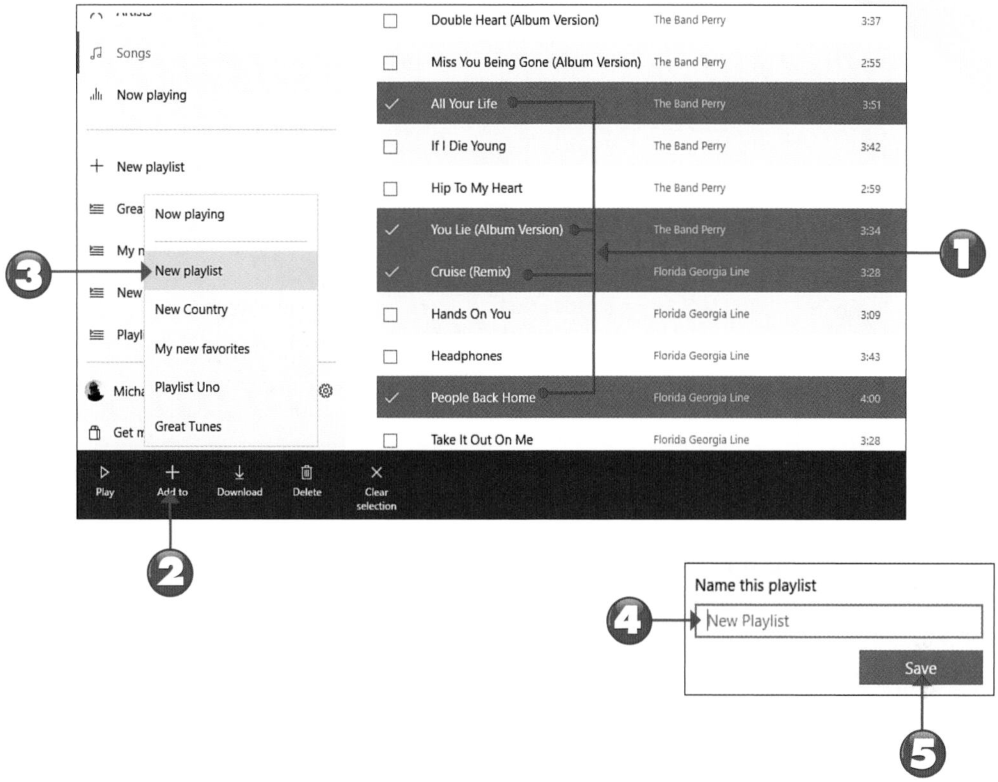

Start

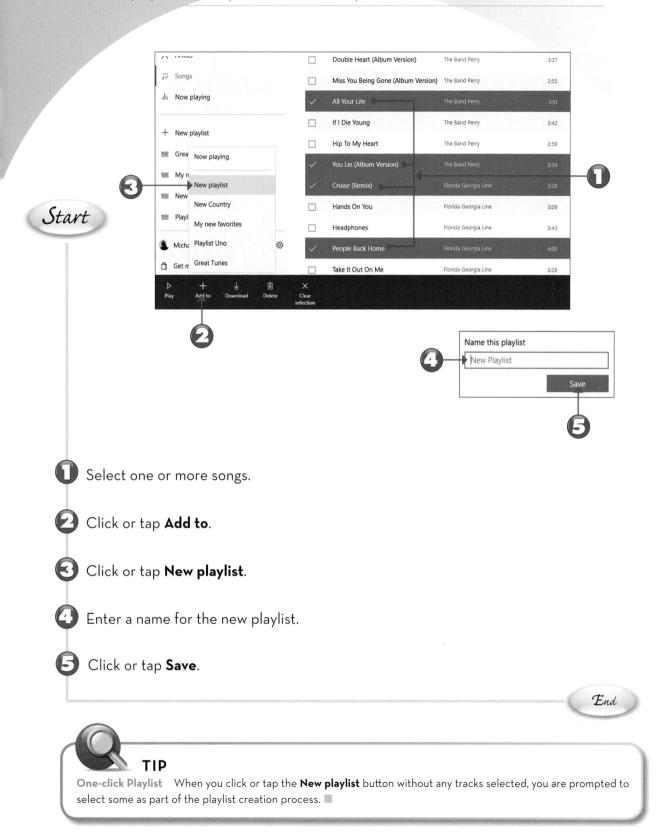

1. Select one or more songs.
2. Click or tap **Add to**.
3. Click or tap **New playlist**.
4. Enter a name for the new playlist.
5. Click or tap **Save**.

End

TIP

One-click Playlist When you click or tap the **New playlist** button without any tracks selected, you are prompted to select some as part of the playlist creation process.

PLAYING A PLAYLIST

Playing a playlist is as easy as playing an album or individual track.

Start

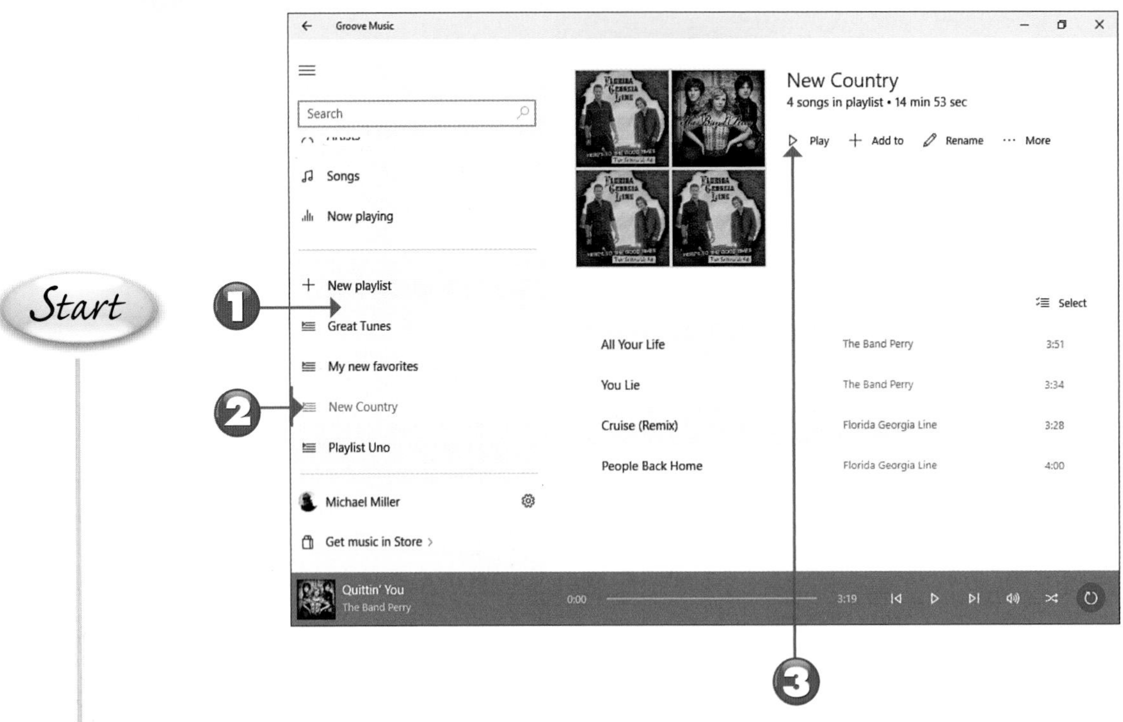

1. In the menu pane, scroll to the playlists section (just beneath the New playlist selection).
2. Click or tap to open the playlist.
3. Click or tap to begin playback.

End

BUYING MUSIC

You can purchase and download music from Microsoft's Windows Store to play back in the Groove Music app.

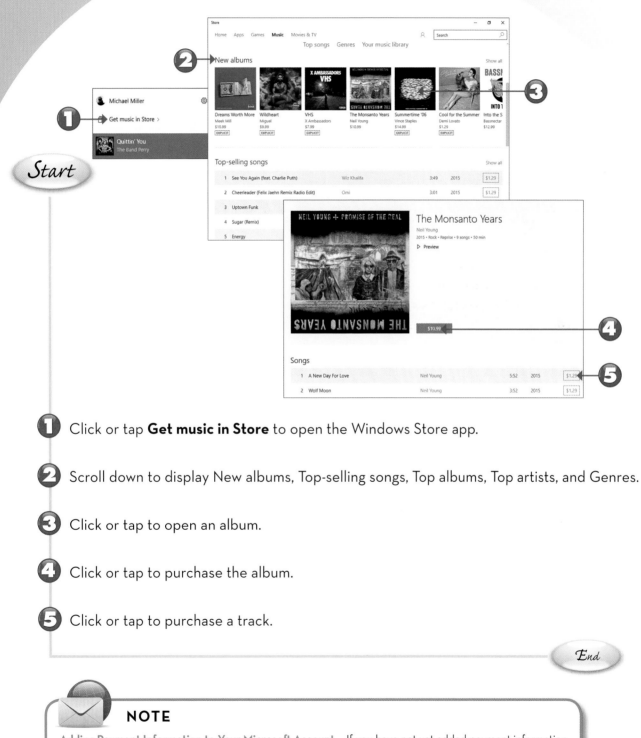

1. Click or tap **Get music in Store** to open the Windows Store app.
2. Scroll down to display New albums, Top-selling songs, Top albums, Top artists, and Genres.
3. Click or tap to open an album.
4. Click or tap to purchase the album.
5. Click or tap to purchase a track.

NOTE

Adding Payment Information to Your Microsoft Account If you have not yet added payment information to your Microsoft account, you will be prompted to do so when you buy an album or a track.

RECORDING AUDIO WITH VOICE RECORDER

You can use your device's built-in or connected microphone to record sounds with Voice Recorder. Here's how to start Voice Recorder from the All Apps menu and use it.

Start

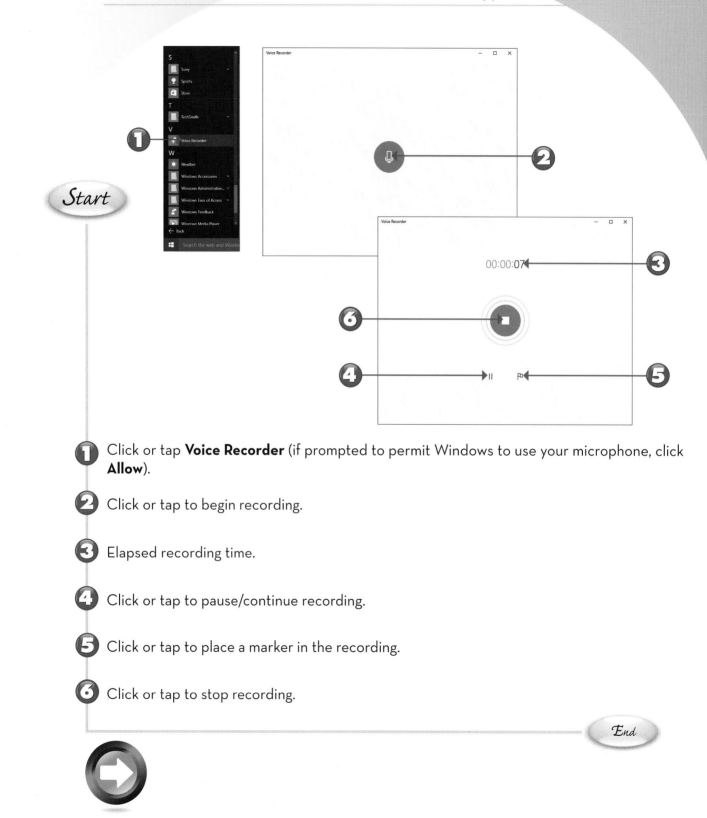

1. Click or tap **Voice Recorder** (if prompted to permit Windows to use your microphone, click **Allow**).
2. Click or tap to begin recording.
3. Elapsed recording time.
4. Click or tap to pause/continue recording.
5. Click or tap to place a marker in the recording.
6. Click or tap to stop recording.

End

PLAYING AND RENAMING A RECORDING

After you create a recording, you can play it back or change its name. You can perform these steps immediately after making a recording, or you can select a recording as described in the "Editing Recorded Audio" exercise.

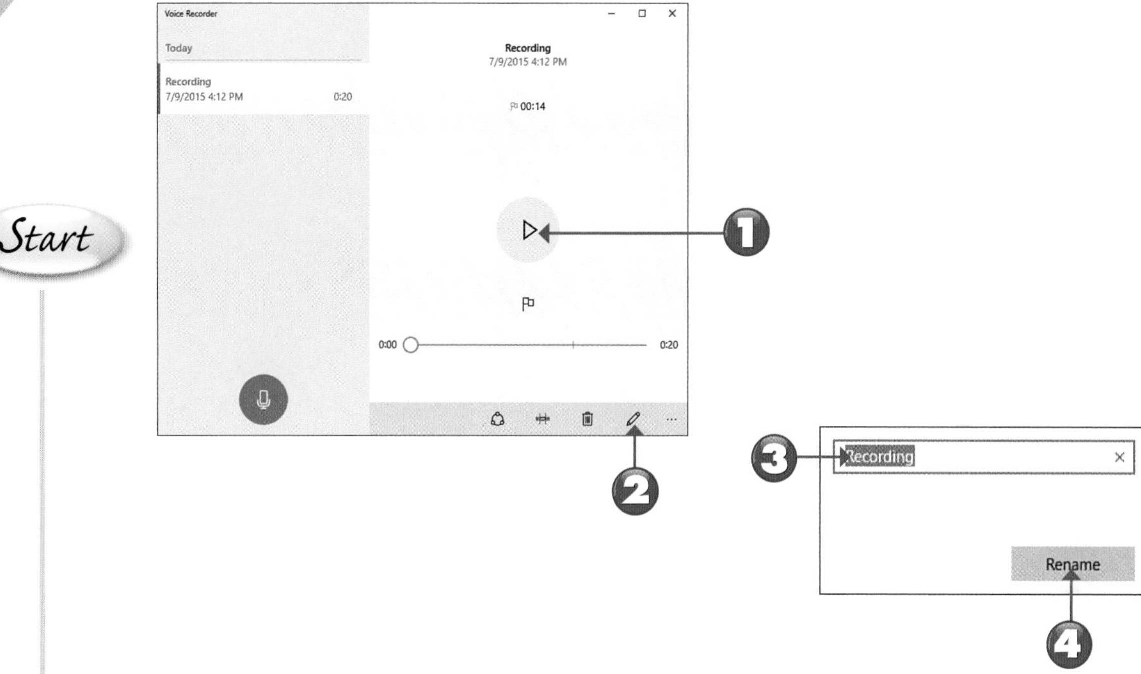

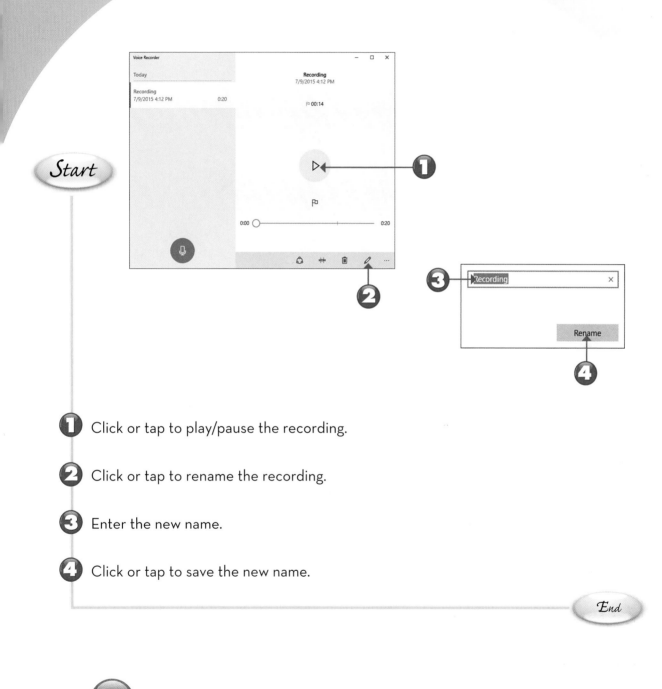

1. Click or tap to play/pause the recording.
2. Click or tap to rename the recording.
3. Enter the new name.
4. Click or tap to save the new name.

End

NOTE

Finding Your Recordings To play your recordings without restarting Voice Recorder, use Cortana/Search to locate your recordings. Windows 10 uses the Groove Music app to play them.

EDITING RECORDED AUDIO

You can cut out unwanted portions of a recording you make with Voice Recorder and save the remainder as a new file. In this example, we'll discard the part of the recording after the flag marker at 14 seconds (00:14).

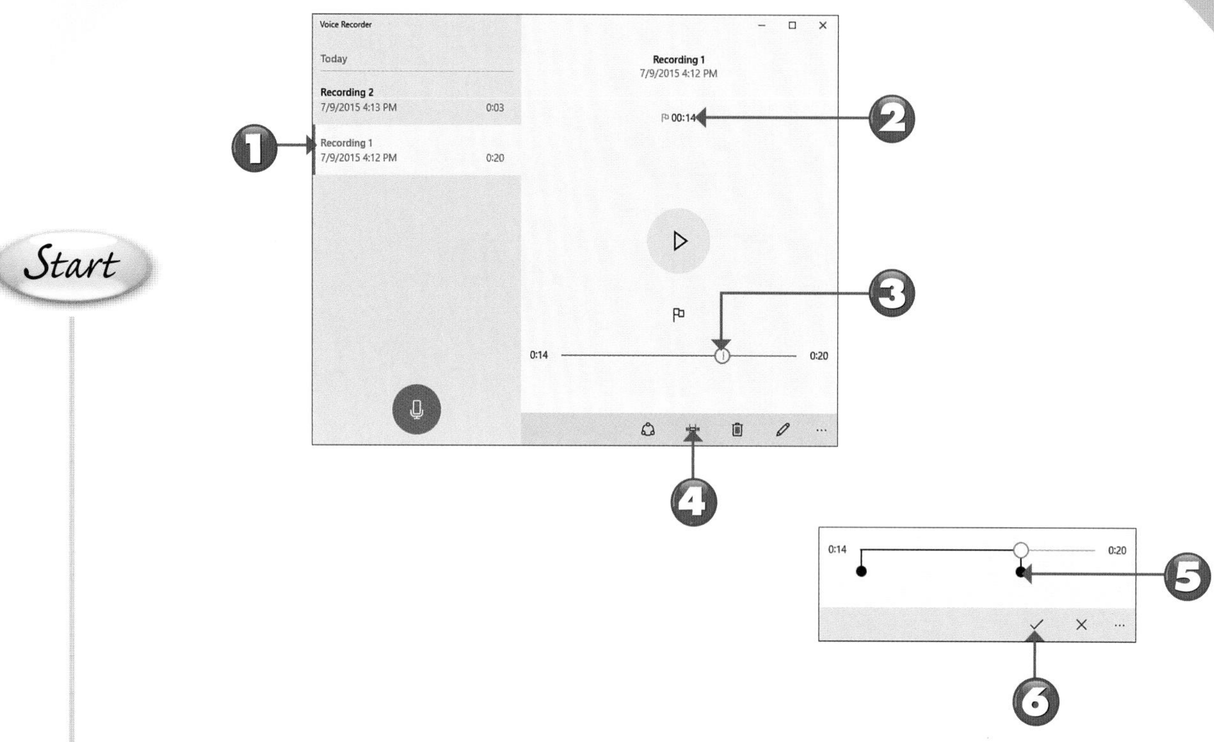

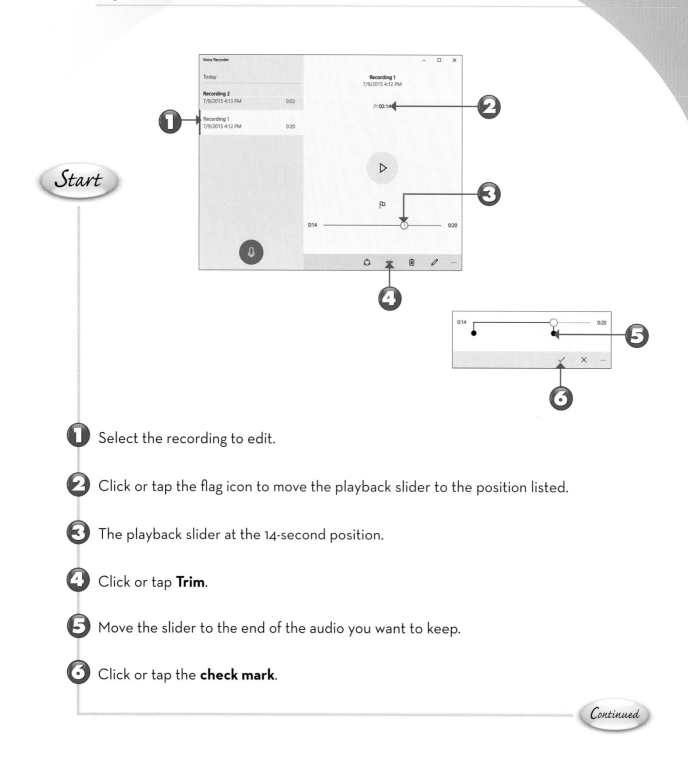

Start

1. Select the recording to edit.
2. Click or tap the flag icon to move the playback slider to the position listed.
3. The playback slider at the 14-second position.
4. Click or tap **Trim**.
5. Move the slider to the end of the audio you want to keep.
6. Click or tap the **check mark**.

Continued

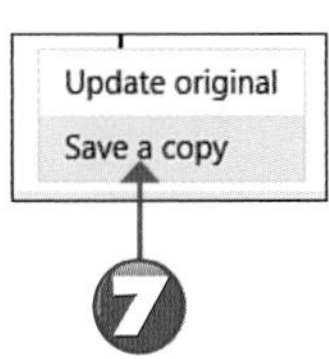

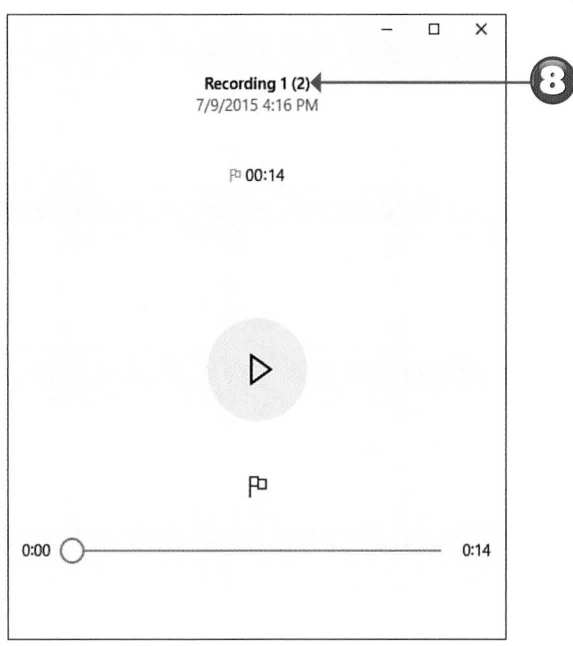

7 Click or tap **Save a copy**.

8 The edited copy of the recording.

End

NOTE

The Microphone Matters For the highest-quality recording, use a headset microphone. If you use the microphone built in to your laptop, it's likely to pick up extraneous noise.

ENJOYING VIDEOS

Windows 10 includes the easy-to-use Movies & TV app, which helps you view both homemade and commercial video (TV, movie) content. In this chapter, you learn how to use Movies & TV to find and play your own video content, hit the Windows Store for TV and movie content, and solve playback problems.

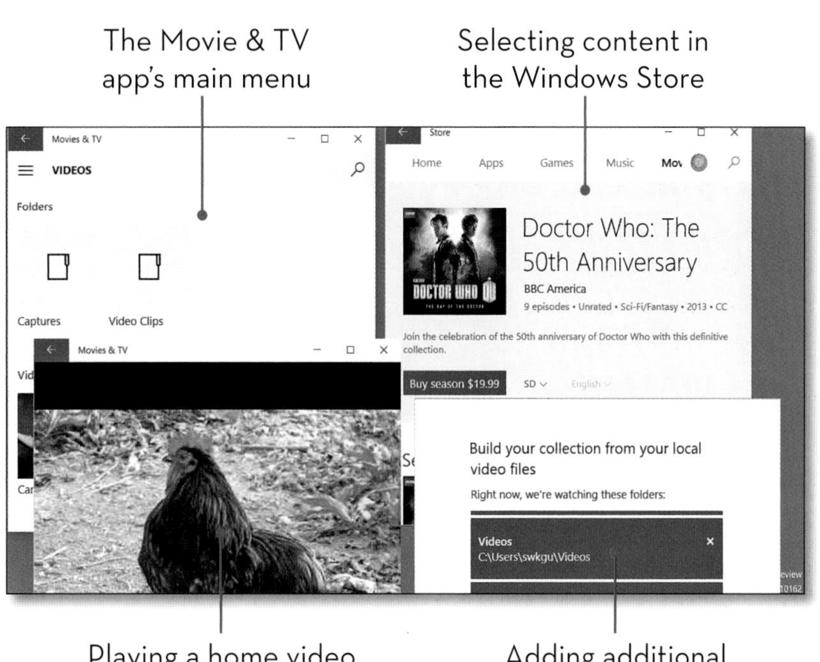
The Movie & TV app's main menu
Selecting content in the Windows Store
Movies & TV
VIDEOS
Folders
Captures
Video Clips
Store
Home
Apps
Games
Music
Doctor Who: The 50th Anniversary
BBC America
9 episodes • Unrated • Sci-Fi/Fantasy • 2013 • CC
Join the celebration of the 50th anniversary of Doctor Who with this definitive collection.
Buy season $19.99
SD
Build your collection from your local video files
Right now, we're watching these folders:
Videos
C:\Users\swkgu\Videos
Playing a home video
Adding additional folders to watch for video content

STARTING THE MOVIES & TV APP

You can use the Movies & TV app to preview, download, and buy video content from the Microsoft store as well as to view video content you create. The app groups your video content into several categories: Movies, TV, and Videos (your own video content). Here's how to get started using the app.

Start

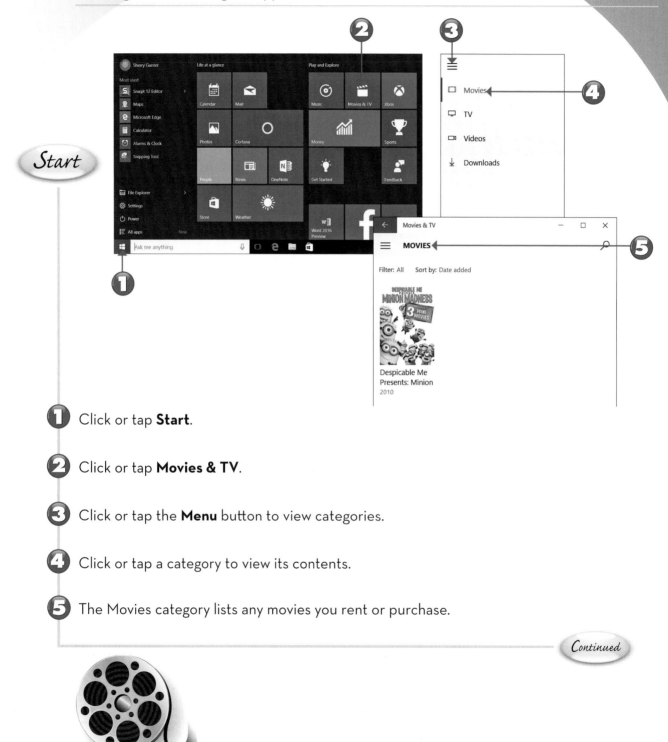

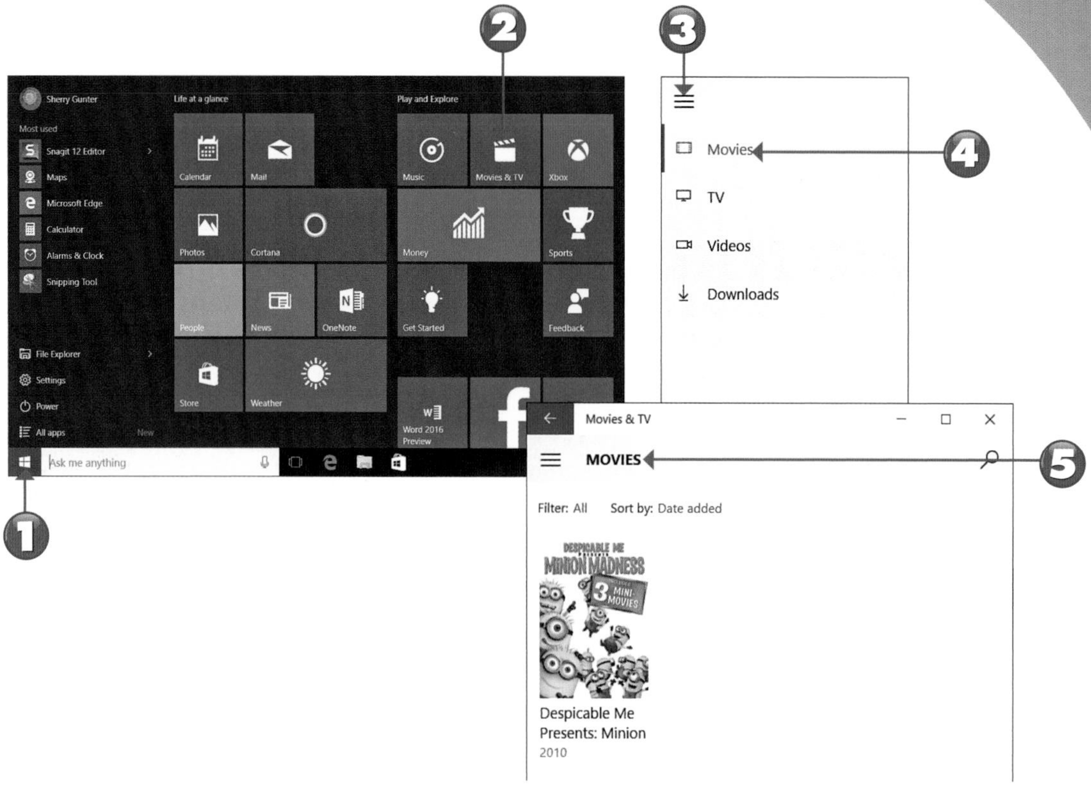

1. Click or tap **Start**.
2. Click or tap **Movies & TV**.
3. Click or tap the **Menu** button to view categories.
4. Click or tap a category to view its contents.
5. The Movies category lists any movies you rent or purchase.

Continued

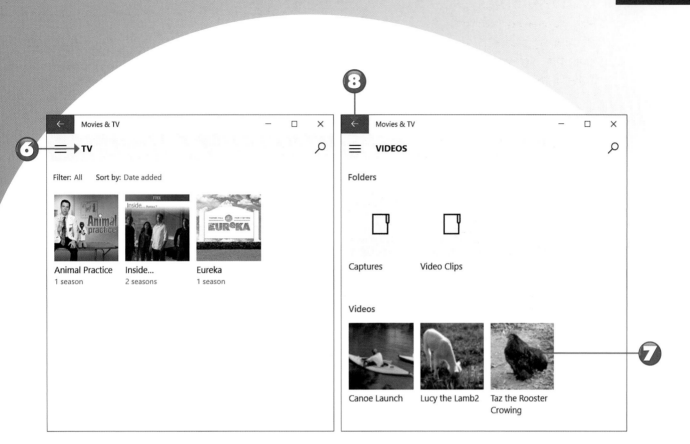

6 The TV category lists TV shows you have purchased.

7 The Videos category lists your video files and folders.

8 Click or tap the navigation button to return to the previous window.

End

NOTE

Downloads Category You can check your movie downloads by clicking or tapping the Downloads category in the Movies & TV app's menu. This window lists any downloading files and displays their progress. ■

ADDING A LOCATION TO LOOK FOR VIDEOS

The Movies & TV app looks in the current user's Videos folder for videos. However, you can also check other folders, such as external drives, network locations, and Camera Roll (the folder used for storing photos and videos shot with your device's onboard camera). Here's how to configure Movies & TV to find videos in other folders.

Start

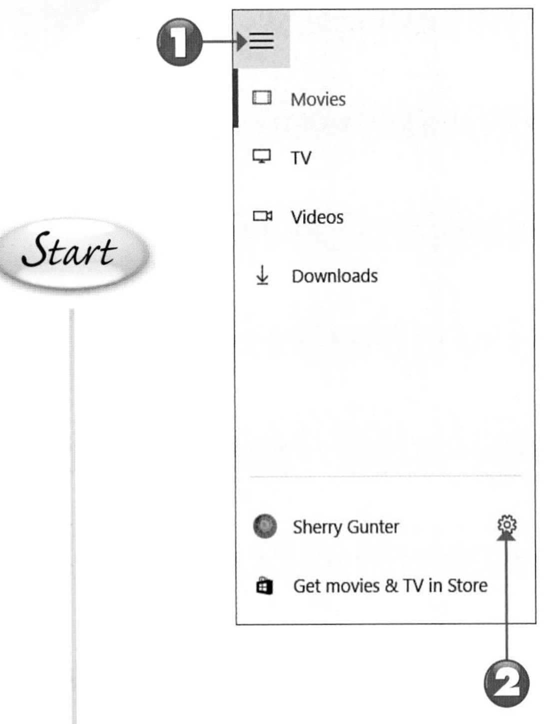

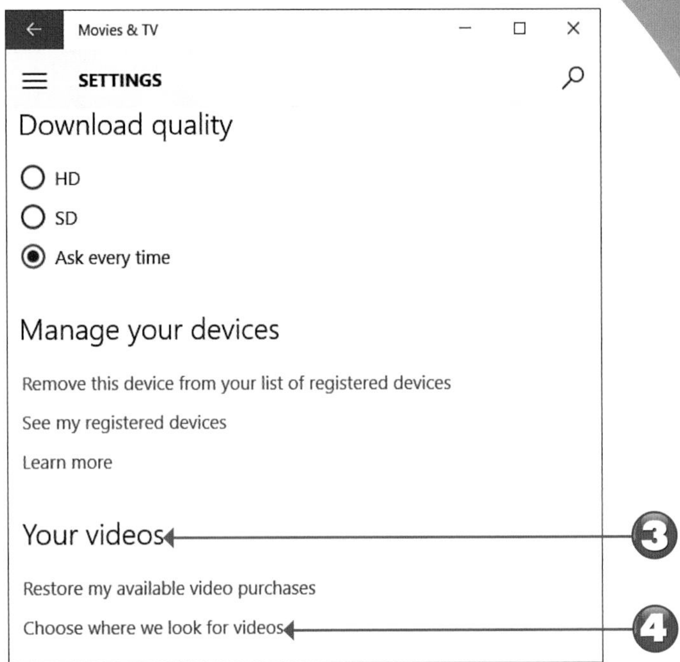

1. Click or tap the **Menu** button.
2. Click or tap **Settings**.
3. Scroll to the **Your Videos** section.
4. Click or tap **Choose where we look for videos**.

Continued

NOTE

Video Folders The Windows 10 default folder for video content, named Videos, also offers a subfolder named Captures, for content you capture with a recording device on your computer. You can also add as many folders as you want to keep your video content organized and easy to find. ■

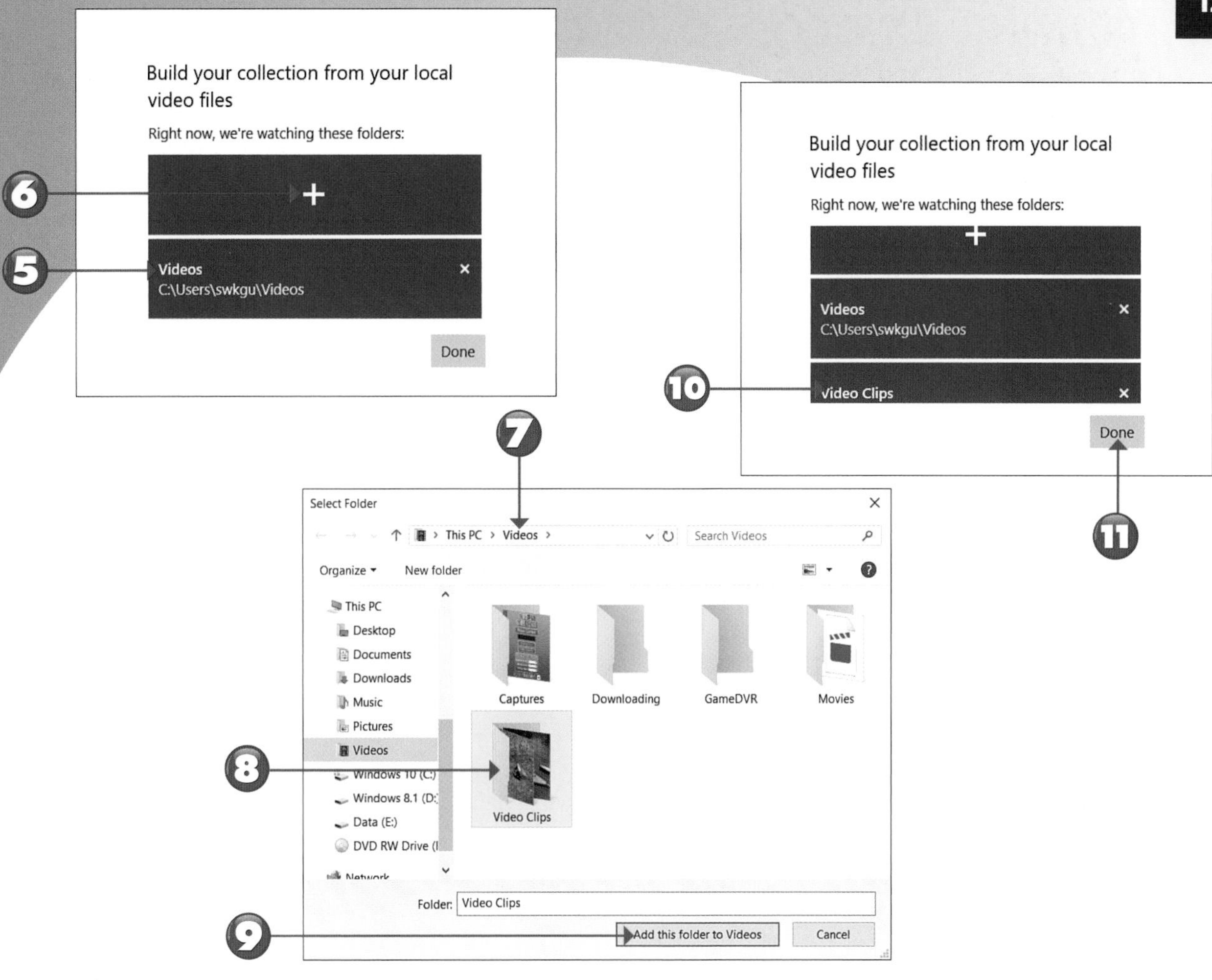

5. Current folder used by the Video app.
6. Click or tap to add a folder.
7. Navigate to the location containing the folder you want to add.
8. Click or tap the folder.
9. Click or tap **Add this folder to Videos**.
10. The new source is added to the list.
11. Click or tap **Done** when finished.

End

PLAYING A VIDEO, MOVIE, OR TV SHOW

You can play a video, movie, or TV show in a window or full screen using the Movies & TV app. You can quickly display playback controls to help you adjust volume, change aspect ratio, or pause the video. This example shows you how to play a video from the Videos collection.

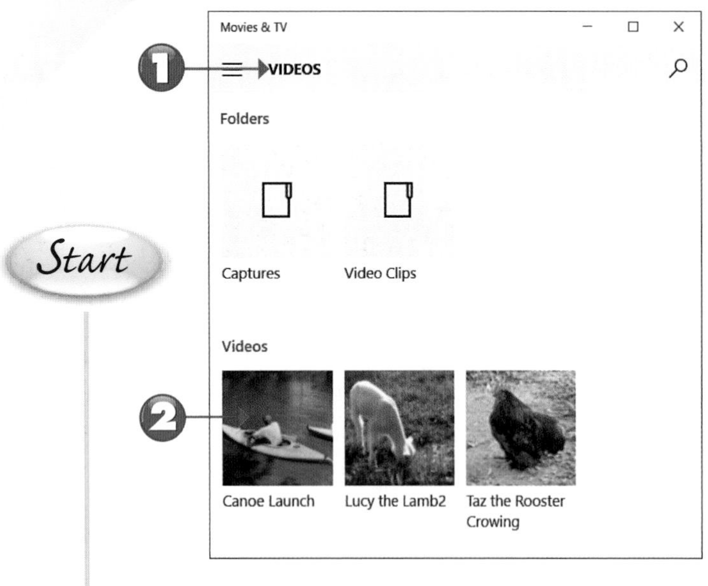

Start

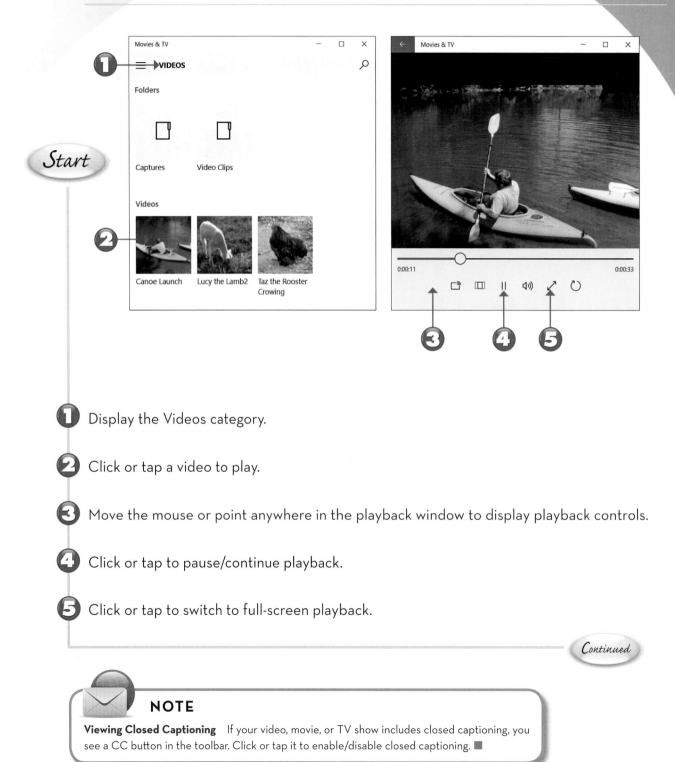

1. Display the Videos category.
2. Click or tap a video to play.
3. Move the mouse or point anywhere in the playback window to display playback controls.
4. Click or tap to pause/continue playback.
5. Click or tap to switch to full-screen playback.

Continued

NOTE

Viewing Closed Captioning If your video, movie, or TV show includes closed captioning, you see a CC button in the toolbar. Click or tap it to enable/disable closed captioning. ■

6 Full-screen view fills the entire screen.

7 Click or tap to change the aspect ratio between full-screen or letterbox format.

8 Click or tap to switch to windowed playback.

9 Click or tap to adjust the volume.

10 Click or tap to repeat.

11 Click or tap to return to the Videos category.

End

NOTE

Viewing Movies and TV Shows To start a movie or TV show, first click or tap the movie or show name, and then click or tap the **Play** button listed on the movie or show's information window. When the movie starts, you can move the mouse to display playback controls.

USING SEARCH TO FIND LOCAL AND WINDOWS STORE MEDIA

The Movies & TV app's powerful search feature can look for matches within your existing collection of videos, movies, or TV shows as well as matches in the Windows Store. In this example, you learn how this feature makes finding your favorite content easier.

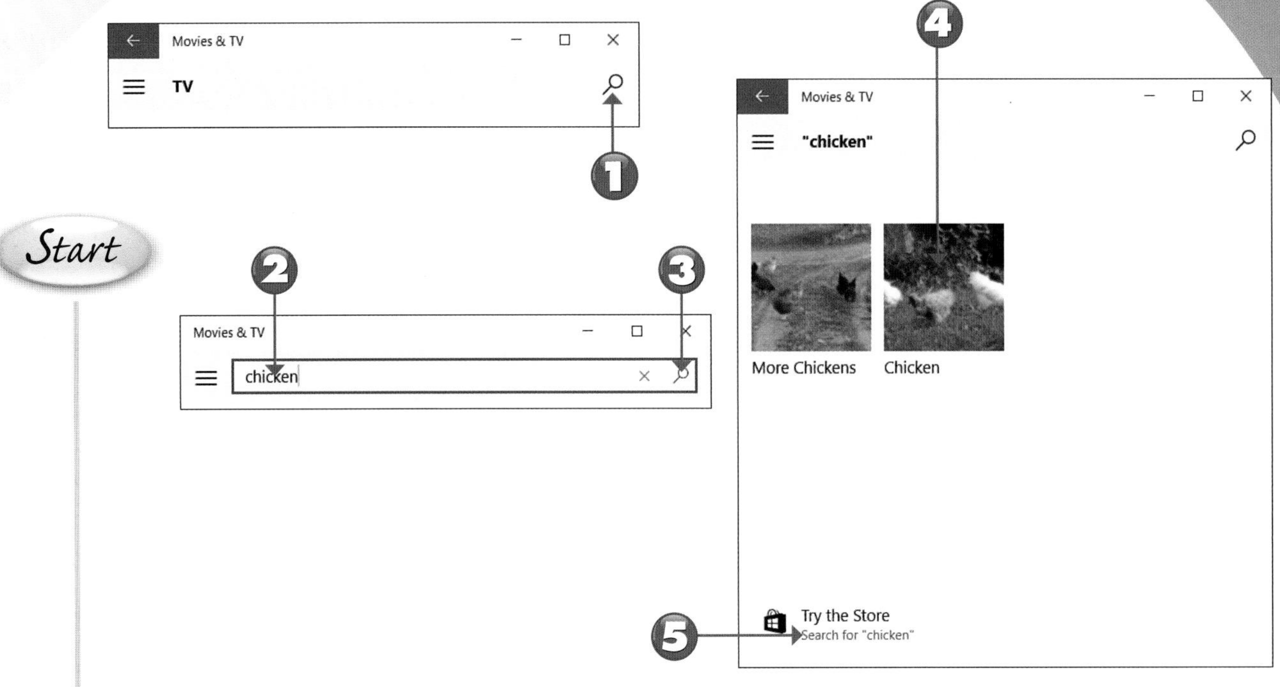

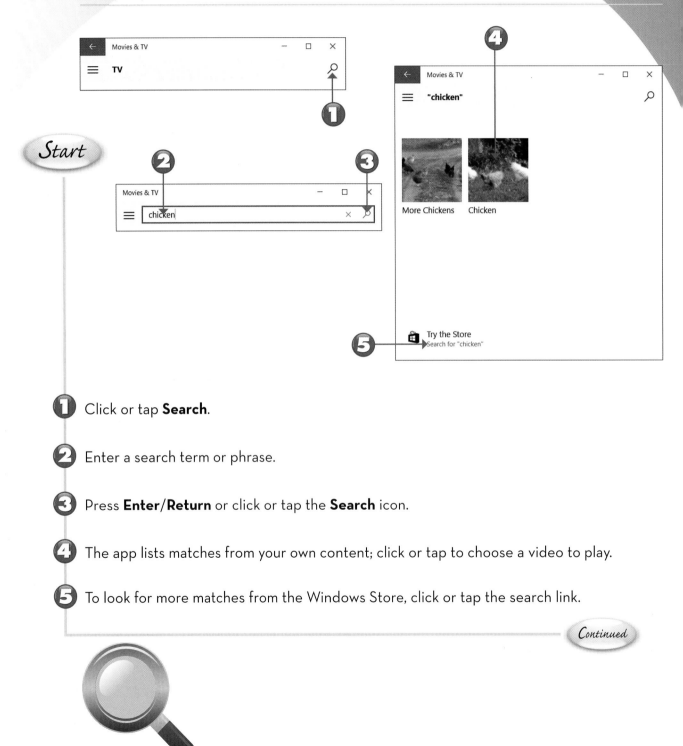

1. Click or tap **Search**.
2. Enter a search term or phrase.
3. Press **Enter/Return** or click or tap the **Search** icon.
4. The app lists matches from your own content; click or tap to choose a video to play.
5. To look for more matches from the Windows Store, click or tap the search link.

Continued

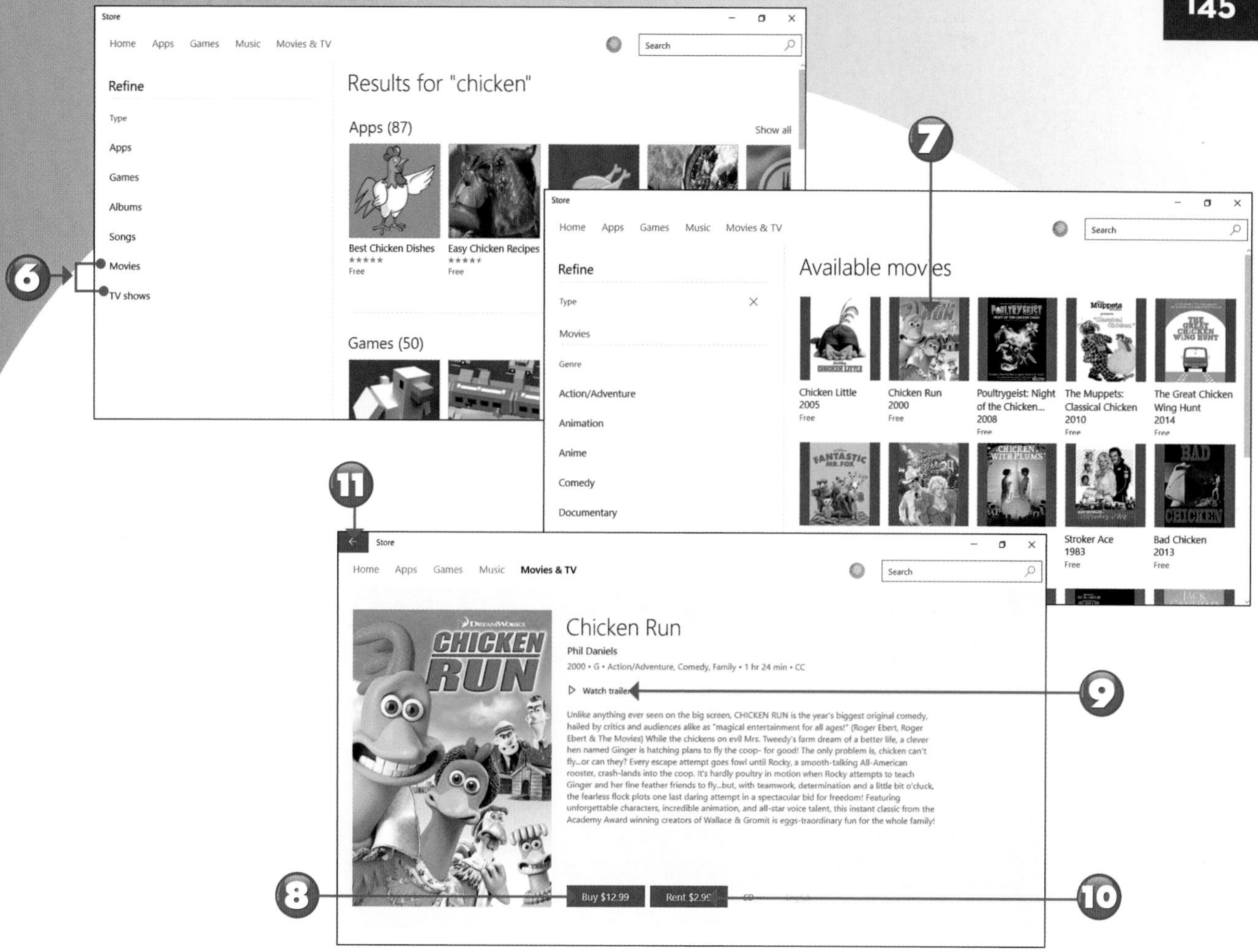

6 Click or tap **Movies** or **TV Shows** to filter results to video content.

7 Click or tap to select a movie or TV show.

8 Standard definition (SD) pricing.

9 Click or tap to view trailer.

10 Click or tap to see pricing for other formats.

11 Click or tap to return to the previous screen.

End

BUYING OR RENTING A MOVIE OR TV SHOW

You can shop for music and videos online from within the Movies & TV app. Using your Microsoft account, you can purchase items for downloading or streaming. This example demonstrates buying an episode of a TV series.

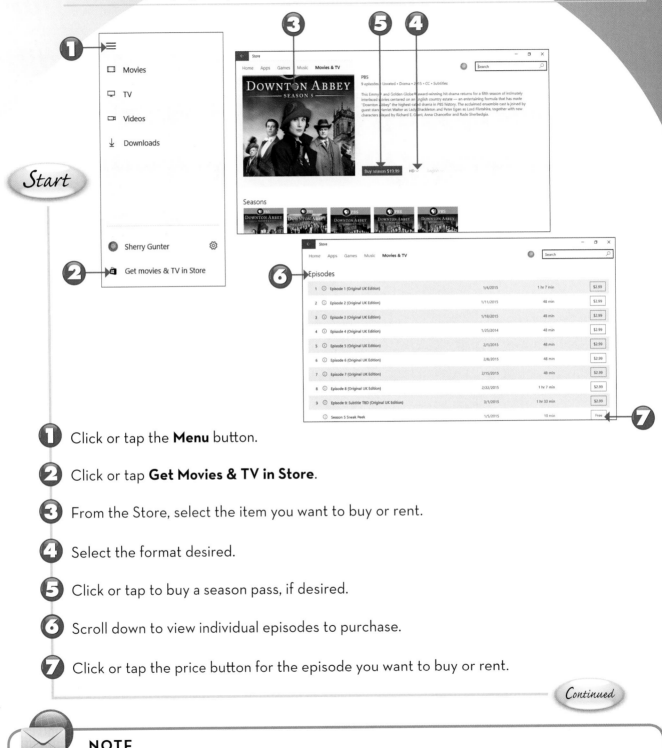

Start

1. Click or tap the **Menu** button.
2. Click or tap **Get Movies & TV in Store**.
3. From the Store, select the item you want to buy or rent.
4. Select the format desired.
5. Click or tap to buy a season pass, if desired.
6. Scroll down to view individual episodes to purchase.
7. Click or tap the price button for the episode you want to buy or rent.

Continued

NOTE

Microsoft Account and Your Payment Information If you did not set up payment information when you set up your Microsoft account, you are prompted to provide a form of payment before you can complete your purchase. Follow the prompts to set up payment options. ■

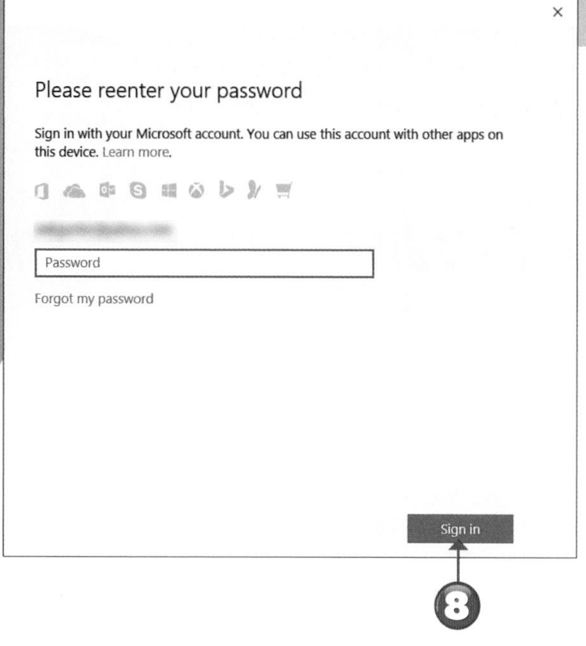

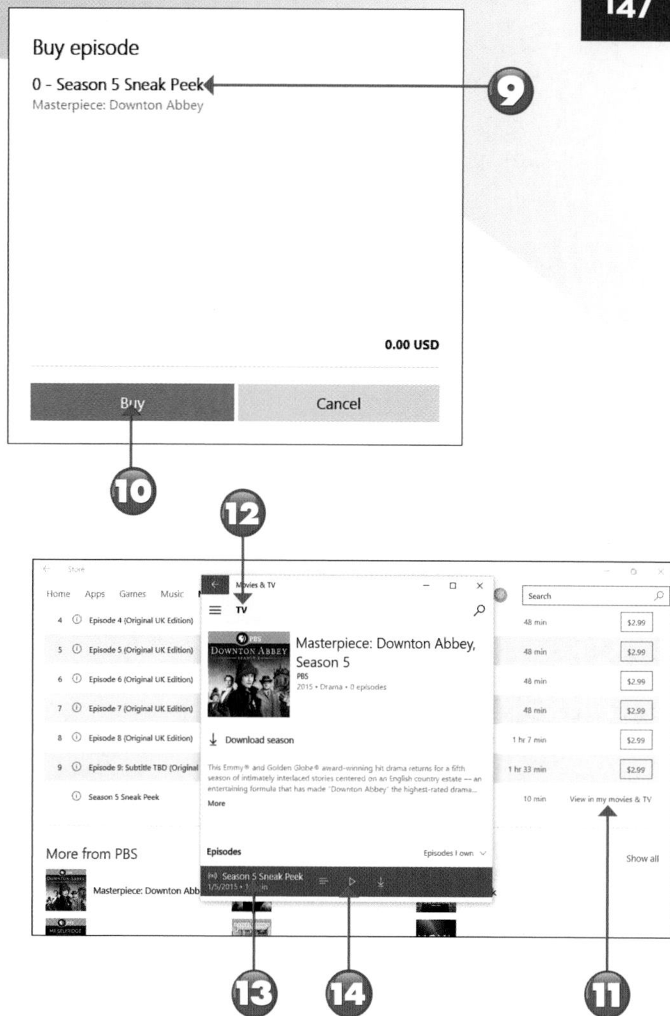

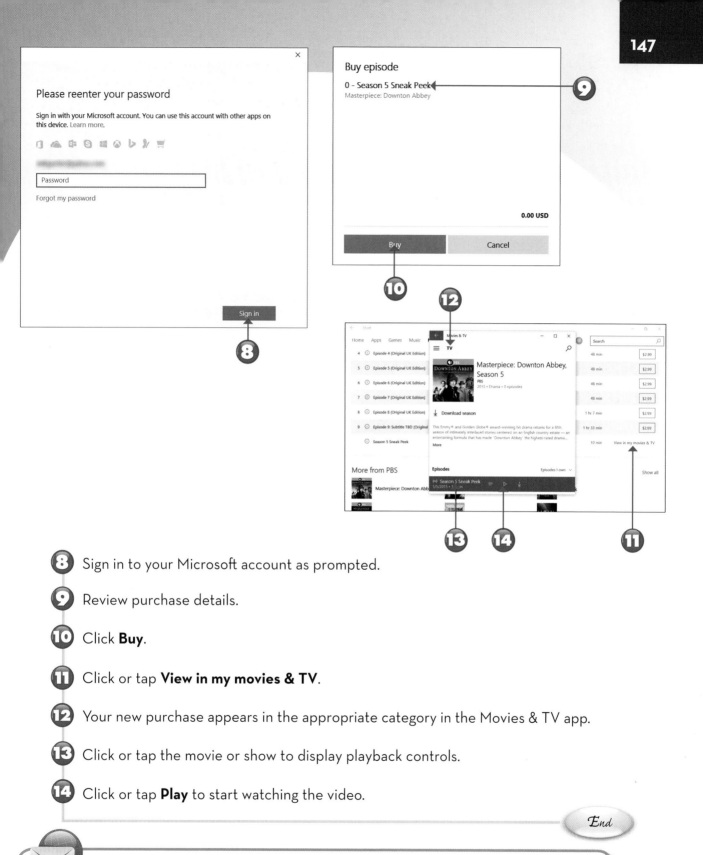

8 Sign in to your Microsoft account as prompted.

9 Review purchase details.

10 Click **Buy**.

11 Click or tap **View in my movies & TV**.

12 Your new purchase appears in the appropriate category in the Movies & TV app.

13 Click or tap the movie or show to display playback controls.

14 Click or tap **Play** to start watching the video.

End

NOTE

Video Issues If video (TV or movie) purchases aren't showing up or won't play, click or tap **Restore my available video purchases** on the Settings screen (click or tap the **Menu** button and then click or tap **Settings**). ■

USING SETTINGS TO REVIEW BILLING

The Settings menu in Movies & TV can help you with account information and issues. You can review media content you've purchased, change billing information, and more.

Start

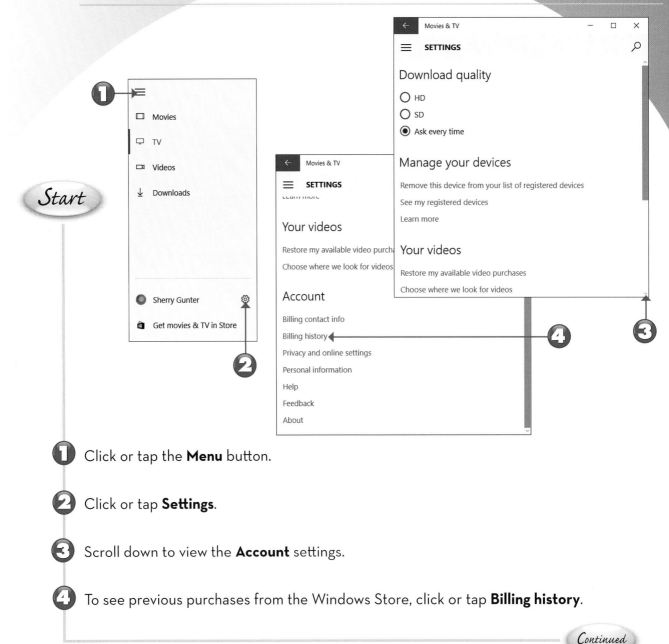

1. Click or tap the **Menu** button.

2. Click or tap **Settings**.

3. Scroll down to view the **Account** settings.

4. To see previous purchases from the Windows Store, click or tap **Billing history**.

Continued

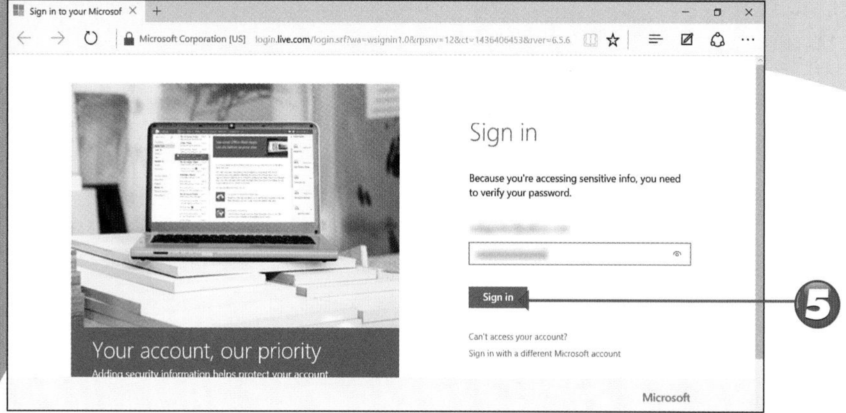

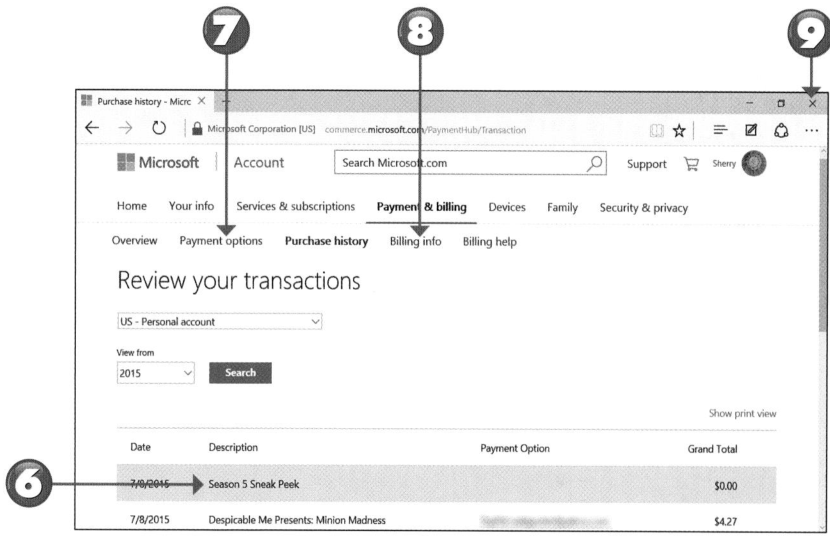

5 The browser window opens to your Microsoft Account's Sign In page. Sign in to your account as directed.

6 The **Purchase history** page shows recent media purchases.

7 Click or tap **Payment options** to make changes to how you pay for purchases.

8 Click or tap **Billing info** to make changes to your billing email, address, or phone number.

9 Click or tap to close the browser window and return to the Movies & TV app.

End

VIEWING AND TAKING PHOTOS WITH CAMERA

Windows 10 helps you take digital photos and videos with your device's webcam, front-facing camera, or rear-facing camera, edit them, and view them. In this chapter you learn how to use Camera and its companion photo-viewing app, Photos.

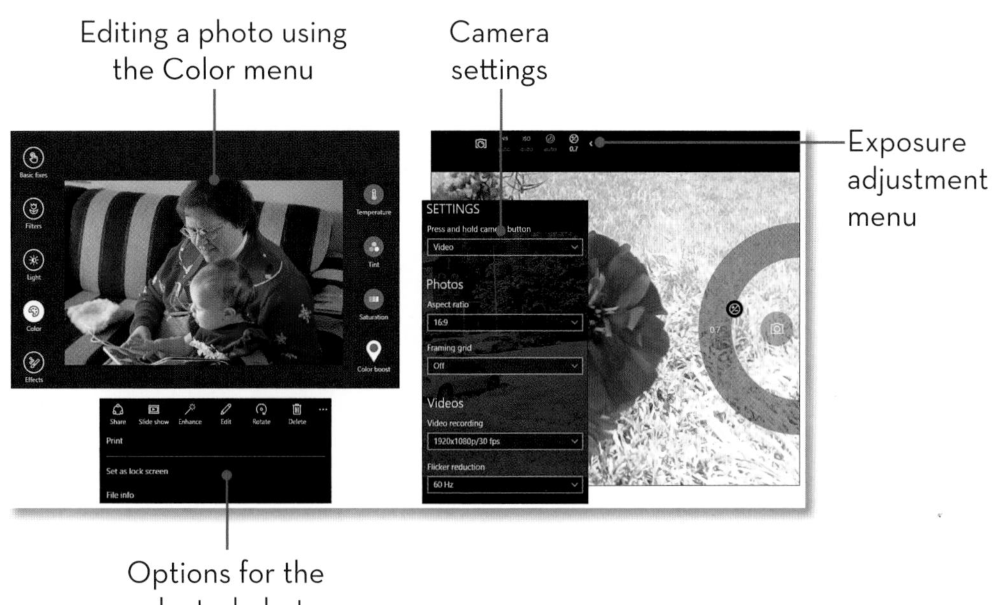
Editing a photo using the Color menu
Camera settings
Exposure adjustment menu
Options for the selected photo
SETTINGS
Press and hold camera button
Video
Photos
Aspect ratio
16:9
Framing grid
Off
Videos
Video recording
1920x1080p/30 fps
Flicker reduction
60 Hz
Share
Slide show
Enhance
Edit
Rotate
Delete
Print
Set as lock screen
File info

STARTING THE CAMERA APP

The Camera app is listed in the All Apps menu. Here's how to locate it and start it.

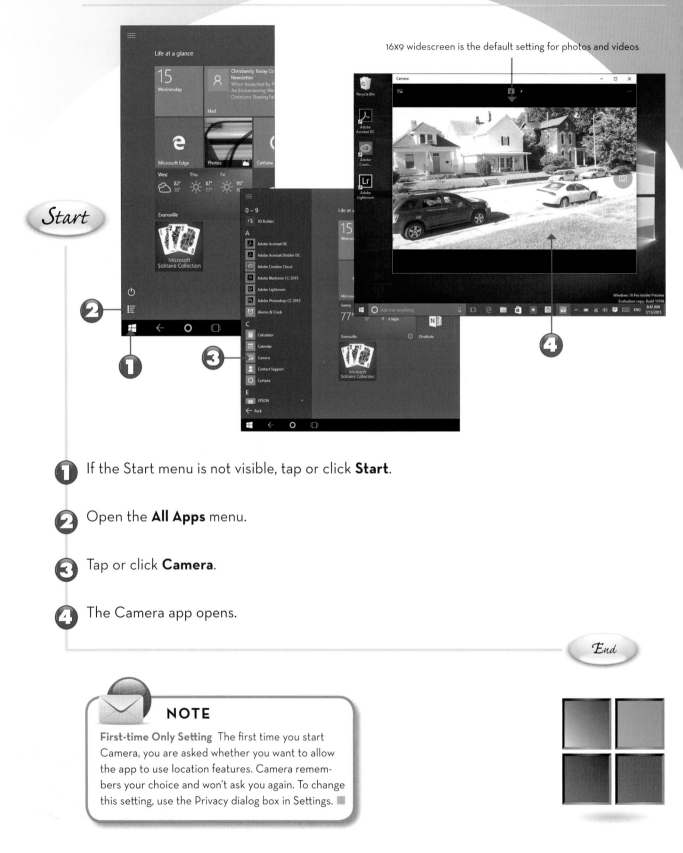

16x9 widescreen is the default setting for photos and videos

Start

1. If the Start menu is not visible, tap or click **Start**.
2. Open the **All Apps** menu.
3. Tap or click **Camera**.
4. The Camera app opens.

End

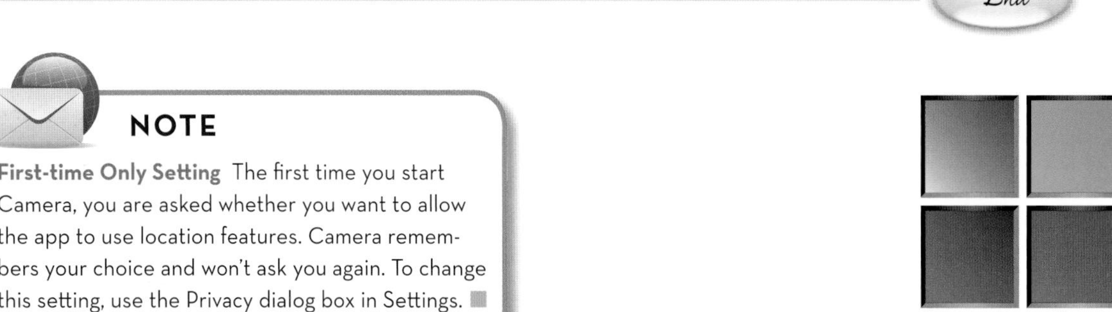

NOTE

First-time Only Setting The first time you start Camera, you are asked whether you want to allow the app to use location features. Camera remembers your choice and won't ask you again. To change this setting, use the Privacy dialog box in Settings.

SWITCHING BETWEEN CAMERAS AND TAKING PICTURES

If you run Windows 10 on a tablet, your device probably has both front-facing and rear-facing cameras. Here's how to use either camera to take pictures.

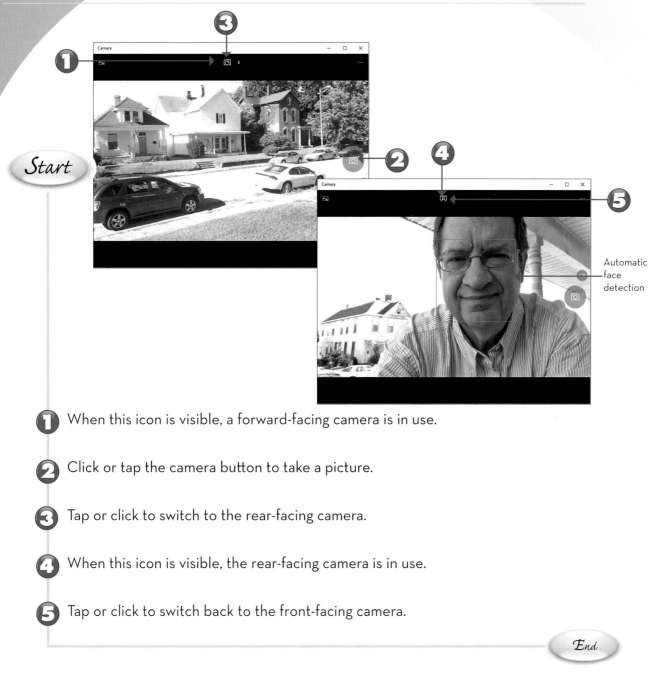

Automatic face detection

Start

1. When this icon is visible, a forward-facing camera is in use.
2. Click or tap the camera button to take a picture.
3. Tap or click to switch to the rear-facing camera.
4. When this icon is visible, the rear-facing camera is in use.
5. Tap or click to switch back to the front-facing camera.

End

SELECTING CAMERA SETTINGS

Some tablets have cameras that have advanced exposure and color settings. Here's how to open the advanced menu and its typical options.

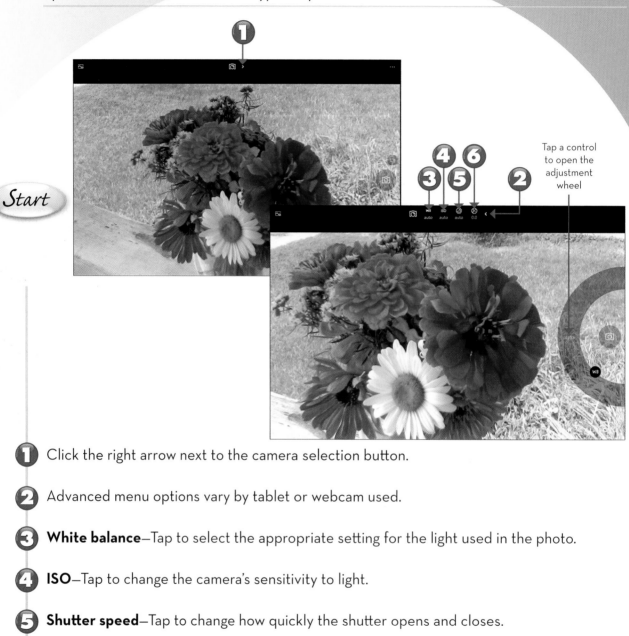

1 Click the right arrow next to the camera selection button.

2 Advanced menu options vary by tablet or webcam used.

3 **White balance**—Tap to select the appropriate setting for the light used in the photo.

4 **ISO**—Tap to change the camera's sensitivity to light.

5 **Shutter speed**—Tap to change how quickly the shutter opens and closes.

6 **EV adjustment**—Tap to adjust exposure.

End

NOTE

Adjustments Vary by Camera Some built-in cameras don't have adjustments. If no right arrow is visible next to the camera switch button, the camera doesn't have any adjustable features.

USING VIDEO MODE

When you select Video mode, you can shoot MPEG4 video files with your device. Here's how to use this feature.

Start

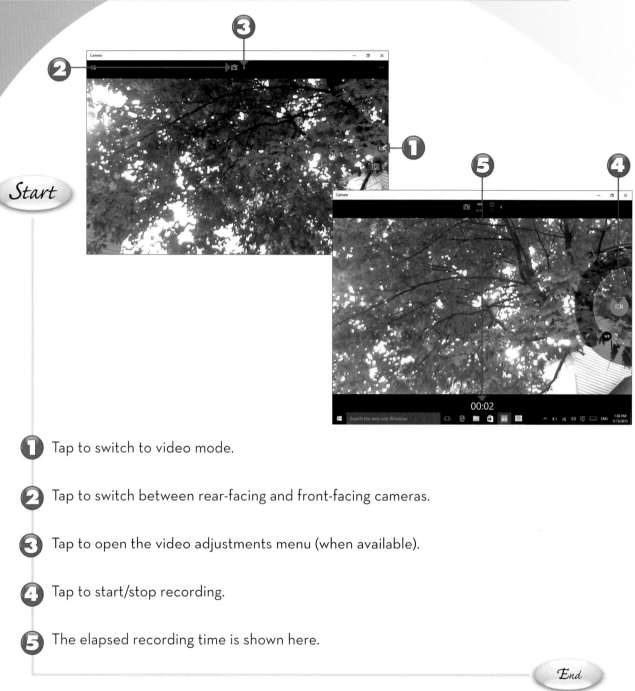

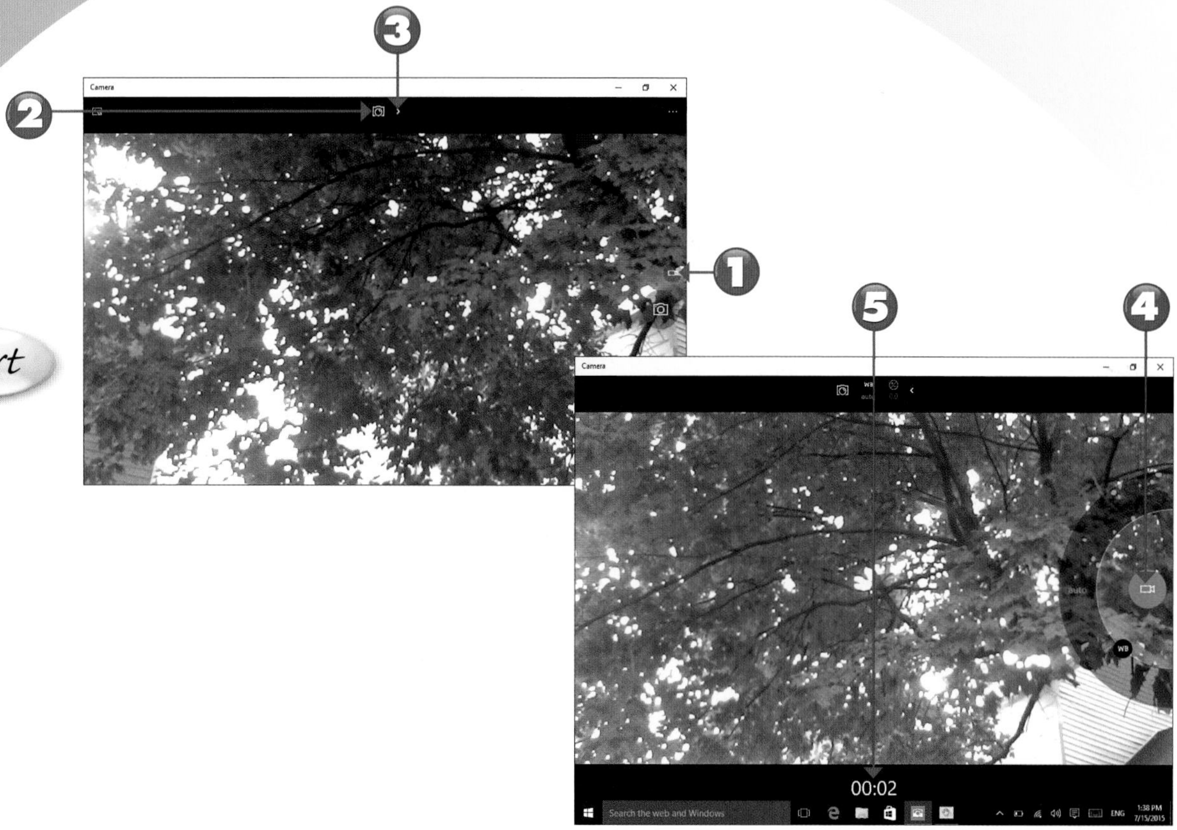

1. Tap to switch to video mode.

2. Tap to switch between rear-facing and front-facing cameras.

3. Tap to open the video adjustments menu (when available).

4. Tap to start/stop recording.

5. The elapsed recording time is shown here.

End

CHANGING CAMERA APP SETTINGS

You can change the proportions (widescreen or standard), recording quality, and other settings with the Settings menu. Here's how.

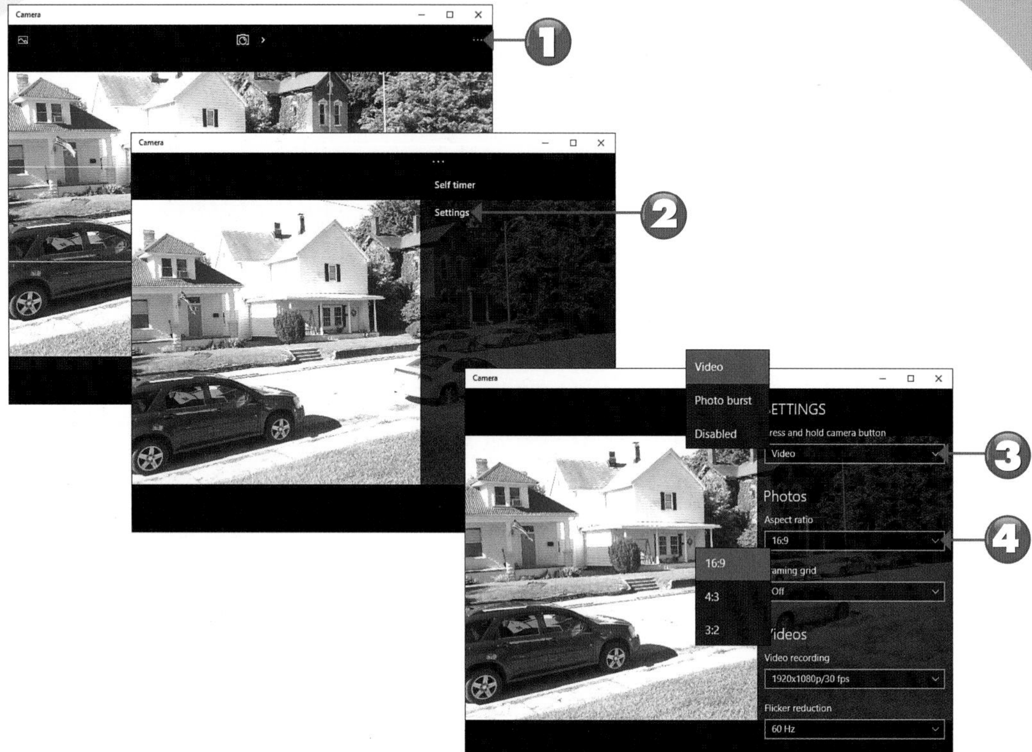

Start

1. Tap the **Menu** button.
2. Tap **Settings**.
3. Tap to select how to use a long press on the shooting key.
4. Tap to adjust the proportions of your photos and videos.

Continued

NOTE

Self Timer The self-timer option (shown in step 2) is set the same way as other options discussed in this lesson.

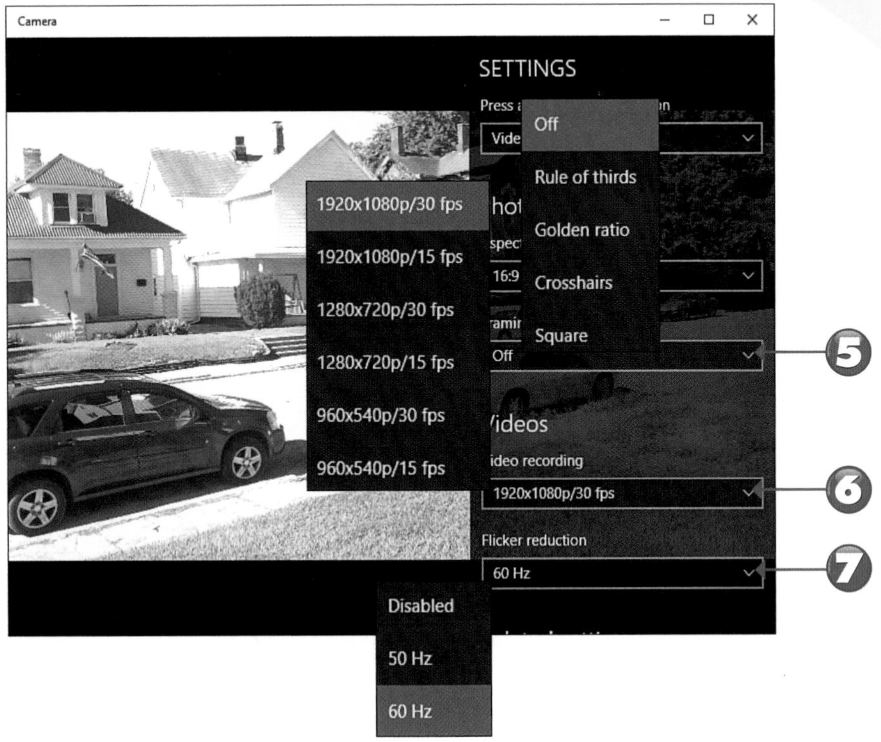

5 Tap to select a framing grid type.

6 Tap to select the video size and frames per second shooting rate.

7 Tap to select a flicker reduction rate (if needed).

End

NOTE

Why Available Resolutions Vary The options shown in this exercise are based on the Microsoft Surface Pro 3 Windows tablet using its rear-facing camera. Other tablets, laptops, and webcams might have different settings, and available resolution settings might vary depending on whether you have selected the front or rear camera.

OPENING THE PHOTOS APP FROM CAMERA

Windows 10 uses the Photos app to display your photos and videos, and you can start it from the Camera app. Here's how.

Start

1. Tap the **Photos** button.
2. The most recent photo or video is shown first.
3. If you are viewing a video, tap the screen or the keyboard to pause playback.
4. Tap or click **View collection** to see older photos and videos.

End

VIEWING YOUR PHOTO AND VIDEO COLLECTION

When you select View collection, you have a variety of ways to move through your photos and videos and add more from other devices. Here's an overview.

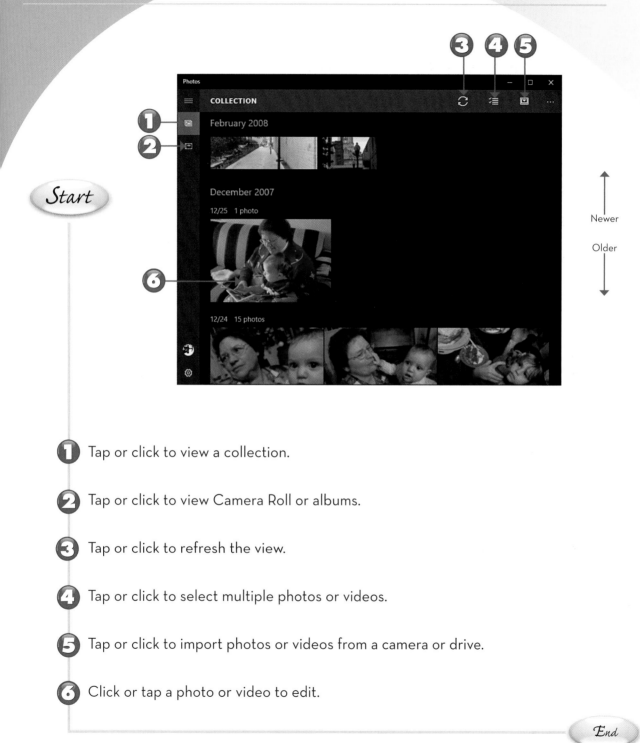

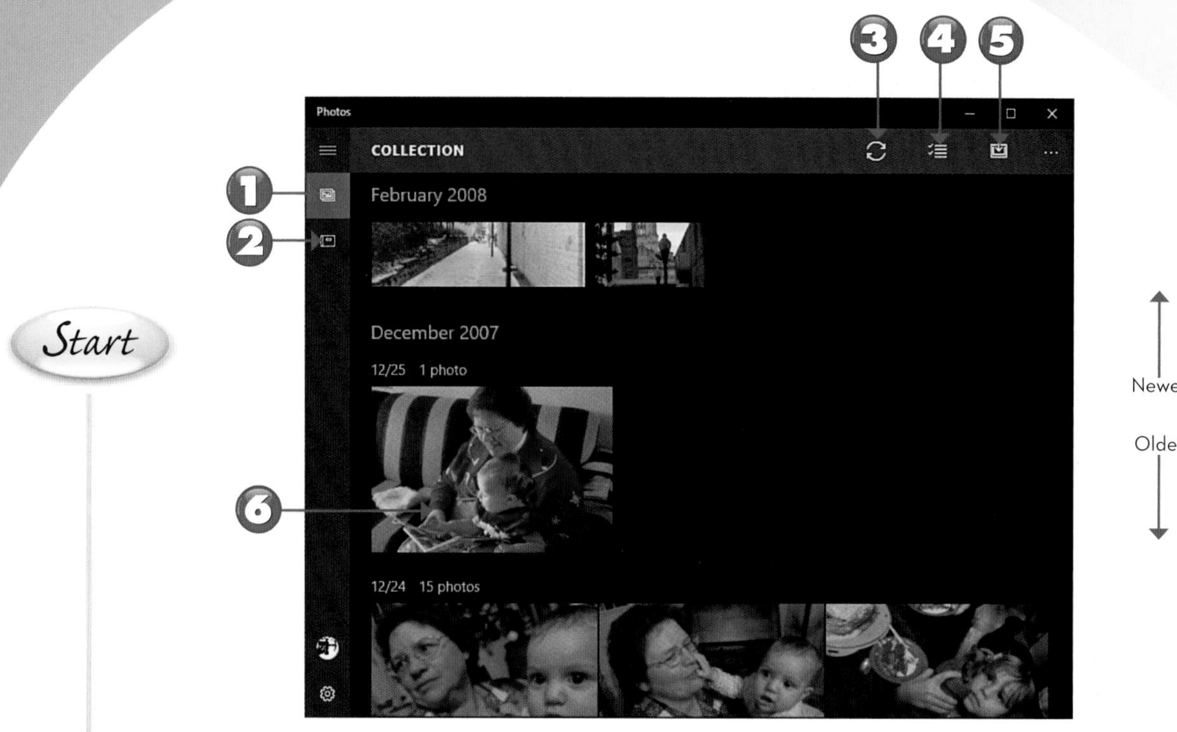

1. Tap or click to view a collection.
2. Tap or click to view Camera Roll or albums.
3. Tap or click to refresh the view.
4. Tap or click to select multiple photos or videos.
5. Tap or click to import photos or videos from a camera or drive.
6. Click or tap a photo or video to edit.

End

BASIC OPTIONS FOR YOUR PHOTOS

After you select a photo, you can rotate it or use it in various places on your device. Here's what you can do.

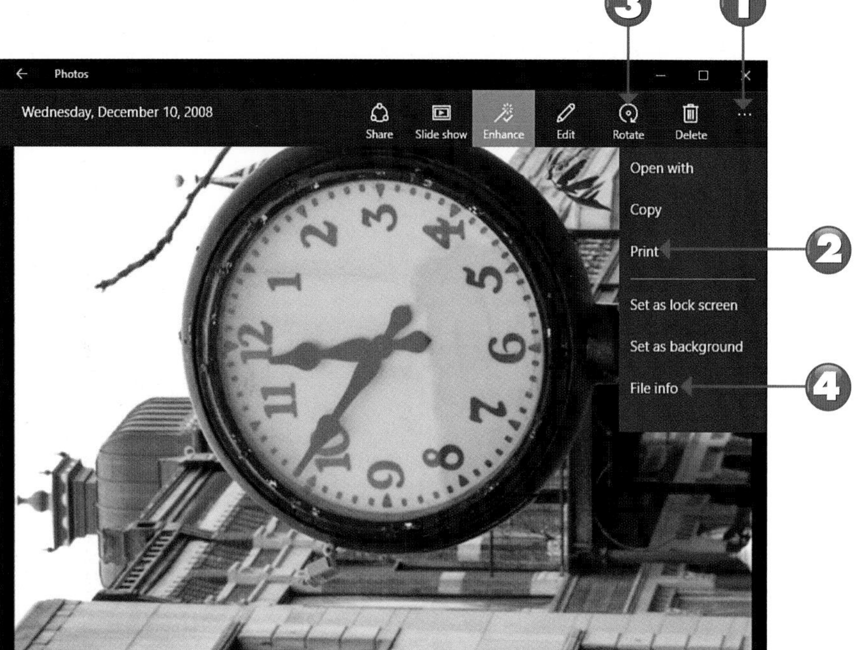

Start

1. Tap the **Menu** button.
2. Tap to print this photo.
3. Tap to rotate the photo.
4. Tap to see file information.

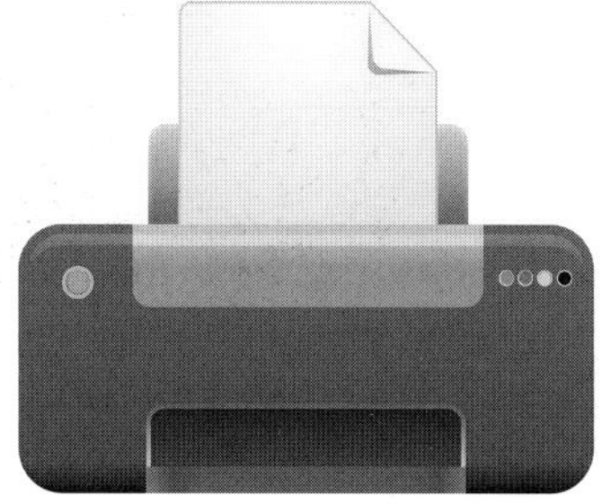

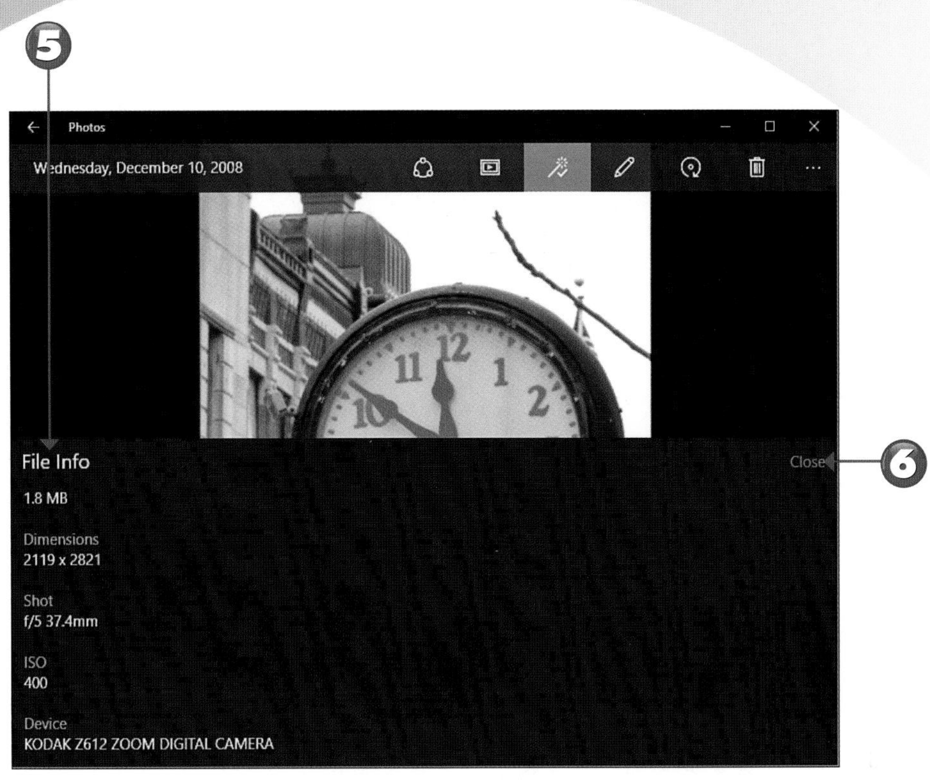

5. Review the exposure and camera information.

6. Click or tap to close information.

End

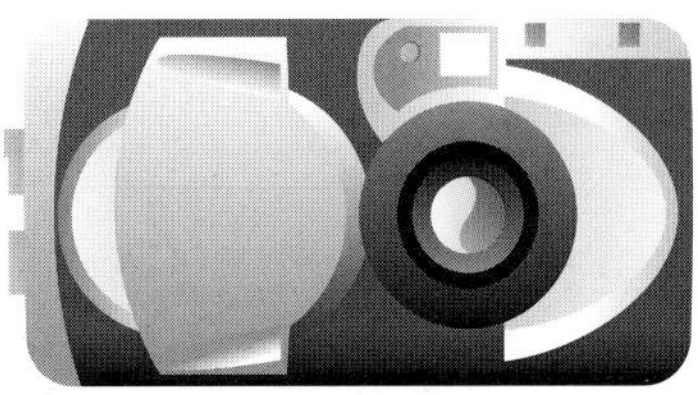

VIEWING YOUR VIDEOS WITH PHOTOS

When you view a video with Photos, you can select how much to play back and whether to trim the length of your video. Here's what the menus look like.

Start

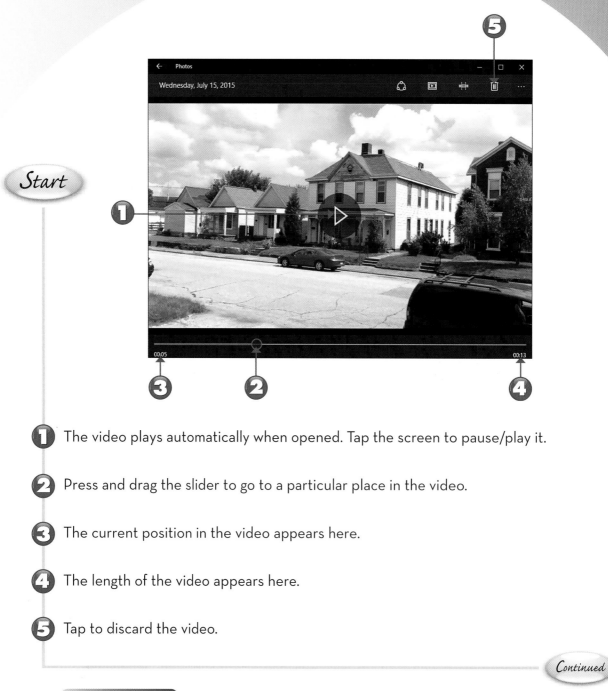

1. The video plays automatically when opened. Tap the screen to pause/play it.
2. Press and drag the slider to go to a particular place in the video.
3. The current position in the video appears here.
4. The length of the video appears here.
5. Tap to discard the video.

Continued

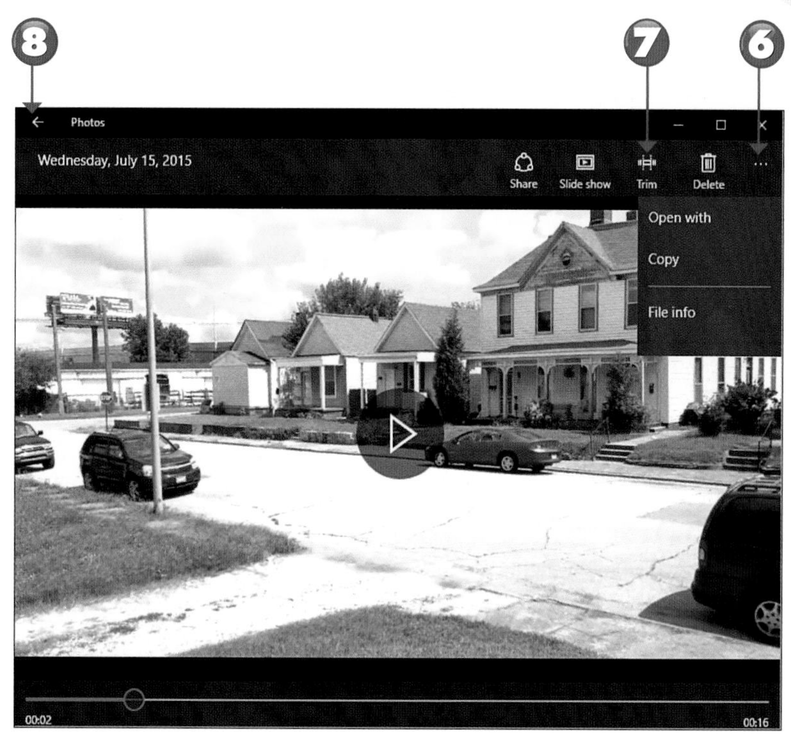

6 Tap to see the **Open with** (app), **Copy**, and **File Info** options.

7 Tap to trim the video.

8 Tap to return to the collection.

End

CROPPING A PICTURE WITH PHOTOS

Photos enables you to crop, change colors, adjust brightness, and add effects to your photos. Here's how to crop a photo to the size desired.

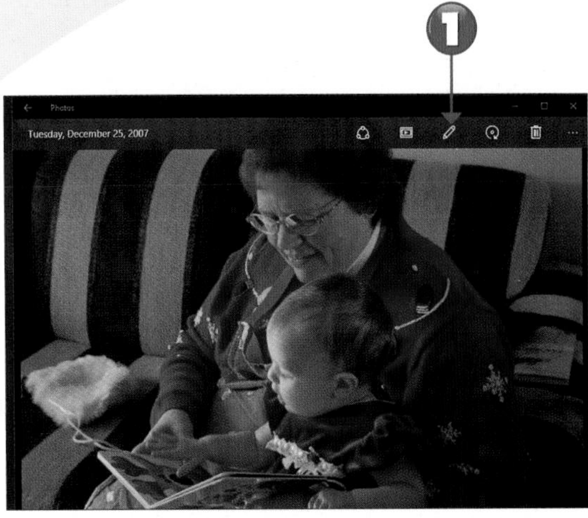

Start

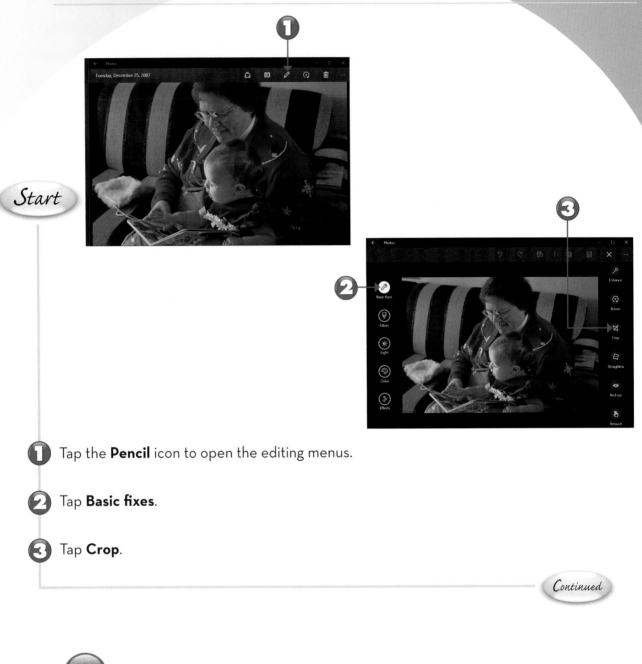

1. Tap the **Pencil** icon to open the editing menus.
2. Tap **Basic fixes**.
3. Tap **Crop**.

Continued

NOTE

Other Basic Edits You Can Make Use **Enhance** to automatically fix a bad picture. Use **Rotate** to turn a picture 90 degrees at a time. Use **Straighten** to fix a crooked photo. Fix red eye in people (but not pets) with **Red eye**. Use **Retouch** to fix surface imperfections.

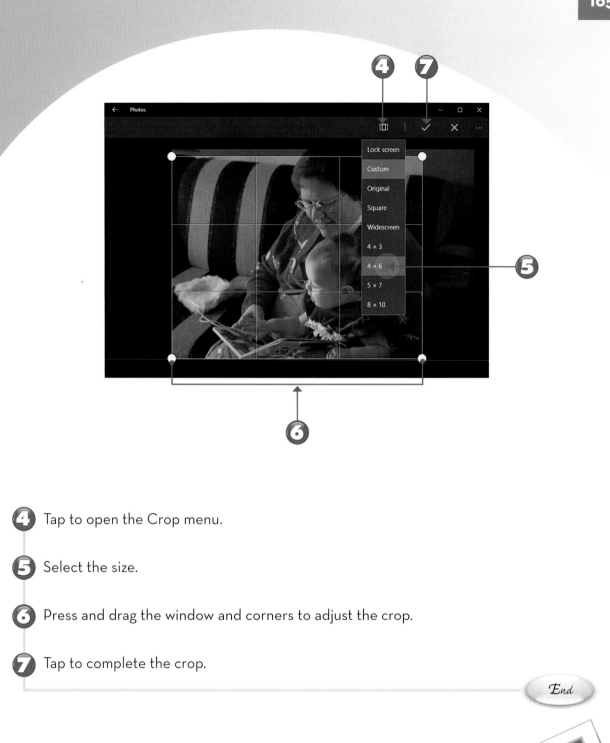

4. Tap to open the Crop menu.
5. Select the size.
6. Press and drag the window and corners to adjust the crop.
7. Tap to complete the crop.

End

IMPROVING BRIGHTNESS AND ADDING EFFECTS WITH PHOTOS

Photos also enables you to brighten or darken a photo and add effects. Here's an example of what you can do.

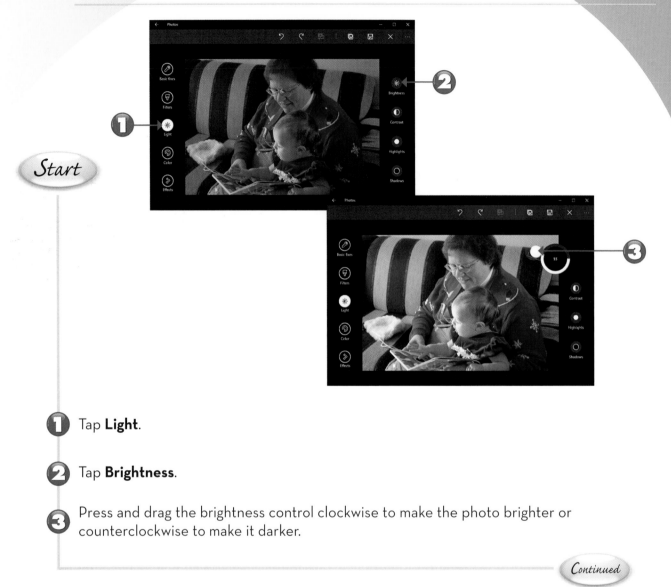

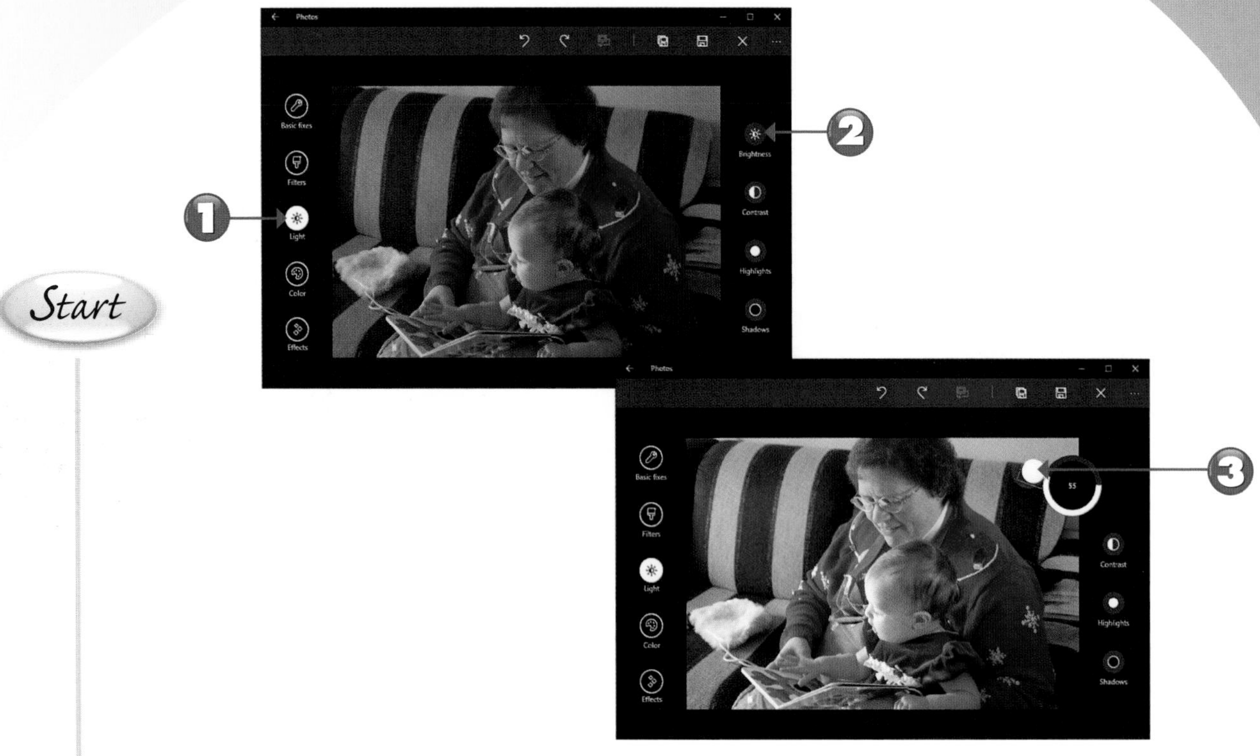

1. Tap **Light**.
2. Tap **Brightness**.
3. Press and drag the brightness control clockwise to make the photo brighter or counterclockwise to make it darker.

Continued

NOTE

Additional Editing Options Use **Contrast** to increase or decrease the differences between light and dark areas in your photo. Use **Highlights** to lighten or darken bright areas in your photo. Use **Shadows** to lighten or darken dark areas in your photo.

4 Tap **Effects**.

5 Tap **Vignette**.

6 Press and drag the Vignette control clockwise to darken the corners of the photo, or counterclockwise to brighten the corners.

End

NOTE

Undo/Redo Each time you tap **Undo** (left-curving button), an edit to your photo is reversed. After you undo at least one edit, you can tap **Redo** (right-curving button) to redo an edit. You can undo/redo multiple changes.

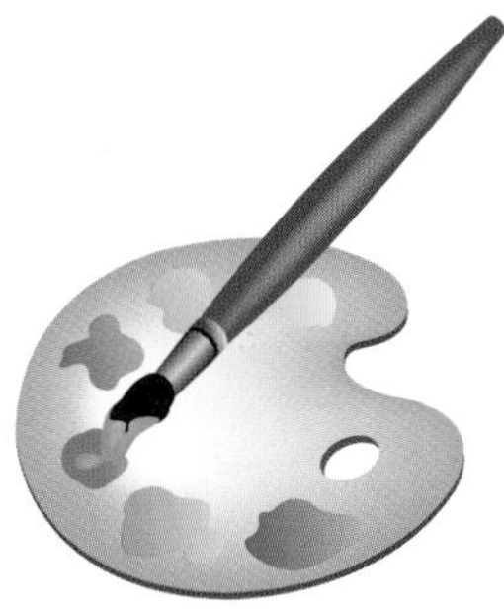

COMPARING EDITED AND ORIGINAL VERSIONS

Before you save your changes, you can quickly compare your edited photo to the original. Here's how.

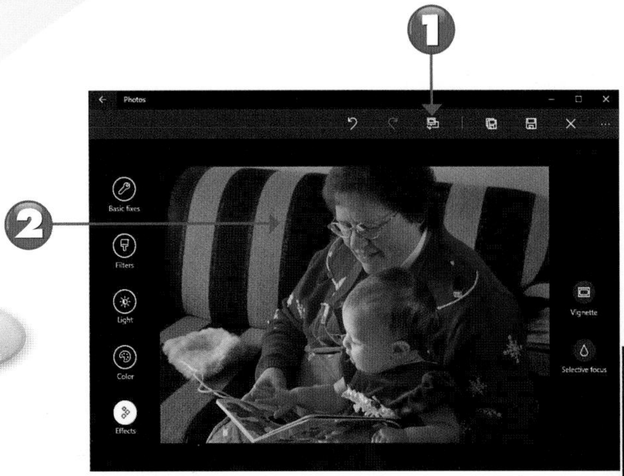

Start

1. Press and hold **Compare**.
2. The photo appears as it did before you made changes.
3. Tap **Compare** again to see the photo after your changes.
4. The edited version of the photo.

End

NOTE

Color and Effects Menu Options On the color menu settings, use **Temperature** to fix problems with a photo being too warm (yellow) or too cool (blue); use **Tint** to tweak color balance; use **Saturation** to make all colors more or less intense; use Color boost to increase or reduce the intensity of the selected color. On the effects menu settings, use **Selective focus** to blur less-important parts of the photo.

SAVING CHANGES

Do you like the improvements you made in your photo? Save your changes. Here's how.

Start

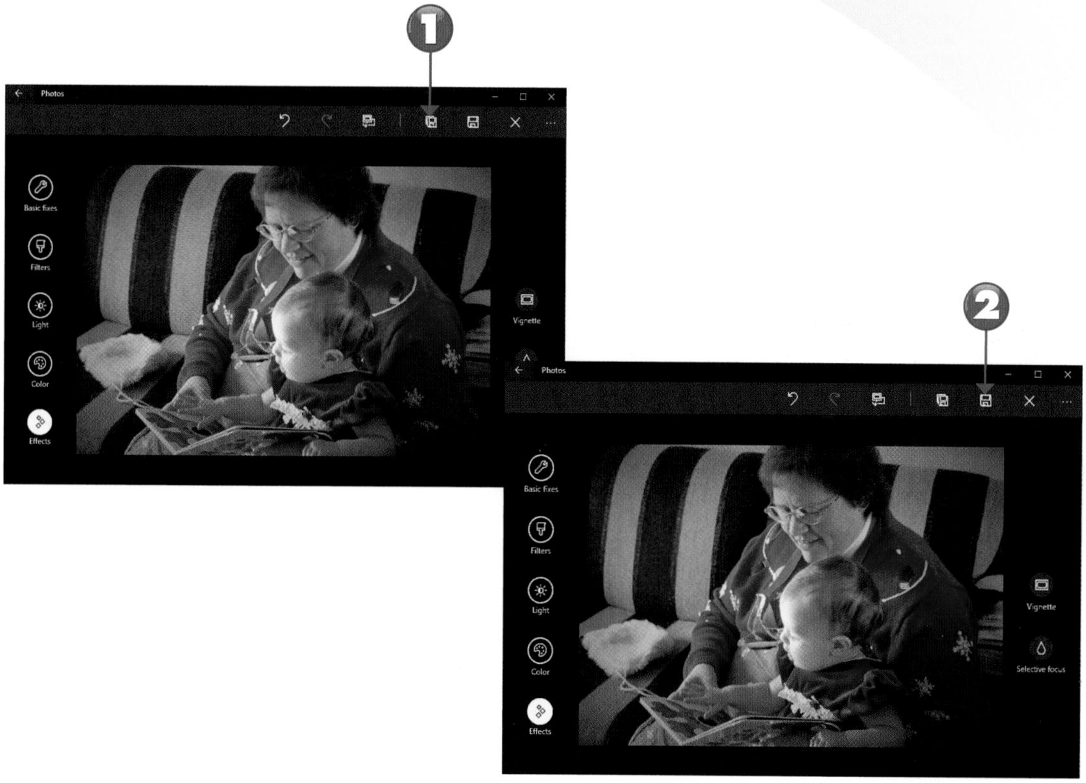

1. Tap **Save a copy**. A copy is saved in the same location as your original. Your original is not changed.
2. Tap **Save** if you want to save your photo into a different folder (the default is Pictures) or if you want to replace your old version.

CONNECTING WITH FRIENDS

Windows 10 offers a variety of ways you can connect with people, ranging from email to social media to face-to-face connections over your computer. In this chapter, you learn how to make use of several of the key communications apps and features.

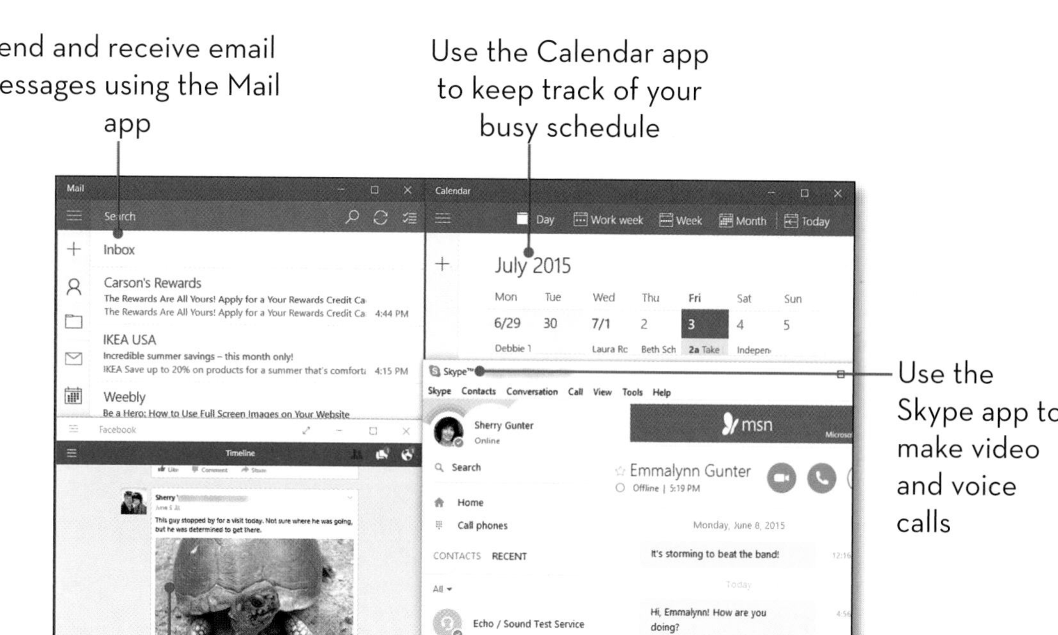
Send and receive email messages using the Mail app
Use the Calendar app to keep track of your busy schedule
Use the Skype app to make video and voice calls
The Facebook app keeps you in touch with friends and family

USING THE PEOPLE APP

You can use the People app to compile and maintain a list of contacts. Behaving like a digital address book, the People app keeps a list of people you contact the most, including email contacts. You can add as many contacts as you like and view each with just a click.

Start

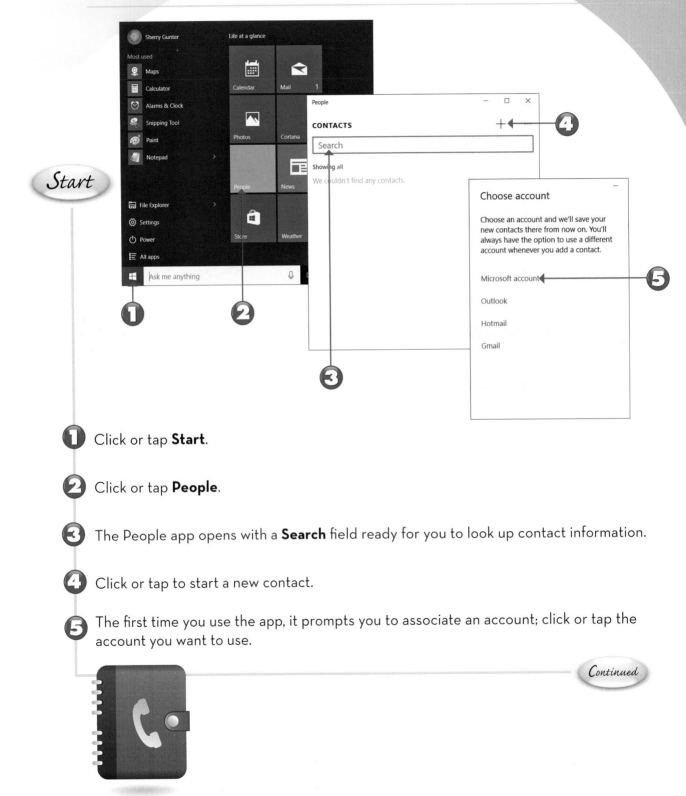

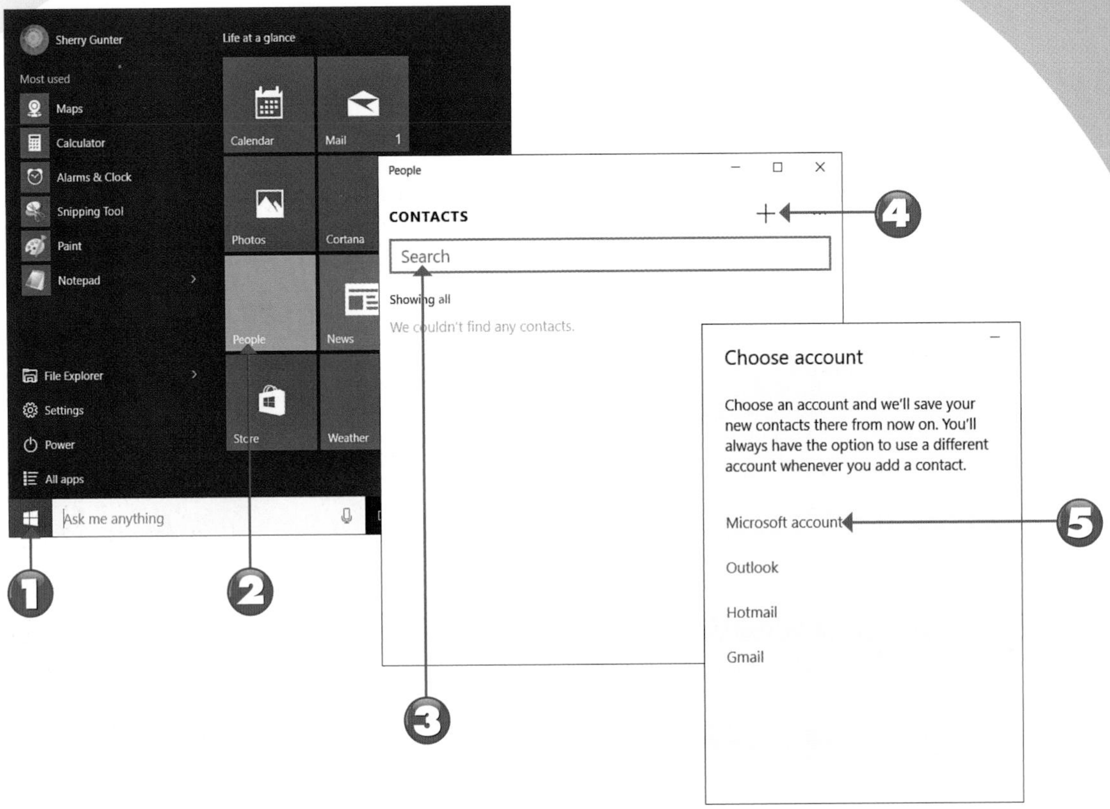

1. Click or tap **Start**.

2. Click or tap **People**.

3. The People app opens with a **Search** field ready for you to look up contact information.

4. Click or tap to start a new contact.

5. The first time you use the app, it prompts you to associate an account; click or tap the account you want to use.

Continued

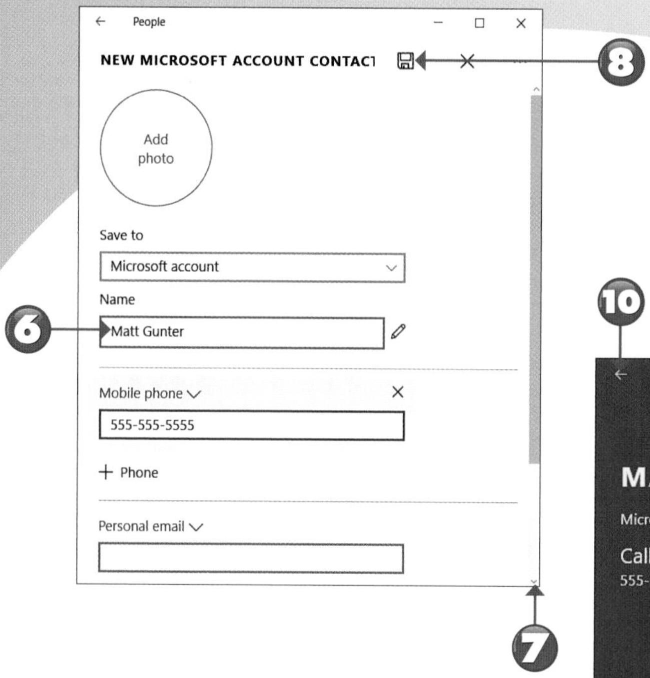

6 Fill out the contact form; click or tap a text box or field and enter the contact information.

7 Scroll down the form to view more fields.

8 Click or tap **Save** when you finish entering contact information.

9 The contact is added to your digital address book.

10 Click or tap here to return to the People app's main page to add more contacts.

End

TIP

Edit Contacts To make changes to a contact's information, click or tap the contact, and then click or tap the **Edit** icon (looks like a pencil). Make your changes to the form fields and click or tap **Save**.

CONNECTING TO FACEBOOK WITH THE FACEBOOK APP

You can use the free Facebook app in the Windows Store to keep up with the latest Facebook postings, add status updates, and upload photos to your profile page. If you don't already have the Facebook app, you must install it first.

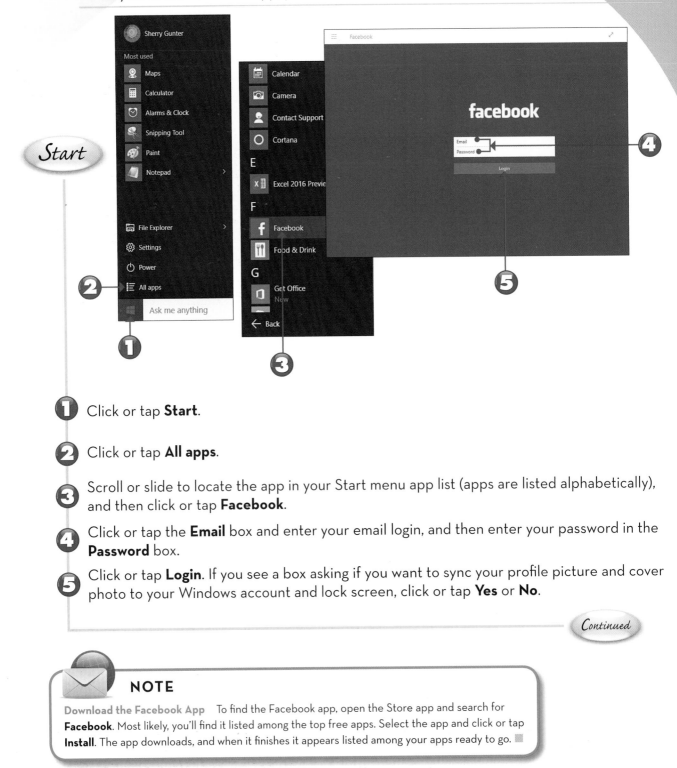

Start

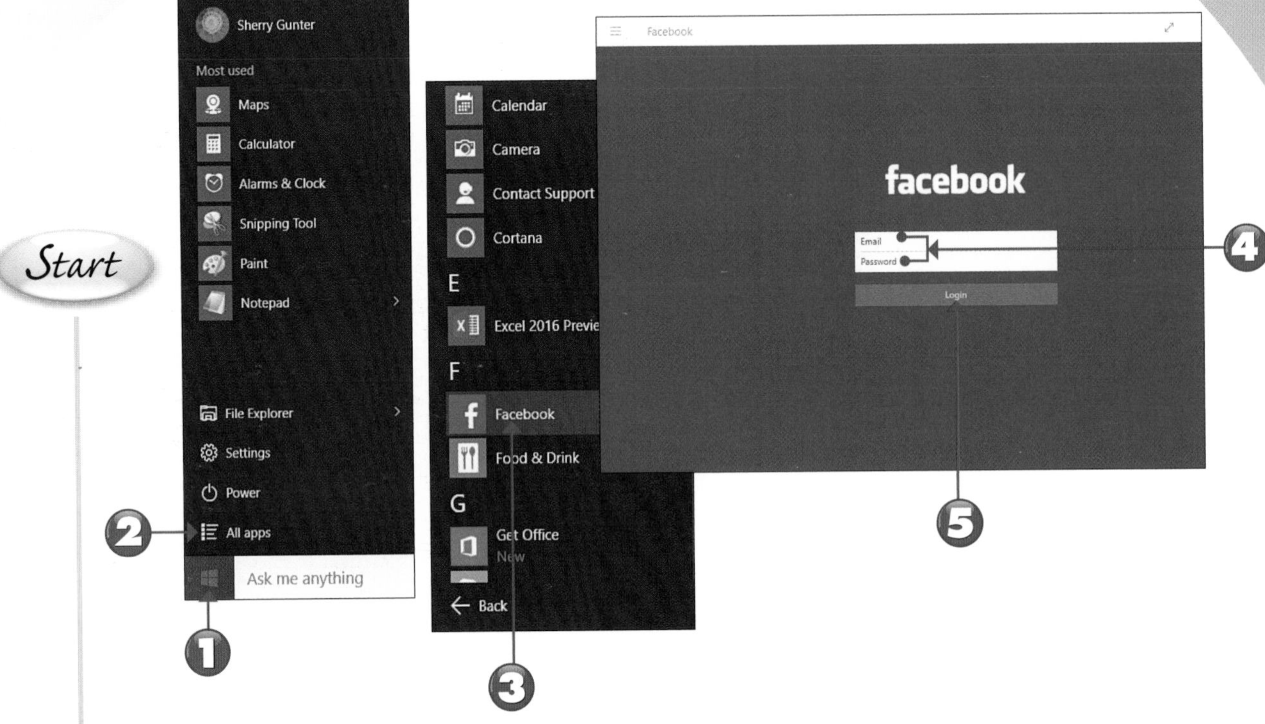

1 Click or tap **Start**.

2 Click or tap **All apps**.

3 Scroll or slide to locate the app in your Start menu app list (apps are listed alphabetically), and then click or tap **Facebook**.

4 Click or tap the **Email** box and enter your email login, and then enter your password in the **Password** box.

5 Click or tap **Login**. If you see a box asking if you want to sync your profile picture and cover photo to your Windows account and lock screen, click or tap **Yes** or **No**.

Continued

NOTE

Download the Facebook App To find the Facebook app, open the Store app and search for **Facebook**. Most likely, you'll find it listed among the top free apps. Select the app and click or tap **Install**. The app downloads, and when it finishes it appears listed among your apps ready to go.

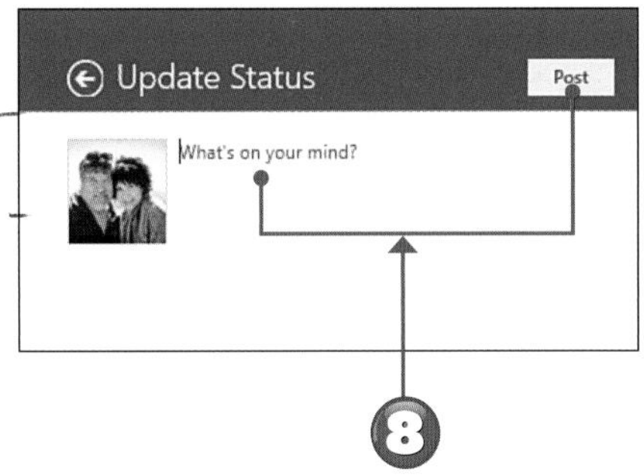

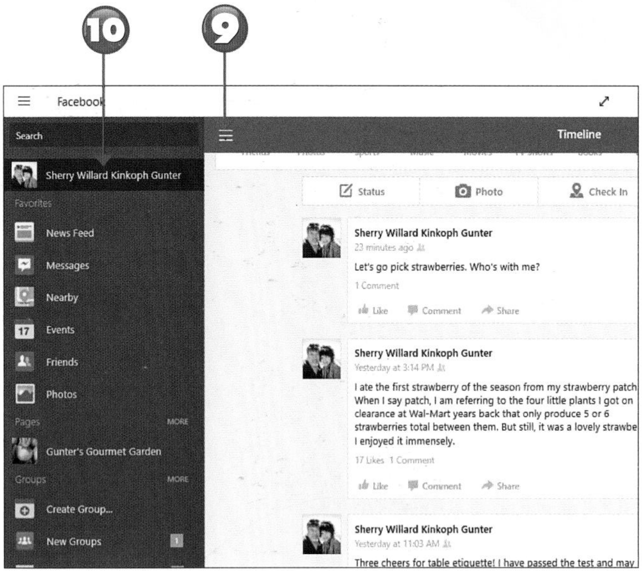

6 By default, the app shows your News Feed. Scroll to view more news.

7 To update your status, click or tap here.

8 Type your status update, and then click or tap **Post**.

9 To view other features, click or tap here.

10 Click or tap here to view your profile page.

End

TIP

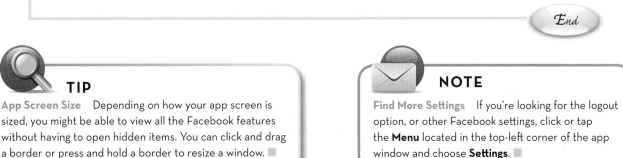

App Screen Size Depending on how your app screen is sized, you might be able to view all the Facebook features without having to open hidden items. You can click and drag a border or press and hold a border to resize a window.

NOTE

Find More Settings If you're looking for the logout option, or other Facebook settings, click or tap the **Menu** located in the top-left corner of the app window and choose **Settings**.

STARTING MAIL

Windows Mail works with Microsoft's web-based email service (now called Outlook.com) and many other email services, including Gmail, Yahoo! Mail, and Exchange. Mail automatically detects the email you used to create your Microsoft account and adds it as your first account. In this task, you learn how to navigate the Mail app.

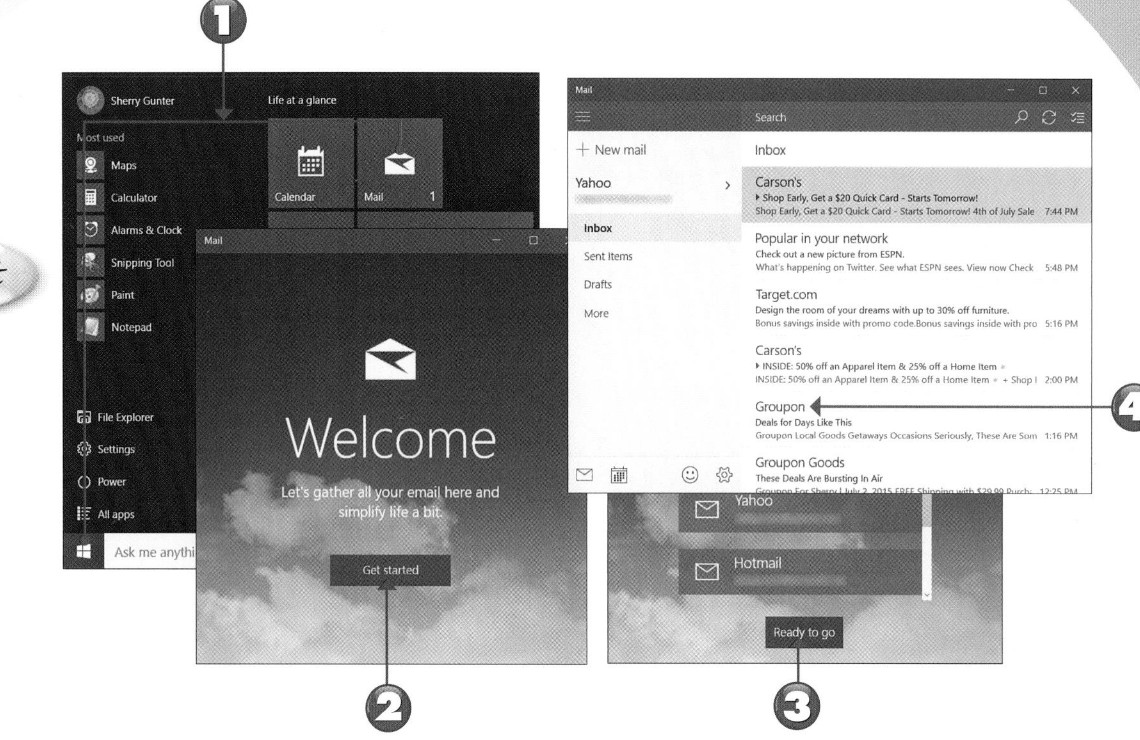

Start

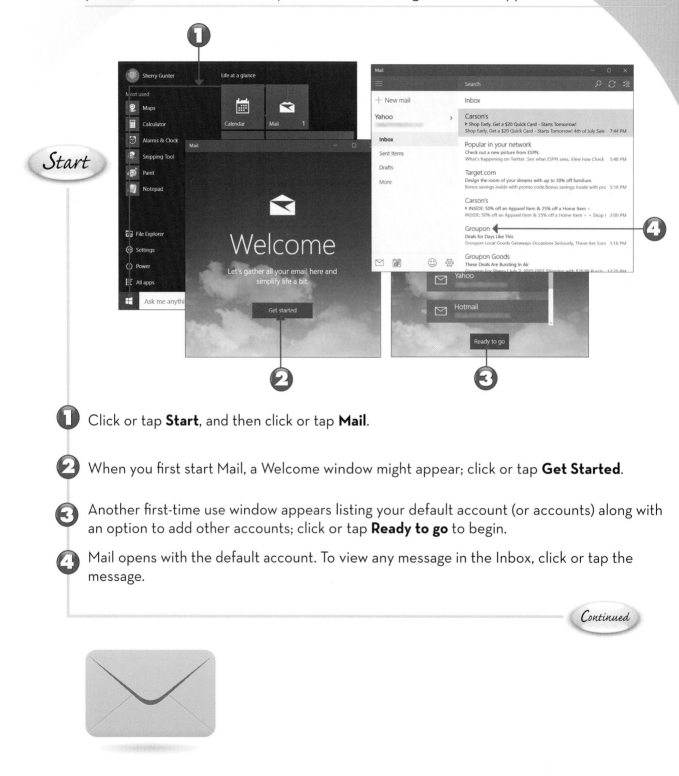

1. Click or tap **Start**, and then click or tap **Mail**.
2. When you first start Mail, a Welcome window might appear; click or tap **Get Started**.
3. Another first-time use window appears listing your default account (or accounts) along with an option to add other accounts; click or tap **Ready to go** to begin.
4. Mail opens with the default account. To view any message in the Inbox, click or tap the message.

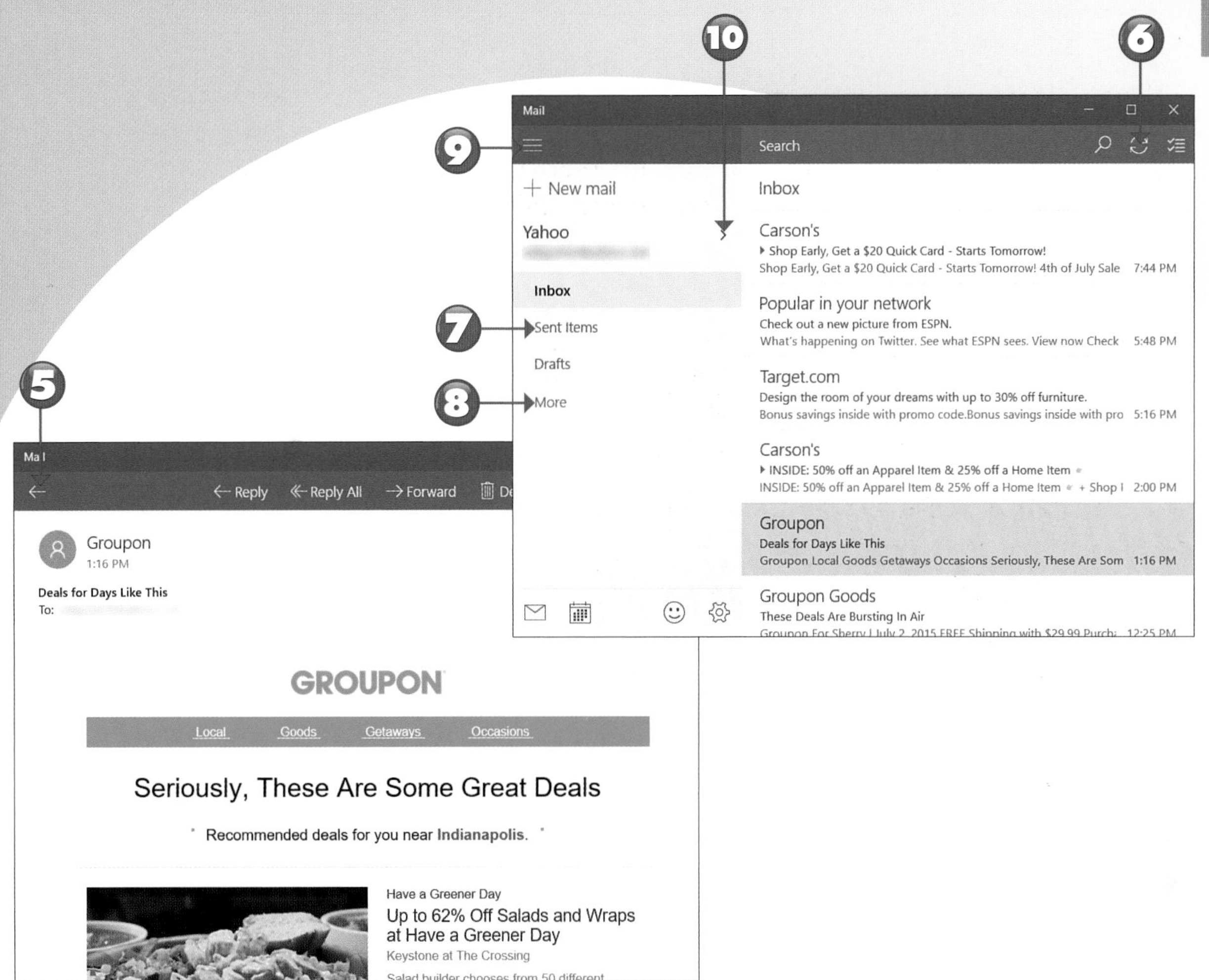

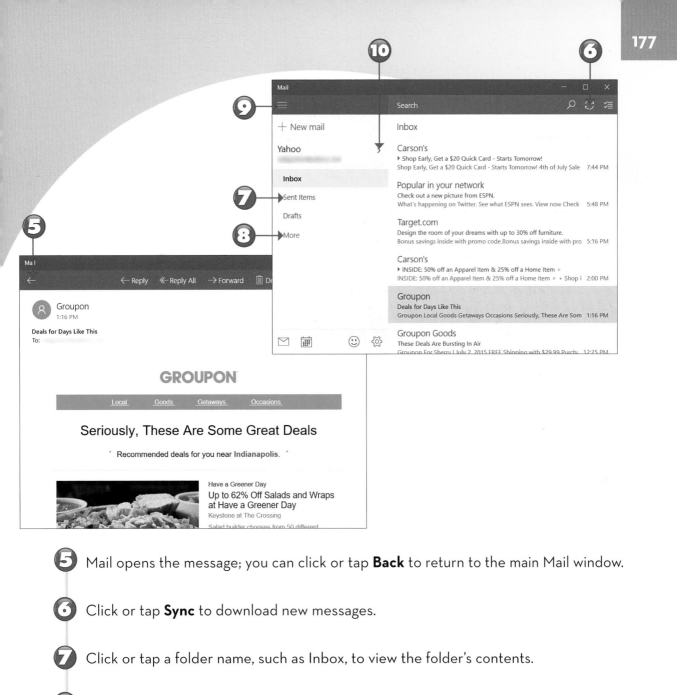

5. Mail opens the message; you can click or tap **Back** to return to the main Mail window.

6. Click or tap **Sync** to download new messages.

7. Click or tap a folder name, such as Inbox, to view the folder's contents.

8. Click or tap **More** to view additional Mail folders.

9. Click or tap **Menu** to hide or display the left pane listing the main Mail components.

10. Click or tap the arrow to view additional email accounts.

Continued

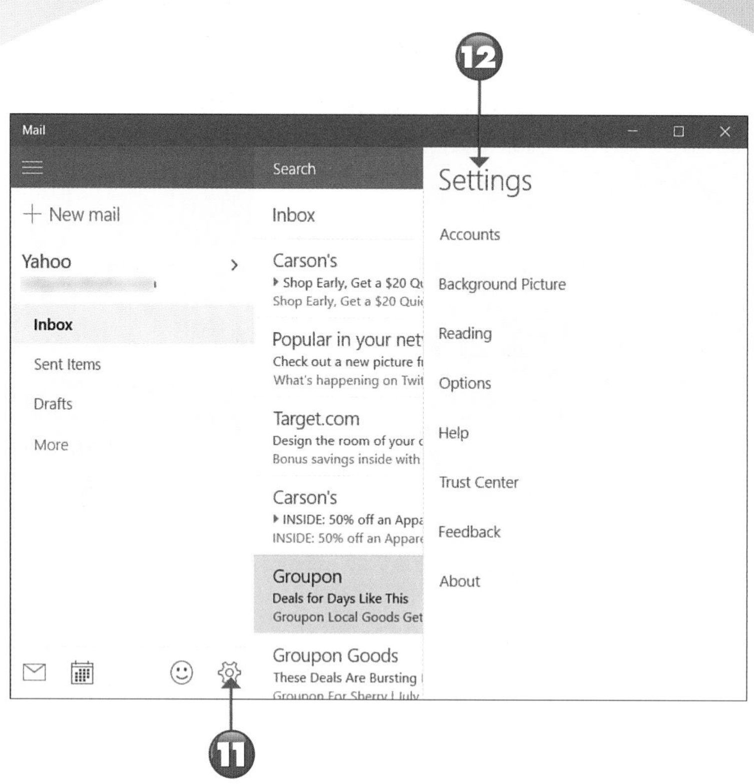

11 Click or tap **Settings**.

12 The Settings panel opens; use this panel to find settings for controlling accounts, adding a signature, specifying how email is marked, and more.

End

TIP

Using Another Email Client? If you're using a web-based email client, such as Yahoo! or Google, you can use your web browser to access messages rather than using the Mail app.

NOTE

Setup Help If you're using an Outlook email account, one of the easiest ways to start setting up your email is to utilize the links found in the Outlook.com Team's introductory email. Just click or tap the message to open it, and then follow the instructions and links provided.

ADDING AN EMAIL ACCOUNT

You can add other email providers to the Windows 10 Mail app and check your messages in one convenient spot. You might have a work email and a home email account, for example, or a Google and a Yahoo! Mail account. You can add them to Mail.

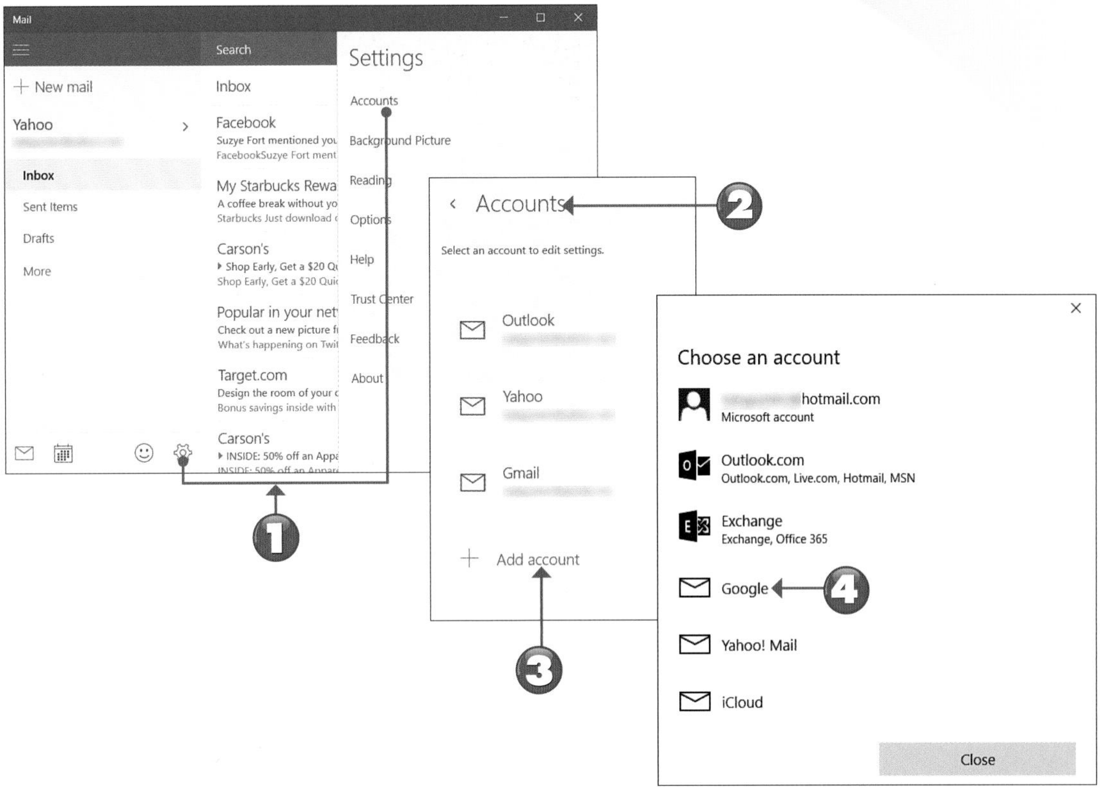

Start

1. With the Mail app open, click or tap **Settings**, and then tap **Accounts**.

2. Click or tap an account to make changes to its settings.

3. To add an email account, click or tap **Add account**.

4. Click or tap an account type.

Continued

NOTE

Mail and Calendar The Windows 10 Mail and Calendar apps are designed to work together, making it easy to email a schedule, set up appointments with other users, and more. That's why there's a Calendar app icon at the bottom of the folder list in Mail. You can click the icon to open the Calendar app. You learn more about Calendar later in this chapter.

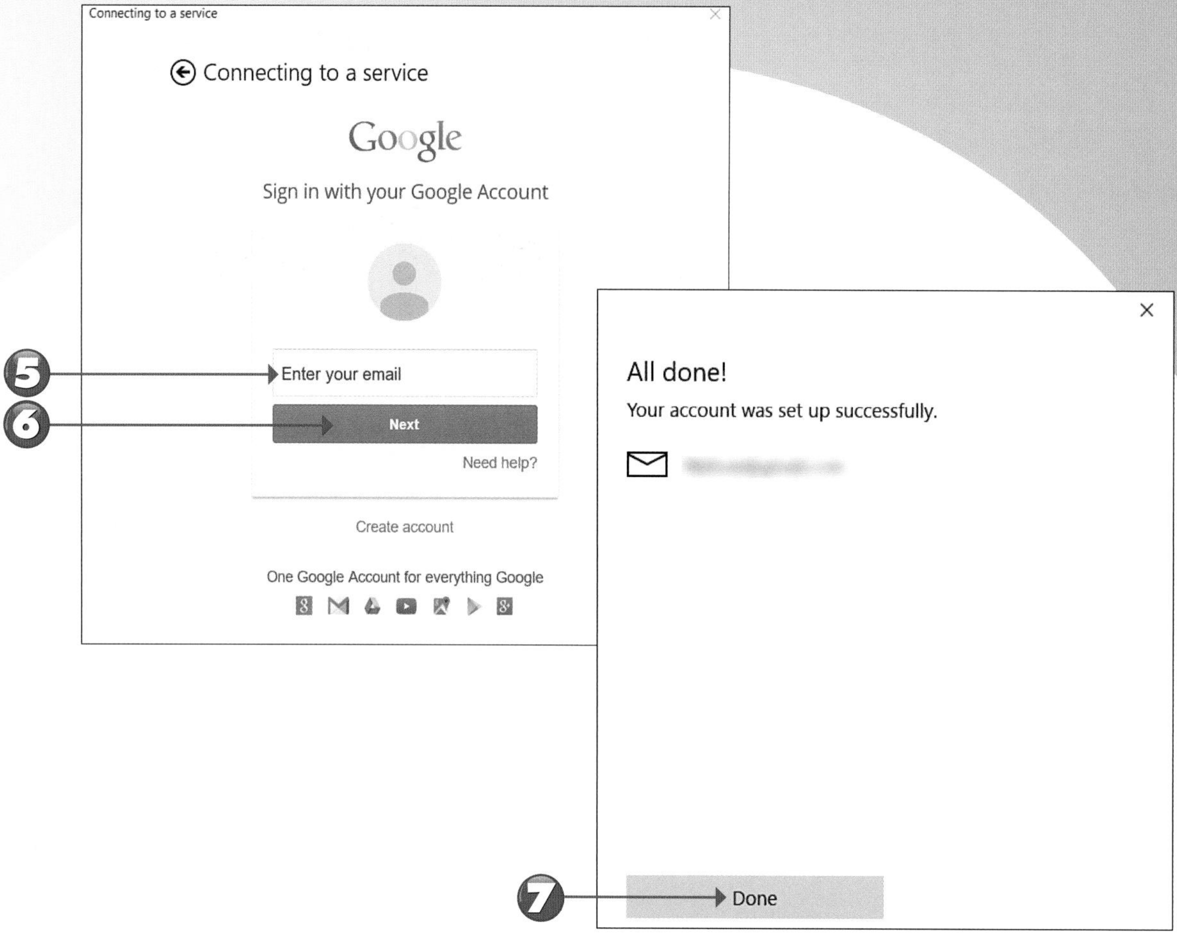

Connecting to a service

Connecting to a service

Google

Sign in with your Google Account

Enter your email

Next

Need help?

Create account

One Google Account for everything Google

All done!

Your account was set up successfully.

Done

5. Fill out the form, as needed; enter the account's email address and password.

6. Click or tap **Next**.

7. Depending on your email provider, you might encounter additional windows to finish the process. Click or tap **Done** when the account is successfully added.

Continued

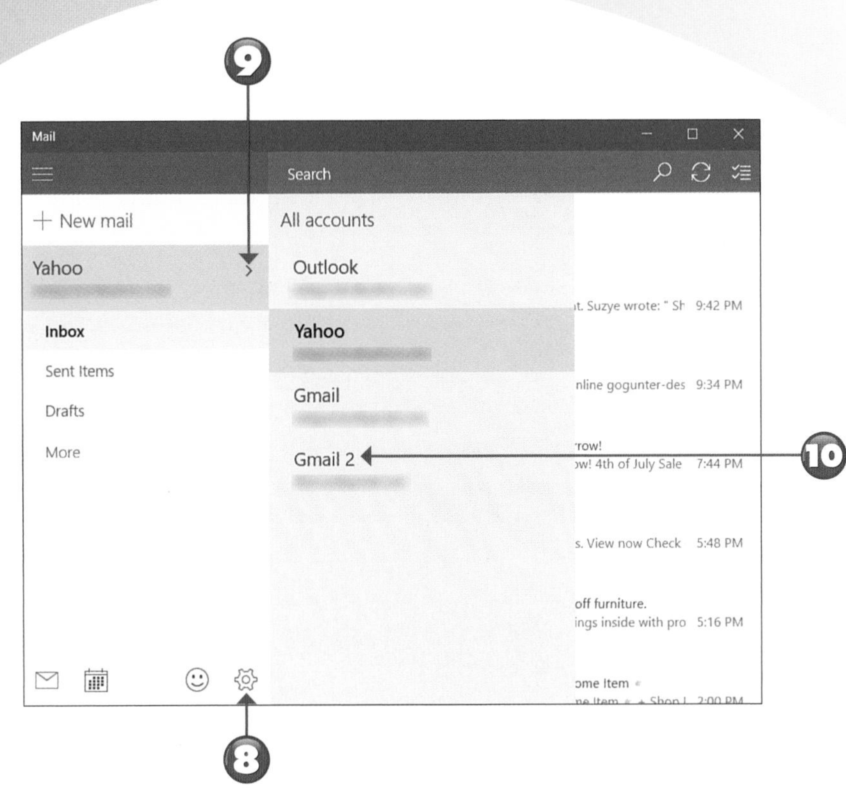

8 Click or tap outside the Accounts pane to close the pane, or click or tap the **Settings** icon.

9 Click here to display a list of accounts.

10 Click or tap an account to use it.

End

NOTE

Edit an Account If you need to make changes to an account's settings, or delete the account entirely, display the Accounts pane and click or tap the account. This opens a window with the account's name, settings, and an option for removing the account from your Mail app. Simply make your changes and click or tap **Save** when finished.

COMPOSING AND SENDING A MESSAGE

You can easily compose a new email message and send it on its way. The Mail app lets you add simple formatting, insert pictures or links, attach files, and even check your spelling before you hit the Send button. In this task, you learn to quickly create a message and add a file attachment.

Start

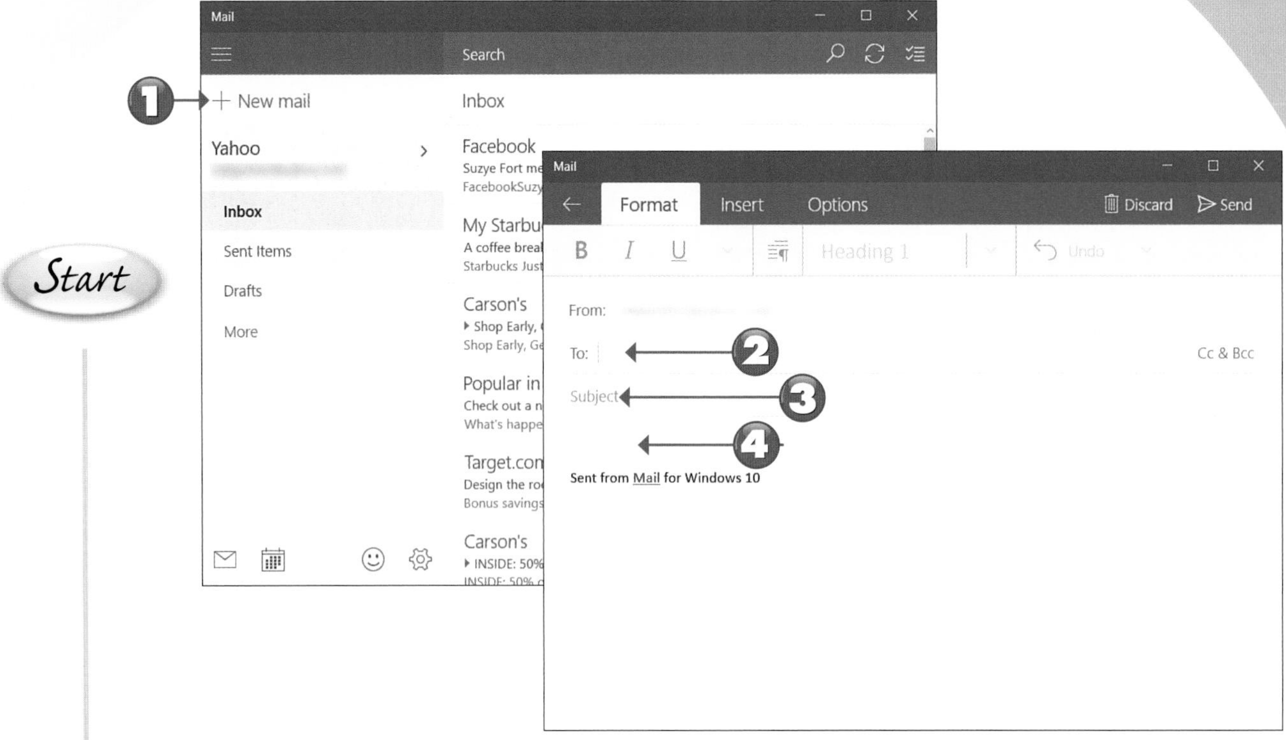

1. With the Mail app open, click or tap **New mail**.
2. Click or tap the **To** field and enter the email address for the person you want to send a message to. If you're sending the email to multiple people, include a semicolon between addresses.
3. Click or tap the **Subject** field and give your message a heading or title.
4. Click or tap the blank area below the Subject field and enter your message text.

Continued

TIP

Use a Contact As you're typing an email address in the To field, a list of possible matches might appear courtesy of the People app (your digital address book of contacts). If the name matches a contact, you can click or tap it to finish the entry.

NOTE

Check Your Folders To see a list of sent emails for an account, click or tap the **Sent Items** folder in the Folder pane. Mail pins the Sent Items and Drafts folders to the Folders pane by default. To pin other folders, first click or tap the **More** button at the bottom of the account listed in the Folder pane (you might need to scroll to view the option). Next, right-click or press and hold a folder name and click or tap **Favorites**. You can also use the same technique to unpin folders from the pane, but you should choose **Remove from Favorites**.

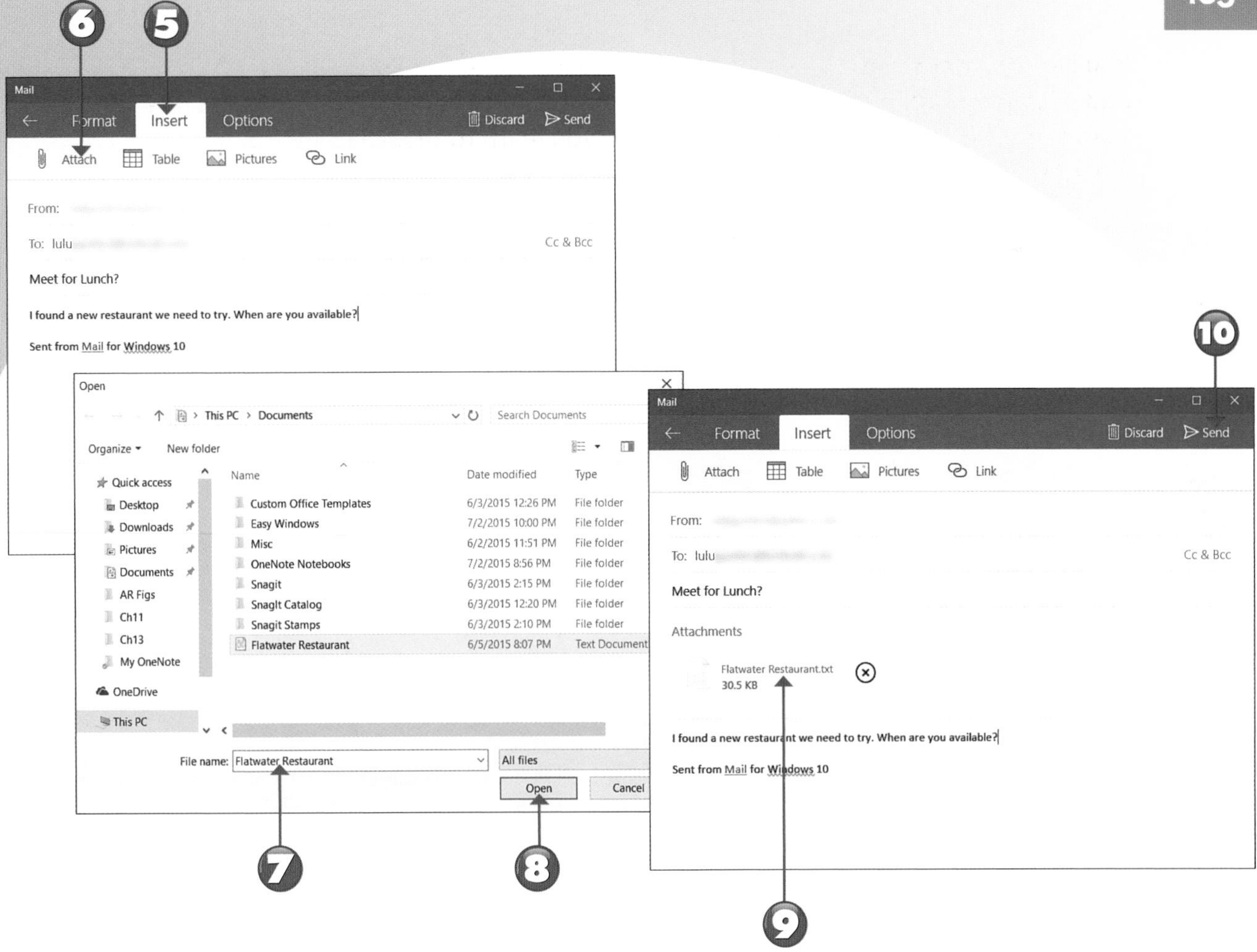

5. To add a file attachment, click or tap the **Insert** menu.

6. Click or tap **Attach**.

7. Navigate to the file you want to attach; click or tap the file name.

8. Click or tap **Open**.

9. Mail adds the file attachment.

10. Click or tap **Send** when you're ready to send the file.

End

READING AND REPLYING TO MESSAGES

Mail lists the email messages for each account in the main window, along with a brief peek at the content of each. You can read individual messages in their entirety in a separate window. You can also reply to a message from within the message window.

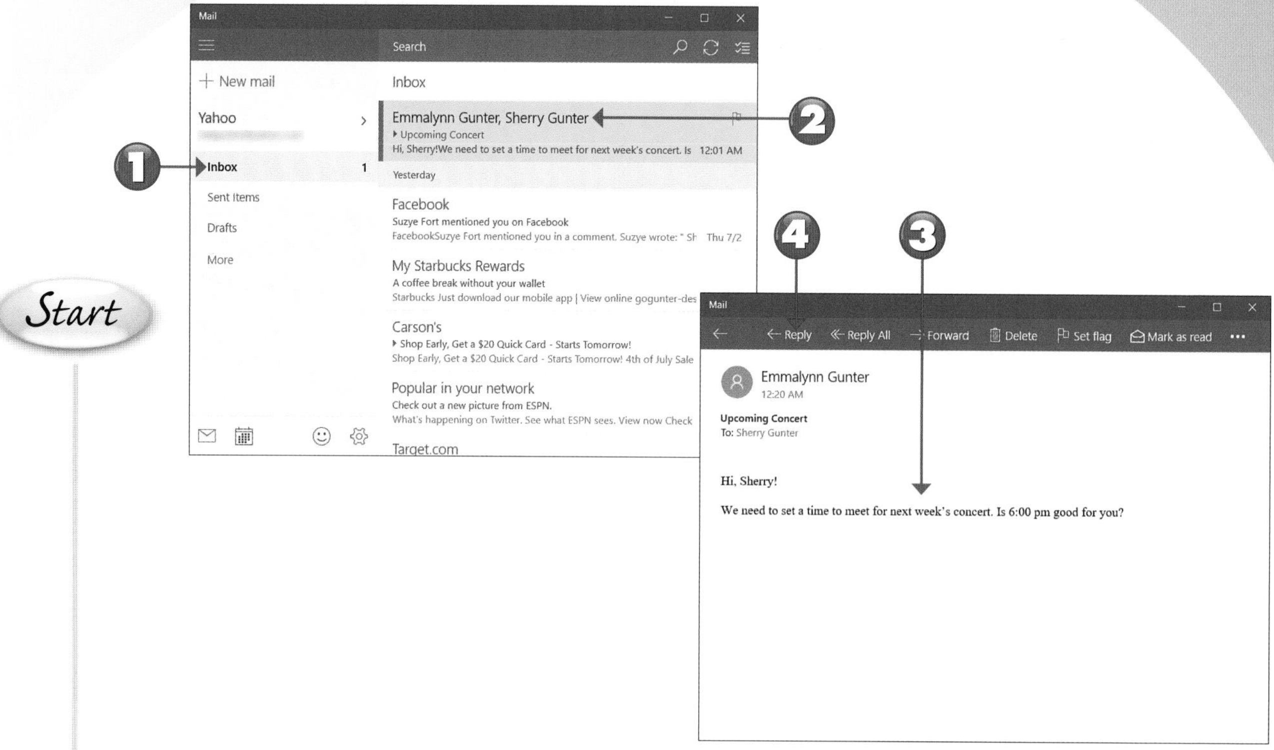

1. From the Folders pane, click or tap the email account or Inbox you want to view.
2. Click or tap the message you want to read.
3. The message opens, along with a toolbar of commands.
4. To reply to a message, click or tap **Reply**. If the message went to multiple people, you can reply to all of them using **Reply All**.

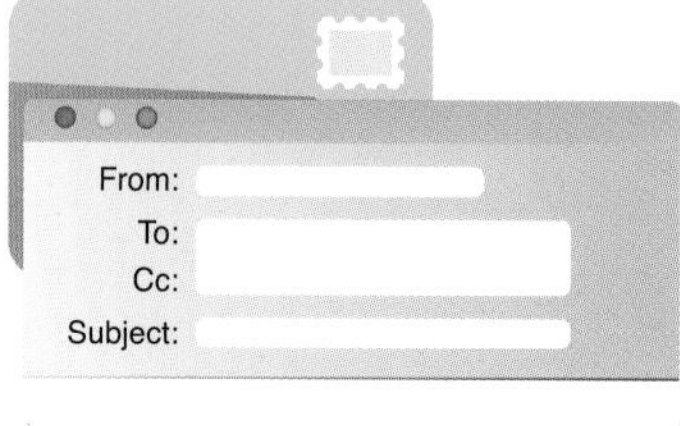

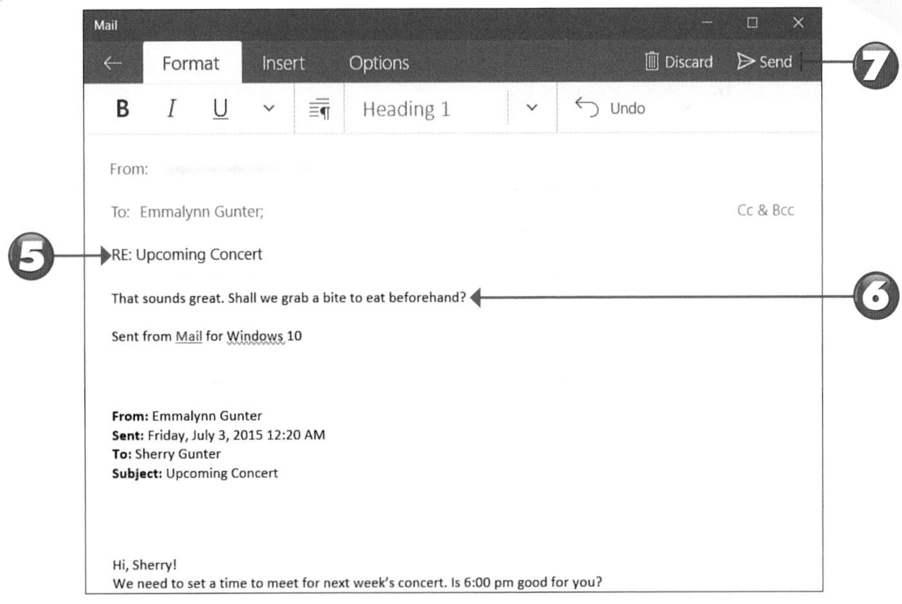
Mail
Format
Insert
Options
Discard
Send
Heading 1
Undo
From:
To: Emmalynn Gunter;
Cc & Bcc
RE: Upcoming Concert
That sounds great. Shall we grab a bite to eat beforehand?
Sent from Mail for Windows 10
From: Emmalynn Gunter
Sent: Friday, July 3, 2015 12:20 AM
To: Sherry Gunter
Subject: Upcoming Concert
Hi, Sherry!
We need to set a time to meet for next week's concert. Is 6:00 pm good for you?
5
6
7

5. Mail automatically fills in the sender's email address and adds "RE:" to the subject line to indicate the message is a reply. Mail also includes the original message text.
6. Type your message reply here.
7. Click or tap **Send**.

End

NOTE

Reading Conversations If you're corresponding with the same person (or persons) with replies back and forth, you can click or tap the message in the main Mail window to view each reply as a submessage to the original message. This lets you see the conversation's progress as each person responds.

FORWARDING MESSAGES

It's easy to forward a message to another person. Mail automatically inserts "FW:" in the subject title to indicate a forwarded message.

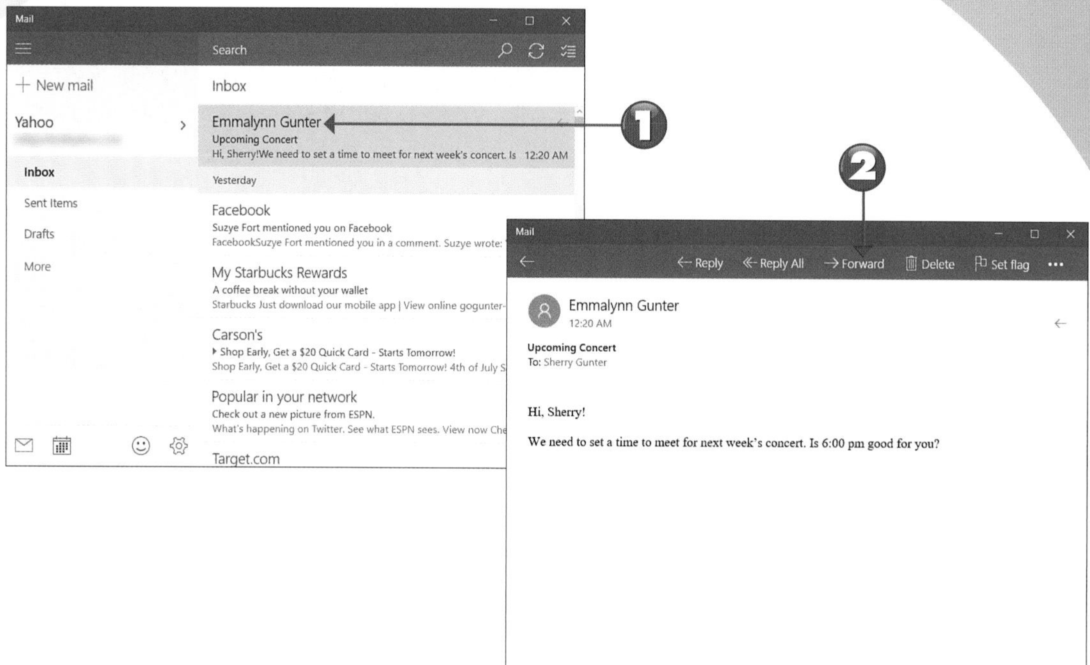

1. From your account's Inbox, click or tap the message you want to forward.
2. Click or tap **Forward**.

Continued

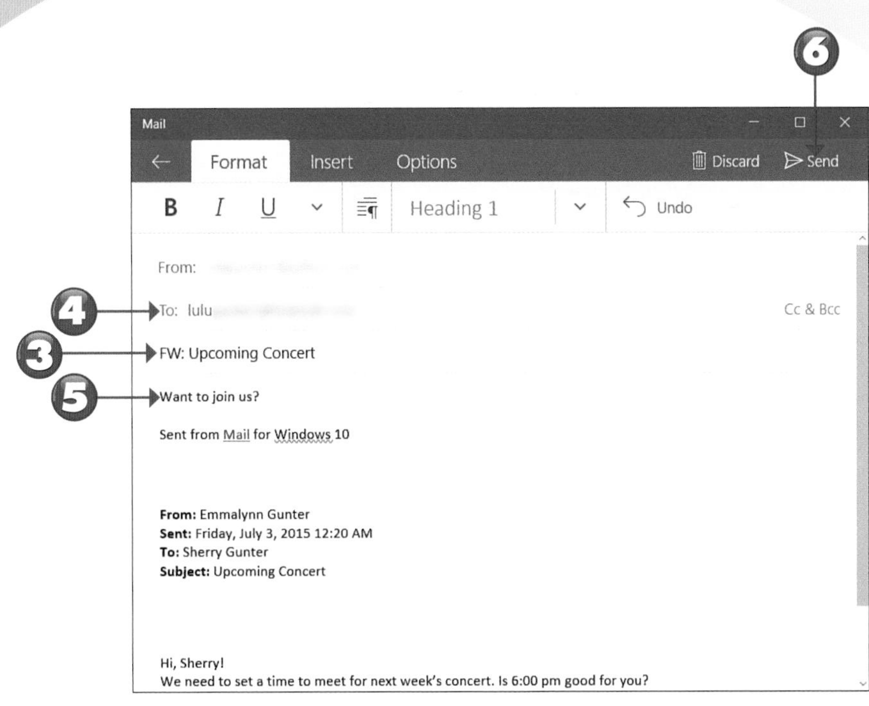
Mail
Format
Insert
Options
Discard
Send
Heading 1
Undo
From:
To: lulu
Cc & Bcc
FW: Upcoming Concert
Want to join us?
Sent from Mail for Windows 10
From: Emmalynn Gunter
Sent: Friday, July 3, 2015 12:20 AM
To: Sherry Gunter
Subject: Upcoming Concert
Hi, Sherry!
We need to set a time to meet for next week's concert. Is 6:00 pm good for you?

3. Mail automatically adds "FW:" to the subject line to indicate the email is a forwarded message.

4. Click or tap the **To** box and type in the email address you want to send to.

5. You can add any additional message text here.

6. Click or tap **Send**.

End

TIP

Adding Formatting You can use the Format menu to add simple formatting to your message text, such as bold and italics, or assign a preformatted style. Click or tap **Format** to view the formatting options.

FLAGGING MESSAGES

You can use Mail's flagging tool to flag a message. When you add a flag, it's easier to spot the message in the list later, such as flagging an important message you want to reread or respond to at a later time. Start by opening the email account you want to use.

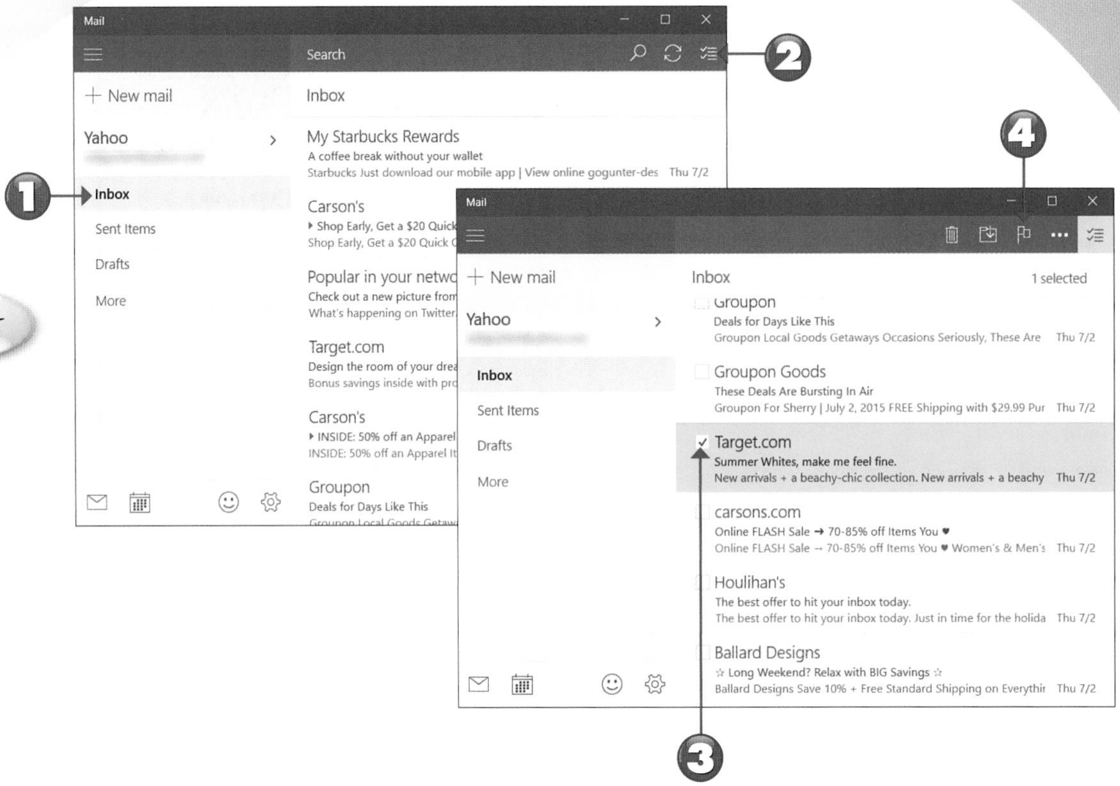

1. From the account's Folders pane, click or tap the Inbox or folder you want to view.
2. Click or tap **Select**.
3. Click or tap the check box for the message you want to mark.
4. Click or tap **Set Flag**.

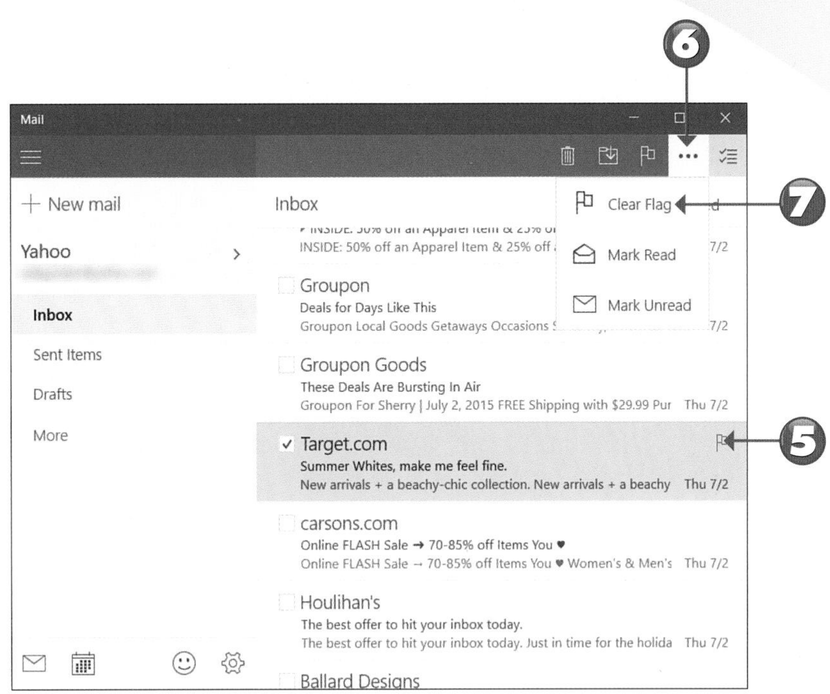

5 Mail adds a flag icon to the message.

6 To clear a flag, click or tap **More Options**. (You might need to click or tap **Select** again to display the More Options icon.)

7 Click or tap **Clear Flag**.

End

TIP

Quick Flagging You can also hover the mouse pointer or move your finger over an email message to reveal a Trash icon (for deleting messages) and a Flag icon. You can click or tap the **Flag** icon to flag the highlighted message.

DELETING MESSAGES

To help keep your Inbox lean and clean, it's a good practice to delete messages you no longer want to keep. You can use the Select feature to check multiple messages for deletion.

Start

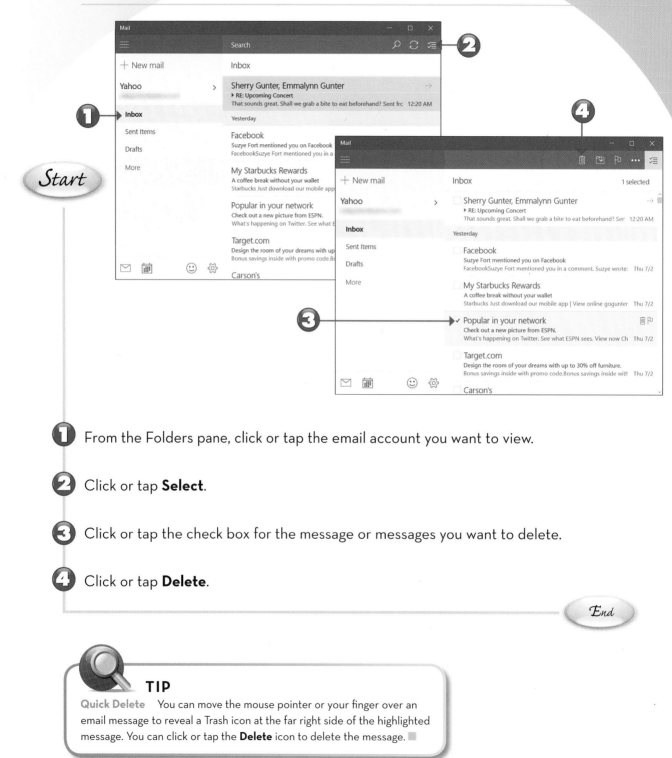

1. From the Folders pane, click or tap the email account you want to view.
2. Click or tap **Select**.
3. Click or tap the check box for the message or messages you want to delete.
4. Click or tap **Delete**.

TIP

Quick Delete You can move the mouse pointer or your finger over an email message to reveal a Trash icon at the far right side of the highlighted message. You can click or tap the **Delete** icon to delete the message.

CREATING AN EMAIL SIGNATURE

A signature is information, typically text, that appears appended to every email message you send, rather like a sign-off to your message. A signature can be as simple as your name and contact information, a website URL, your favorite quote, or your company name and number.

Start

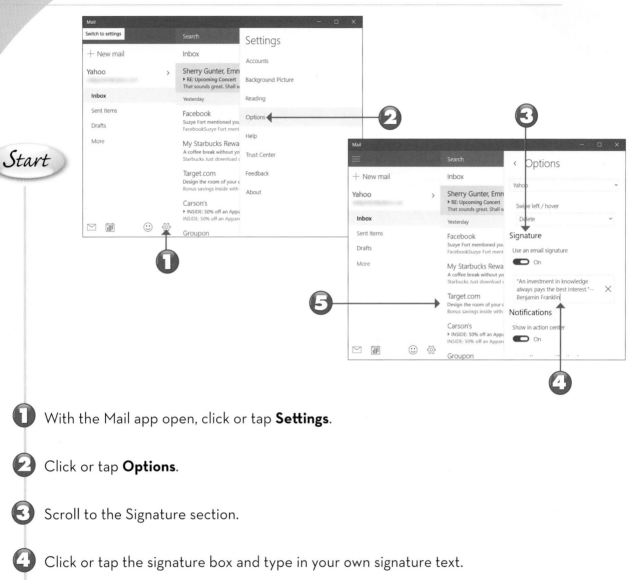

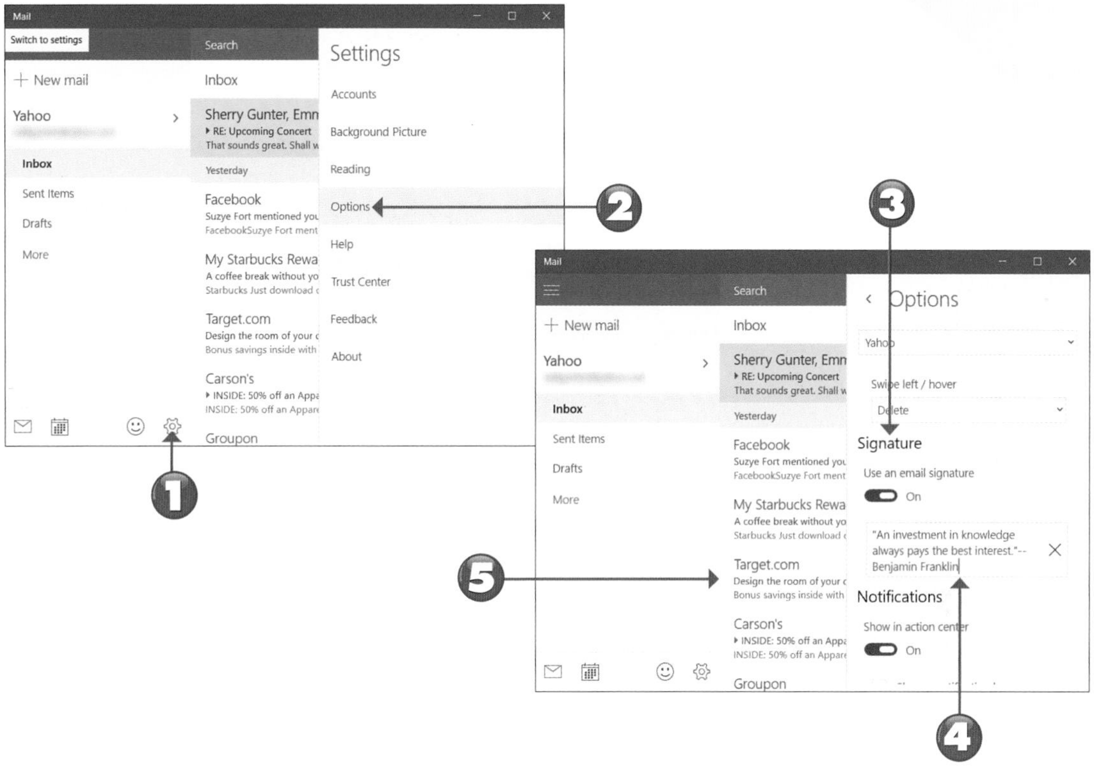

1. With the Mail app open, click or tap **Settings**.

2. Click or tap **Options**.

3. Scroll to the Signature section.

4. Click or tap the signature box and type in your own signature text.

5. Click or tap anywhere outside the Settings pane to return to the Mail window.

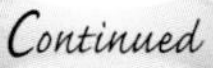

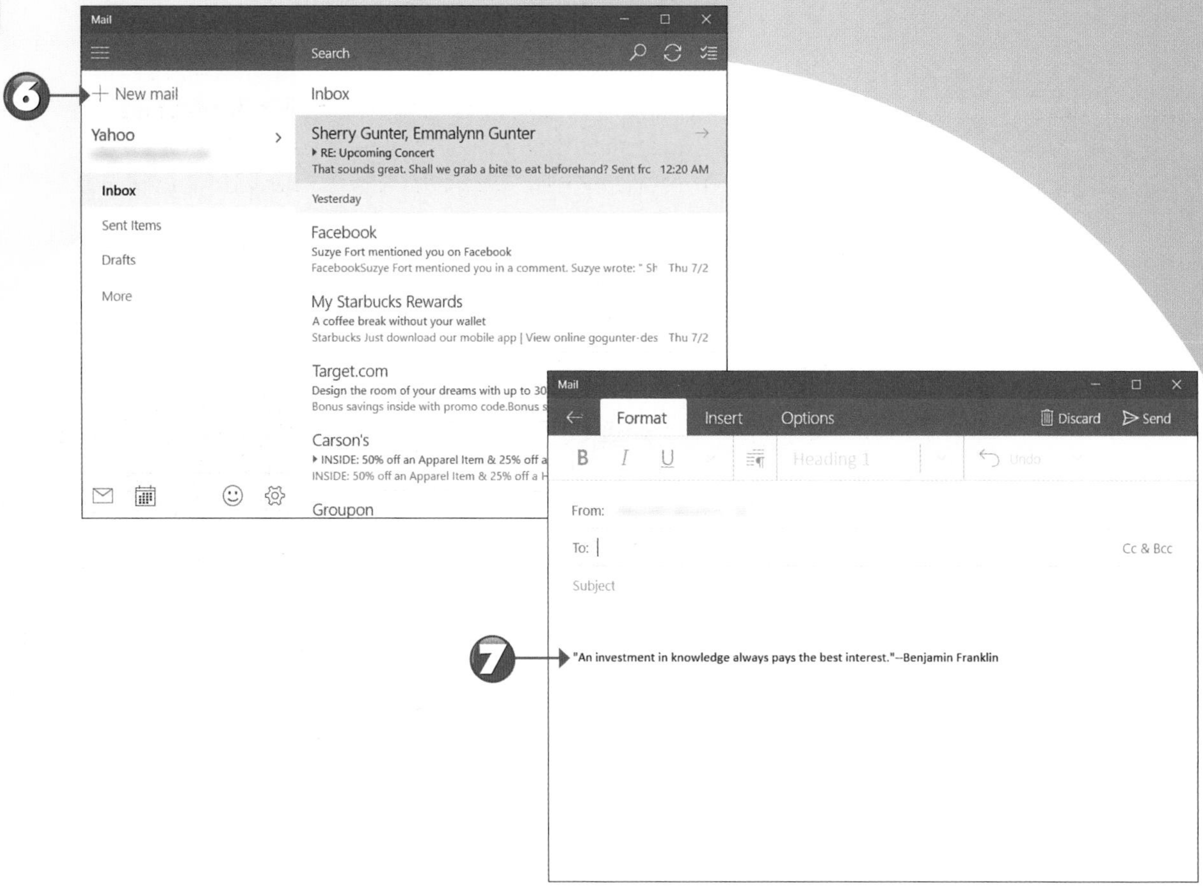

Mail

Search

6 + New mail

Inbox

Yahoo

Sherry Gunter, Emmalynn Gunter
RE: Upcoming Concert
That sounds great. Shall we grab a bite to eat beforehand? Sent frc 12:20 AM

Inbox

Yesterday

Sent Items

Facebook
Suzye Fort mentioned you on Facebook
FacebookSuzye Fort mentioned you in a comment. Suzye wrote: " Sh Thu 7/2

Drafts

More

My Starbucks Rewards
A coffee break without your wallet
Starbucks Just download our mobile app | View online gogunter-des Thu 7/2

Target.com
Design the room of your dreams with up to 30
Bonus savings inside with promo code.Bonus s

Carson's
INSIDE: 50% off an Apparel Item & 25% off a
INSIDE: 50% off an Apparel Item & 25% off a H

Groupon

Mail

Format Insert Options Discard Send

B I U Heading 1 Undo

From:

To: Cc & Bcc

Subject

7 "An investment in knowledge always pays the best interest."--Benjamin Franklin

6 To view your new signature, click or tap **New mail**.

7 The signature automatically appears at the bottom of the new message.

End

NOTE

Turn Off Signatures If you don't want to include a signature with your emails, you can turn off the feature. Click or tap **Settings**, **Options**, and then scroll to the Signature feature. Click or tap the **On/Off** button to the Off position.

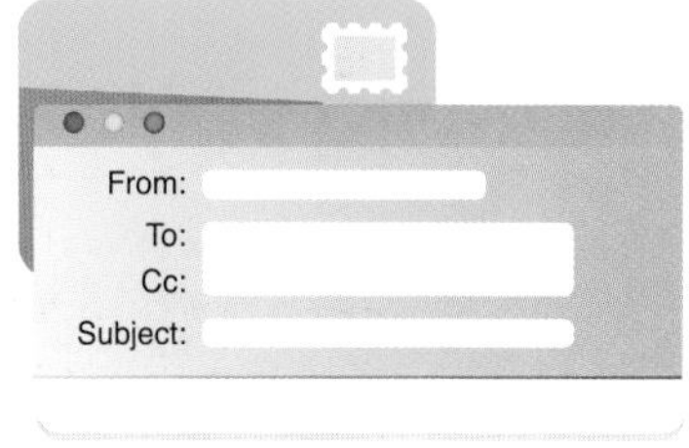

USING THE CALENDAR APP

You can use the Calendar app to keep track of appointments you make with friends, colleagues, and others. Calendar helps you remember important birthdays and special occasions, events, and other daily, weekly, or monthly activities you pursue. You can flip back and forth between daily, weekly, or monthly view and check out your work-week schedule, too.

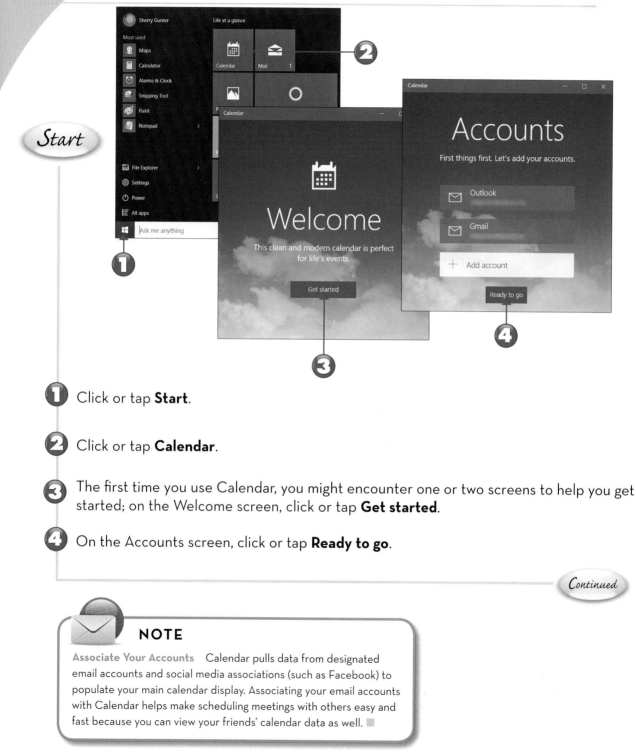

1. Click or tap **Start**.
2. Click or tap **Calendar**.
3. The first time you use Calendar, you might encounter one or two screens to help you get started; on the Welcome screen, click or tap **Get started**.
4. On the Accounts screen, click or tap **Ready to go**.

Continued

NOTE

Associate Your Accounts Calendar pulls data from designated email accounts and social media associations (such as Facebook) to populate your main calendar display. Associating your email accounts with Calendar helps make scheduling meetings with others easy and fast because you can view your friends' calendar data as well.

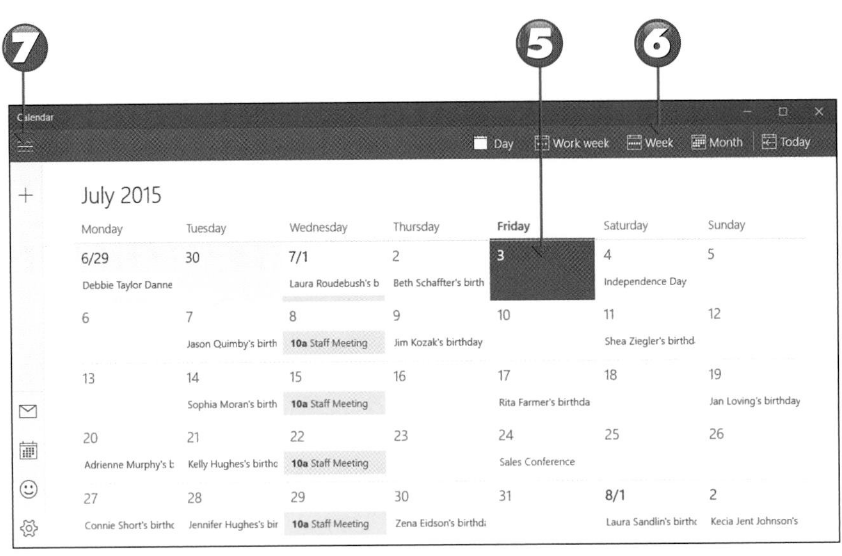

5. Calendar opens to the current date. If you're using several email and social media accounts, Calendar already inserts items such as birthdays and anniversaries for you.

6. To change views, click or tap a view: **Day**, **Work week**, **Week**, or **Month**.

7. To view the navigation bar, click or tap the Menu button.

Continued

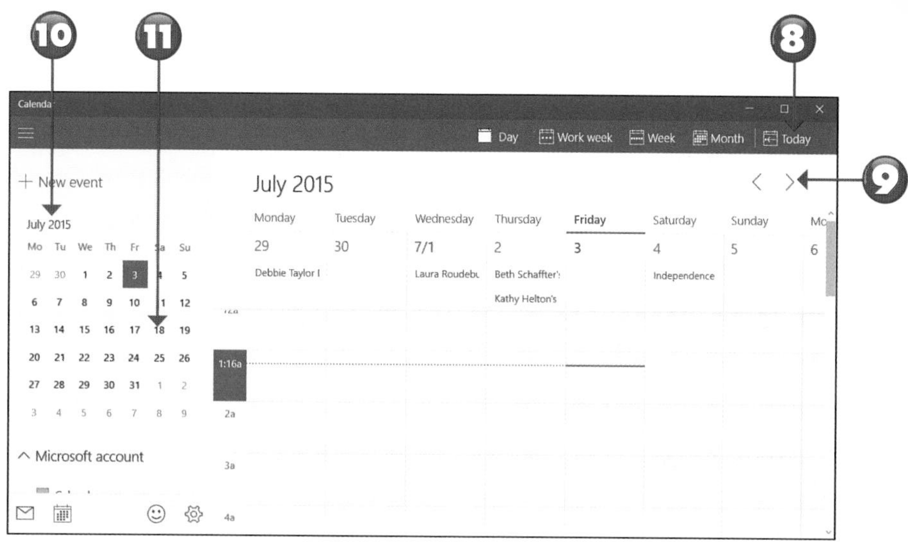

8 To display the current date, click or tap **Today**.

9 To move between days, weeks, or months, move the mouse pointer over the corner of the calendar display and click or tap a navigation arrow.

10 Use the navigation calendar to view a particular date; move the mouse pointer over the corner and click or tap the arrows to change the calendar display.

11 Click or tap the date you want to view.

End

NOTE

Turn Off Calendars Account calendars are listed below the navigation calendar, including the Birthday calendar with Facebook birthdays. You can uncheck a calendar to turn off its display as part of your main calendar. For example, if you uncheck the Birthday calendar, you no longer see your friends' birthdays listed in the calendar display.

SCHEDULING AN APPOINTMENT WITH CALENDAR

It's easy to set up an appointment using Calendar. Appointments are called *events* in Calendar's lingo. You can set up a quick event using the pop-up box, or you can fill out more details for an event using a form. In this task, you learn how to schedule a detailed appointment.

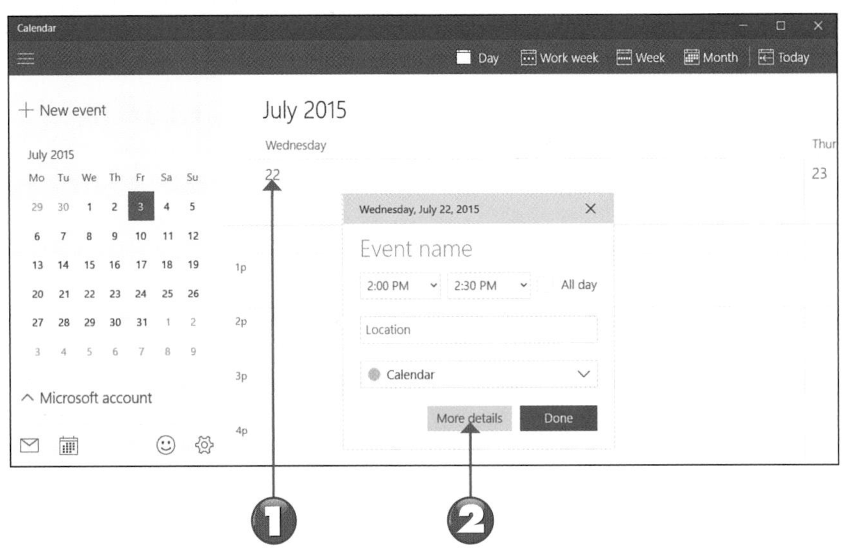

1. Navigate to the date to which you want to add an appointment, and click or tap the date. If you're in Day, Work week, or Week view, you can click or tap a specific time.
2. Click or tap **More details**.

Continued

NOTE

Set a Quick Appointment In Day, Work week, or Week view, you can set a quick appointment without having to open the Event form. Just fill out the start and end times for the appointment and a location, and then click or tap **Done**. Keep in mind, however, that the appointment won't have a title, so you won't know exactly what it's for when you glance at it on the calendar display.

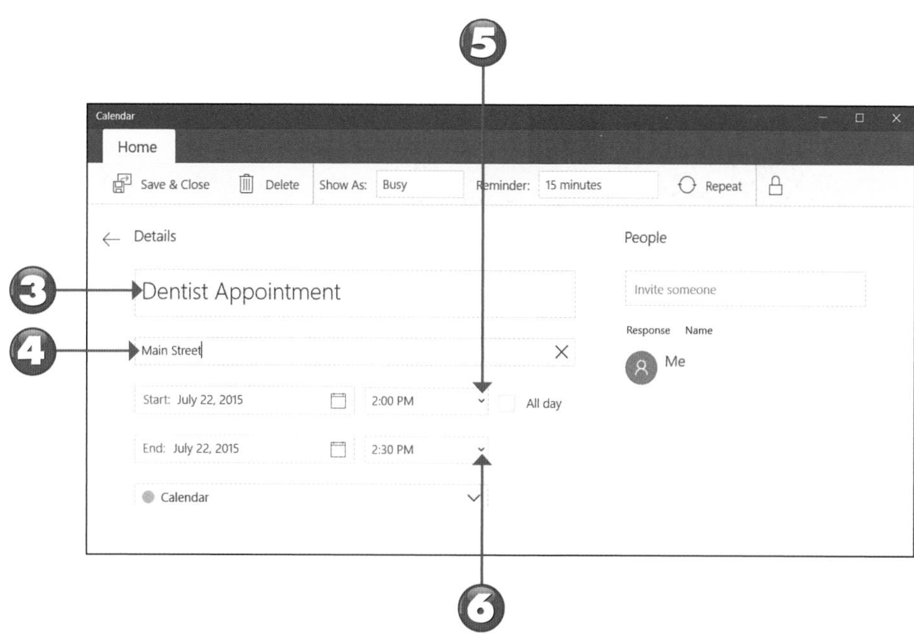

3. Calendar opens a form window for filling out more details. Click or tap the **Event name** box and enter a title for the appointment, such as Doctor Appointment or Staff Meeting.

4. Optionally, click or tap the **Location** box to enter a place for the appointment.

5. Click or tap the **Start time** arrow and choose a start time.

6. Click or tap the **End time** arrow and choose an end time.

Continued

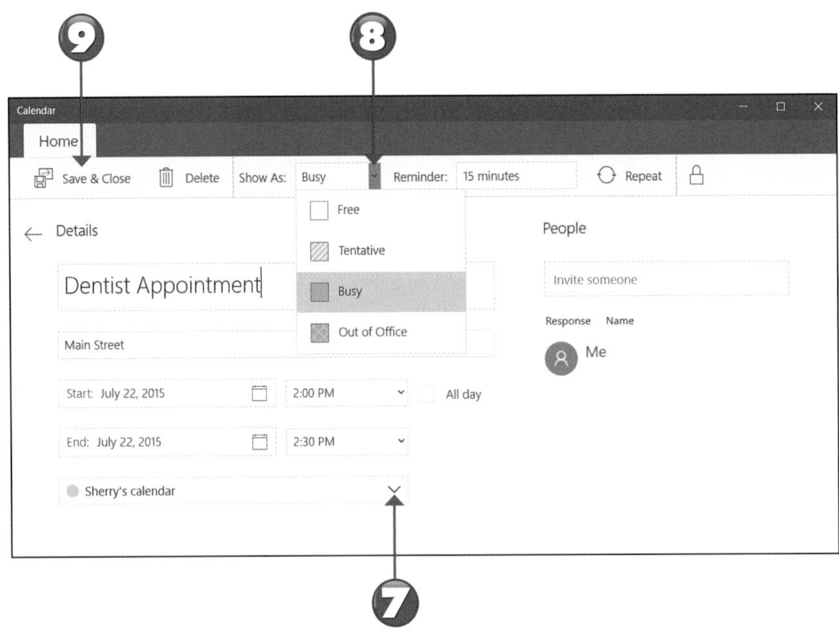

7. Optionally, to choose a different calendar to post the event to, click or tap here and choose another calendar.
8. To change how the event appears on shared calendars, click or tap the **Show As** arrow and choose a setting.
9. Click or tap **Save & Close** to add the event to your schedule.

Continued

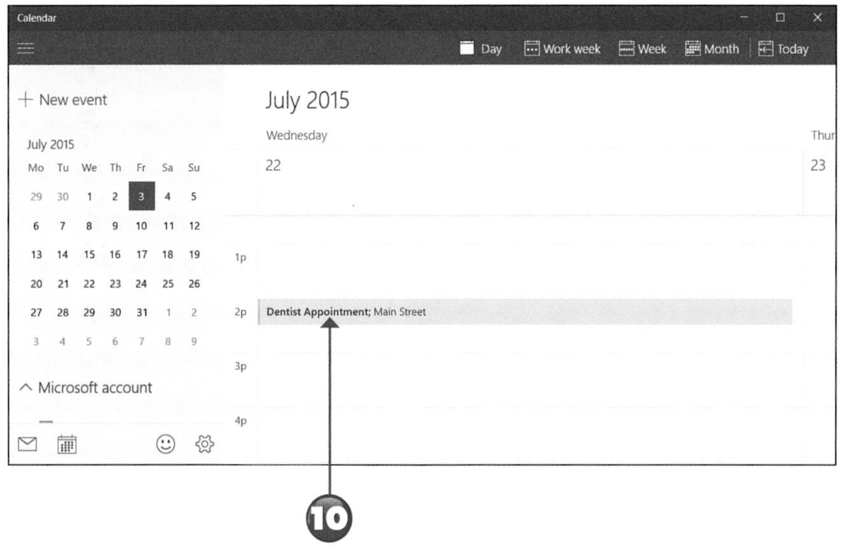

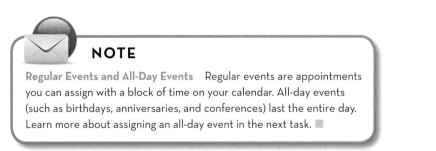

10 The appointment is added to your calendar. To make changes to the appointment, simply click or tap it to reopen the form.

End

NOTE

Regular Events and All-Day Events Regular events are appointments you can assign with a block of time on your calendar. All-day events (such as birthdays, anniversaries, and conferences) last the entire day. Learn more about assigning an all-day event in the next task.

SCHEDULING AN ALL-DAY EVENT

An all-day event is anything that lasts for the entire day, such as a birthday or a conference you're attending. All-day events appear listed at the top of a date in Day, Week, or Work week view.

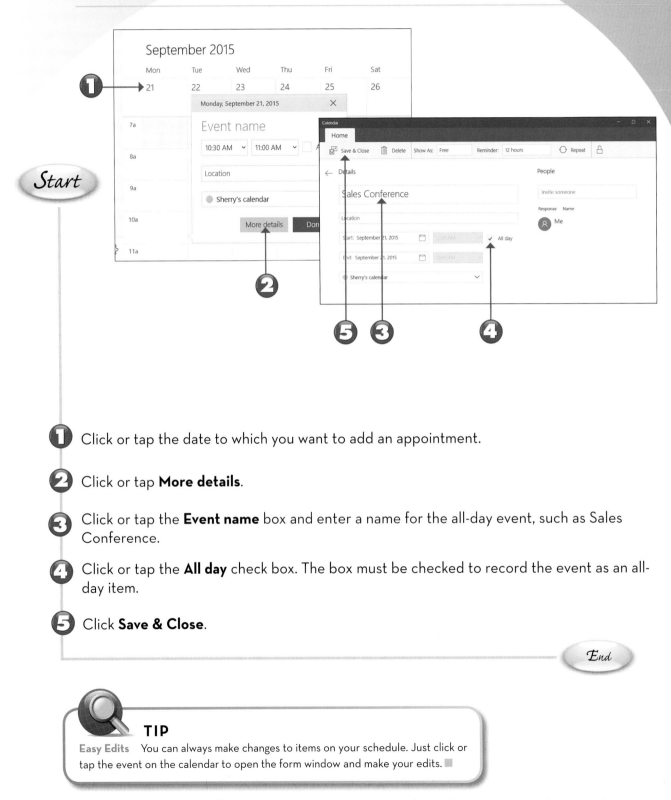

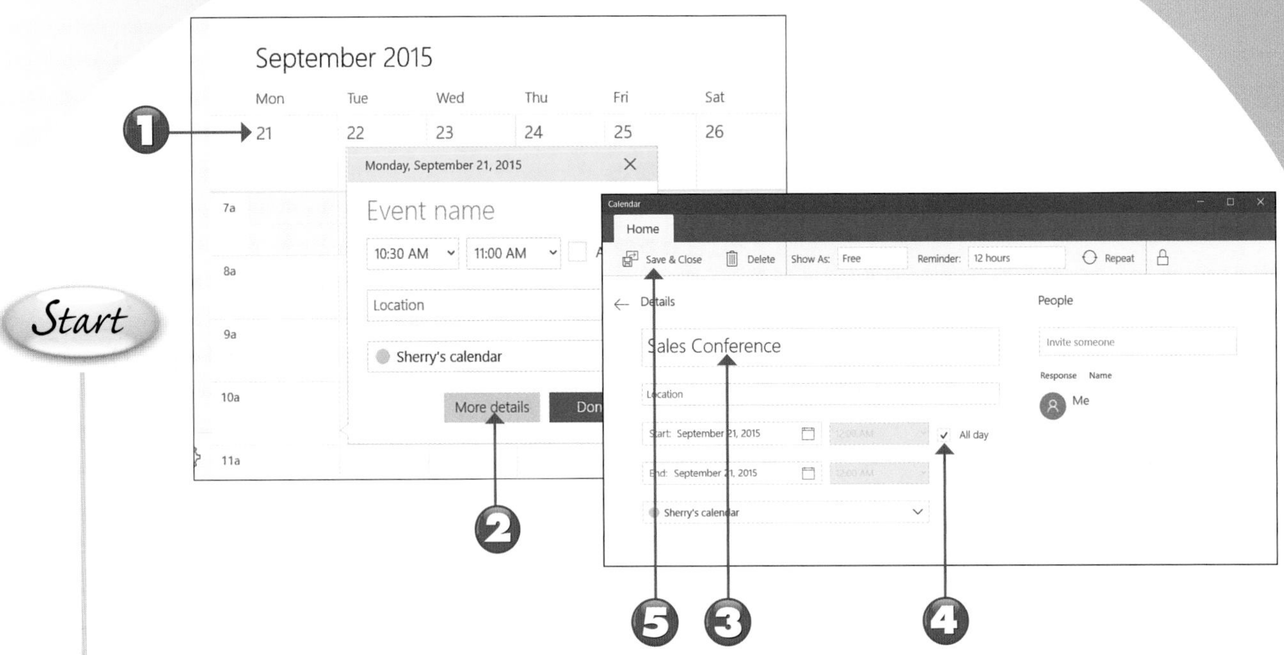

1. Click or tap the date to which you want to add an appointment.
2. Click or tap **More details**.
3. Click or tap the **Event name** box and enter a name for the all-day event, such as Sales Conference.
4. Click or tap the **All day** check box. The box must be checked to record the event as an all-day item.
5. Click **Save & Close**.

TIP

Easy Edits You can always make changes to items on your schedule. Just click or tap the event on the calendar to open the form window and make your edits.

SCHEDULING A RECURRING APPOINTMENT

If your schedule involves regular appointments, such as a weekly staff meeting, you can set a recurring event. Using the Repeat feature, you can specify how often the event occurs and when it stops recurring.

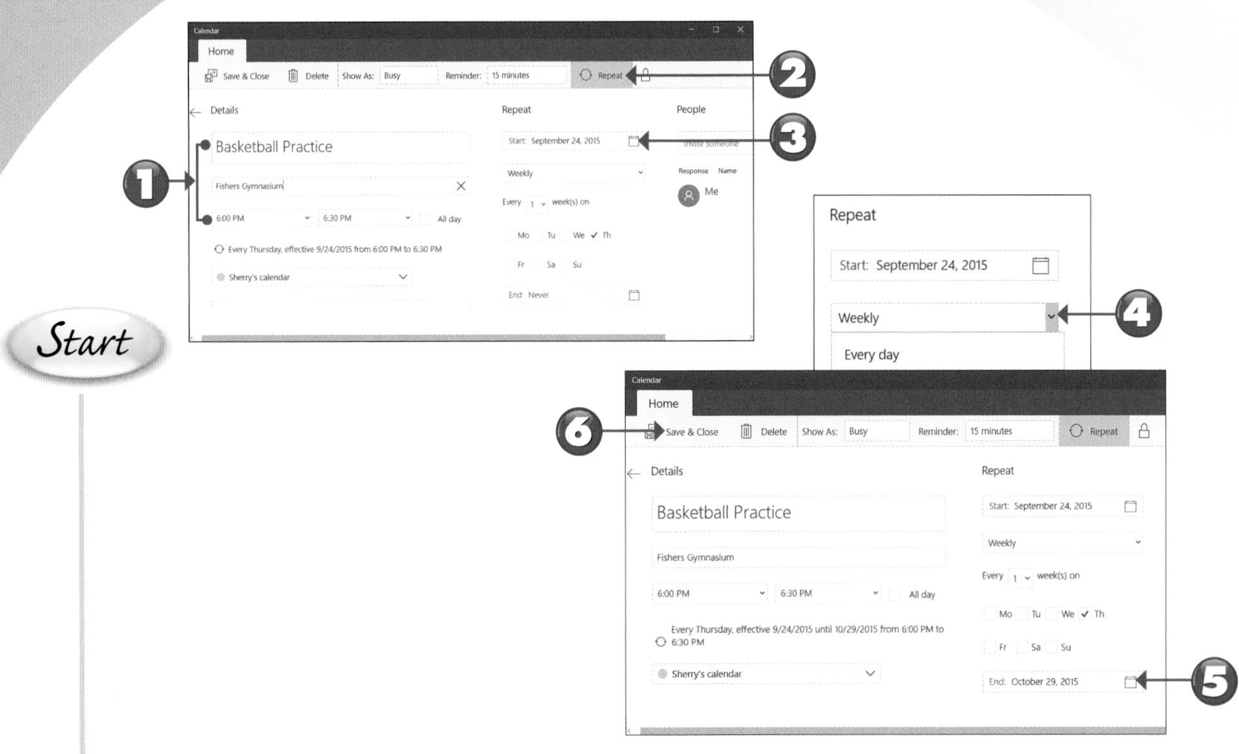

1. Open the Event form and fill out the appropriate appointment details.
2. Click or tap **Repeat**.
3. Click or tap **Start** to choose a date when the recurring event begins.
4. Click or tap the **Occurrence** arrow and choose how often the event repeats.
5. To set an end date for the event, click or tap **End** and choose a date.
6. Click or tap **Save & Close**.

End

NOTE

Editing Recurrences You can make changes to a repeating appointment by clicking or tapping the event on the calendar. This opens the form where you can click or tap **Edit series** to change how often the appointment repeats. To remove the appointment entirely, click or tap **Delete**.

SETTING AN APPOINTMENT REMINDER

Calendar has a handy feature for helping you remember upcoming events on your calendar. The Reminder feature lets you set an alarm that notifies you with a prompt box when the appointment draws near.

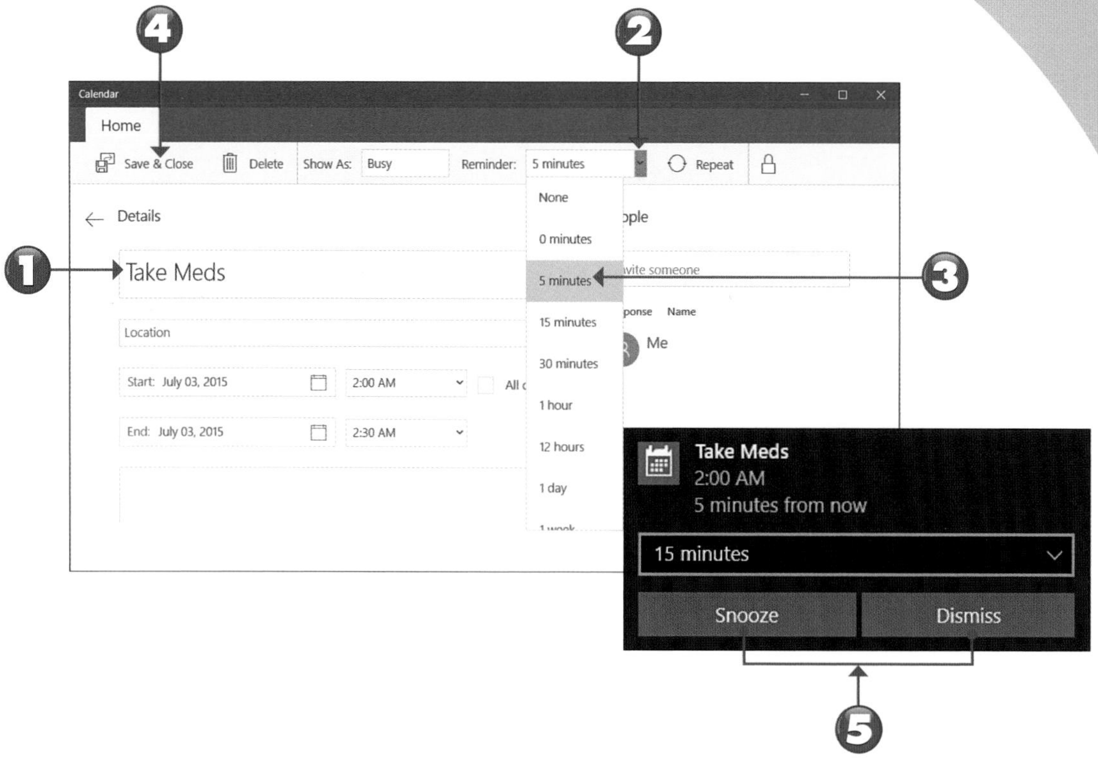

Start

1. Open the event's form.
2. Click or tap **Reminder**.
3. Click or tap a reminder time.
4. Click or tap **Save & Close**.
5. When the specified reminder time arrives, a notification reminder box pops up onscreen; click or tap Snooze to ignore it for a few minutes, or click or tap Dismiss to close the reminder.

TIP

Removing a Reminder To remove a reminder, reopen the form, click or tap **Reminder**, and choose **None** from the drop-down menu.

HIDING AND DISPLAYING CALENDAR'S FOLDERS PANE

The left side of the Calendar app lists your folders, a navigation calendar, and icons for accessing Mail, Settings, and more. You can hide the pane to free up more viewing space for the calendar display.

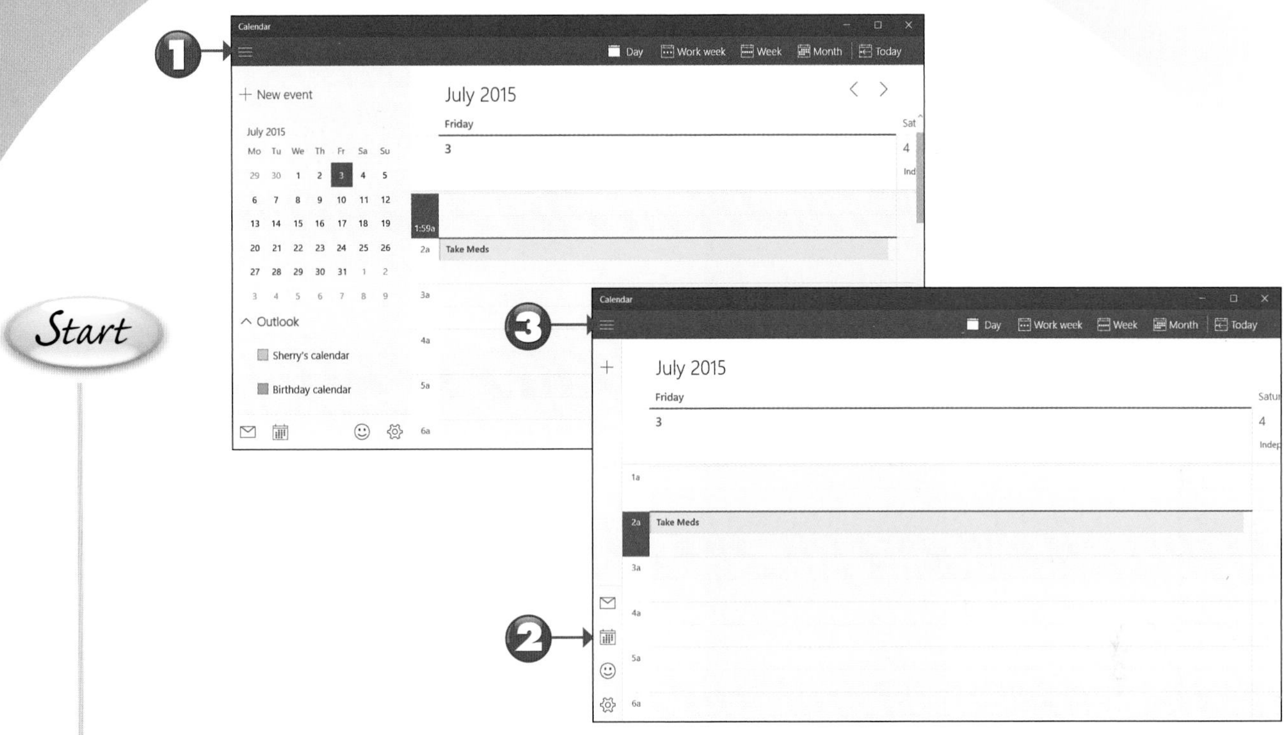

Start

1. Click or tap here to hide the pane.

2. Calendar hides the pane but still offers access to the icons.

3. Click or tap to display the pane again.

End

TIP

Switching You can switch back and forth between the Calendar app and the Mail app. Click or tap the **Mail** icon to view mail; click or tap the **Calendar** icon to view your schedule.

STARTING SKYPE

You can use the free Skype app to make face-to-face video calls over the Internet. You can also use Skype to send and receive text messages and voice calls around the world. You need a webcam and a microphone to use Skype. If you're new to Skype, you also must create an account. This task focuses on the new Skype for Desktop program.

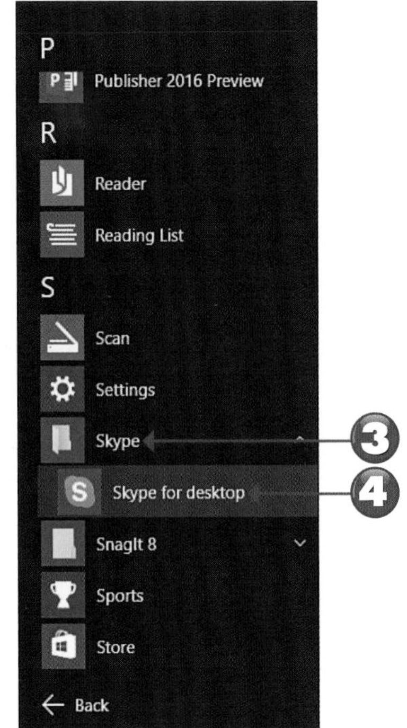

Start

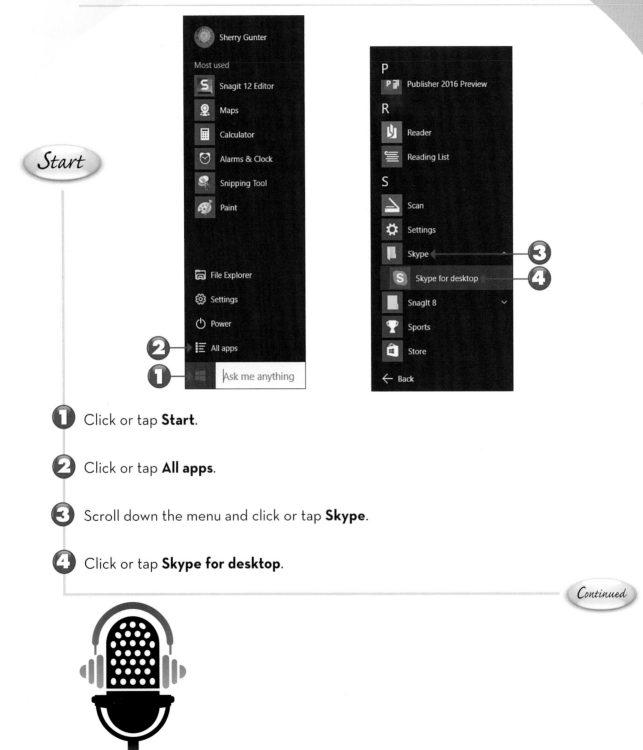

1. Click or tap **Start**.
2. Click or tap **All apps**.
3. Scroll down the menu and click or tap **Skype**.
4. Click or tap **Skype for desktop**.

Continued

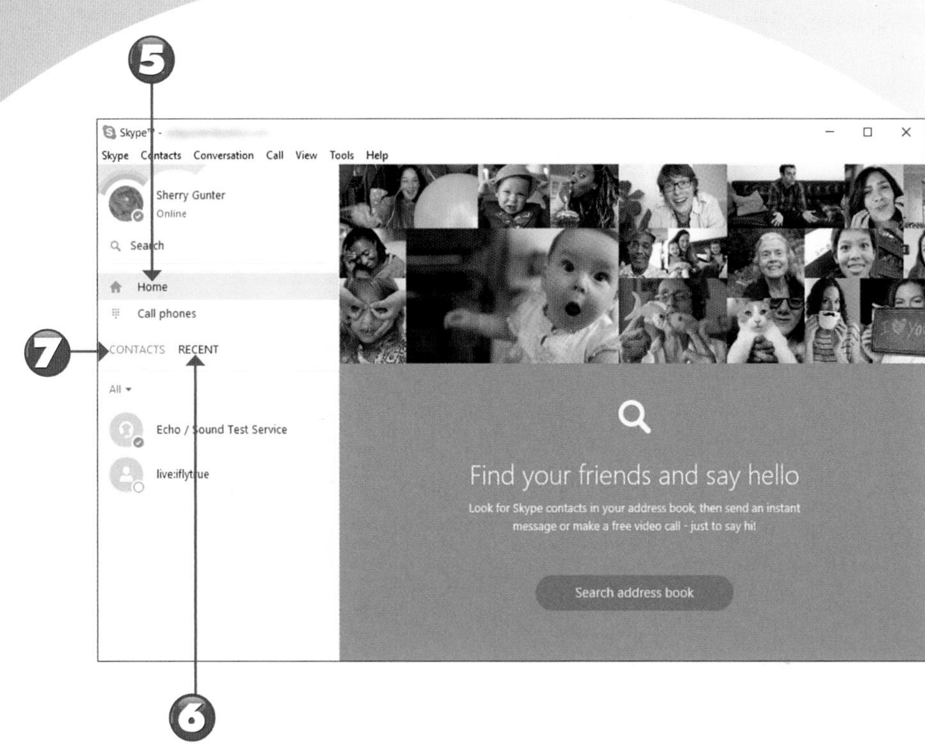

5 The Skype window opens to your account's Home page.

6 Click or tap **Recent** to view recent activity.

7 Click or tap **Contacts** to view your contacts list.

Continued

TIP

Testing, Testing To quickly test your device's sound, click or tap **Echo/Sound Test Service** located under the Contacts category on the main Skype window. Click or tap the **Call** button and follow the instructions to conduct a sound test.

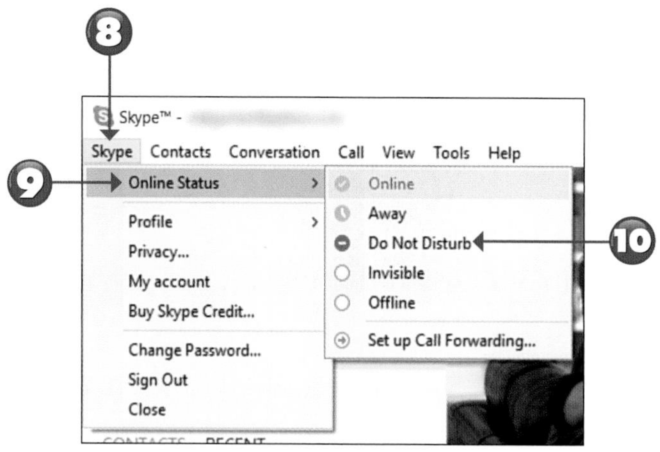

8 To change your online status, click or tap the Skype menu.

9 Click or tap **Online Status**.

10 Click or tap a status.

Continued

NOTE

No Skype? If you can't find the Skype app on your computer, tablet, or smartphone, you can download the app from the Store. Click or tap **Start**, and click or tap **Store**. Using the **Search** box, type **Skype** and locate the app. Select the app and click or tap the **Free** button to download and install it. During the installation, Skype helps you get everything set up to use the app. After you have everything ready, you can open Skype any time you want from the Start menu's apps list.

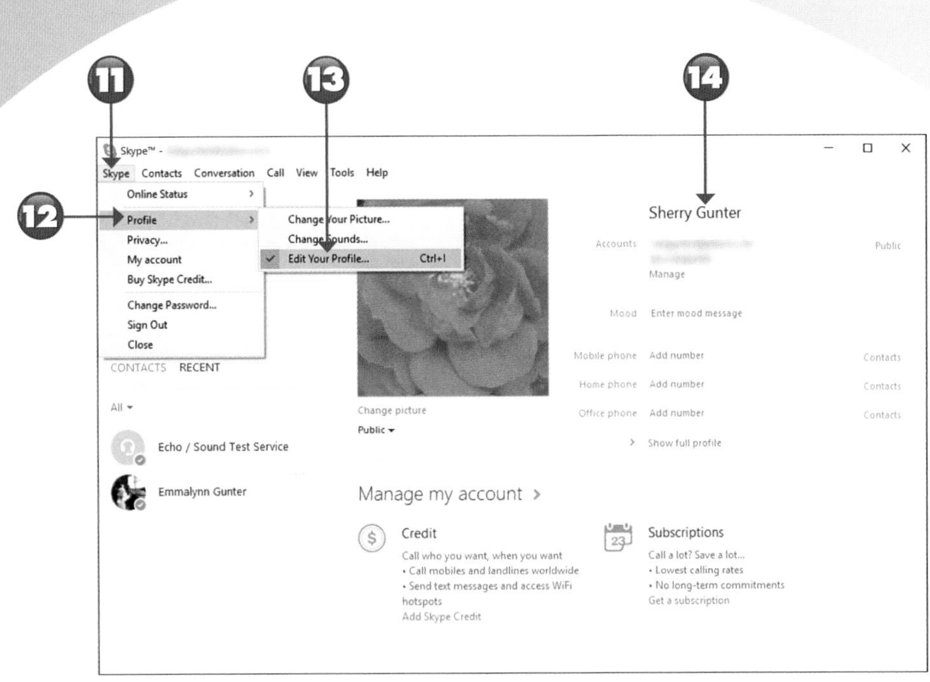

11. To edit your profile, such as change profile picture or add contact numbers, click or tap **Skype**.

12. Click or tap **Profile**.

13. Click or tap **Edit Your Profile**.

14. Skype opens your profile page with settings you can edit, such as changing your profile picture.

End

ADDING CONTACTS WITH SKYPE

You can add contacts to Skype for people you communicate with the most.

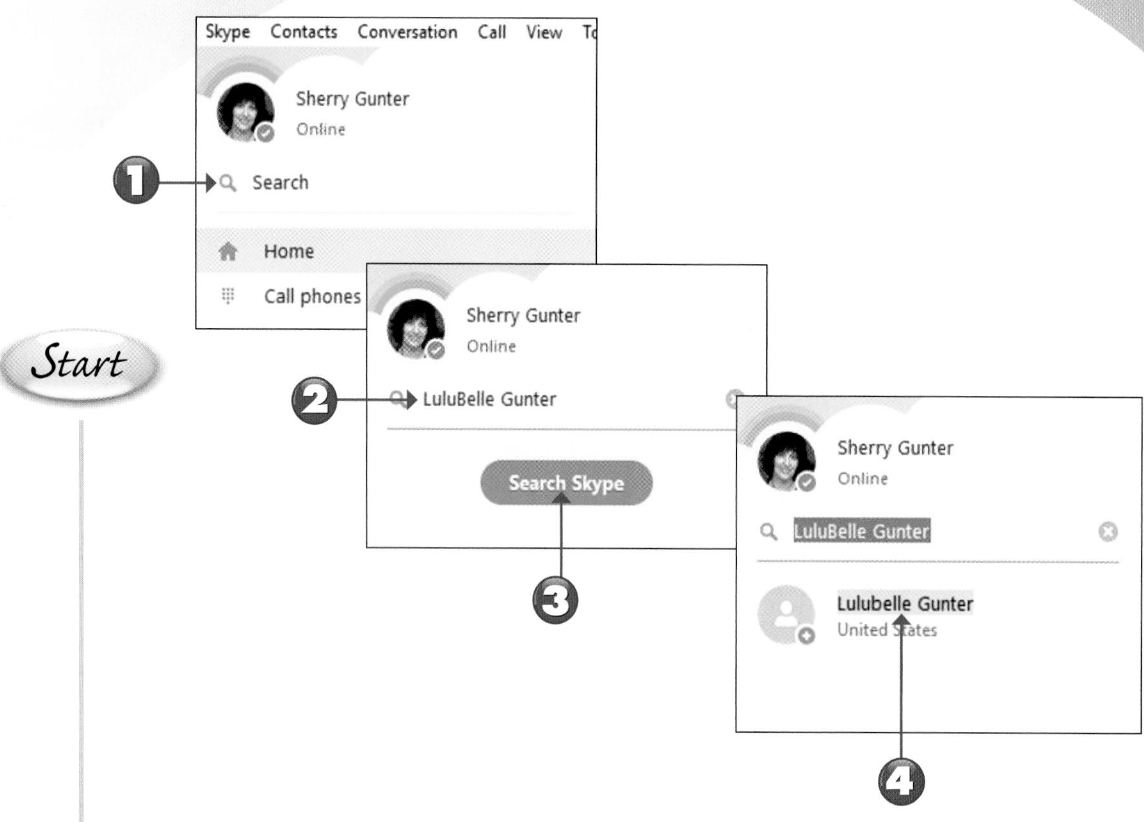

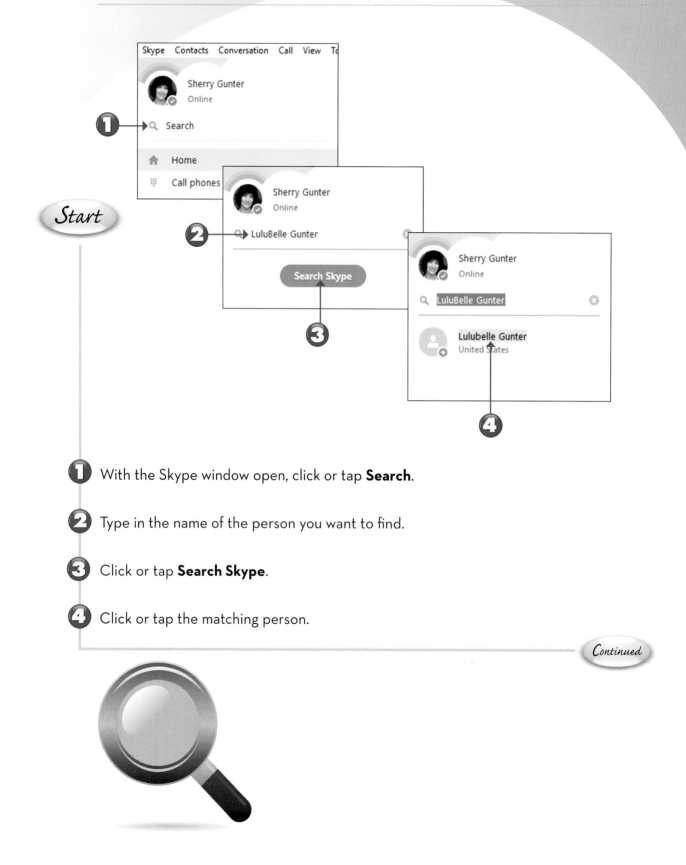

1. With the Skype window open, click or tap **Search**.
2. Type in the name of the person you want to find.
3. Click or tap **Search Skype**.
4. Click or tap the matching person.

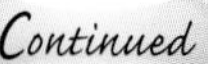
Continued

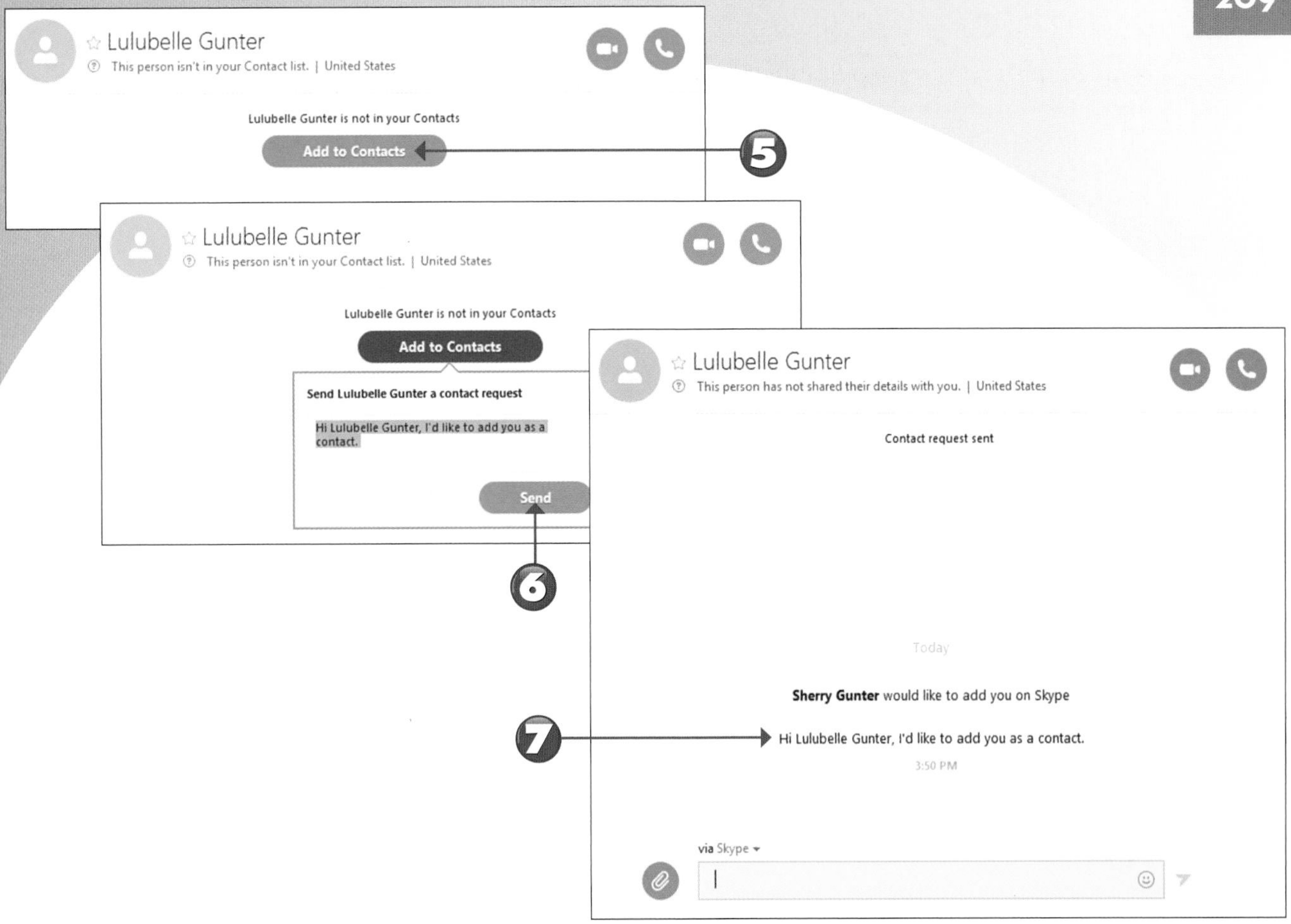

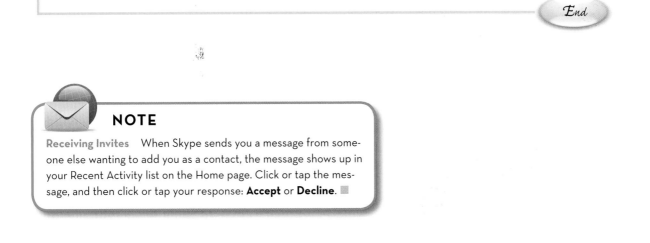

5 Click or tap **Add to Contacts**.

6 Skype displays a Contact Request form; type out a message, if desired, or use the default message and click or tap **Send**.

7 The recipient receives a message and can accept or decline your invitation. If it is accepted, the contact is added to your list and Skype lets you know.

End

NOTE

Receiving Invites When Skype sends you a message from someone else wanting to add you as a contact, the message shows up in your Recent Activity list on the Home page. Click or tap the message, and then click or tap your response: **Accept** or **Decline**.

PLACING A VIDEO CALL WITH SKYPE

With your webcam, you can place a face-to-face video call. When making a video call, Skype displays a few tools you can use, and it keeps track of the call duration.

Start

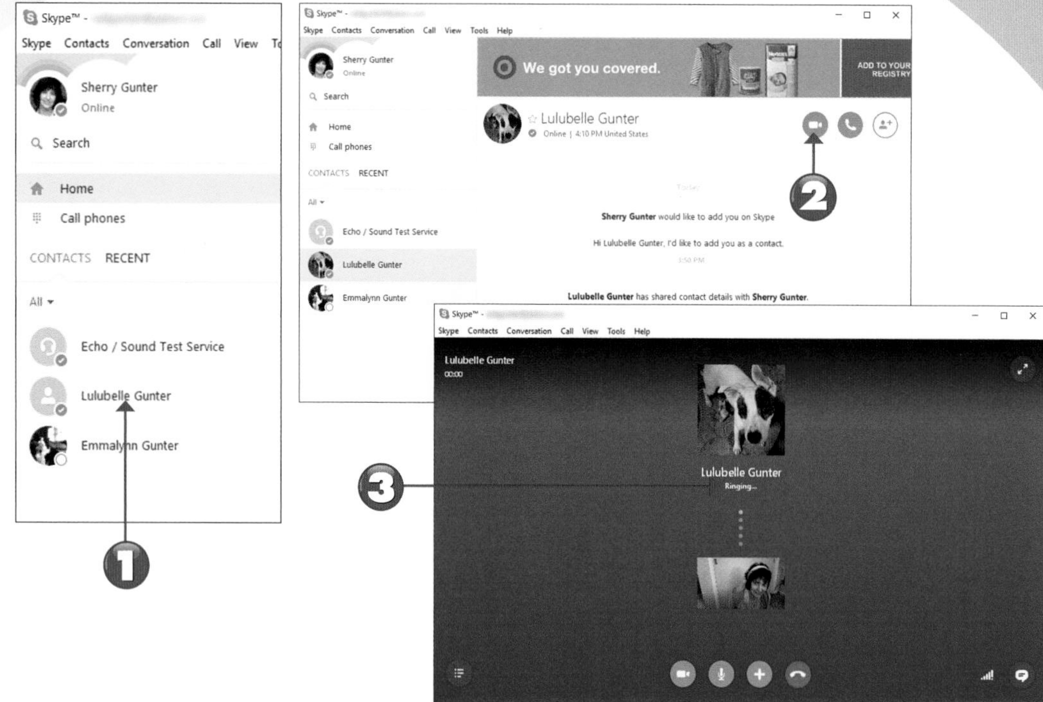

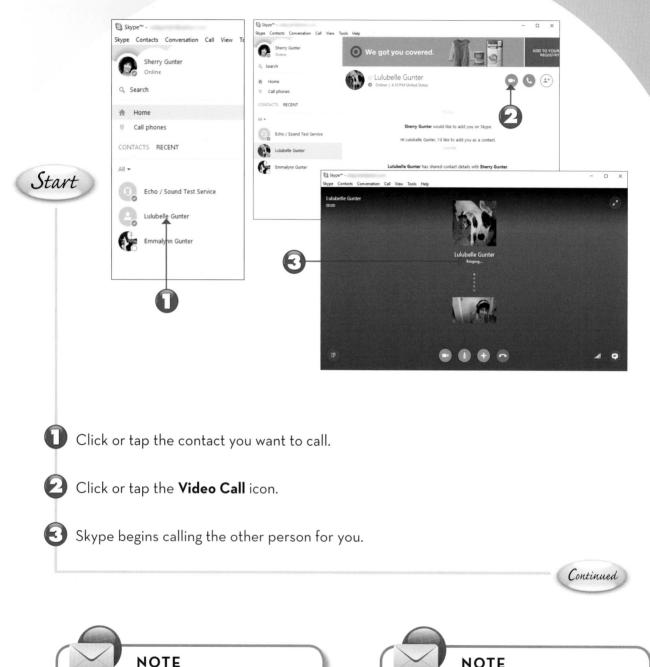

1. Click or tap the contact you want to call.
2. Click or tap the **Video Call** icon.
3. Skype begins calling the other person for you.

Continued

NOTE

Voice Calls A voice call works the same way as a video call in Skype. Click or tap the **Voice Call** icon instead of the **Video Call** icon to place your call. When you're connected, only the microphone works; the video feed is turned off.

NOTE

Find Settings To find settings for Skype, click or tap the **Tools** menu and choose **Options**. The Options dialog box includes general program settings, audio and web camera settings, notifications, and more.

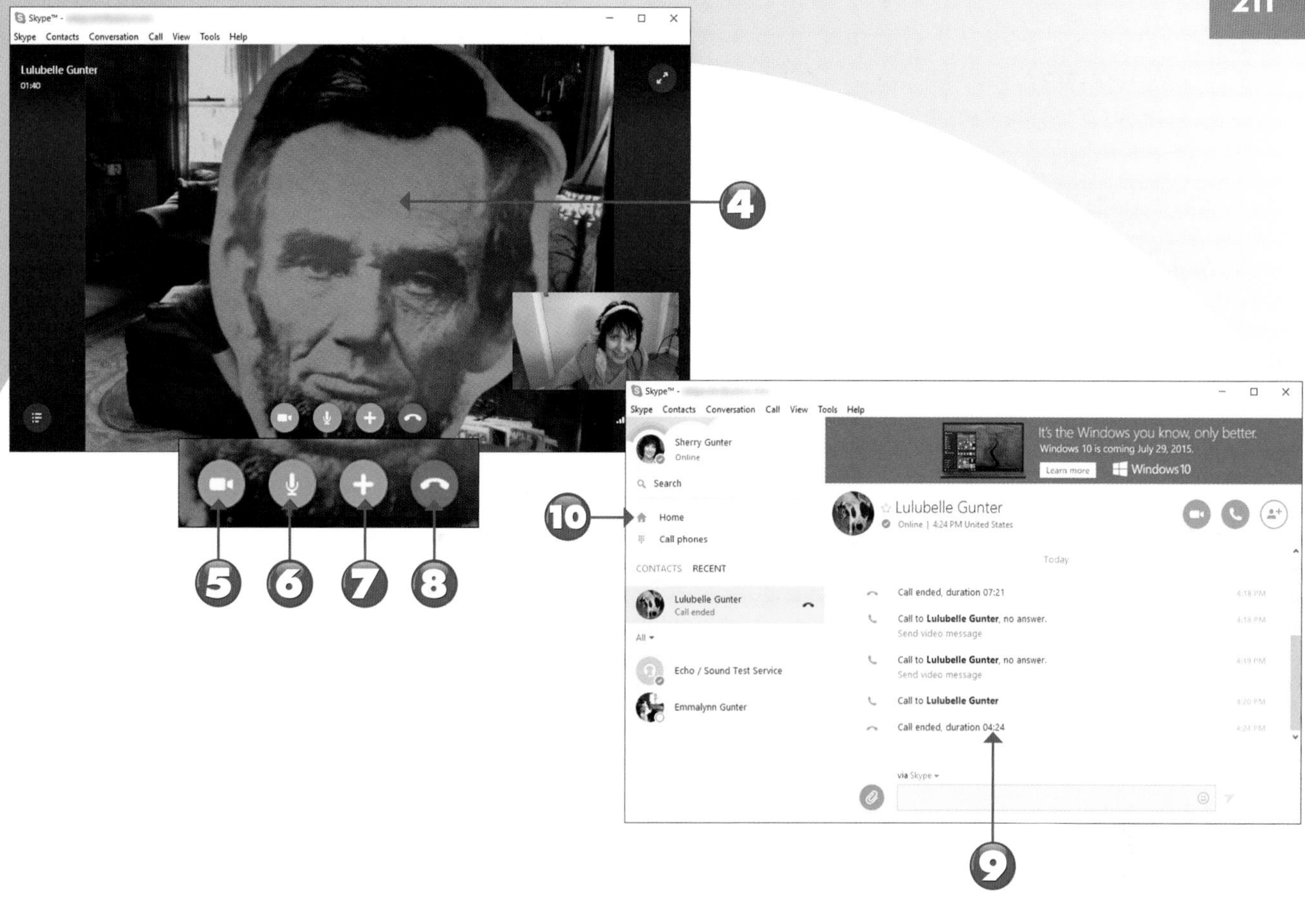

4. When the person accepts your call, the screen shows the view from their webcam along with some call tools.
5. Click or tap here to turn off your video feed; the other user will see your profile picture instead.
6. Click or tap here to mute your microphone.
7. To view more tools, such as for adding more participants or sending files, click or tap here.
8. Click or tap **End** to end the call.
9. Skype lists the call duration here.
10. Click or tap here to return to the Home screen.

End

RECEIVING A CALL WITH SKYPE

When you receive a Skype call, a notification box pops up and you can choose to accept or decline the call. You can choose between taking a video call or a voice call.

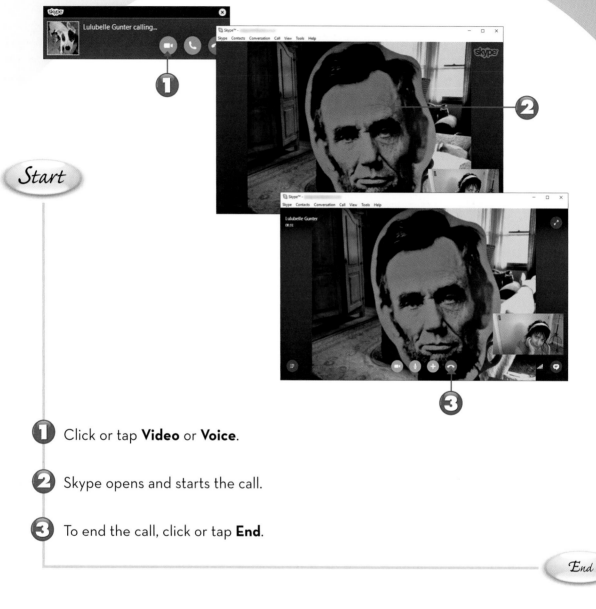

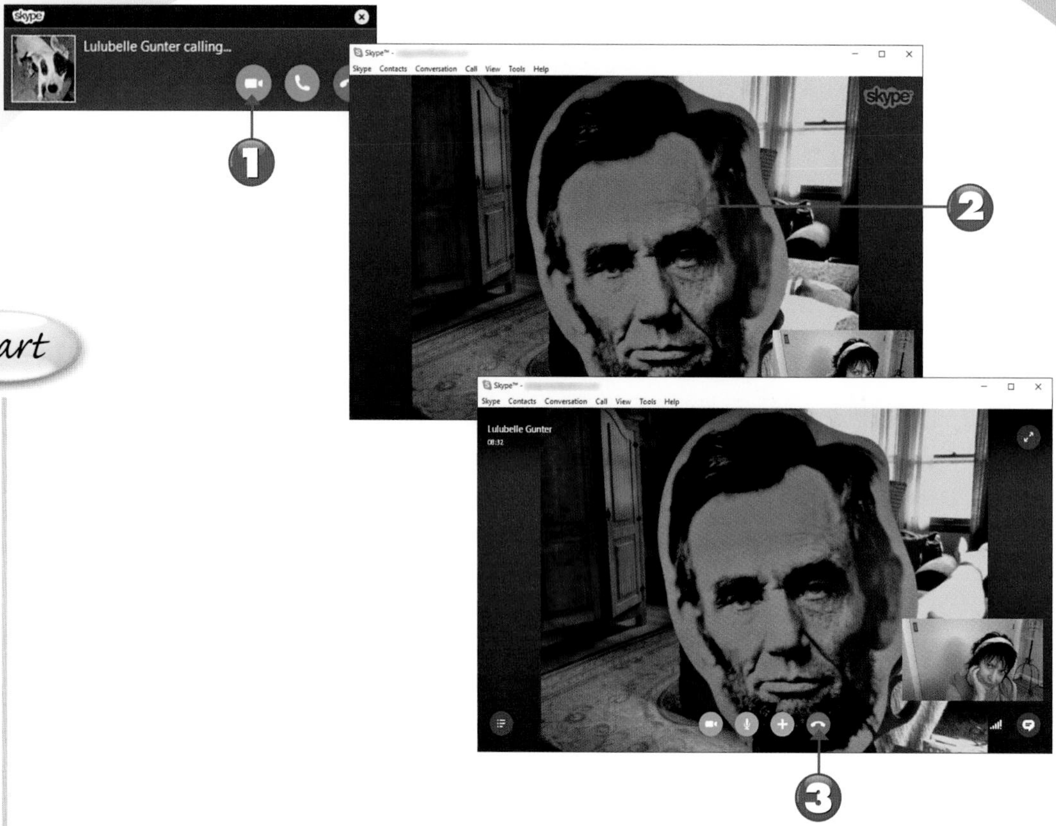

Start

1. Click or tap **Video** or **Voice**.
2. Skype opens and starts the call.
3. To end the call, click or tap **End**.

End

TIP

Alternatively, Choose a Voice Call You can also choose the **Voice Call** option in the notification box to start a voice call instead of a video call.

TEXT MESSAGING WITH SKYPE

You can also use Skype to send instant messages to your friends and family. Text messages appear as a conversation in the contact window.

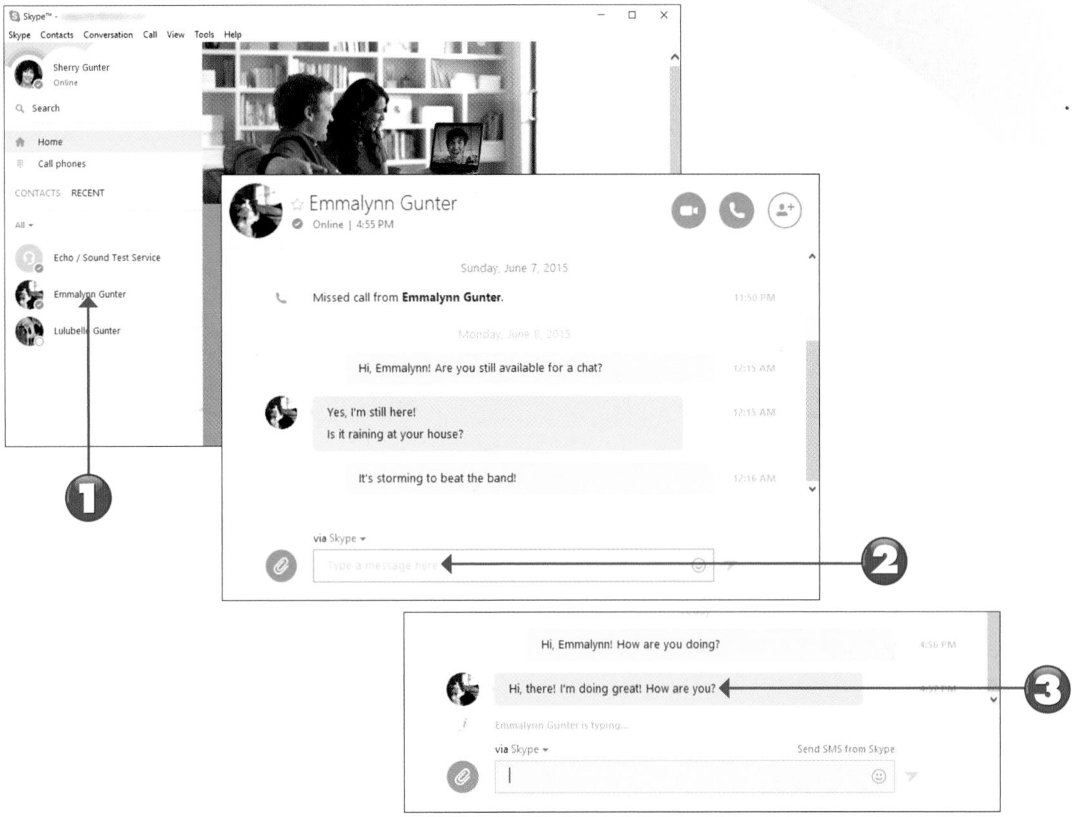

Start

1. Click or tap the contact you want to message.

2. Click or tap the **Type a message here** box and enter your message text and press **Enter/Return**.

3. When the other person responds, the conversation scrolls up the window, with the latest message appearing at the bottom.

End

TIP

Send an SMS Message You can also send a text message from Skype to a contact's cell phone. Click or tap the drop-down arrow directly above the **Type a message here** box and choose **SMS**. Next, type in your message text as you normally would and press **Enter/Return**.

CONTROLLING NOTIFICATIONS

By default, notifications are turned on for all the communication apps you use, such as People, Facebook, Mail, and Skype. You might prefer not to see so many notifications from these apps. You can control notifications through the Notifications & Actions settings.

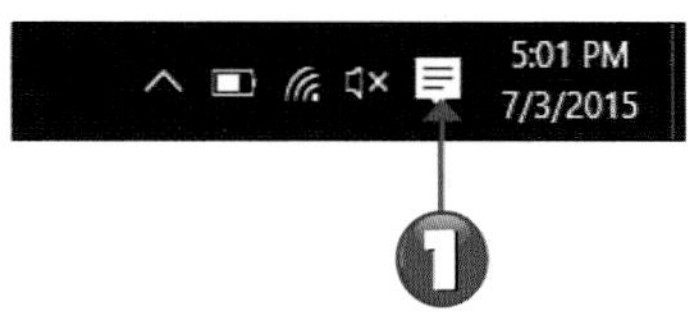

Start

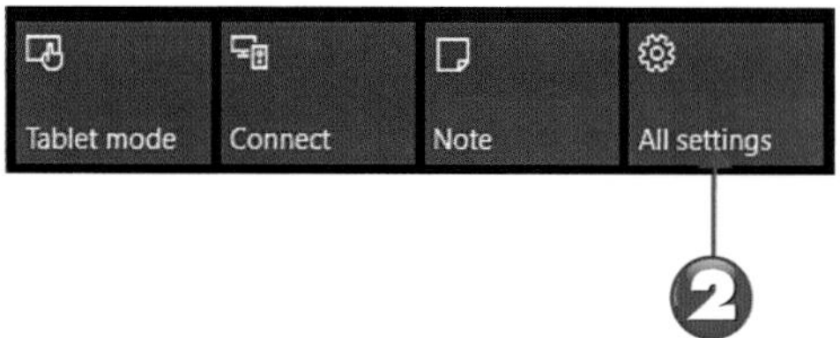

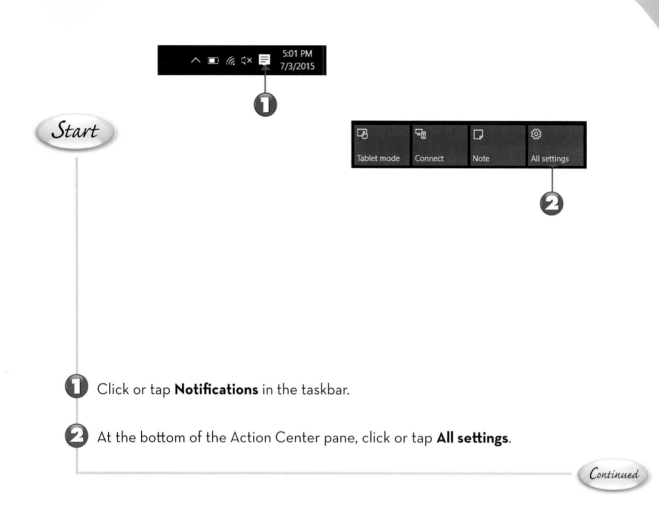

1. Click or tap **Notifications** in the taskbar.
2. At the bottom of the Action Center pane, click or tap **All settings**.

Continued

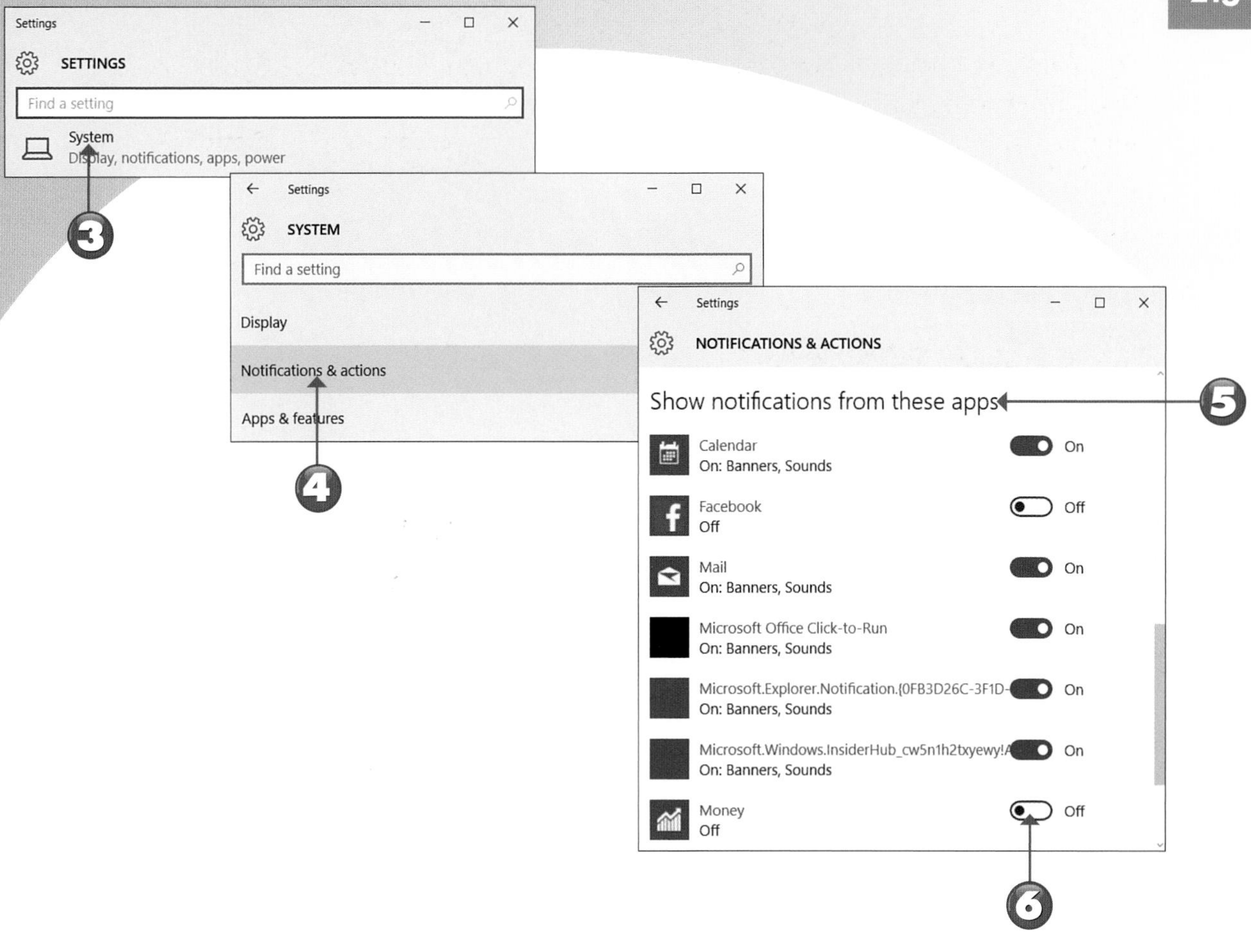

3 Click or tap **System**.

4 Click or tap **Notifications & actions**.

5 Scroll down the window to view the **Show notifications from these apps** settings.

6 Click or tap the toggle to turn an app's notifications on or off.

End

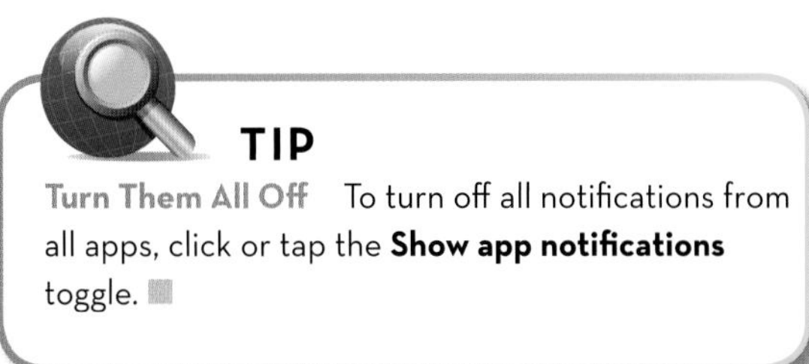

TIP

Turn Them All Off To turn off all notifications from all apps, click or tap the **Show app notifications** toggle.

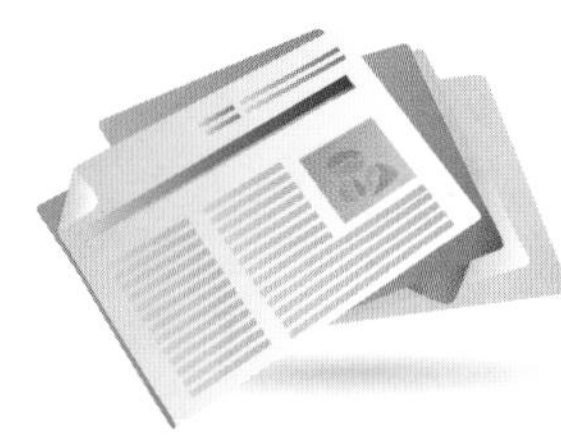

NEWS AND INFORMATION

You can use Windows 10 to keep abreast of the latest news and information the Internet has to offer. This chapter shows you how to use the Windows 10 apps to access headlines, local news, maps, and weather.

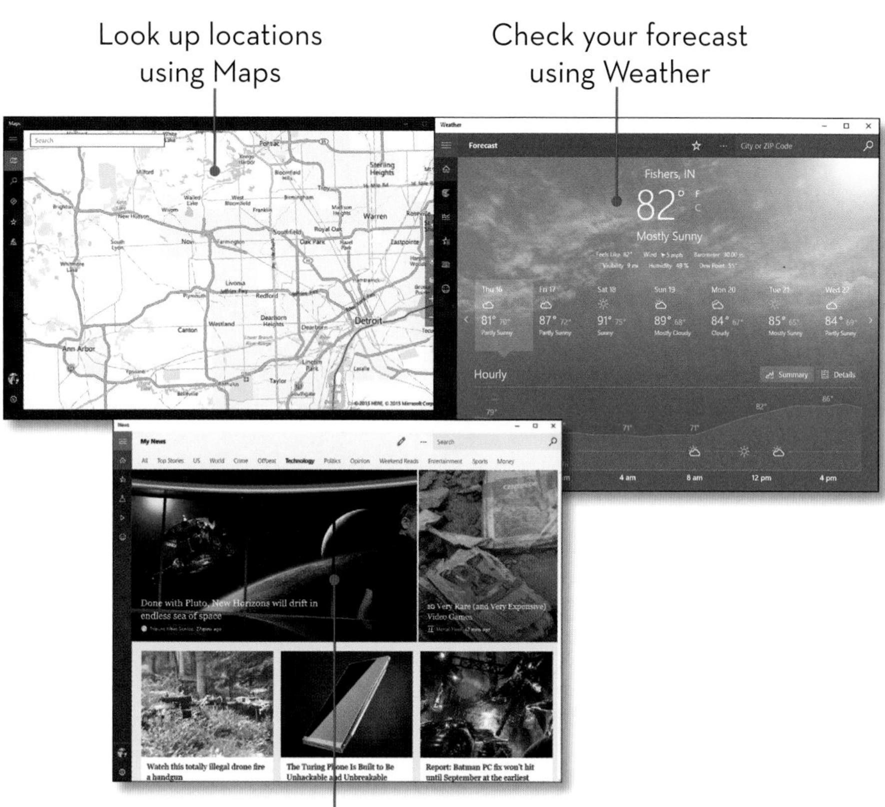
Look up locations using Maps
Check your forecast using Weather
Use News to view local, national, and global news

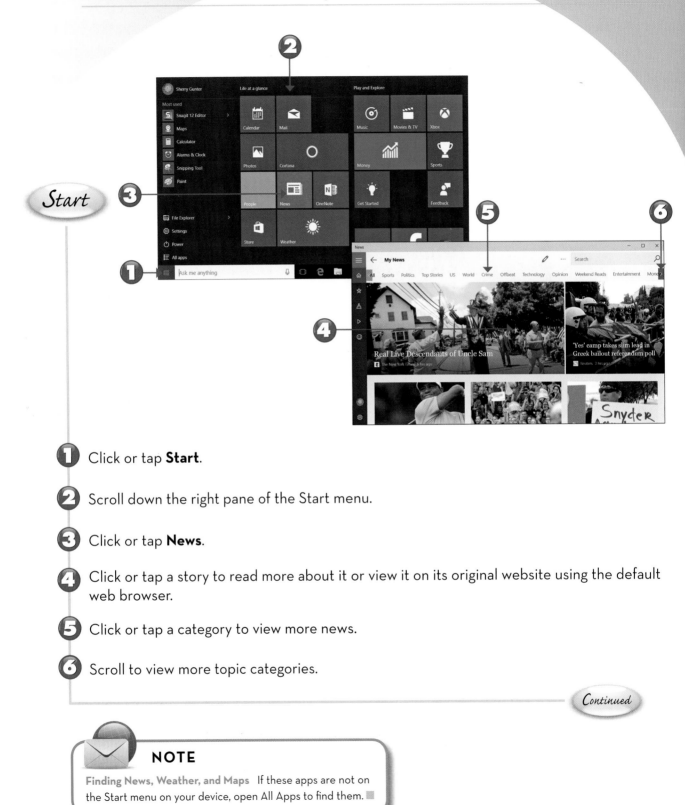

USING THE NEWS APP

The News app taps into the powerful Bing search engine to bring you the latest news and headlines from around the world or in your own locale.

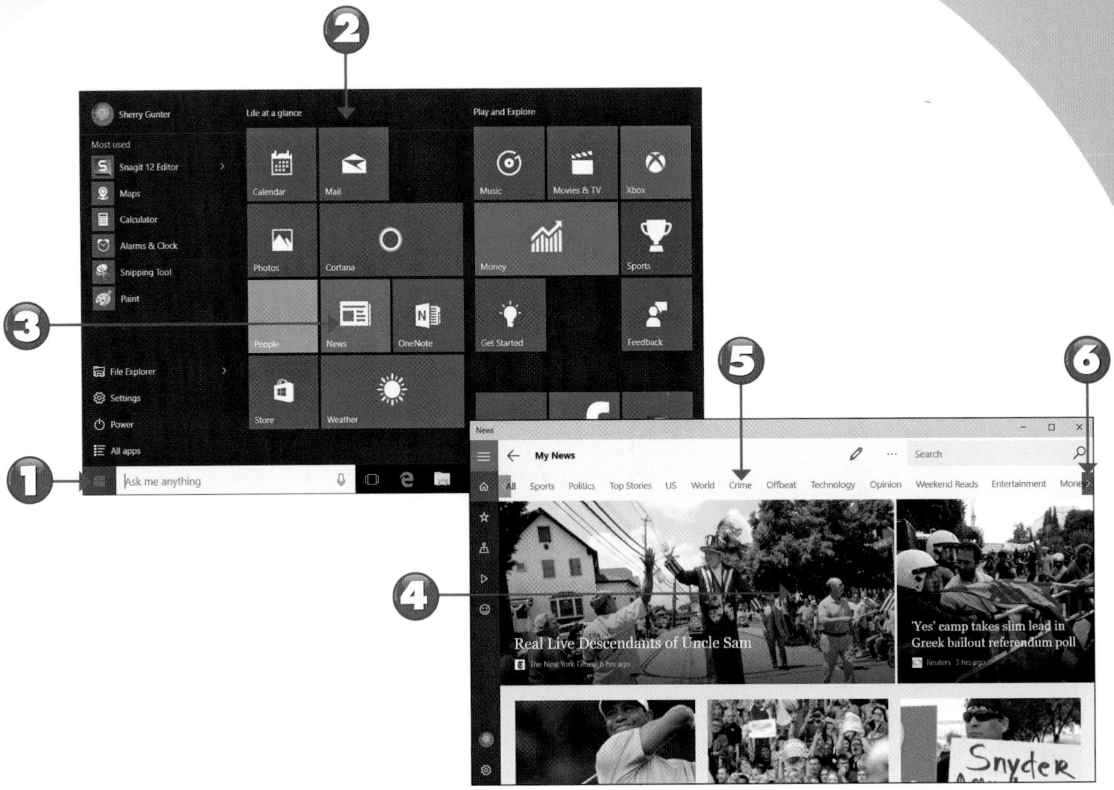

Start

1. Click or tap **Start**.
2. Scroll down the right pane of the Start menu.
3. Click or tap **News**.
4. Click or tap a story to read more about it or view it on its original website using the default web browser.
5. Click or tap a category to view more news.
6. Scroll to view more topic categories.

Continued

NOTE

Finding News, Weather, and Maps If these apps are not on the Start menu on your device, open All Apps to find them.

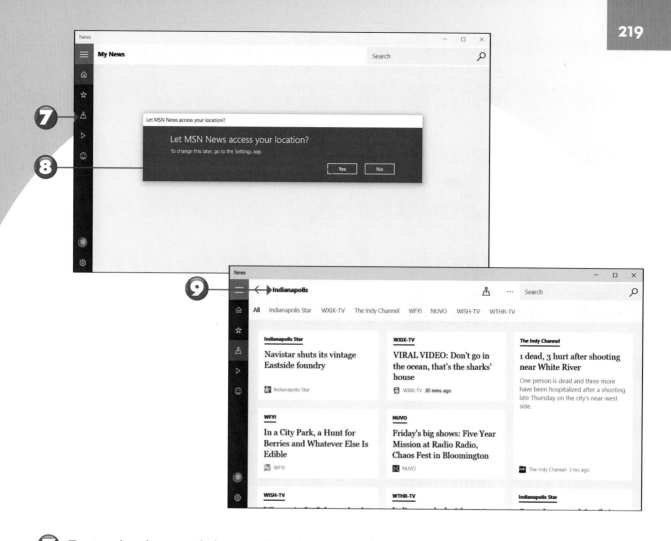

7 To view local news, click or tap **Local**. You can also click or tap the menu and choose **Local**.

8 A prompt box appears; click or tap **Yes** to let the app access your location.

9 The News app displays headlines for your location.

End

TIP

Look Up Specific Topics You can use the Search box to look up specific news topics. For example, you might look up stories about a particular politician or celebrity. Click or tap the **Search** box and type in your keyword or words.

CUSTOMIZING NEWS SOURCES

You can look up your favorite news sources and add them to the News app's Interests list. News stories from your favorite sites appear listed among the default content on the Home page. You can toggle the default topics on or off to control which news topics appear listed across the screen.

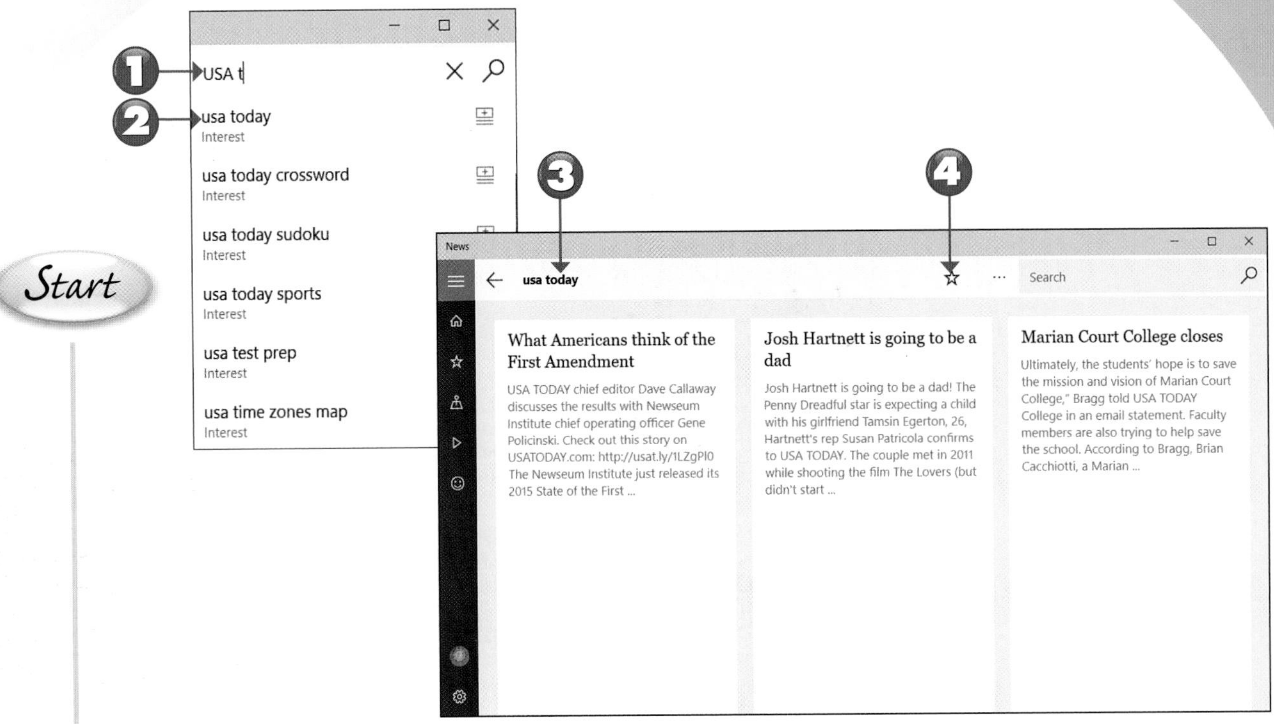

Start

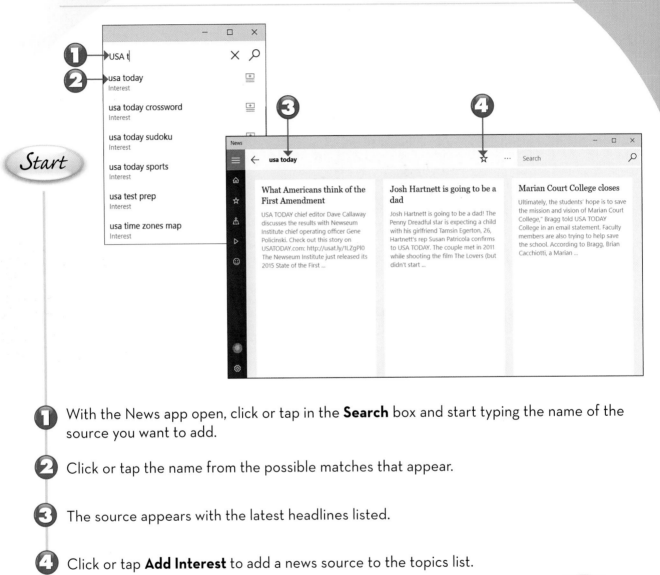

1. With the News app open, click or tap in the **Search** box and start typing the name of the source you want to add.
2. Click or tap the name from the possible matches that appear.
3. The source appears with the latest headlines listed.
4. Click or tap **Add Interest** to add a news source to the topics list.

Continued

TIP

More Customizing You can also customize your news topics within the Interests window. Click or tap the **Add an Interest** icon at the top of the window and type in the news source you want to add.

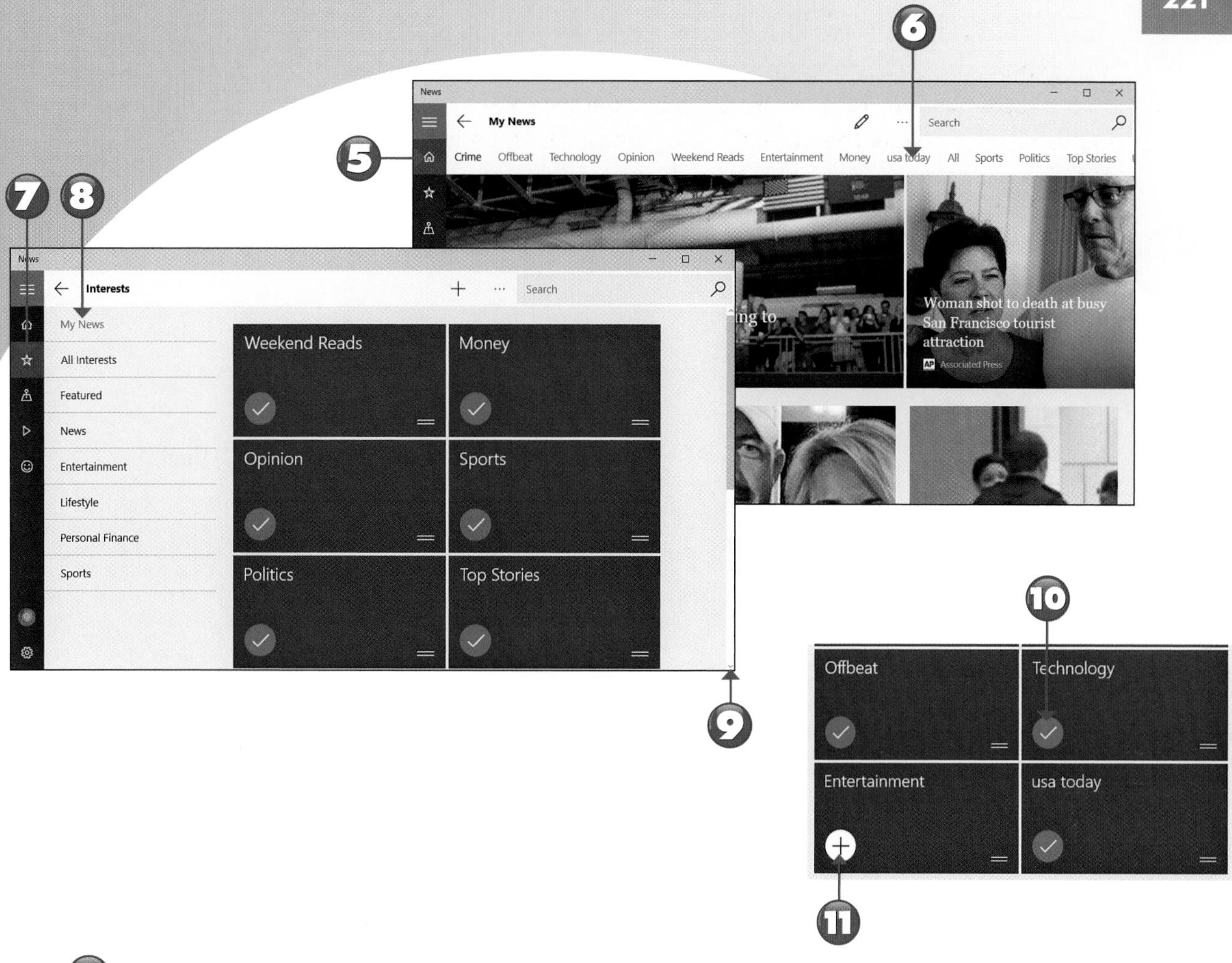

5 Click or tap **Home**.

6 Scroll to view the newly added source among the topics listed.

7 To control which sources are listed, click or tap **Interests**.

8 Click or tap **My News**.

9 Scroll to the bottom of the list to see your newly added source.

10 Click or tap a check box to turn off a source's display in your news list. If you select the check box for a custom source you've added to the list, it's permanently removed from the list.

11 A plus sign appears for the deselected source. When you exit the Interests window, the source is removed from the list.

End

CHECKING WEATHER WITH THE WEATHER APP

You can use the Weather app to check your local weather report, view forecasts, and track the weather in your favorite locations.

Start

1. Click or tap **Start**.
2. Scroll down the right pane of the Start menu.
3. Click or tap **Weather**.
4. Weather shows the current forecast for your location; scroll down the window to view more details.
5. Click or tap an icon to view weather news, maps, weather history, or saved favorite locations.

TIP

Celsius or Fahrenheit? To toggle your view of temperature in the Forecast window to Celsius or Fahrenheit, click or tap the appropriate symbol next to the current temperature.

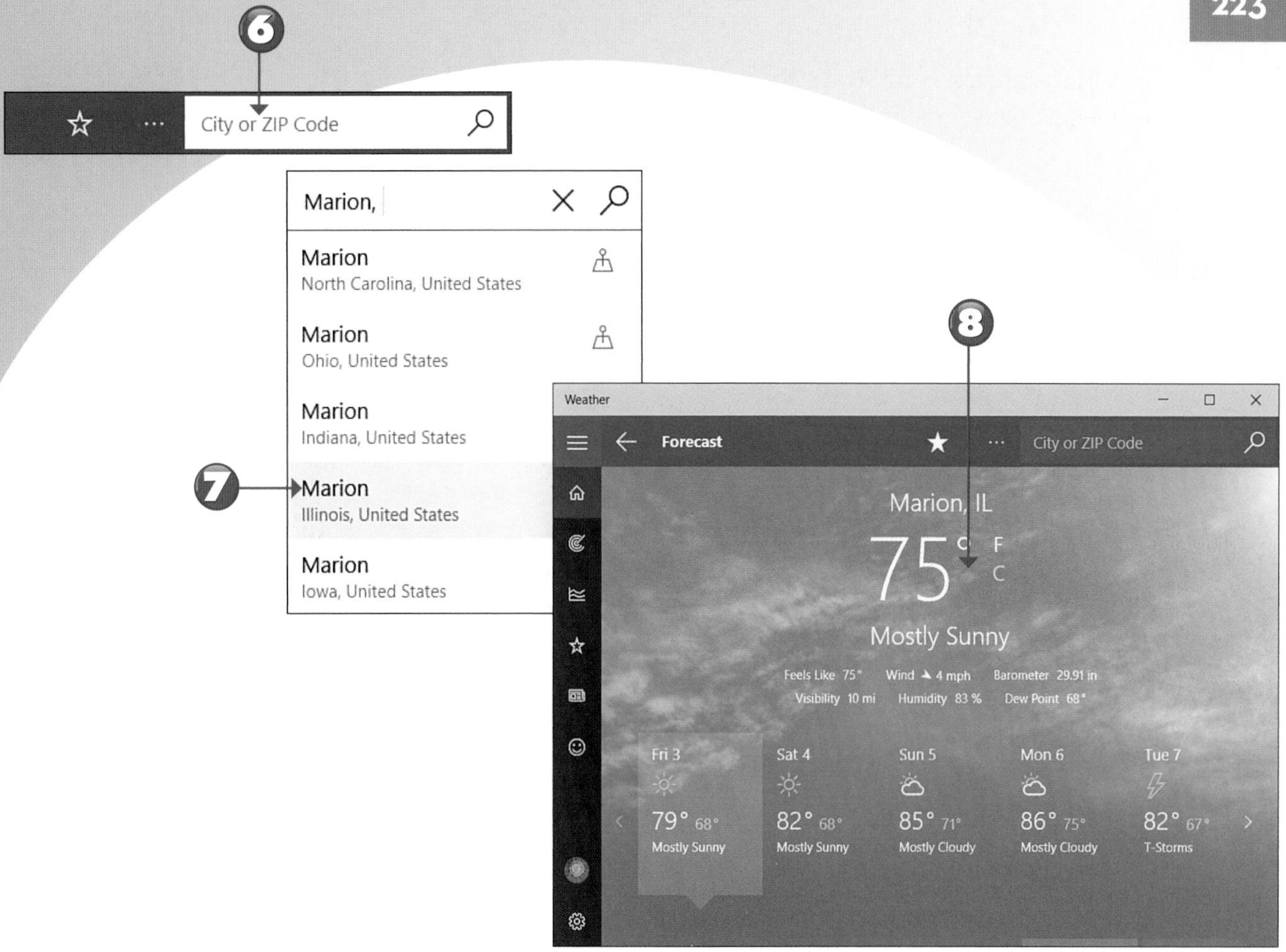

6. To check weather for a specific location, click or tap in the **City or ZIP Code** box and type the location.

7. Click or tap the location from the list, or click or tap the **Search** icon to conduct a search.

8. The Weather app window displays the current information and forecast for the designated place.

End

TIP

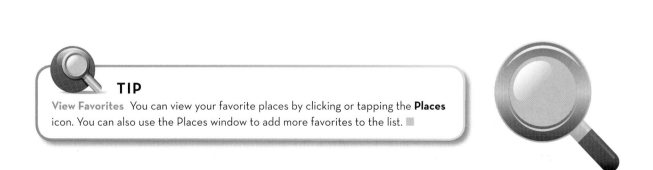

View Favorites You can view your favorite places by clicking or tapping the **Places** icon. You can also use the Places window to add more favorites to the list.

GETTING DIRECTIONS WITH MAPS

The Maps app works with Microsoft's Bing website to help you find locations around the world or down the street. You can find directions, look up an address, or view your own current location using this app. In this task, you learn how to find directions between two locations.

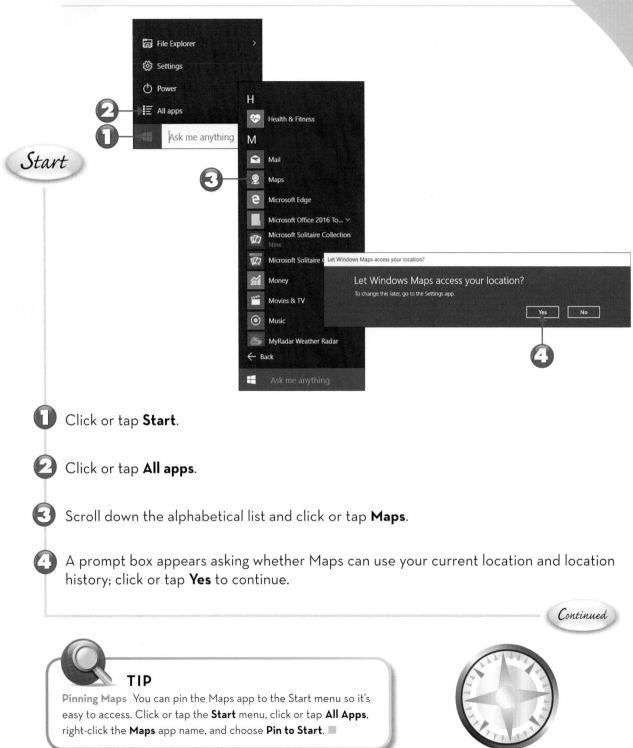

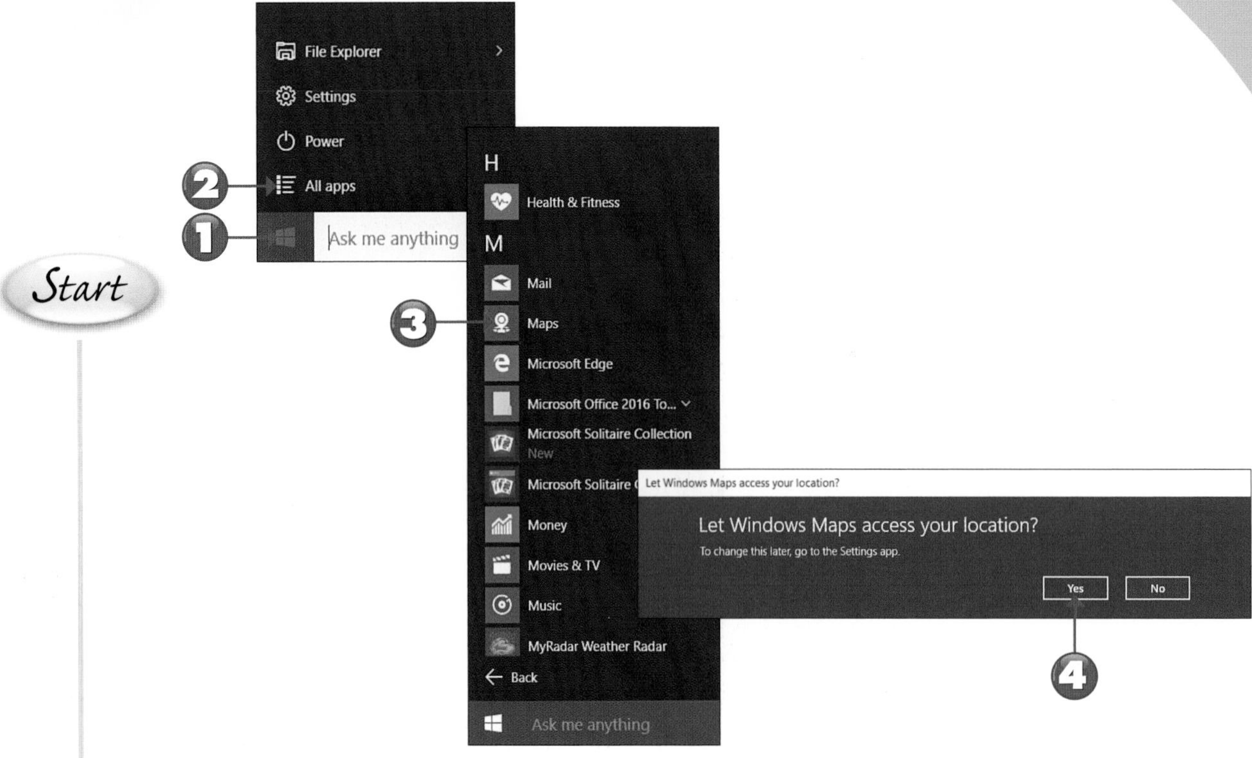

1. Click or tap **Start**.
2. Click or tap **All apps**.
3. Scroll down the alphabetical list and click or tap **Maps**.
4. A prompt box appears asking whether Maps can use your current location and location history; click or tap **Yes** to continue.

Continued

TIP

Pinning Maps You can pin the Maps app to the Start menu so it's easy to access. Click or tap the **Start** menu, click or tap **All Apps**, right-click the **Maps** app name, and choose **Pin to Start**.

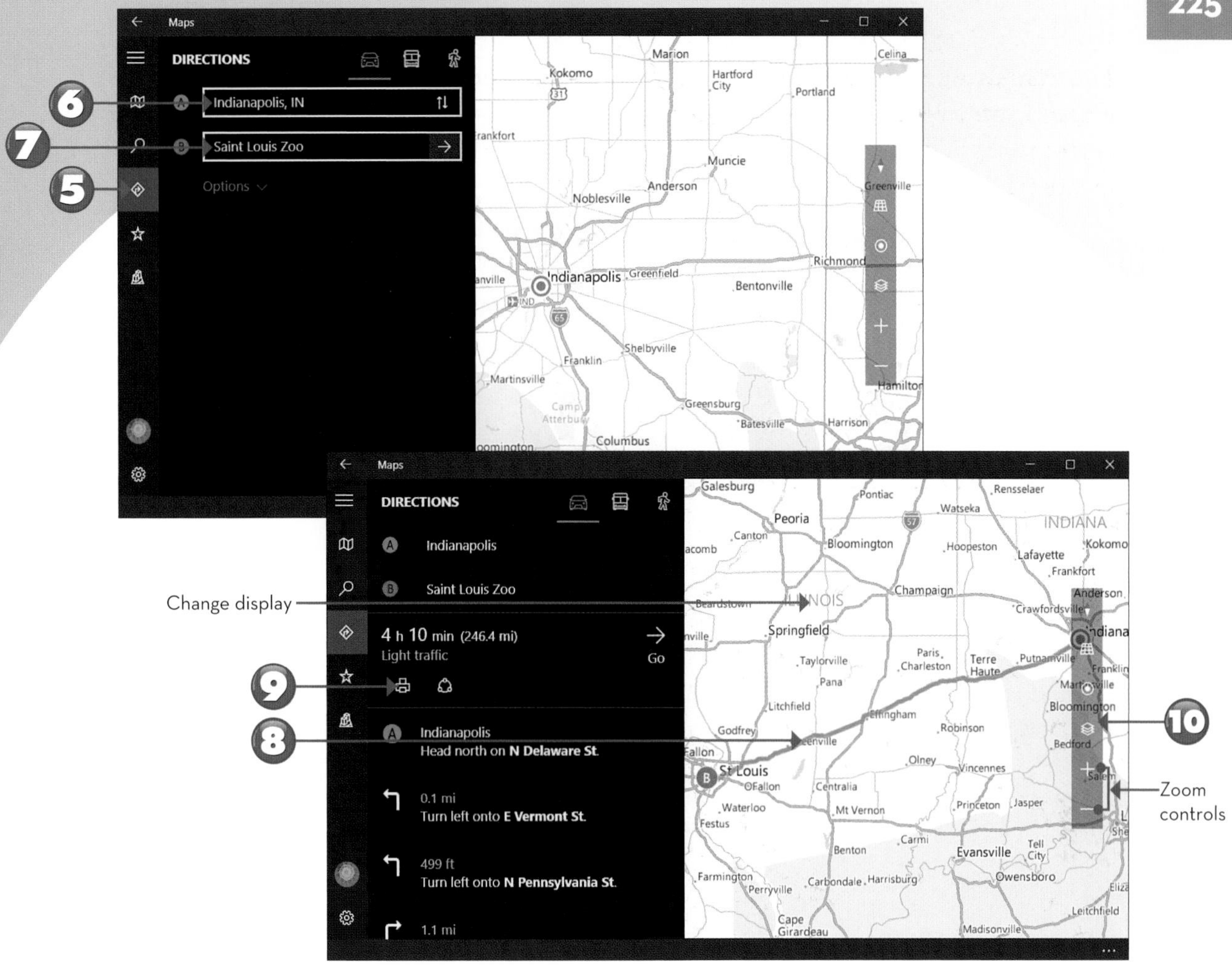

5. Click or tap the **Directions** icon.

6. Enter a starting point and destination point, such as an address or city.

7. Click or tap **Get Directions**.

8. Maps displays the path on the map as well as a list of instructions to your destination.

9. Click or tap here to print directions.

10. Click or tap map controls to change how the map is displayed.

End

TIP

Driving or Walking? When you activate Map's Directions feature, you can specify whether you're driving, taking public transit, or walking by clicking the appropriate icon at the top of the Directions window.

TRIP PLANNING WITH MAPS

You can use the Maps app to plan a trip, including finding where to stay, eat, or find attractions.

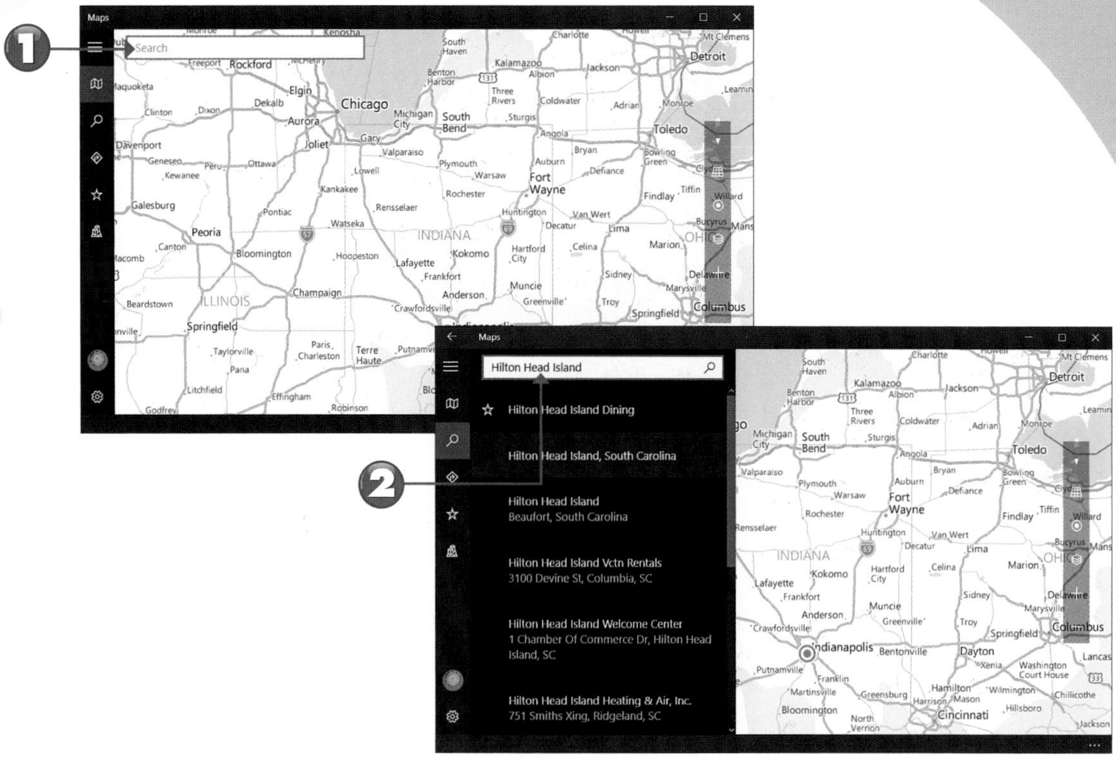

Start

1. Open the Maps app, and click or tap the **Search** box.

2. Enter the location you want to look up.

Continued

TIP

Move Your Map View You can click and drag or flick to scroll around a map display, moving left, right, up, or down to change the map data. To always return to your original Home destination, click or tap the **Show my location** icon on the map navigation toolbar, or press **Ctrl+Home** on the keyboard.

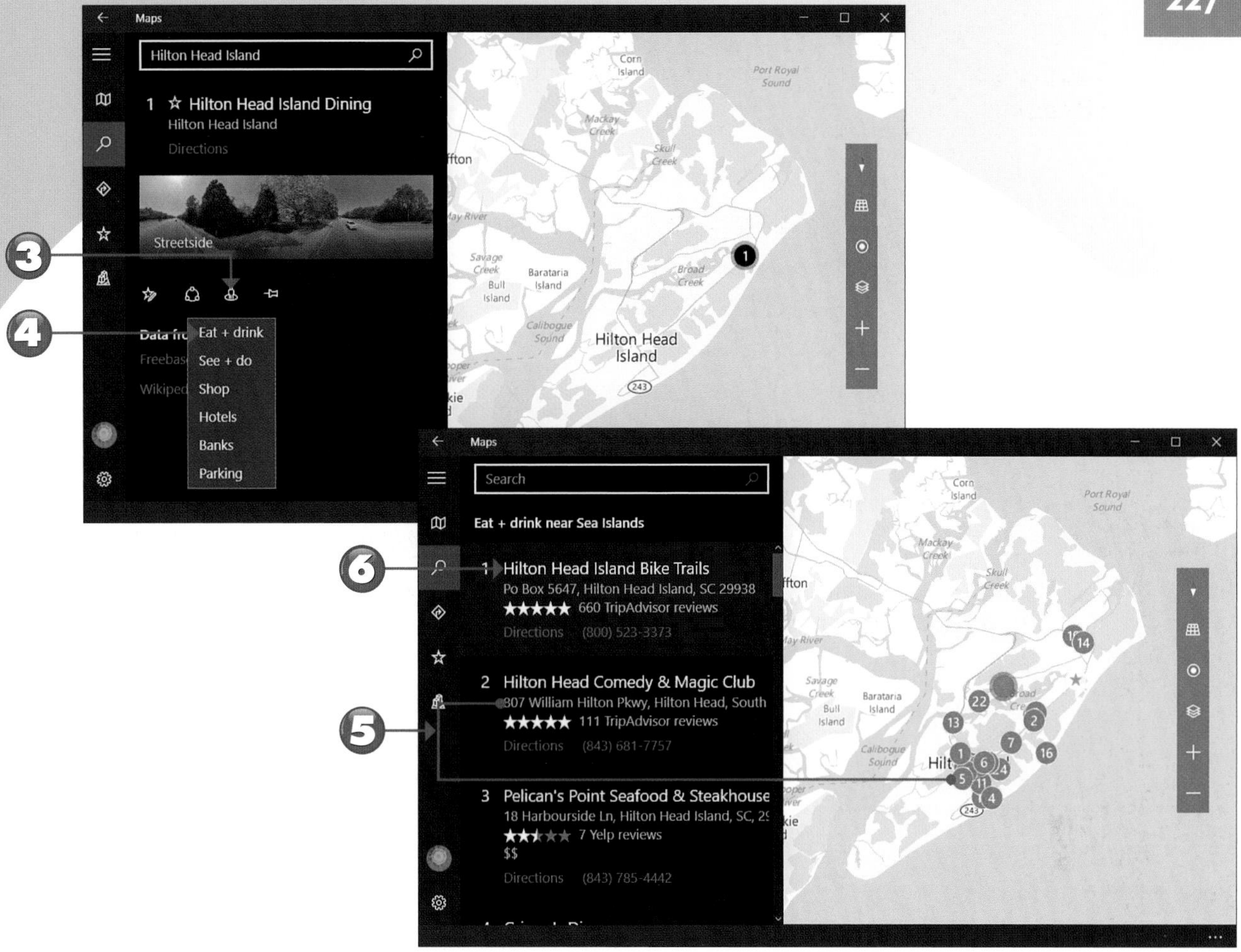

3. Click or tap the **Nearby** icon.

4. Click or tap the type of point of interest youv want to look up.

5. Maps displays a list of options and marks their location on the map.

6. Click or tap a link or marker to view more details.

End

TIP

Save It To save a destination option, such as a restaurant or hotel you look up on the map, click or tap the **Add to Favorites** icon that appears listed when you look up a destination. A pop-up box appears and you can assign a nickname for the information; click or tap **Save**. To view favorites later, click or tap the **Favorites** in the left-side tool panel.

TRACKING MONEY AND SPORTS NEWS

Everyone has his or her favorite sources for keeping up with financial news and local sports teams. The Money and Sports apps help you find the financial and team updates you're looking for.

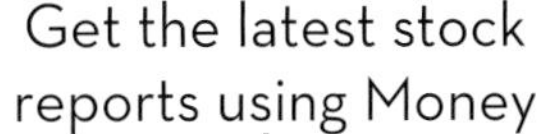

Get the latest stock reports using Money

Check your favorite sports teams with the Sports app

USING THE MONEY APP

Whether you're browsing financial news or focusing on a single company, the Money app (formerly called Finance) is ready to help.

Start

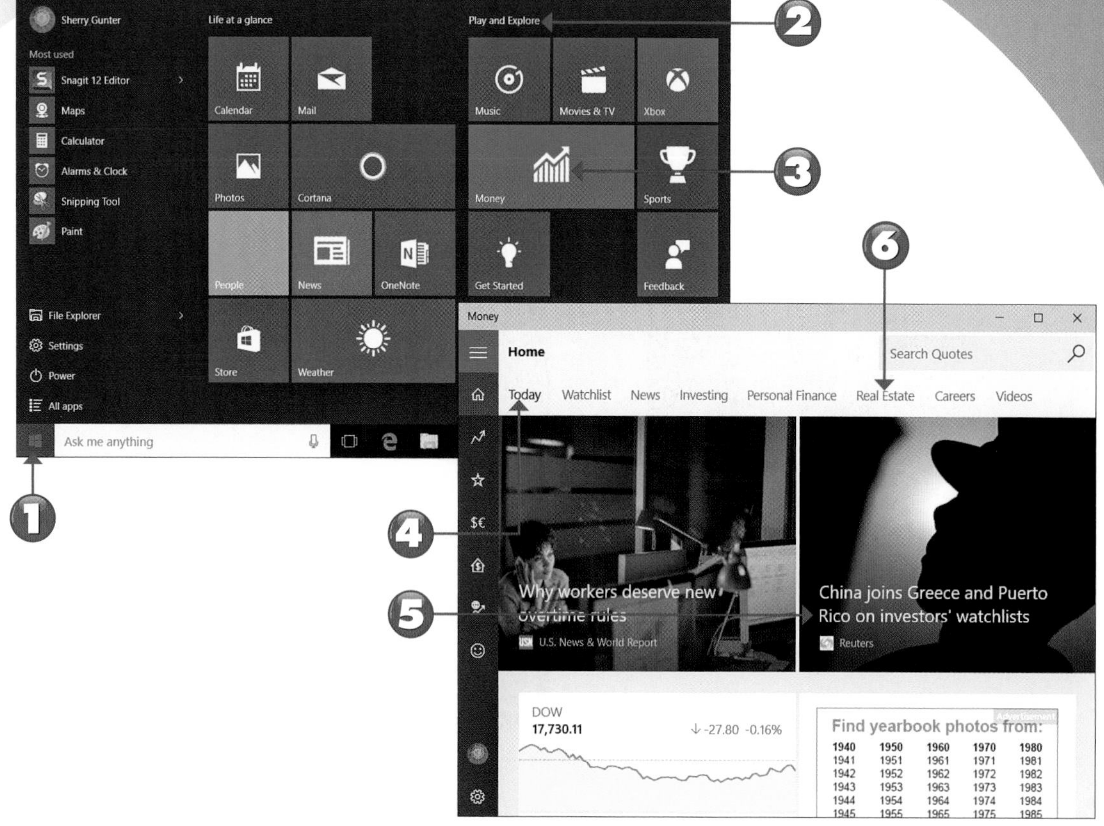

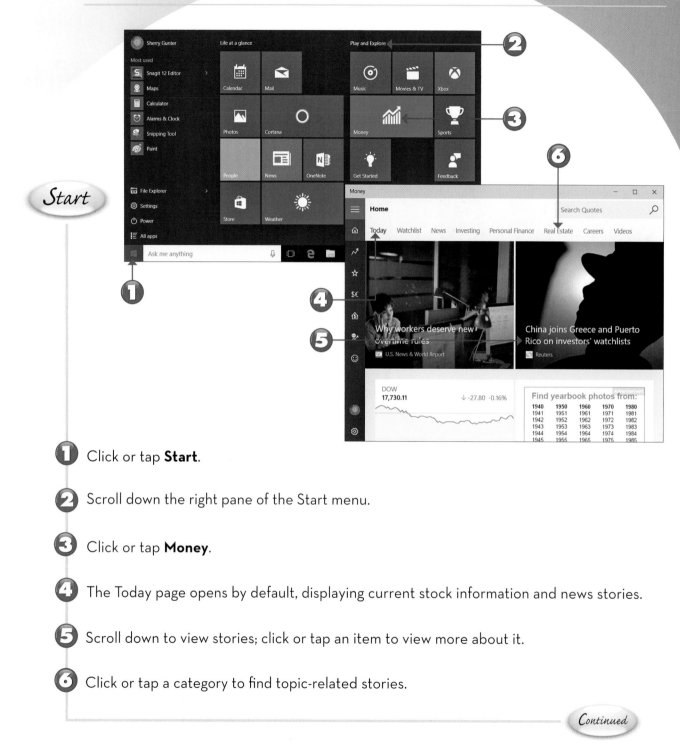

1. Click or tap **Start**.
2. Scroll down the right pane of the Start menu.
3. Click or tap **Money**.
4. The Today page opens by default, displaying current stock information and news stories.
5. Scroll down to view stories; click or tap an item to view more about it.
6. Click or tap a category to find topic-related stories.

Continued

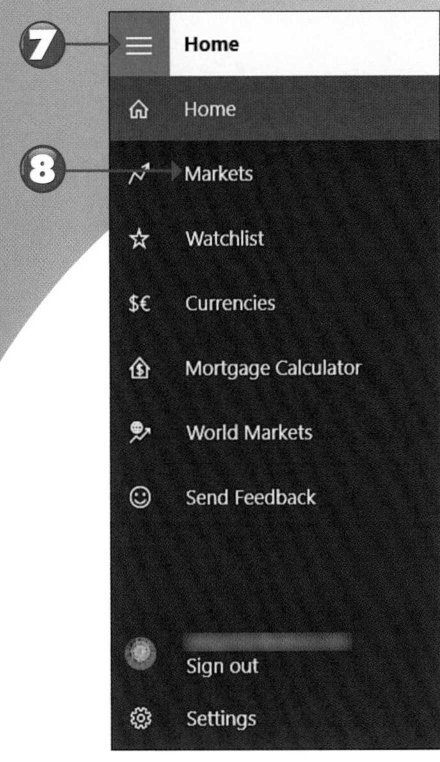

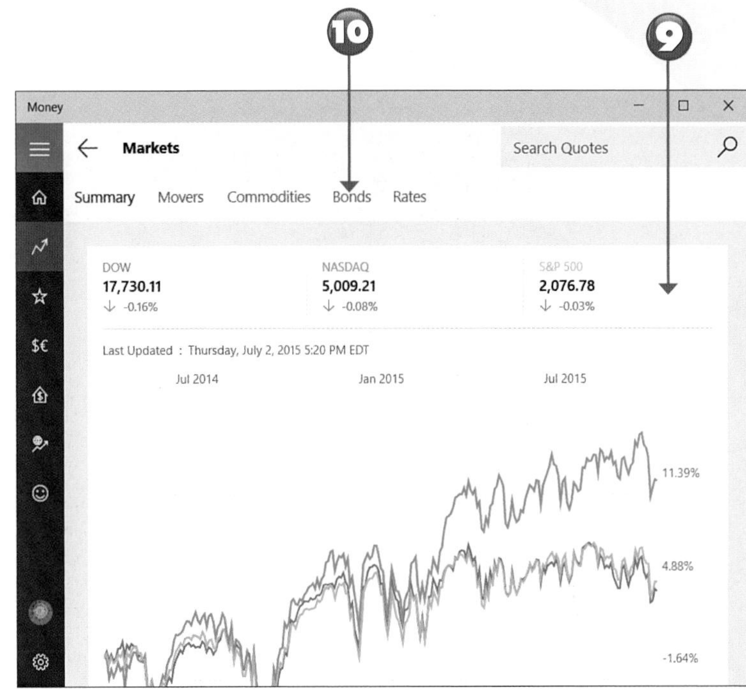

7 To view the latest market data, click or tap the **Menu** button.

8 Click or tap **Markets**.

9 Money opens a page with a live market data summary.

10 Click or tap a category to view more market data.

Continued

NOTE

First Time? The very first time you use the Money app, it might take a bit longer to load. It must download features and updates before you start using it. Just give it a minute to refresh the window with current information. ■

NOTE

Other Locations for Money and Sports If the Money or Sports apps are not in the Start menu on your device, you will find them in All Apps. ■

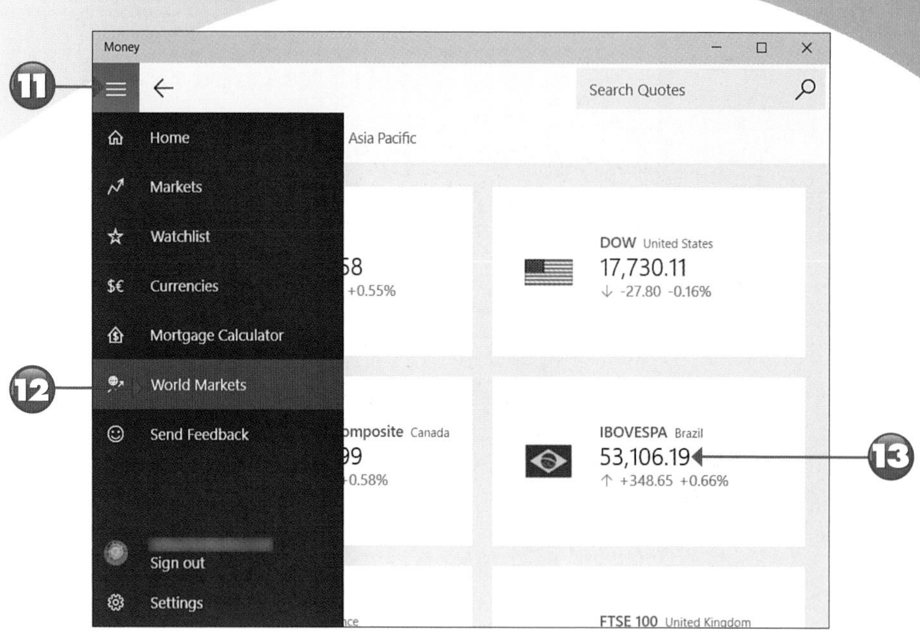

11 To view world markets, click or tap the **Menu** button.

12 Click or tap **World Markets**.

13 Money displays world market data.

Continued

NOTE

More Features You can also use the Money app to look up currency exchange rates, personal finance news, and world markets and even to calculate a mortgage. Just click or tap the **Menu** button and choose a feature. ■

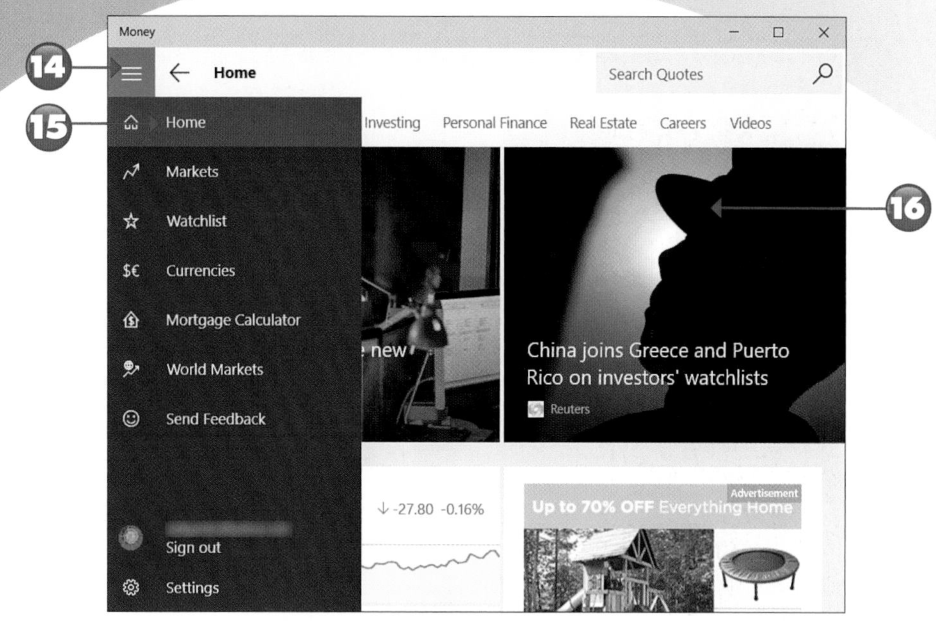

14 To return to Money's home screen again, click or tap the **Menu** button.

15 Click or tap **Home**.

16 The home window reappears.

End

TIP

Using Cortana If you've activated Cortana (the Windows 10 digital assistant), you can view news by clicking or tapping the **Ask me anything** box next to the Start menu. Cortana lists the day's top headlines, displays any stocks you're watching, and shows your local weather report, all in a scrollable pop-up menu. ■

LOOK UP A STOCK

You can use the Money app to look up specific stock symbols, companies, or index names. You can also pin your favorite stock to the watchlist.

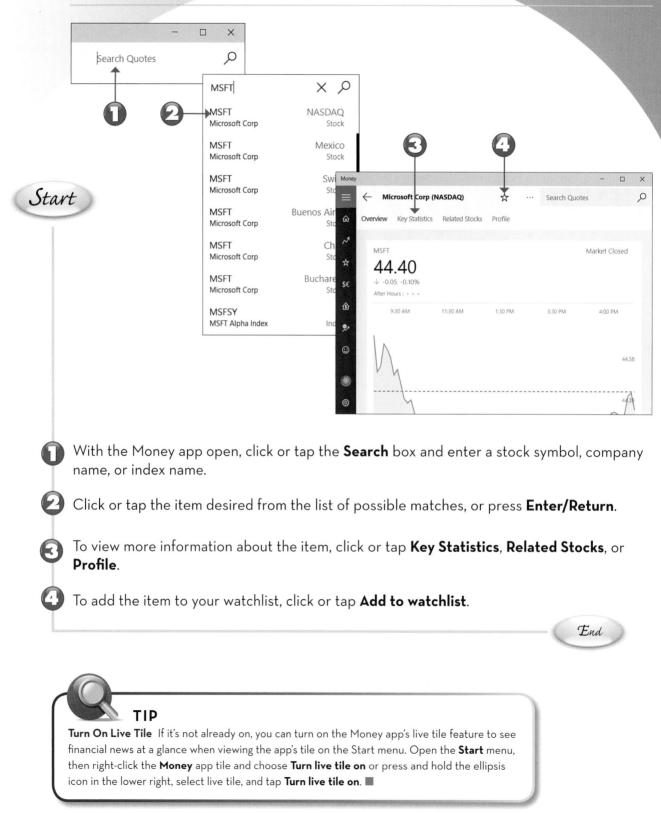

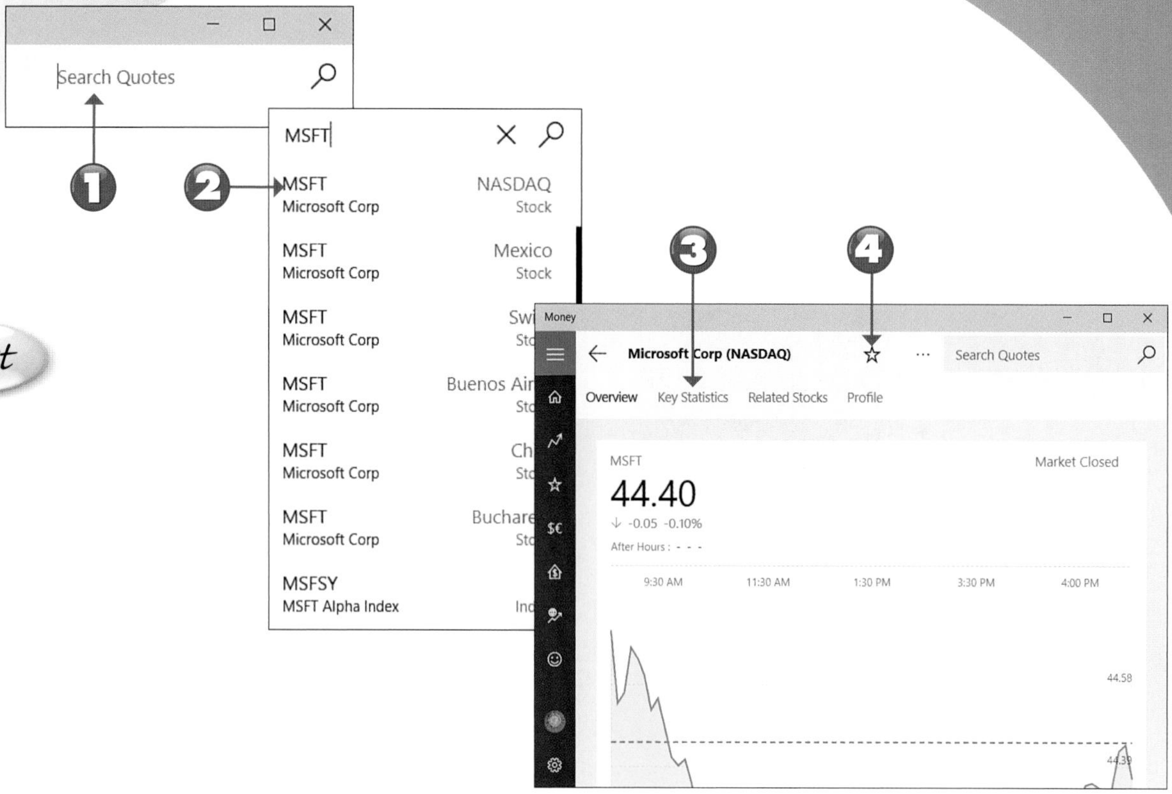

Start

1. With the Money app open, click or tap the **Search** box and enter a stock symbol, company name, or index name.
2. Click or tap the item desired from the list of possible matches, or press **Enter/Return**.
3. To view more information about the item, click or tap **Key Statistics**, **Related Stocks**, or **Profile**.
4. To add the item to your watchlist, click or tap **Add to watchlist**.

End

TIP

Turn On Live Tile If it's not already on, you can turn on the Money app's live tile feature to see financial news at a glance when viewing the app's tile on the Start menu. Open the **Start** menu, then right-click the **Money** app tile and choose **Turn live tile on** or press and hold the ellipsis icon in the lower right, select live tile, and tap **Turn live tile on**. ■

VIEW YOUR WATCHLIST

You can view your favorite stocks on the Money app's watchlist. The watchlist appears on the Watchlist window or in the Today window along with the other financial news highlights.

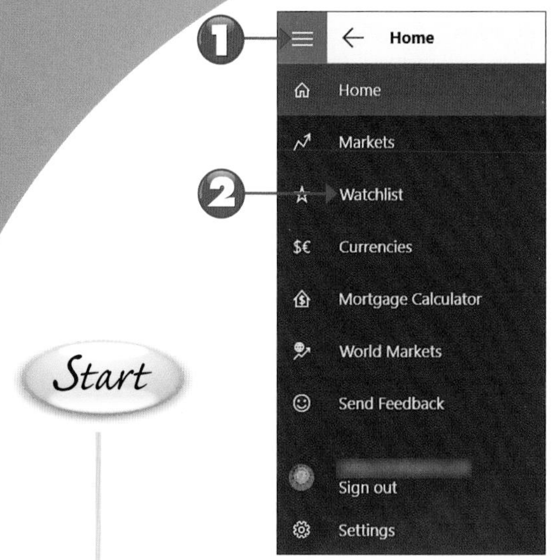

Start

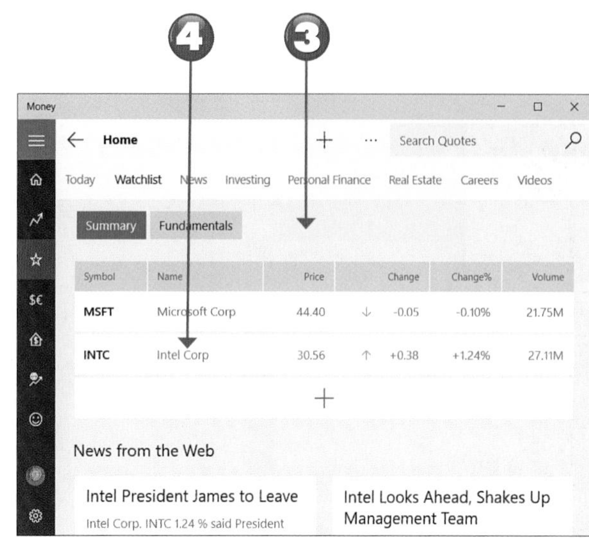

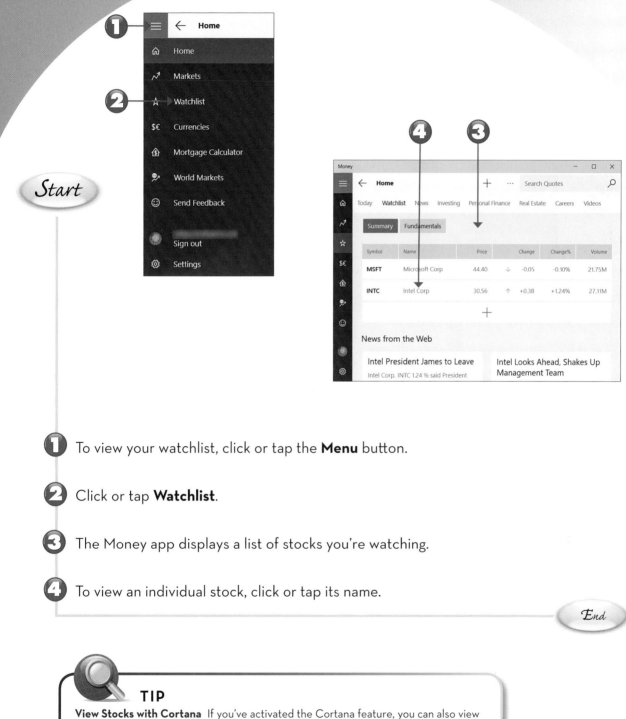

1. To view your watchlist, click or tap the **Menu** button.
2. Click or tap **Watchlist**.
3. The Money app displays a list of stocks you're watching.
4. To view an individual stock, click or tap its name.

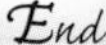

TIP

View Stocks with Cortana If you've activated the Cortana feature, you can also view your watchlist by clicking or tapping the **Ask me anything** box. Scroll down the menu to view your saved stocks. ■

USING THE SPORTS APP

You can use the Sports app to view the latest news and scores from athletic events around the world, including video clips and slideshows of the latest events.

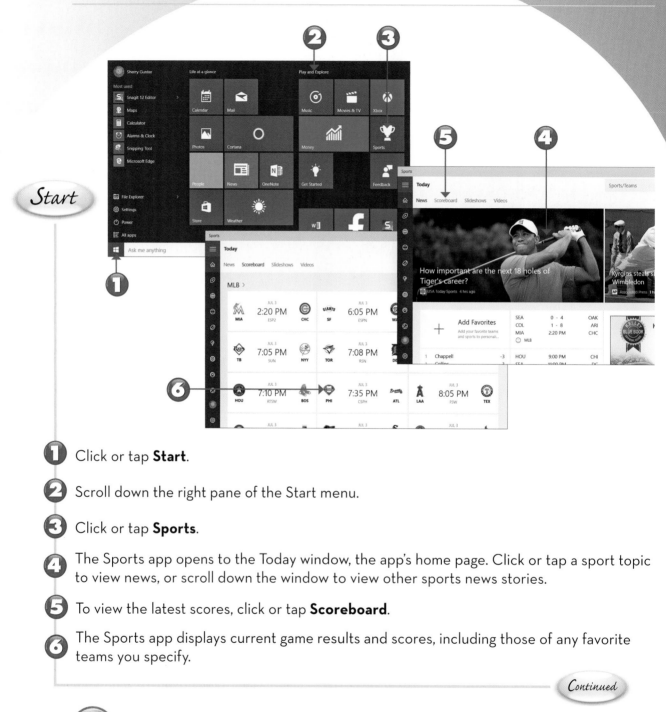

Start

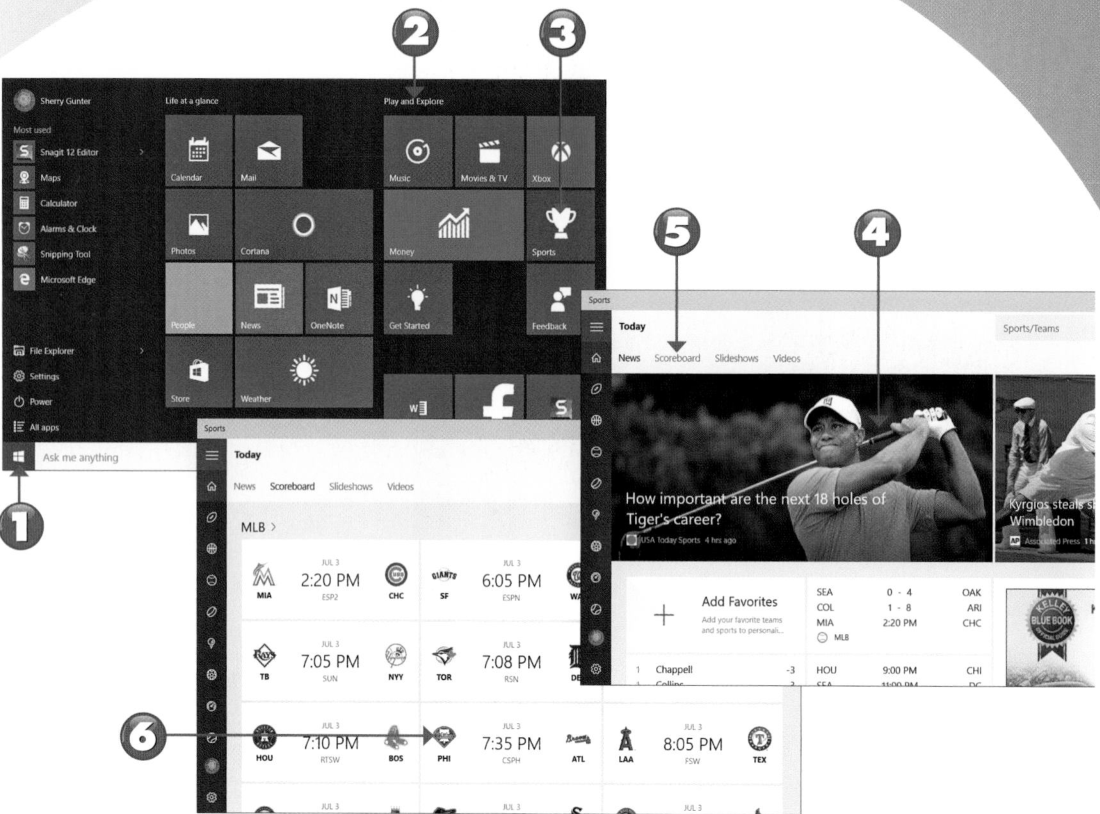

1. Click or tap **Start**.
2. Scroll down the right pane of the Start menu.
3. Click or tap **Sports**.
4. The Sports app opens to the Today window, the app's home page. Click or tap a sport topic to view news, or scroll down the window to view other sports news stories.
5. To view the latest scores, click or tap **Scoreboard**.
6. The Sports app displays current game results and scores, including those of any favorite teams you specify.

Continued

TIP

View Specific Sports Click or tap the **Menu** button to view sports categories, such as NFL or Golf. When you select a specific sport from the list, a page opens with scores and news pertaining just to that sport. ■

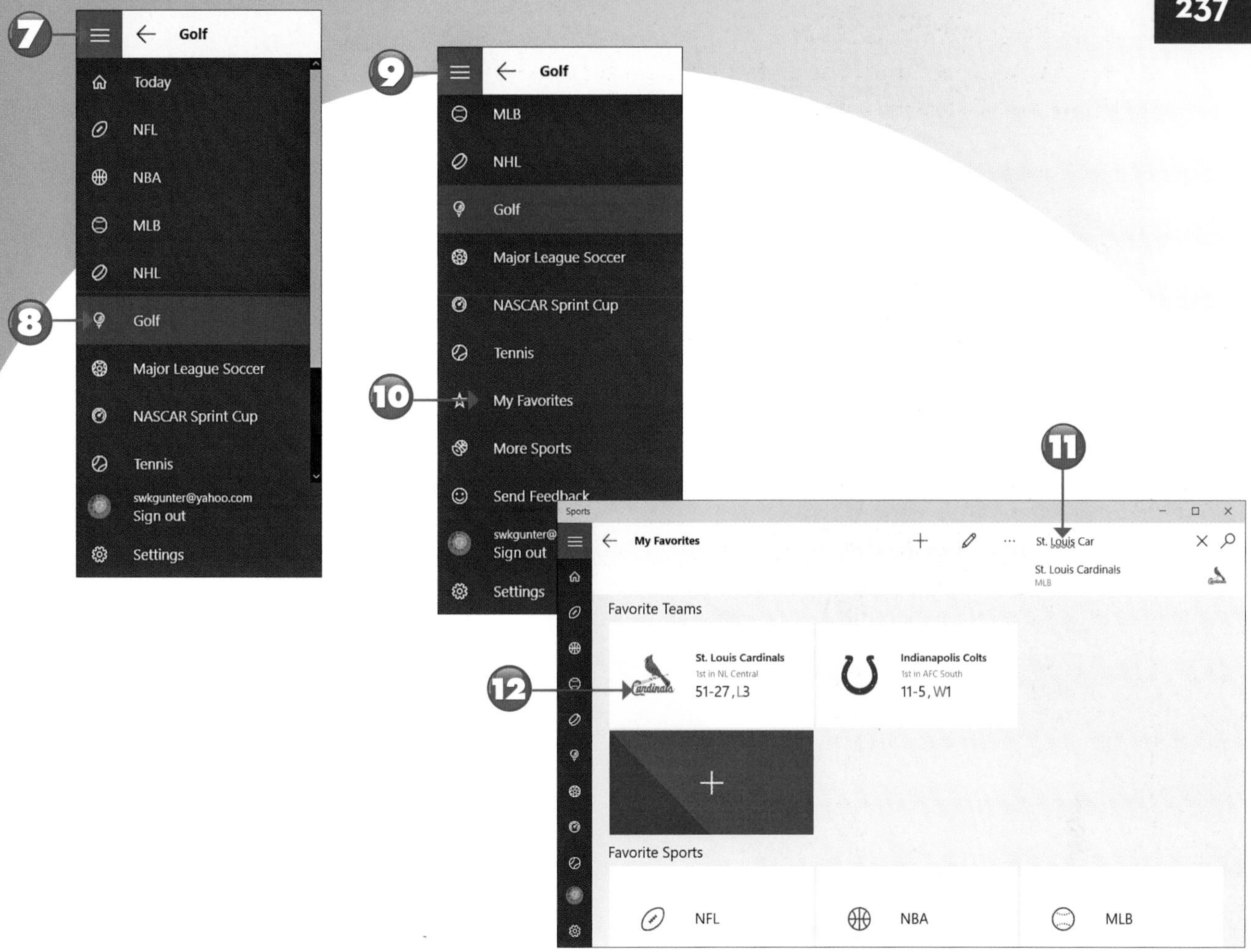

7 You can use the scrollable menu to view news for different sports categories; click or tap the **Menu** button.

8 Click or tap a sport category.

9 To add your own favorite sport or team to the list, click or tap the **Menu** button and scroll to the **My Favorites** category.

10 Click or tap **My Favorites**.

11 Click or tap the **Sports/Teams** box and type in the team you want to add or select it from the list of possible matches.

12 The Sports app adds the team to the Favorite Teams list and the Scoreboard window.

End

TIP

Edit Your Favorites You can easily edit your Favorite Teams list; click or tap the **Menu** button and choose **My Favorites** to display the list. Click or tap the team you want to remove, click or tap the **Remove from Favorites** icon (looks like a pencil), and select X on the team's box.

STORING AND FINDING YOUR FILES

Windows 10's File Explorer provides access to both local files and OneDrive cloud-based storage. File Explorer makes it easier than ever to locate and use recently used folders and files. In this chapter, you learn how to use File Explorer to learn more about your files and find ways to make them more useful.

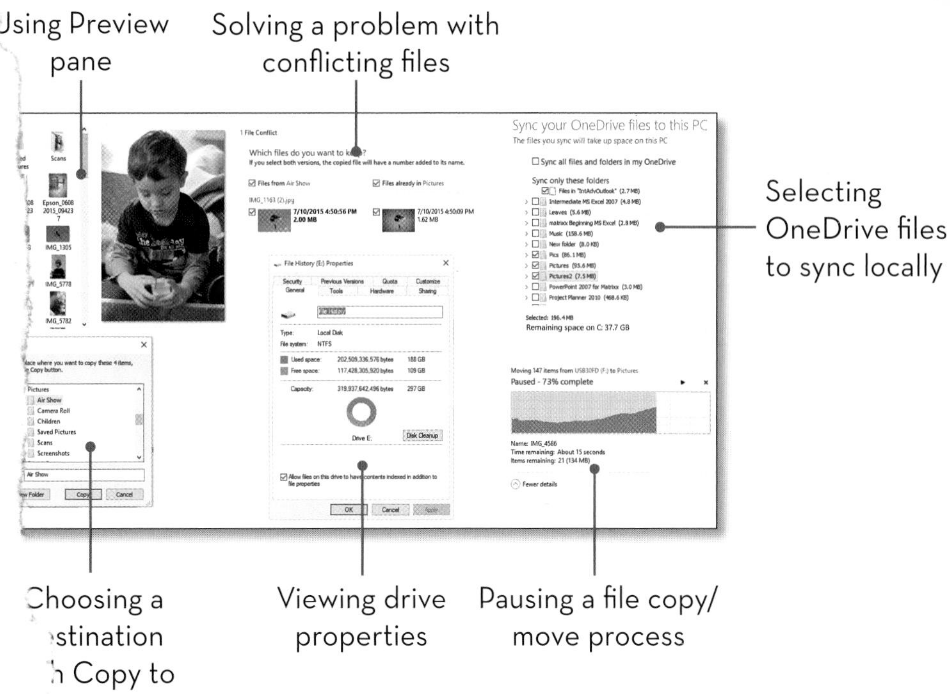

sing Preview pane
Solving a problem with conflicting files
Selecting OneDrive files to sync locally
hoosing a
stination
Copy to
Viewing drive properties
Pausing a file copy/ move process

OPENING FILE EXPLORER

File Explorer is Windows 10's version of the venerable Windows Explorer file and drive management interface. Follow these steps to open File Explorer.

Start

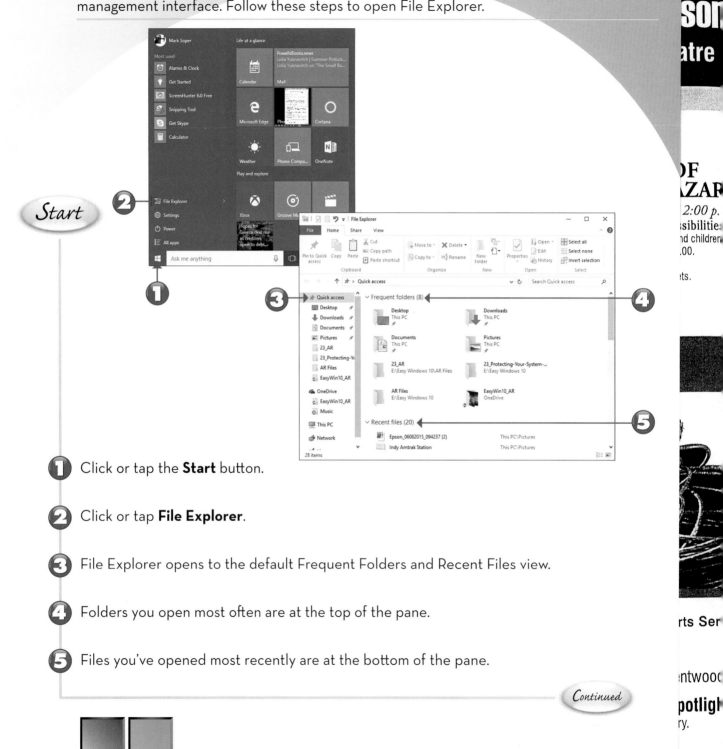

1. Click or tap the **Start** button.
2. Click or tap **File Explorer**.
3. File Explorer opens to the default Frequent Folders and Recent Files view.
4. Folders you open most often are at the top of the pane.
5. Files you've opened most recently are at the bottom of the pane.

Continued

6 Click or tap **This PC** to see the folders and drives on your computer.

7 Double-click or double-tap the **Pictures** folder.

8 Click or tap to switch to the details view.

9 The details view lists additional information about each file.

10 Click or tap to switch to the large thumbnails view.

11 The large thumbnails view shows a preview of each file.

End

USING THE VIEW TAB

The File Explorer's View tab helps you select from a variety of settings so you can view drives, files, folders, and network locations in the most appropriate ways. Here are some examples of how to use the View tab.

Start

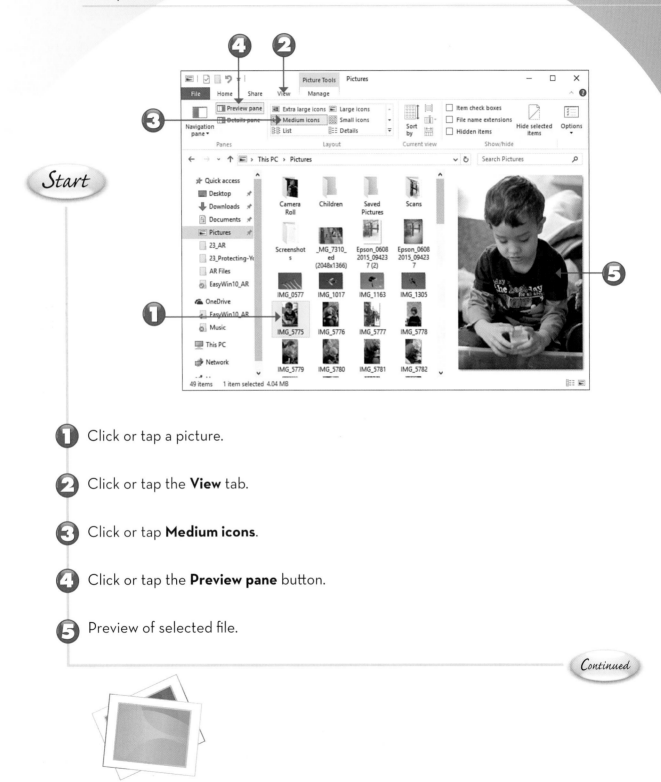

1. Click or tap a picture.
2. Click or tap the **View** tab.
3. Click or tap **Medium icons**.
4. Click or tap the **Preview pane** button.
5. Preview of selected file.

Continued

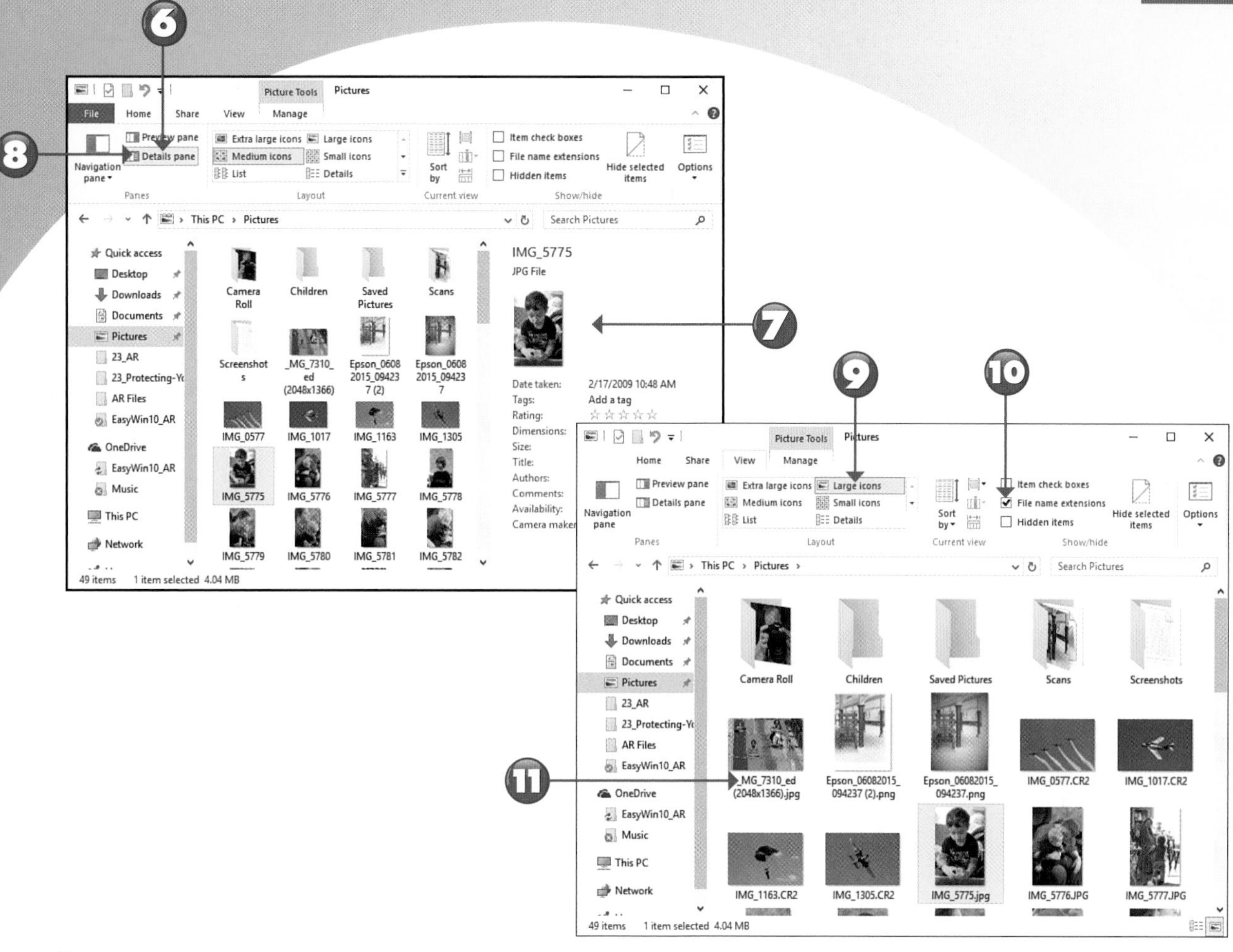

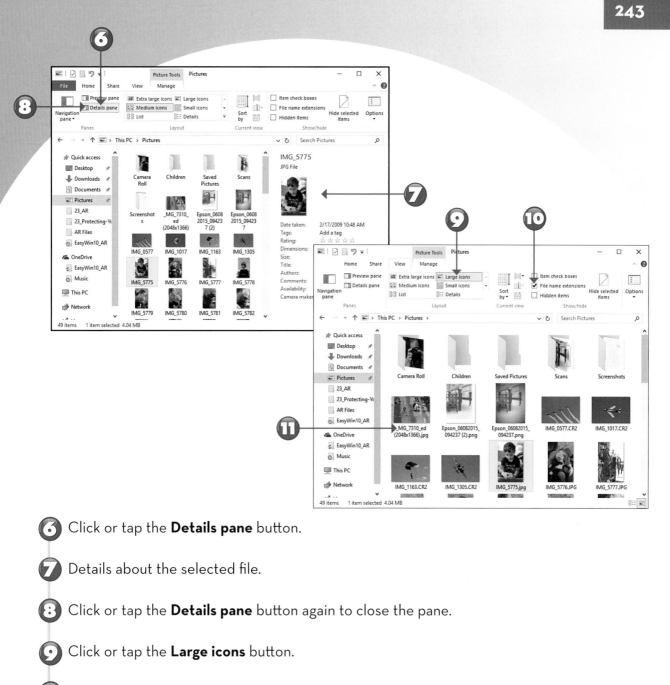

6 Click or tap the **Details pane** button.

7 Details about the selected file.

8 Click or tap the **Details pane** button again to close the pane.

9 Click or tap the **Large icons** button.

10 Click or tap the empty **File name extensions** check box.

11 Files with various file name extensions.

End

NOTE

File Name Extensions Displaying file name extensions is useful when you have similar-looking files. For example, CR2 files are very large and need special software to be viewed, but JPG (JPEG) and PNG files use less disk space and can be viewed in web browsers and by email apps. To turn off file name extensions, clear the **File name extensions** check box.

USING COPY TO

In this exercise, you create a new folder in the Pictures folder and copy files to it.

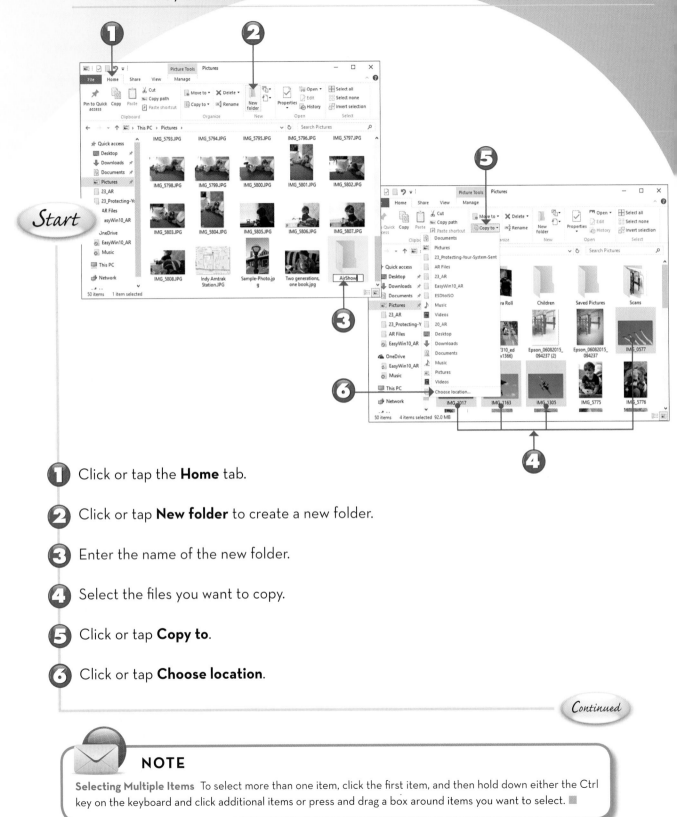

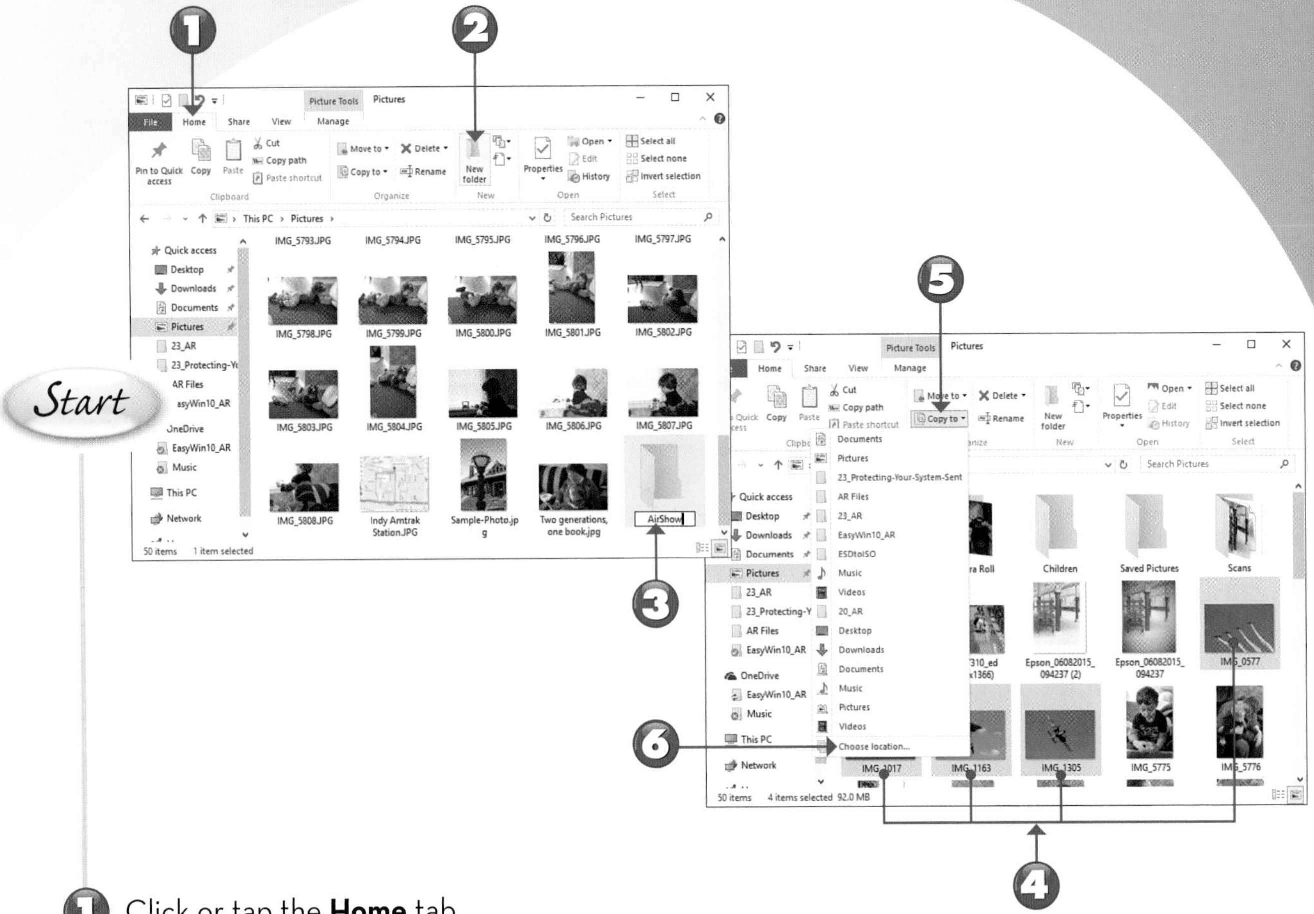

Start

1. Click or tap the **Home** tab.
2. Click or tap **New folder** to create a new folder.
3. Enter the name of the new folder.
4. Select the files you want to copy.
5. Click or tap **Copy to**.
6. Click or tap **Choose location**.

Continued

NOTE

Selecting Multiple Items To select more than one item, click the first item, and then hold down either the Ctrl key on the keyboard and click additional items or press and drag a box around items you want to select.

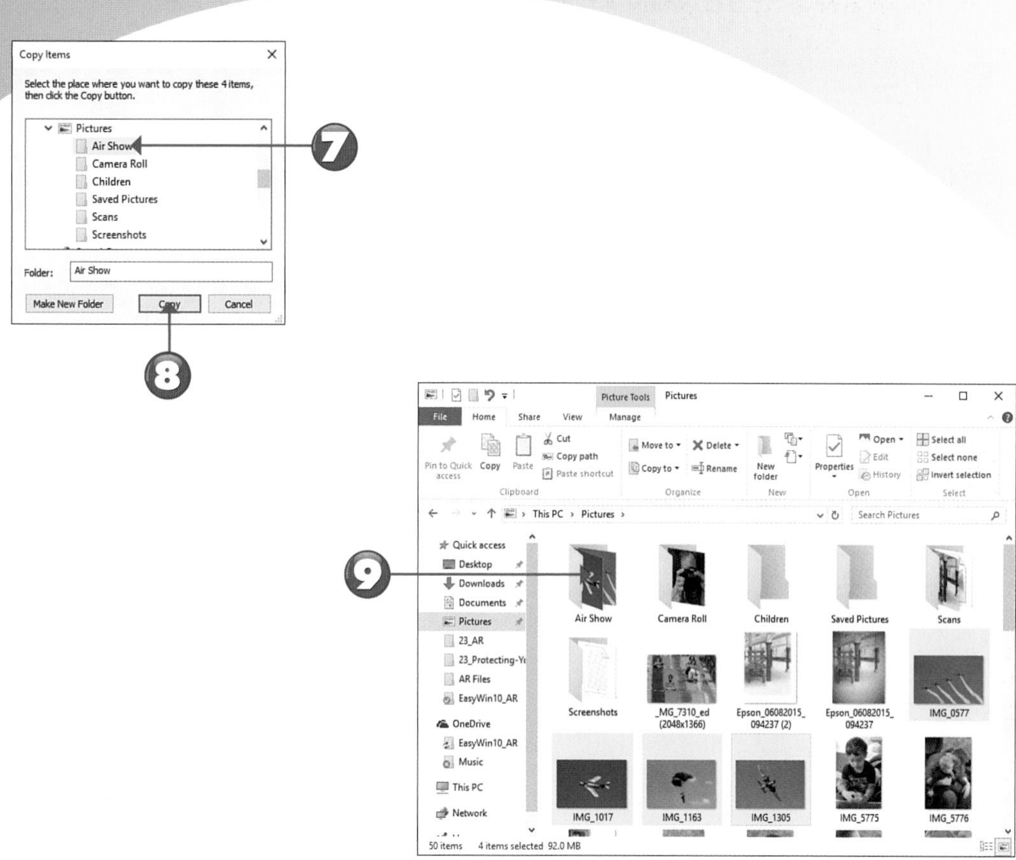

7. Navigate to and click or tap the folder you created in steps 2 and 3.

8. Click or tap **Copy**.

9. The files are copied into the folder.

End

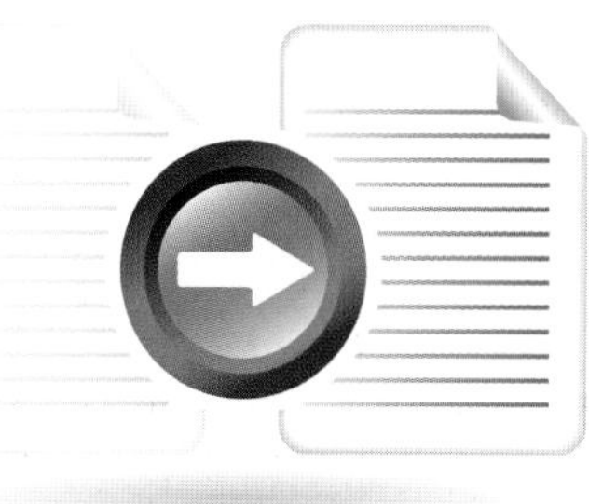

RENAMING FILES

In this exercise, you rename a file you copied in the previous exercise.

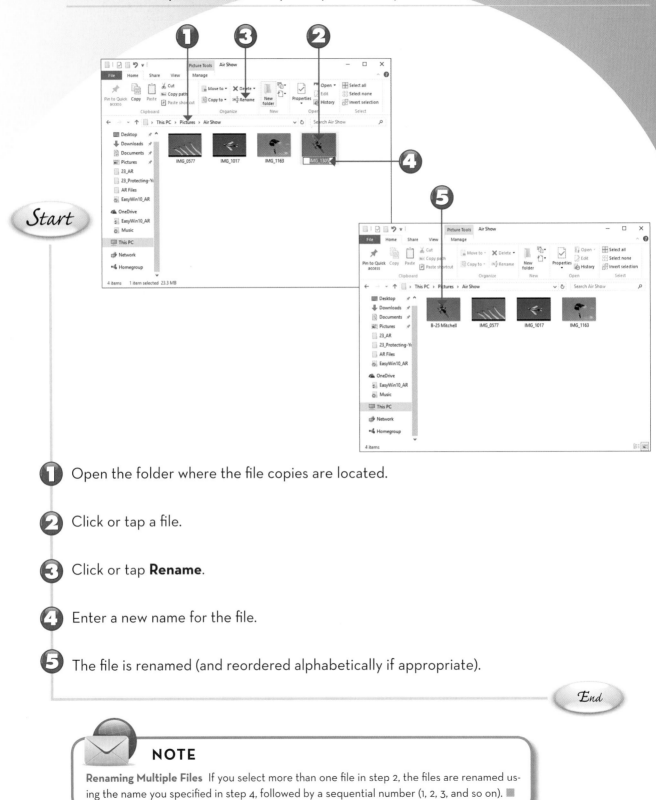

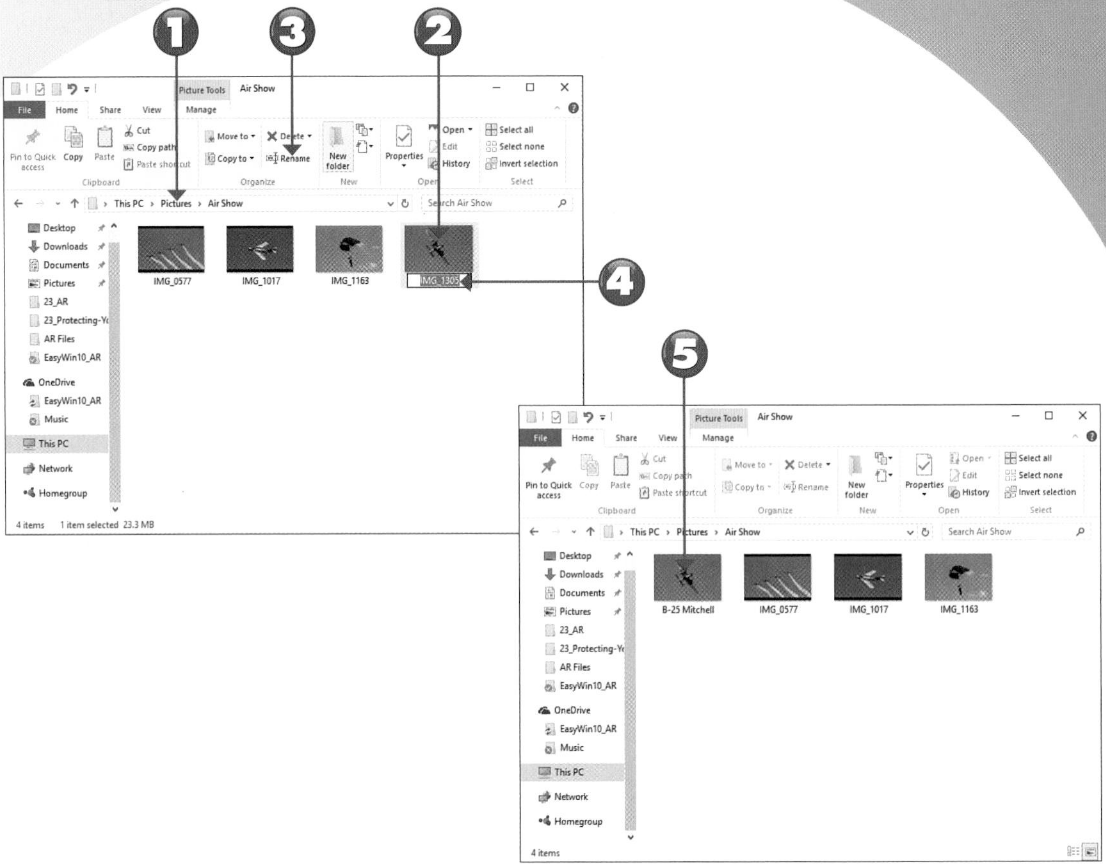

1. Open the folder where the file copies are located.
2. Click or tap a file.
3. Click or tap **Rename**.
4. Enter a new name for the file.
5. The file is renamed (and reordered alphabetically if appropriate).

NOTE

Renaming Multiple Files If you select more than one file in step 2, the files are renamed using the name you specified in step 4, followed by a sequential number (1, 2, 3, and so on).

SELECTING FILES

This exercise demonstrates how to select files.

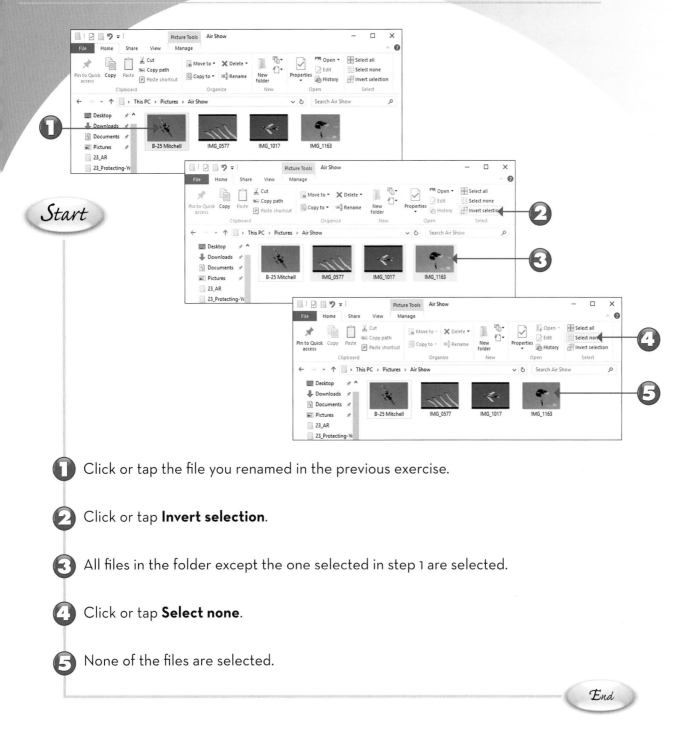

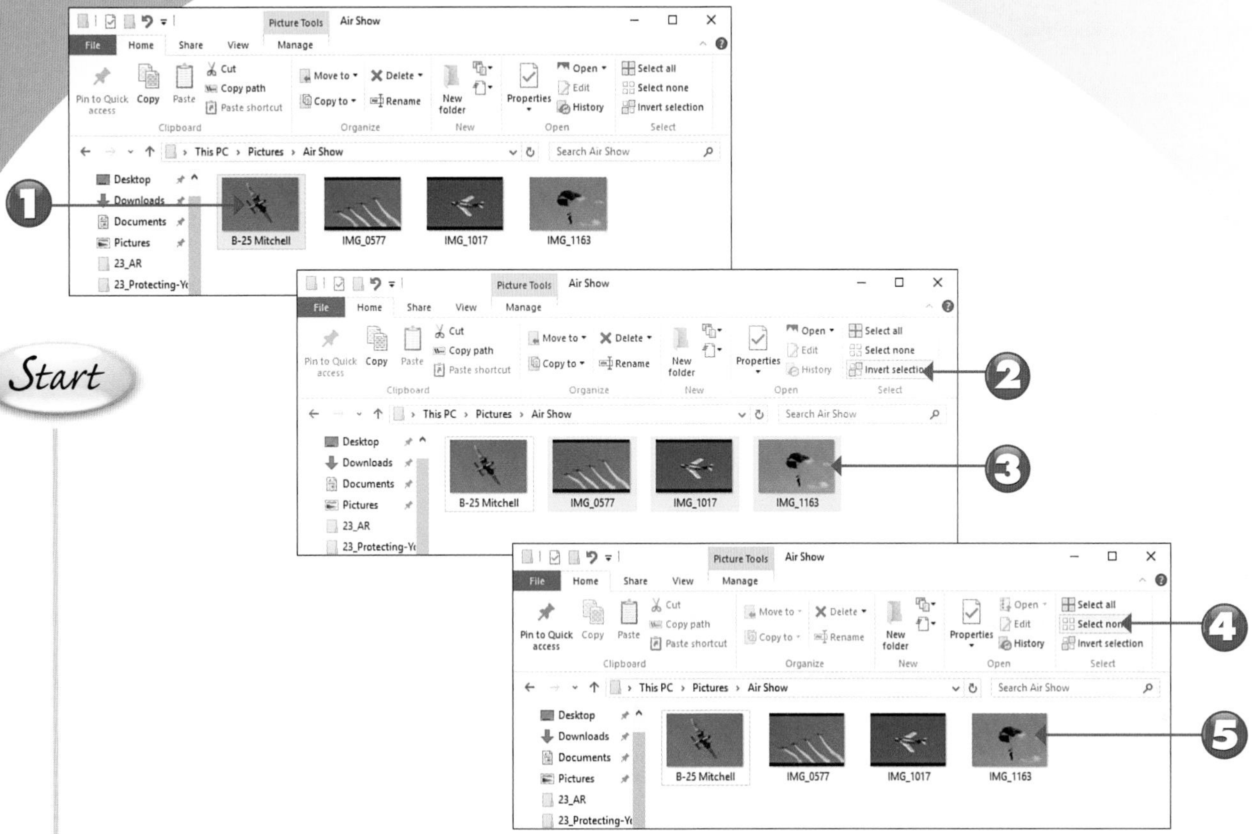

Start

1. Click or tap the file you renamed in the previous exercise.
2. Click or tap **Invert selection**.
3. All files in the folder except the one selected in step 1 are selected.
4. Click or tap **Select none**.
5. None of the files are selected.

End

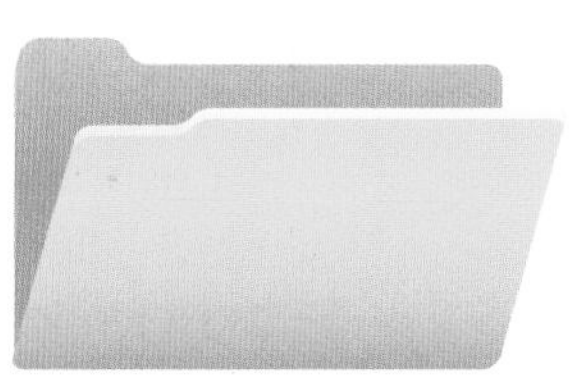

DELETING FILES

This exercise demonstrates how to select and delete all files in a location.

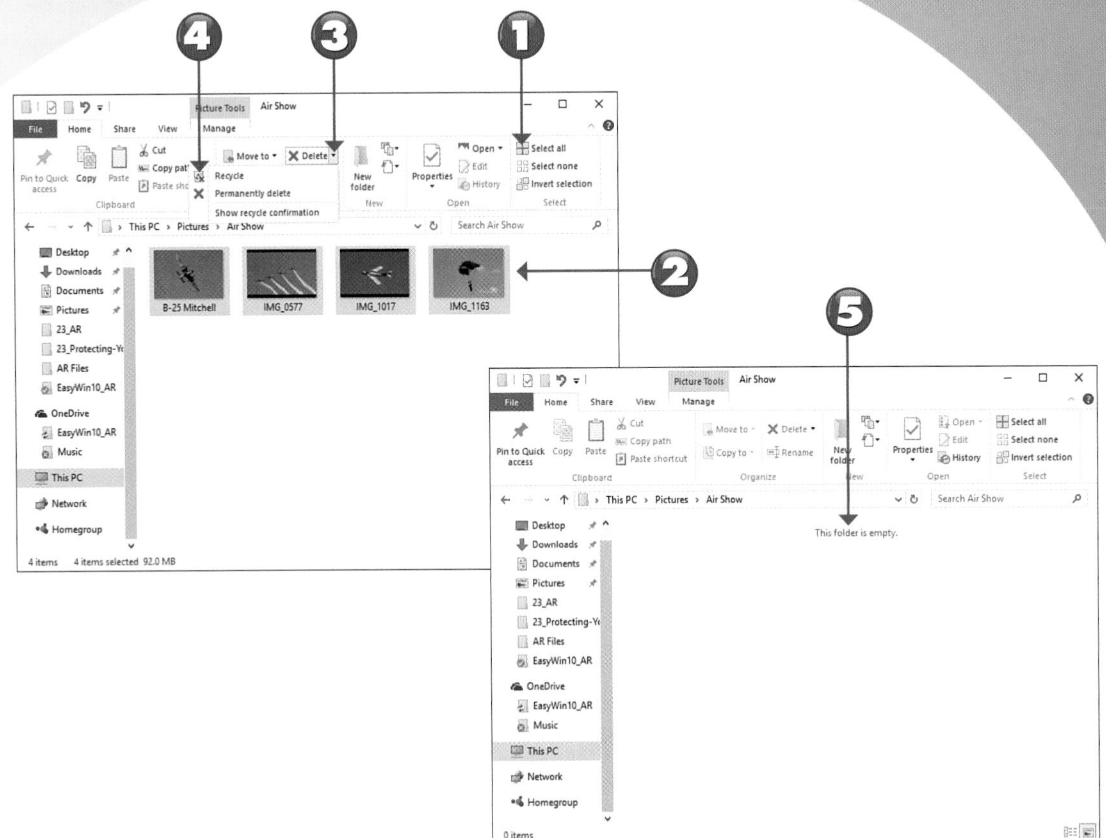

Start

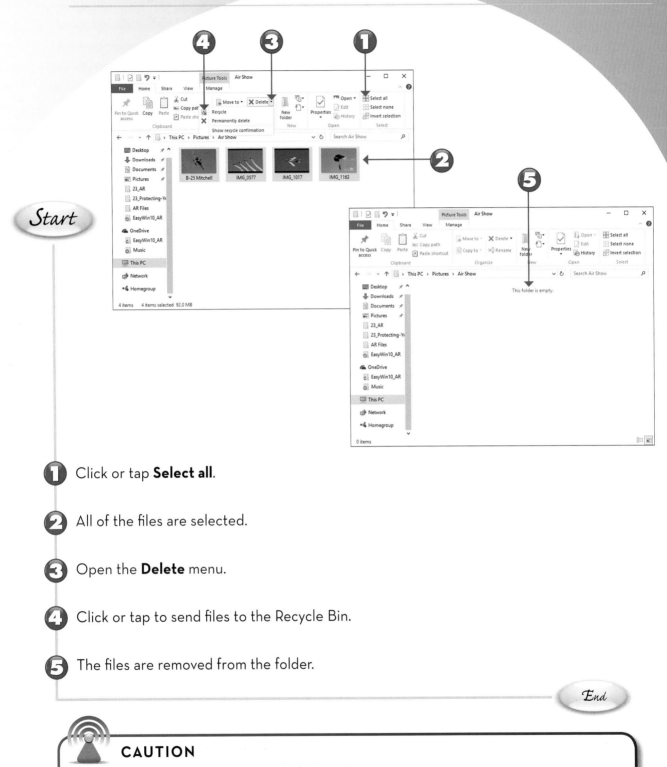

1. Click or tap **Select all**.
2. All of the files are selected.
3. Open the **Delete** menu.
4. Click or tap to send files to the Recycle Bin.
5. The files are removed from the folder.

End

CAUTION

Permanently Delete Versus Recycle If you permanently delete files, the space they occupy on the drive can be reused by new files. If you decide you need to retrieve those files, you must use a third-party data-recovery utility.

RETRIEVING FILES FROM THE RECYCLE BIN

If you delete files you should have kept, the Recycle Bin is here to help. In this lesson, you learn how to restore files from the Recycle Bin to their original location.

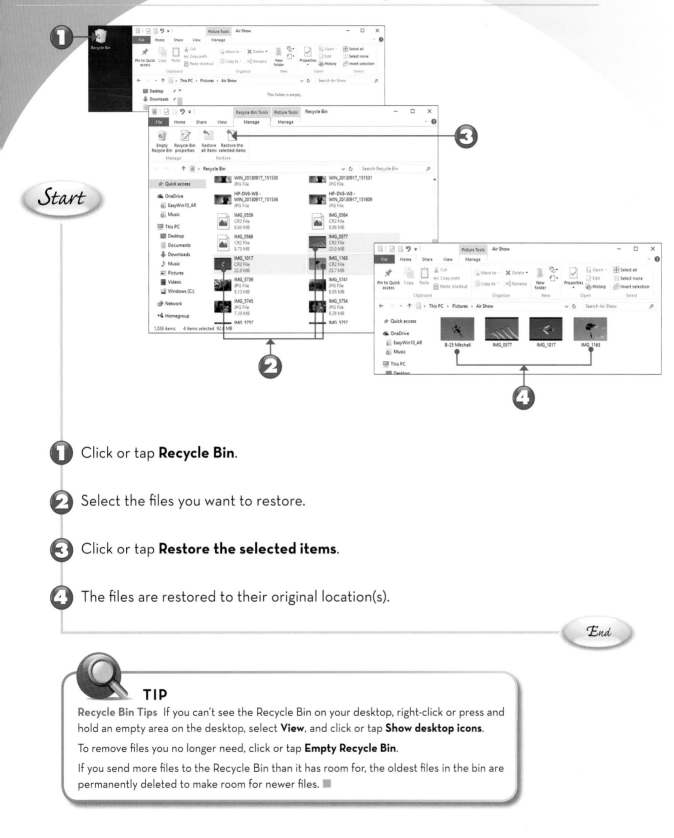

Start

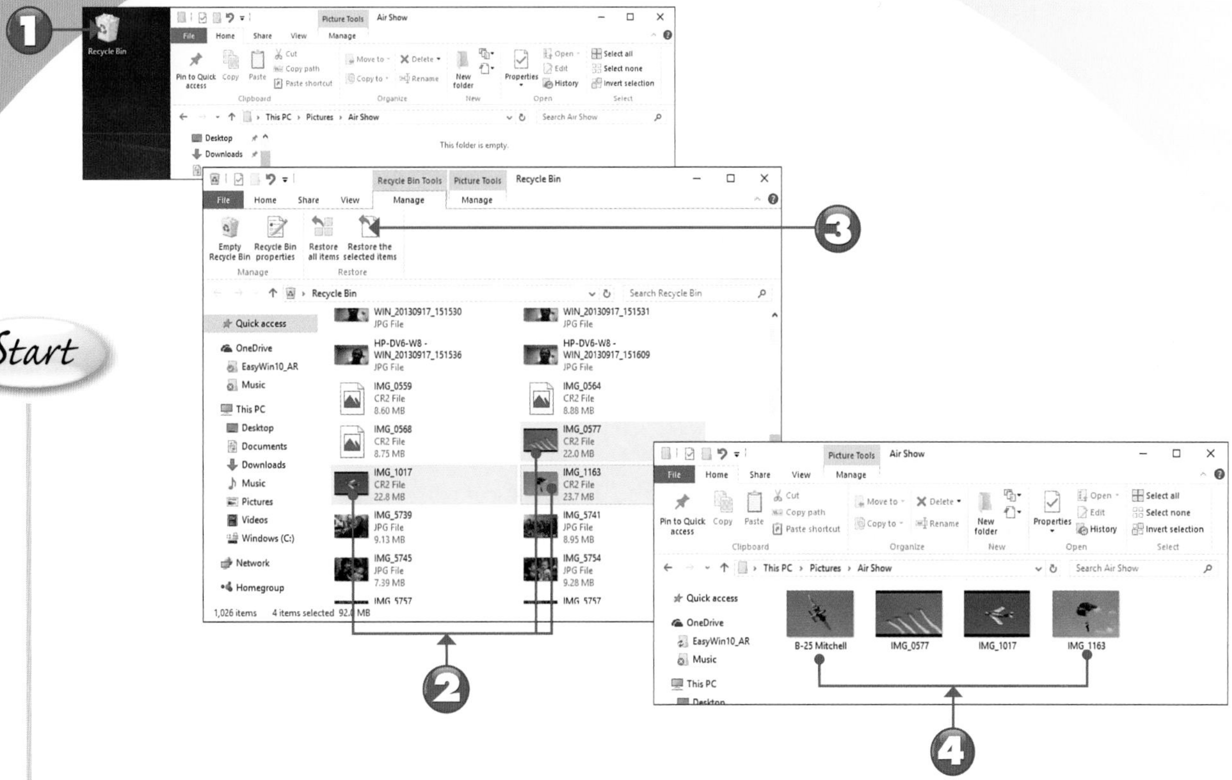

1. Click or tap **Recycle Bin**.
2. Select the files you want to restore.
3. Click or tap **Restore the selected items**.
4. The files are restored to their original location(s).

End

TIP

Recycle Bin Tips If you can't see the Recycle Bin on your desktop, right-click or press and hold an empty area on the desktop, select **View**, and click or tap **Show desktop icons**.

To remove files you no longer need, click or tap **Empty Recycle Bin**.

If you send more files to the Recycle Bin than it has room for, the oldest files in the bin are permanently deleted to make room for newer files.

MOVING FILES OR FOLDERS

The Move To command enables you to easily move files or folders to a different location. You can select from a listed destination (as in this example) or choose another location. With either Copy To or Move To, you might be able to pause and continue the process if the process takes more than a few seconds. In this example, you see how to move a folder containing many photos from an external drive to your Pictures folder.

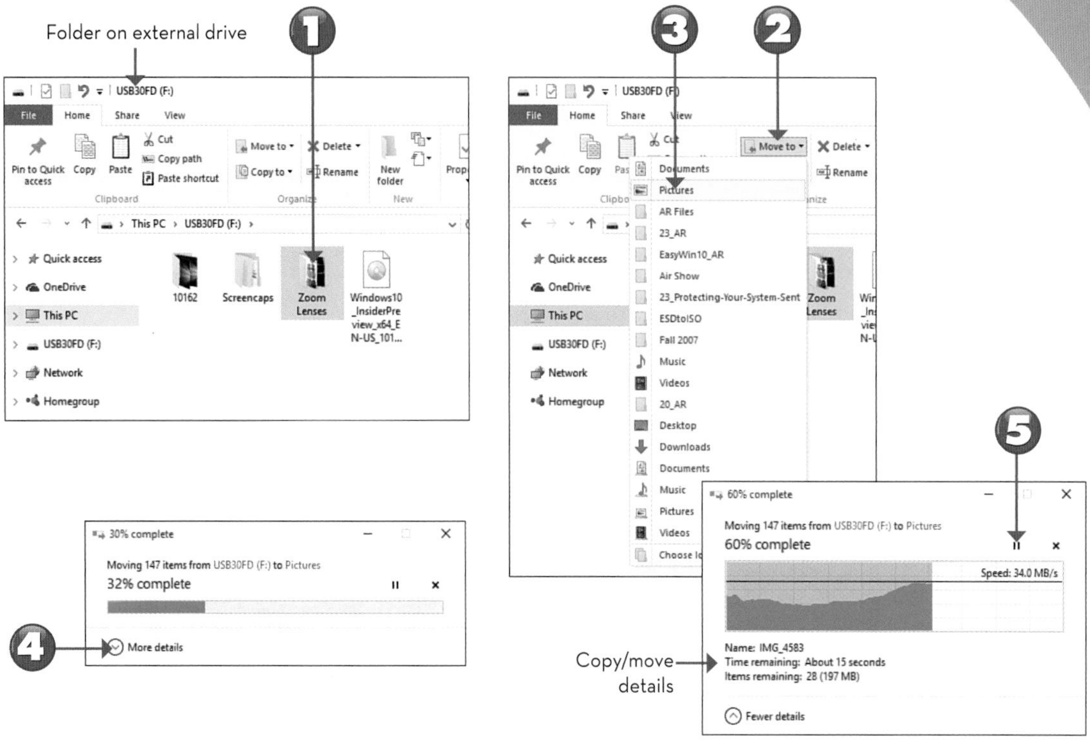

Folder on external drive

Copy/move details

Start

1. Select the folder you want to move.
2. Open the **Move to** menu.
3. Click or tap **Pictures**.
4. To see more information about the process, click the down arrow next to **More details**.
5. To pause the process, click the **Pause** button.

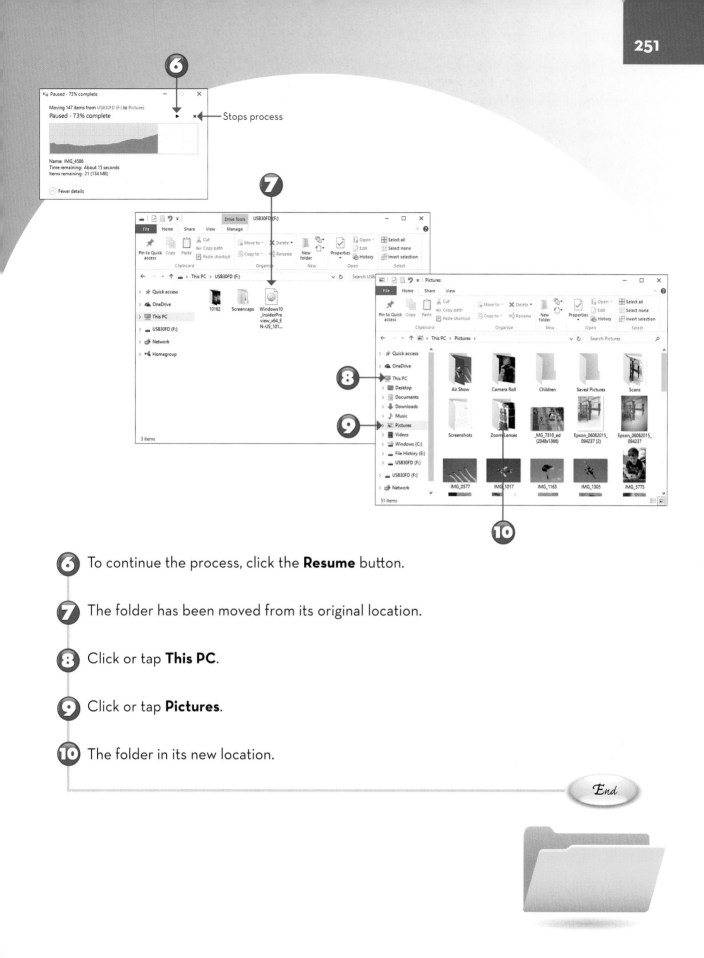

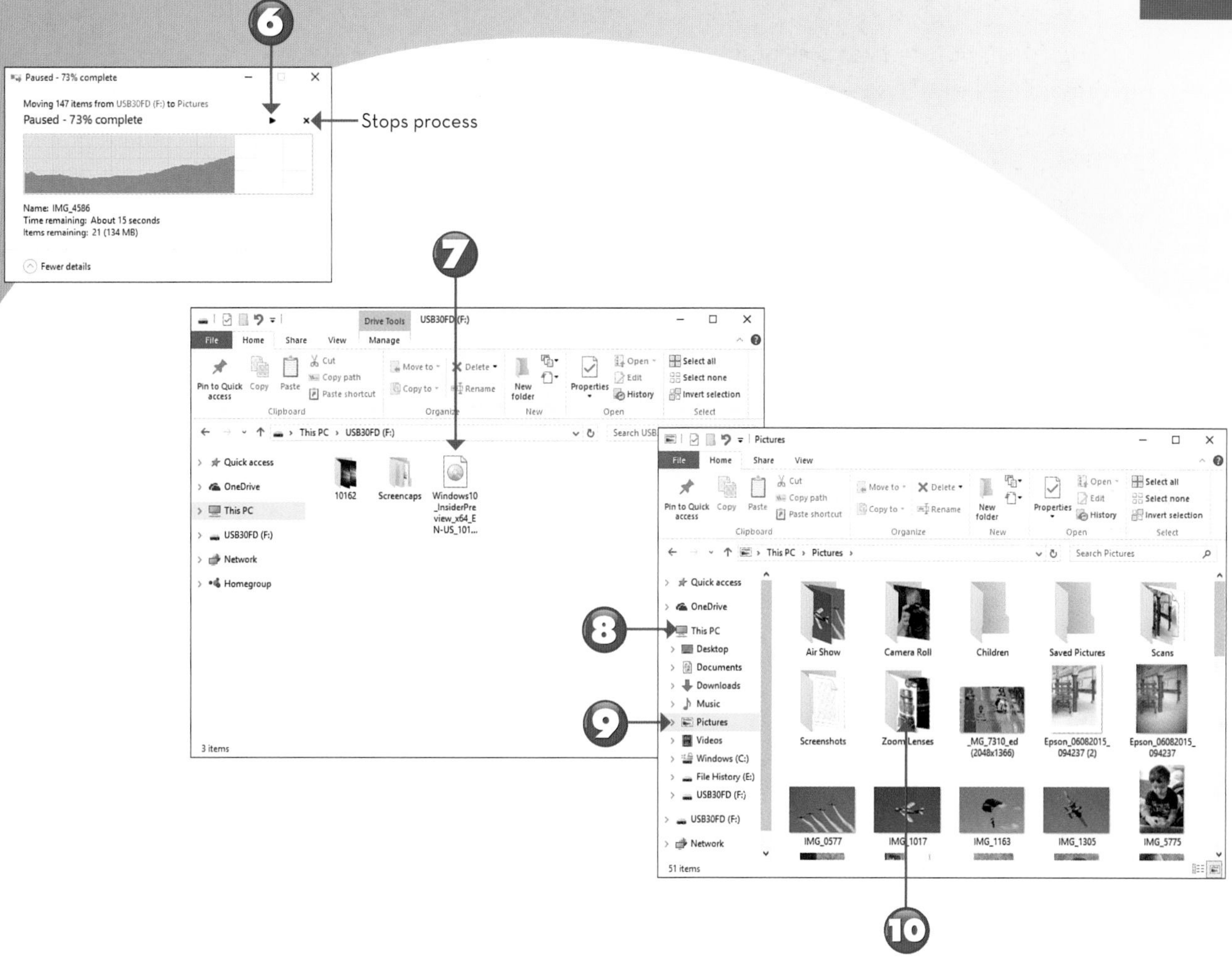

Stops process

6. To continue the process, click the **Resume** button.

7. The folder has been moved from its original location.

8. Click or tap **This PC**.

9. Click or tap **Pictures**.

10. The folder in its new location.

End

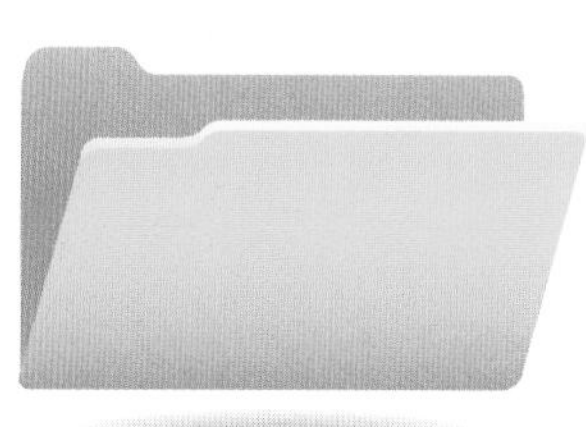

DEALING WITH FILE NAME CONFLICTS

When you copy or move files with File Explorer, you might discover that some files being copied or moved have the same names as files already in the destination location. Here's what to do.

Start

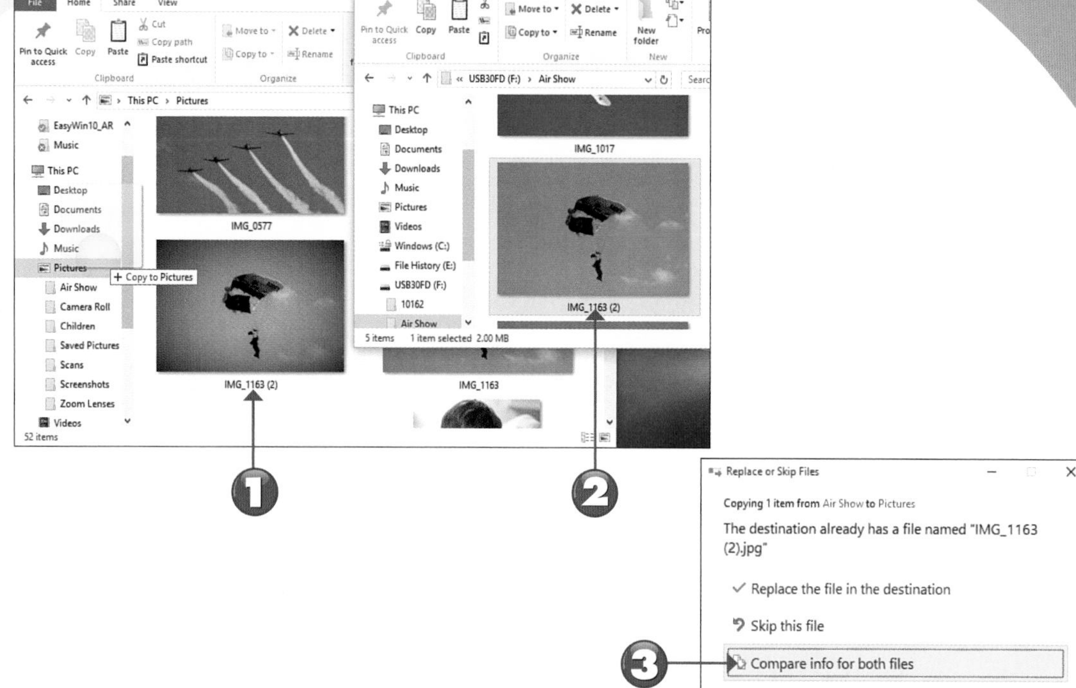

1. A photo in the Pictures folder.
2. Copy a different photo with the same name to that folder.
3. Click or tap **Compare info for both files**.

Continued

NOTE

Using Drag and Drop In step 2, the file is copied using drag and drop. To drag and drop a file, click or press and hold the file, drag it to the destination, and release it. Use the **Ctrl** key to switch between copying and moving the file. ■

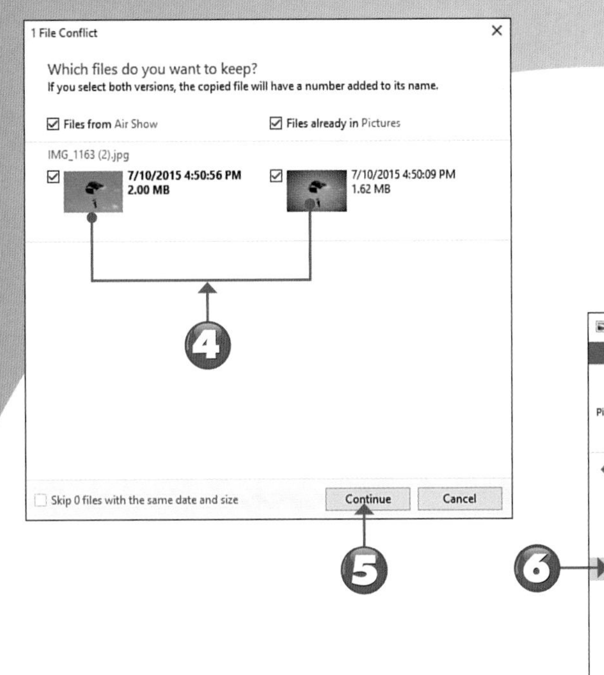

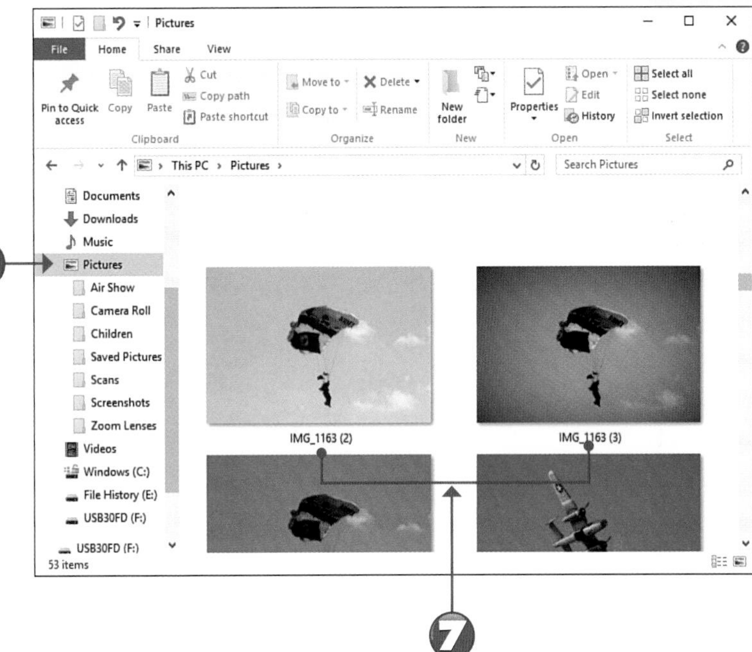

4. To keep both files, click both check boxes.
5. Click or tap **Continue**.
6. Click or tap the destination folder.
7. The copied file with the name conflict is renamed to avoid replacing the original file.

End

NOTE

Dealing with Multiple File Name Conflicts If you copy or move more than one file or folder with a name conflict, choose **Let me decide for each** in step 3. You are then prompted to choose what to do with each file.

BURNING DATA DISCS

You can use options on the Share tab in File Explorer to easily burn CDs or DVDs of your favorite files. Here's how.

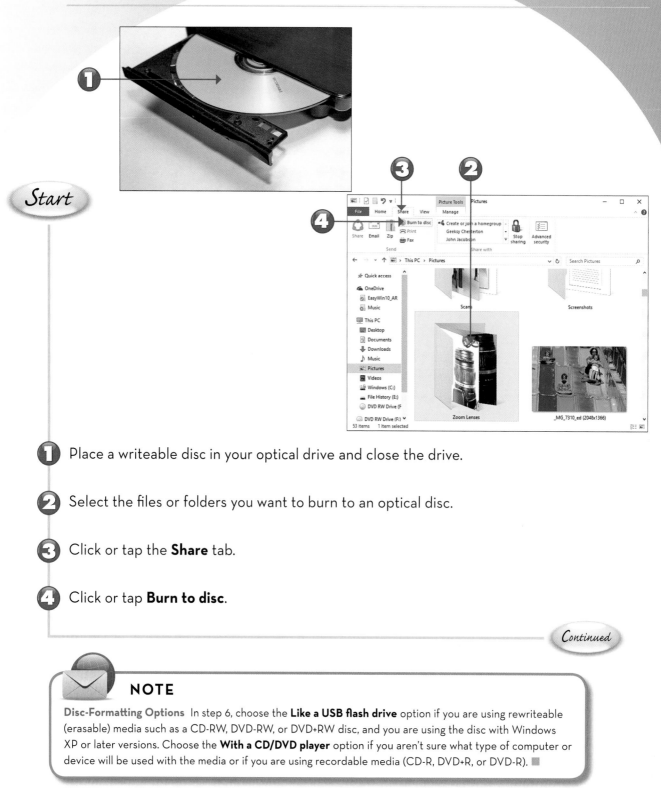

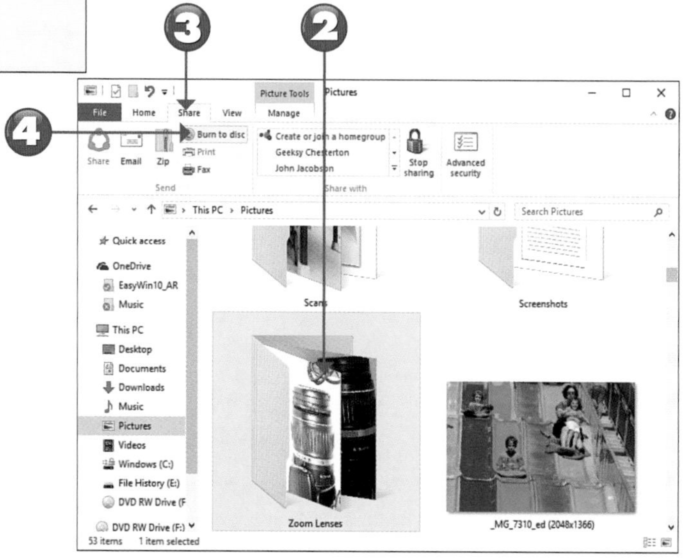

Start

1. Place a writeable disc in your optical drive and close the drive.
2. Select the files or folders you want to burn to an optical disc.
3. Click or tap the **Share** tab.
4. Click or tap **Burn to disc**.

Continued

NOTE

Disc-Formatting Options In step 6, choose the **Like a USB flash drive** option if you are using rewriteable (erasable) media such as a CD-RW, DVD-RW, or DVD+RW disc, and you are using the disc with Windows XP or later versions. Choose the **With a CD/DVD player** option if you aren't sure what type of computer or device will be used with the media or if you are using recordable media (CD-R, DVD+R, or DVD-R).

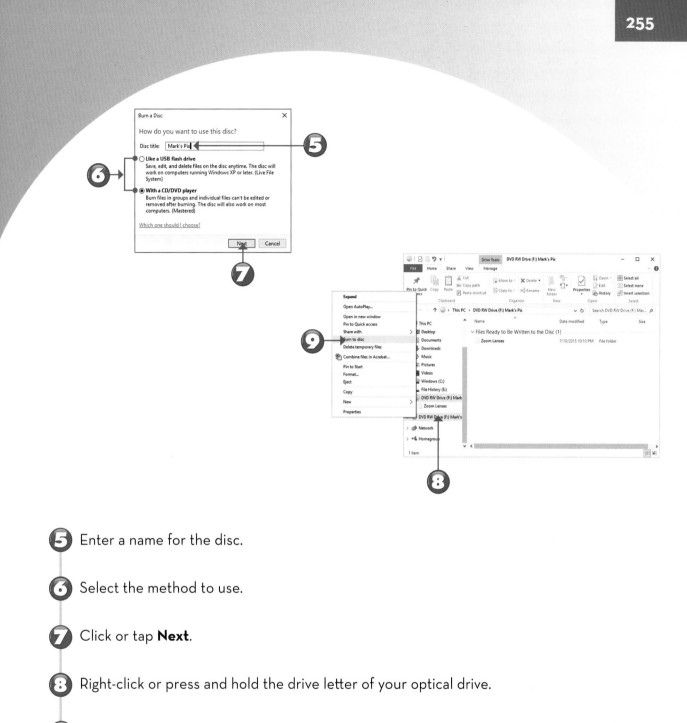

5. Enter a name for the disc.

6. Select the method to use.

7. Click or tap **Next**.

8. Right-click or press and hold the drive letter of your optical drive.

9. Click or tap **Burn to disc**.

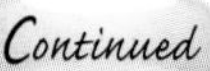

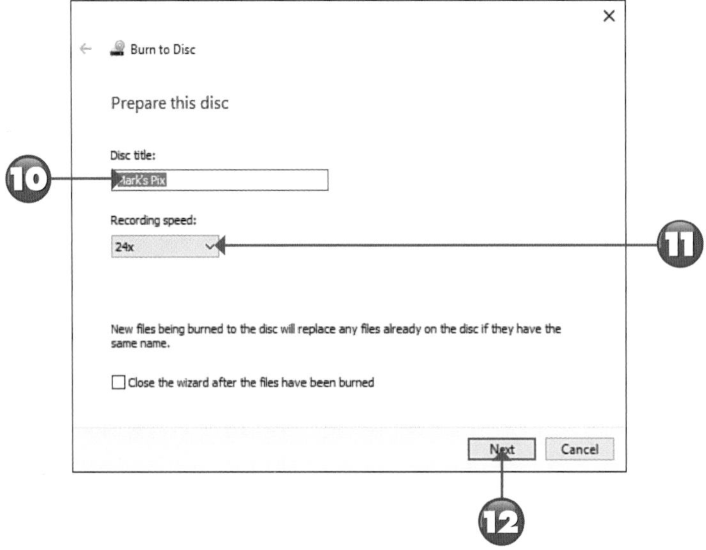

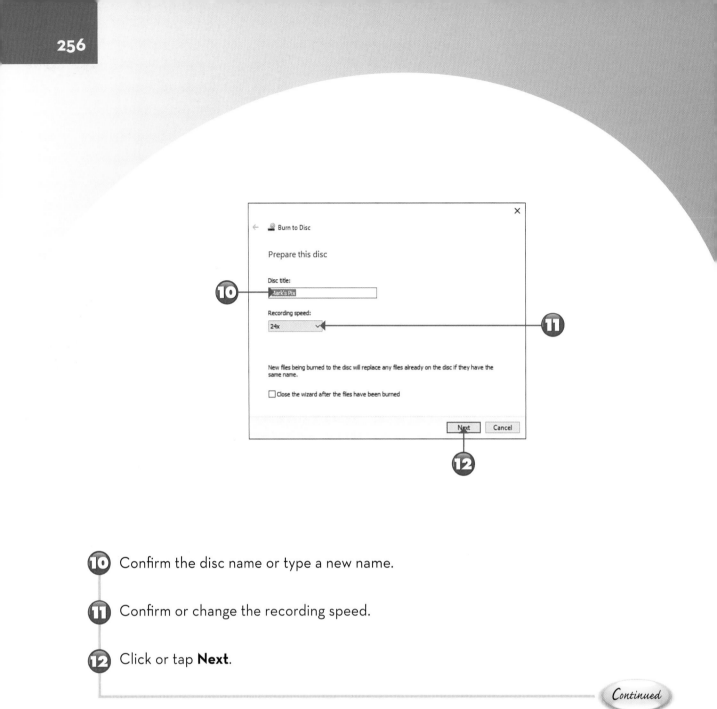

10 Confirm the disc name or type a new name.

11 Confirm or change the recording speed.

12 Click or tap **Next**.

Continued

NOTE

Burning One Disc Only If you don't want the opportunity to burn additional discs from the files you selected, click or tap the empty **Close the wizard after the files have been burned** check box shown in steps 10–12.

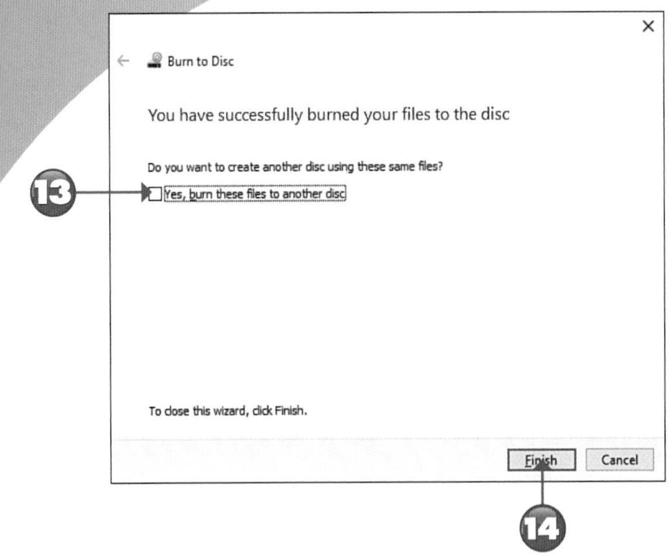

13 Click or tap the **Yes, burn these files to another disc** check box if you want to burn another copy of the disc.

14 Click or tap **Finish**.

15 Remove the disc from the drive.

End

TIP

Recording Speeds Choose a slower recording speed in step 11 if you have had problems using recorded media from your computer on another device, such as a CD player.

SORTING AND GROUPING FILES

Windows 10 provides a variety of ways to sort and group files to make it easier to find the files you want. This lesson uses some folders containing photos. However, the methods described here can also be used with music files, videos, or other types of documents.

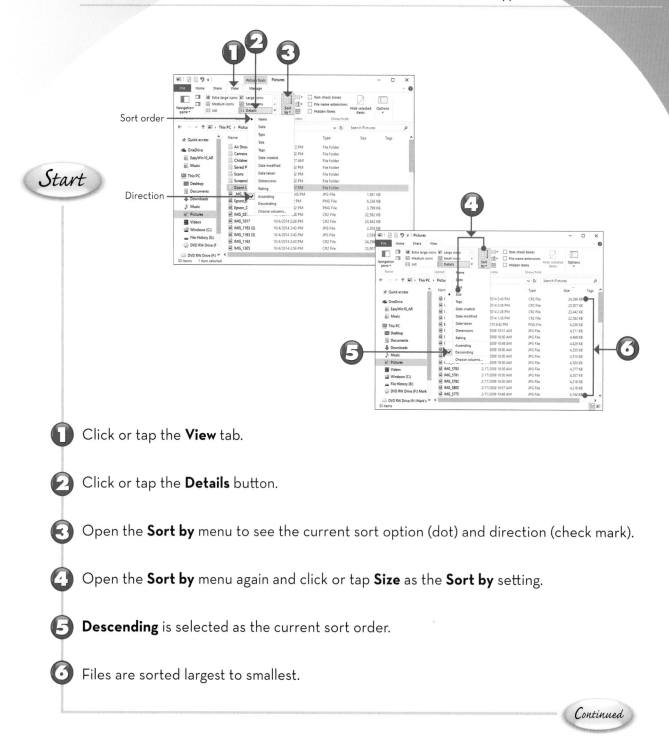

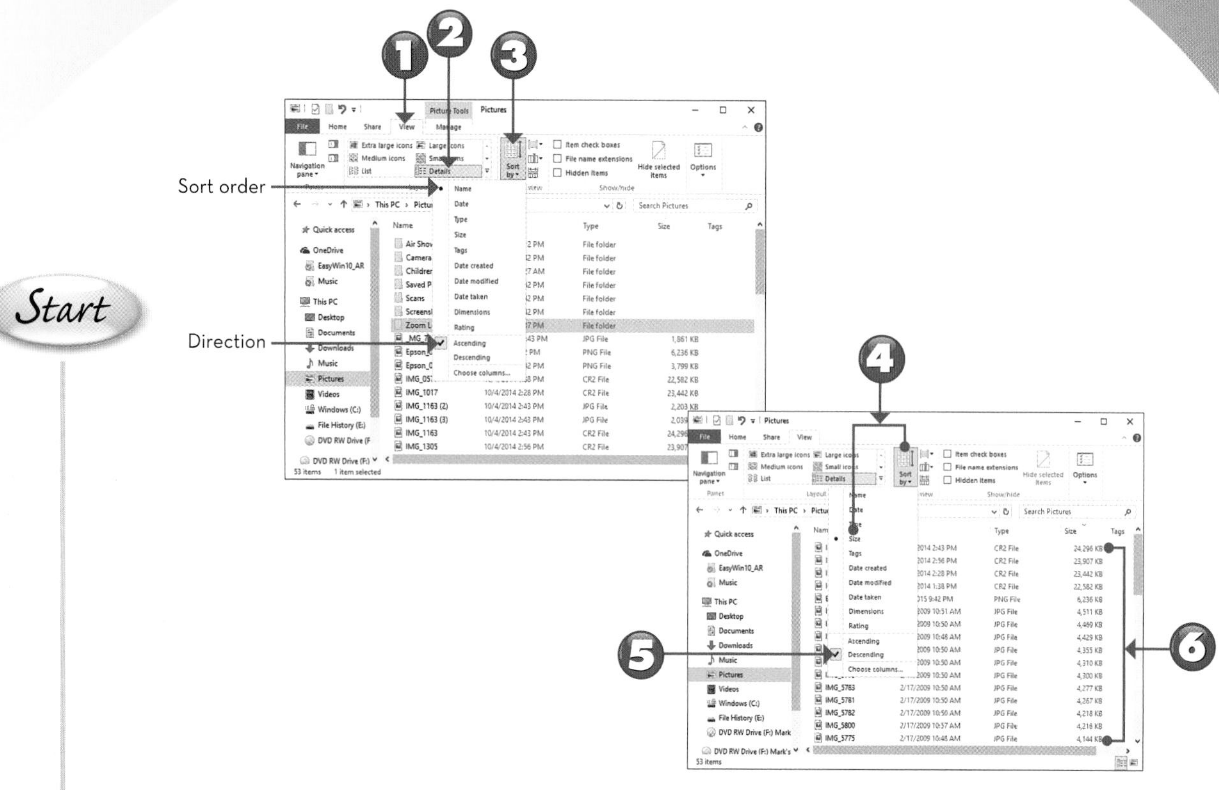

1. Click or tap the **View** tab.
2. Click or tap the **Details** button.
3. Open the **Sort by** menu to see the current sort option (dot) and direction (check mark).
4. Open the **Sort by** menu again and click or tap **Size** as the **Sort by** setting.
5. **Descending** is selected as the current sort order.
6. Files are sorted largest to smallest.

Continued

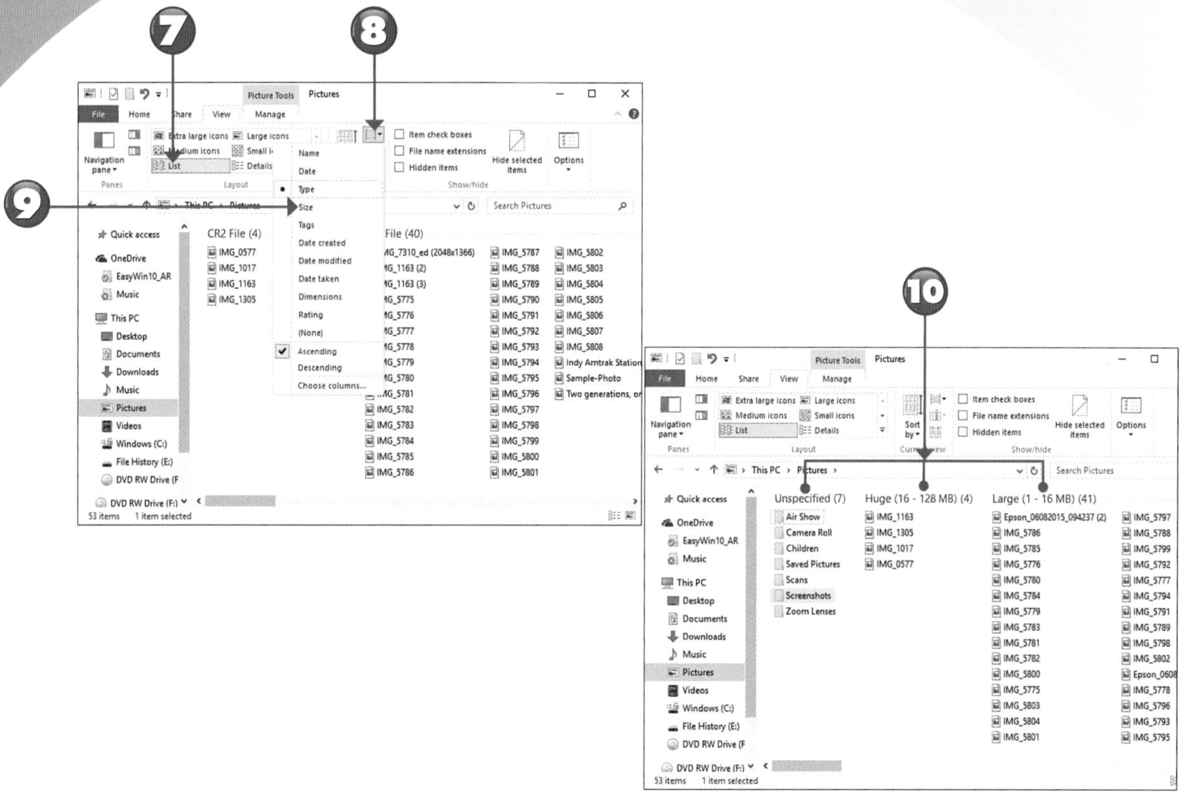

7 Select **List** as the view.

8 Open the **Group by** menu.

9 Click or tap **Size**.

10 Files grouped by size.

End

TIP

Adding Group Columns and Ungrouping Files To choose other items to group files by or to display in Details view, click or tap **Choose columns** in the Group menu. To stop grouping items, click or tap **(None)** in the Group menu.

CREATING ZIP FILES WITH THE SHARE TAB

Zip files are handy because you can store multiple files and folders into a single file that's usually smaller than the combined size of the original files. The resulting file is also easier to email. Zip file creation is available from the Share tab in File Explorer.

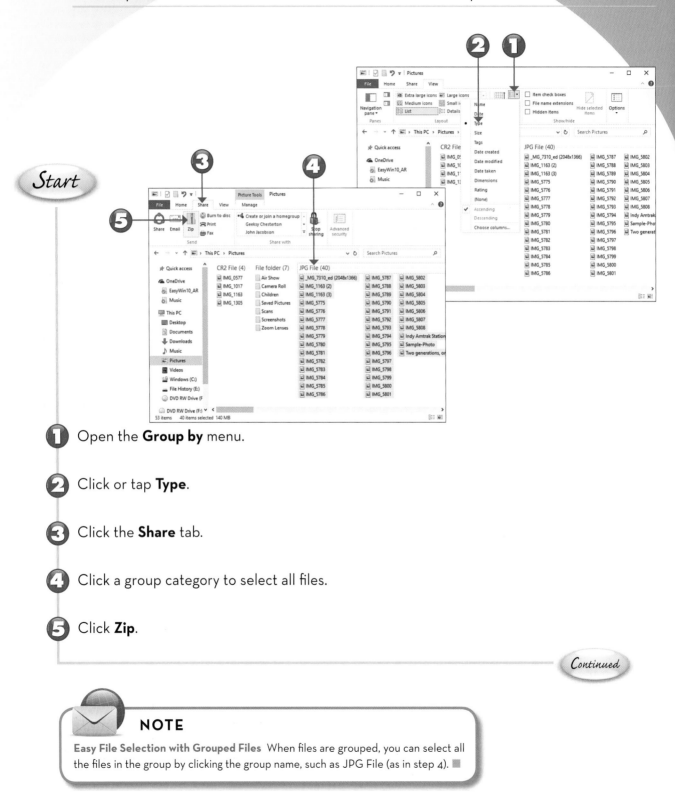

Start

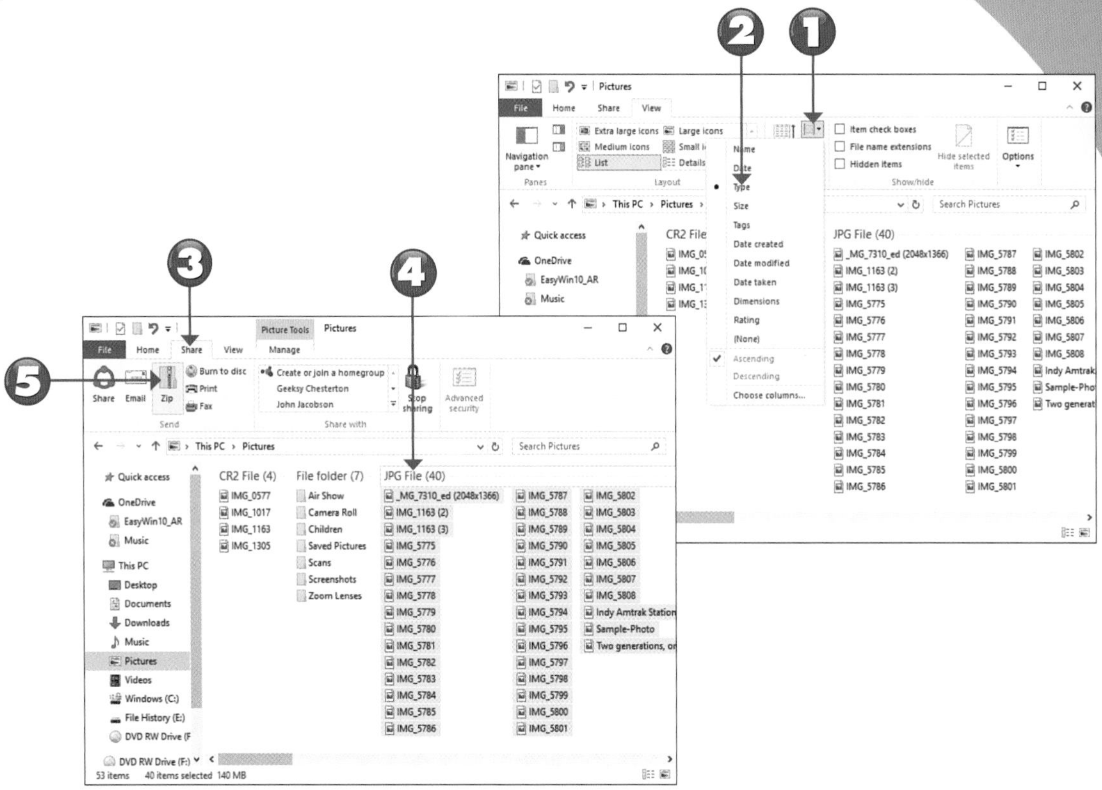

1. Open the **Group by** menu.
2. Click or tap **Type**.
3. Click the **Share** tab.
4. Click a group category to select all files.
5. Click **Zip**.

Continued

NOTE

Easy File Selection with Grouped Files When files are grouped, you can select all the files in the group by clicking the group name, such as JPG File (as in step 4).

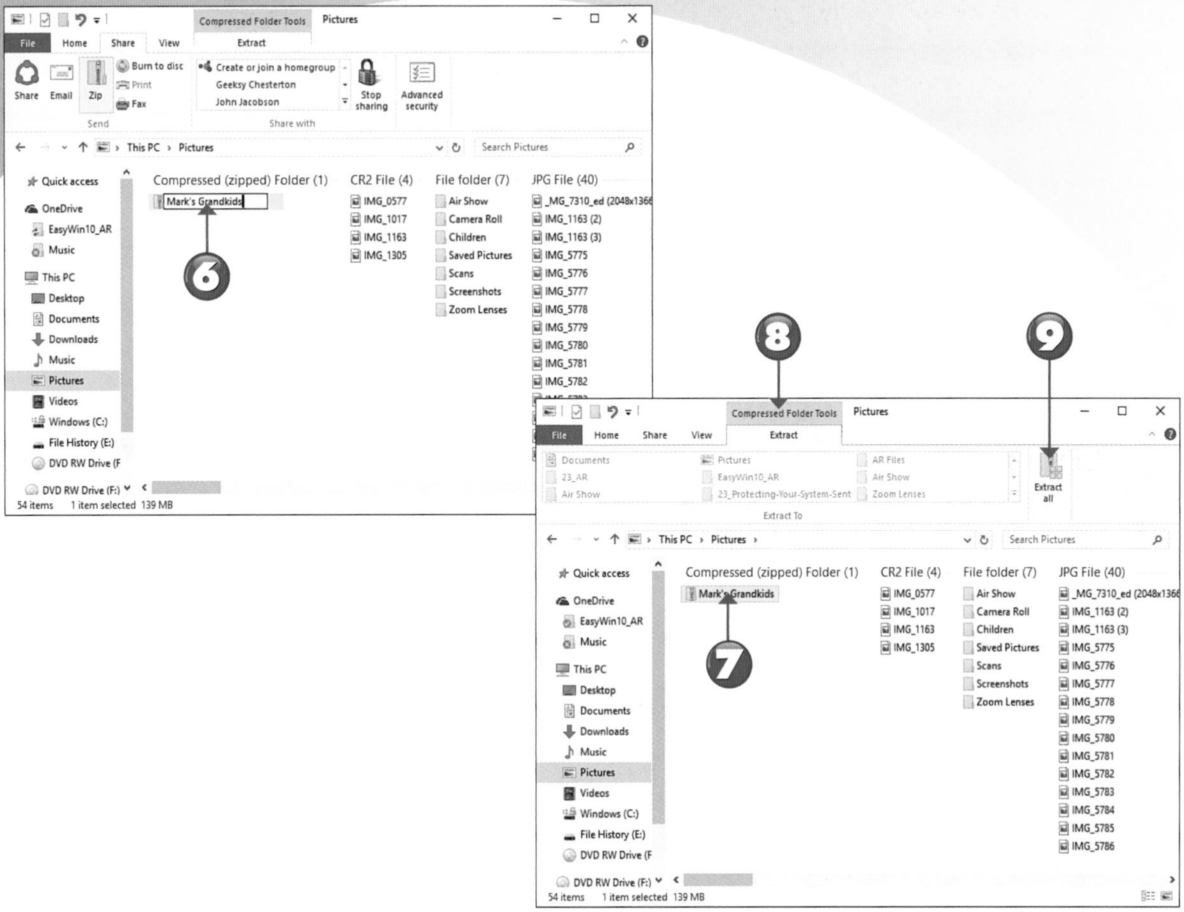

6. Enter a new name for the Zip file.

7. Click or tap the Zip file.

8. Click or tap **Compressed Folder Tools**.

9. Click or tap the **Extract all** button when you need to extract files from the Zip file.

End

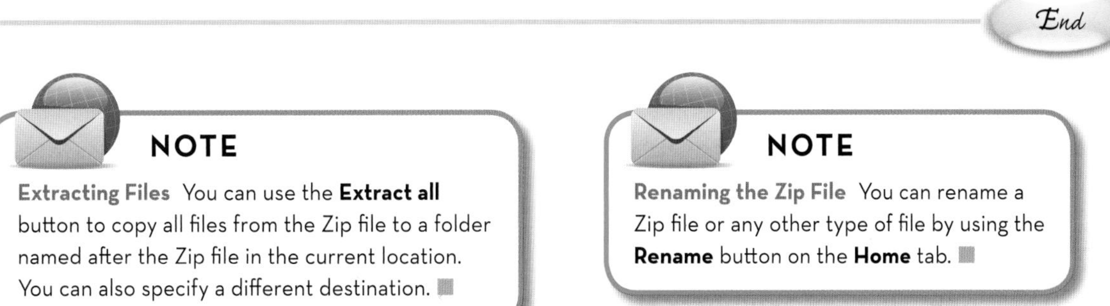

NOTE

Extracting Files You can use the **Extract all** button to copy all files from the Zip file to a folder named after the Zip file in the current location. You can also specify a different destination.

NOTE

Renaming the Zip File You can rename a Zip file or any other type of file by using the **Rename** button on the **Home** tab.

SYNCING A FOLDER WITH ONEDRIVE

Microsoft provides OneDrive cloud-based storage to everyone with a Microsoft account. You can synchronize local files and folders with OneDrive. Here's how.

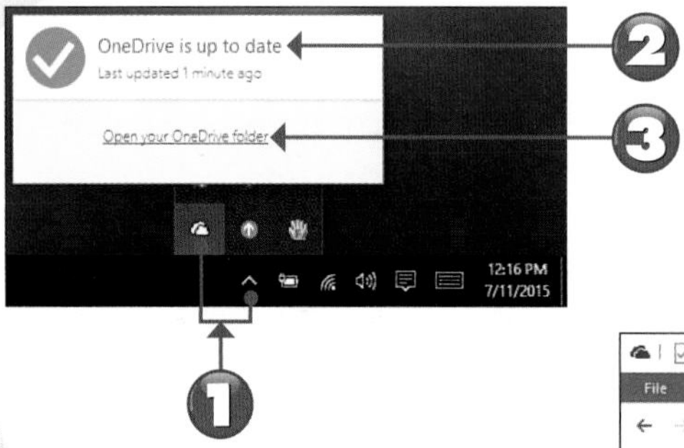

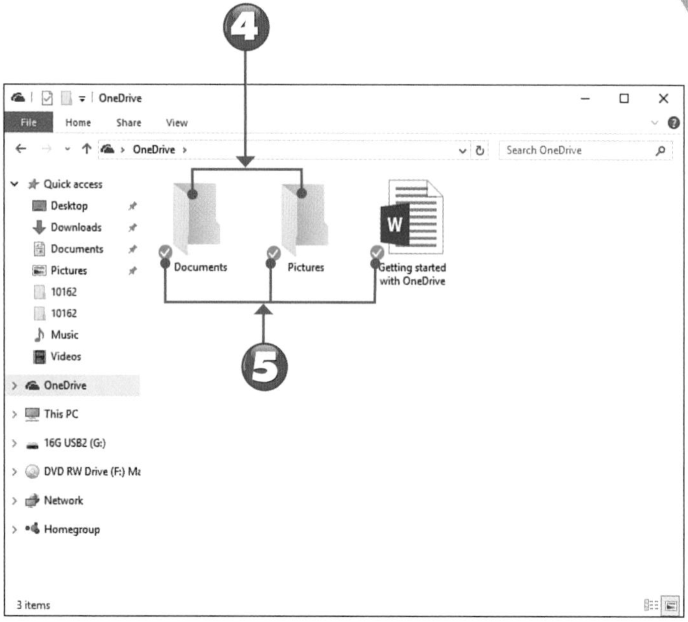

Start

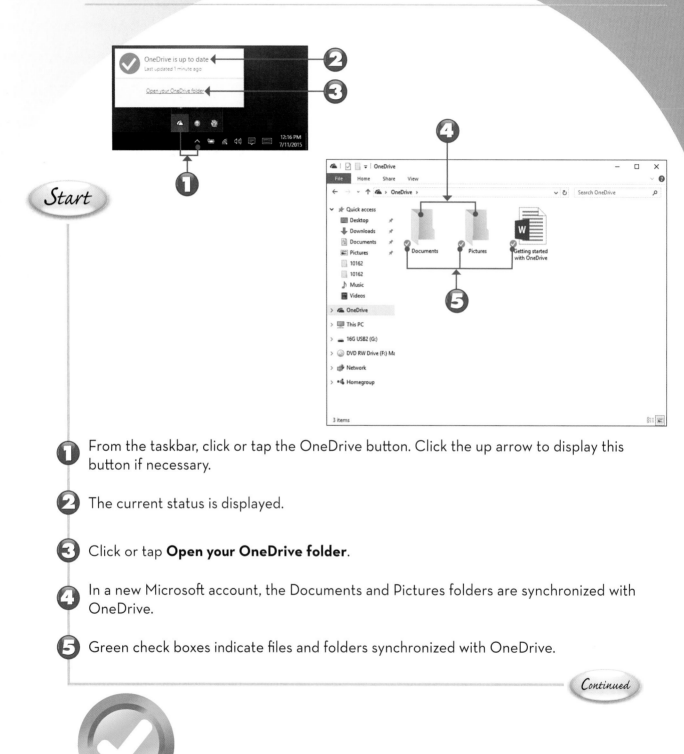

1. From the taskbar, click or tap the OneDrive button. Click the up arrow to display this button if necessary.
2. The current status is displayed.
3. Click or tap **Open your OneDrive folder**.
4. In a new Microsoft account, the Documents and Pictures folders are synchronized with OneDrive.
5. Green check boxes indicate files and folders synchronized with OneDrive.

Continued

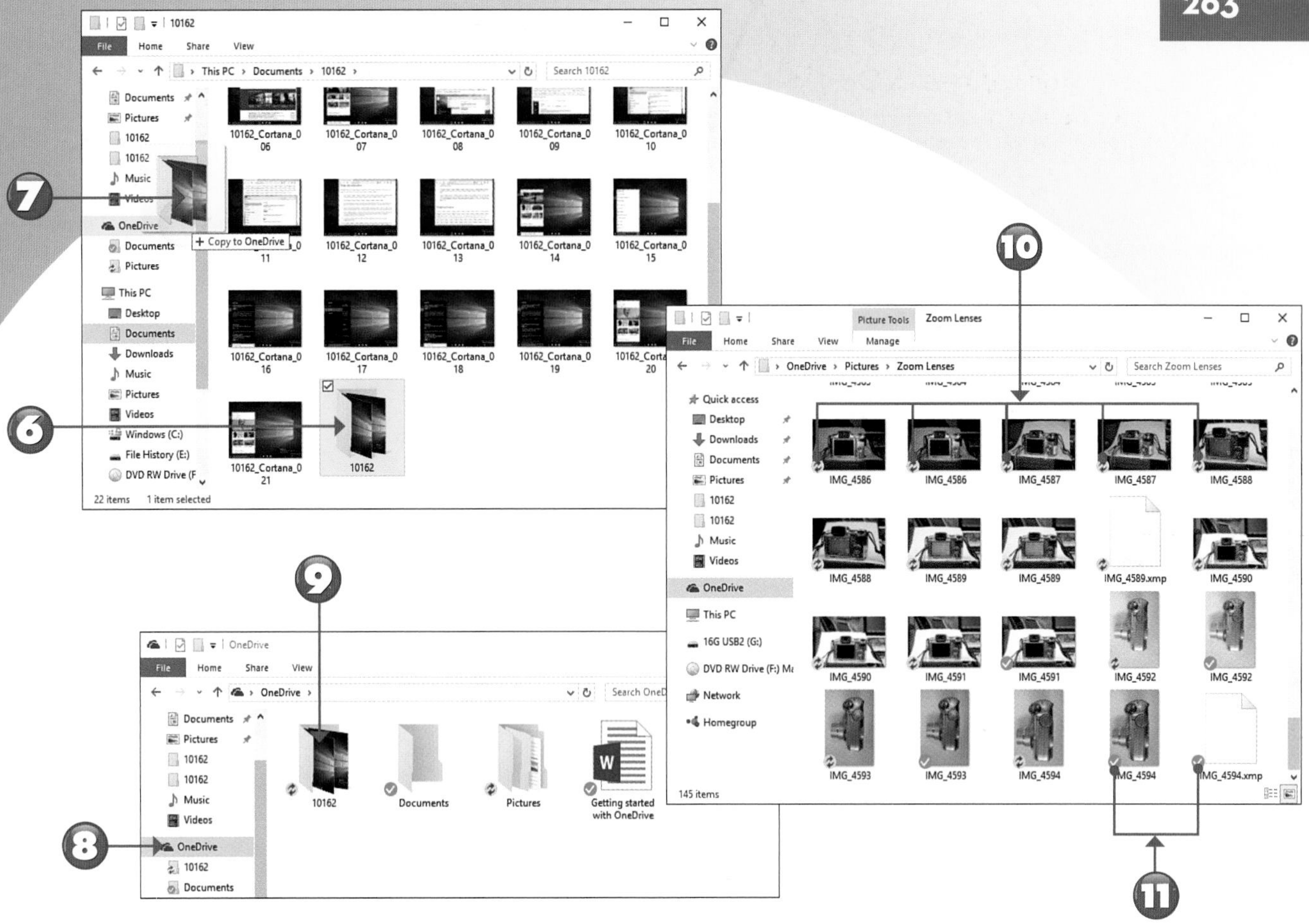

6. Click or tap a folder to sync.
7. Copy it to OneDrive by dragging it to the OneDrive item on the left.
8. Click or tap **OneDrive**.
9. Click or tap the folder you copied in step 7.
10. Files being synced to OneDrive are indicated with the double arrow symbol.
11. Files already synced to OneDrive have a green check mark.

End

CONFIGURING ONEDRIVE

If you have already used OneDrive on a different device, you can use it to sync files and folders stored on OneDrive with your device and configure other options. Here's how.

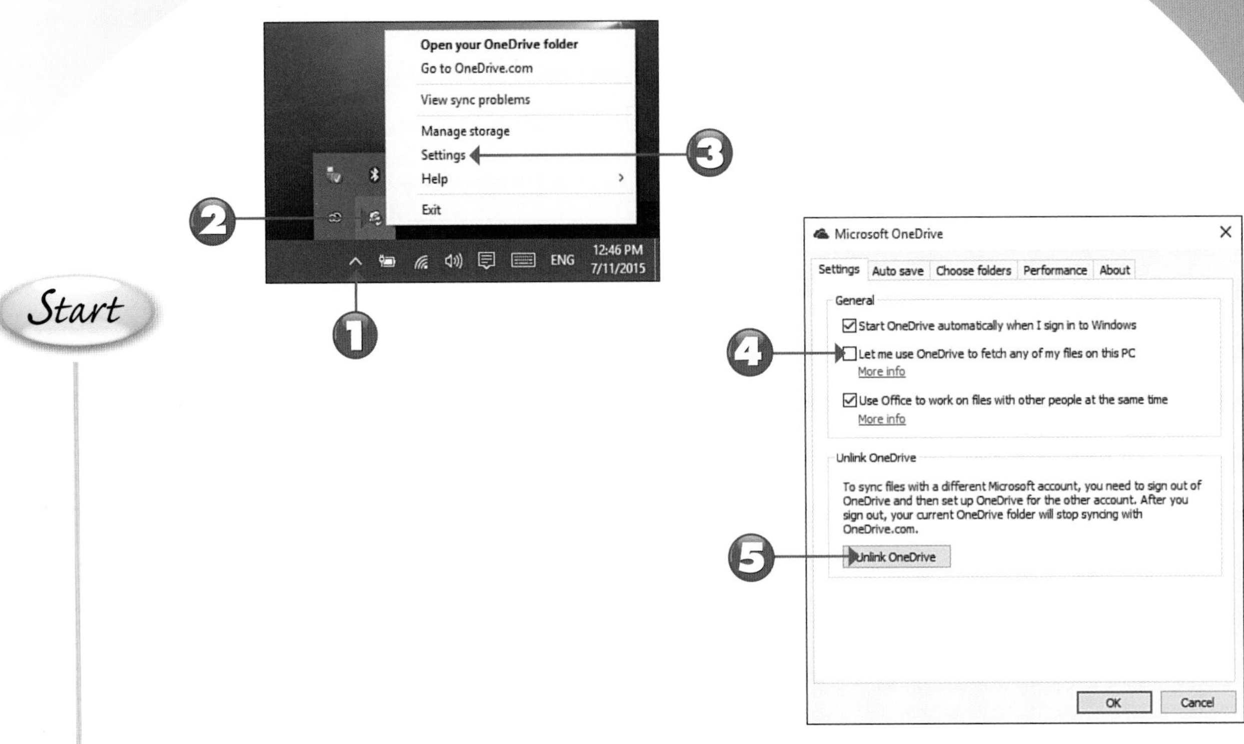

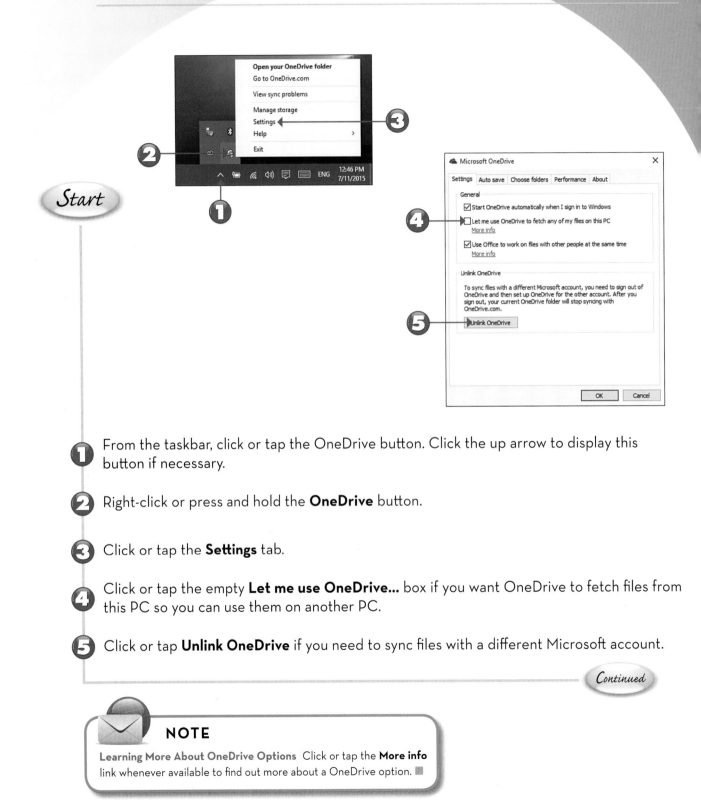

1. From the taskbar, click or tap the OneDrive button. Click the up arrow to display this button if necessary.
2. Right-click or press and hold the **OneDrive** button.
3. Click or tap the **Settings** tab.
4. Click or tap the empty **Let me use OneDrive...** box if you want OneDrive to fetch files from this PC so you can use them on another PC.
5. Click or tap **Unlink OneDrive** if you need to sync files with a different Microsoft account.

NOTE

Learning More About OneDrive Options Click or tap the **More info** link whenever available to find out more about a OneDrive option.

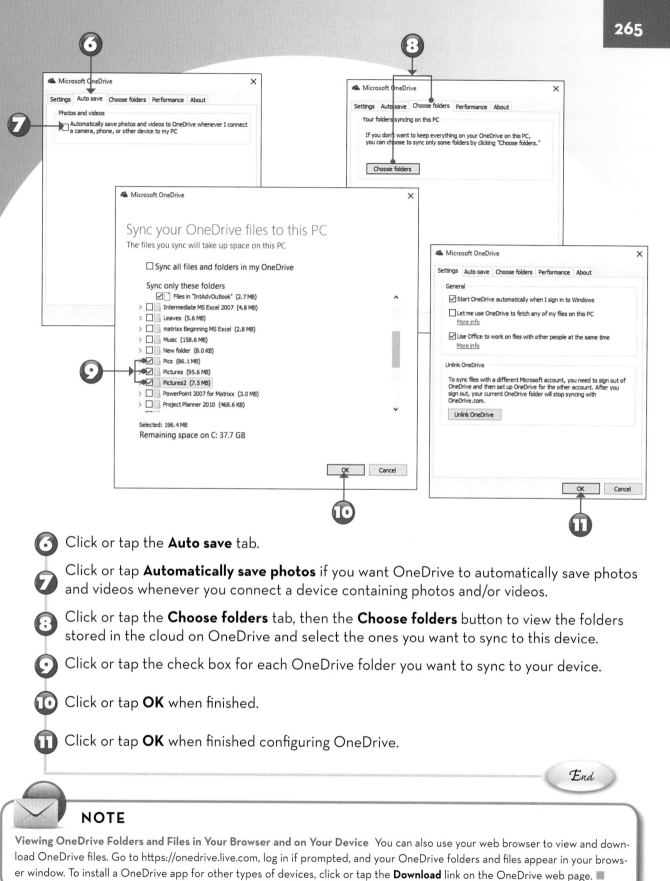

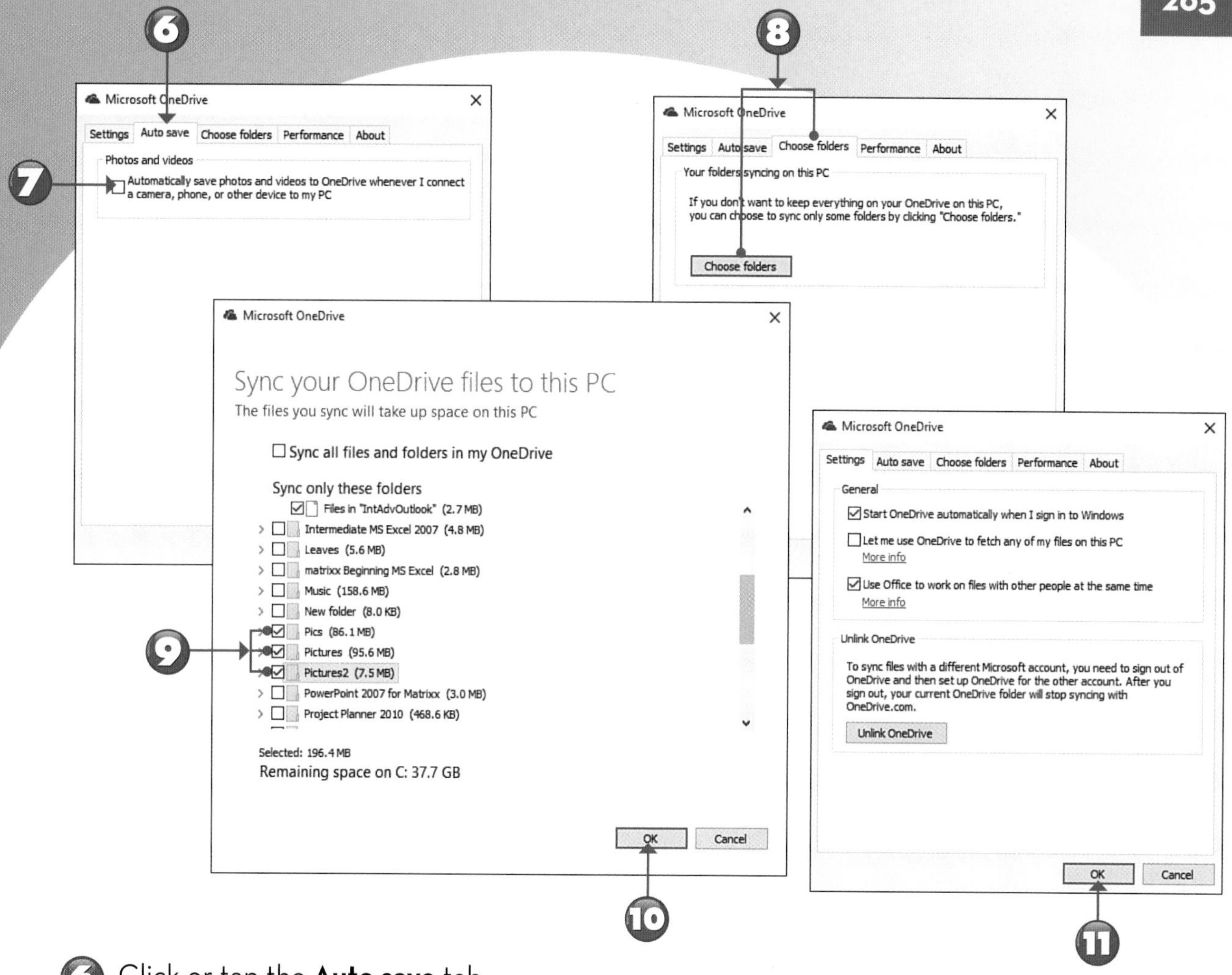

6. Click or tap the **Auto save** tab.
7. Click or tap **Automatically save photos** if you want OneDrive to automatically save photos and videos whenever you connect a device containing photos and/or videos.
8. Click or tap the **Choose folders** tab, then the **Choose folders** button to view the folders stored in the cloud on OneDrive and select the ones you want to sync to this device.
9. Click or tap the check box for each OneDrive folder you want to sync to your device.
10. Click or tap **OK** when finished.
11. Click or tap **OK** when finished configuring OneDrive.

End

NOTE

Viewing OneDrive Folders and Files in Your Browser and on Your Device You can also use your web browser to view and download OneDrive files. Go to https://onedrive.live.com, log in if prompted, and your OneDrive folders and files appear in your browser window. To install a OneDrive app for other types of devices, click or tap the **Download** link on the OneDrive web page.

DISCOVERING AND USING WINDOWS 10'S TOOLS AND ACCESSORIES

Windows 10 includes a variety of apps. Some apps, such as Money and Sports, are designed to perform a variety of tasks and are covered in other chapters. This chapter focuses on Windows accessories such as Notepad and the Snipping Tool as well as Universal apps designed for specialized tasks, such as Calculator and Alarms & Clock. Although there are differences, most apps work similarly after you open them.

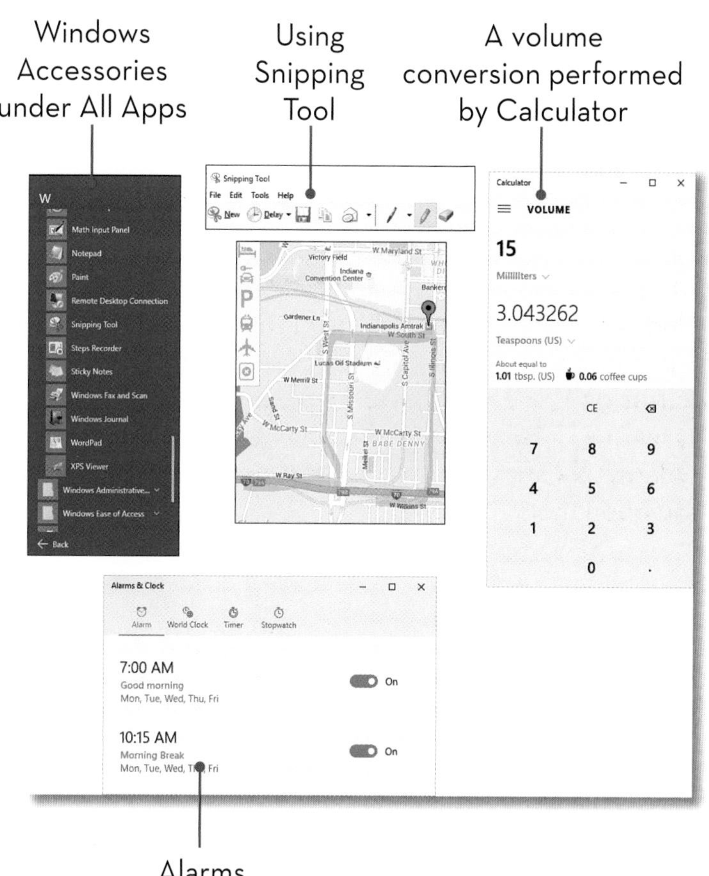
Windows Accessories under All Apps
Using Snipping Tool
A volume conversion performed by Calculator
Alarms
Snipping Tool
File Edit Tools Help
Calculator
VOLUME
15
Milliliters
3.043262
Teaspoons (US)
Alarms & Clock
Alarm World Clock Timer Stopwatch
7:00 AM
Good morning
Mon, Tue, Wed, Thu, Fri
10:15 AM
Morning Break

FINDING ACCESSORIES AND TOOLS FROM THE START MENU

To find Windows tools from the Start menu, you must dig into the All Apps menu. Here's what you'll find.

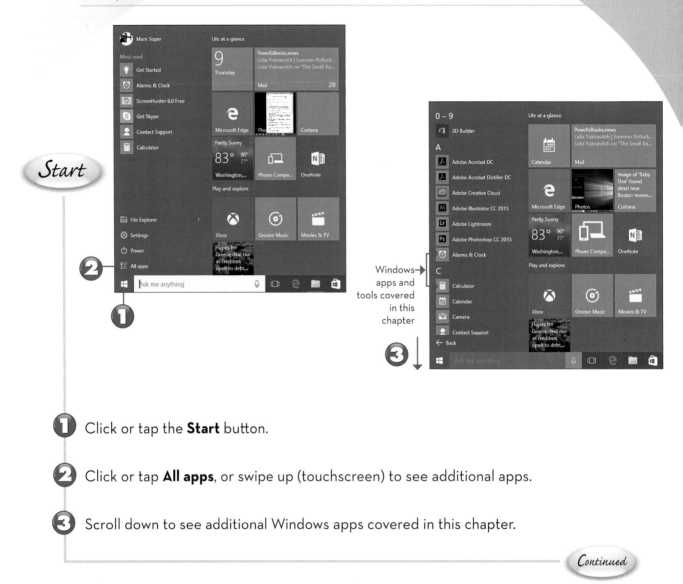

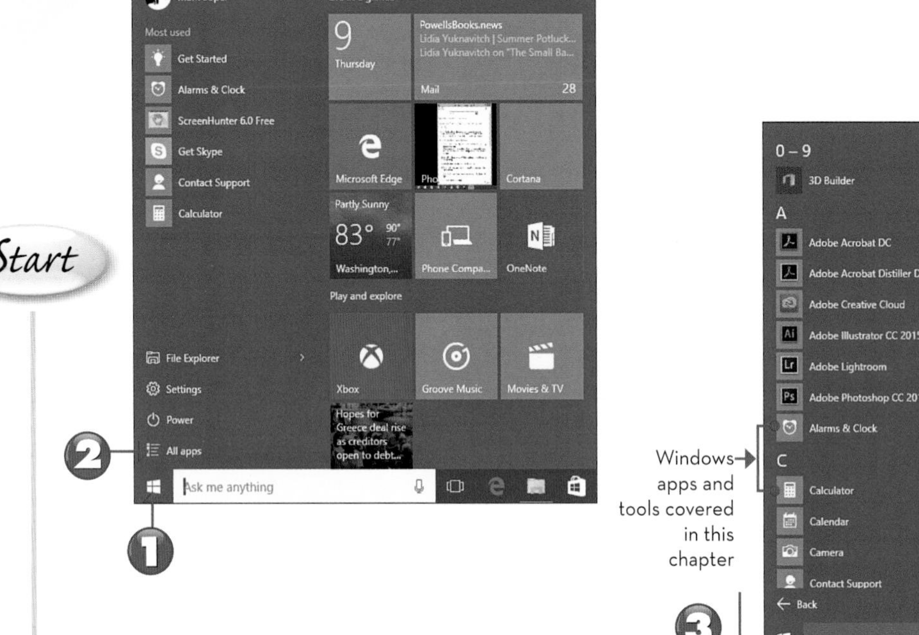

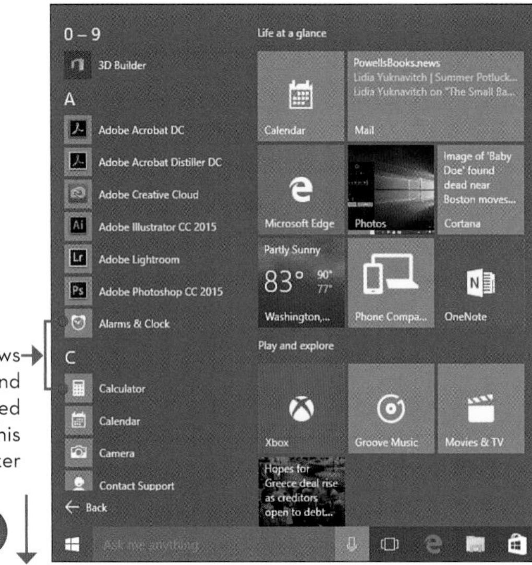

1. Click or tap the **Start** button.
2. Click or tap **All apps**, or swipe up (touchscreen) to see additional apps.
3. Scroll down to see additional Windows apps covered in this chapter.

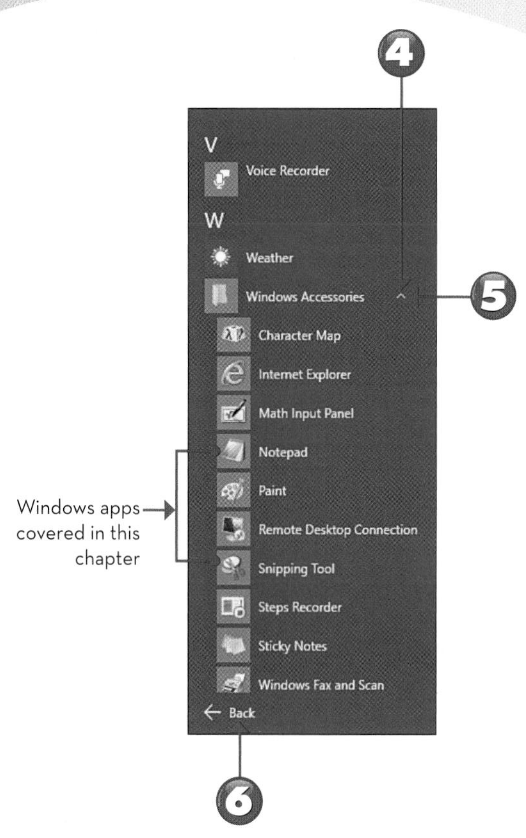

4. Click or tap the arrow for **Windows Accessories** folder to see more Windows tools.
5. Click or tap the arrow to close the folder.
6. Click or tap to return to Start.

End

SETTING ALARMS WITH THE ALARMS & CLOCK APP

You can use the Alarms & Clock app as a stopwatch, an alarm clock, or a timer. Here's how to use it as an alarm clock for a morning break Monday through Friday.

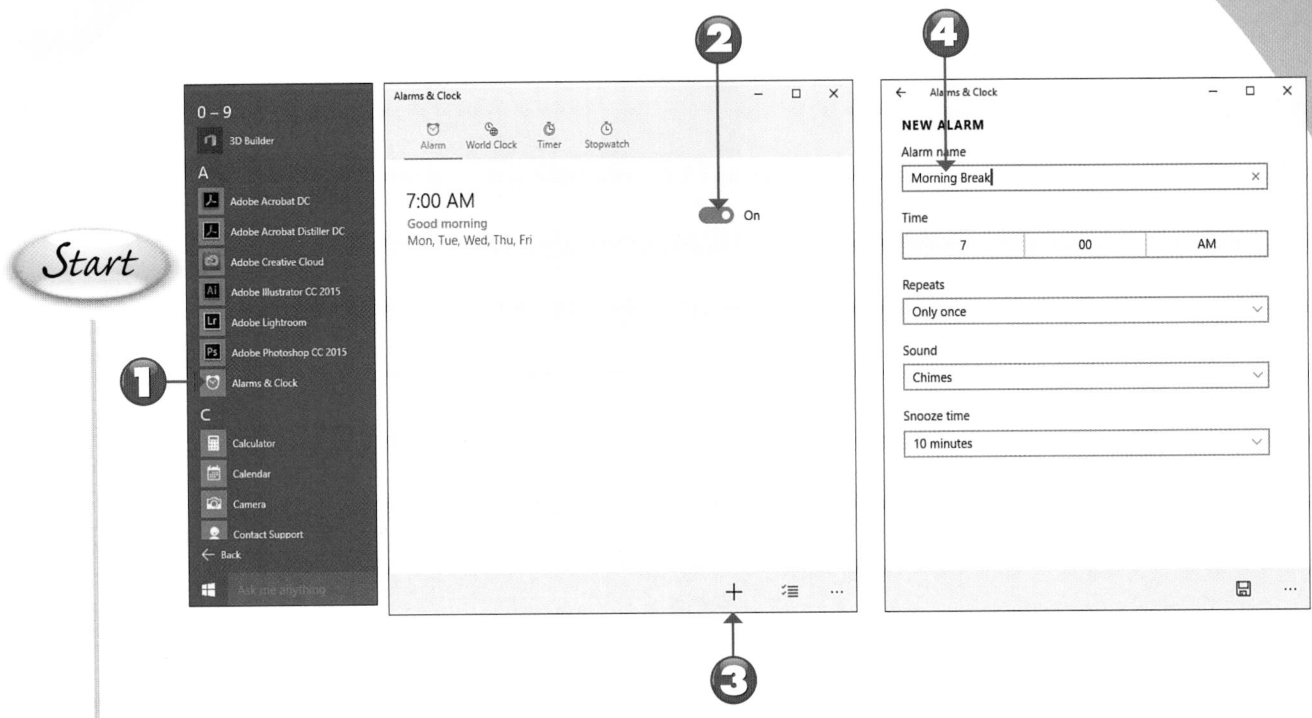

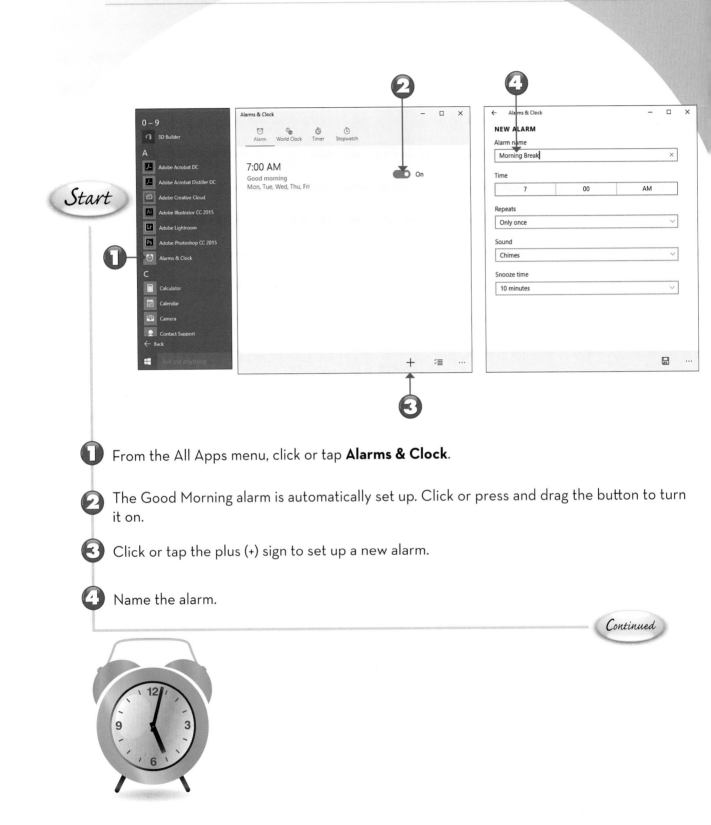

1. From the All Apps menu, click or tap **Alarms & Clock**.
2. The Good Morning alarm is automatically set up. Click or press and drag the button to turn it on.
3. Click or tap the plus (+) sign to set up a new alarm.
4. Name the alarm.

Continued

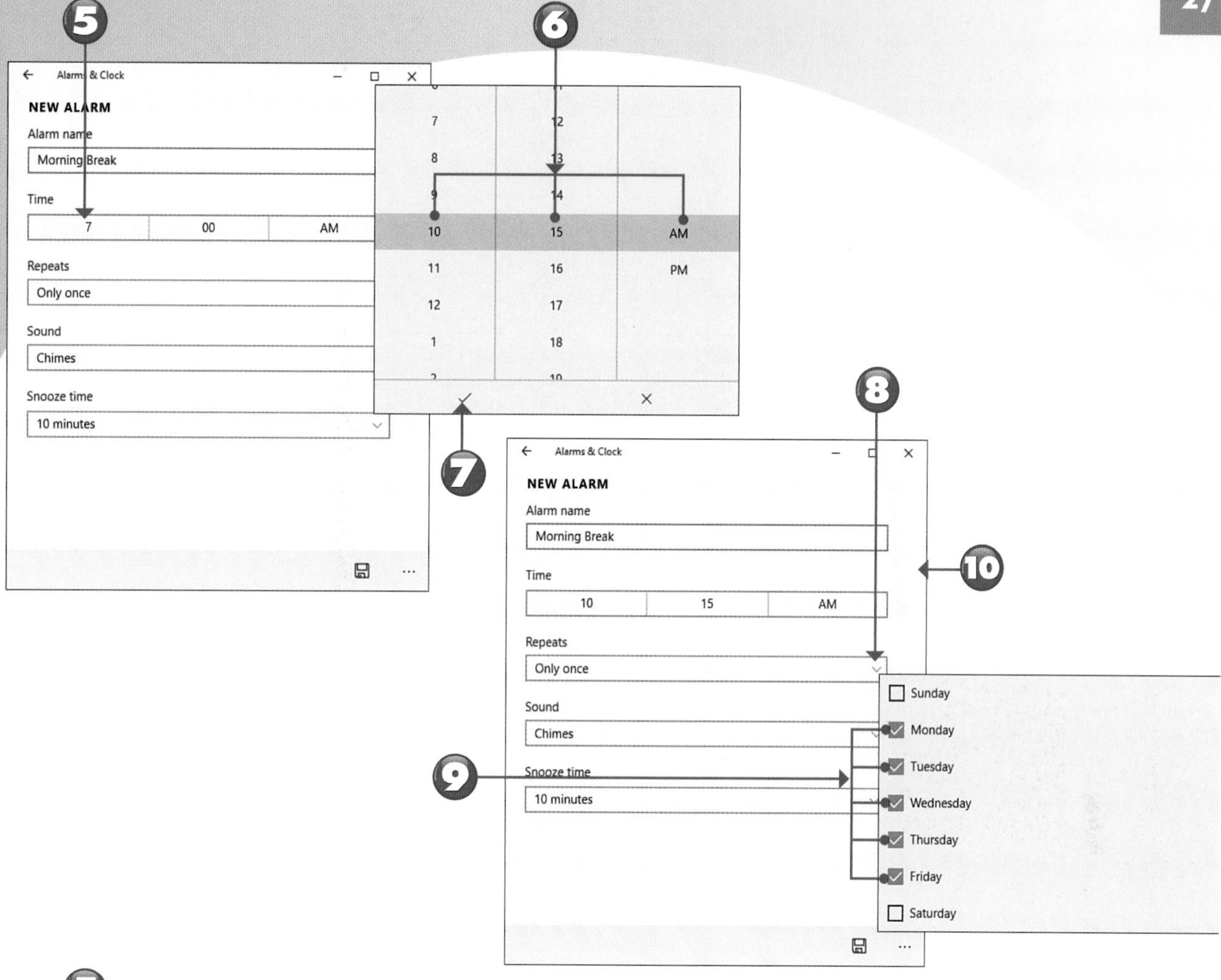

5 Click or tap to change the time.

6 Click or tap each column and scroll with finger or mouse to select hour, minute, and AM/PM.

7 Click or tap the check mark when done.

8 Click or tap to select which day(s) of the week the alarm repeats.

9 Click or tap the check box for each day of the week.

10 Click or tap outside the day field to accept changes.

Continued

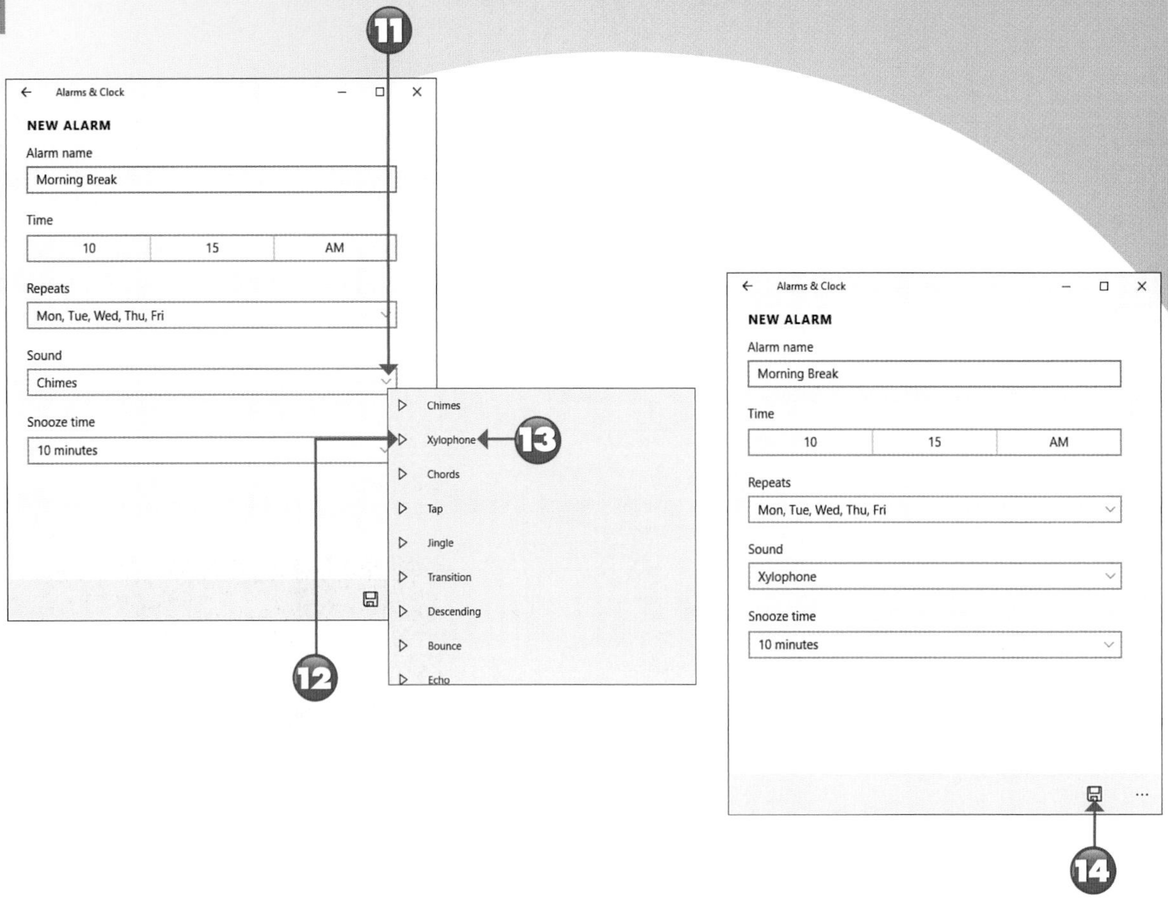

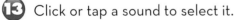

11 Click or tap to select a different sound.

12 Click or tap to preview a sound.

13 Click or tap a sound to select it.

14 Click the **Save** icon to save the alarm.

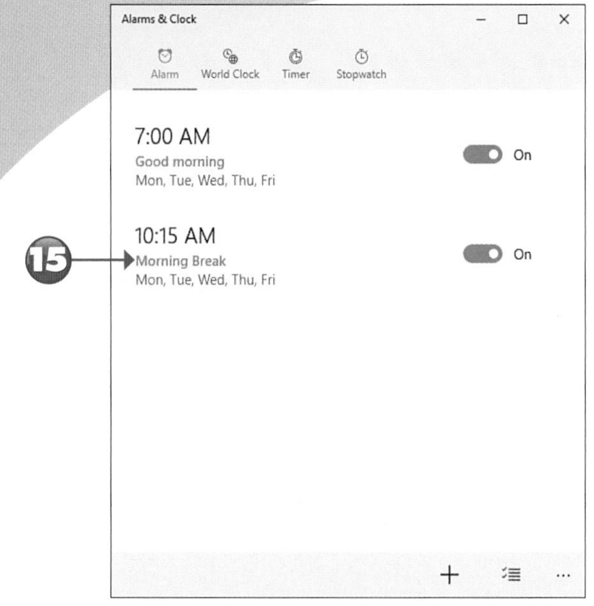

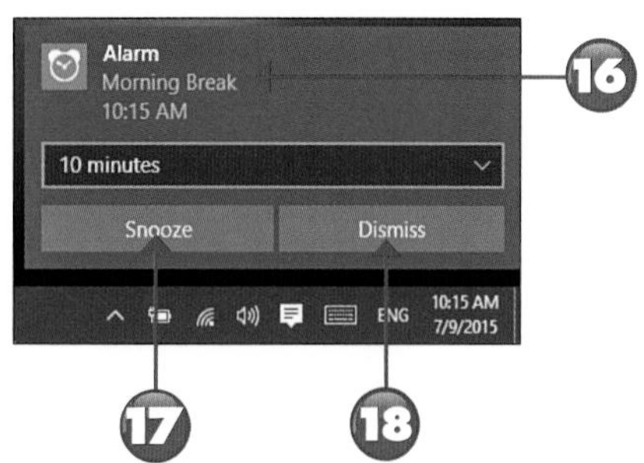

15 You see the new alarm on the Alarms & Clock app screen.

16 The alarm is displayed in the Notification area when triggered.

17 Click or tap to snooze the alarm.

18 Click or tap to shut off the alarm.

End

CONVERTING NUMBER VALUES WITH CALCULATOR

Windows 10's Calculator includes a powerful conversion feature as well as standard and scientific calculations. Here's how to use it.

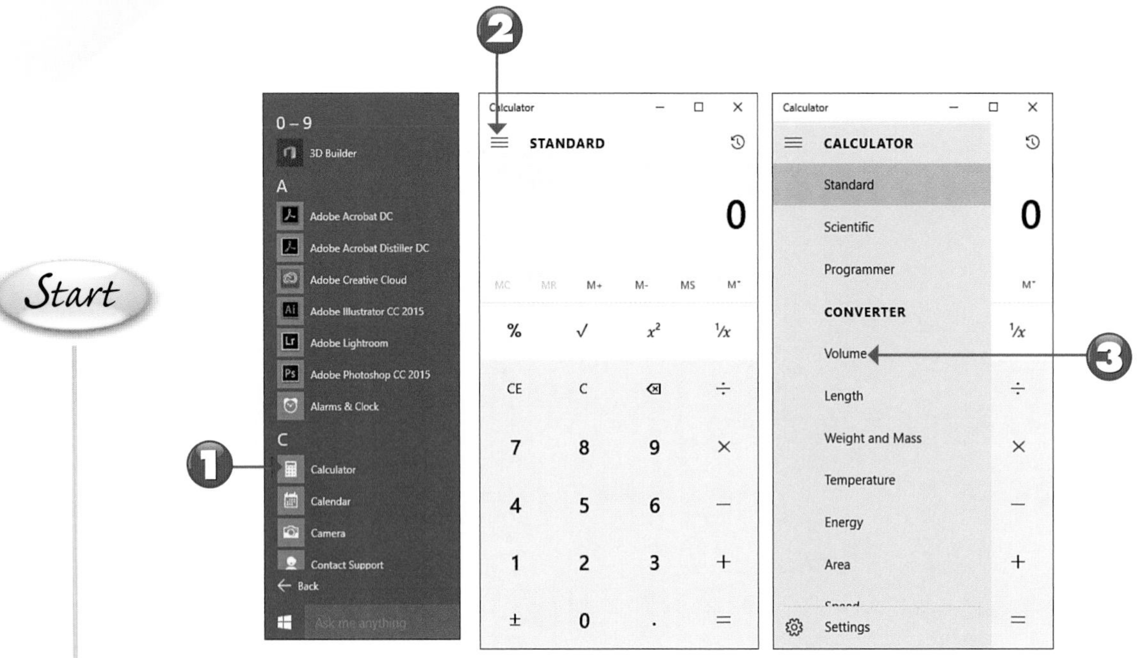

1. Click or tap **Calculator** from the All Apps menu.
2. Click or tap the **Menu** button.
3. Select the type of conversion to perform.

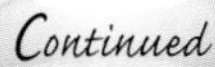

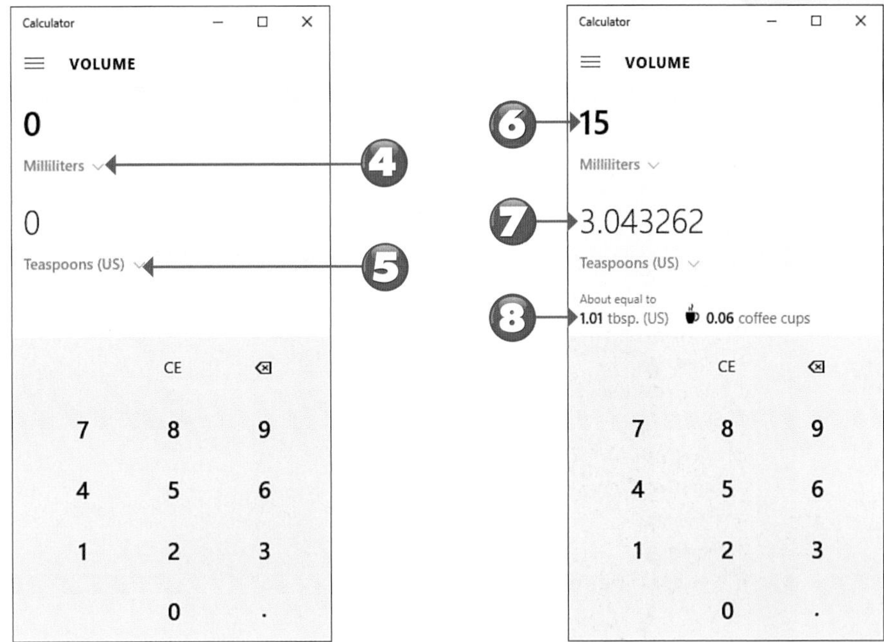

4. Select the units to convert from.
5. Select the units to convert to.
6. Enter the value.
7. The answer appears.
8. Other common measurements for the value.

End

ENABLING WORD WRAP IN NOTEPAD

Notepad is a simple text editor included in Windows 10. You can use it for note taking and for creating lists of items. When you type a long line of text into Notepad, the text might extend past the right edge of the window. Here's how to search for an app and set Notepad so you can see all of the text.

Start

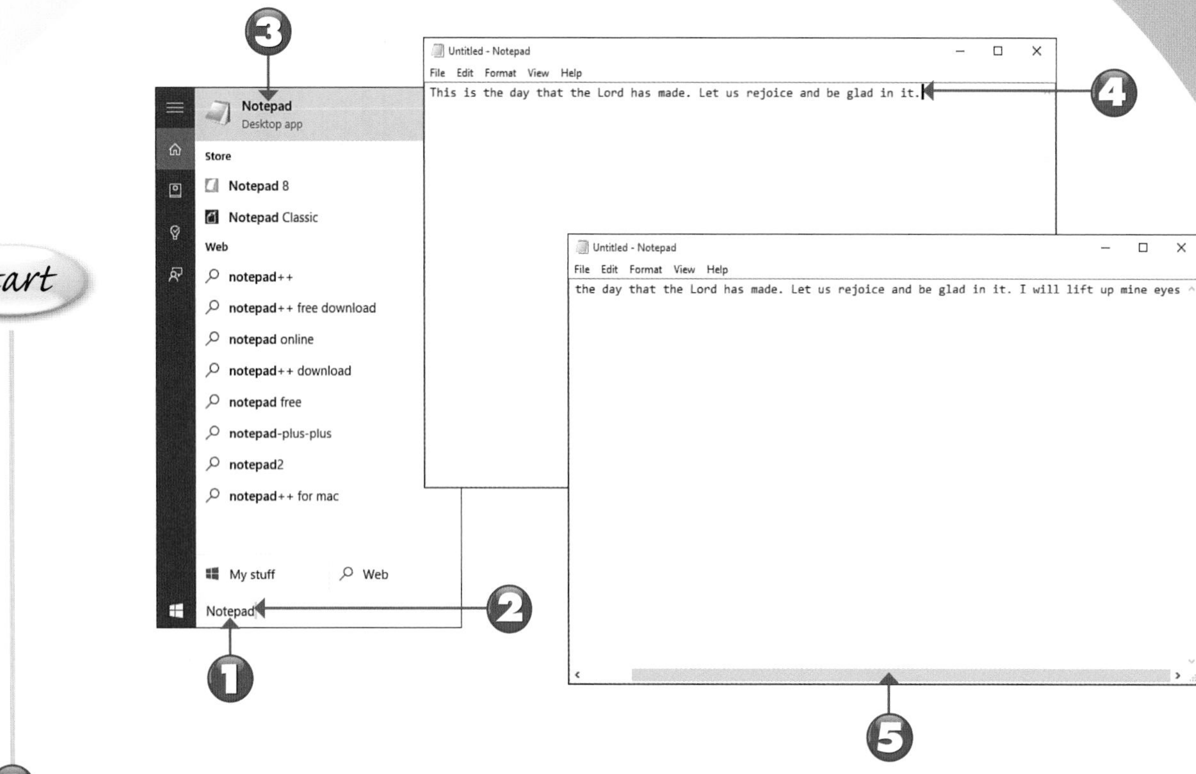

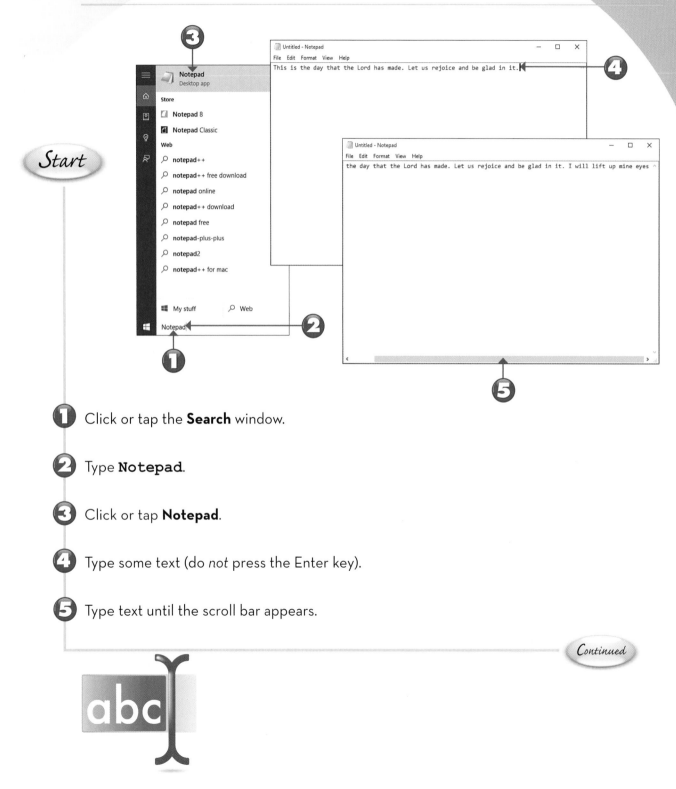

1. Click or tap the **Search** window.
2. Type **`Notepad`**.
3. Click or tap **Notepad**.
4. Type some text (do *not* press the Enter key).
5. Type text until the scroll bar appears.

Continued

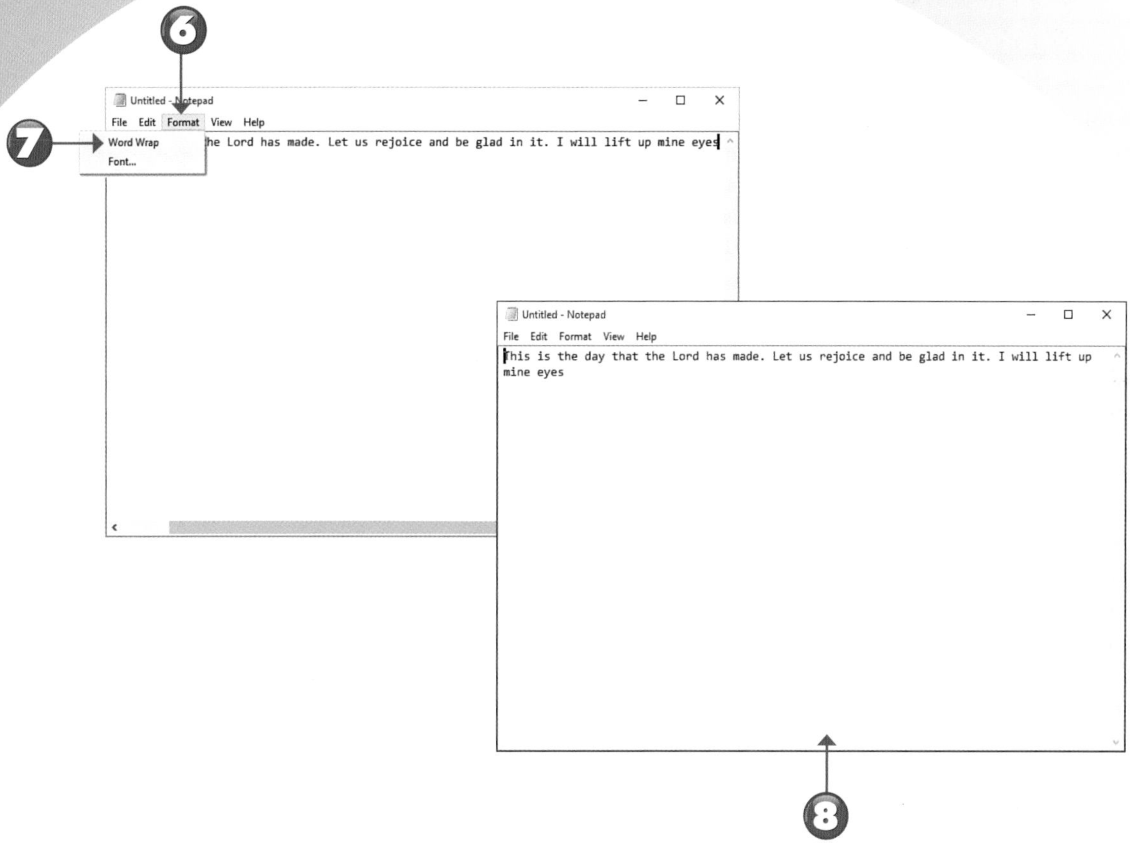

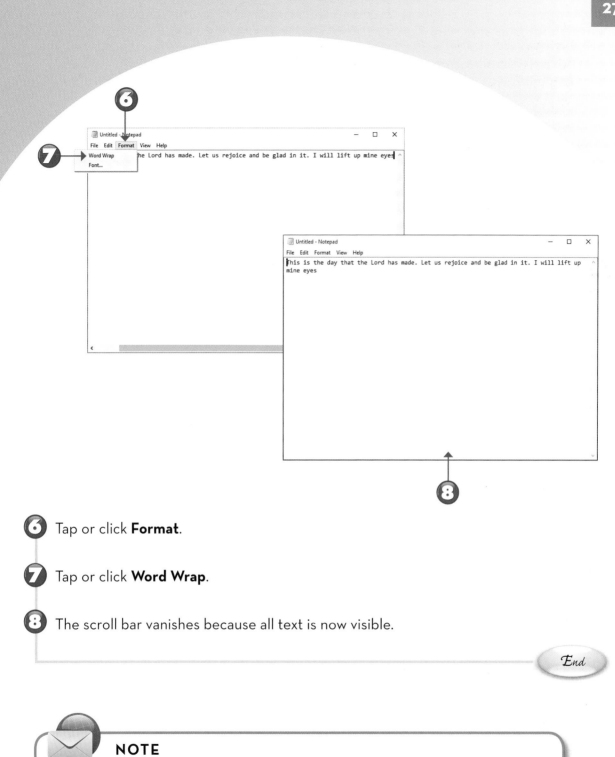

6. Tap or click **Format**.

7. Tap or click **Word Wrap**.

8. The scroll bar vanishes because all text is now visible.

End

NOTE

Word Wrap Benefits and Drawbacks Enable Word Wrap to see an entire paragraph without scrolling or if you want to print your Notepad text. However, if you are using Notepad along with another app, such as WordPad, Word, or a web browser, be sure to disable Word Wrap before copying and pasting text. If you leave Word Wrap enabled, the line breaks you see onscreen will also be used when the text is pasted.

CAPTURING SCREENS WITH SNIPPING TOOL

If you want to turn what you see on your Windows desktop into a picture file, give Snipping Tool a try. This example shows you how to use Snipping Tool to capture part of a web page that's already open.

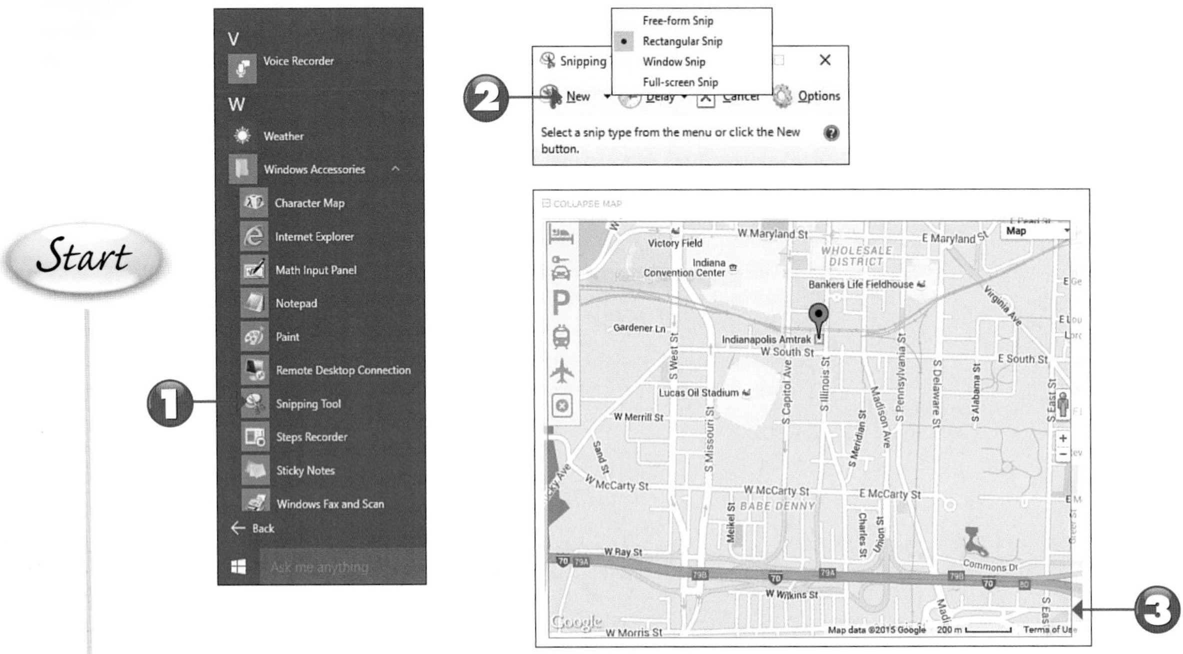

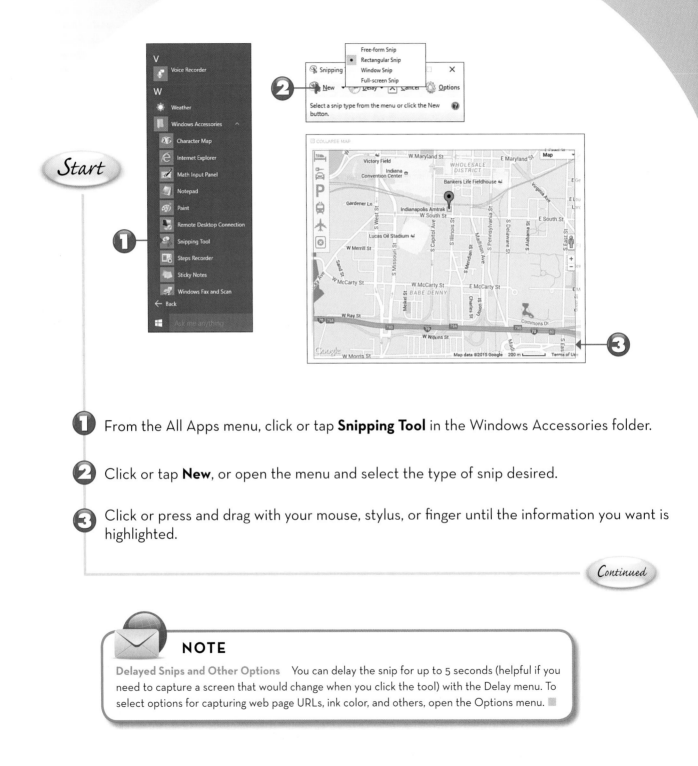

1. From the All Apps menu, click or tap **Snipping Tool** in the Windows Accessories folder.

2. Click or tap **New**, or open the menu and select the type of snip desired.

3. Click or press and drag with your mouse, stylus, or finger until the information you want is highlighted.

Continued

NOTE

Delayed Snips and Other Options You can delay the snip for up to 5 seconds (helpful if you need to capture a screen that would change when you click the tool) with the Delay menu. To select options for capturing web page URLs, ink color, and others, open the Options menu.

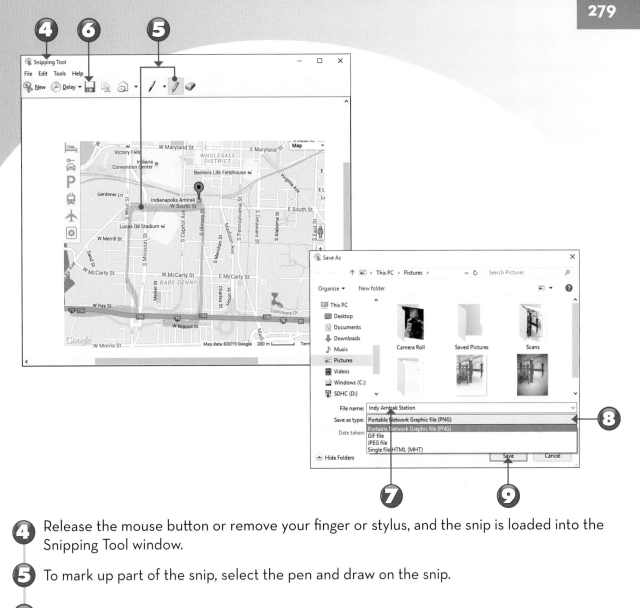

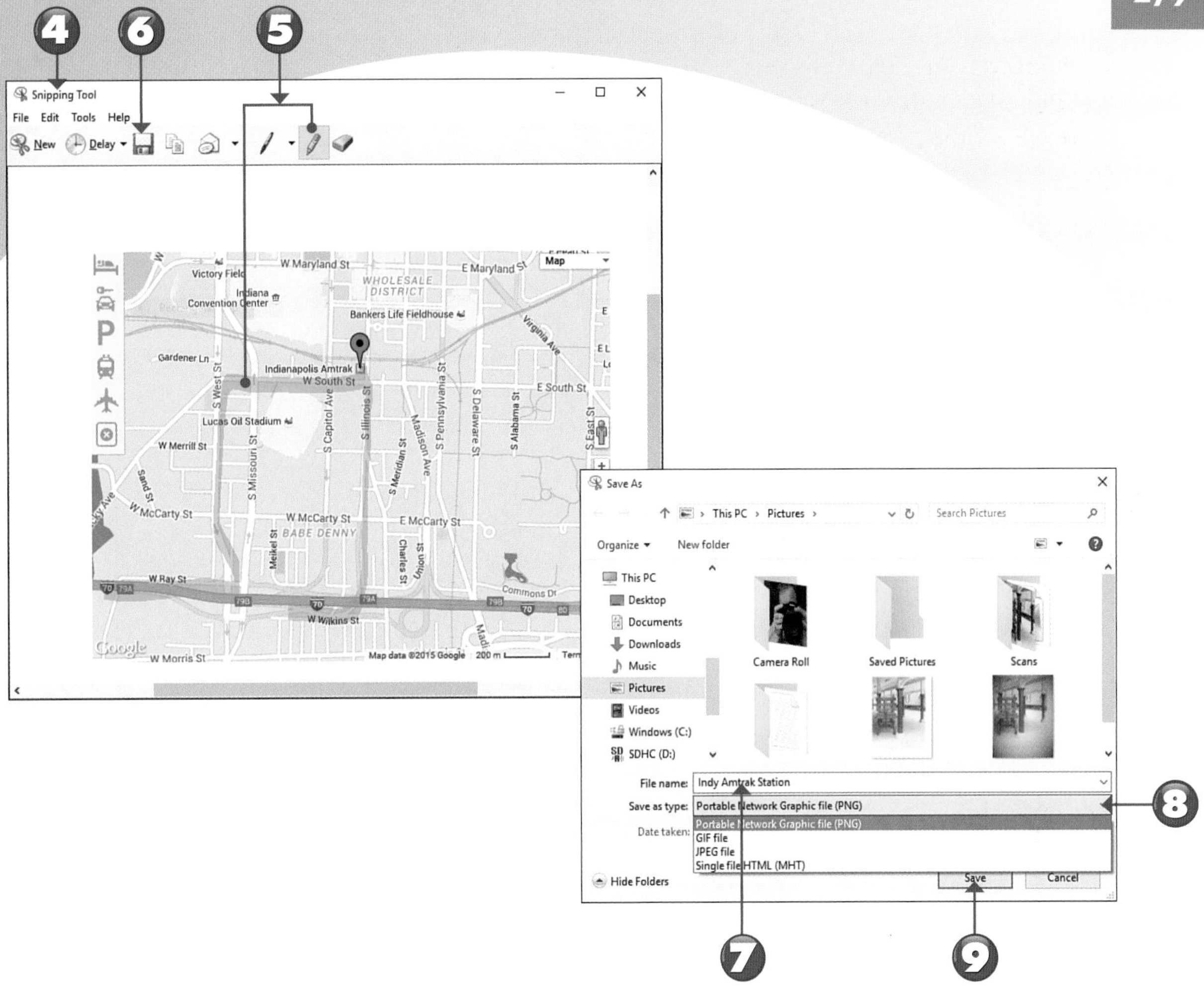

4. Release the mouse button or remove your finger or stylus, and the snip is loaded into the Snipping Tool window.
5. To mark up part of the snip, select the pen and draw on the snip.
6. Click or tap **Save**.
7. Enter a new name for the capture (the default is Capture).
8. To change the file type, click or tap and select the file type desired.
9. Click or tap **Save**.

End

NOTE

Ink Colors, Highlight, and Erase To change the ink color when drawing, open the Pen menu. To highlight part of the snip, use the Highlight tool. To erase ink or highlighting, use the Eraser tool.

USING THE WINDOWS STORE

You can use the Windows Store app to shop online for more apps and for TV shows and movies. The Windows Store features a variety of apps and media content, for a variety of uses, and it has been streamlined in Windows 10. You can find plenty of free apps, paid apps, and trial versions in the Store using the Search or Categories view. In this chapter, you learn how to navigate the Store to find just the right apps for you and your device.

Windows Store Home screen

Rating an app

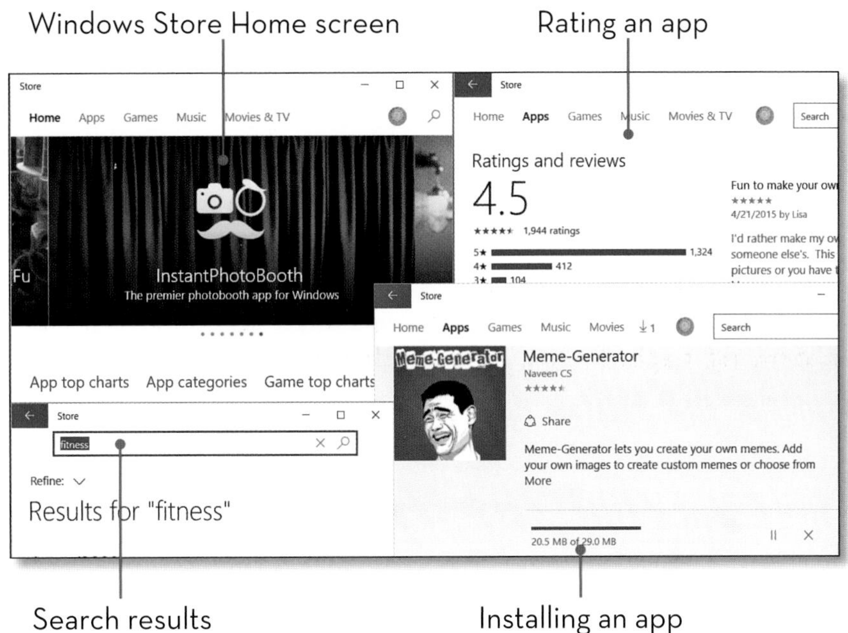

Search results

Installing an app

GOING TO THE STORE

When you initially open the Windows Store app, the first screen displays the currently featured app and links to the most popular apps and new releases. As you scroll through the Store, you can find new apps and the most popular paid and free apps.

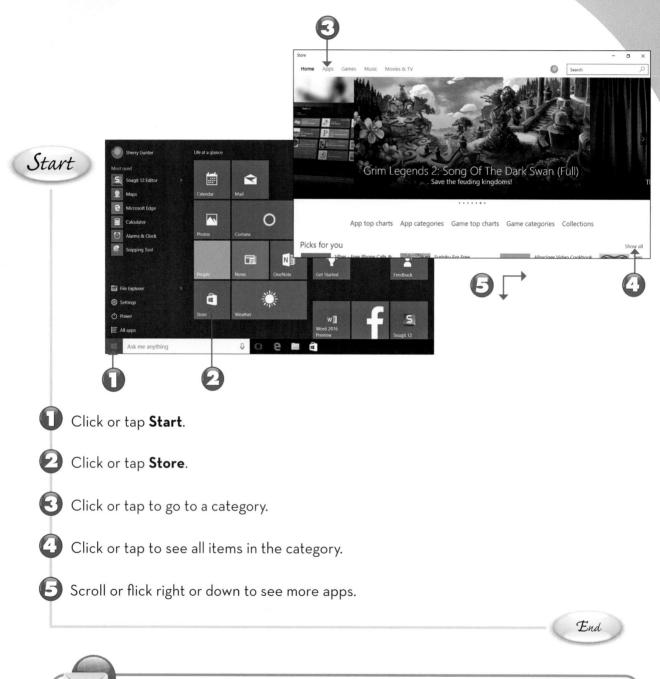

Start

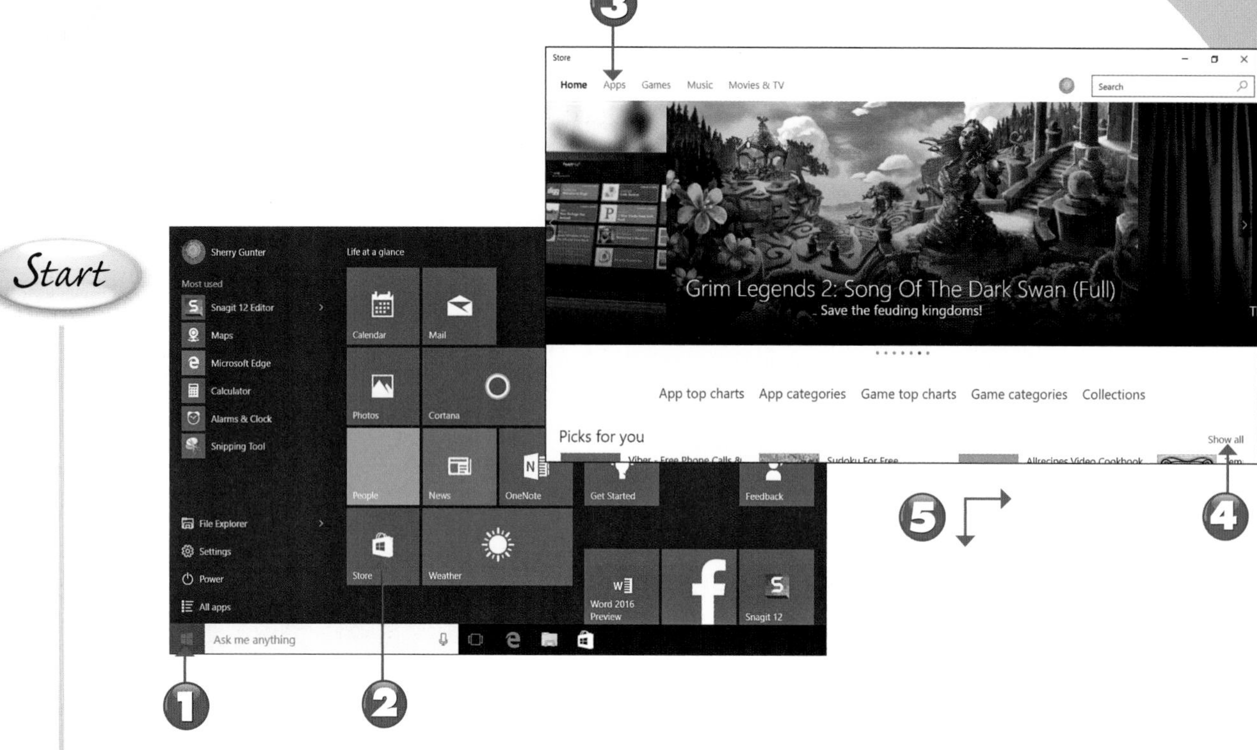

1. Click or tap **Start**.
2. Click or tap **Store**.
3. Click or tap to go to a category.
4. Click or tap to see all items in the category.
5. Scroll or flick right or down to see more apps.

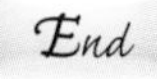

NOTE

Picks for You After you visit the Store and download or purchase content, the next time you open the Store, you see a "Picks for You" category below the app categories (see the next exercise). These choices are based on the apps you have downloaded or what people with similar interests are downloading or purchasing.

SEARCHING FOR APPS BY NAME

You can use the Windows Store Search window to search the Store for a specific app or type of app. Here's how to search for your favorite app.

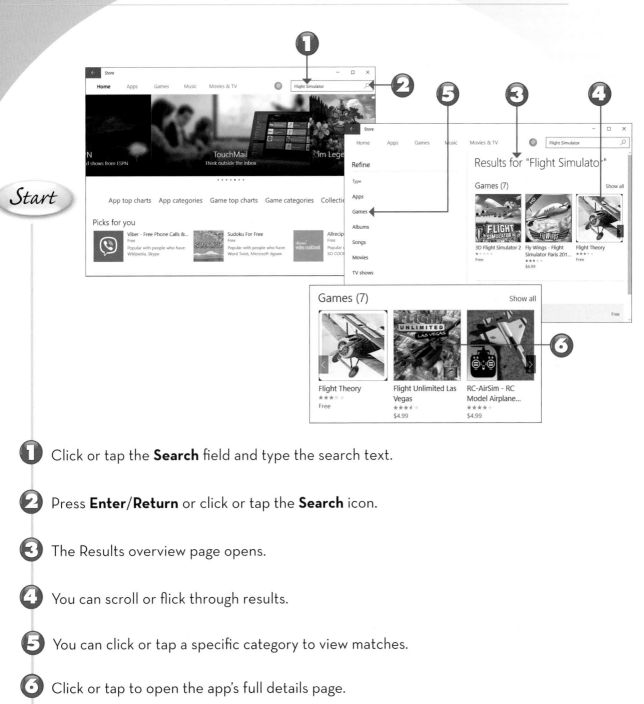

1. Click or tap the **Search** field and type the search text.
2. Press **Enter/Return** or click or tap the **Search** icon.
3. The Results overview page opens.
4. You can scroll or flick through results.
5. You can click or tap a specific category to view matches.
6. Click or tap to open the app's full details page.

End

REVIEWING AN APP

When you go to an app's details page, here's what to look for as you decide whether to download or buy the app.

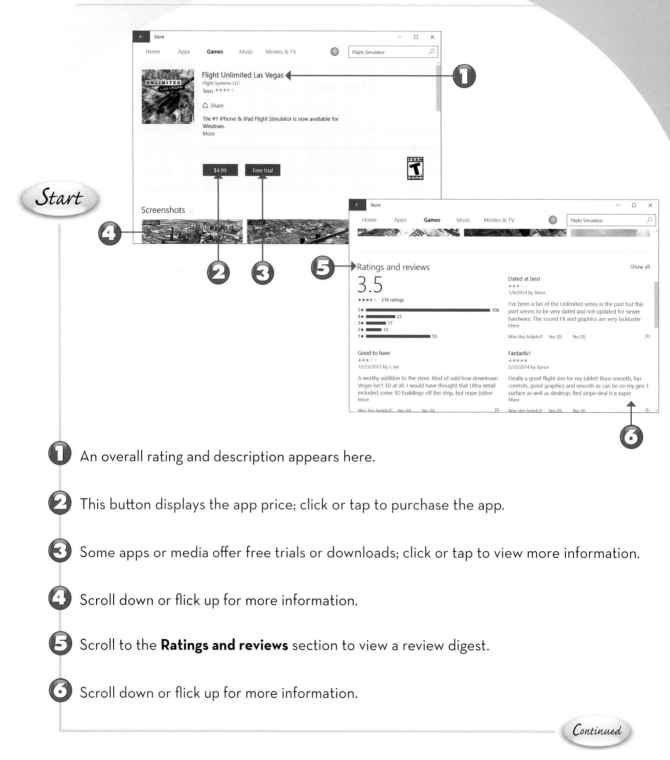

Start

1. An overall rating and description appears here.
2. This button displays the app price; click or tap to purchase the app.
3. Some apps or media offer free trials or downloads; click or tap to view more information.
4. Scroll down or flick up for more information.
5. Scroll to the **Ratings and reviews** section to view a review digest.
6. Scroll down or flick up for more information.

Continued

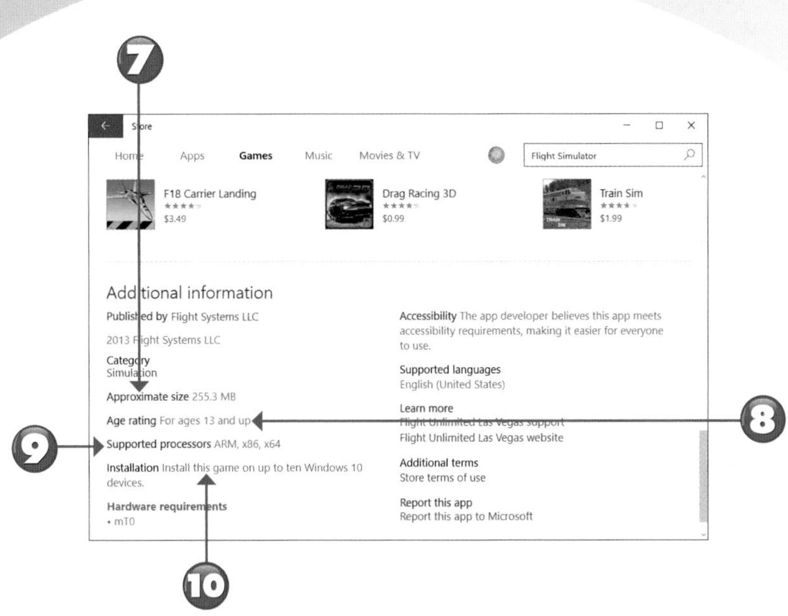

7. The app size is listed here.
8. View the app's age rating here.
9. You can read which processors work with the app.
10. Installation details appear here.

NOTE

Supported Processors x86 and x64 work on PCs and devices with 32-bit or 64-bit Intel or AMD processors; ARM works on Windows RT devices such as Microsoft Surface and Surface 2.

BROWSING FOR APPS BY CATEGORY

The Windows Store also enables you to browse by category or collection. Here's how to open the category view from the Home page.

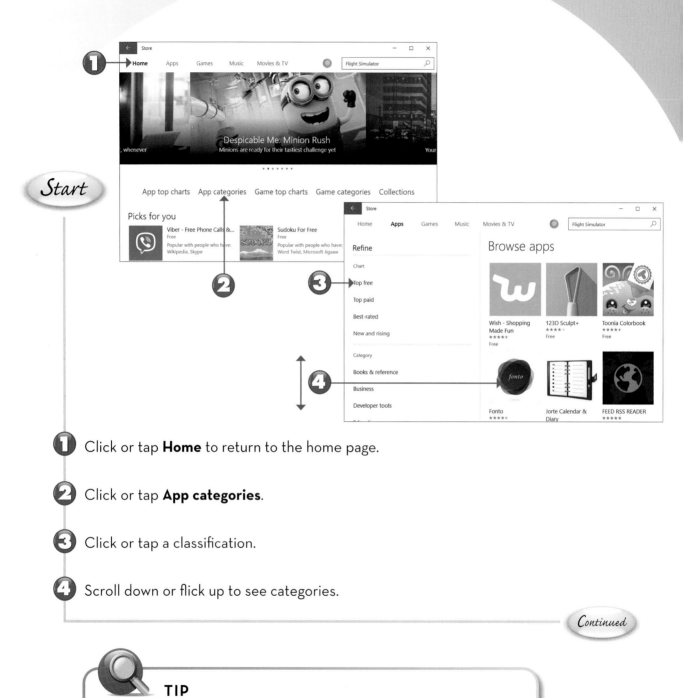

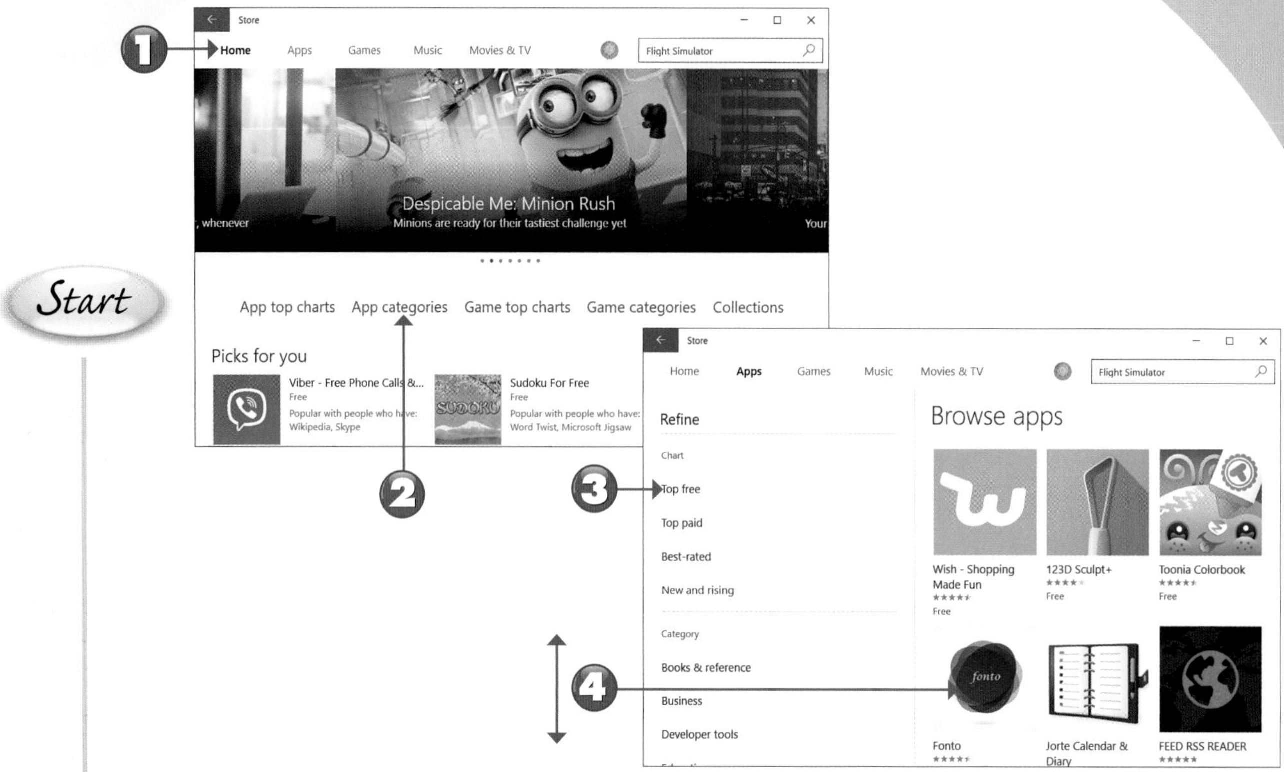

Start

1. Click or tap **Home** to return to the home page.
2. Click or tap **App categories**.
3. Click or tap a classification.
4. Scroll down or flick up to see categories.

Continued

TIP

Turning Your Local Account into a Microsoft Account To turn your local account into a Microsoft account, open **Settings**, click or tap **Accounts**, click or tap **Your account**, click or tap **Sign in with a Microsoft account instead**, and **Create one**! The process that follows is similar to the one used to create a Microsoft account for another user. See "Adding a User Who Needs a Microsoft Account," starting with step 4, Chapter 22, p. 412.

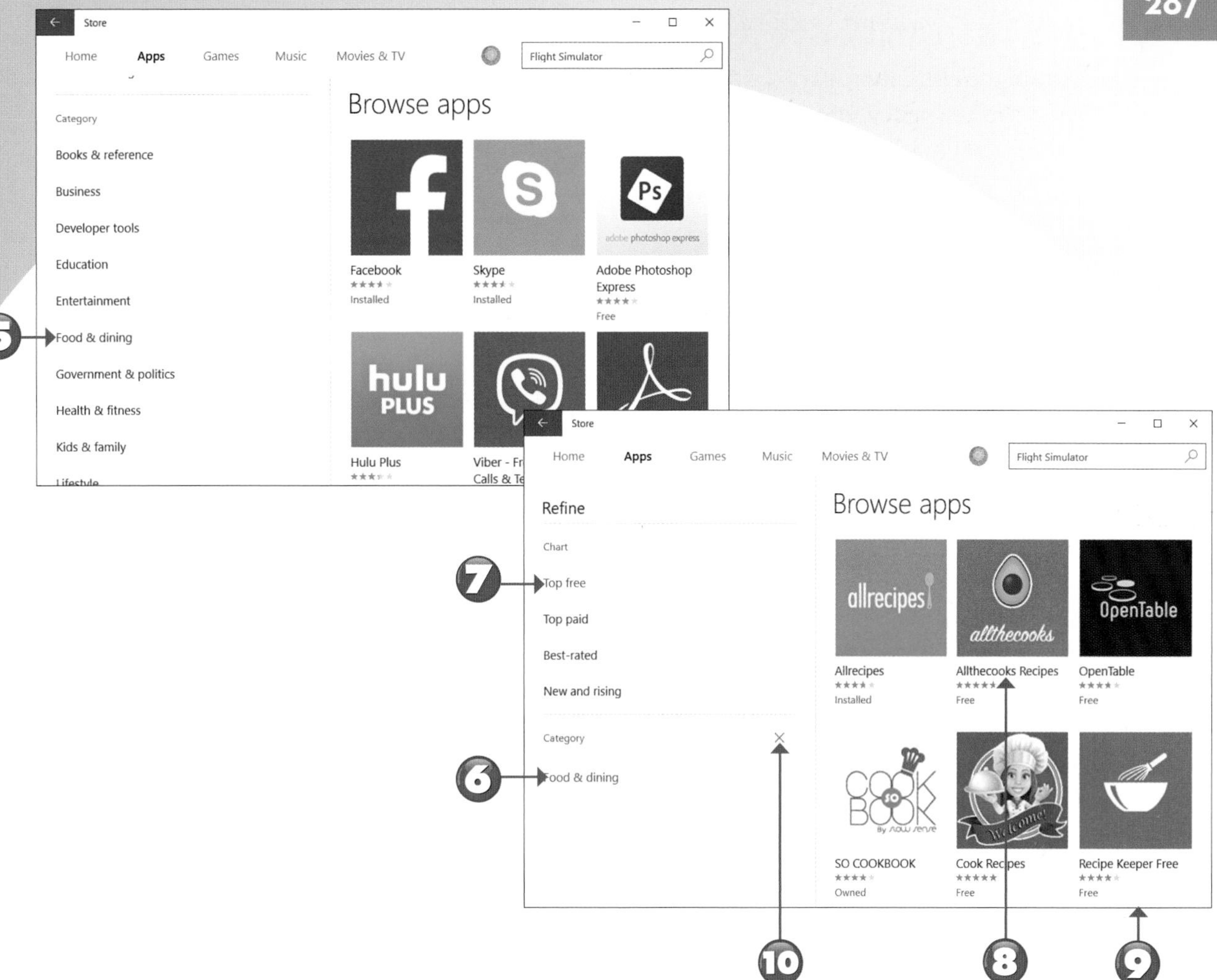

5. Click or tap a category.
6. The selected category is highlighted here.
7. The selected classification is highlighted here.
8. View the name, rating, and price of an app here.
9. Scroll or flick to see more matches.
10. Click or tap to see all categories listed again.

End

INSTALLING AN APP

When you find an app you want, you can easily install it in just a few clicks. Windows does most of the hard work for you. When you install an app, the app is added to the Windows All apps menu.

Start

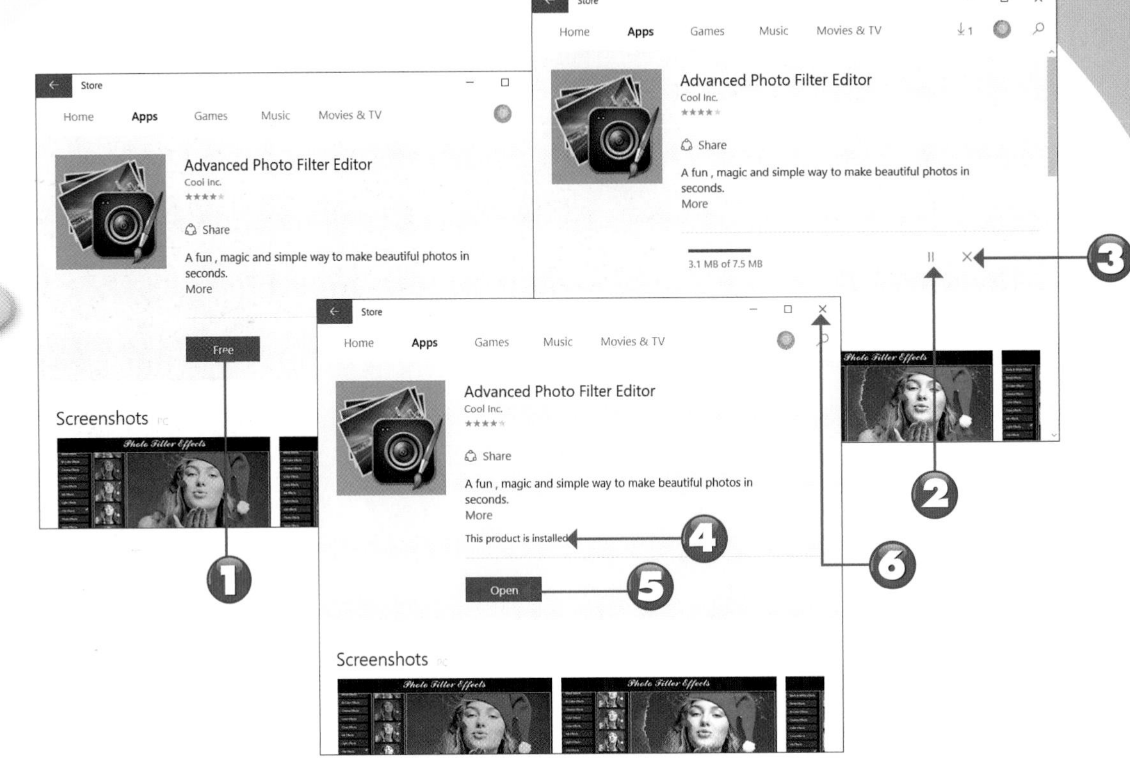

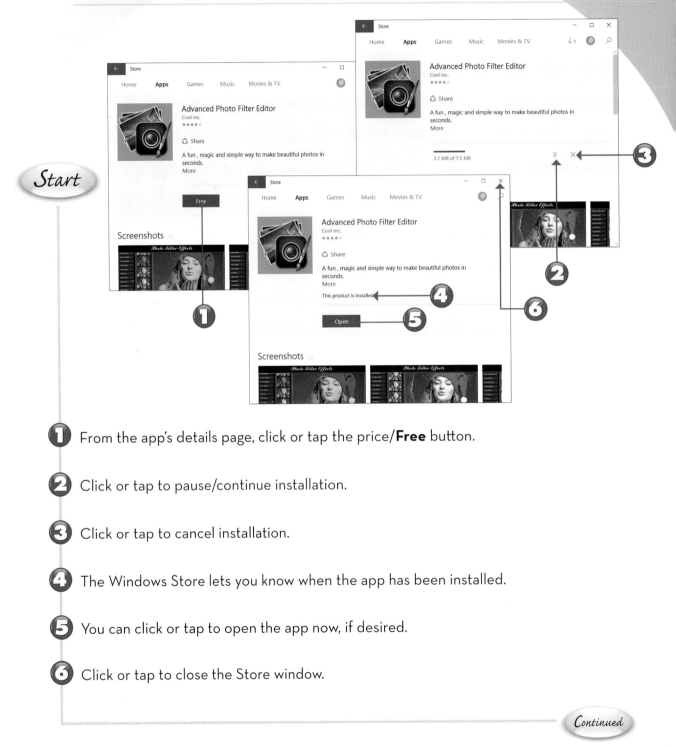

1. From the app's details page, click or tap the price/**Free** button.
2. Click or tap to pause/continue installation.
3. Click or tap to cancel installation.
4. The Windows Store lets you know when the app has been installed.
5. You can click or tap to open the app now, if desired.
6. Click or tap to close the Store window.

Continued

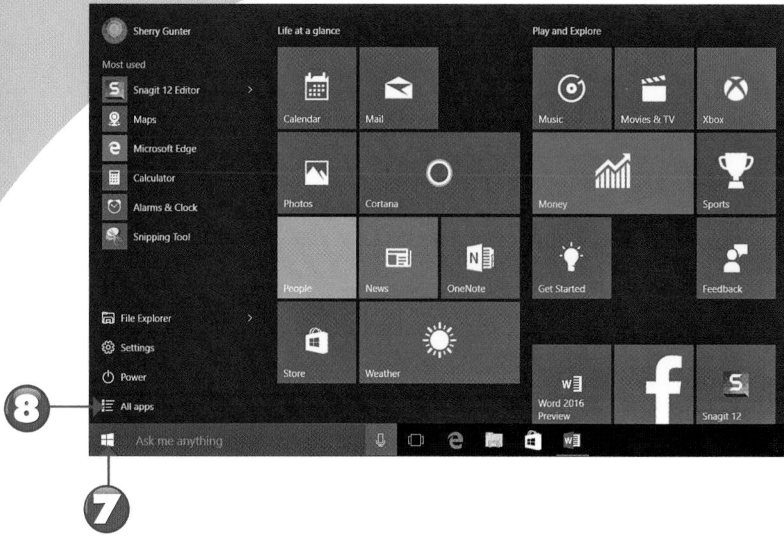

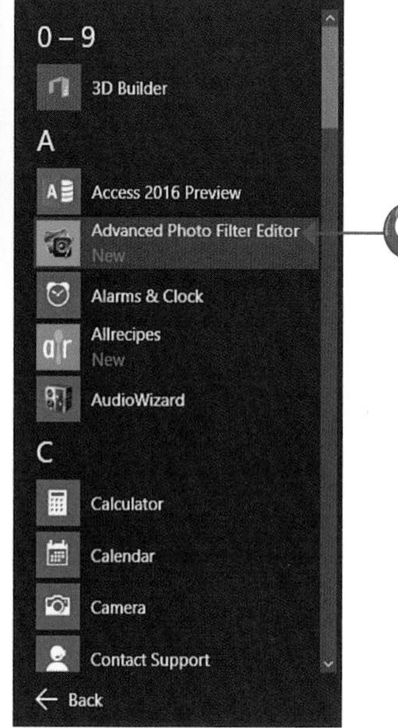

7 To locate the app later, click or tap **Start**.

8 Click or tap **All apps**.

9 Scroll to locate the app, and click or tap the app to open it.

End

NOTE

Installing Paid Apps When you install a paid app, Windows directs you to a login screen where you can log in to your Microsoft account and choose a payment method. Windows might also prompt you to log in to your Microsoft account before continuing with the download.

RATING AN APP

The Windows Store includes user reviews. This information is helpful when you're deciding whether you want to try an app. By rating an app, you help other potential users know how it worked for you.

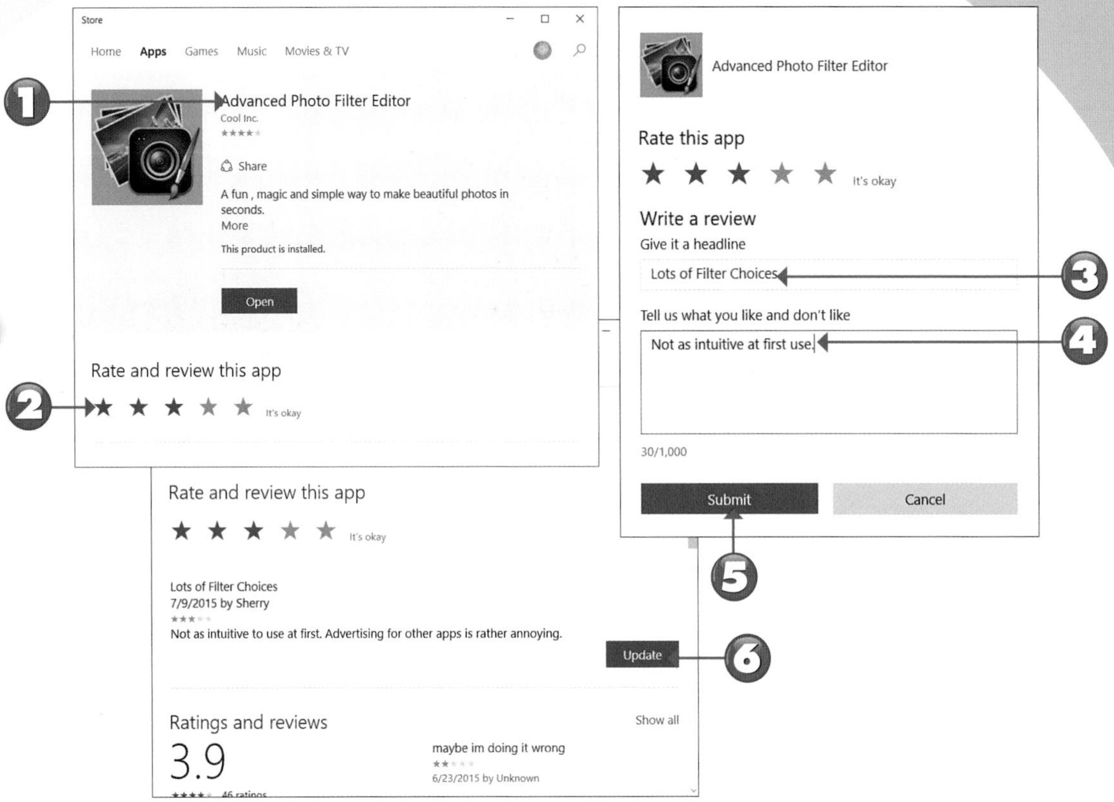

Store

Home Apps Games Music Movies & TV

Advanced Photo Filter Editor
Cool Inc.

Share

A fun , magic and simple way to make beautiful photos in seconds.
More

This product is installed.

Open

Rate and review this app

It's okay

Advanced Photo Filter Editor

Rate this app

It's okay

Write a review

Give it a headline

Lots of Filter Choices

Tell us what you like and don't like

Not as intuitive at first use.

30/1,000

Submit Cancel

Rate and review this app

It's okay

Lots of Filter Choices
7/9/2015 by Sherry
Not as intuitive to use at first. Advertising for other apps is rather annoying.

Update

Ratings and reviews Show all

3.9

maybe im doing it wrong
6/23/2015 by Unknown

Start

1. Go to the app's page in the Windows Store.
2. Click or drag across the stars to rate the app.
3. Enter a title for your review.
4. Enter review text.
5. Click or tap **Submit**
6. Click or tap **Update** if you want to change your review at any time.

End

NOTE

Rating Shortcut Some apps include a rating button or link you can click or tap to open a review window for rating the app.

UNINSTALLING AN APP FROM THE START SCREEN

You can easily remove an app you no longer use or want. Uninstalling an app removes it from your computer and deletes the app from your Start menu.

Start

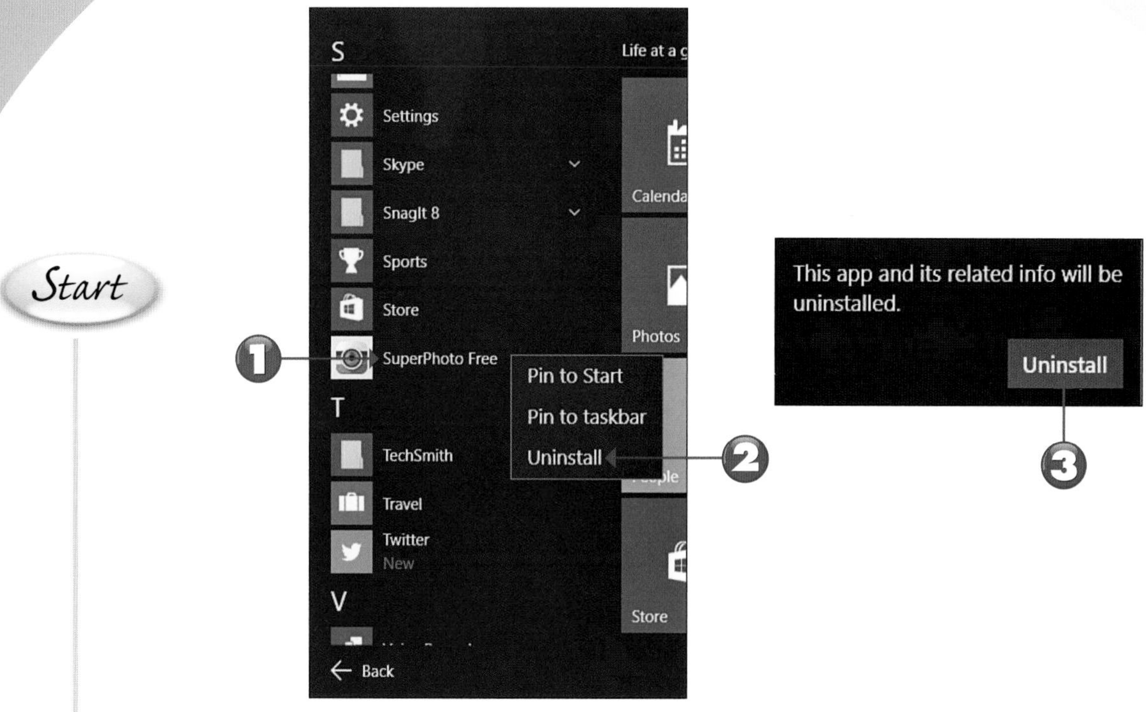

1. Right-click or press and hold the app you want to uninstall.
2. Click or tap **Uninstall**.
3. Click or tap **Uninstall**, and the app is removed.

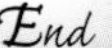

GAMING

Windows 10 continues to improve upon PC gaming, offering a variety of favorite games for all kinds of users and player levels. Whether you're just taking a break with a quick round of Solitaire or battling it out with rivals with the latest online game, you can find games for downloading in the Windows Store. If you're an Xbox user, you can use the Xbox app to enhance your online experience, connect with friends, view gaming achievements, and much more.

Connect and play with friends using the Xbox app

Shop for games in the Windows 10 Store

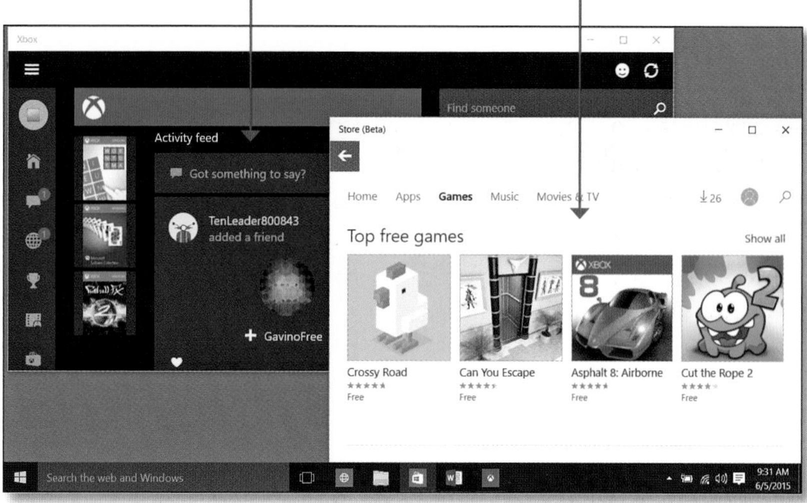

FINDING GAMES WITH THE STORE APP

If you're looking for games to play on your computer or smartphone, visit the Windows Store. The Store offers all kinds of games you can download—both free and paid games for single or multiple players.

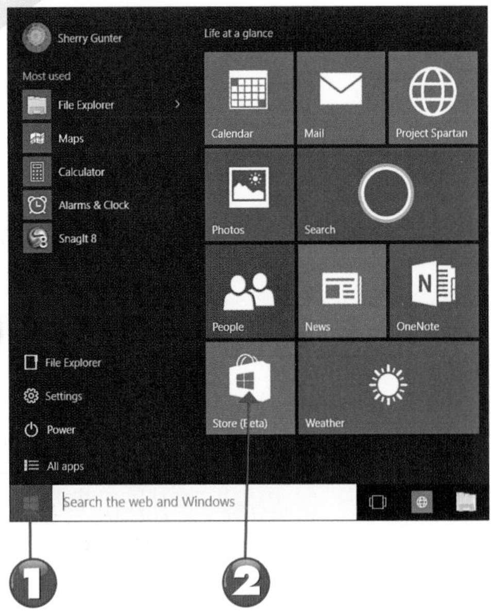

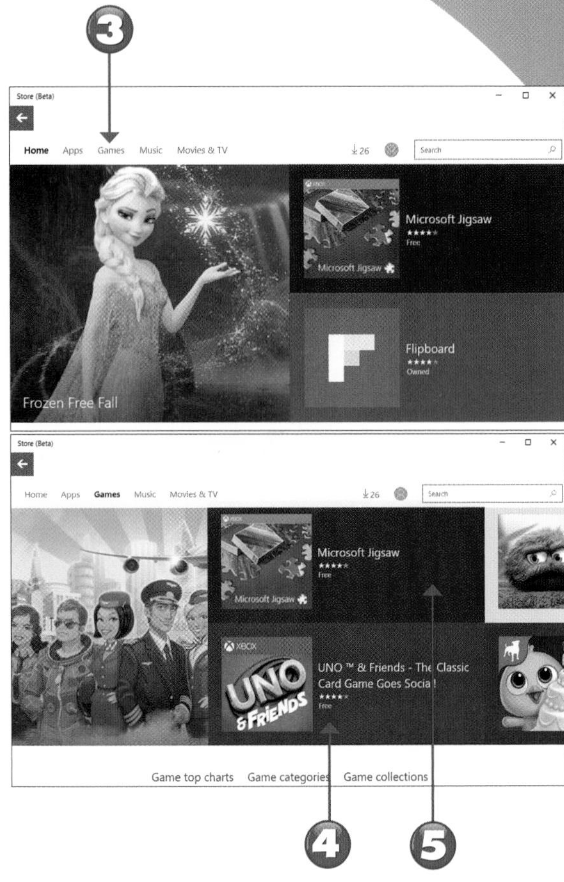

Start

1. Click or tap **Start**.
2. Click or tap **Store**.
3. Click or tap the **Games** category.
4. Scroll through the list of available games to find one you like.
5. Click or tap a game to learn more about it.

Continued

TIP

Xbox Gamers You can also access the Windows Store through the Xbox app. Learn more about Xbox games in the next task. ■

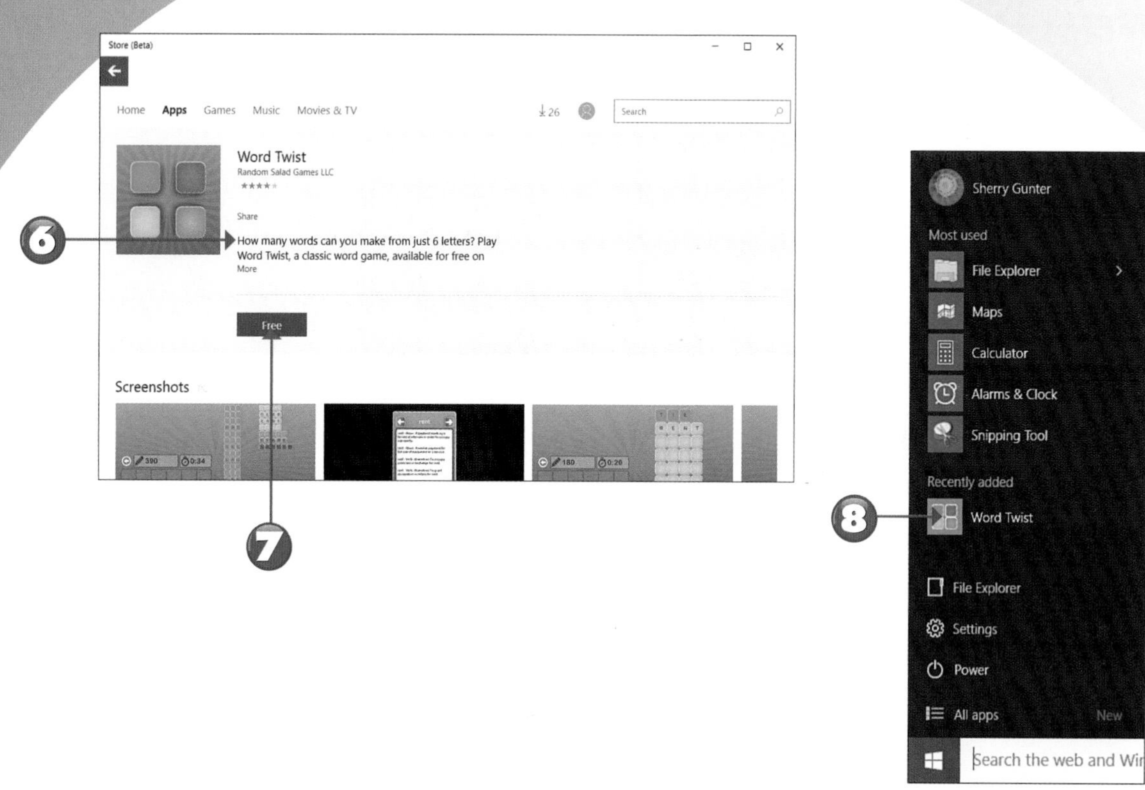

6 When you select a game to view, a description of the game opens along with screenshots of what the game looks like.

7 If it's a free game, click or tap the **Free** button to start the download.

8 Windows 10 installs the game automatically and adds it to the Apps list. Click or tap the **Start** menu to see it listed under **Recently added** items.

End

NOTE

Buying a Game? If you're buying a game, you see a price button instead of the Free button. You also go through some extra steps before downloading the game, such as logging in to your Microsoft account and choosing a payment option. ■

STARTING THE XBOX APP

The Xbox app is your gaming headquarters for all things Xbox. You can use the app to log in to your gaming account, chat with friends, play games, track your achievements, and more. This task shows you how to get started with the app.

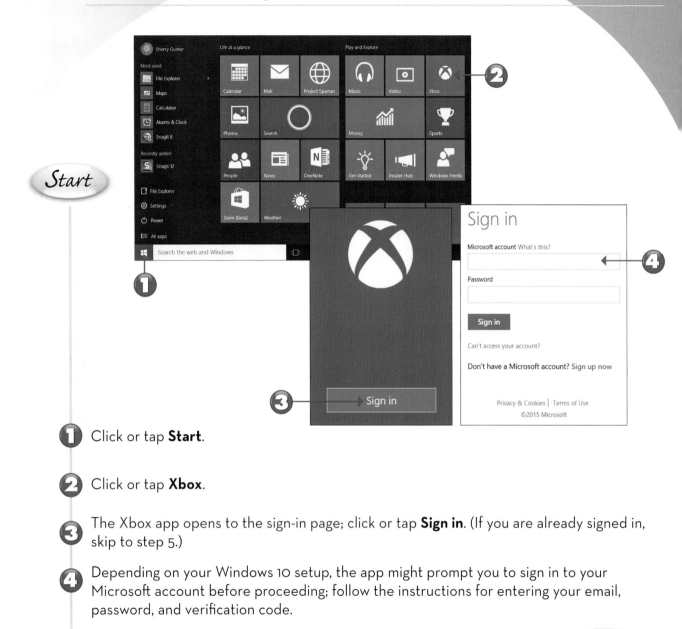

Start

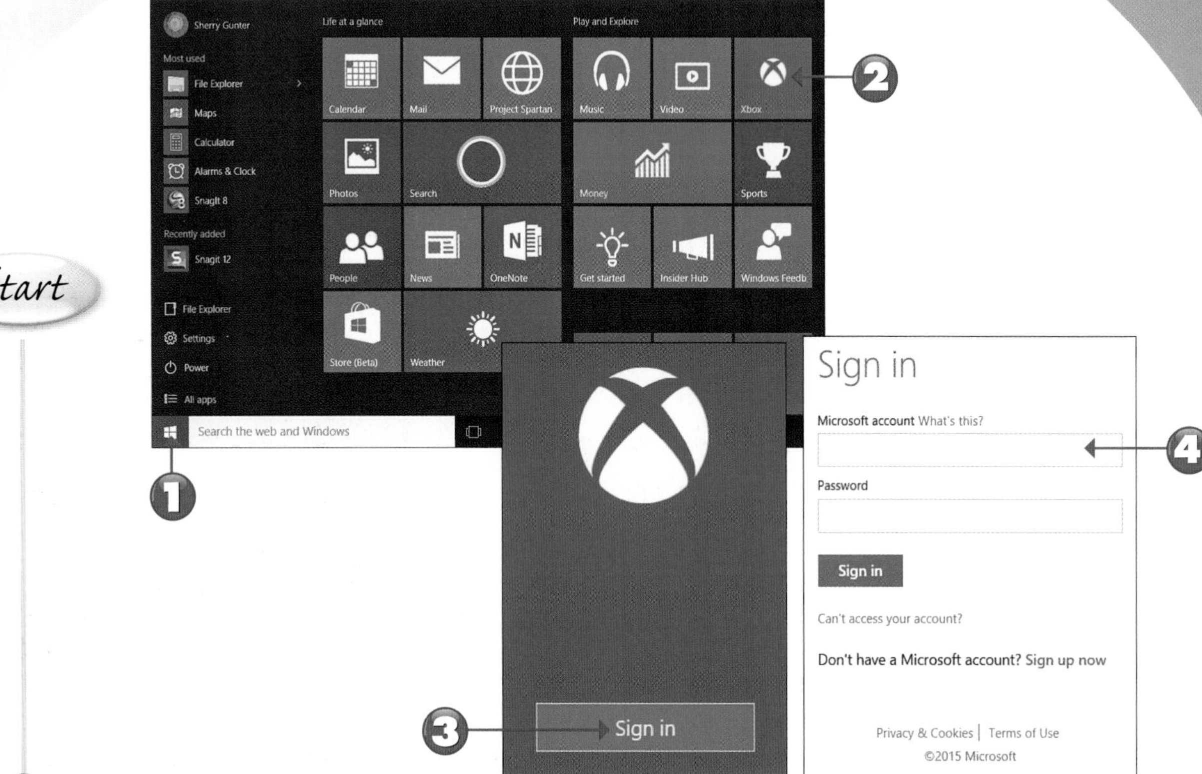

1. Click or tap **Start**.

2. Click or tap **Xbox**.

3. The Xbox app opens to the sign-in page; click or tap **Sign in**. (If you are already signed in, skip to step 5.)

4. Depending on your Windows 10 setup, the app might prompt you to sign in to your Microsoft account before proceeding; follow the instructions for entering your email, password, and verification code.

Continued

TIP

First-time User? If this is your first time using Xbox.com, you must create an account. See the next task to learn how to create a new user account. ■

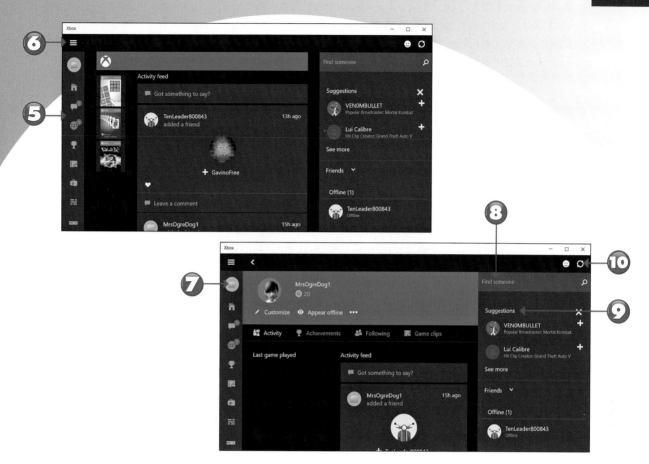

5 The Xbox app opens to your Home page, displaying any recent activity. Use the menu bar on the left side of the app to access features such as messaging, activity alerts, and the Windows Store.

6 You can also click or tap here to display the menu.

7 Click or tap your avatar picture to view customizing and offline options.

8 To find a friend online, click or tap **Find someone** and type your friend's gamertag (username).

9 Friends and suggested friends are listed in this pane.

10 To refresh the information shown on any window, click or tap here.

End

TIP

Need to Sign Out? The Xbox app keeps you signed in as soon as you start using the app unless you specify otherwise. You can find the sign-out option listed among the Xbox app's settings. Click or tap the **Settings** icon on the menu, and then click or tap **Sign Out** to officially log off of your connection. ■

CREATING A NEW XBOX ACCOUNT

You can create a new account to play games online. An Xbox account is free, and you can sign up through the Xbox app and the Xbox.com website. The browser window opens to help you complete the process.

Start

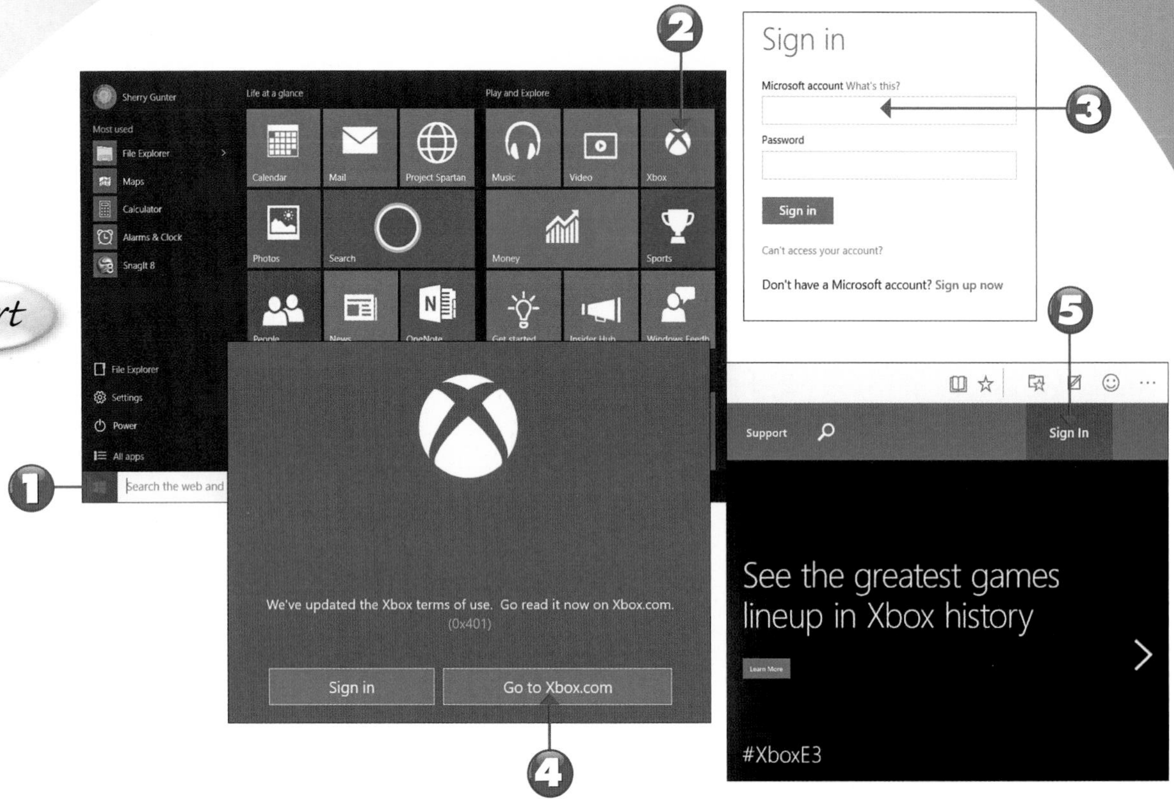

1. Click or tap **Start**.
2. Click or tap **Xbox**.
3. The app might prompt you to sign in to your Microsoft account before proceeding; follow the instructions for entering your email, password, and verification code.
4. Click or tap **Go to Xbox.com**.
5. The default browser window opens to the site; click or tap the **Sign In** link.

Continued

TIP

Customizing Options Not only can you change your gamertag, you can also customize your avatar. The easiest way to do this is to log in to the Xbox website (live.xbox.com) and choose from a wide variety of characters, costumes, and more. ■

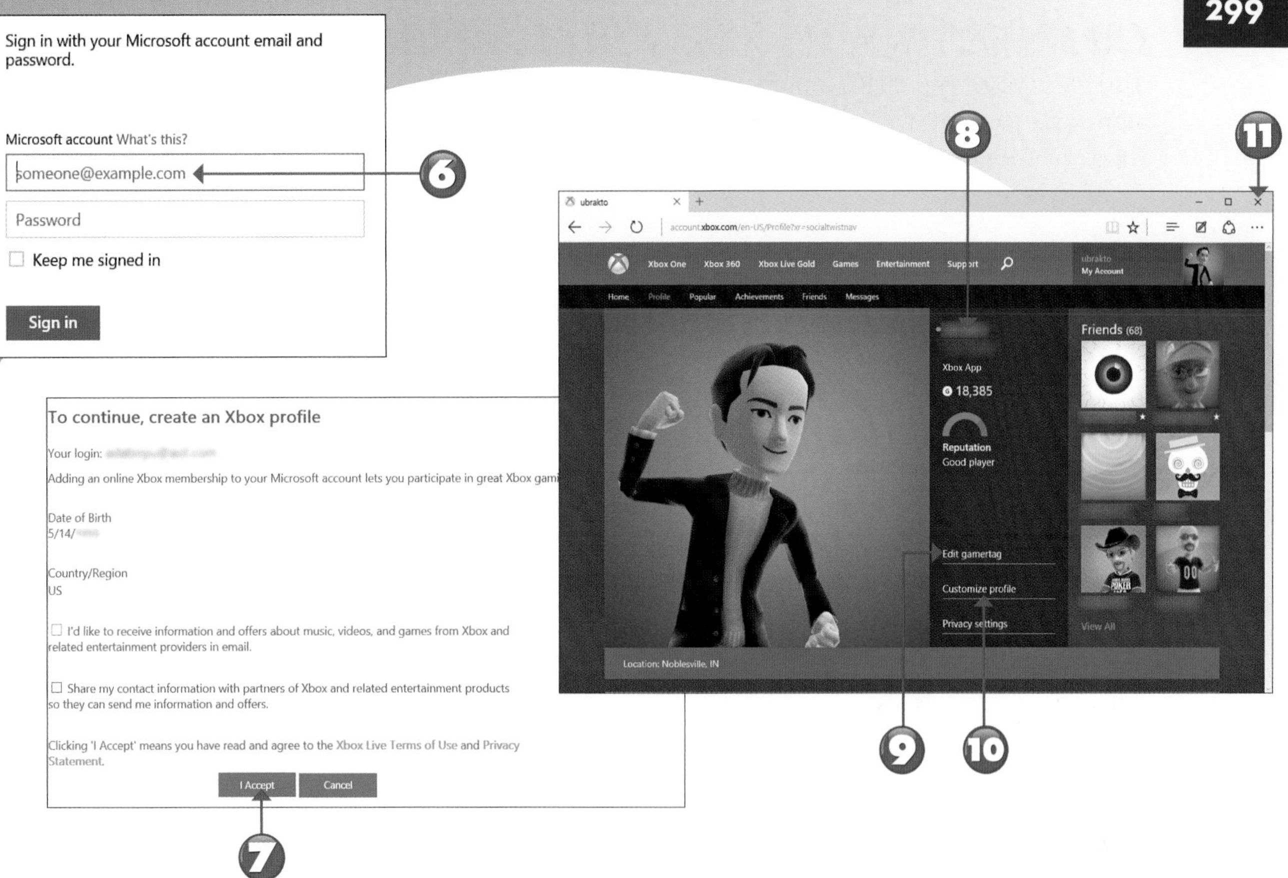

6. Sign in to your Microsoft account again; enter your email and password, and then click or tap **Sign in**.

7. Click or tap **I Accept**.

8. A default username (or gamertag) is created, and your profile page opens.

9. To change your username, scroll down the page and click or tap **Edit gamertag**.

10. To customize your profile, such as change your avatar, click or tap **Customize profile**.

11. When finished, click or tap here to close the browser window. The next time you open the Xbox app or sign in, your new account is ready to go.

End

CONNECTING TO XBOX ONE

The Xbox One has been enhanced with several new features for better integration with Windows 10. To use these features, you must connect your Windows 10 device with the Xbox One on your network from within the Xbox app. After you connect to your Xbox One, you can stream compatible games from your Xbox One to your Windows 10 device.

Start

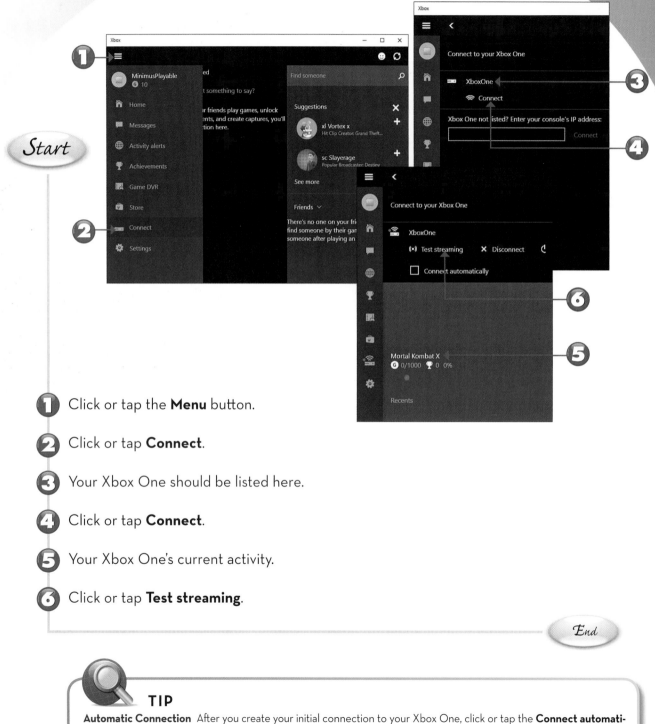

1. Click or tap the **Menu** button.
2. Click or tap **Connect**.
3. Your Xbox One should be listed here.
4. Click or tap **Connect**.
5. Your Xbox One's current activity.
6. Click or tap **Test streaming**.

End

TIP

Automatic Connection After you create your initial connection to your Xbox One, click or tap the **Connect automatically** check box. When this box is checked, your Windows 10 device automatically connects to your Xbox One. ■

VIEWING GAMING CLIPS

The Xbox One can capture gaming clips, which can be shared. You can view them with your Windows 10 device. Here's how.

Start

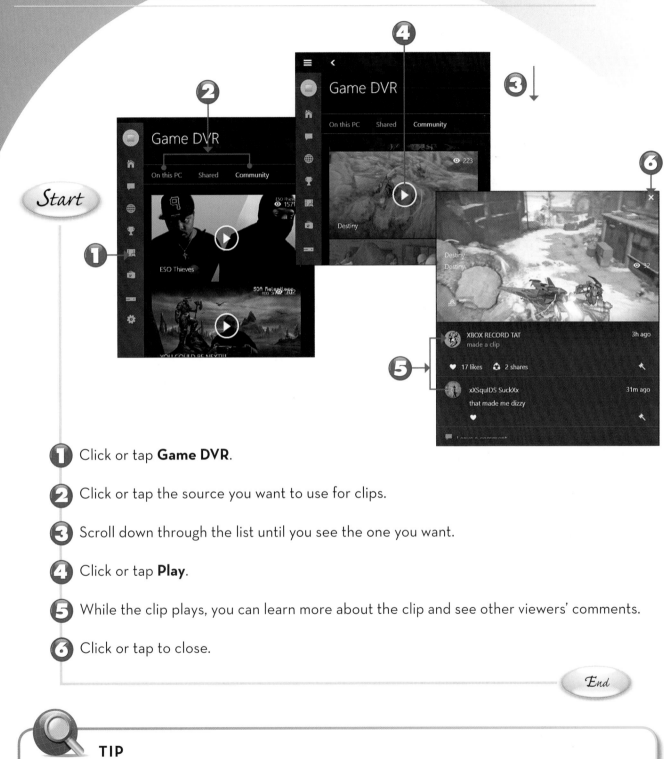

1. Click or tap **Game DVR**.
2. Click or tap the source you want to use for clips.
3. Scroll down through the list until you see the one you want.
4. Click or tap **Play**.
5. While the clip plays, you can learn more about the clip and see other viewers' comments.
6. Click or tap to close.

End

TIP

Choosing a Clip Source Click or tap **On this PC** to view clips you created with your own Xbox One. Click or tap **Shared** to view clips other users have shared with you. Click or tap **Community** (used in this example) to view clips shared with all Xbox users. ■

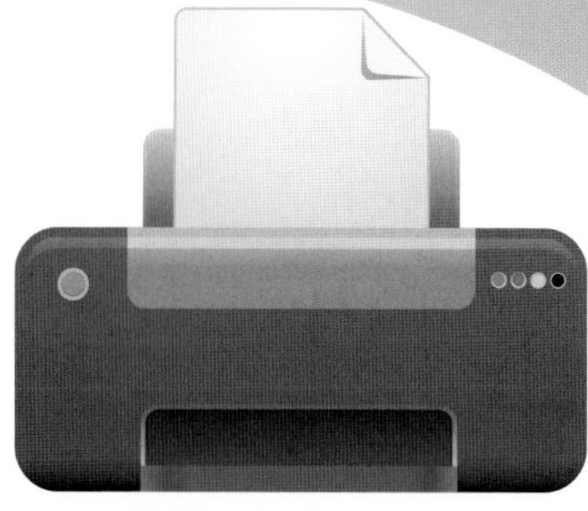

PRINTING AND SCANNING

Windows 10 can use most existing printers, scanners, and all-in-one units. Here's how to use these devices with Windows 10's built-in apps and features.

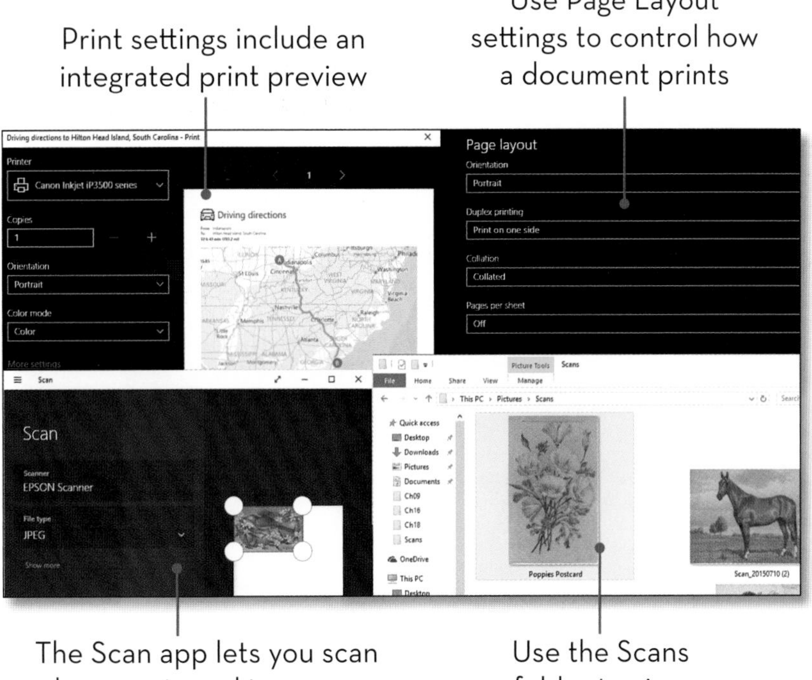
Print settings include an integrated print preview
Use Page Layout settings to control how a document prints
The Scan app lets you scan documents and images as different file types
Use the Scans folder to view scanned files

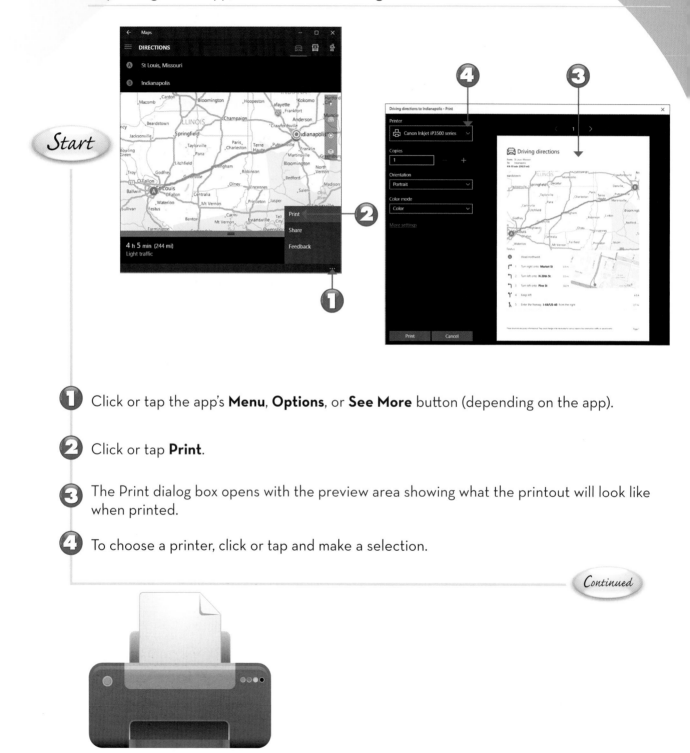

PRINTING A DOCUMENT

Windows 10 includes virtual printers that can create PDF (Adobe Reader) or XPS files. You can also install printers through the Settings app (see Chapter 19, "Managing Windows 10," for details). After your printer is installed, you can change the normal settings as needed, depending on the print job. Here's how to print a document from a typical Windows app. Depending on the app, the Print command might be located in a different location.

1. Click or tap the app's **Menu**, **Options**, or **See More** button (depending on the app).
2. Click or tap **Print**.
3. The Print dialog box opens with the preview area showing what the printout will look like when printed.
4. To choose a printer, click or tap and make a selection.

Continued

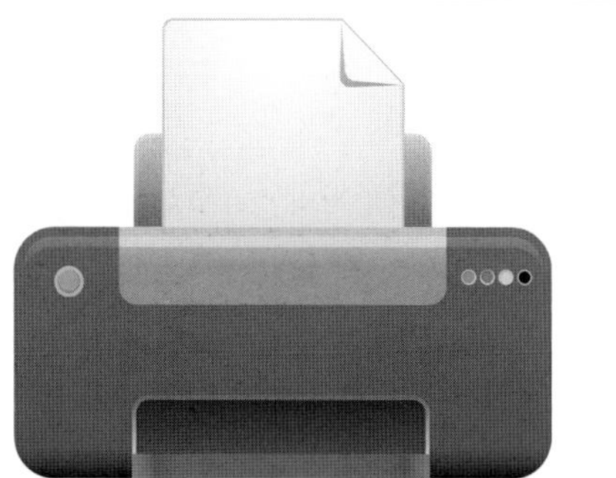

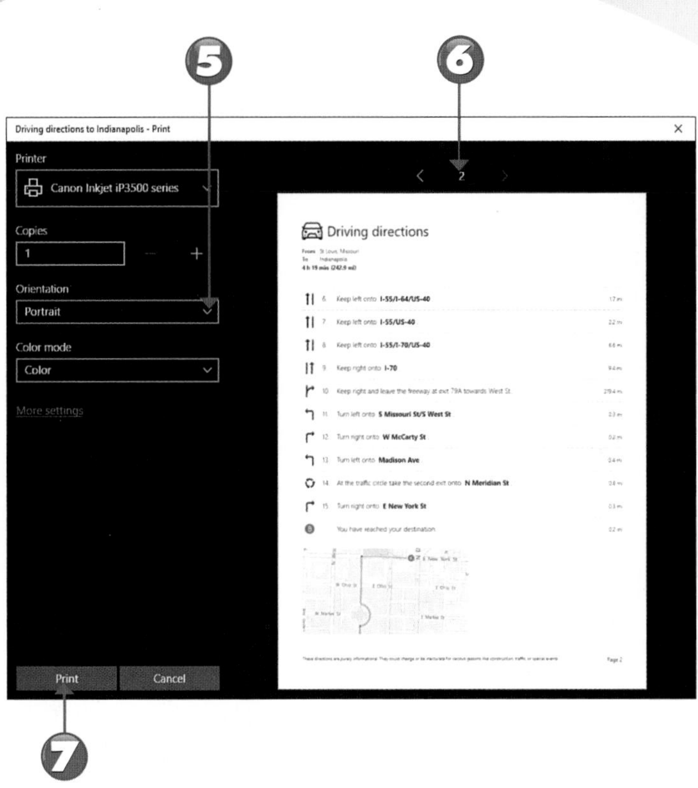

5 To change page orientation, click or tap **Orientation** and make a selection.

6 Click or tap to preview additional pages in the document, if applicable.

7 Click or tap **Print** to print the document.

End

TIP

Different Printer Options Don't expect to see the same print options every time you open the Print dialog box. Depending on which printer you select from the drop-down list, the options vary.

SELECTING A DIFFERENT PRINTER

Even before you install a physical printer, Windows 10 includes virtual printer apps that can create a PDF (Adobe Reader) or XPS (Microsoft XPS) file. Use this lesson to learn how to choose the right printer from those installed.

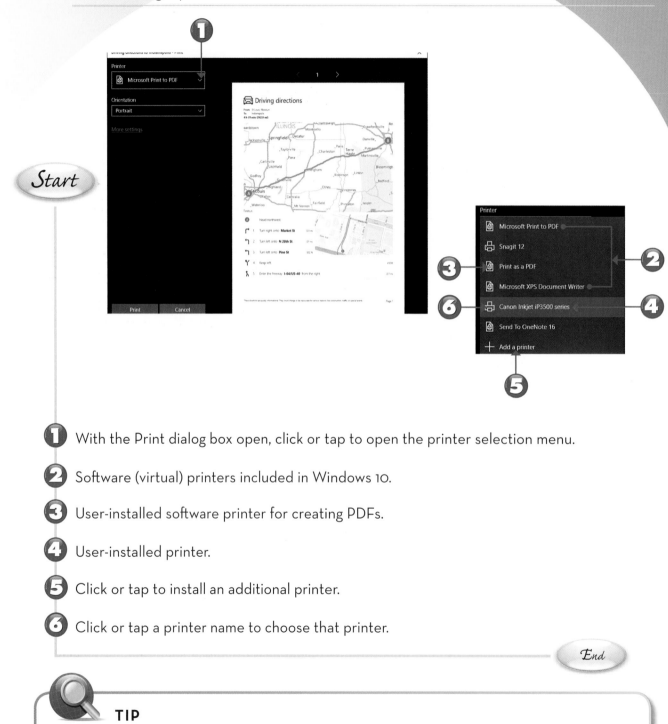

Start

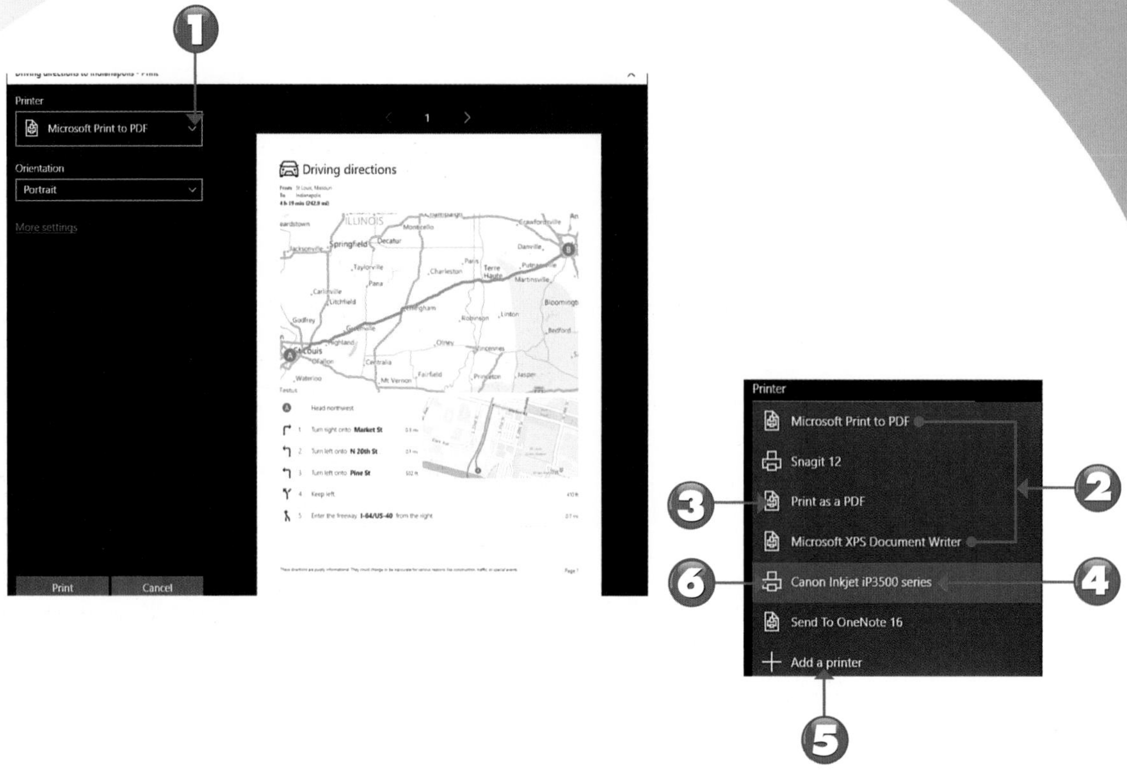

1. With the Print dialog box open, click or tap to open the printer selection menu.
2. Software (virtual) printers included in Windows 10.
3. User-installed software printer for creating PDFs.
4. User-installed printer.
5. Click or tap to install an additional printer.
6. Click or tap a printer name to choose that printer.

End

TIP

Set a Default Printer You can designate a printer as the default. When you do, the apps that allow printing list the chosen printer without needing to specify a printer every time. Conduct a Windows search for Devices and Printers (found in the Control Panel). Locate your printer, and right-click or press and hold the printer name, and choose **Set as default printer**.

MORE PRINTER SETTINGS

The basic printer settings are all you need for document printing onto standard 8.5x11 or A4 letter-size paper. However, if you need to use a different paper size or a different type of paper for printing photos, or adjust how your printer prints, you must use the More settings link. Here's what to expect with a typical inkjet printer.

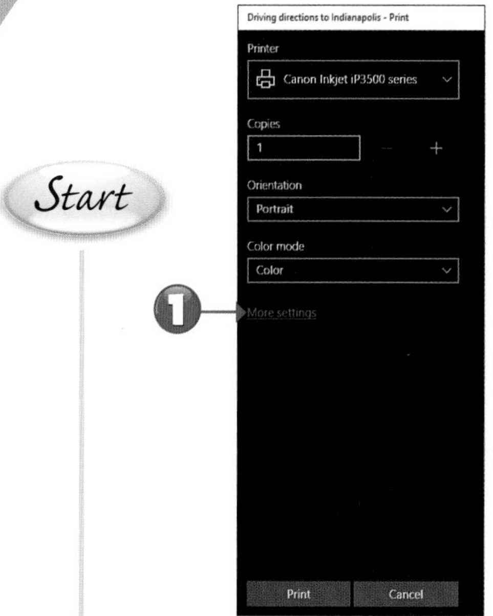

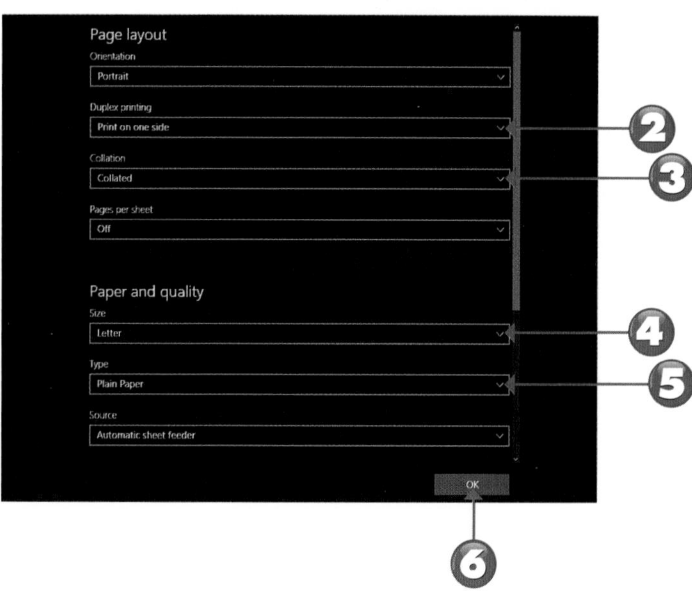

1. Click or tap **More settings**.
2. Click or tap **Duplex printing** if your printer can print on both sides of the paper.
3. Click or tap **Collation** if you want options for printing a multipage document.
4. Click or tap **Size** if you need to change the paper size.
5. Click or tap **Type** to use matte or photo paper instead of plain paper.
6. Click or tap **OK** to return to the main print menu.

End

NOTE

More About Printer Options Use the **Duplex printing** menu to select whether to print one side only or to flip the paper on the long or short edge to print the reverse side. Select **Uncollated** in the Collation menu if you want the printer to print all copies of page 1 before page 2, and so on. Available paper sizes and paper types vary by printer.

PHOTO PRINTING SETTINGS

If you want to print a photo on 4x6 photo paper, here are typical options to select. You can select these options in any order, and some printers offer slightly different options or wording.

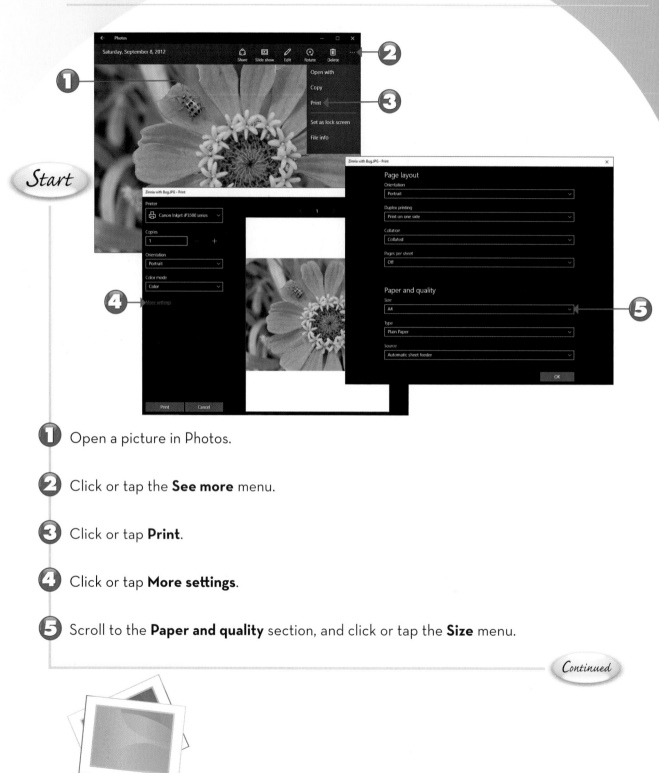

Start

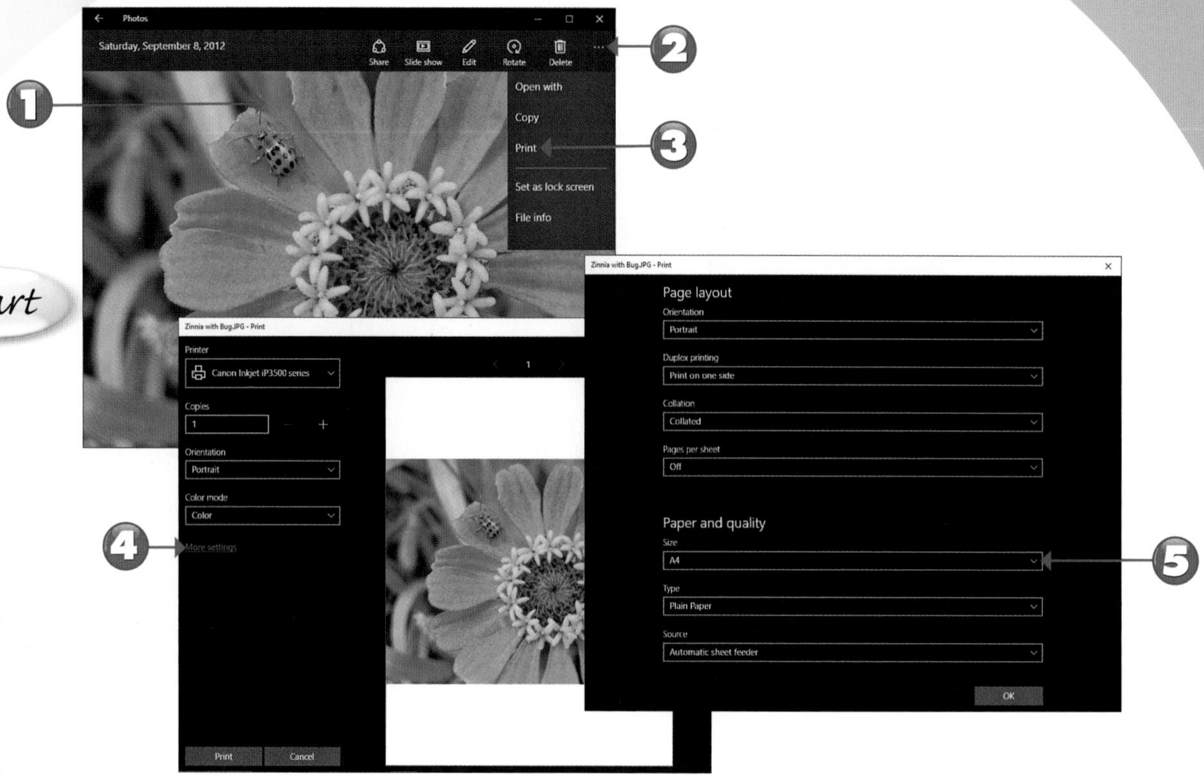

1. Open a picture in Photos.
2. Click or tap the **See more** menu.
3. Click or tap **Print**.
4. Click or tap **More settings**.
5. Scroll to the **Paper and quality** section, and click or tap the **Size** menu.

Continued

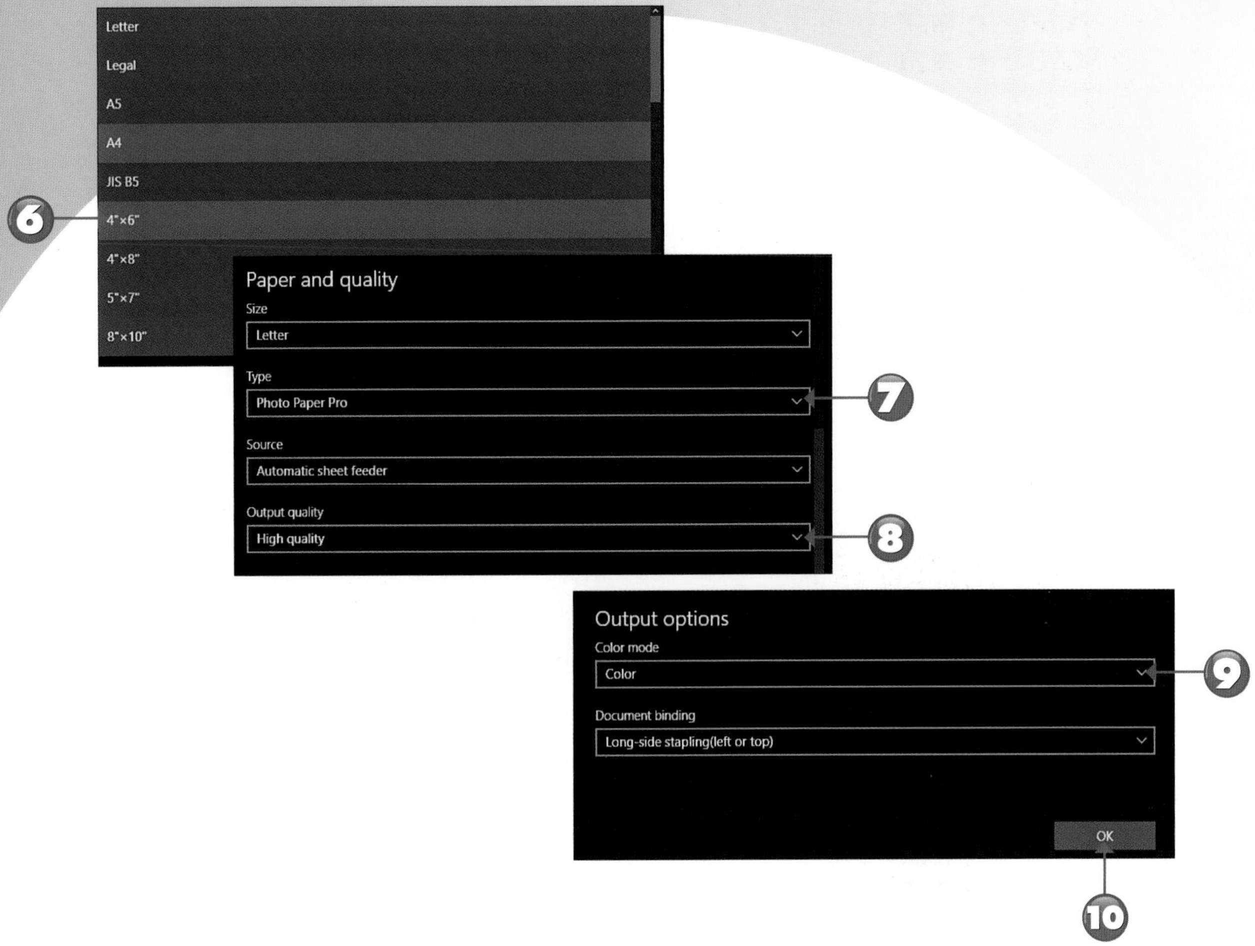

6. Click or tap **4"x6"** or another appropriate paper size for your photo printout.

7. Click or tap **Type** to change paper type.

8. Click or tap **Output quality** to change print quality.

9. Scroll to the **Output options** section and click or tap to choose **Color** or **Monochrome** printing.

10. Click **OK** and you're ready to print the photo.

End

USING SCAN

If you have a flatbed scanner or multifunction device, you can use Windows 10's simple scanning utility to convert prints or documents into electronic form.

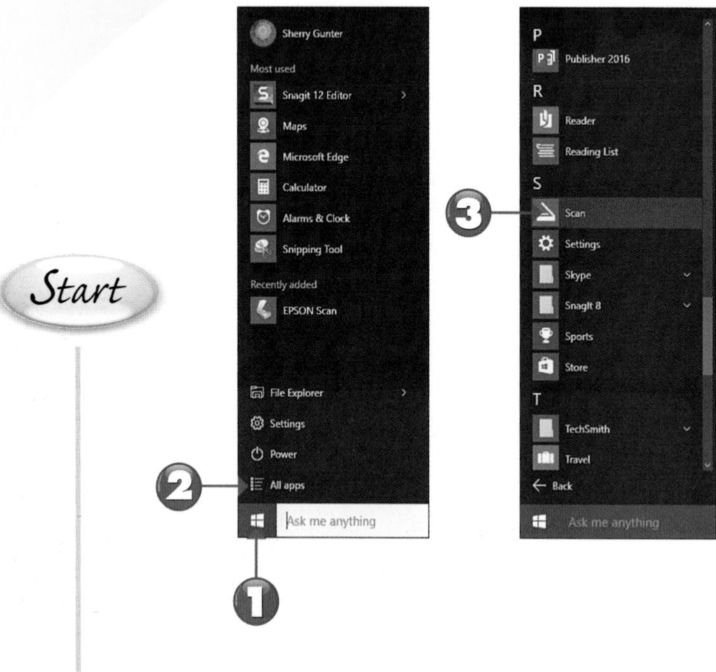

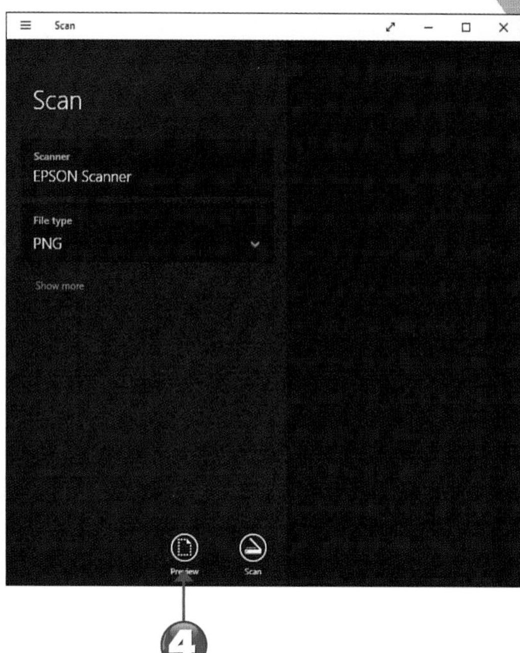

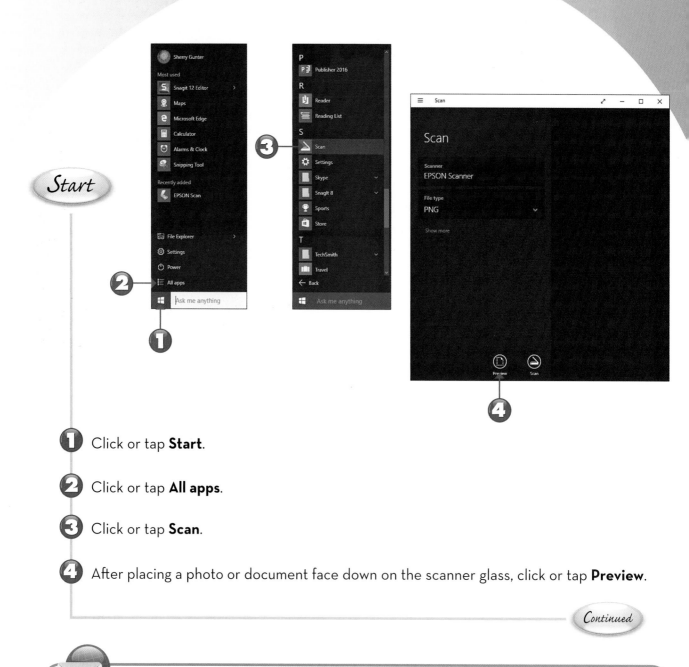

1. Click or tap **Start**.
2. Click or tap **All apps**.
3. Click or tap **Scan**.
4. After placing a photo or document face down on the scanner glass, click or tap **Preview**.

Continued

NOTE

Scan Versus Vendor-Supplied Tools The Scan app performs basic scanning with flatbed scanner or all-in-one units. However, if you need to adjust exposure or contrast, restore color to faded originals, use a sheet feeder or transparency unit, or use dust or scratch removal tools, you must use software provided by the scanner vendor or third-party scanning software. Note that vendor-supplied apps available in the Store are typically much more limited than the drivers you can obtain directly from the vendors' websites. If a Windows 10 version is not available, you can usually install and use the Windows 8.1 version.

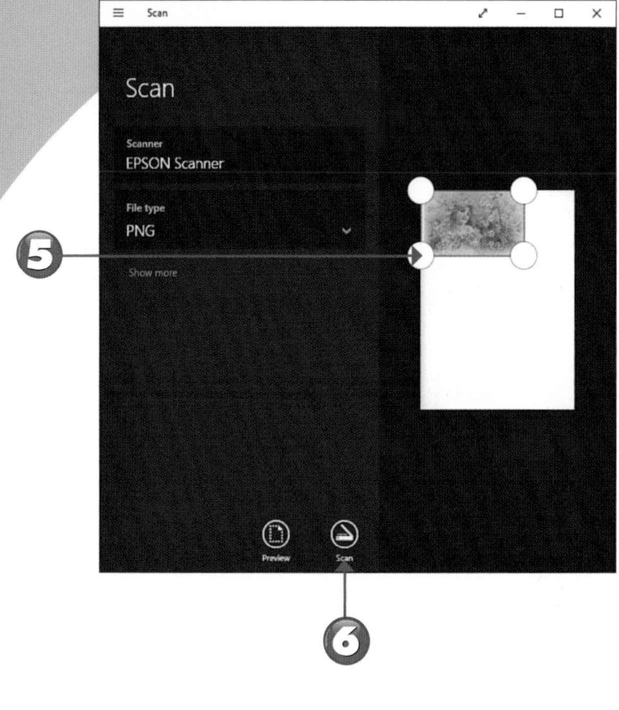

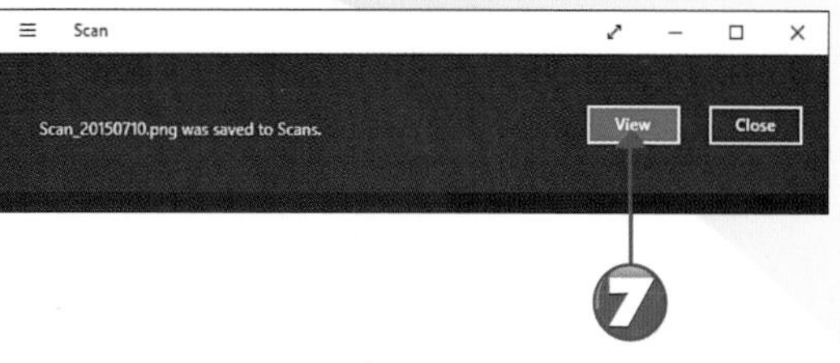

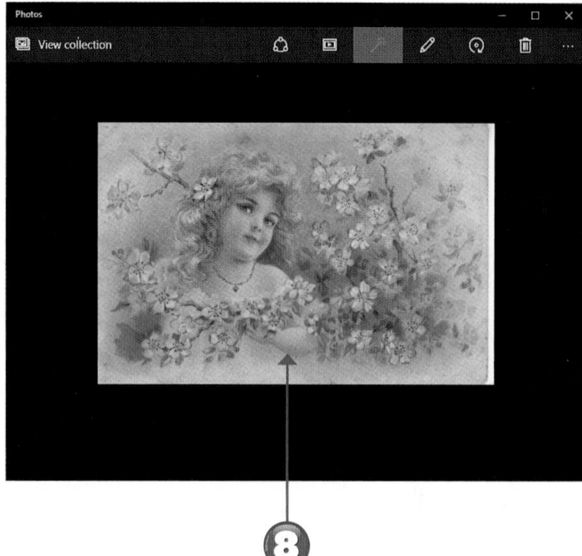

5 Drag the crop tools as desired around the preview. The area inside the rectangle will be scanned.

6 Click or tap **Scan**.

7 Click or tap **View**.

8 Your scan is opened by the default app for the file type.

End

NOTE

What Scan Uses to View Your Scans If you use only the apps included in Windows 10, Scan uses the Photos app for most file types. For XPS and OpenXPS files, Scan uses the Reader app. For PDF files, Scan uses Reader or Microsoft Edge. If you install third-party apps that use these file types, your results might vary.

ADJUSTING SCAN SETTINGS

By default, Scan uses the PNG file type. However, you can select other file types if they are more suitable for your needs. By default, Scan uses a resolution of 100dpi. This is sufficient for scanning images that you plan to view or email. However, if you want to print a scan, you should use a resolution of 300dpi (for same-size prints) or 600dpi (for small documents or photos you want to print at a larger size). You can also scan color or black-and-white photos or documents using different settings. In this lesson, you learn how to use these features.

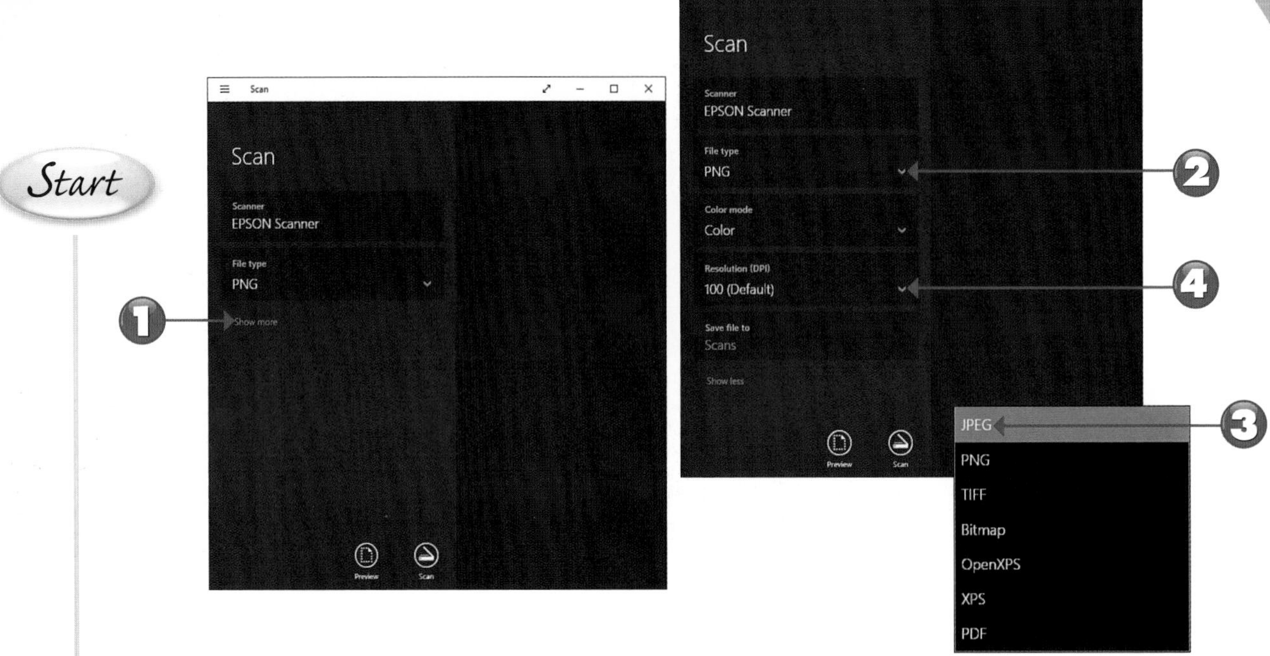

1. With the Scan app open, click or tap **Show more**.

2. Click or tap to change file type.

3. Choose a file type. In this example, we chose JPEG because it is compatible with online photo printing services and photo-editing programs.

4. Click or tap to change resolution.

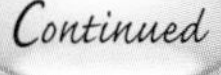

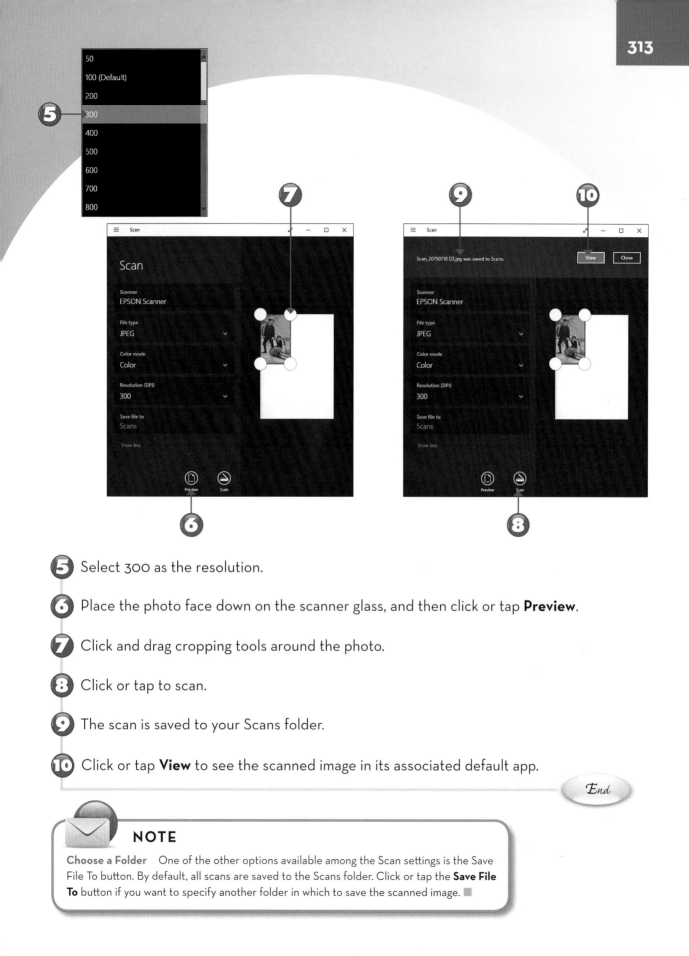

5 Select 300 as the resolution.

6 Place the photo face down on the scanner glass, and then click or tap **Preview**.

7 Click and drag cropping tools around the photo.

8 Click or tap to scan.

9 The scan is saved to your Scans folder.

10 Click or tap **View** to see the scanned image in its associated default app.

End

NOTE

Choose a Folder One of the other options available among the Scan settings is the Save File To button. By default, all scans are saved to the Scans folder. Click or tap the **Save File To** button if you want to specify another folder in which to save the scanned image.

SELECTING COLOR, GRAYSCALE, OR BLACK-AND-WHITE MODES

Normally, you want to use the default Color mode to scan color photos or documents. However, you can use Grayscale to create a so-called "black-and-white" version of a color photo. The black-and-white mode uses only black and white. This mode is primarily intended for scanning printed or typed documents, but as you learn in this lesson, you can turn ordinary photos into graphic designs with this mode. For this example, we compare grayscale and black-and-white modes.

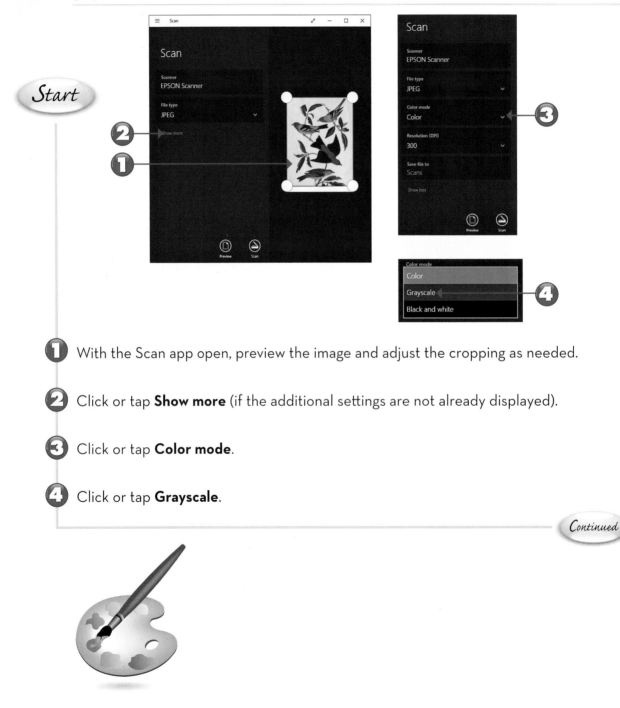

1. With the Scan app open, preview the image and adjust the cropping as needed.
2. Click or tap **Show more** (if the additional settings are not already displayed).
3. Click or tap **Color mode**.
4. Click or tap **Grayscale**.

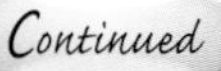
Continued

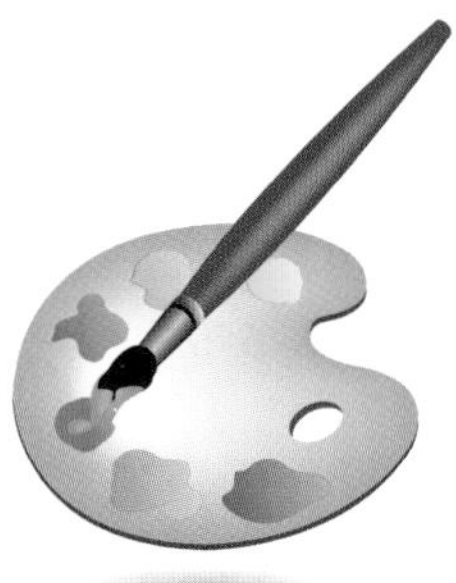

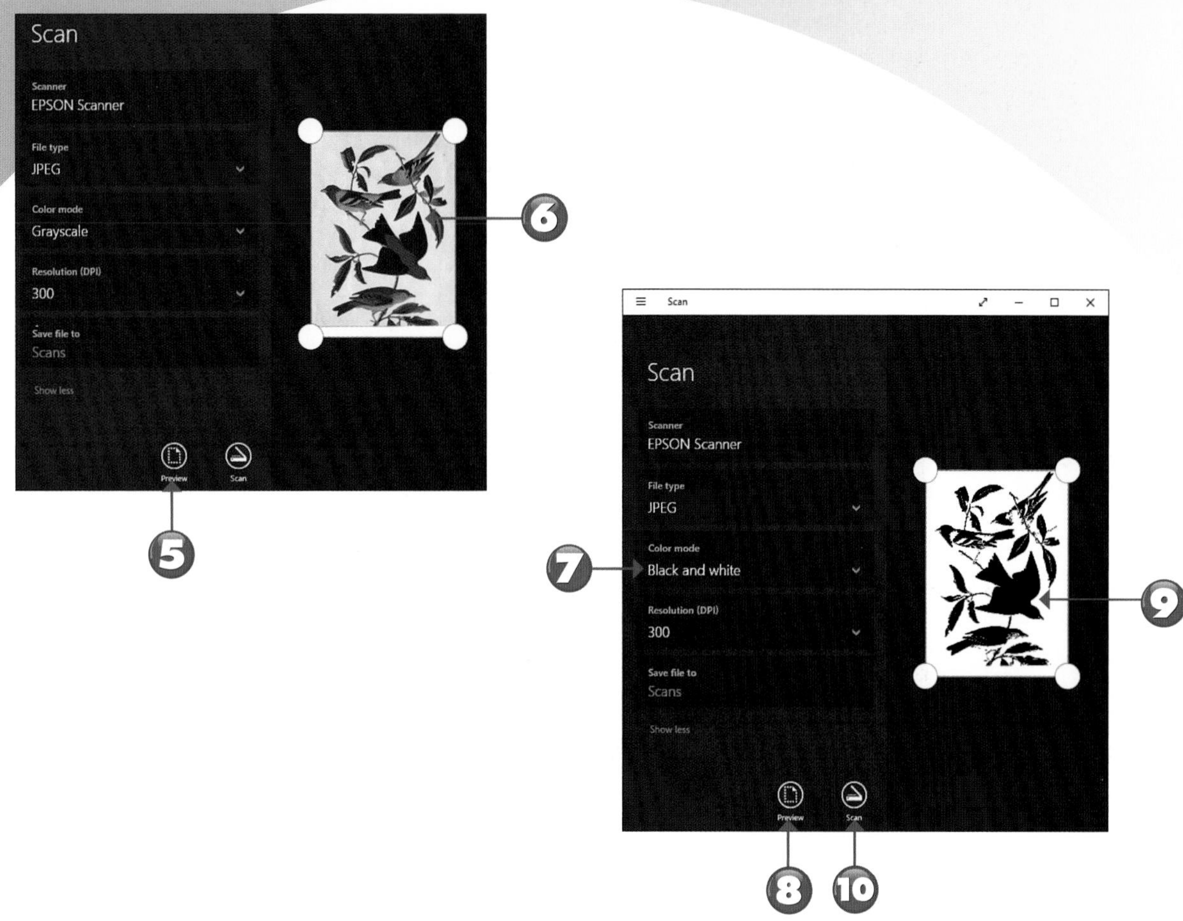

5 Click or tap **Preview**.

6 The image appears in grayscale in the preview area.

7 Change the Color mode to **Black and white**.

8 Click or tap **Preview**.

9 The image appears as black and white in the preview area.

10 You can scan the image, or reset to a preferred color mode before scanning.

End

OPENING THE SCANS FOLDER

Unless you change the default setting for Scan, all scans are stored in the Scans folder by default. You can view all your scans by opening this folder with File Manager.

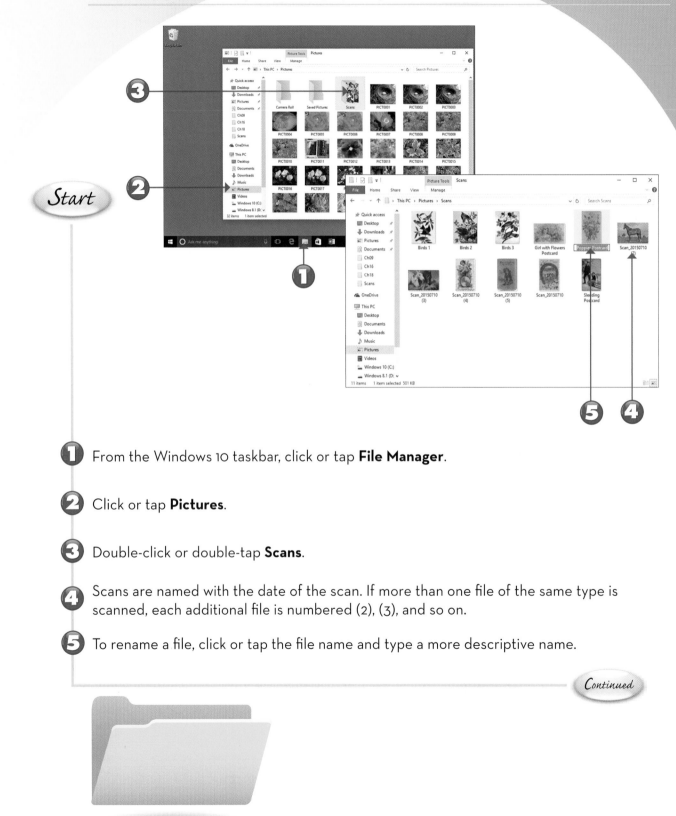

Start

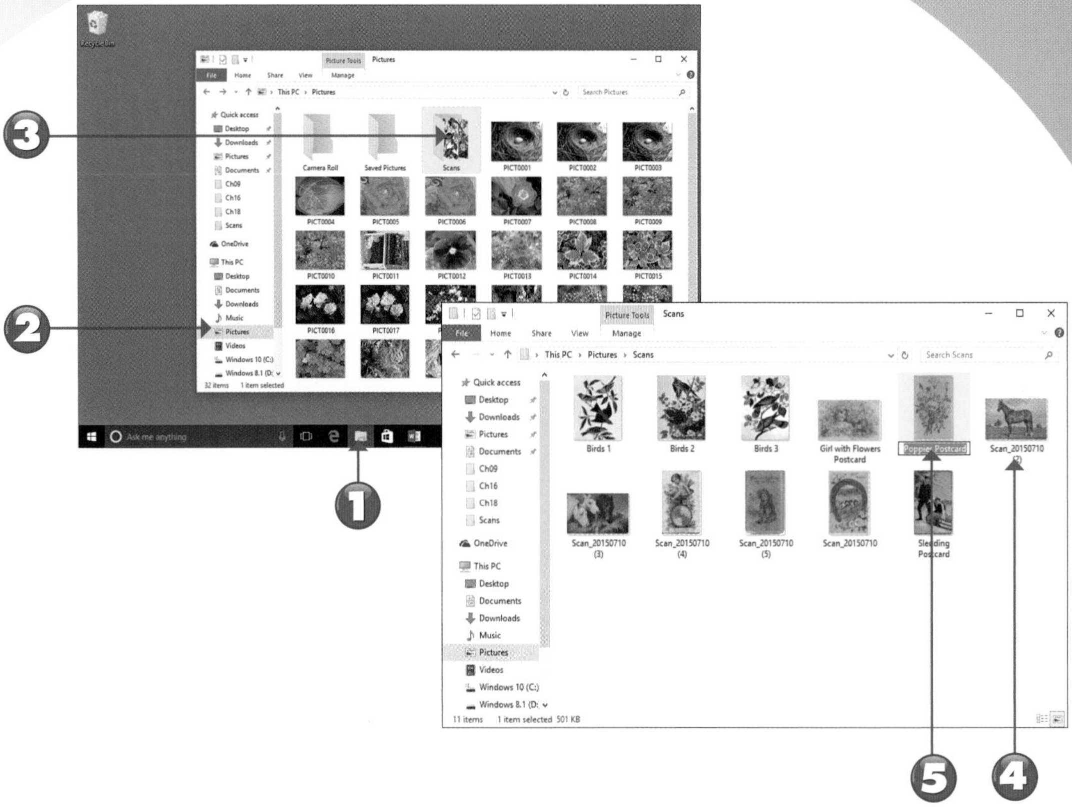

1. From the Windows 10 taskbar, click or tap **File Manager**.
2. Click or tap **Pictures**.
3. Double-click or double-tap **Scans**.
4. Scans are named with the date of the scan. If more than one file of the same type is scanned, each additional file is numbered (2), (3), and so on.
5. To rename a file, click or tap the file name and type a more descriptive name.

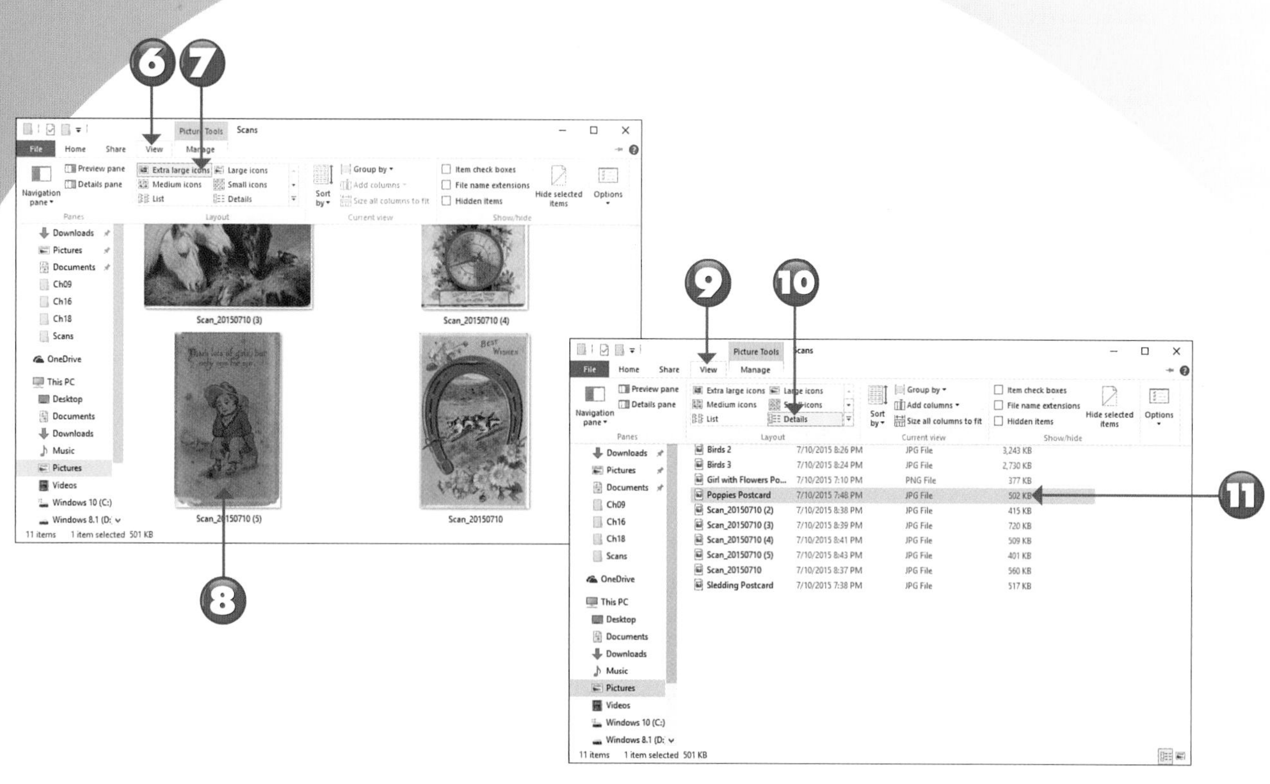

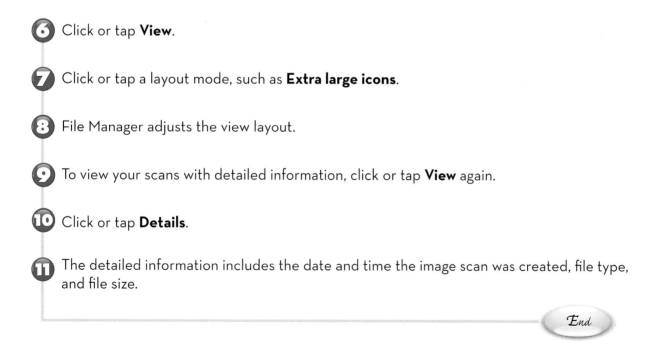

6 Click or tap **View**.

7 Click or tap a layout mode, such as **Extra large icons**.

8 File Manager adjusts the view layout.

9 To view your scans with detailed information, click or tap **View** again.

10 Click or tap **Details**.

11 The detailed information includes the date and time the image scan was created, file type, and file size.

End

MANAGING WINDOWS 10

The Settings dialog box in Windows 10 is where to go to make basic settings of all types. This chapter focuses on configuring system and privacy options as well as the volume control.

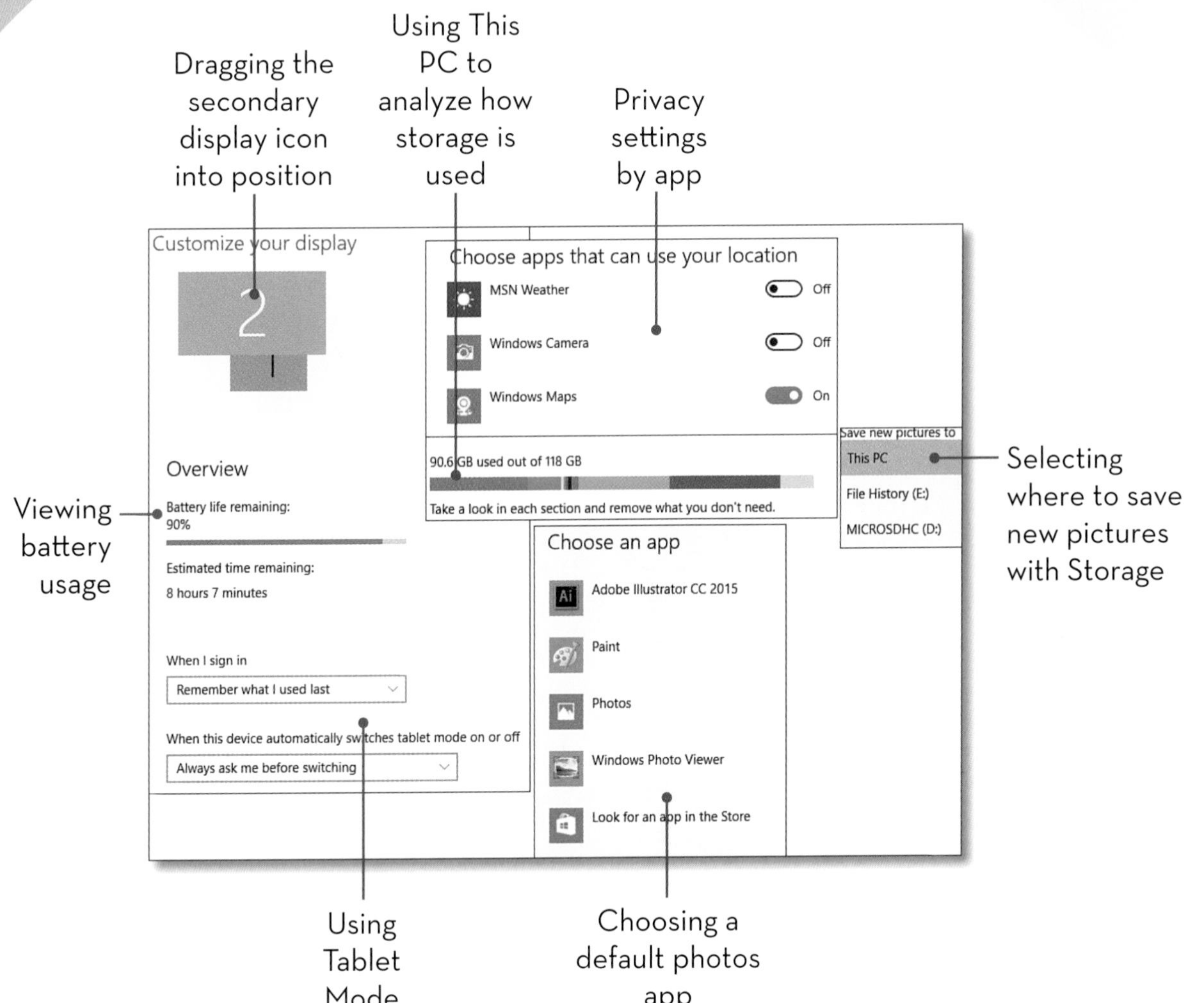
Dragging the secondary display icon into position
Using This PC to analyze how storage is used
Privacy settings by app
Customize your display
2
1
Choose apps that can use your location
MSN Weather
Off
Windows Camera
Off
Windows Maps
On
Save new pictures to
This PC
File History (E:)
MICROSDHC (D:)
Selecting where to save new pictures with Storage
Overview
Viewing battery usage
Battery life remaining:
90%
Estimated time remaining:
8 hours 7 minutes
90.6 GB used out of 118 GB
Take a look in each section and remove what you don't need.
Choose an app
Adobe Illustrator CC 2015
Paint
Photos
Windows Photo Viewer
Look for an app in the Store
When I sign in
Remember what I used last
When this device automatically switches tablet mode on or off
Always ask me before switching
Using Tablet Mode
Choosing a default photos app

ADJUSTING SYSTEM VOLUME

If your music is too loud or you can't hear the audio in the YouTube video you're playing, it's time to adjust the volume. Here's how.

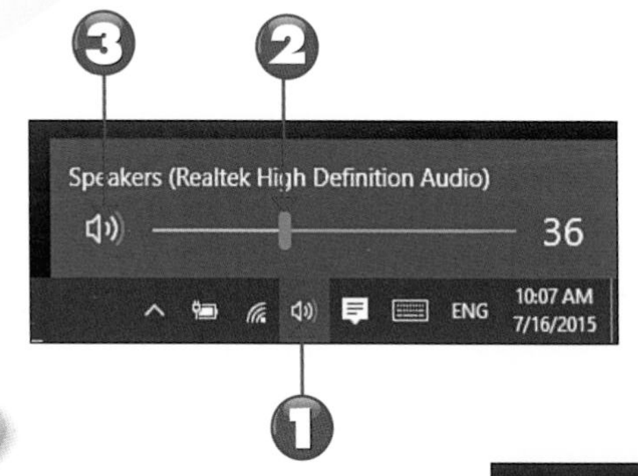

Start

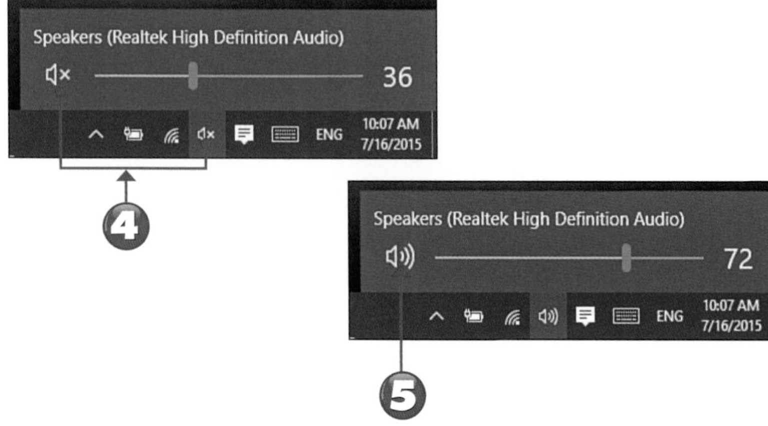

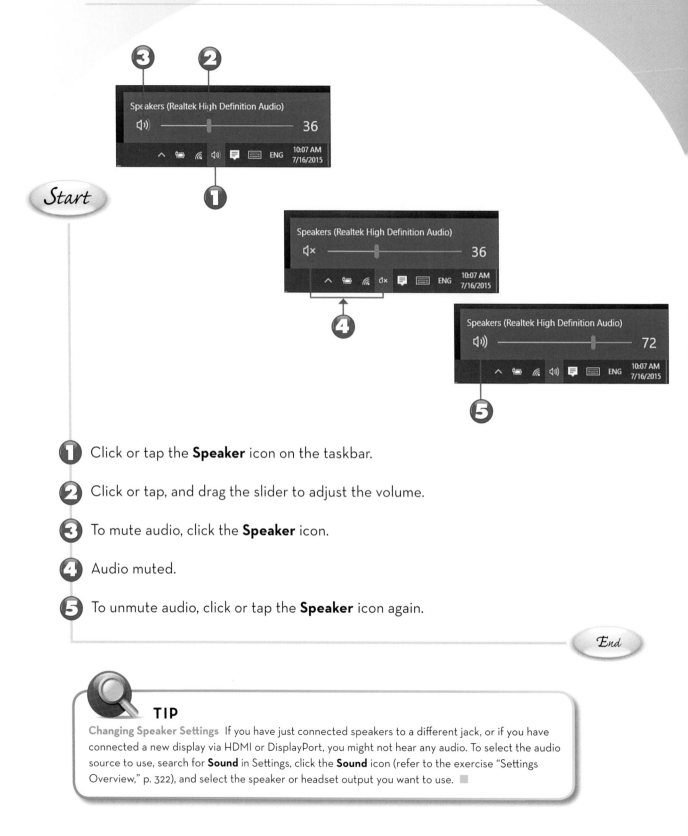

1. Click or tap the **Speaker** icon on the taskbar.
2. Click or tap, and drag the slider to adjust the volume.
3. To mute audio, click the **Speaker** icon.
4. Audio muted.
5. To unmute audio, click or tap the **Speaker** icon again.

End

TIP

Changing Speaker Settings If you have just connected speakers to a different jack, or if you have connected a new display via HDMI or DisplayPort, you might not hear any audio. To select the audio source to use, search for **Sound** in Settings, click the **Sound** icon (refer to the exercise "Settings Overview," p. 322), and select the speaker or headset output you want to use.

ACCESSING THE SETTINGS MENU

You use the Settings menu to make most of the adjustments discussed in this chapter. Here's how to open the Settings menu.

Start

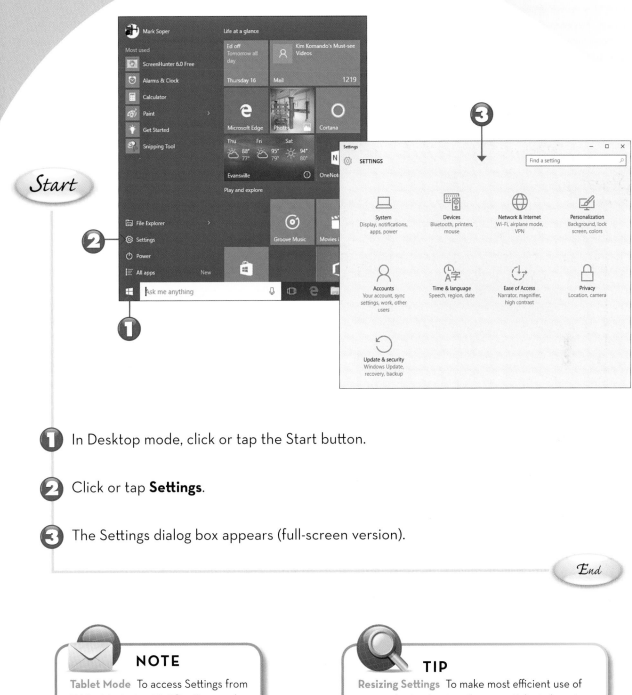

1. In Desktop mode, click or tap the Start button.
2. Click or tap **Settings**.
3. The Settings dialog box appears (full-screen version).

End

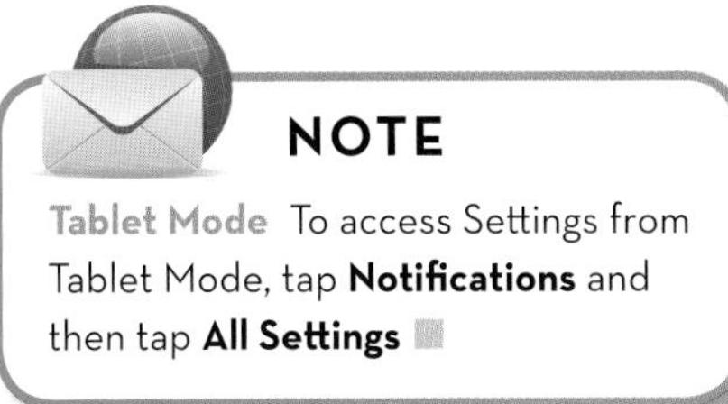

NOTE

Tablet Mode To access Settings from Tablet Mode, tap **Notifications** and then tap **All Settings**

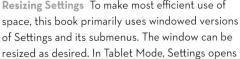

TIP

Resizing Settings To make most efficient use of space, this book primarily uses windowed versions of Settings and its submenus. The window can be resized as desired. In Tablet Mode, Settings opens full screen.

SETTINGS OVERVIEW

The Settings dialog box provides a useful way to access the settings you're most likely to change. Let's look at the menus covered in this chapter and learn how to search for a setting. When you use the Settings Search box, some matches point to portions of the Control Panel, which is still present in Windows 10 (for example, **Sound** in Step 5).

Start

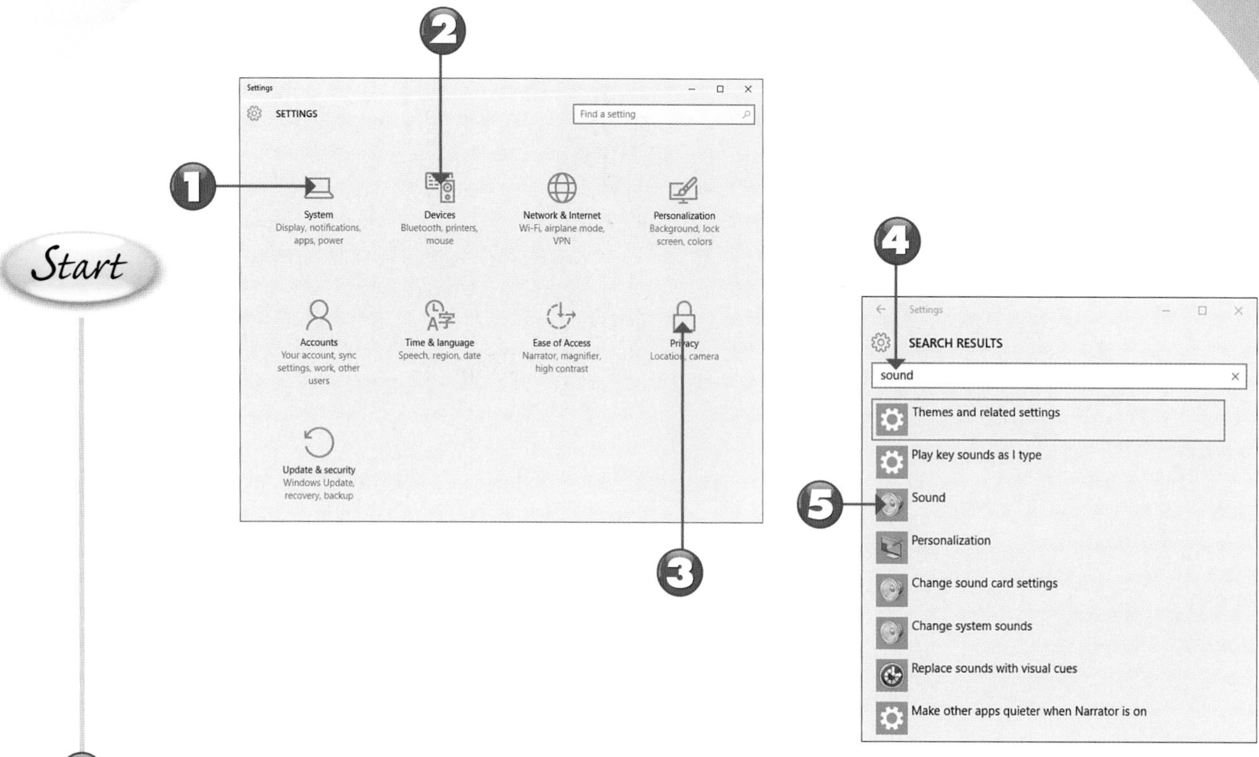

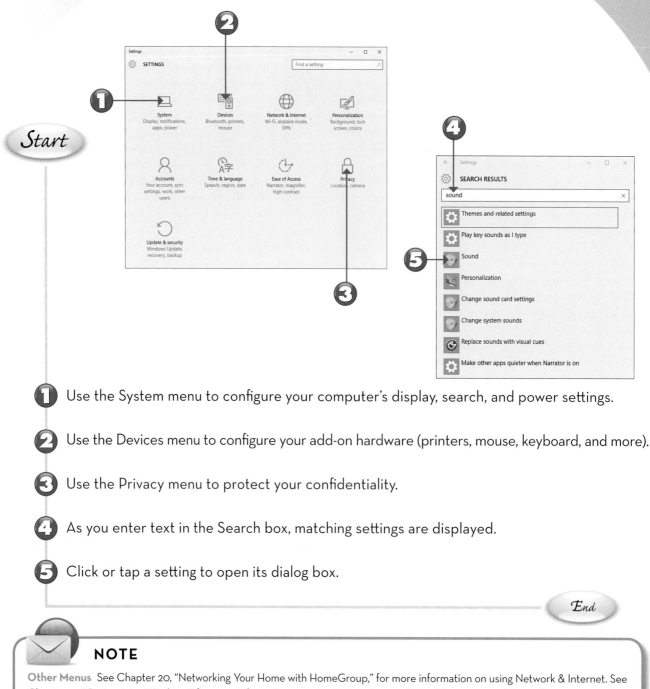

1. Use the System menu to configure your computer's display, search, and power settings.
2. Use the Devices menu to configure your add-on hardware (printers, mouse, keyboard, and more).
3. Use the Privacy menu to protect your confidentiality.
4. As you enter text in the Search box, matching settings are displayed.
5. Click or tap a setting to open its dialog box.

End

NOTE

Other Menus See Chapter 20, "Networking Your Home with HomeGroup," for more information on using Network & Internet. See Chapter 21, "Customizing Windows," for more information on using Personalization, Time & language, and Ease of Access. See Chapter 22, "Adding and Managing Users," for more information on using Accounts. See Chapter 23, "Protecting Your System," and Chapter 24, "System Maintenance and Performance," for more information on using Windows Update, backup, and recovery options.

ADJUSTING DISPLAY BRIGHTNESS AND ROTATION

Use the System submenu to change display settings, including brightness, additional displays, and more. It's easy to adjust display brightness and rotation, as this exercise points out.

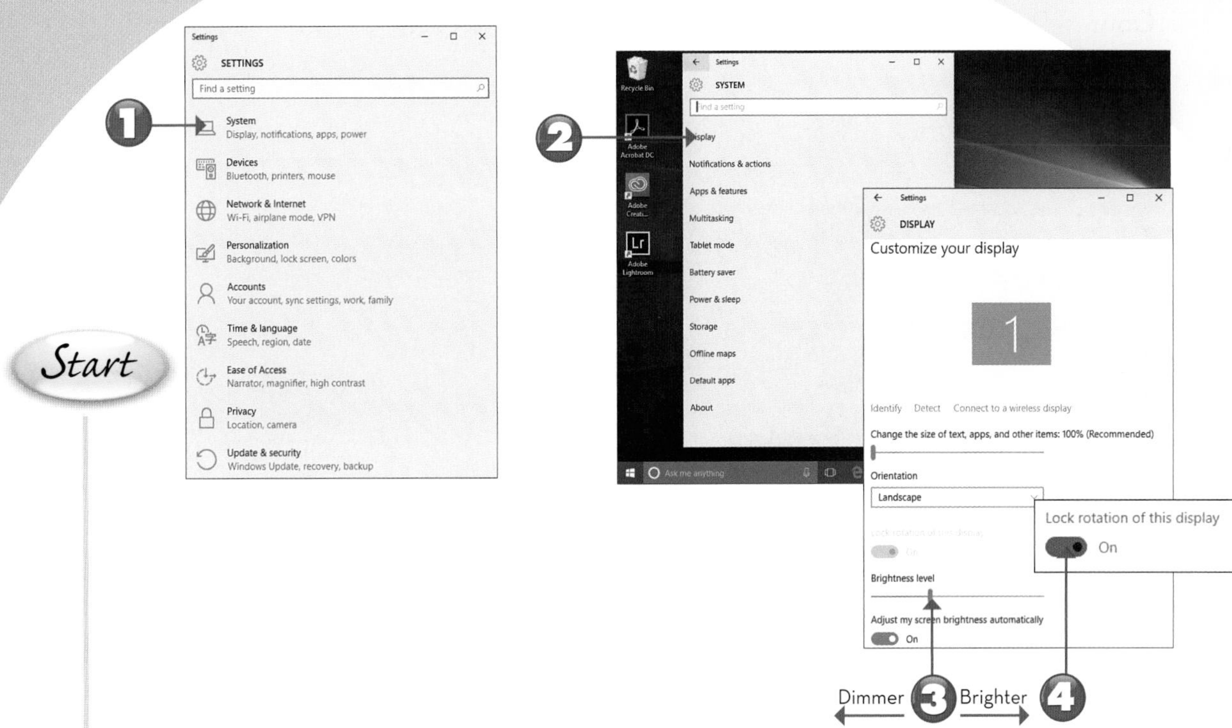

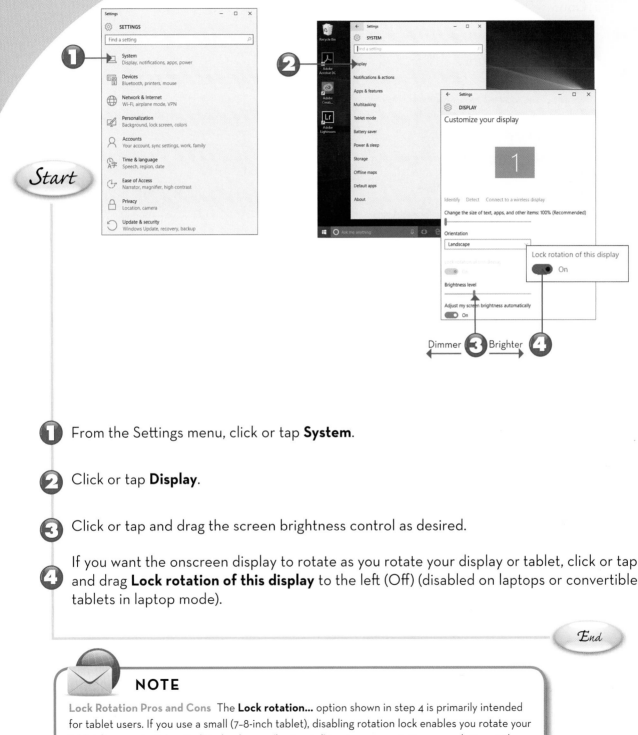

1. From the Settings menu, click or tap **System**.

2. Click or tap **Display**.

3. Click or tap and drag the screen brightness control as desired.

4. If you want the onscreen display to rotate as you rotate your display or tablet, click or tap and drag **Lock rotation of this display** to the left (Off) (disabled on laptops or convertible tablets in laptop mode).

End

NOTE

Lock Rotation Pros and Cons The **Lock rotation...** option shown in step 4 is primarily intended for tablet users. If you use a small (7-8-inch tablet), disabling rotation lock enables you rotate your tablet from portrait (vertical) to landscape (horizontal) to view presentations or websites at the largest possible size. However, disabling rotation lock could use up battery power faster.

ADDING A SECOND DISPLAY

Have an extra display? Windows 10 makes using it easier than ever. We start from the Display dialog box you learned about in the previous exercise.

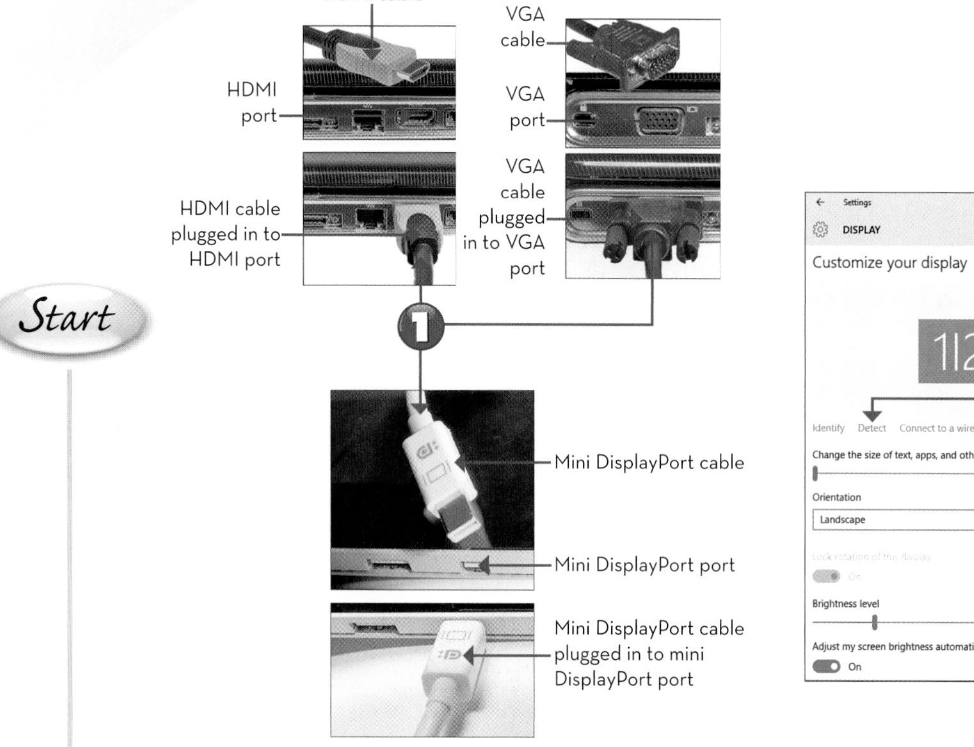

Start

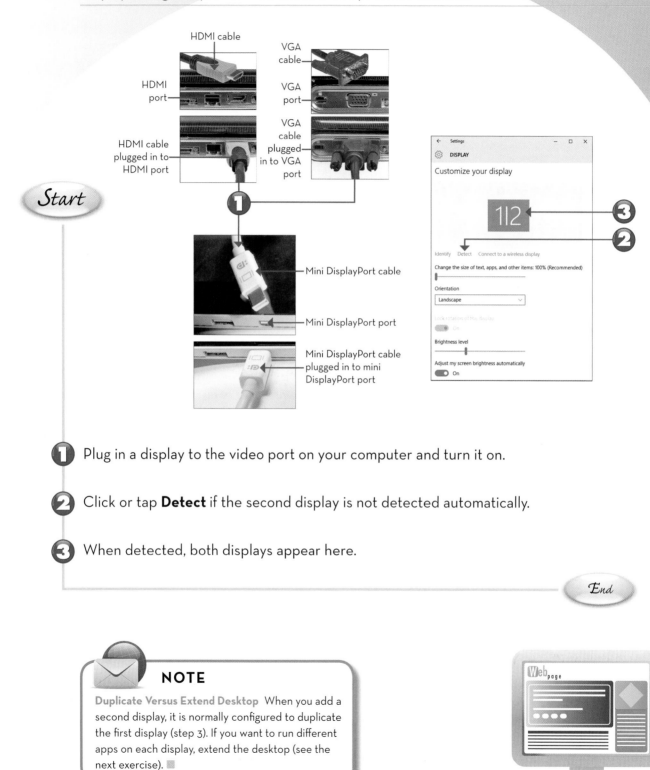

1. Plug in a display to the video port on your computer and turn it on.
2. Click or tap **Detect** if the second display is not detected automatically.
3. When detected, both displays appear here.

End

NOTE

Duplicate Versus Extend Desktop When you add a second display, it is normally configured to duplicate the first display (step 3). If you want to run different apps on each display, extend the desktop (see the next exercise).

EXTENDING YOUR DESKTOP

In most cases, if you add an additional display, it's because you want more onscreen space for apps. Here's how to configure your additional display as an extended desktop.

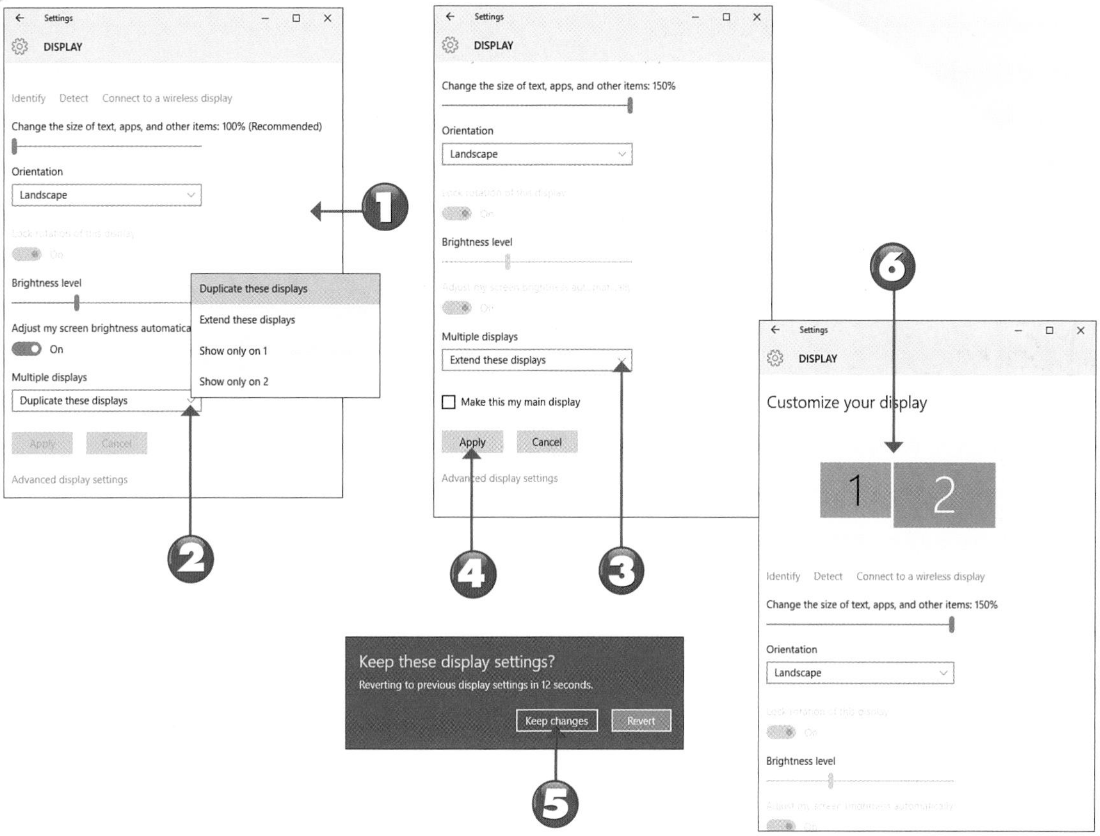

Start

1. Scroll down or flick up until the **Multiple displays** menu is visible (if necessary).
2. Open the **Multiple displays** menu.
3. Select **Extend these displays**.
4. Click or tap **Apply**.
5. Click or tap **Keep changes**.
6. The first and second display icons are now separate.

End

NOTE

Using the Extended Desktop Drag a program to the second display, and when you close that program, Windows remembers which display was last used for the program. When you open the program again, Windows uses the additional display to run the program.

ADJUSTING SCREEN RESOLUTION

In the Display dialog box, the relative sizes of the display icons indicate the resolution; higher-resolution displays have larger icons than lower-resolution displays. If any display is not using the correct resolution (horizontal and vertical pixel settings), follow this procedure to change its resolution.

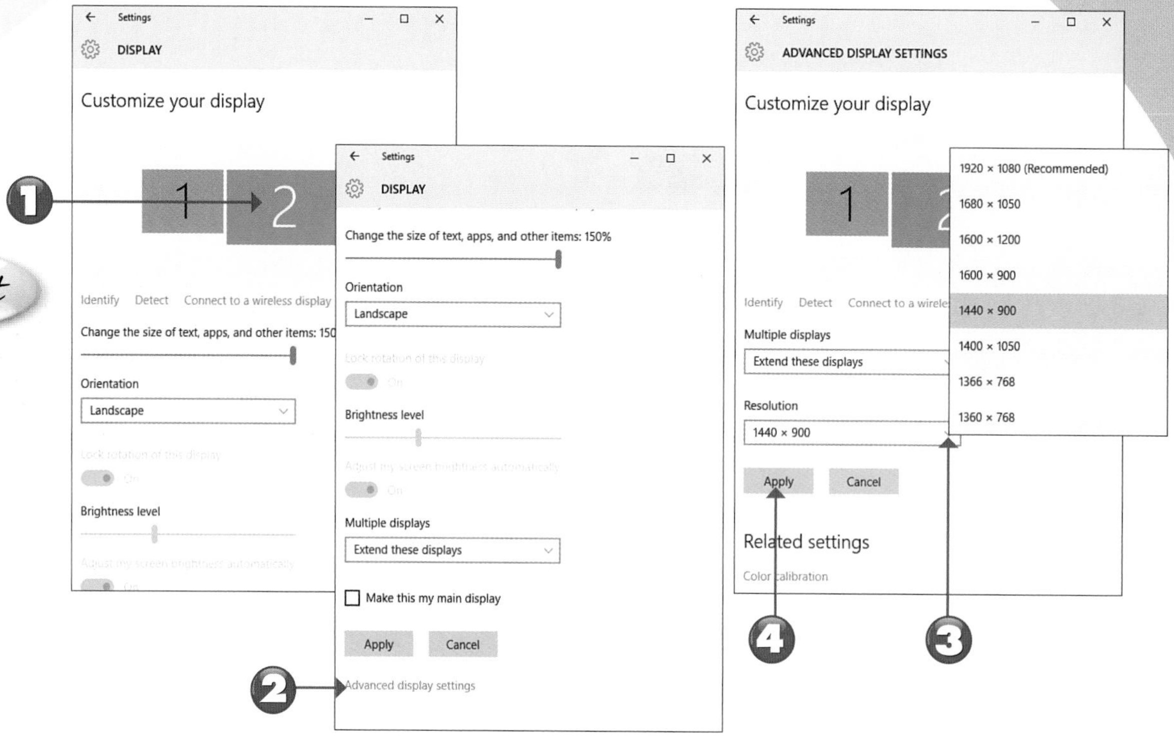

Start

1. Click or tap the display to change.
2. Click or tap **Advanced display settings**.
3. Click or press and drag the resolution setting to (Recommended).
4. Click or tap **Apply**.

Continued

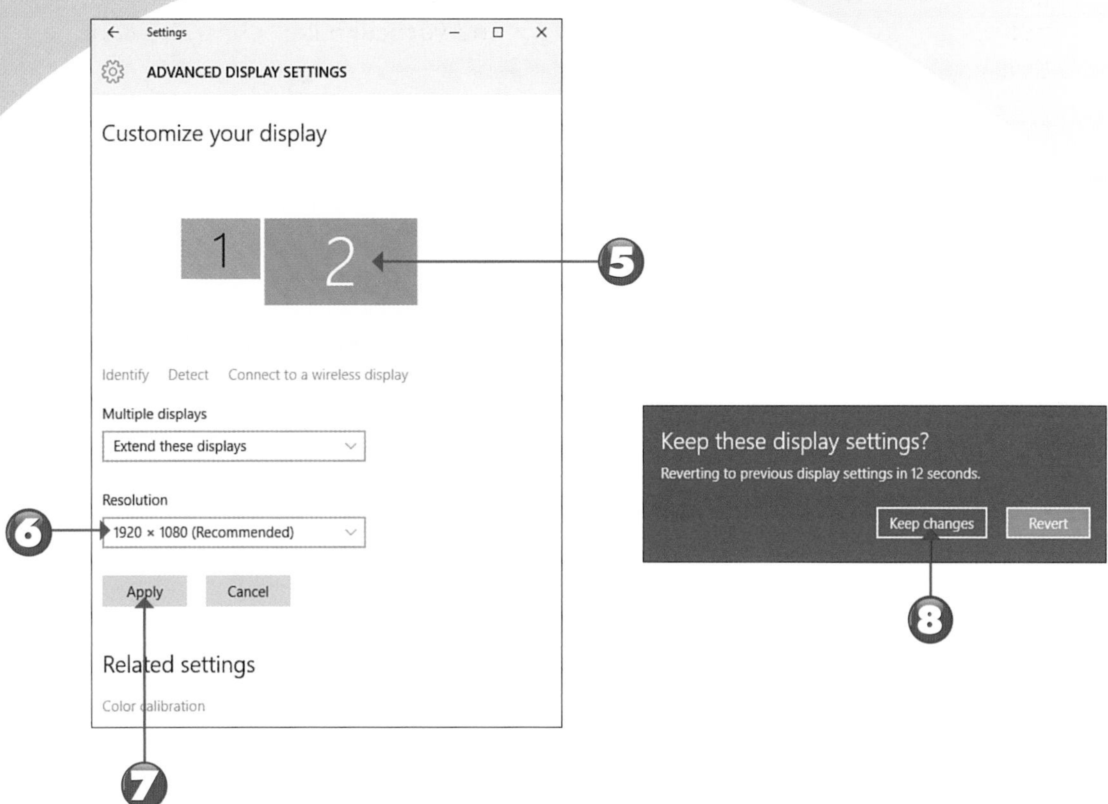

5. The display icon changes in size according to the resolution setting selected in step 3.

6. The new display resolution.

7. Click or tap **Apply**.

8. Click or tap **Keep changes**.

End

NOTE

Recommended = Optimal Windows 10 refers to the optimal resolution for your display as "Recommended." However, if you find the desktop objects or web pages are too small onscreen, use the **Change the size of text, apps, and other items** slider (Display dialog box) to choose a larger size or a lower resolution.

ADJUSTING SCREEN POSITION

When you add an additional display, Windows assumes that it is located to the right of your original display. If your additional display is in some other relative position, you should move the display icon accordingly. In this example, the additional display is placed to the left of the original. Here's how to change its position.

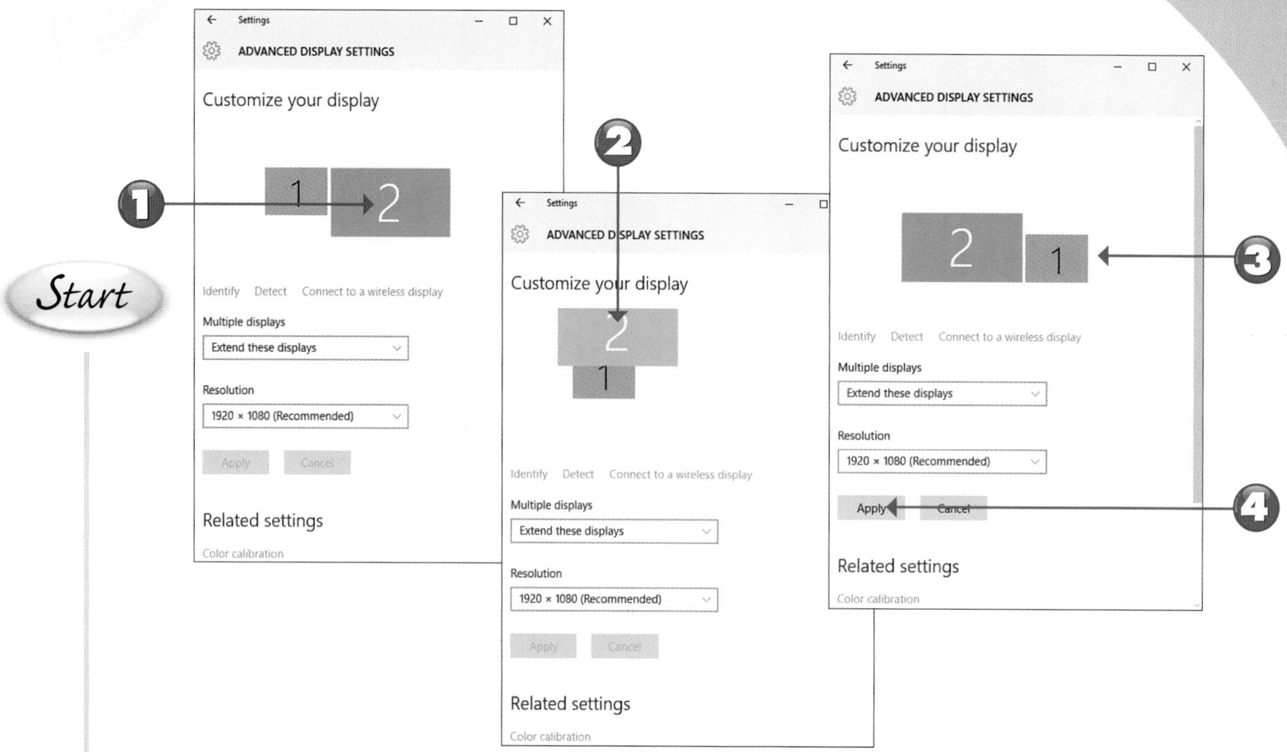

Start

1. The additional display icon (2) is not in the correct position relative to the original display (1).
2. Click or press and drag the display icon to the correct relative position.
3. The additional display icon is now in the correct location.
4. Click or tap **Apply**.

Continued

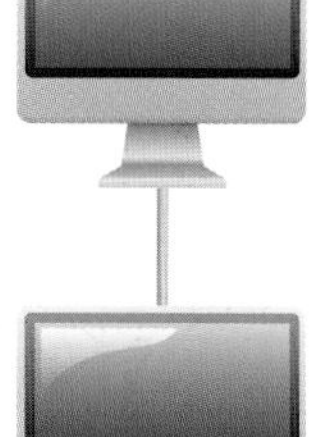

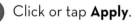

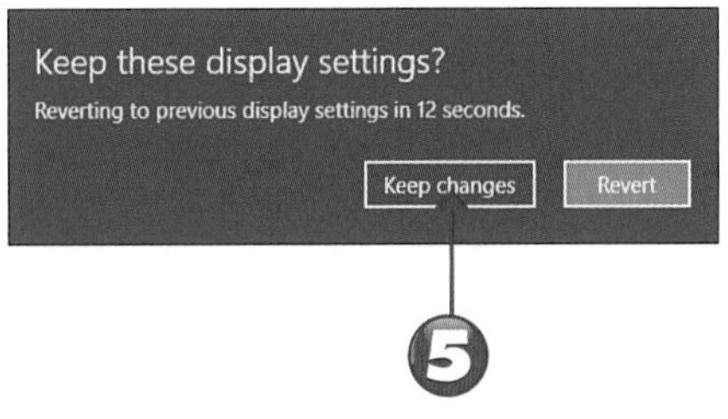
Keep these display settings?
Reverting to previous display settings in 12 seconds.
Keep changes
Revert
5

5 Click or tap **Keep changes**.

End

TIP

Back Arrow and Gearbox Icons From any menu in Settings, click the gearbox icon to return to the Settings dialog box. To return to the previous dialog, click the back arrow. To go back two levels, click the back arrow twice.

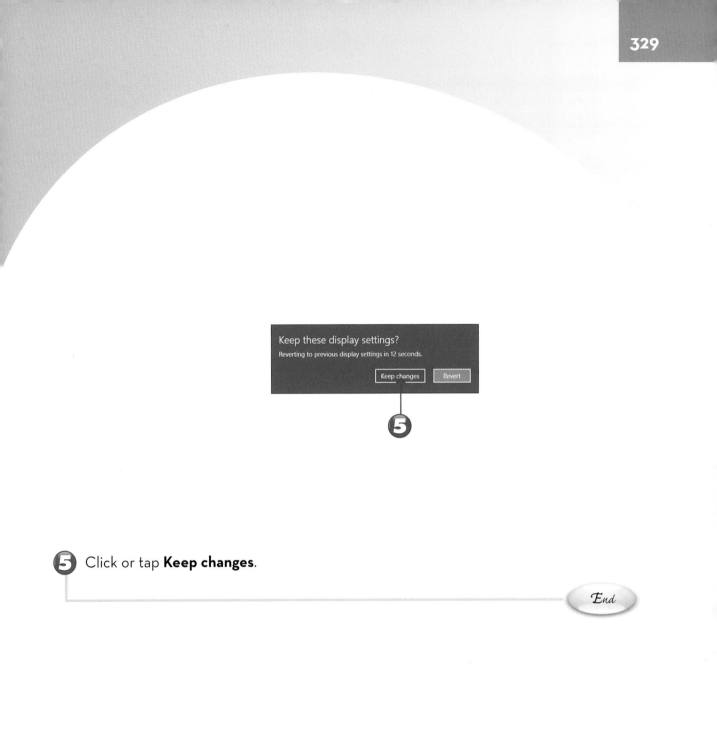

CHANGING QUICK ACTIONS

The Action Center button near the clock in the Windows taskbar displays quick action icons when clicked or tapped that provide access to features you use frequently. Use the Notifications & Actions dialog box to select the icons you prefer.

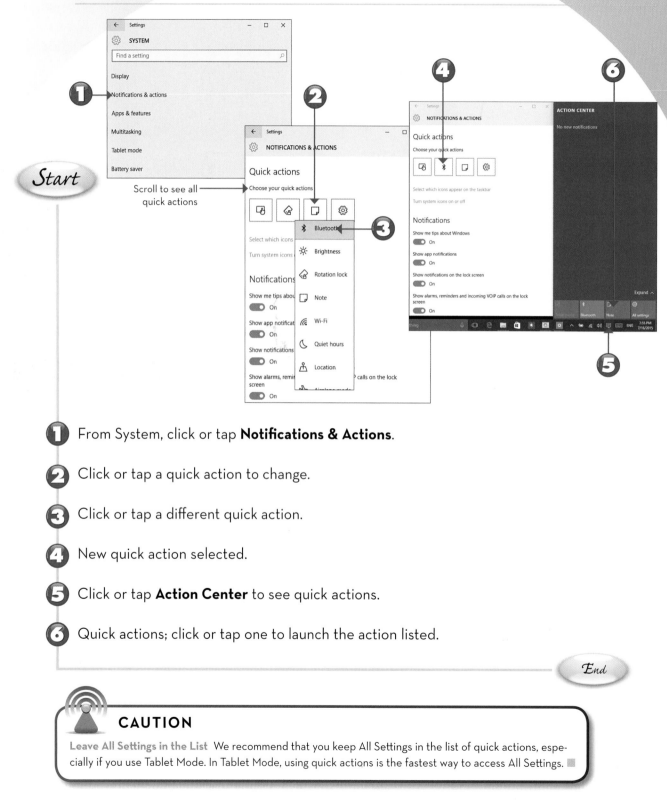

Start

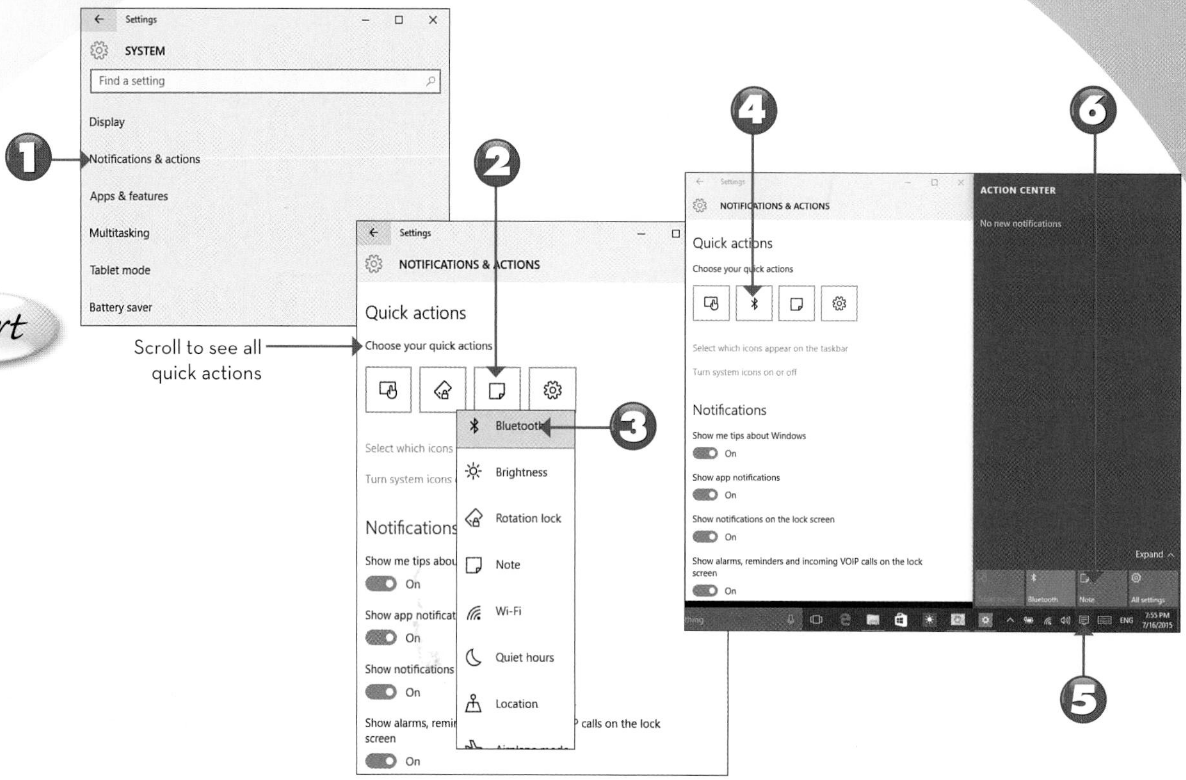

Scroll to see all quick actions

1. From System, click or tap **Notifications & Actions**.
2. Click or tap a quick action to change.
3. Click or tap a different quick action.
4. New quick action selected.
5. Click or tap **Action Center** to see quick actions.
6. Quick actions; click or tap one to launch the action listed.

End

CAUTION

Leave All Settings in the List We recommend that you keep All Settings in the list of quick actions, especially if you use Tablet Mode. In Tablet Mode, using quick actions is the fastest way to access All Settings.

CONFIGURING THE TASKBAR

The Windows 10 taskbar is also a great place to manage your system. Use Notifications & Actions to specify the settings you prefer.

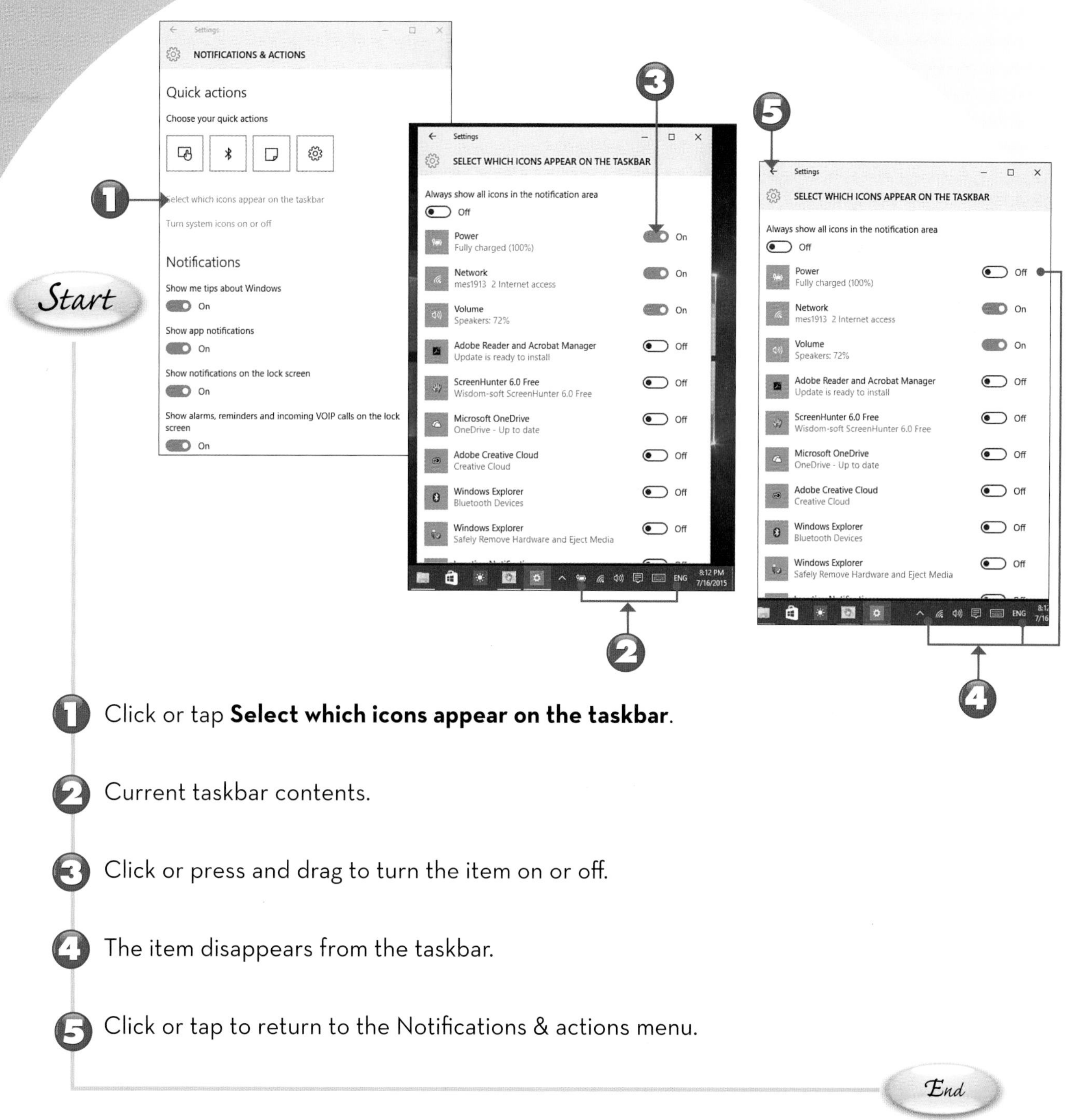

1. Click or tap **Select which icons appear on the taskbar**.
2. Current taskbar contents.
3. Click or press and drag to turn the item on or off.
4. The item disappears from the taskbar.
5. Click or tap to return to the Notifications & actions menu.

CONFIGURING SYSTEM ICONS

Some icons on the right side of the taskbar Windows designates specifically as system icons. In this exercise, you learn how to choose the ones that appear.

Start

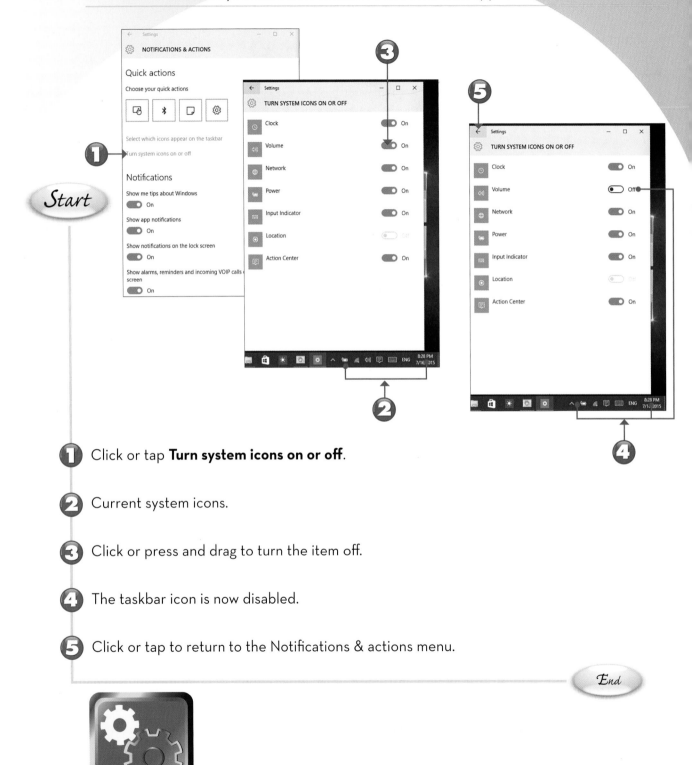

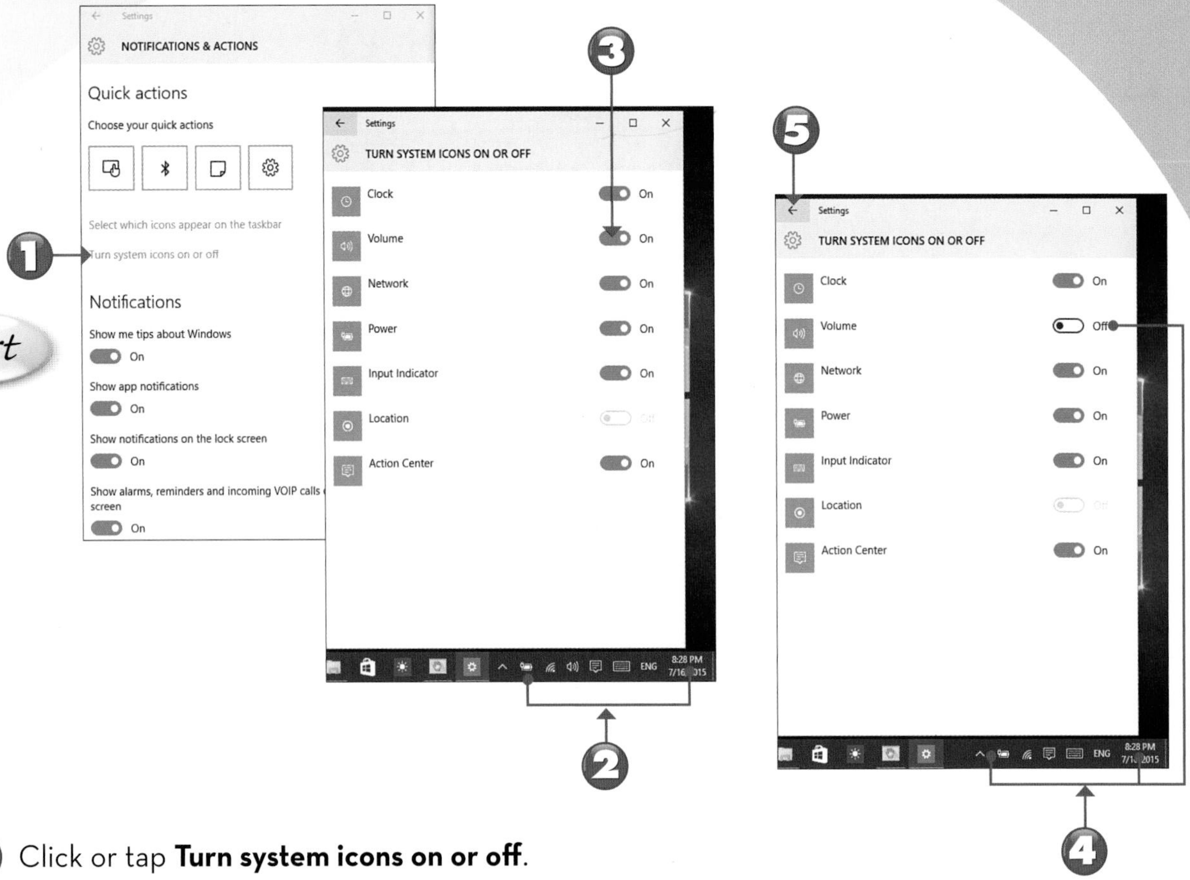

1. Click or tap **Turn system icons on or off**.
2. Current system icons.
3. Click or press and drag to turn the item off.
4. The taskbar icon is now disabled.
5. Click or tap to return to the Notifications & actions menu.

End

CONFIGURING APP-SPECIFIC NOTIFICATIONS

Many of the apps included in Windows 10 (and some you can install) can display notifications. In this exercise, you learn how to turn off notifications you do not need.

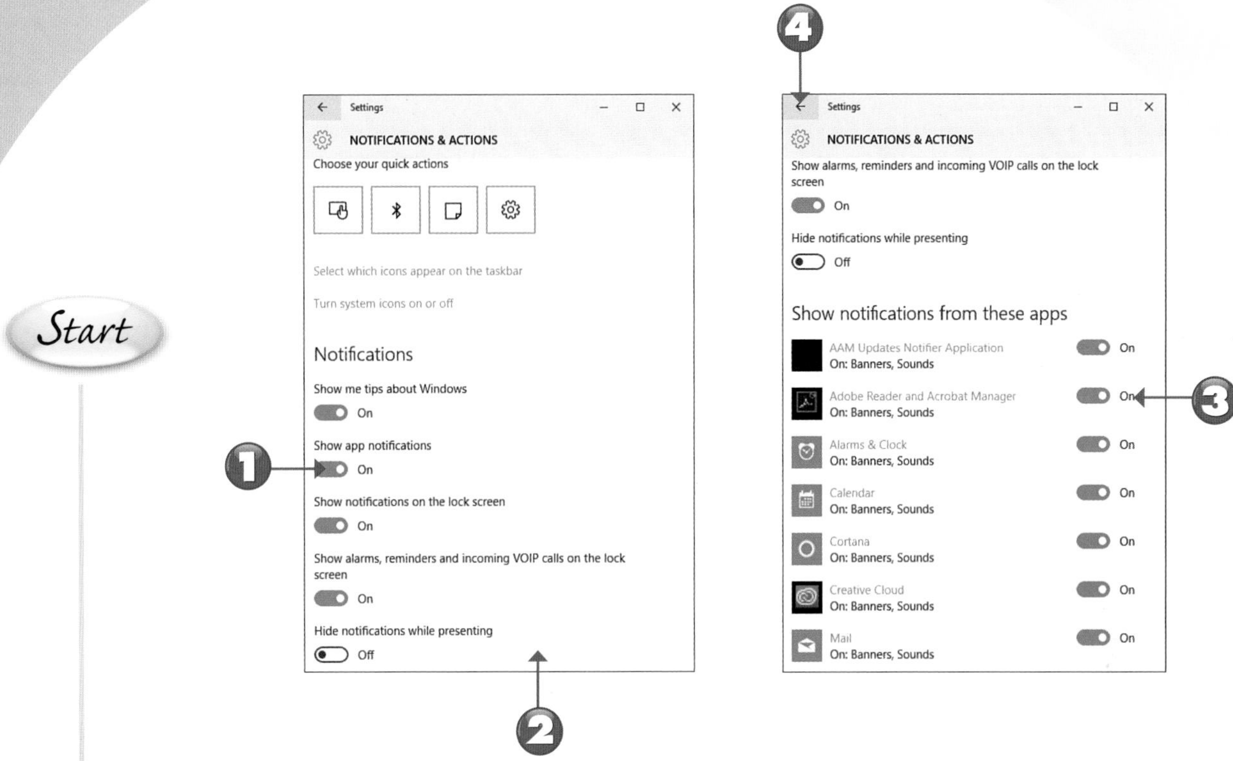

1. If you want to turn off all app notifications, click or tap to turn the switch to **Off**.
2. Scroll down or flick up to see all apps with notification options.
3. To turn off notifications for an app, click or tap to turn the switch **Off**.
4. Click or tap to return to the **System** dialog box.

End

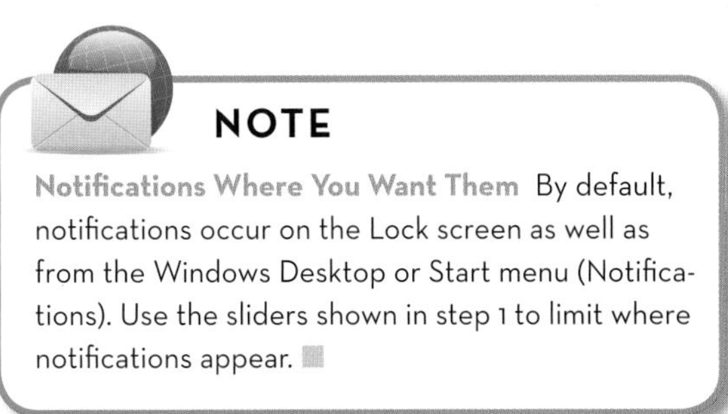

NOTE

Notifications Where You Want Them By default, notifications occur on the Lock screen as well as from the Windows Desktop or Start menu (Notifications). Use the sliders shown in step 1 to limit where notifications appear.

APPS & FEATURES

Particularly with Ultrabooks and tablets, both of which use small-capacity SSD storage, knowing how much space an app uses can be very helpful, especially if you also have the ability to uninstall apps that you don't need anymore. The Apps & Features dialog box provides you with both features.

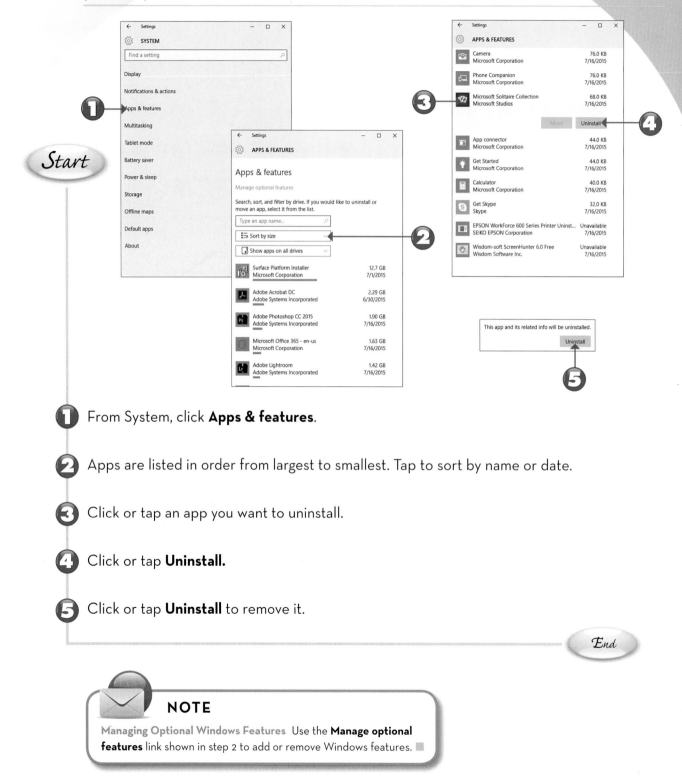

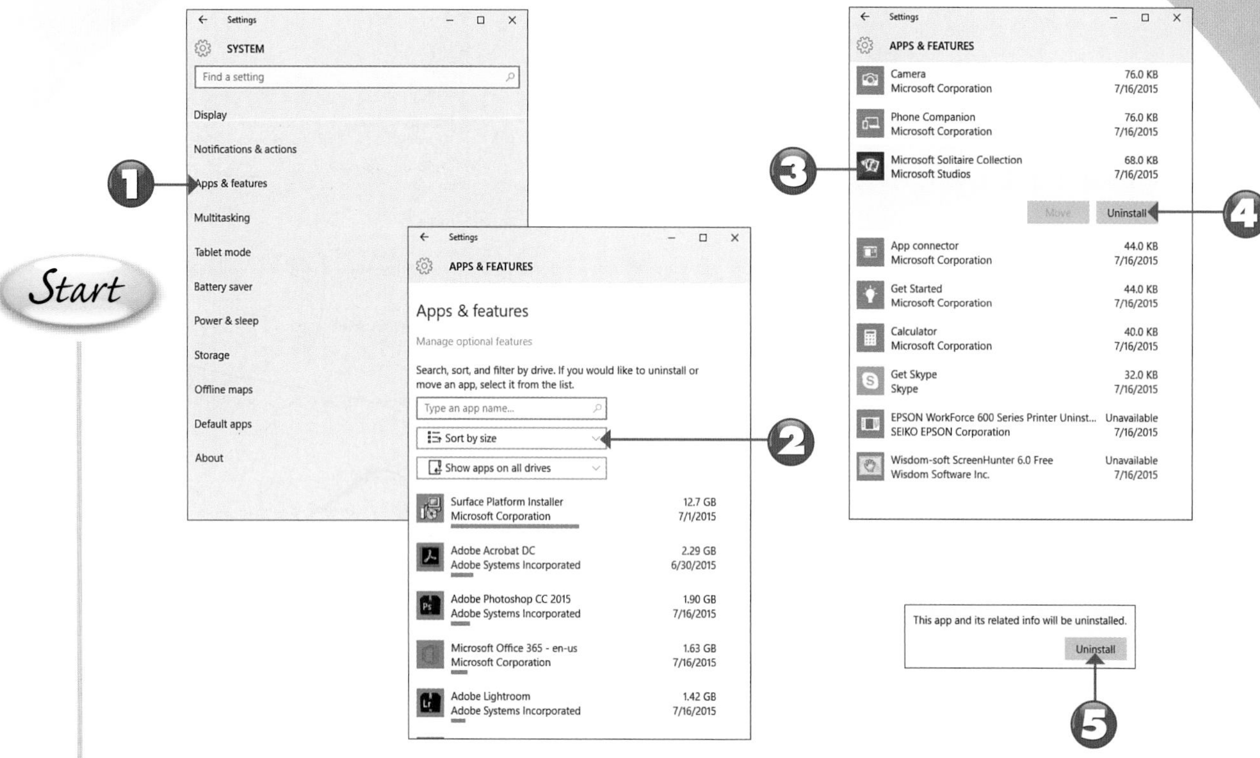

1. From System, click **Apps & features**.
2. Apps are listed in order from largest to smallest. Tap to sort by name or date.
3. Click or tap an app you want to uninstall.
4. Click or tap **Uninstall.**
5. Click or tap **Uninstall** to remove it.

End

NOTE

Managing Optional Windows Features Use the **Manage optional features** link shown in step 2 to add or remove Windows features.

CONFIGURING SNAP

Windows 10's Multitasking dialog box enables you to configure how your screen functions when you are using two or more apps. In this exercise, you learn how to configure the Snap feature, which controls how app windows behave.

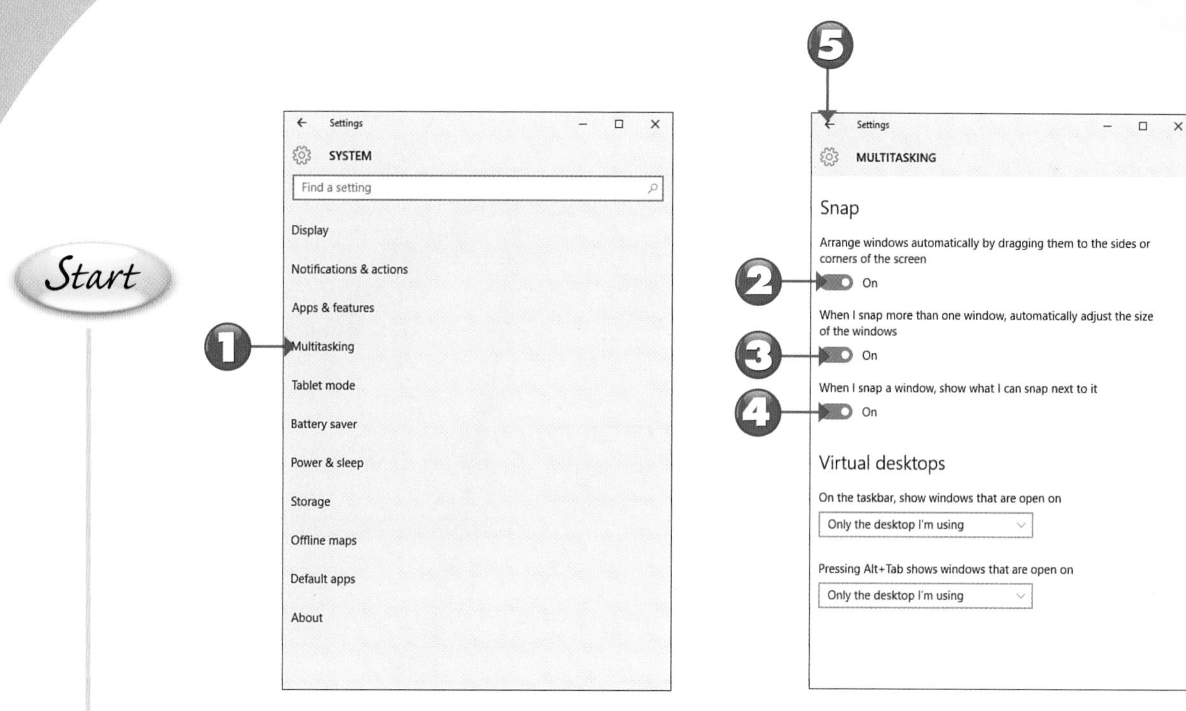

1. From System, click or tap **Multitasking**.

2. If you don't want a window that you drag to the top of the screen to expand to full screen, click or press and drag to **Off**.

3. If you prefer to arrange window sizes manually, click or press and drag to **Off**.

4. If you don't want to see additional running apps you can snap when you snap a window to one side, click or press and drag to **Off**.

5. Click or tap to return to the System dialog.

End

CONFIGURING TABLET MODE

If you use a tablet or a convertible tablet/laptop device (a device with a quick-release keyboard or a keyboard that flips out of the way so you can use the touchscreen as a tablet), the Tablet Mode dialog box helps you optimize your device for touch use.

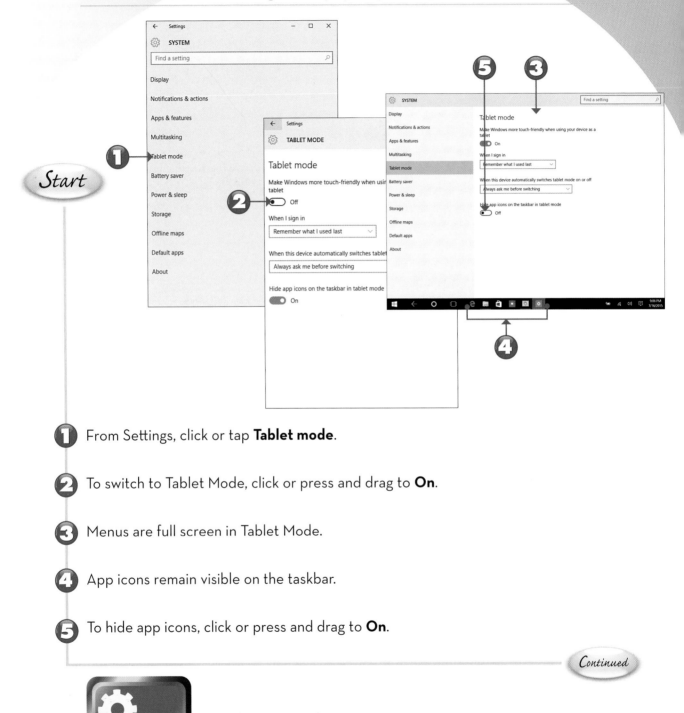

Start

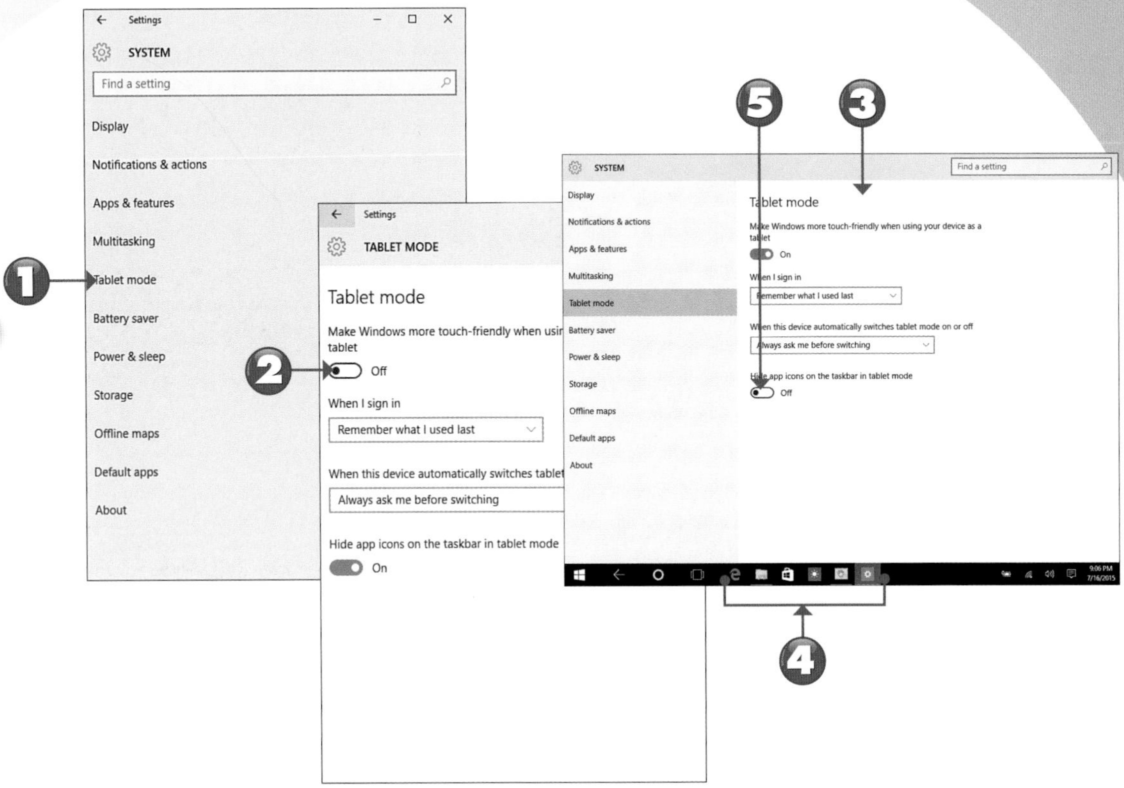

1. From Settings, click or tap **Tablet mode**.
2. To switch to Tablet Mode, click or press and drag to **On**.
3. Menus are full screen in Tablet Mode.
4. App icons remain visible on the taskbar.
5. To hide app icons, click or press and drag to **On**.

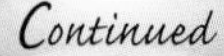

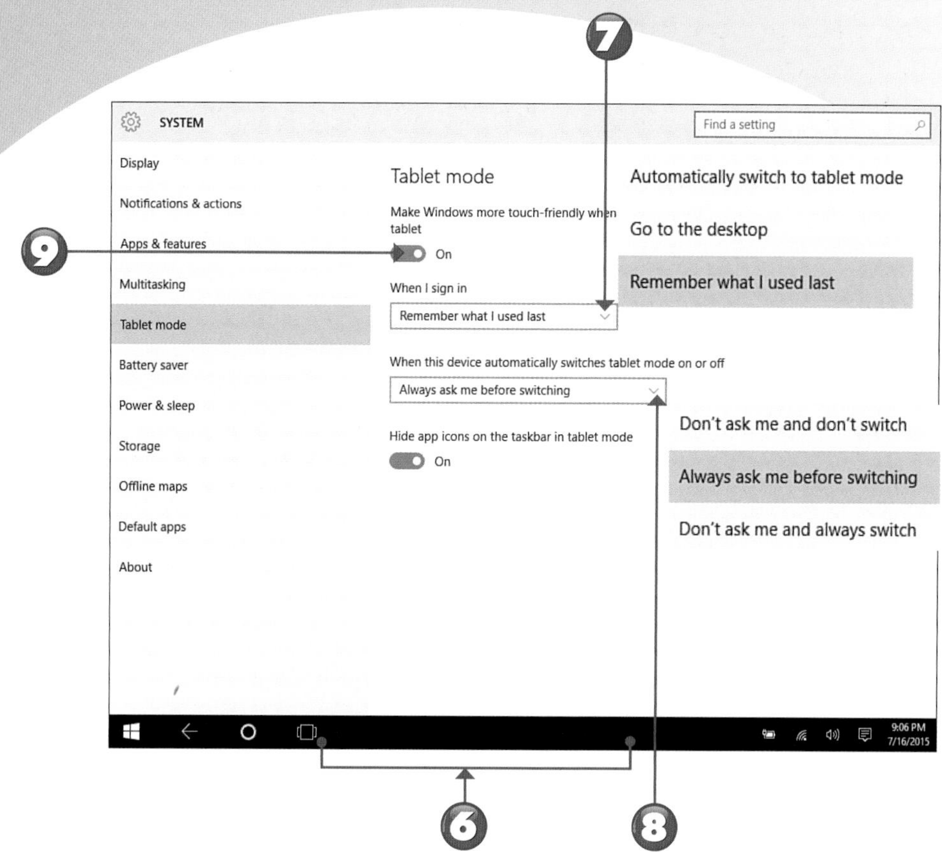

6. App icons are no longer visible.
7. Click or tap to change login options.
8. Click or tap to change mode-switching options.
9. To disable Tablet Mode, click or press and drag to **Off**.

End

NOTE

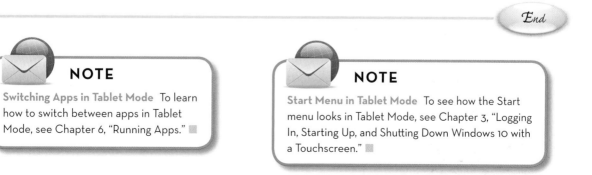

Switching Apps in Tablet Mode To learn how to switch between apps in Tablet Mode, see Chapter 6, "Running Apps."

NOTE

Start Menu in Tablet Mode To see how the Start menu looks in Tablet Mode, see Chapter 3, "Logging In, Starting Up, and Shutting Down Windows 10 with a Touchscreen."

USING BATTERY SAVER

If you use Windows 10 on a laptop or tablet, Battery Saver shows you how your system uses battery power. Here's how to use it.

Start

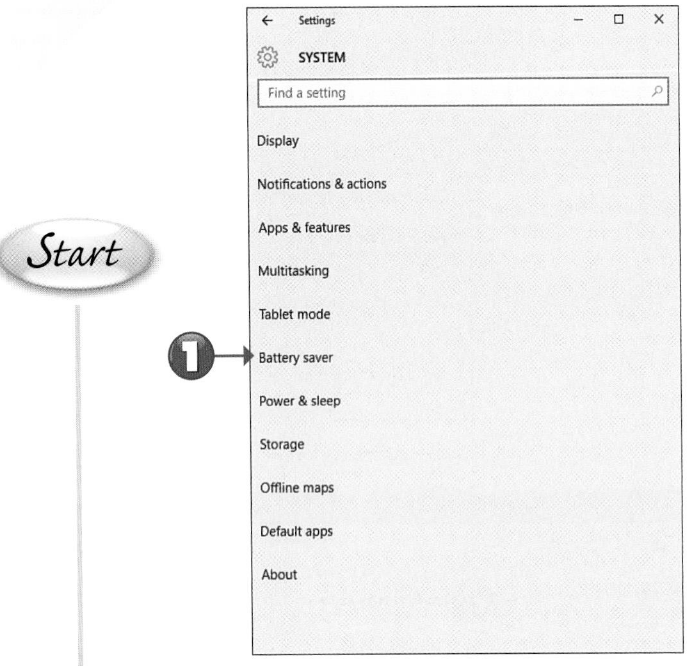

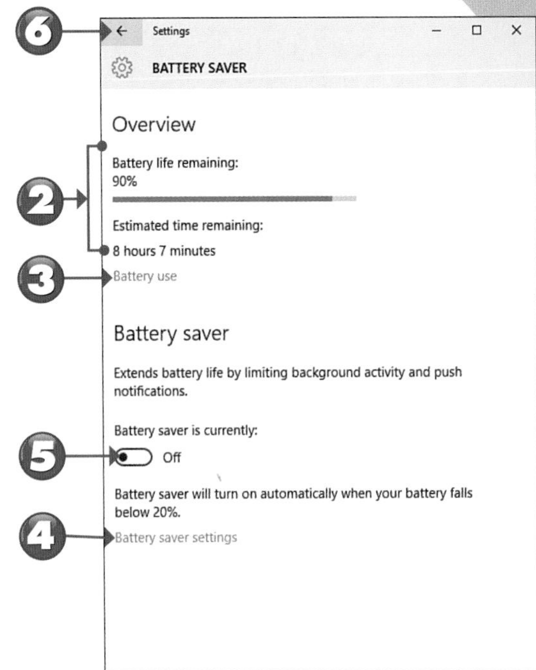

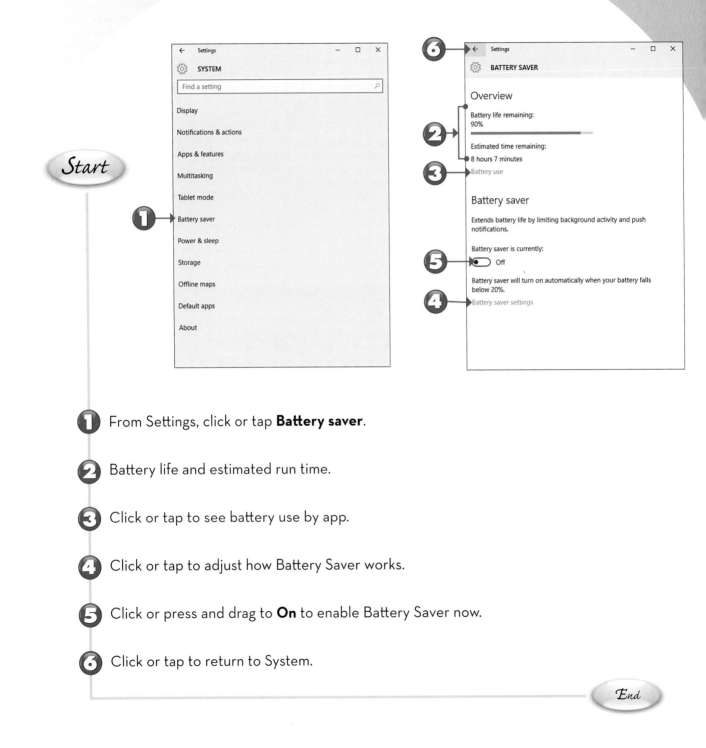

1. From Settings, click or tap **Battery saver**.
2. Battery life and estimated run time.
3. Click or tap to see battery use by app.
4. Click or tap to adjust how Battery Saver works.
5. Click or press and drag to **On** to enable Battery Saver now.
6. Click or tap to return to System.

End

POWER & SLEEP

Use the Power & sleep menu to adjust how long your device stays on when idle.

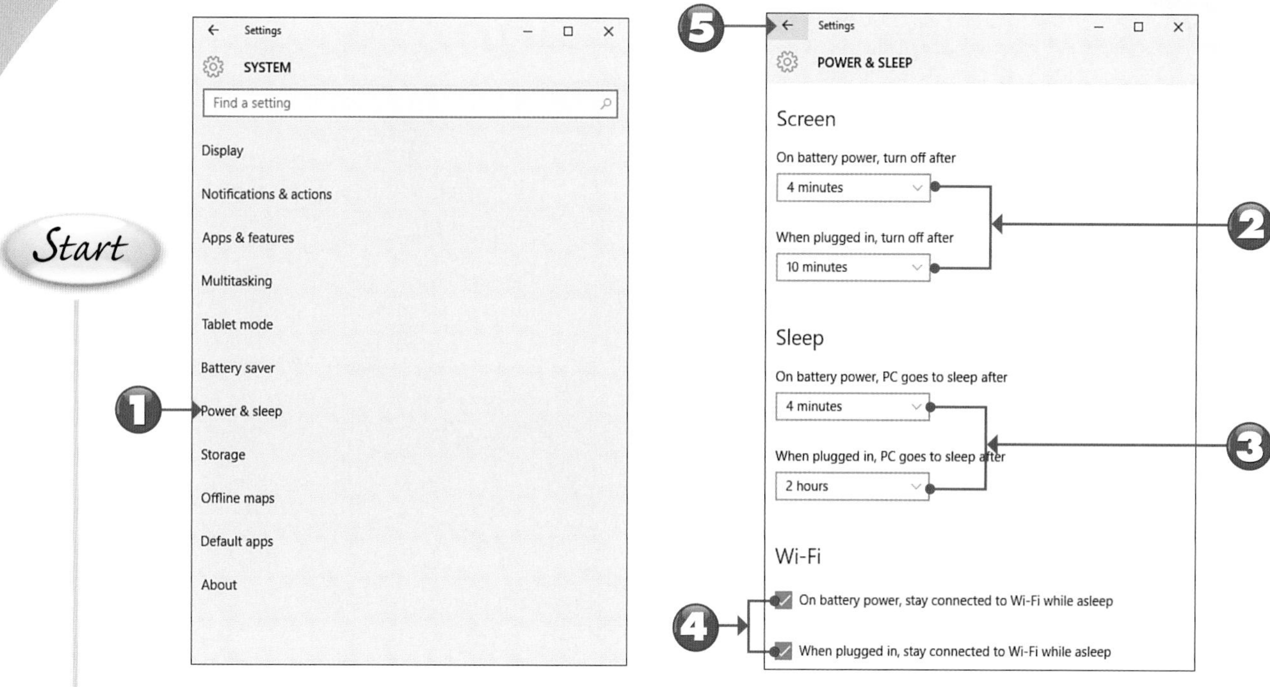

1. From Settings, click or tap **Power & sleep**.
2. Click or tap to select when to turn off the screen on battery or when plugged in (AC power).
3. Click or tap to select when to sleep on battery or when plugged in (AC power).
4. Clear check boxes to drop Wi-Fi connections when the system is sleeping.
5. Click or tap to return to System.

NOTE

Choosing a Power Plan Click the Additional Power Settings link at the bottom of the screen (not shown) and choose the High performance setting if you want your device to run at top speed all the time (uses the most power). Balanced is the normal setting. Power Saver uses the least power by running the device at a lower clock speed than with the High or Balanced settings.

CHECKING DRIVE CAPACITY WITH STORAGE

Use Storage to find out how much and what types of information is stored on the drives connected to your system.

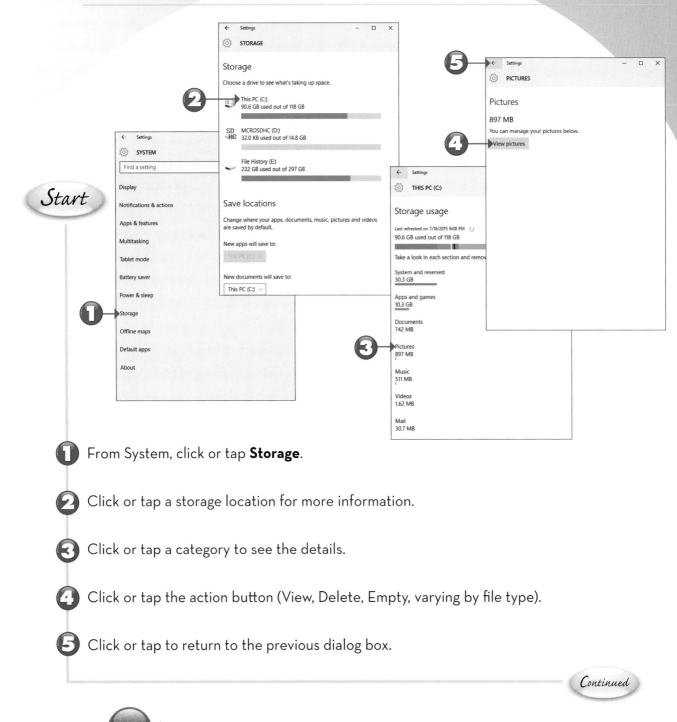

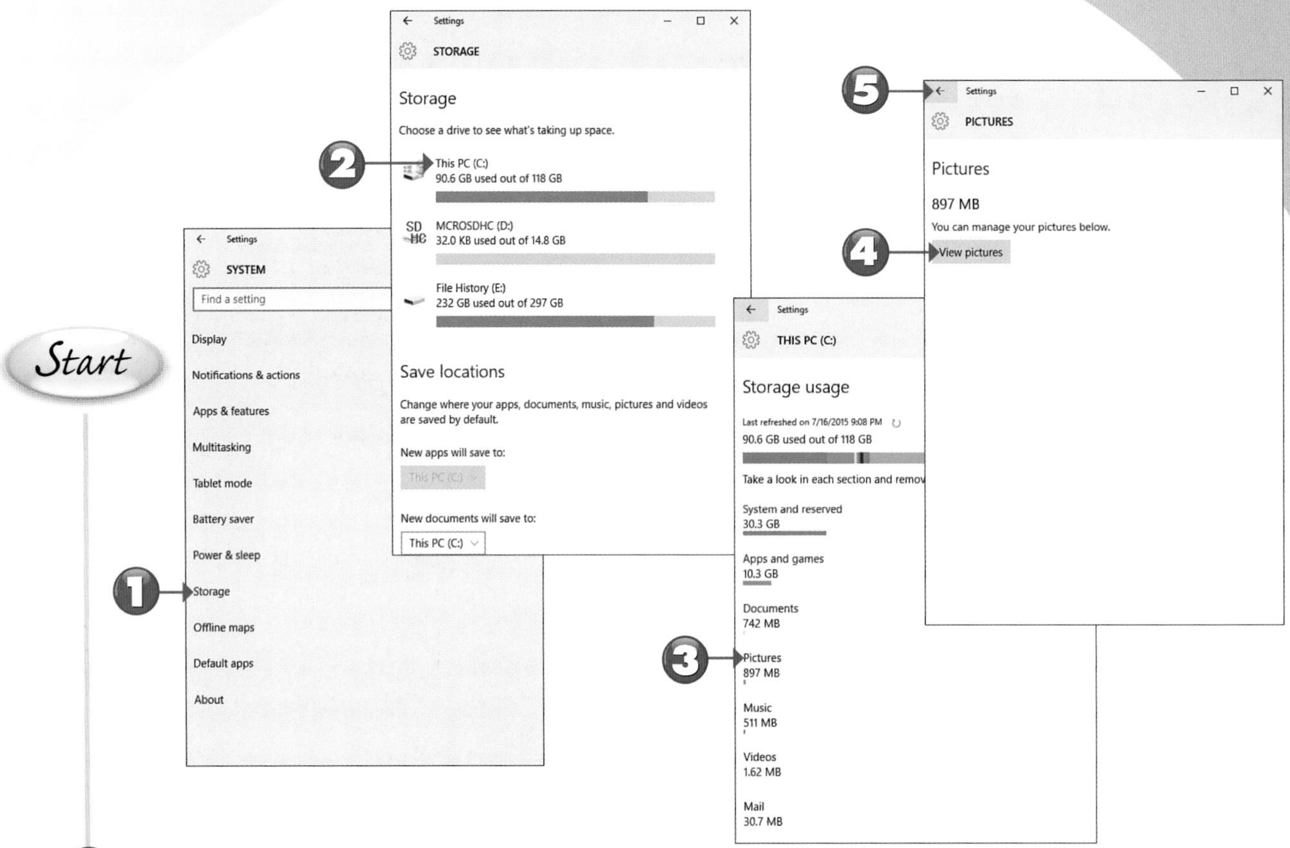

Start

1. From System, click or tap **Storage**.
2. Click or tap a storage location for more information.
3. Click or tap a category to see the details.
4. Click or tap the action button (View, Delete, Empty, varying by file type).
5. Click or tap to return to the previous dialog box.

Continued

NOTE

This PC = Drive C: Windows 10 uses the term "This PC" to refer to your system drive, which is normally the C: drive.

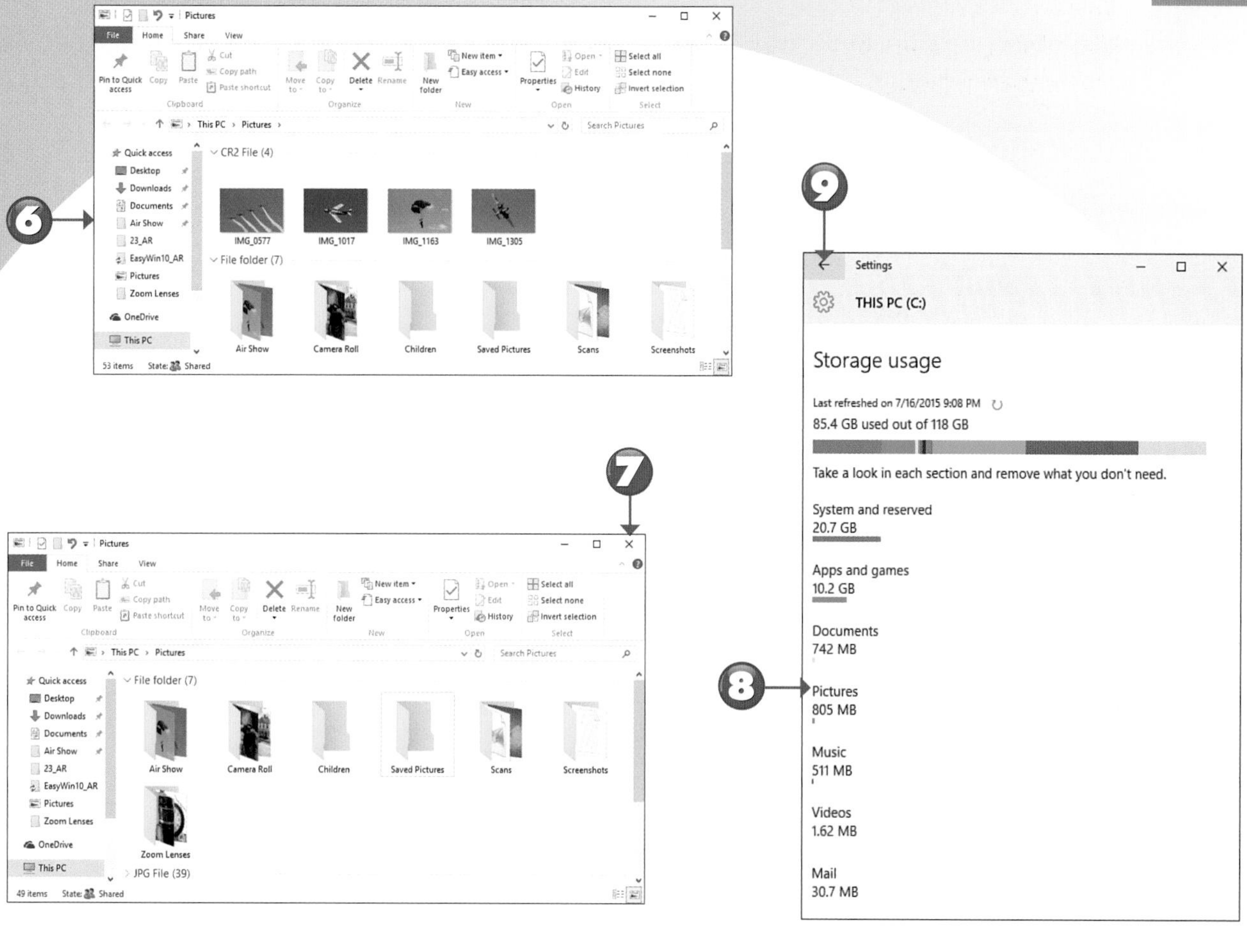

6 In this example, File Explorer opens the Pictures folder.

7 After deleting, copying, or moving files, close the window.

8 The storage location details dialog box shows any change in space used in the category you chose in step 3.

9 Click or tap to return to the previous dialog box.

End

NOTE

Copying, Moving, and Deleting Files and Folders To learn more about working with files and folders, see Chapter 14, “Storing and Finding Your Files.”

CHANGING FILE LOCATIONS WITH STORAGE

Storage can also help you use flash memory and external hard disks for new apps and files. Here's how.

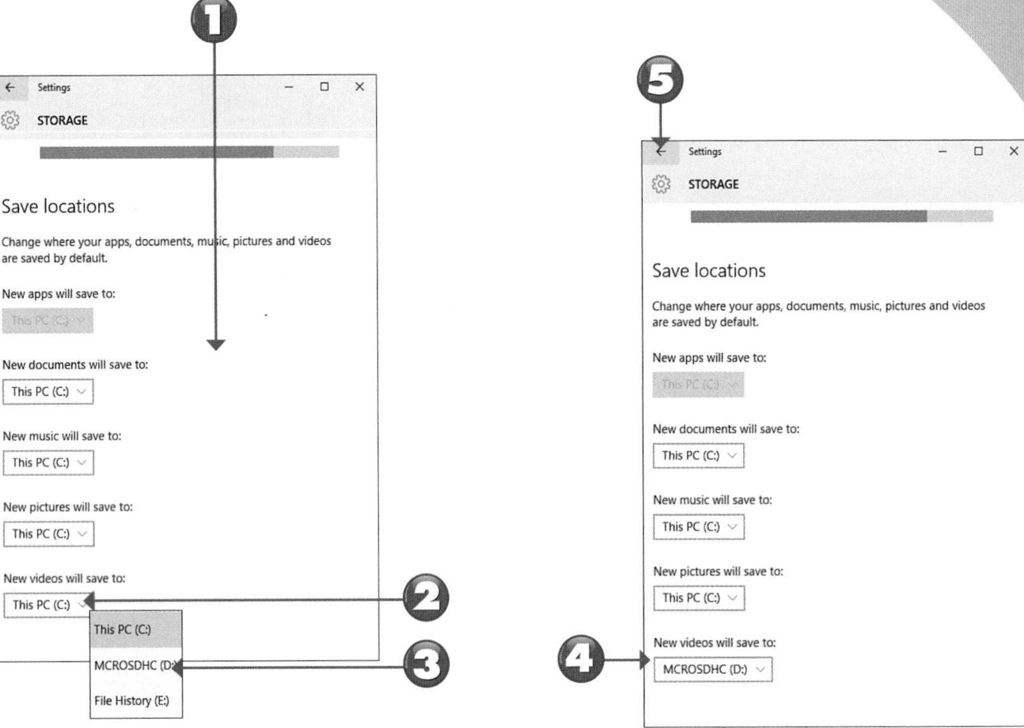

1. Scroll down or flick up to **Save locations**.
2. Choose a file type.
3. Select a new location for the file.
4. New video files will be stored at the new location.
5. Click or tap to return to System.

End

NOTE

Changed Storage Location? Don't Disconnect That Drive! If you disconnect or remove a drive that you set up for apps or files with Storage, Windows can't find your apps or files until you reconnect or insert the drive.

MAKING MAPS AVAILABLE OFFLINE

Thanks to GPS units in smartphones, tablets, and cars, real-time navigation is a great way to get around—unless you don't have a signal. If you want to use your device to navigate no matter your location, use Windows 10's downloadable offline maps feature. You can select maps for most regions of the world.

Start

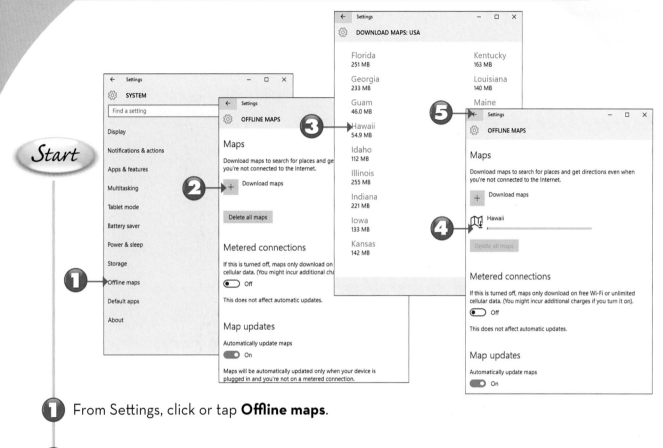

1. From Settings, click or tap **Offline maps**.
2. Click or tap + to select a map (region, country, state or province as listed).
3. After you select a map, it is downloaded to your system.
4. After you download a map, Windows 10's Maps app can use it even when you're not connected to the Internet.
5. Click or tap to return to System.

End

CHANGING DEFAULT APPS

If you have more than one app that can be used for a particular task or to open a particular type of file, use the Default Apps dialog box to specify which app is the one you prefer.

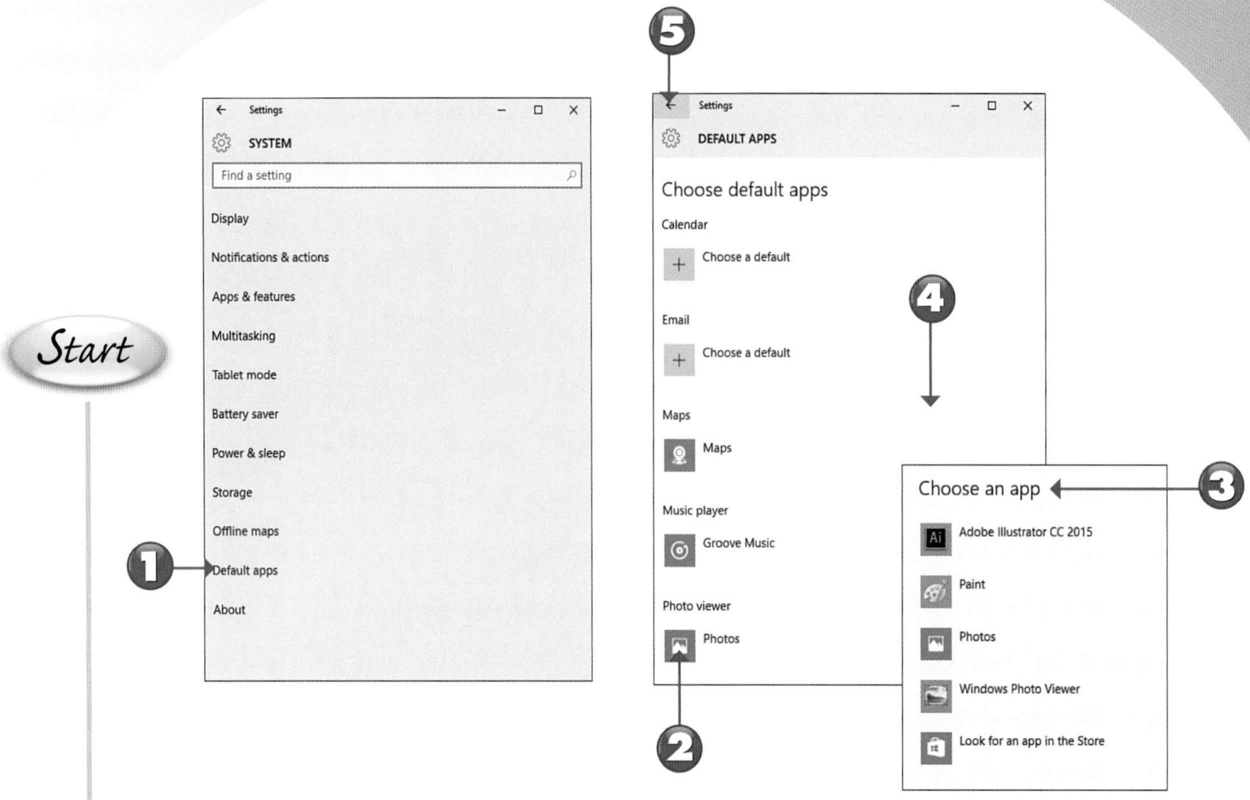

1. From Settings, click or tap **Default apps**.
2. Click or tap a type of app.
3. Select the app to use.
4. Scroll down or flick up for other file types and advanced settings.
5. Click or tap to return to System.

NOTE

Available Apps Vary The exact list of default apps you can choose from depends on the file or app type you choose and the apps installed on your device.

ADDING A DEVICE, PRINTER, OR SCANNER

The Devices category is used to view and add external components such as mice, keyboards, Bluetooth devices, printers, and scanners. You can also manage mouse, keyboard, pen, and AutoPlay settings in the appropriate submenus. Here's how to add a device that's plugged in or has been detected on your network.

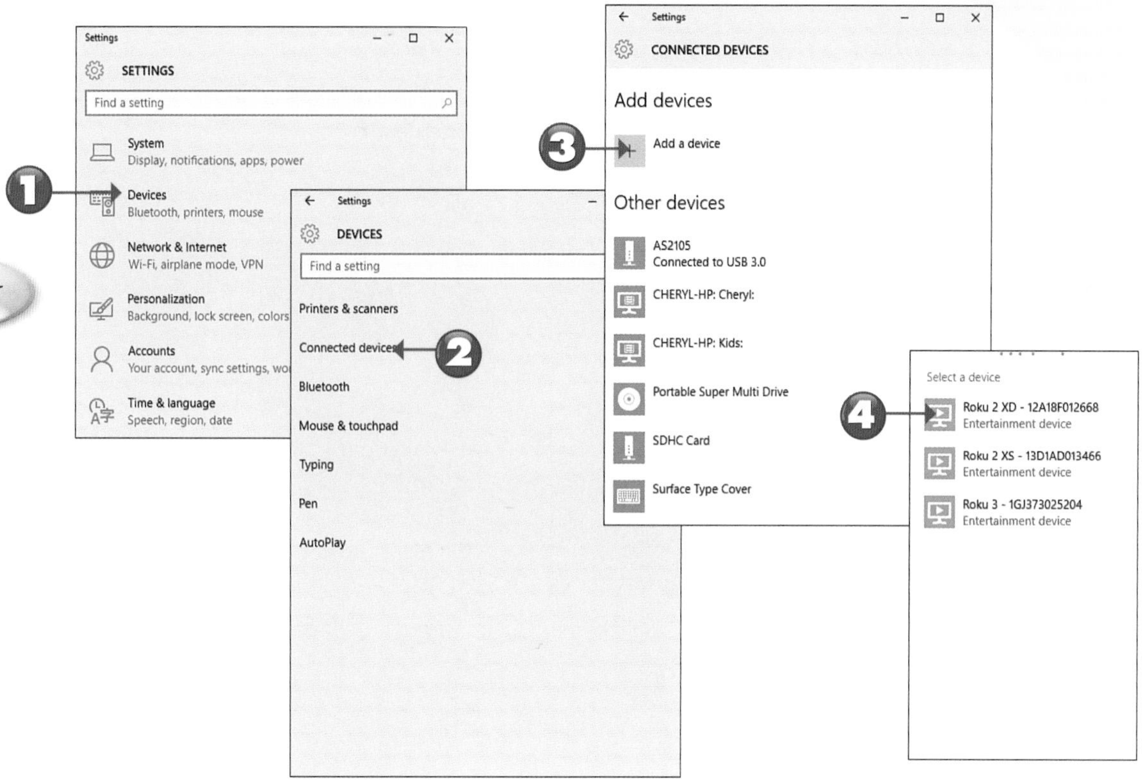

1. From Settings, click or tap **Devices**.
2. From Devices, click or tap **Connected devices**.
3. Click or tap **+** to add a device.
4. Choose a device from those available.

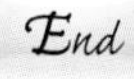

NOTE

Adding or Removing a Printer or Scanner The Printers & scanners category in Devices works the same way as the Connected Devices category. Follow these instructions to add or remove a printer or scanner.

NOTE

Directions Might Vary by Device To install some devices, you might need to install a driver disc or a downloaded installation program. If the device is connected via a network, you might need to press a physical button or click a software button on the device to finish the task.

REMOVING A DEVICE

The Connected devices dialog box is also used to remove a device safely. Using this dialog box is especially important if you want to remove a storage device because it ensures that no data is being written to or read from the device when you disconnect it.

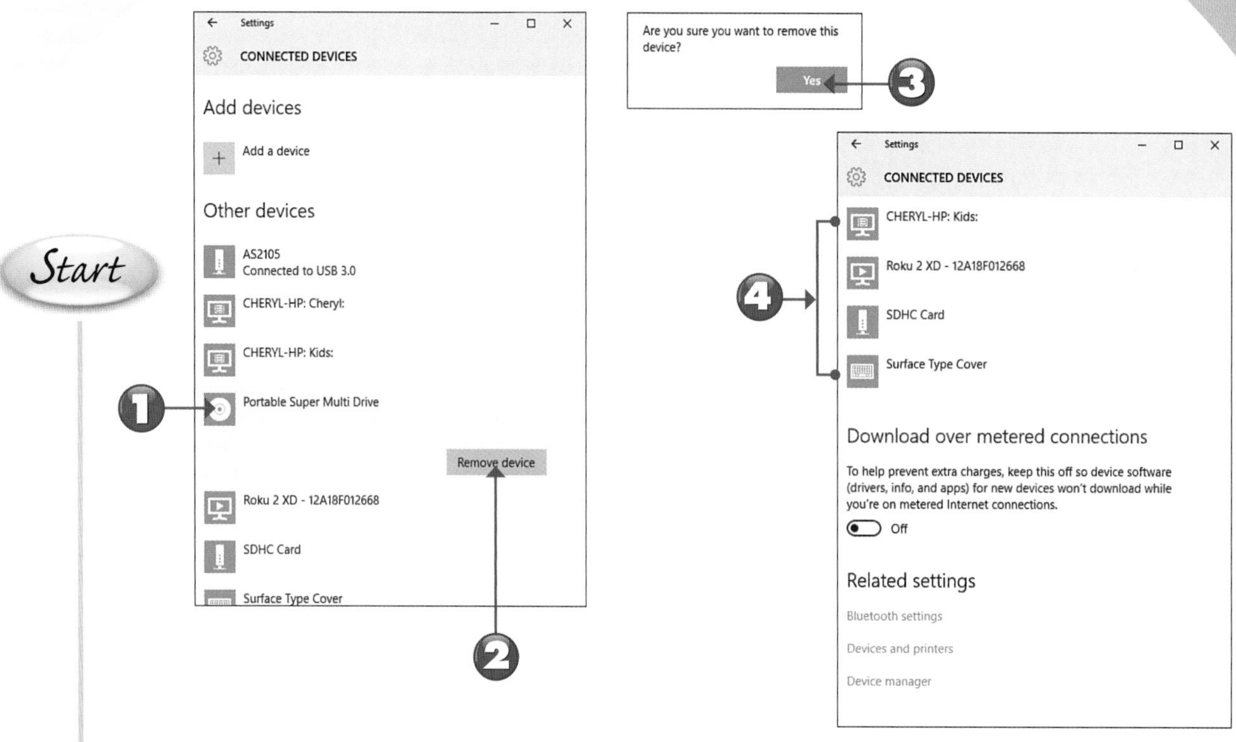

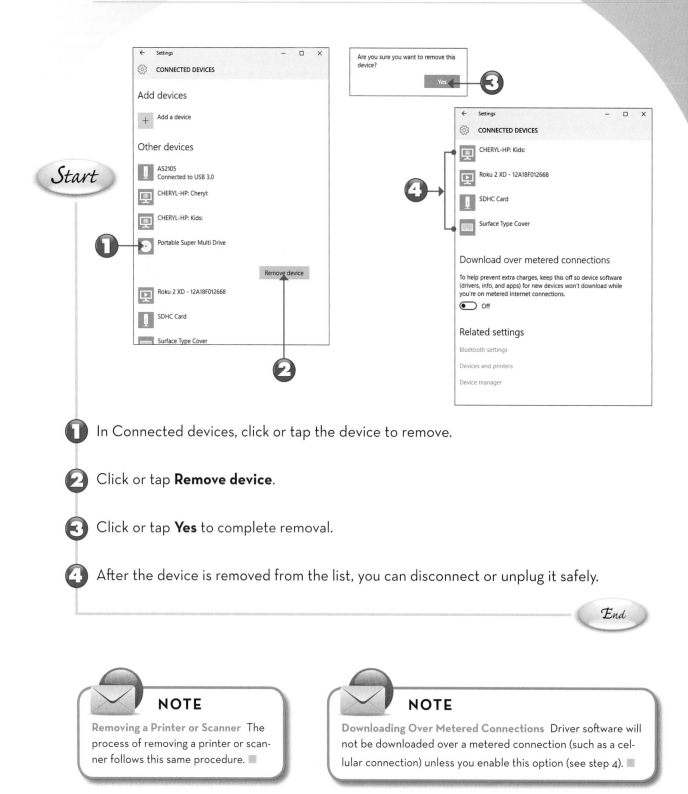

1. In Connected devices, click or tap the device to remove.
2. Click or tap **Remove device**.
3. Click or tap **Yes** to complete removal.
4. After the device is removed from the list, you can disconnect or unplug it safely.

NOTE

Removing a Printer or Scanner The process of removing a printer or scanner follows this same procedure.

NOTE

Downloading Over Metered Connections Driver software will not be downloaded over a metered connection (such as a cellular connection) unless you enable this option (see step 4).

WORKING WITH BLUETOOTH DEVICES

Use the Bluetooth menu to connect to wireless Bluetooth devices such as keyboards, mice, or media players. In this example, we'll connect a Bluetooth mouse to a tablet.

Start

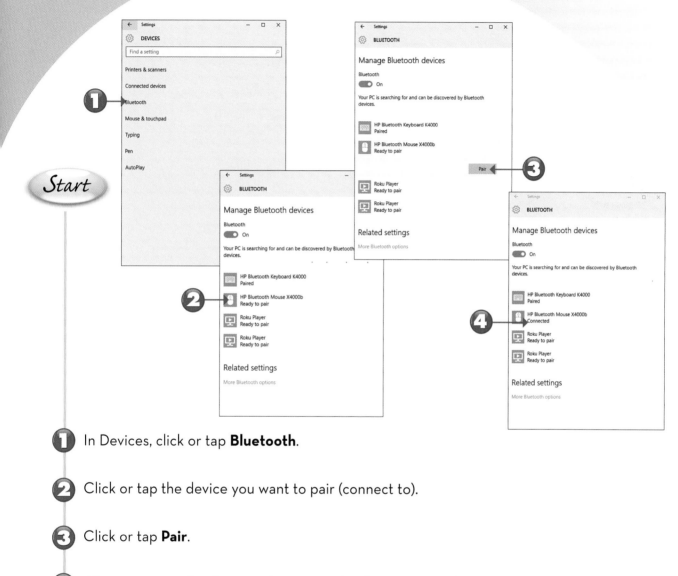

1. In Devices, click or tap **Bluetooth**.
2. Click or tap the device you want to pair (connect to).
3. Click or tap **Pair**.
4. After you press the **Connect** button on the device, it's ready to use.

End

NOTE

Pairing a Keyboard When you pair a keyboard, you might need to enter a code displayed onscreen so that your device "knows" that the keyboard is ready to pair.

CONFIGURING MOUSE & TOUCHPAD

Whether you use a mouse, a touchpad, or both, this menu helps you tweak your pointing devices to work the way you want.

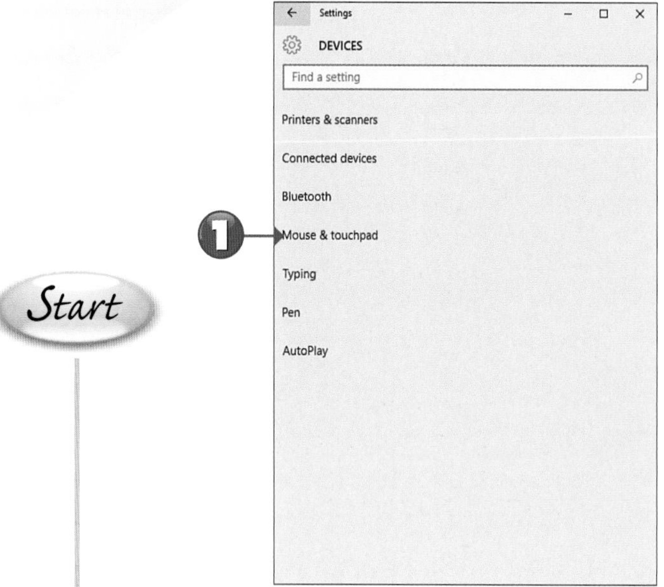

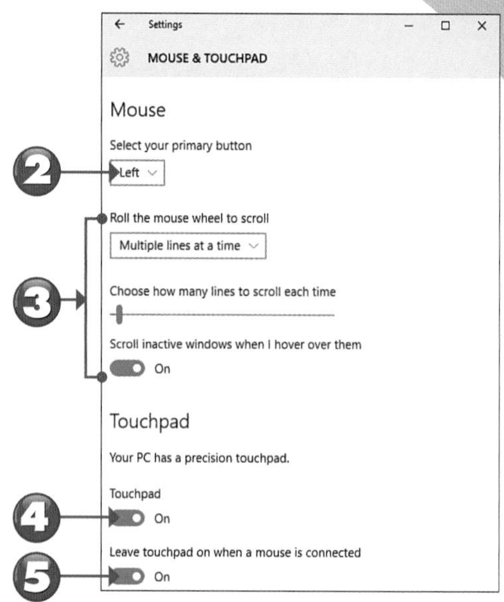

Start

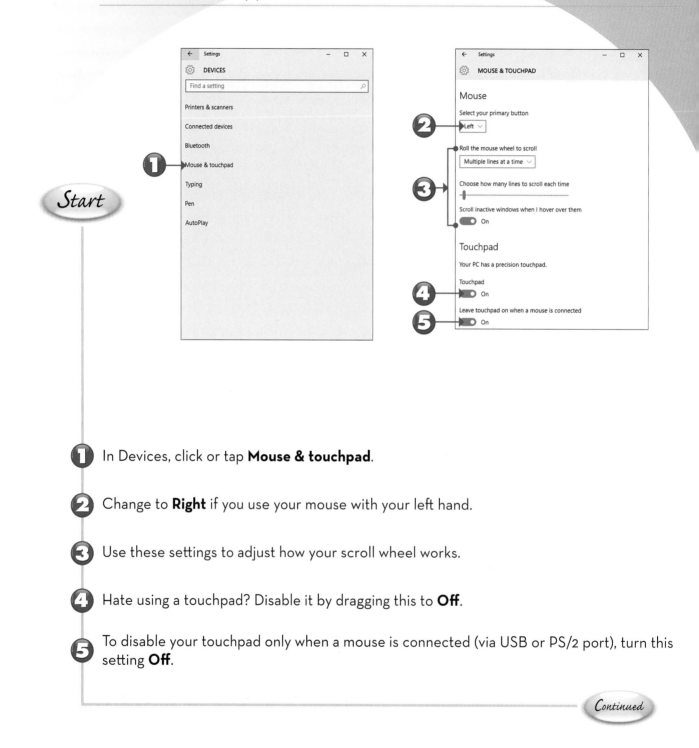

1. In Devices, click or tap **Mouse & touchpad**.
2. Change to **Right** if you use your mouse with your left hand.
3. Use these settings to adjust how your scroll wheel works.
4. Hate using a touchpad? Disable it by dragging this to **Off**.
5. To disable your touchpad only when a mouse is connected (via USB or PS/2 port), turn this setting **Off**.

Continued

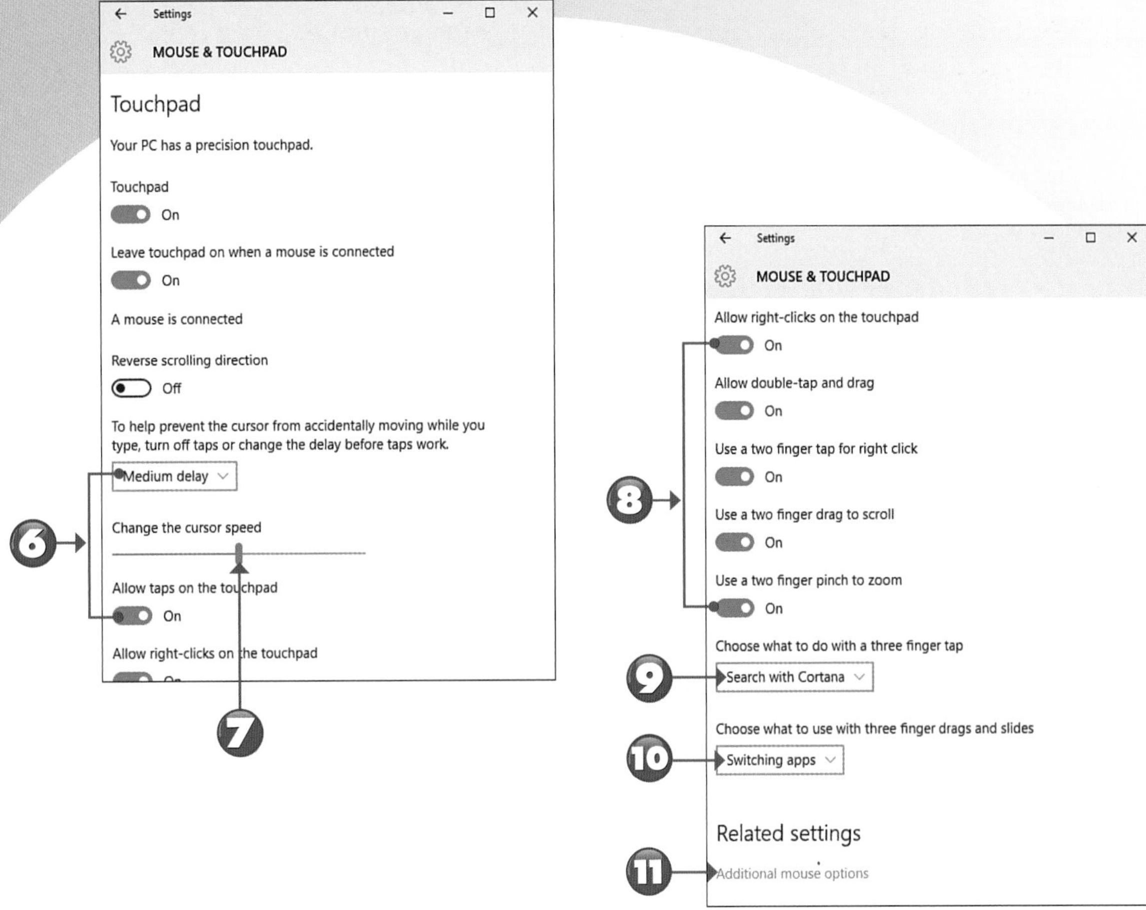

6. If you hit your touchpad accidentally, change the delay or turn off taps.
7. Drag to the left to slow down the mouse cursor; drag to the right to speed it up.
8. Use these settings to configure one-finger and two-finger touchpad operations.
9. To change what a three-finger tap does, click or tap here.
10. To change what a three-finger drag or slide does, click or tap here.
11. To change mouse pointer, pointer size, and double-click speeds, click or tap here.

End

CHANGING TYPING SETTINGS

Use the Typing dialog box to set up spelling, typing, and onscreen keyboard options.

Settings
DEVICES
Find a setting
Printers & scanners
Connected devices
Bluetooth
Mouse & touchpad
Typing
Pen
AutoPlay

Settings
TYPING
Spelling
Autocorrect misspelled words
On
Highlight misspelled words
On
Typing
Show text suggestions as I type
On
Add a space after I choose a text suggestion
On
Add a period after I double-tap the Spacebar
On
Touch keyboard
Play key sounds as I type
On
Capitalize the first letter of each sentence

Settings
TYPING
On
Add a space after I choose a text suggestion
On
Add a period after I double-tap the Spacebar
On
Touch keyboard
Play key sounds as I type
On
Capitalize the first letter of each sentence
On
Use all uppercase letters when I double-tap Shift
On
Add the standard keyboard layout as a touch keyboard option
Off
Automatically show the touch keyboard in windowed apps when there's no keyboard attached to your device
Off

Start

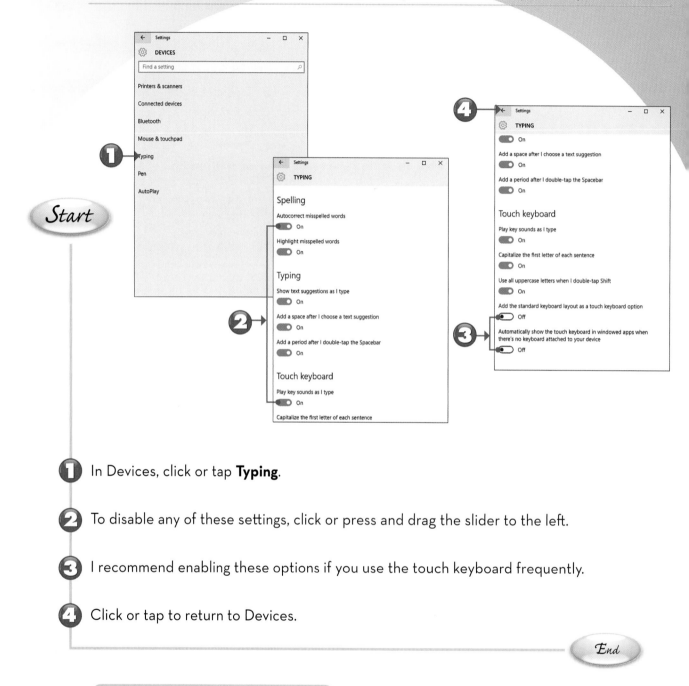

1. In Devices, click or tap **Typing**.
2. To disable any of these settings, click or press and drag the slider to the left.
3. I recommend enabling these options if you use the touch keyboard frequently.
4. Click or tap to return to Devices.

CHANGING PEN SETTINGS

If your computer or tablet uses a pen, you use the Pen menu to configure basic settings.

Start

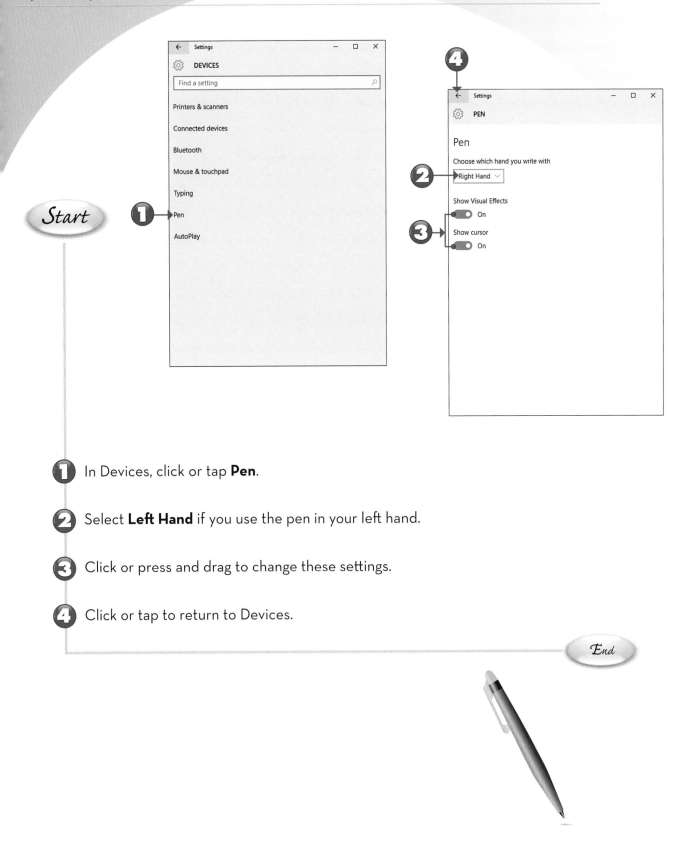

1. In Devices, click or tap **Pen**.
2. Select **Left Hand** if you use the pen in your left hand.
3. Click or press and drag to change these settings.
4. Click or tap to return to Devices.

End

CHANGING AUTOPLAY SETTINGS

Use the AutoPlay menu to determine what happens when you connect a new removable-media drive or flash memory card.

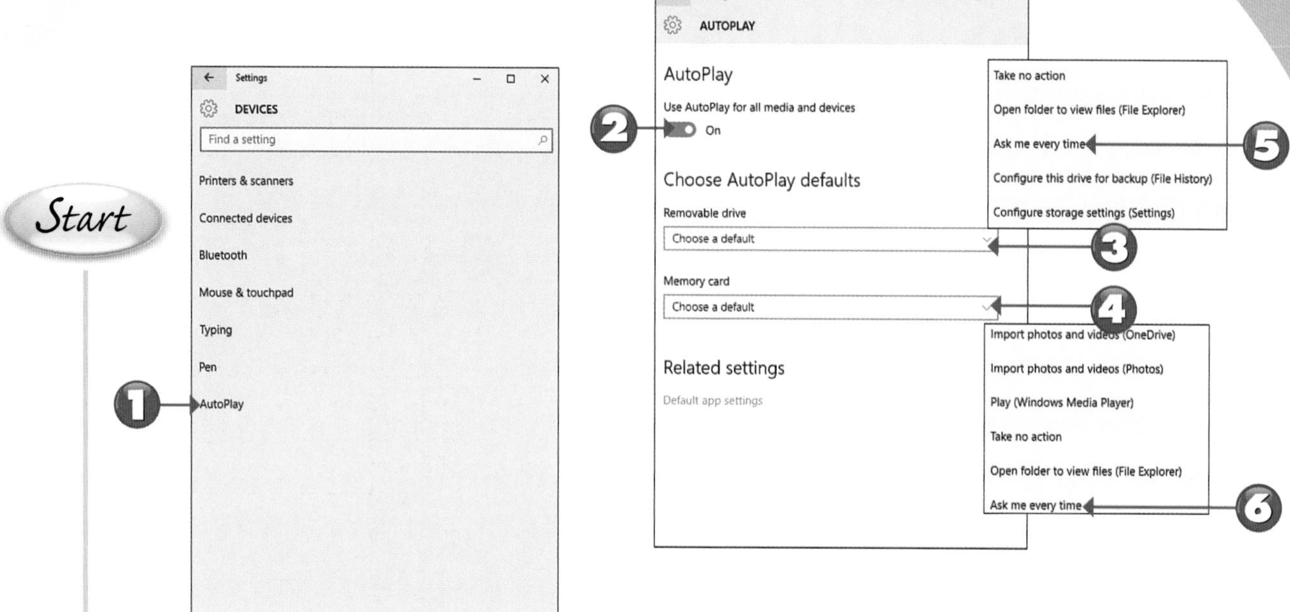

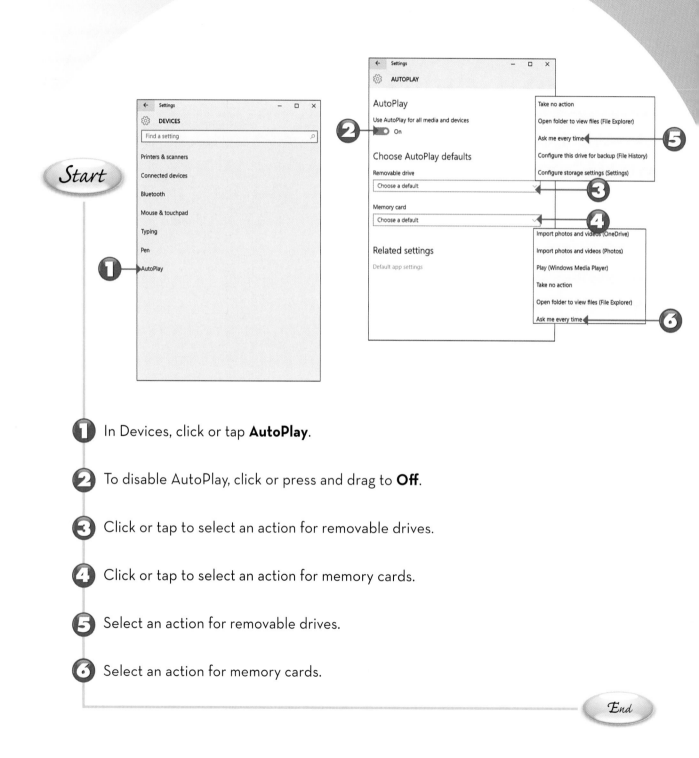

1. In Devices, click or tap **AutoPlay**.
2. To disable AutoPlay, click or press and drag to **Off**.
3. Click or tap to select an action for removable drives.
4. Click or tap to select an action for memory cards.
5. Select an action for removable drives.
6. Select an action for memory cards.

End

GENERAL PRIVACY SETTINGS

In Windows 10, you have much more control over how much information Windows and Windows apps can gather as you use your device than in previous versions. It's a tradeoff: the more information Windows knows about you, the more targeted the information it provides but the less privacy you have. Use the Privacy section of Settings to customize your privacy settings for apps included with Windows 10 or available from the Windows Store. In this example, we'll open the General privacy settings menu and see the available settings.

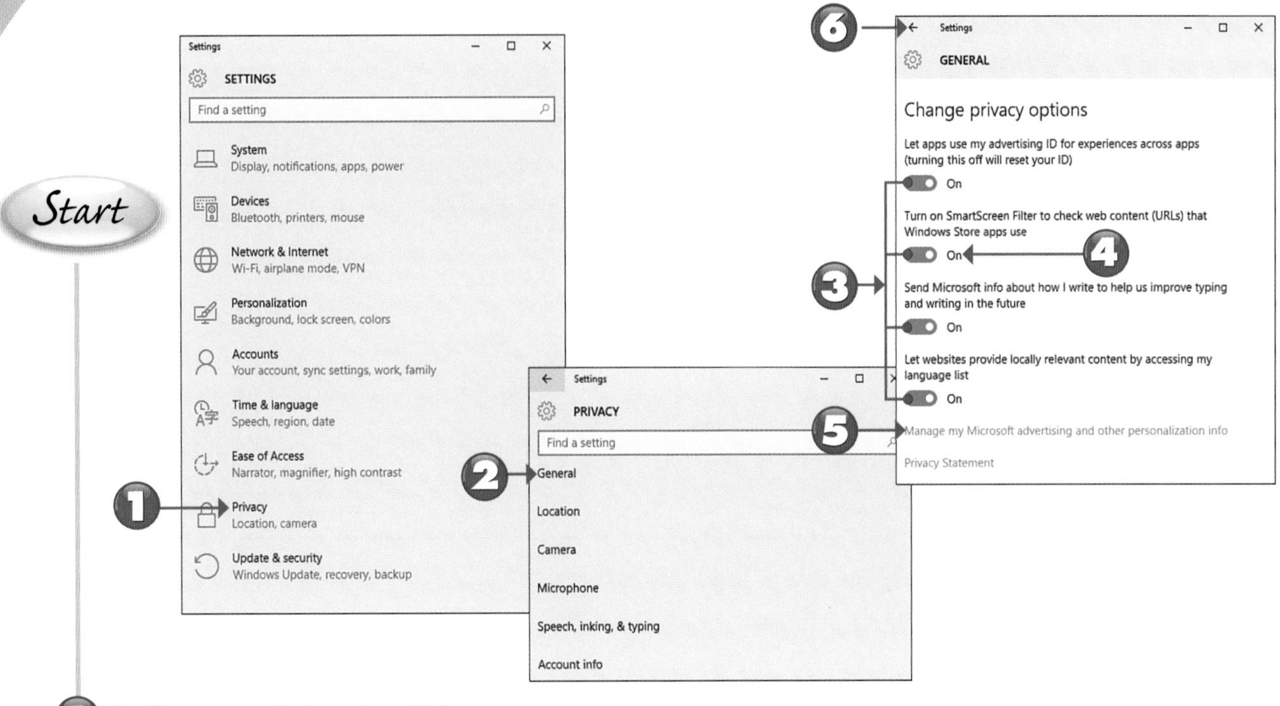

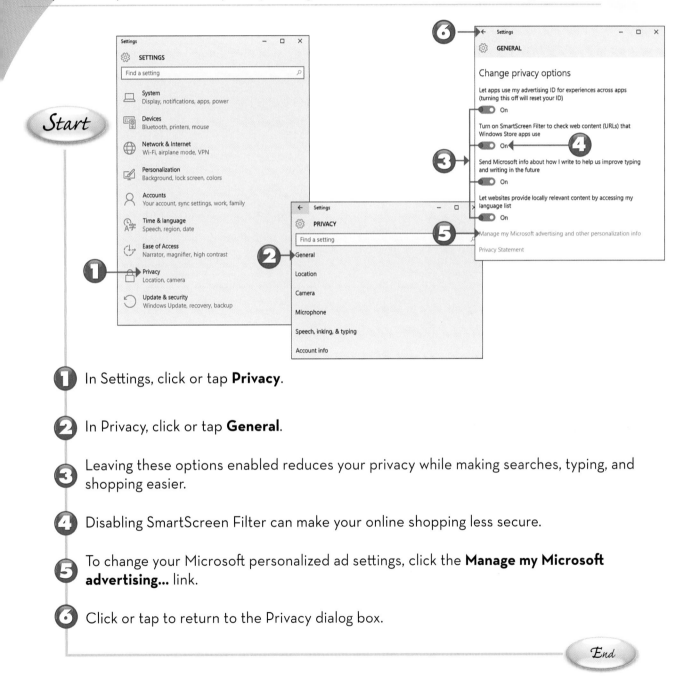

1. In Settings, click or tap **Privacy**.
2. In Privacy, click or tap **General**.
3. Leaving these options enabled reduces your privacy while making searches, typing, and shopping easier.
4. Disabling SmartScreen Filter can make your online shopping less secure.
5. To change your Microsoft personalized ad settings, click the **Manage my Microsoft advertising...** link.
6. Click or tap to return to the Privacy dialog box.

End

CONFIGURING LOCATION SETTINGS

Many apps are designed to use your location to provide you with more relevant information. If you need to change these settings, use the Location dialog box in the Privacy section of Settings.

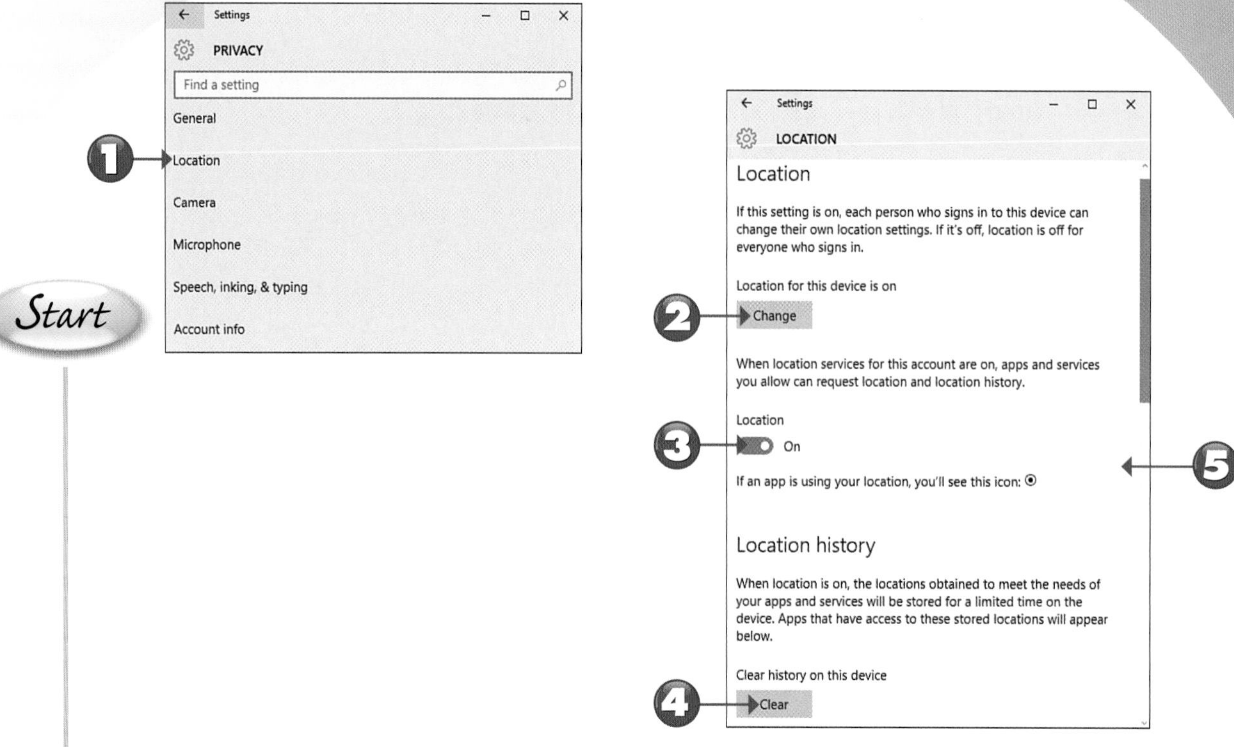

1. From the Privacy category of Settings, click or tap **Location**.
2. If you don't want each user to set individual location settings, click or tap **Change** and select **Off** in the pop-up window.
3. To disable location settings for your account, click or press and drag to **Off**.
4. To clear location history, click or tap **Clear** and confirm your choice when prompted.
5. To change location history settings by app or to see if any apps use geofencing, scroll down or flick up.

Continued

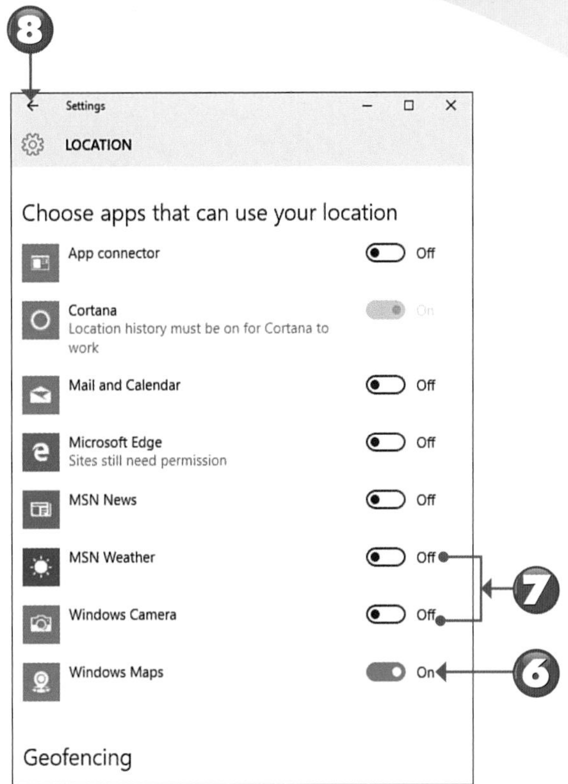

6. Location for this app is enabled.

7. Enabling notification (off by default) can help keep you better informed.

8. Click or tap to return to Privacy.

End

NOTE

Benefits of Enabling Location Settings By enabling location settings for the listed apps, you can find items that apply to your location more quickly. I recommend using location settings for Weather and News.

CHANGING PRIVACY SETTINGS FOR CAMERA, MICROPHONE, CONTACTS, MESSAGING, RADIOS, AND ACCOUNT INFO

You can enable or disable privacy settings for all apps in the category or for individual apps in each category. If there are no apps in a listed category, you are invited to download an app from the Windows Store. In this task, we'll see how privacy settings work for the Camera and Microphone categories of Privacy.

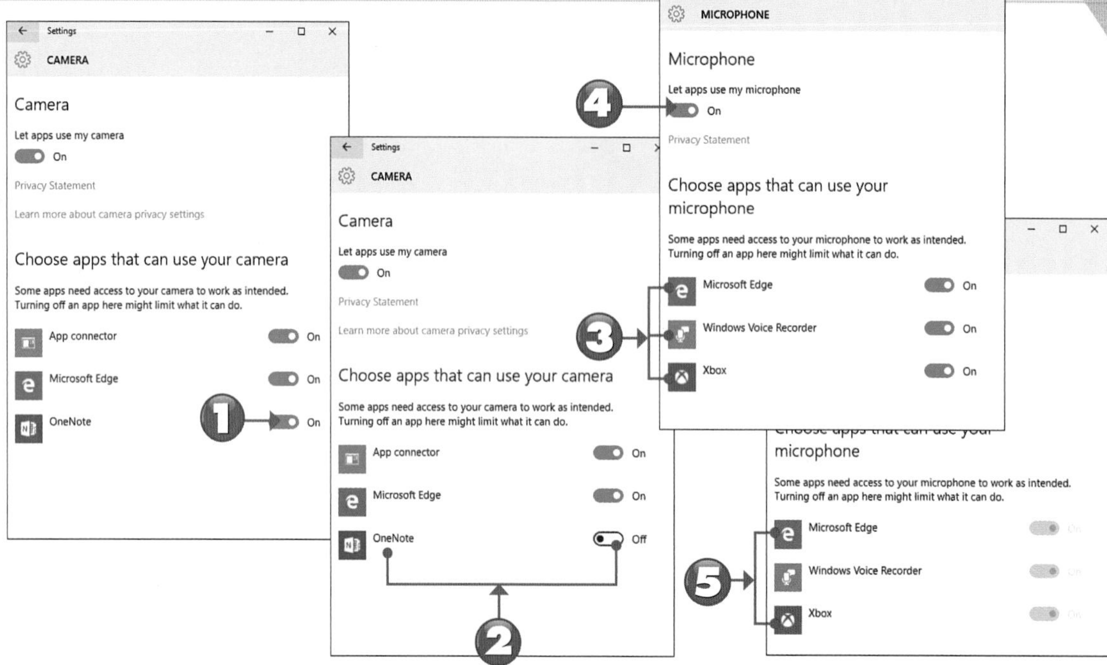

1. To block an app from using a device, click or press and drag the control to **Off**.
2. OneNote is blocked from using the camera.
3. All listed apps can use the microphone.
4. Click or press and drag the Microphone setting to **Off**.
5. No apps can use the microphone.

CAUTION

Privacy and Cameras Even if you block listed apps from using your camera, it's possible for malware to use your camera. If you're concerned about this potential privacy risk, unplug your USB camera when you're not using it, or cover up the lenses of your devices' built-in cameras.

CHANGING SPEECH, INK, AND TYPING PRIVACY SETTINGS

With the introduction of the Cortana search assistant in Windows 10, Windows wants to learn your voice and your writing, and it collects information to serve your search and dictation needs better. If you're not interested, use the Speech, Inking, & Typing dialog box to stop the information gathering. Here's how.

Start

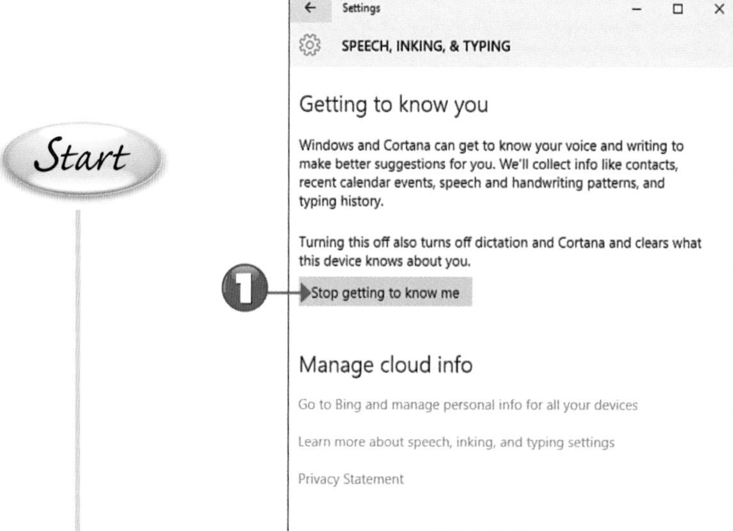

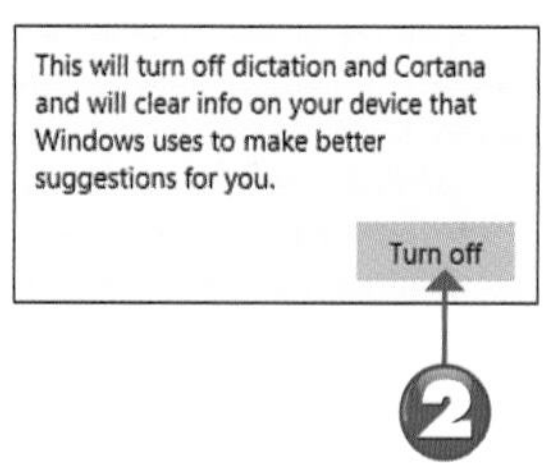

1. After selecting **Speech, inking, & typing** from the Privacy menu, click or tap **Stop getting to know me**.
2. Click or tap **Turn off**, and you turn off Cortana and dictation.

End

MANAGING PERSONAL INFORMATION WITH BING

In Windows 10, the default Microsoft Bing search tool keeps track of a lot of information about you on every device you use with a Windows account, such as your search history. If this is a little too helpful, you can stop it. Here's how.

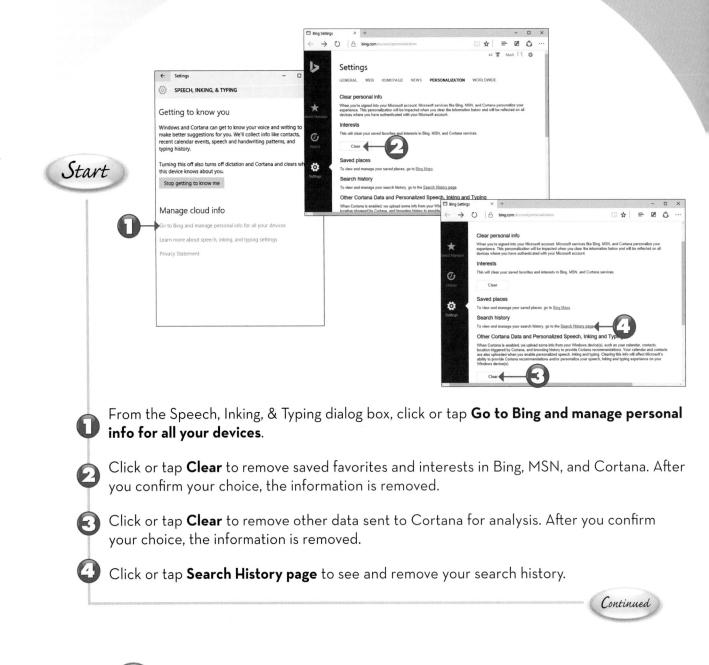

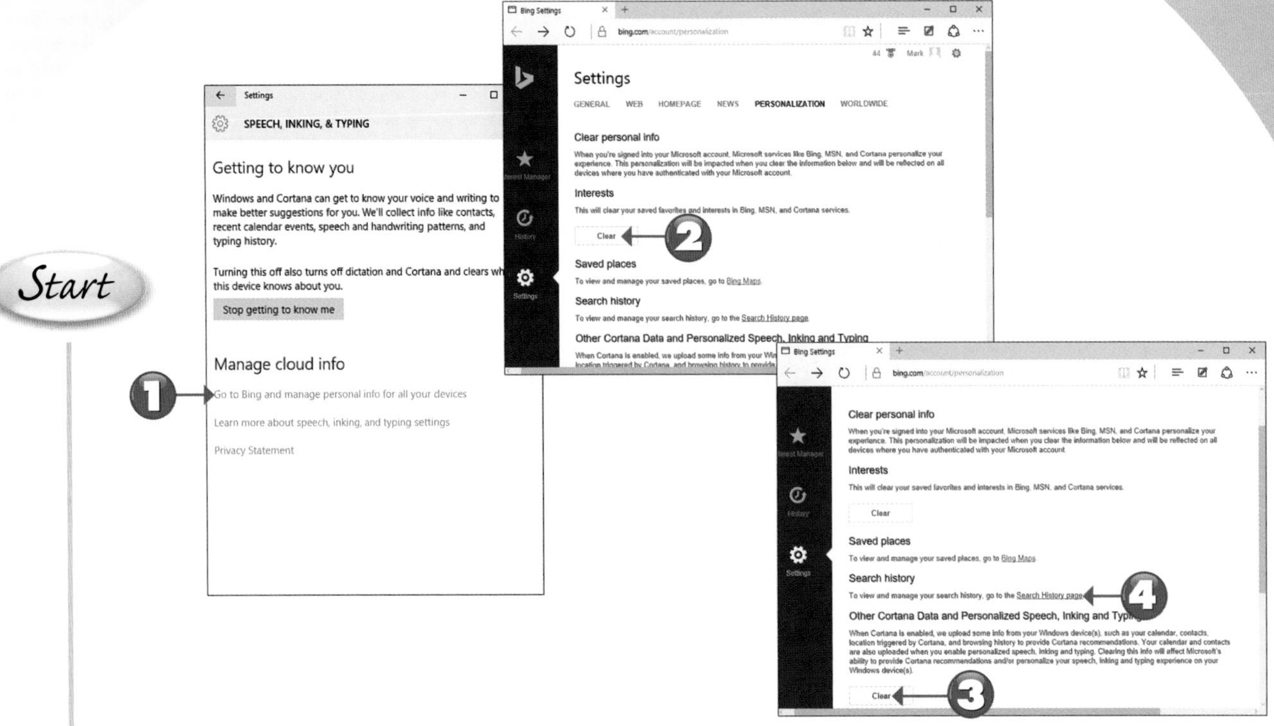

1. From the Speech, Inking, & Typing dialog box, click or tap **Go to Bing and manage personal info for all your devices**.

2. Click or tap **Clear** to remove saved favorites and interests in Bing, MSN, and Cortana. After you confirm your choice, the information is removed.

3. Click or tap **Clear** to remove other data sent to Cortana for analysis. After you confirm your choice, the information is removed.

4. Click or tap **Search History page** to see and remove your search history.

Continued

NOTE

Enter, and Sign In Please If you use a Microsoft account on Windows 10, you are already signed in to all Microsoft services. However, if prompted, provide your Microsoft account information (name and password). You must be signed in before you can make changes to your account settings.

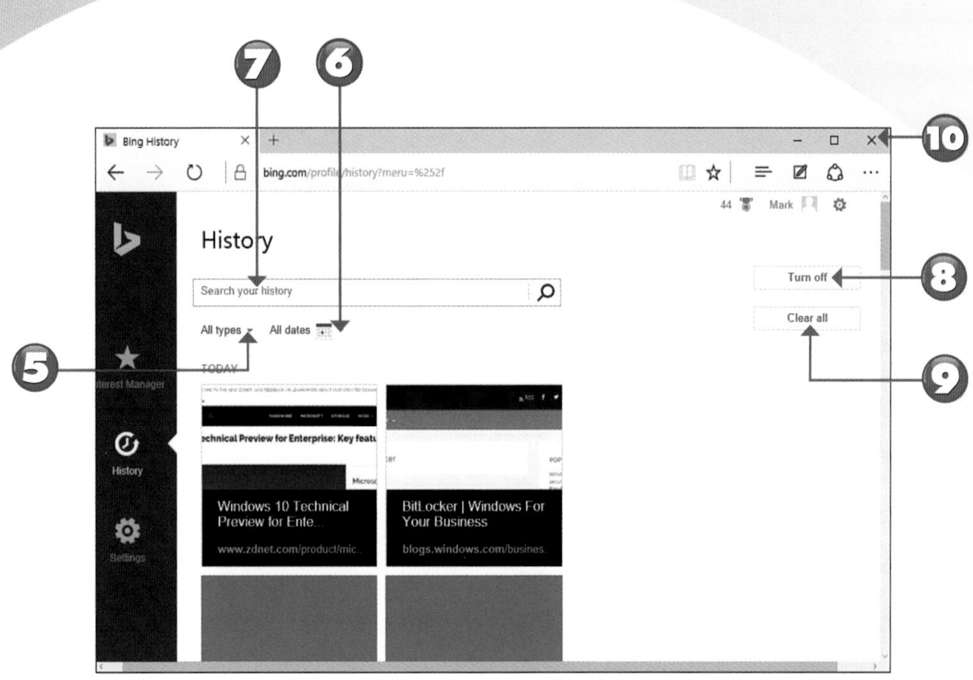

5. Click or tap to view search history by type (web, images, videos).
6. Click or tap to view search history by date.
7. Search for a particular item in search history here.
8. Click or tap **Turn off** to turn off search history. Confirm your choice when prompted.
9. Click or tap **Clear all** to clear search history. Confirm your choice when prompted.
10. Close the browser when you're finished.

End

NETWORKING YOUR HOME WITH HOMEGROUP

Wi-Fi wireless networking and HomeGroup secure networking make it easy to connect your Windows 10 device with the rest of the world. This chapter explains how to create and leave a wireless network and how to use HomeGroup secure home networking.

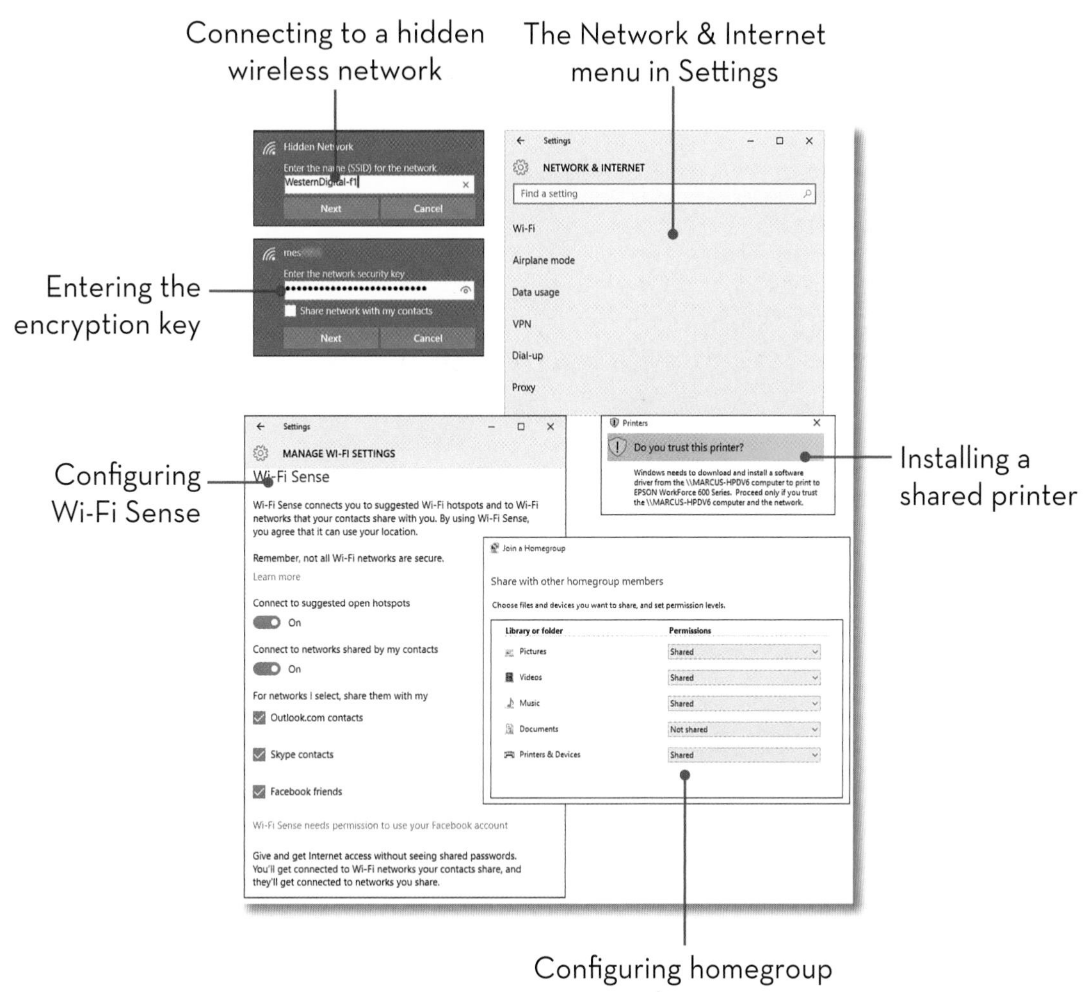

Connecting to a hidden wireless network
The Network & Internet menu in Settings
Entering the encryption key
Configuring Wi-Fi Sense
Installing a shared printer
Configuring homegroup shares
Hidden Network
Enter the name (SSID) for the network
WesternDigital-f1
Next
Cancel
Enter the network security key
Share network with my contacts
Next
Cancel
Settings
NETWORK & INTERNET
Find a setting
Wi-Fi
Airplane mode
Data usage
VPN
Dial-up
Proxy
Settings
MANAGE WI-FI SETTINGS
Wi-Fi Sense
Wi-Fi Sense connects you to suggested Wi-Fi hotspots and to Wi-Fi networks that your contacts share with you. By using Wi-Fi Sense, you agree that it can use your location.
Remember, not all Wi-Fi networks are secure.
Learn more
Connect to suggested open hotspots
On
Connect to networks shared by my contacts
On
For networks I select, share them with my
Outlook.com contacts
Skype contacts
Facebook friends
Wi-Fi Sense needs permission to use your Facebook account
Give and get Internet access without seeing shared passwords. You'll get connected to Wi-Fi networks your contacts share, and they'll get connected to networks you share.
Printers
Do you trust this printer?
Windows needs to download and install a software driver from the \\MARCUS-HPDV6 computer to print to EPSON WorkForce 600 Series. Proceed only if you trust the \\MARCUS-HPDV6 computer and the network.
Join a Homegroup
Share with other homegroup members
Choose files and devices you want to share, and set permission levels.
Library or folder
Permissions
Pictures
Shared
Videos
Shared
Music
Shared
Documents
Not shared
Printers & Devices
Shared

STARTING THE WIRELESS NETWORK CONNECTION PROCESS

To connect to a wireless network, use the Wireless Network button in the taskbar. Here's how.

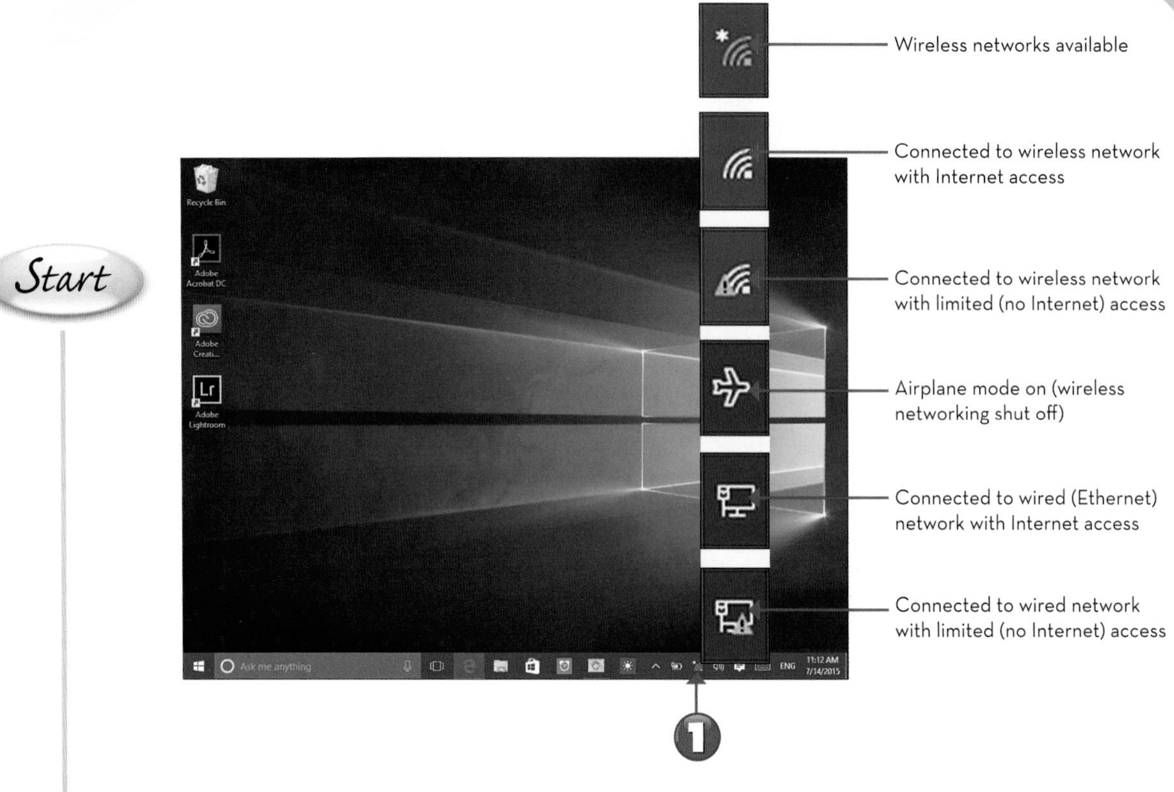

1. Click the wireless network button in the taskbar.

Continued

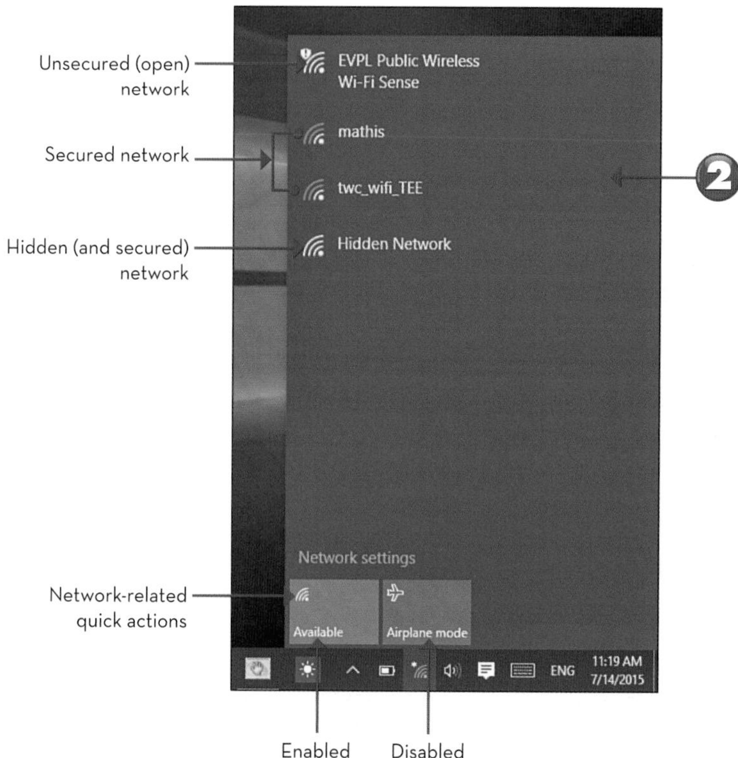

2. The Network Connections dialog appears. Choose one of the listed networks for your connection.

End

NOTE

Secure and Unsecure Network Icons Secure networks use the signal strength icon. Unsecure networks add a shield marked with an exclamation point (!) to the icon, indicating they are not secure (see step 2).

NOTE

Finishing Your Connection To complete the process, see "Connecting to a Secured Private Network," p. 366, "Connecting to an Unsecured Wireless Network," p. 364, or "Connecting to a Hidden Network," on the online PDF.

CONNECTING TO AN UNSECURED WIRELESS NETWORK

Your home and office networks should be secure networks (in other words, you should use a password with your home Wi-Fi network; your work network is probably already secure); however, wireless networks found in locations such as coffee shops, libraries, restaurants, and hotels often are unsecured. Some of these networks also require you to use your web browser to accept the Wi-Fi service's terms. Here's how to connect to these networks using Windows 10.

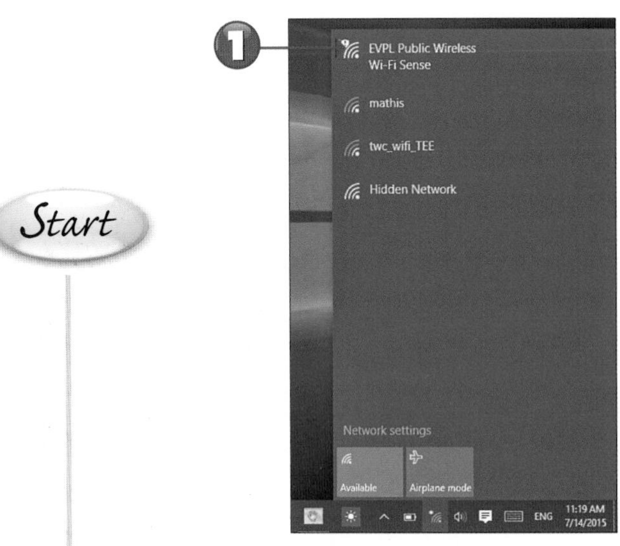

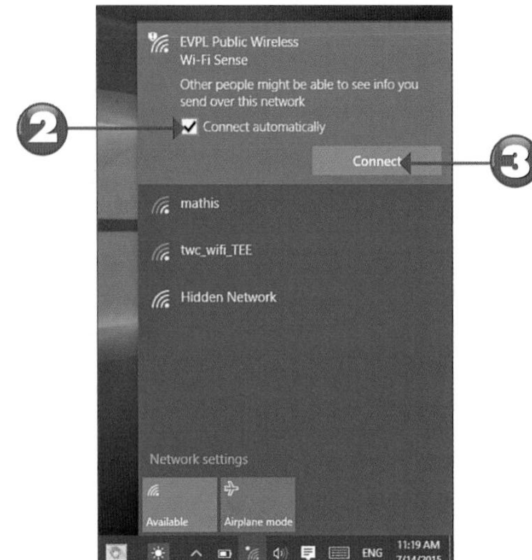

Start

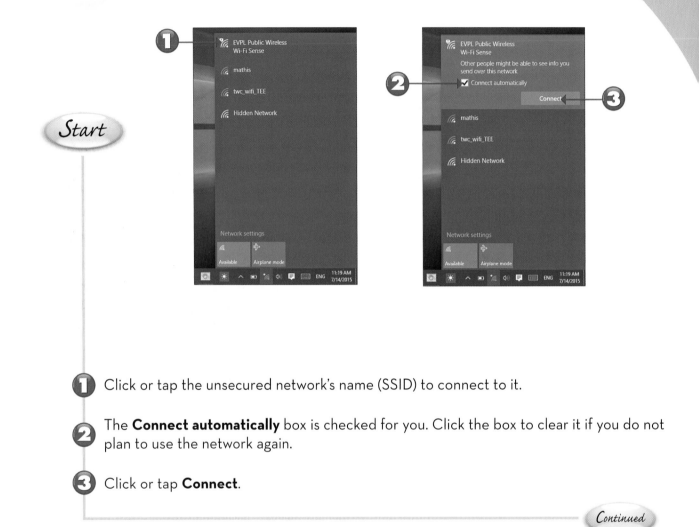

1. Click or tap the unsecured network's name (SSID) to connect to it.
2. The **Connect automatically** box is checked for you. Click the box to clear it if you do not plan to use the network again.
3. Click or tap **Connect**.

Continued

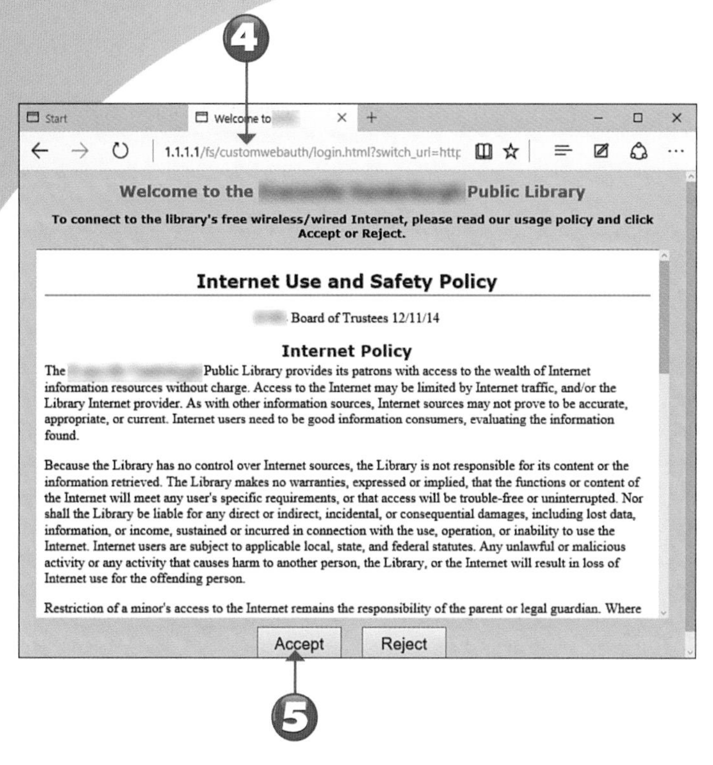

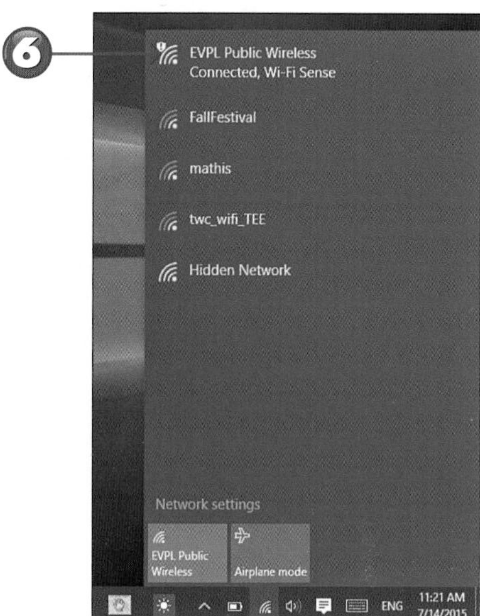

4. If the network requires you to accept terms and conditions, your browser opens the agreement page.

5. Read and agree to the terms and conditions, and click or tap the **Accept** button.

6. Your network connection is listed first and marked “Connected.”

End

CONNECTING TO A SECURED PRIVATE NETWORK

A secured network uses a network security key, also known as an *encryption key*. The first time you connect to a secured network, you must enter the network security key. Windows 10 can remember your network security key and the rest of your connection details for you. Here's how this process works.

Start

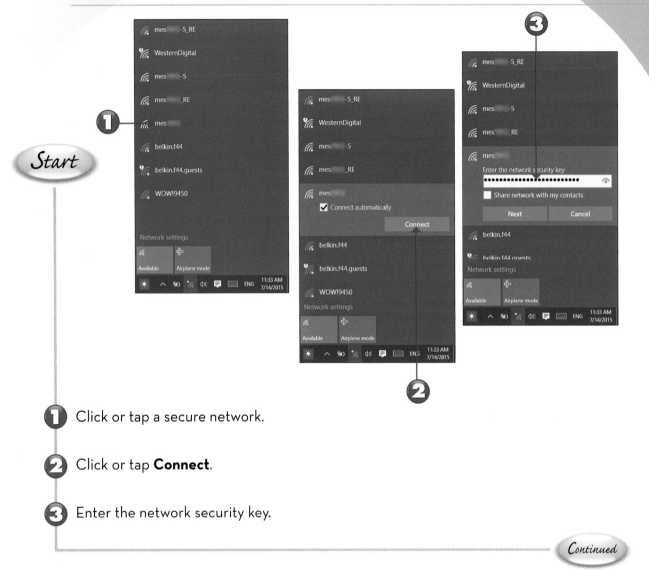

1. Click or tap a secure network.
2. Click or tap **Connect**.
3. Enter the network security key.

Continued

CAUTION

Learning More About Wi-Fi Sense In step 5, you have the option of sharing a network and its encryption key with your contacts, a feature called Wi-Fi Sense. To learn how to configure or disable Wi-Fi Sense, see "Managing Wi-Fi Sense," p. 373.

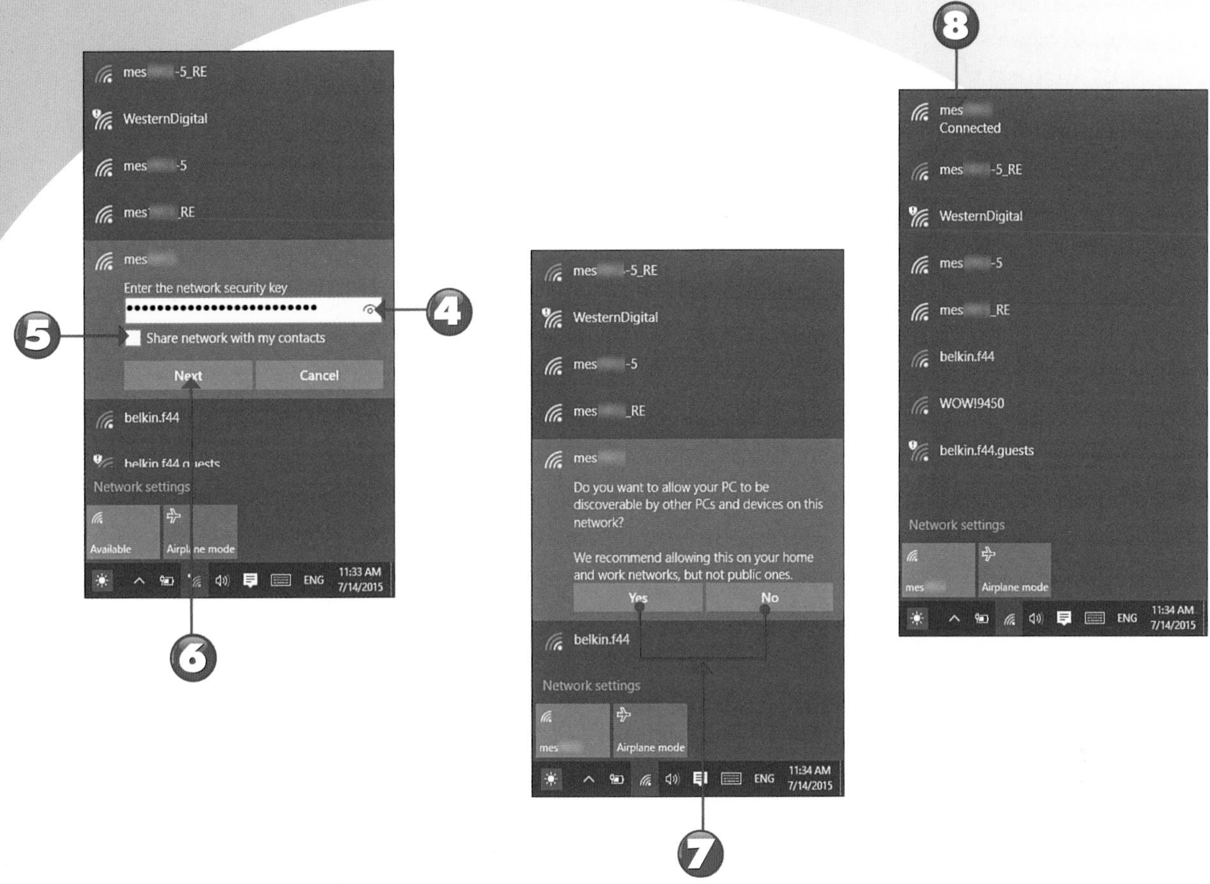

4. To see the hidden characters, click or tap the eye icon.

5. You might be prompted to share your connection with your contacts. If you want to, click or tap the empty **Share network** check box.

6. Click or tap **Next**.

7. Click or tap **Yes** to enable your device to be discovered on your network (recommended for home and office networks). Click or tap **No** if you are connecting to a public network (restaurants, hotels, and so on).

8. Your network connection is listed first.

End

DISCONNECTING A WIRELESS CONNECTION

If you decide that you need to connect to a stronger signal or want to disconnect from Wi-Fi altogether, follow these steps to disconnect from your current Wi-Fi network.

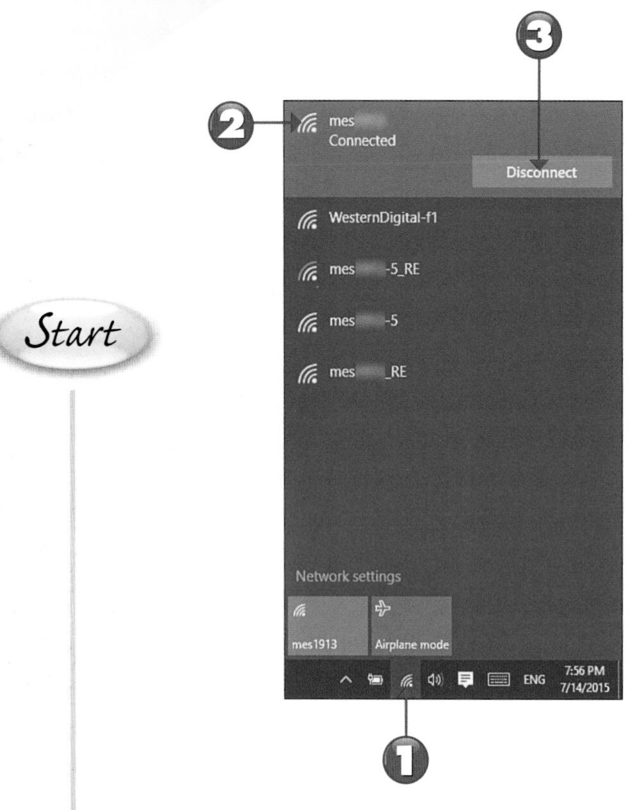

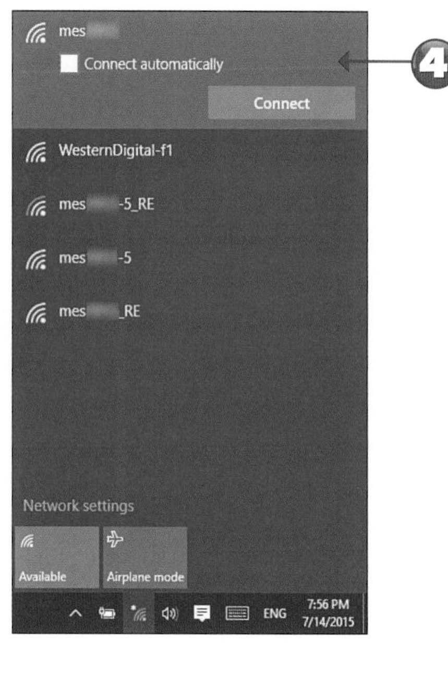

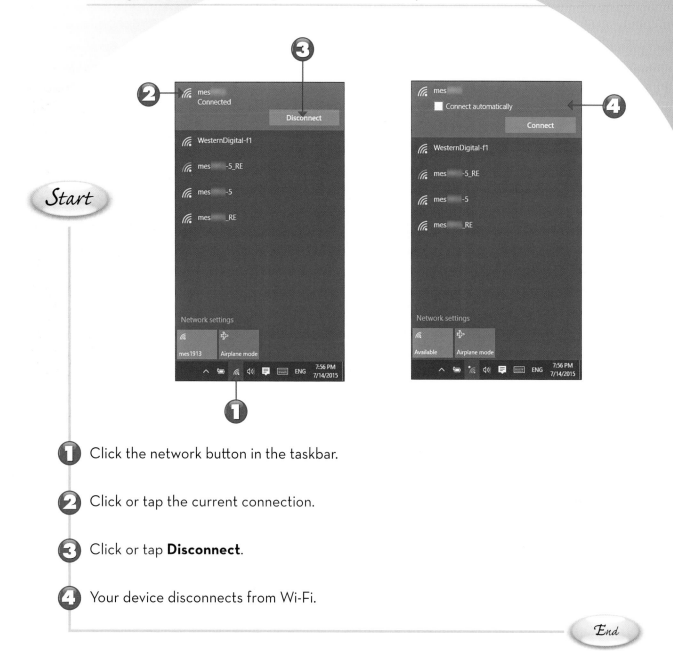

1. Click the network button in the taskbar.
2. Click or tap the current connection.
3. Click or tap **Disconnect**.
4. Your device disconnects from Wi-Fi.

End

NOTE

Disabling Automatic Reconnection In step 3, if you disconnect from a Wi-Fi network that is configured for automatic connections, the **Connect** button appears (as in this example). Click or tap it if you want to reconnect, click or tap a different network, or click or tap an empty part of the desktop if you don't want to connect right now.

USING AIRPLANE MODE

When Wi-Fi access is not needed, you can quickly turn off Wi-Fi (and Bluetooth) to save power. Here's how.

Start

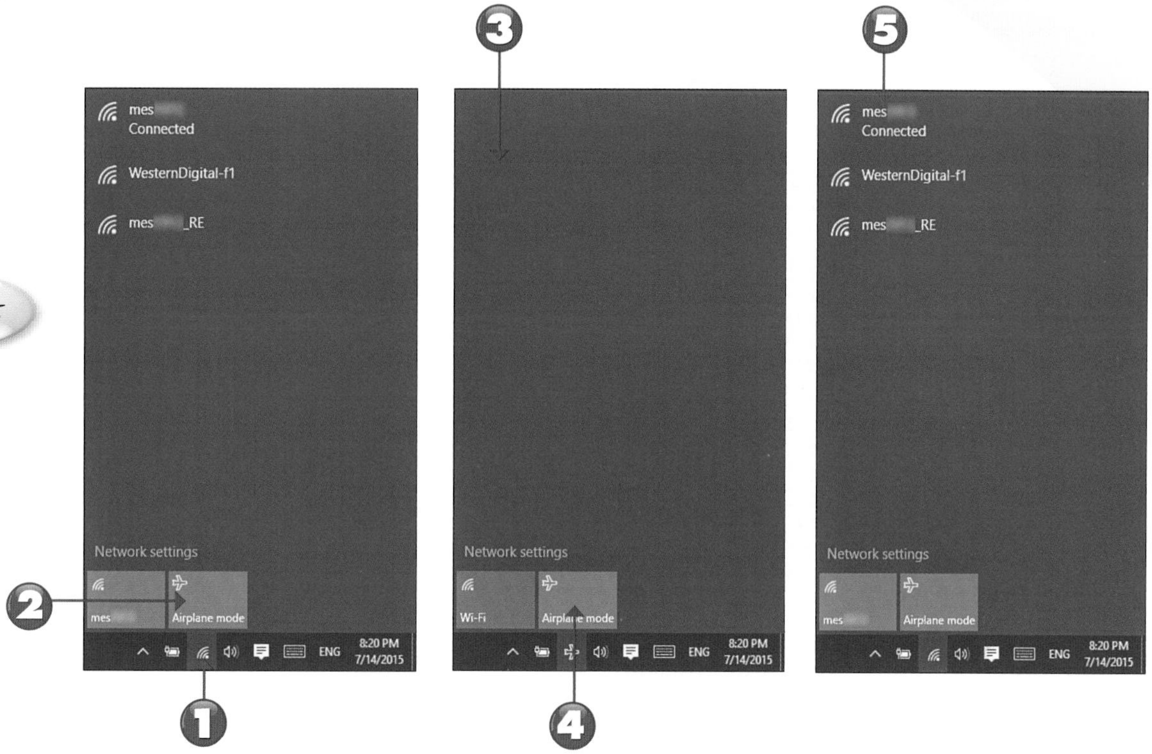

1. Click or tap the **Wireless Network** button in the taskbar.
2. Click or tap the **Airplane mode** button.
3. No wireless connections are available.
4. To re-enable wireless access, click or tap **Airplane mode**.
5. Wireless connections are again available.

End

CAUTION

Selecting Wi-Fi Only Using the Airplane mode quick setting is a fast way to disable Wi-Fi, but it also disables Bluetooth. If you use Bluetooth devices and want to disable only Wi-Fi, you can turn off Wi-Fi without changing Bluetooth settings. For details, see "Disabling and Enabling Wi-Fi," p. 372.

MANAGING NETWORKS

To manage wireless connections, create a HomeGroup, or manage a HomeGroup, use the Network menu available from Settings. Here's how to get to the Network menu from the Start menu.

Start

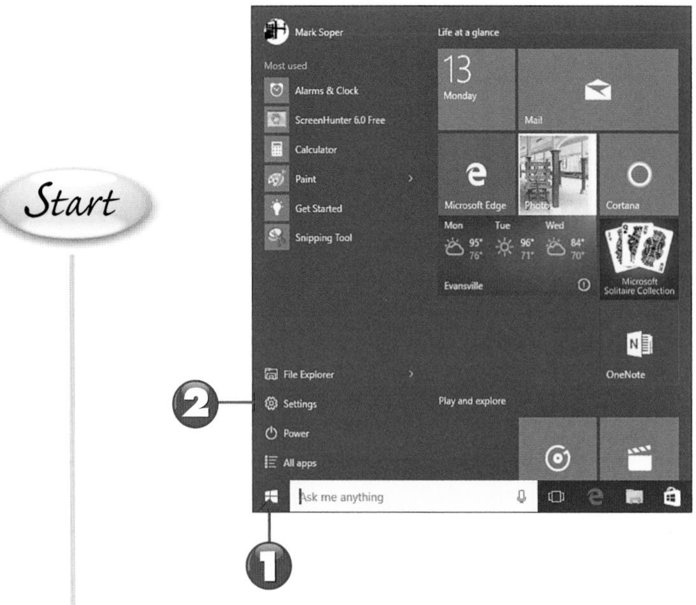

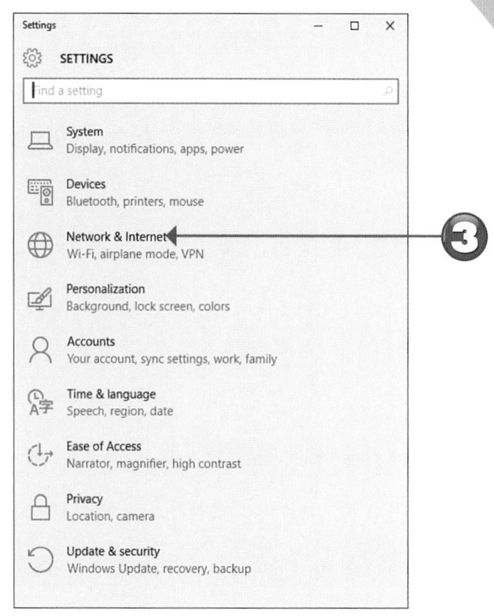

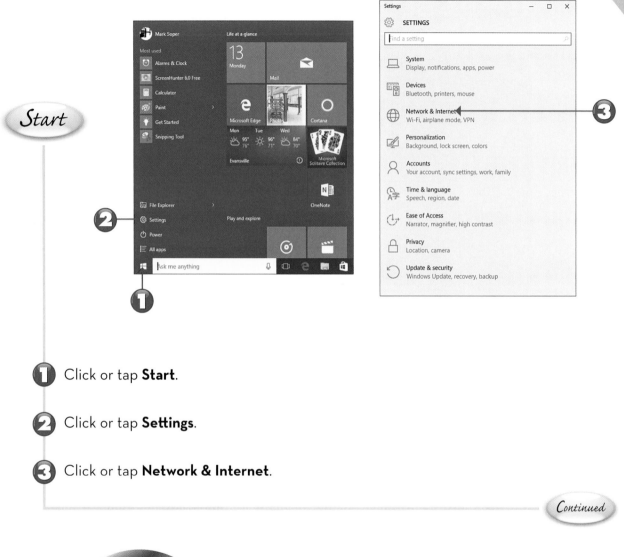

1. Click or tap **Start**.
2. Click or tap **Settings**.
3. Click or tap **Network & Internet**.

Continued

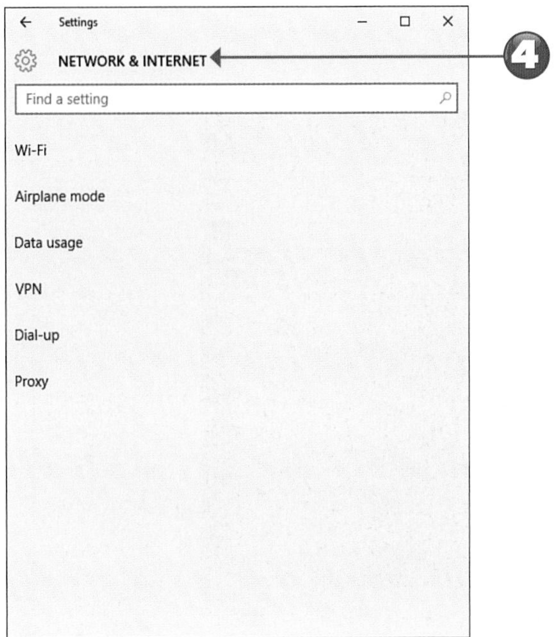

4 The Network & Internet menu.

End

NOTE

Other Network & Internet Topics This chapter focuses on the Wi-Fi and Airplane mode menus. Use the Data usage menu if you use metered connections. Use the VPN menu to help set up or manage a virtual private network (typically used to connect to corporate networks). Use the Dial-up menu to help set up or manage a modem that dials in to a telephone number for Internet connections. Use the Proxy menu if you need to set up or manage a proxy connection (typically used in corporate networks).

DISABLING AND ENABLING WI-FI

You can disable and enable Wi-Fi by using the Wi-Fi menu. By using this menu, your Bluetooth settings are unaffected.

Start

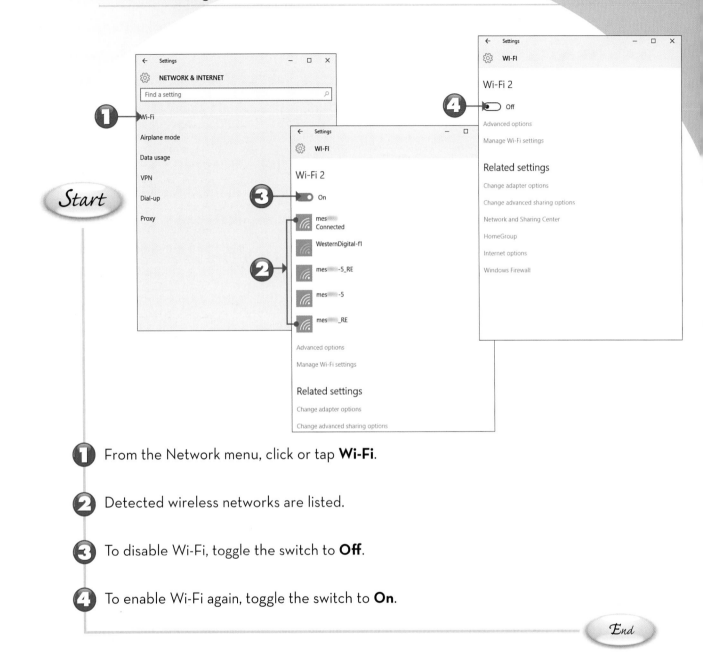

1. From the Network menu, click or tap **Wi-Fi**.
2. Detected wireless networks are listed.
3. To disable Wi-Fi, toggle the switch to **Off**.
4. To enable Wi-Fi again, toggle the switch to **On**.

End

MANAGING WI-FI SENSE

Wi-Fi Sense is a new feature in Windows 10. It enables you to use Wi-Fi connections shared by contacts, including secure connections, and enables you to share connections you make with contacts as well. Here's how to limit what it does.

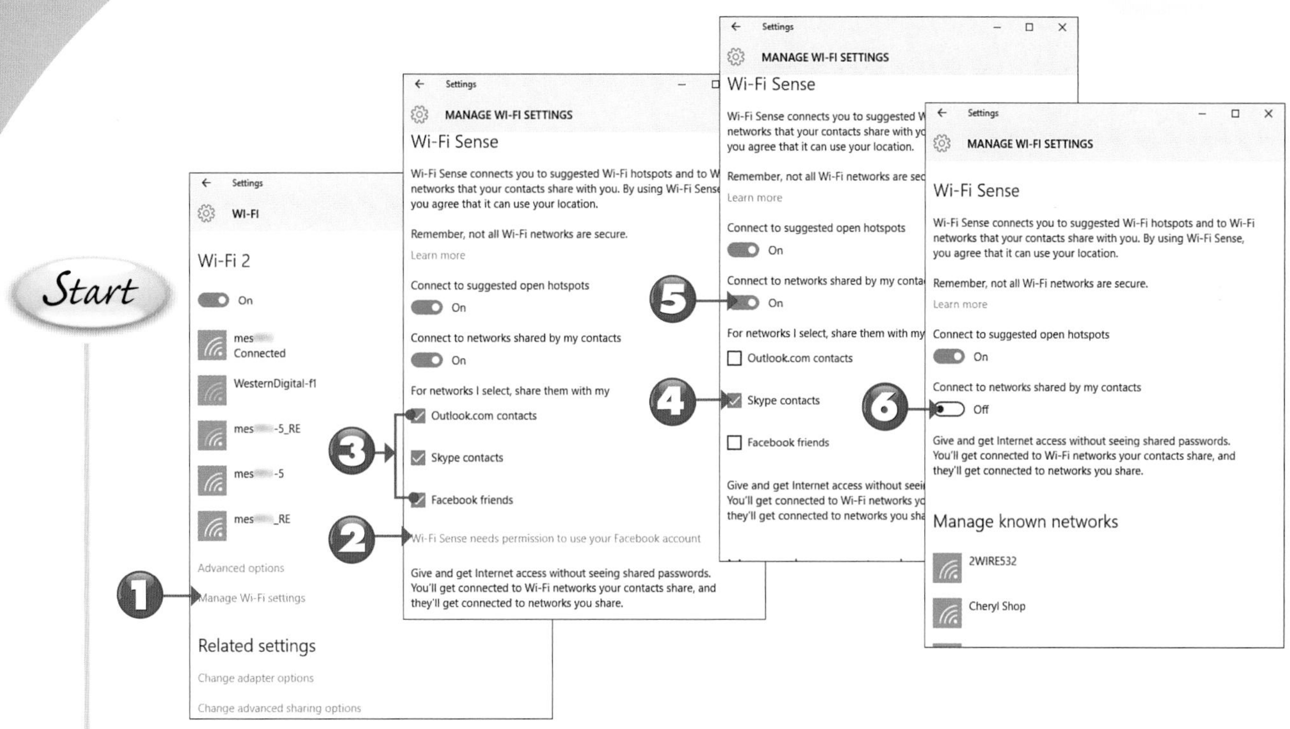

1. From the Wi-Fi menu, click or tap **Manage Wi-Fi settings**.
2. To permit sharing with Facebook contacts, click or tap this link.
3. To disable connection sharing for a group of contacts, click its filled check box.
4. Network connections will be shared only with Skype contacts.
5. To turn off receiving shared connections, click or press and drag to **Off**.
6. If you turn off receiving shared connections, you also turn off sharing connections with your contacts. To share connections with contacts again, click or drag to **On**.

End

NOTE

More About Wi-Fi Sense Suggested hot spots are those suggested by Windows 10. When you share a secure connection or use a shared secure connection, you don't need to provide the encryption key to others or enter it yourself.

MANAGING WIRELESS CONNECTIONS

Windows 10 stores information about each Wi-Fi connection you create. If you travel and use different Wi-Fi networks, the list can become very long. Here's how to remove ("forget") networks you won't be using again.

Start

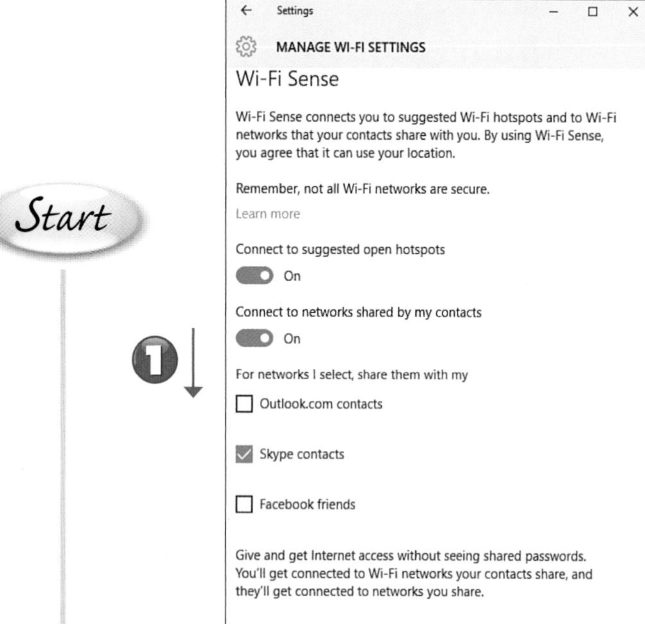

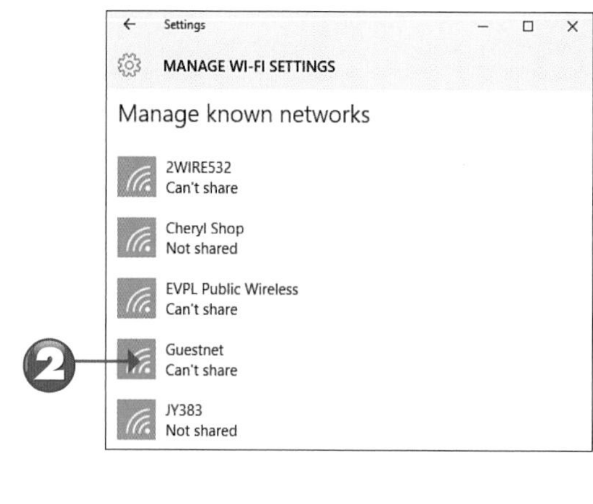

1. From the **Manage Wi-Fi settings** menu, scroll down to the **Manage known networks** section.
2. Click or tap a network you want to forget.

Continued

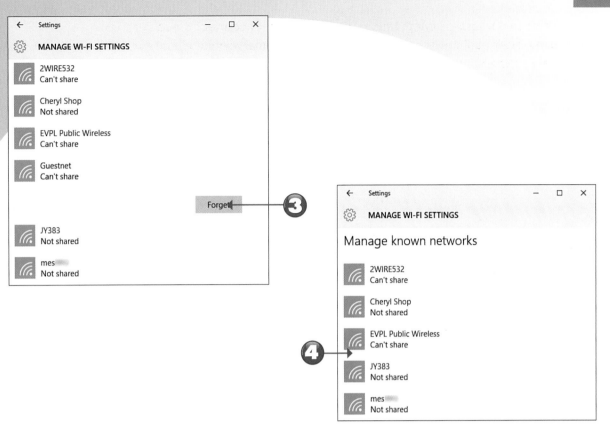

3. Click or tap **Forget**.

4. The network is removed from the list of known networks.

End

NOTE

Reconnecting to a Forgotten Network If you want to reconnect to a wireless network you forgot, you must reenter the SSID (if the network is hidden) and its encryption key (password).

CREATING A HOMEGROUP

Windows 10 supports an easy-to-use, yet secure, type of home and small-business networking feature called a homegroup (also available in Windows 7, 8, and 8.1). Homegroup networking enables home network users to share libraries and printers—you can specify which libraries to share and whether to share printers and devices on a particular system. All users of a homegroup use the same password but don't need to worry about specifying particular folders to share. You can create a new homegroup or join one from the Wi-Fi menu, but it's faster to start the process from the Cortana Search window.

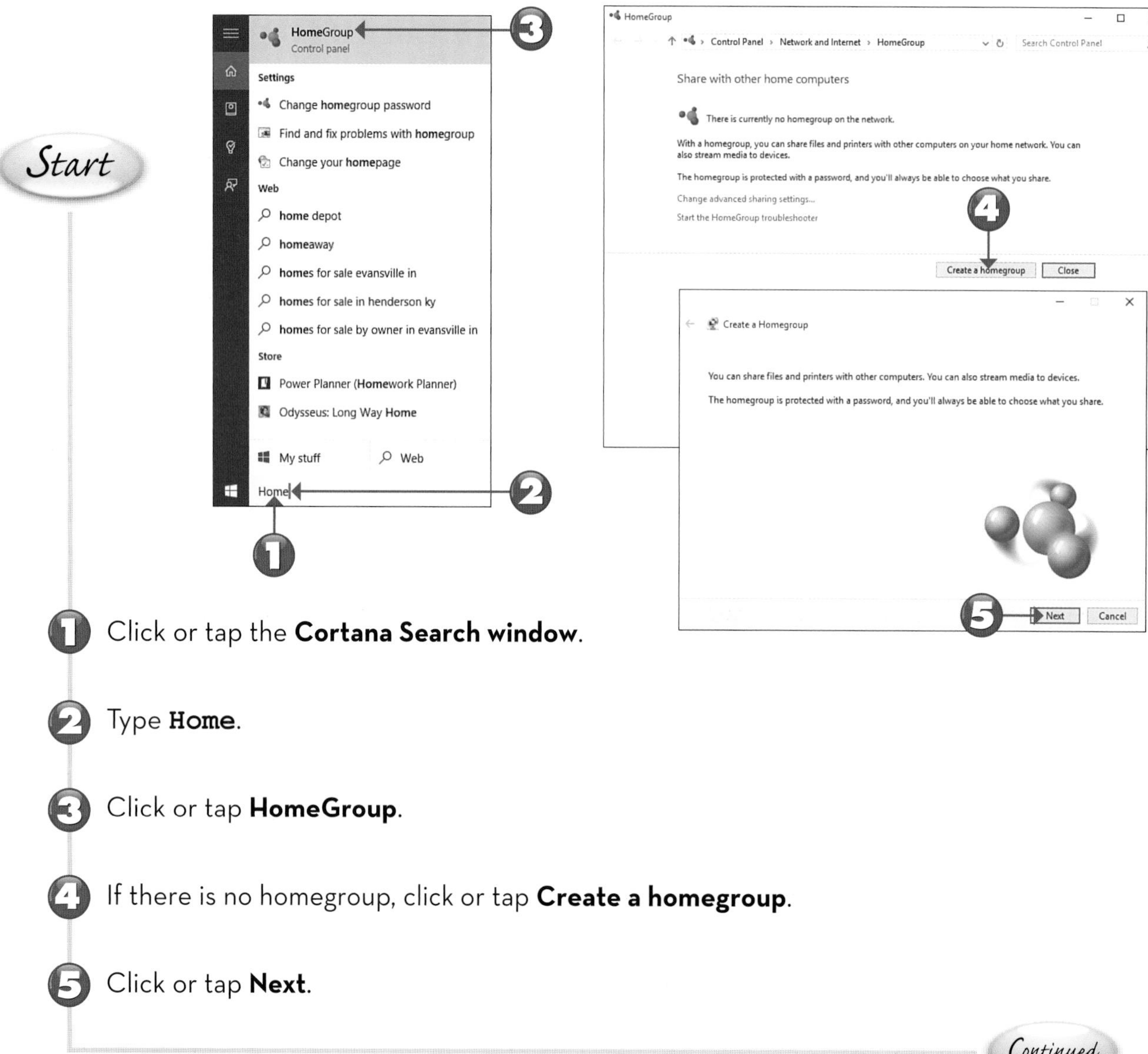

1. Click or tap the **Cortana Search window**.
2. Type **Home**.
3. Click or tap **HomeGroup**.
4. If there is no homegroup, click or tap **Create a homegroup**.
5. Click or tap **Next**.

Continued

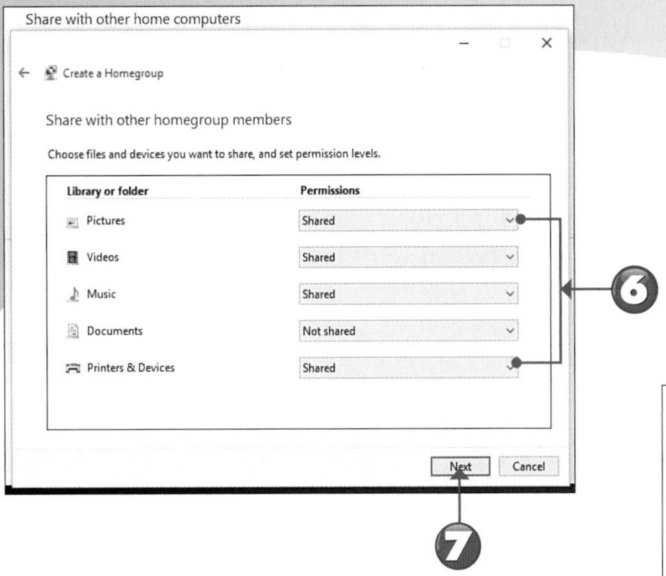

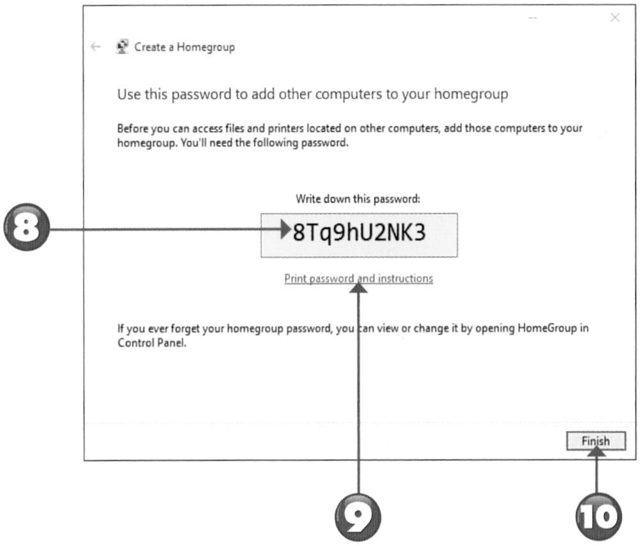

Share with other home computers

Create a Homegroup

Share with other homegroup members

Choose files and devices you want to share, and set permission levels.

Library or folder	Permissions
Pictures	Shared
Videos	Shared
Music	Shared
Documents	Not shared
Printers & Devices	Shared

Next Cancel

Create a Homegroup

Use this password to add other computers to your homegroup

Before you can access files and printers located on other computers, add those computers to your homegroup. You'll need the following password.

Write down this password:

8Tq9hU2NK3

Print password and instructions

If you ever forget your homegroup password, you can view or change it by opening HomeGroup in Control Panel.

Finish

6. Select **Shared** or **Not shared** as desired for the folders and devices on your system (defaults shown here).

7. Click or tap **Next**.

8. Provide this password to others who need to connect to the homegroup.

9. Click or tap to print the password and instructions.

10. Click or tap **Finish** to close the dialog box.

End

JOINING A HOMEGROUP

Microsoft introduced homegroups in Windows 7, so if you have one or more Windows 7, Windows 8/8.1, or Windows 10 computers in your home or small office, you might already have a homegroup. Here's how to add your Windows 10 computer to an existing homegroup. This example starts from the Wi-Fi menu.

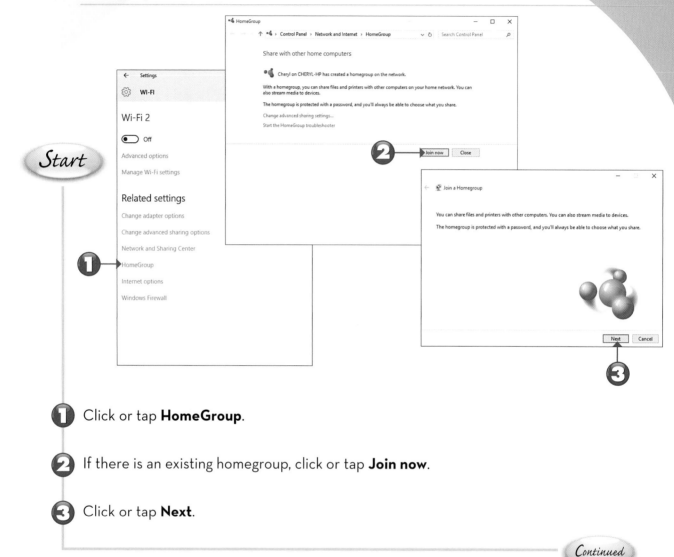

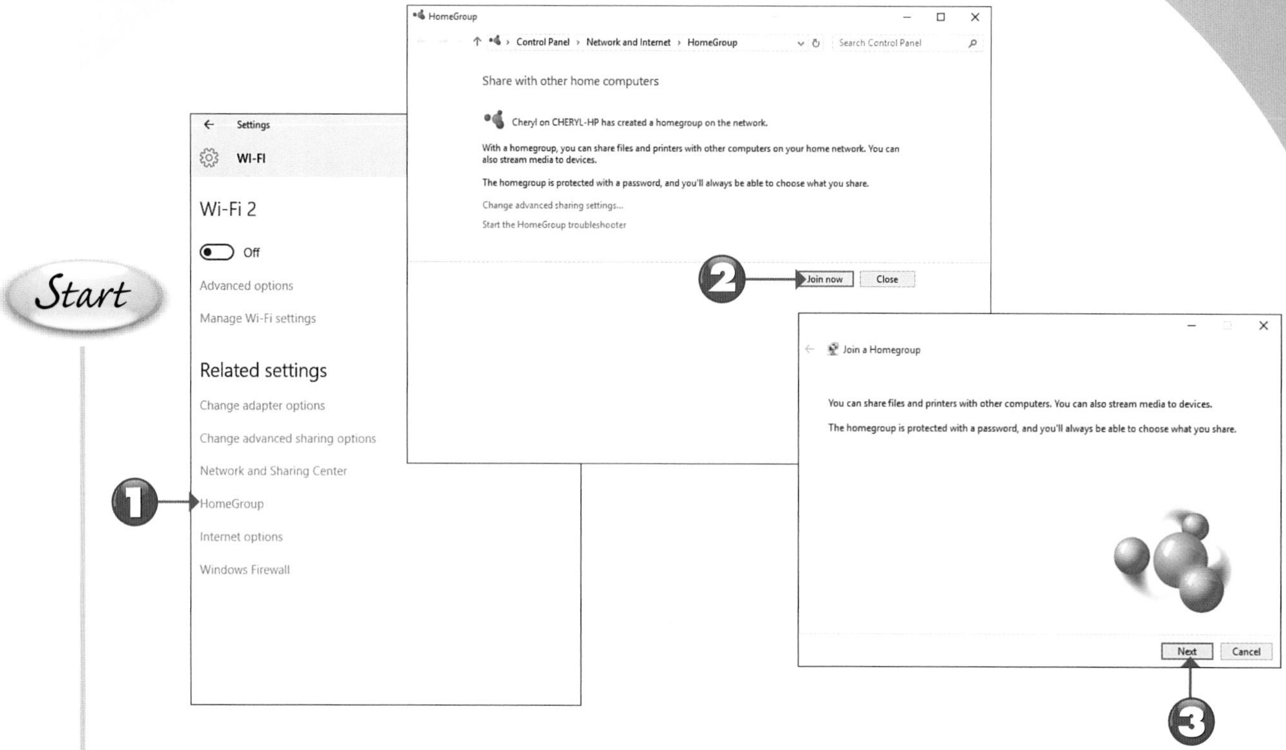

1. Click or tap **HomeGroup**.
2. If there is an existing homegroup, click or tap **Join now**.
3. Click or tap **Next**.

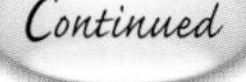

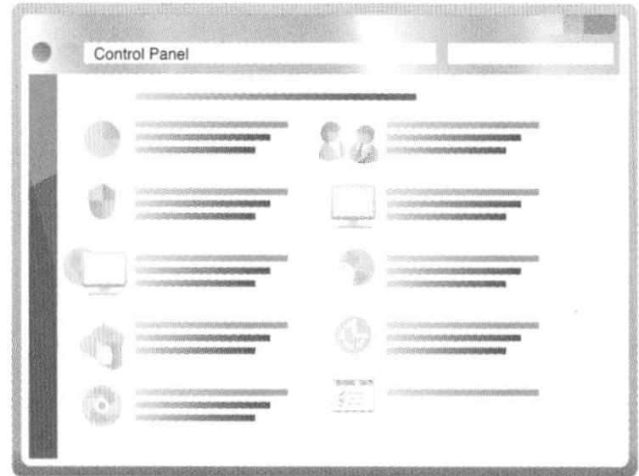

Join a Homegroup
Share with other homegroup members
Choose files and devices you want to share, and set permission levels.
Library or folder
Permissions
Pictures
Shared
Videos
Shared
Music
Shared
Documents
Not shared
Printers & Devices
Shared
Next
Cancel
Join a Homegroup
Type the homegroup password
A password helps prevent unauthorized access to homegroup files and printers. You can get the password from Cheryl on CHERYL-HP or another member of the homegroup.
Type the password:
E4VQ9dk39P
Next
Cancel
Join a Homegroup
You have joined the homegroup
You can begin accessing files and printers shared by other people in the homegroup.
Finish

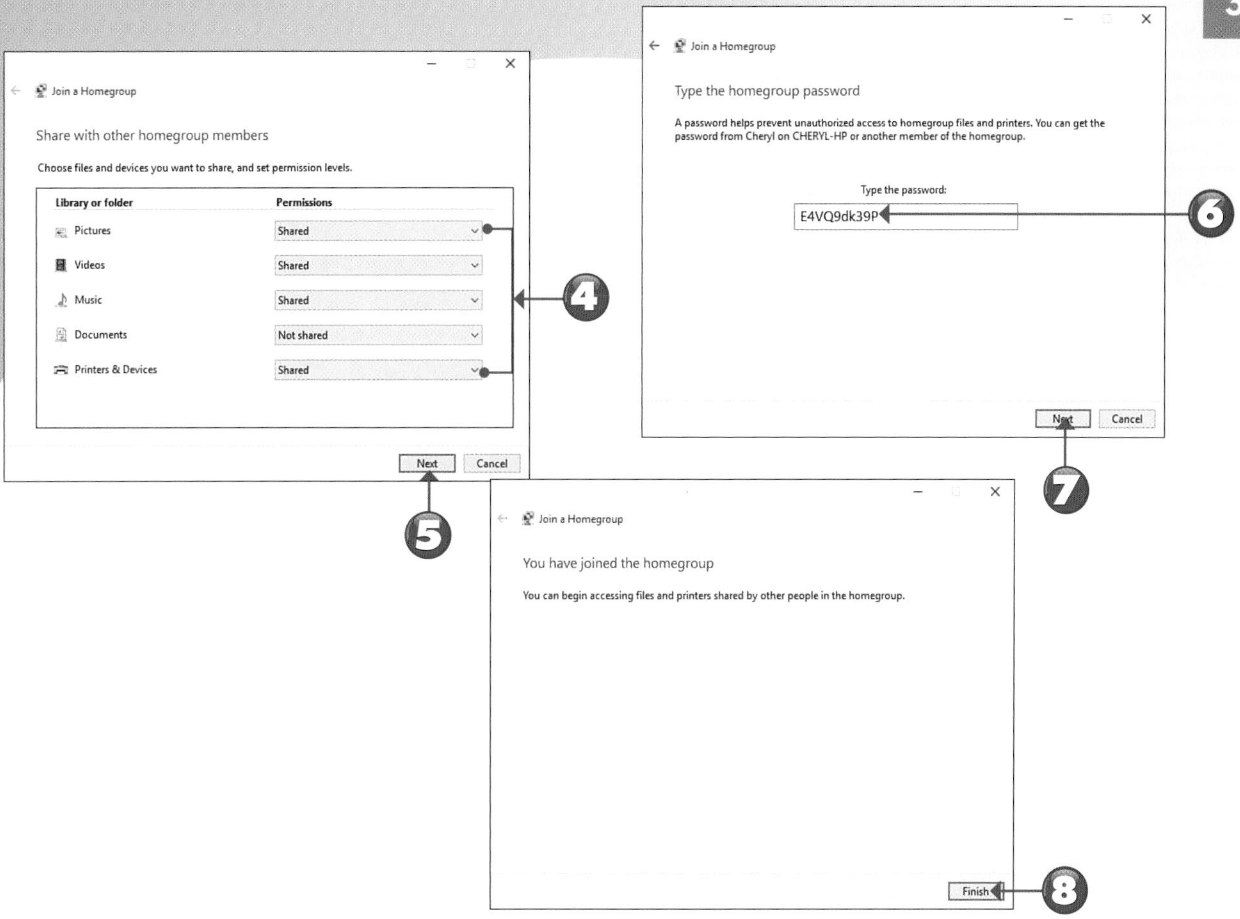

4. Select **Shared** or **Not shared** as desired for the folders and devices on your system (defaults shown here).
5. Click or tap **Next**.
6. Enter the password for the homegroup.
7. Click or tap **Next**.
8. Click or tap **Finish** to close the dialog box.

End

NOTE

Leaving a Homegroup If you want to leave a homegroup you've joined, open the HomeGroup dialog and select the link for **Leave the homegroup**.

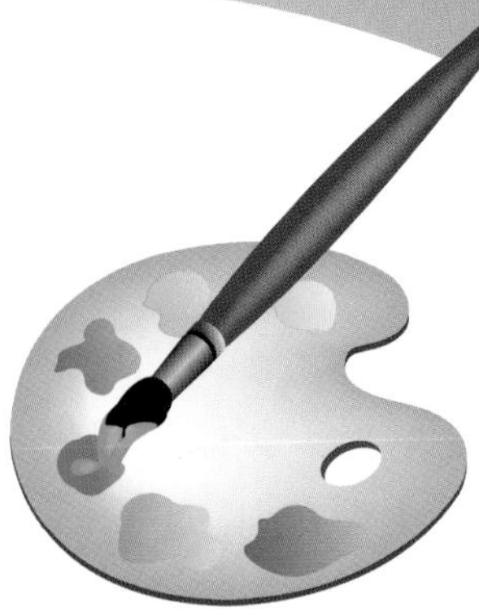

CUSTOMIZING WINDOWS

From tweaking the Start menu and the taskbar to adjusting the desktop and personalizing the Lock screen, Windows 10 provides many ways to make your account uniquely yours.

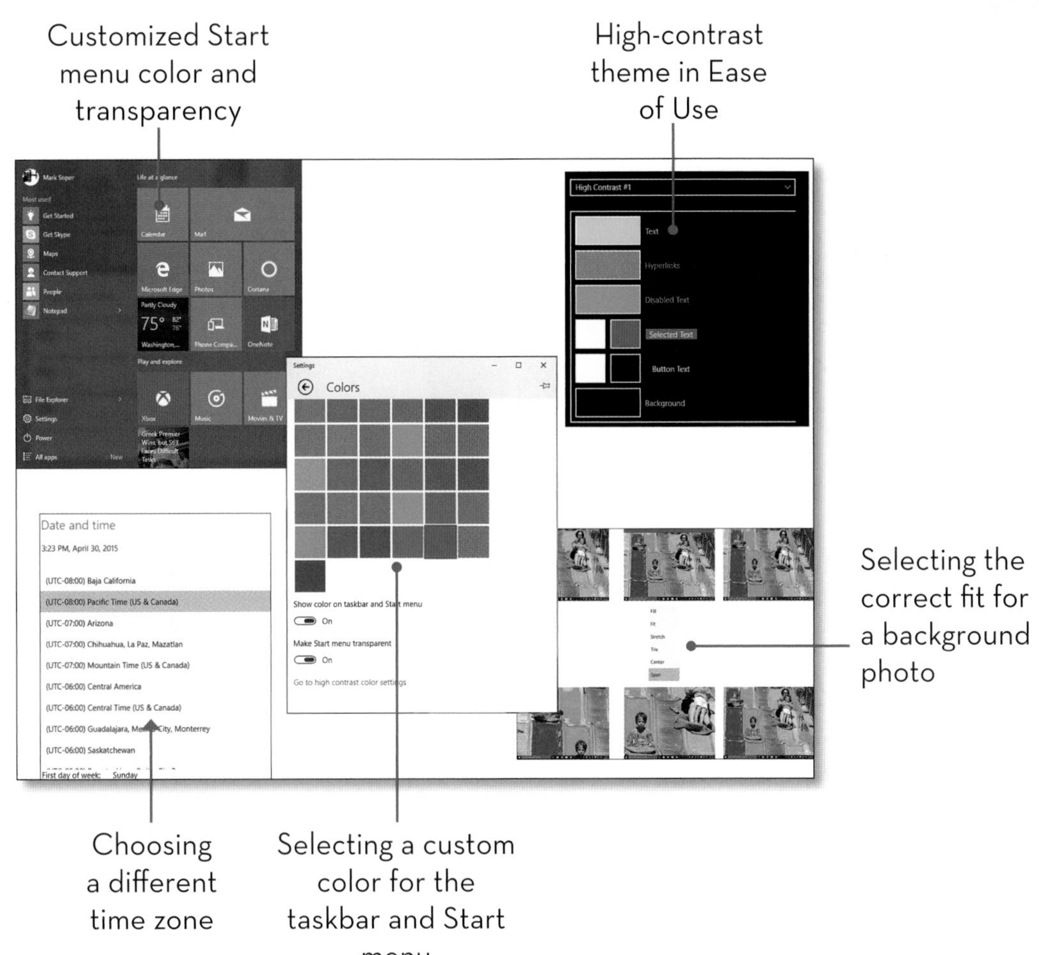

Customized Start menu color and transparency
High-contrast theme in Ease of Use
Selecting the correct fit for a background photo
Choosing a different time zone
Selecting a custom color for the taskbar and Start menu

THE PERSONALIZATION MENU

The Personalization menu enables you to change your desktop background, colors, Lock screen, and themes. Here's how to start the process from the normal Start menu.

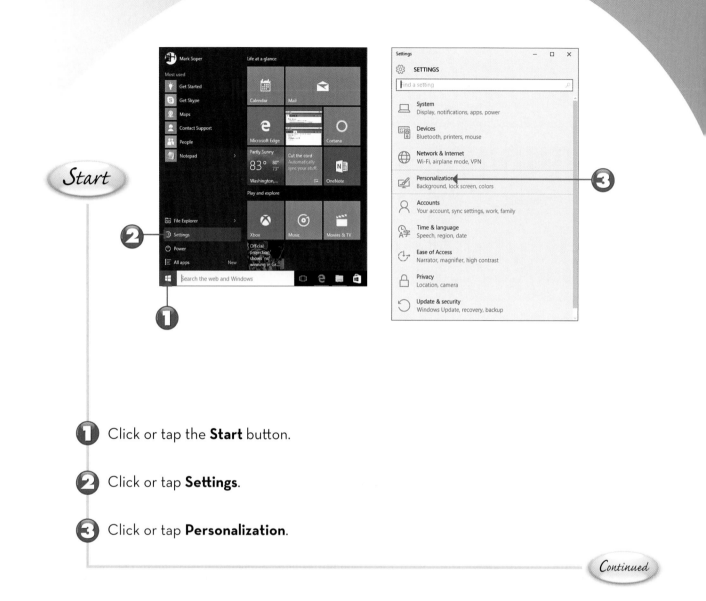

Start

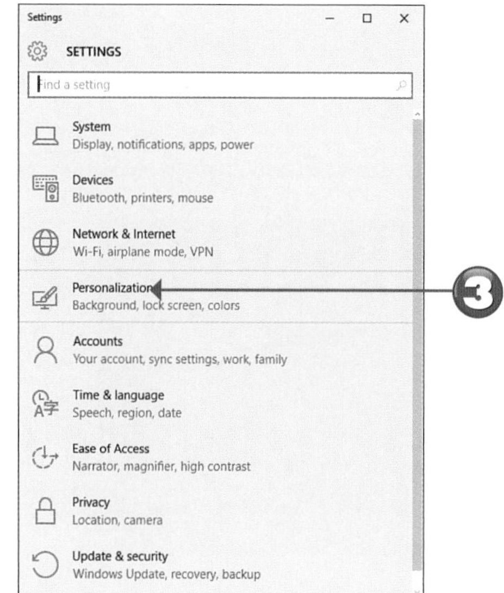

1. Click or tap the **Start** button.
2. Click or tap **Settings**.
3. Click or tap **Personalization**.

Continued

TIP

Opening Settings in Tablet Mode In Tablet Mode, tap the **Notifications** button in the taskbar, then tap **All settings** to open the Settings menu. ■

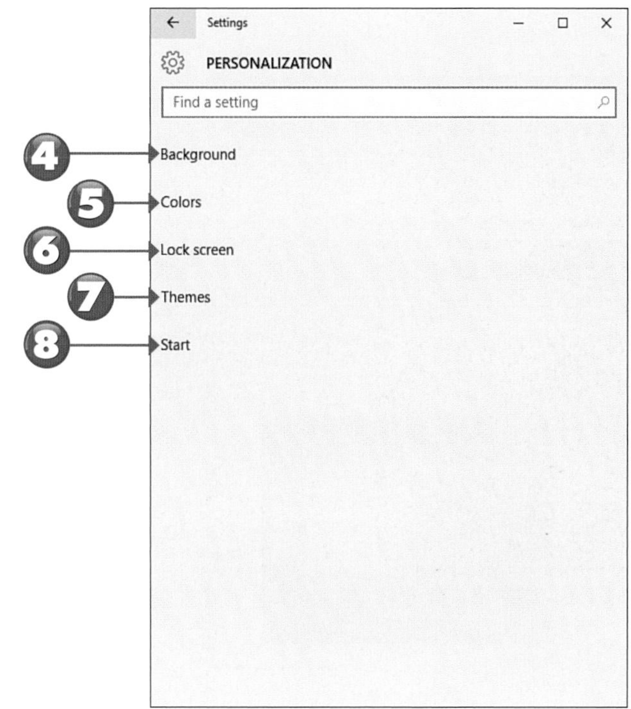

4. Click or tap to change the screen background.

5. Click or tap to change the taskbar and Start menu colors.

6. Click or tap to change the Lock screen.

7. Click or tap to change settings for sounds, mouse pointers, desktop icons, and themes.

8. Click or tap to change Start menu settings.

End

CHANGING THE SCREEN BACKGROUND

Changing the screen background ("wallpaper" for Windows veterans) is one of the most popular ways to personalize your system. In this exercise, you learn how to customize it, Windows 10 style.

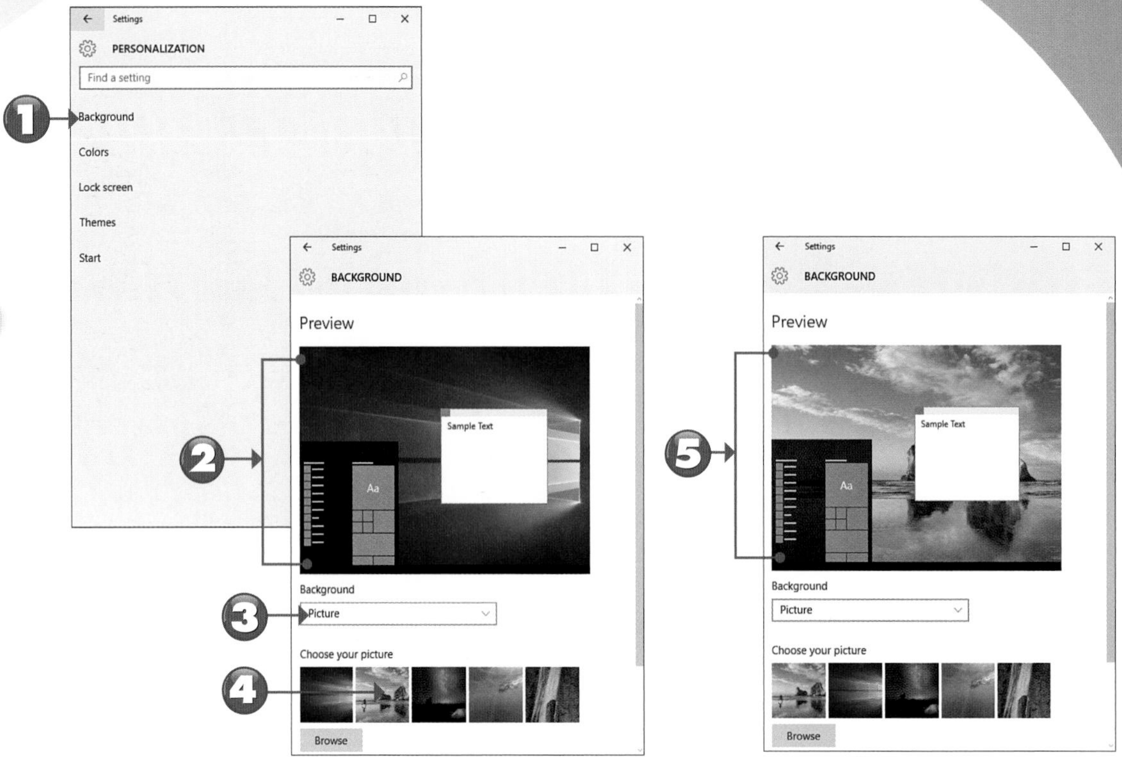

Start

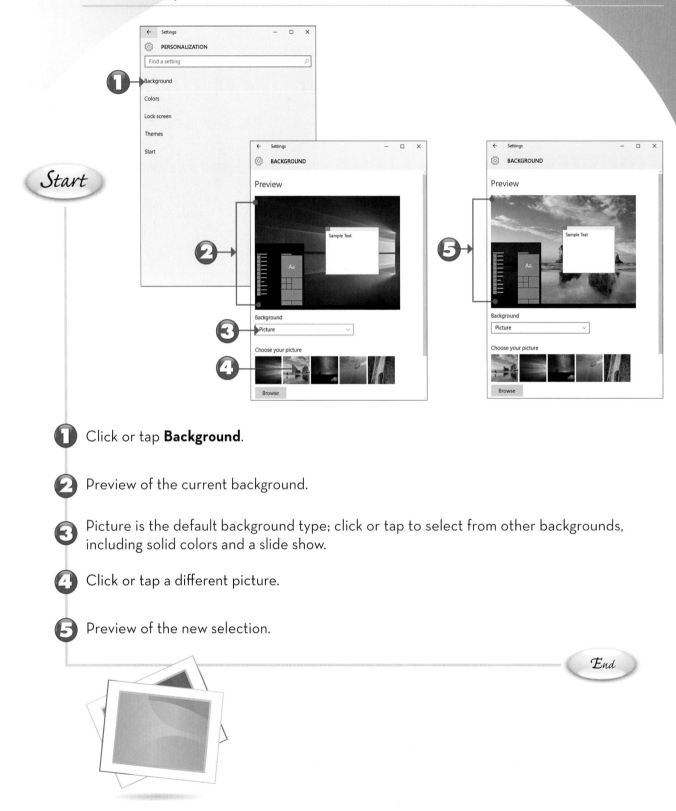

1. Click or tap **Background**.
2. Preview of the current background.
3. Picture is the default background type; click or tap to select from other backgrounds, including solid colors and a slide show.
4. Click or tap a different picture.
5. Preview of the new selection.

End

CHOOSING YOUR OWN PICTURE

Choosing one of Windows 10's spectacular nature photos adds pizazz to your desktop, but if you really want to say, "This is my computer," there's nothing like adding your own photo. Here's how to do that.

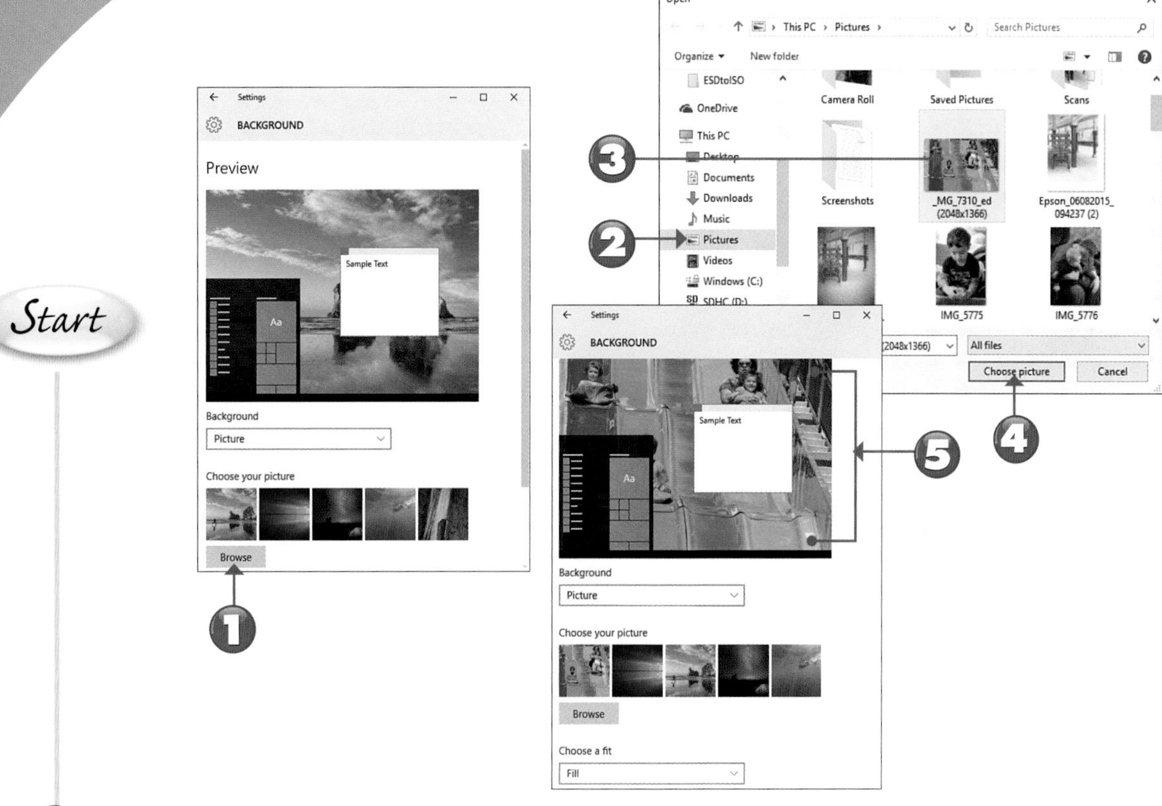

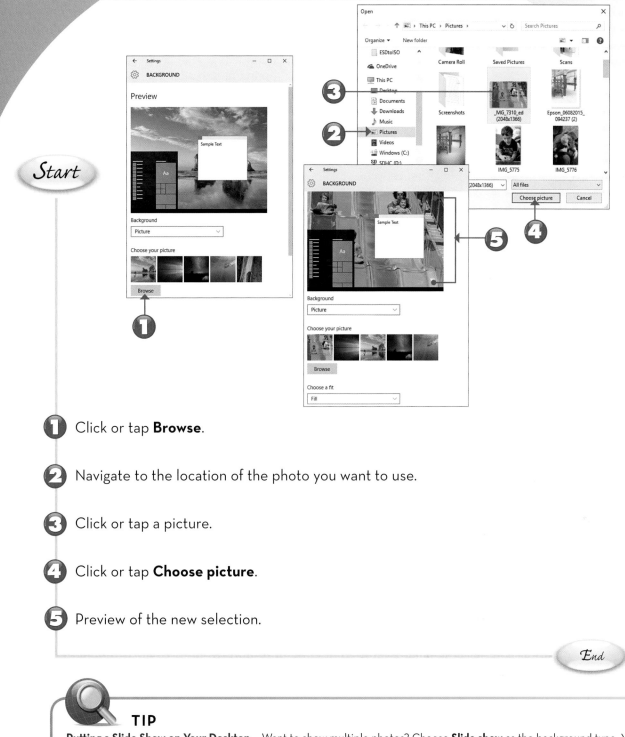

1. Click or tap **Browse**.
2. Navigate to the location of the photo you want to use.
3. Click or tap a picture.
4. Click or tap **Choose picture**.
5. Preview of the new selection.

End

TIP

Putting a Slide Show on Your Desktop Want to show multiple photos? Choose **Slide show** as the background type. You can then navigate to a folder and use its contents. You can also select a picture fit and how often to change photos. ■

CHOOSING A PICTURE FIT

Most of the time, the picture(s) you choose for your background might not be an exact fit. Here's how to use the Choose a Fit menu to select the best setting for your photo.

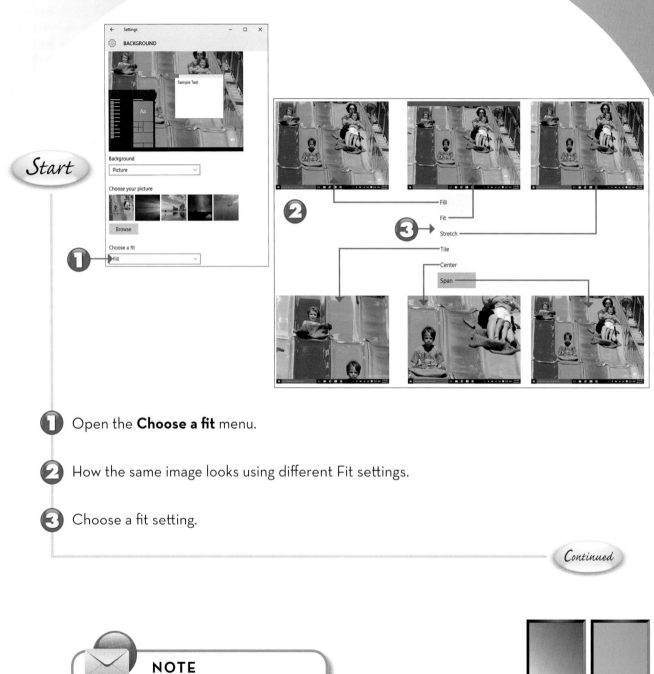

Start

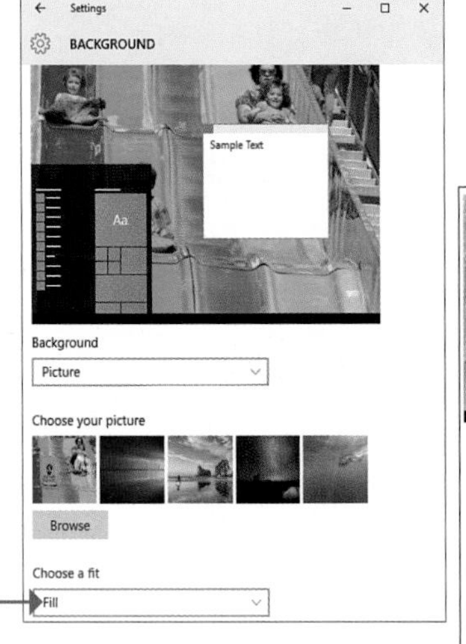

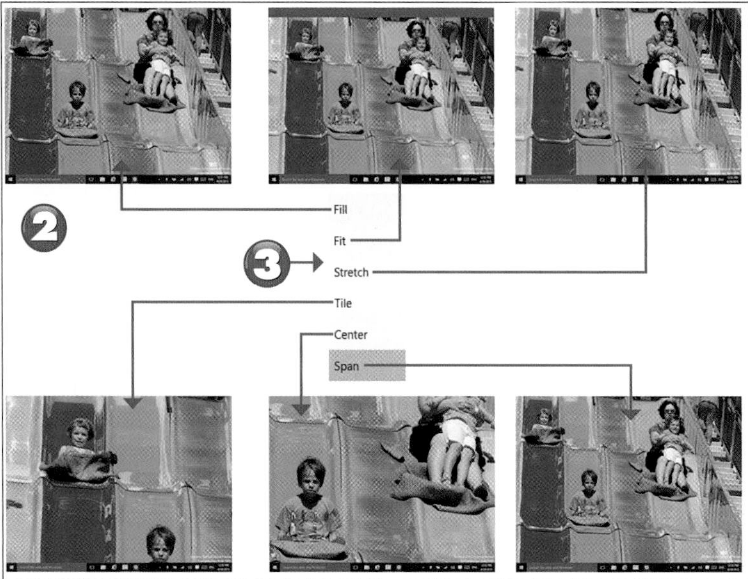

1. Open the **Choose a fit** menu.

2. How the same image looks using different Fit settings.

3. Choose a fit setting.

Continued

NOTE

Spanning Images Use Span when stretching an image across multiple monitors. ■

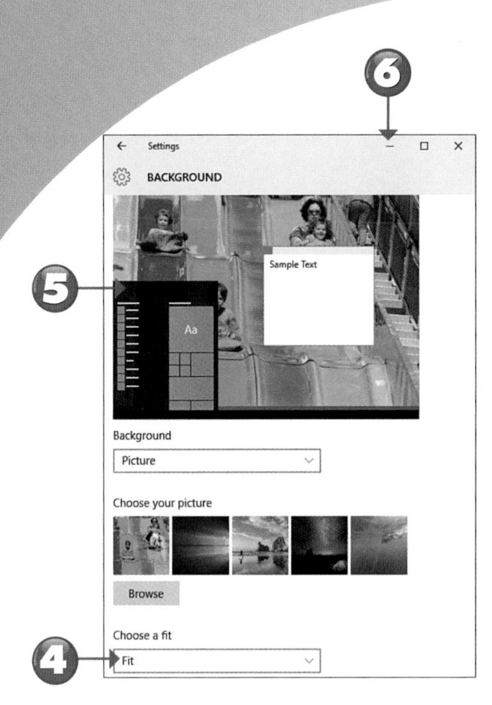

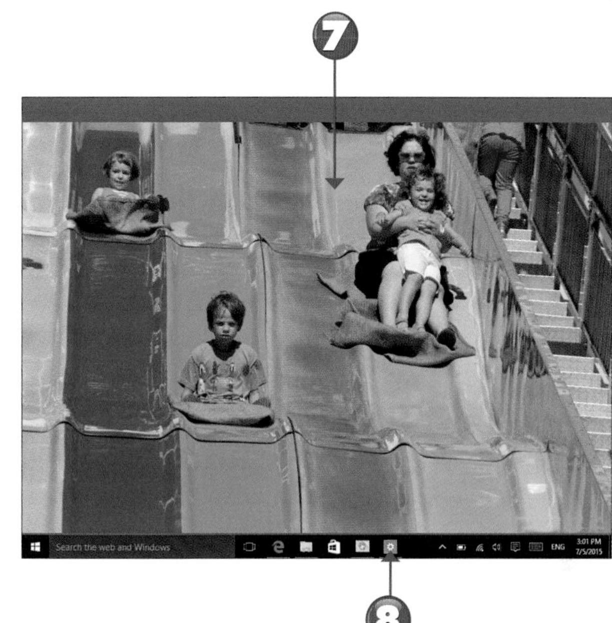

4 Current fit ("Fit").

5 Current background preview.

6 Click or tap to minimize.

7 Windows desktop using personal background.

8 Click or tap to restore the Background menu.

End

CHANGING ACCENT COLORS

Windows 10 adds new ways to customize your taskbar and Start menu colors. Let's start by changing the accent color used for active apps and Start menu tiles from the Personalization menu.

Start

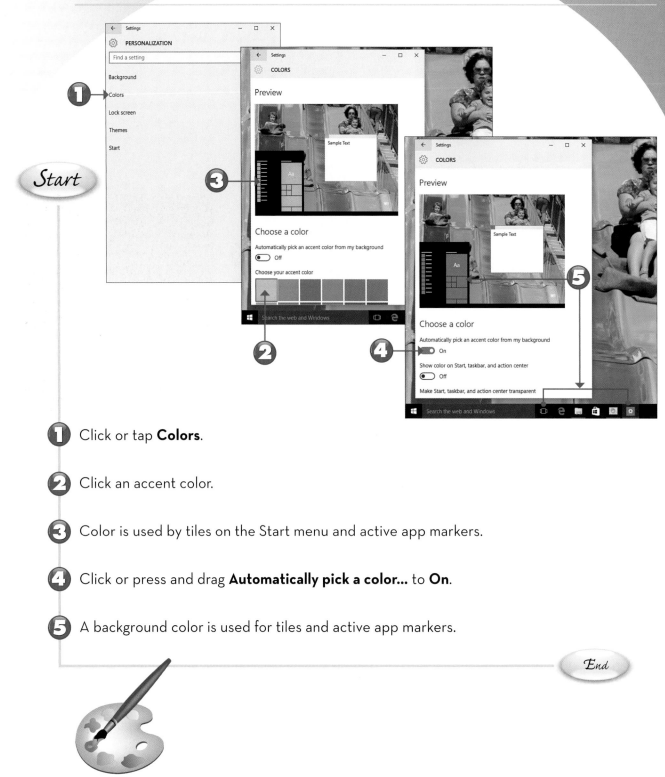

1. Click or tap **Colors**.
2. Click an accent color.
3. Color is used by tiles on the Start menu and active app markers.
4. Click or press and drag **Automatically pick a color...** to **On**.
5. A background color is used for tiles and active app markers.

End

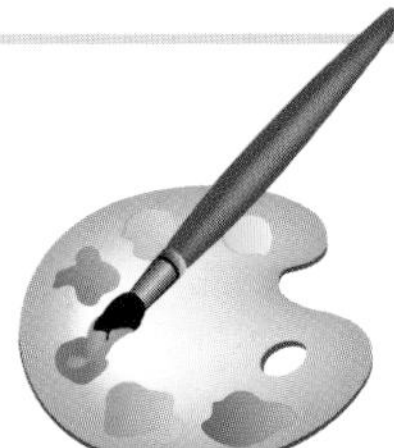

CHANGING TASKBAR AND START MENU COLORS

When you select a color in the Colors menu, you can also use this color in the taskbar and Start menu. Here's how.

Start

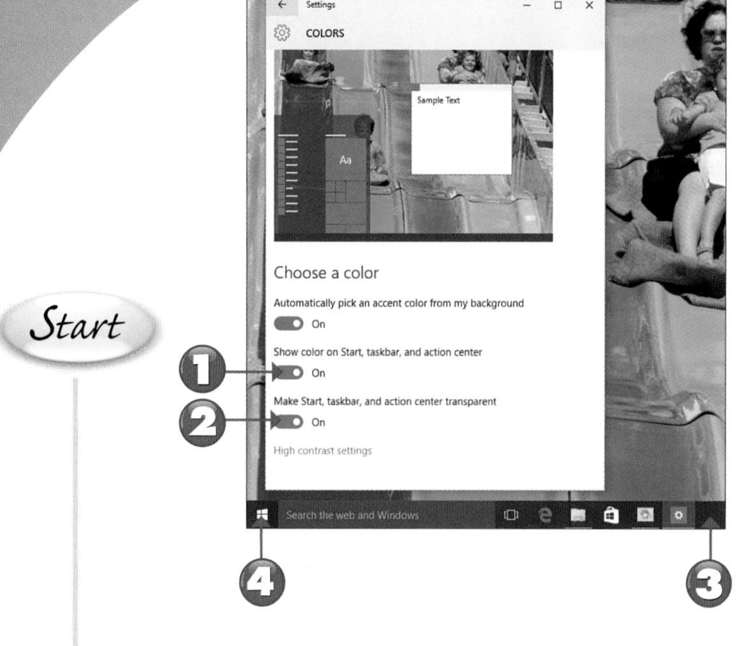

1. Click or press and drag **Show color on Start, taskbar, and action center** to **On**.
2. Click or press and drag **Make Start, taskbar, and action center transparent** to **On**.
3. The taskbar changes to the selected color.
4. Click or tap **Start**.
5. The Start menu changes to the selected color.
6. The Start menu has some transparency.

End

CHANGING START MENU TRANSPARENCY AND COLOR SETTINGS

If you don't like the Start menu transparency feature you saw in the last exercise, it's easy to turn it off from the Colors menu.

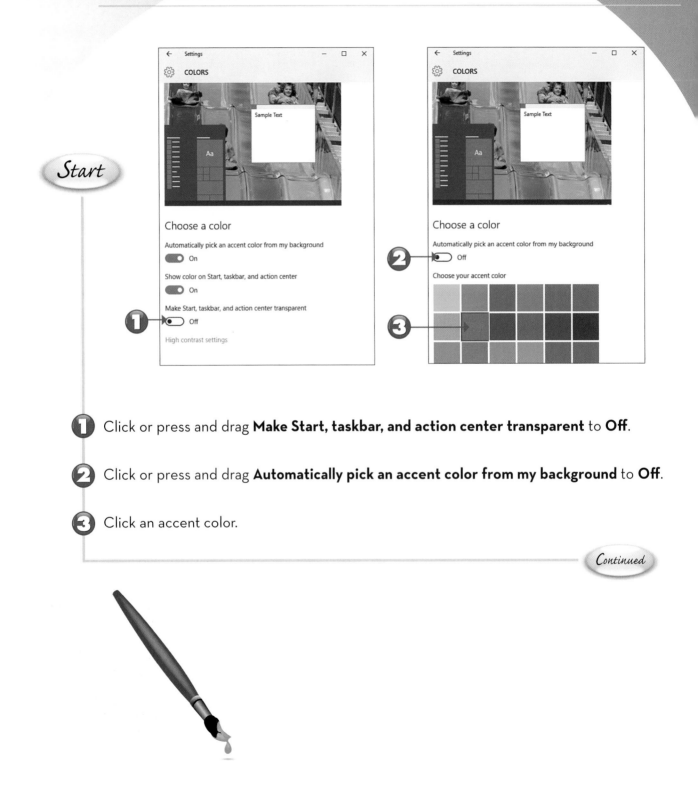

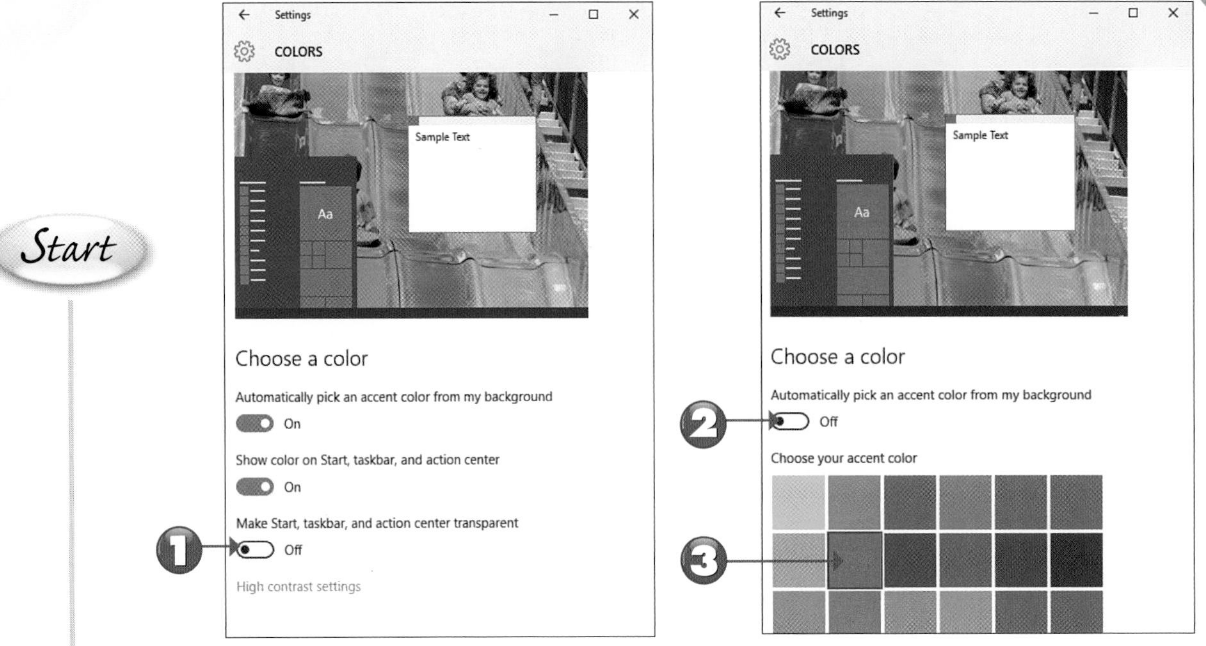

1. Click or press and drag **Make Start, taskbar, and action center transparent** to **Off**.
2. Click or press and drag **Automatically pick an accent color from my background** to **Off**.
3. Click an accent color.

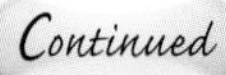

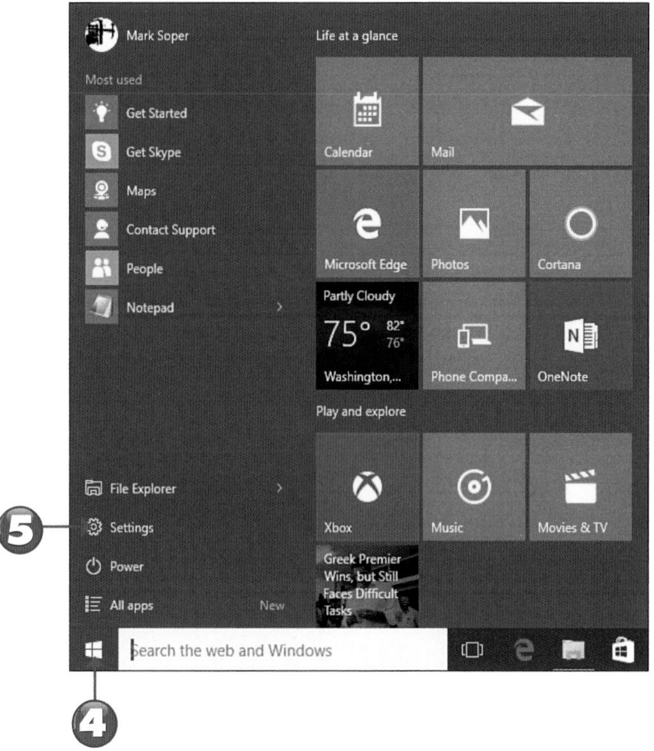

4. Click or tap **Start**.
5. Click or tap **Settings**.

End

CHANGING START MENU SETTINGS

You can also change the items that appear on the Start menu and its on-screen size. In this lesson, you learn how to run Start in full-screen mode and how to add folders to the Start menu.

Start

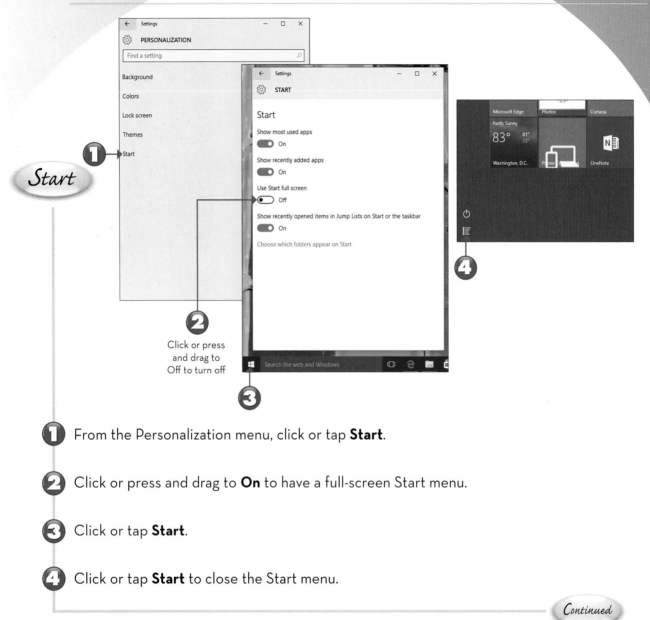

Click or press and drag to Off to turn off

1. From the Personalization menu, click or tap **Start**.
2. Click or press and drag to **On** to have a full-screen Start menu.
3. Click or tap **Start**.
4. Click or tap **Start** to close the Start menu.

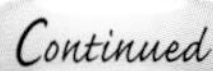

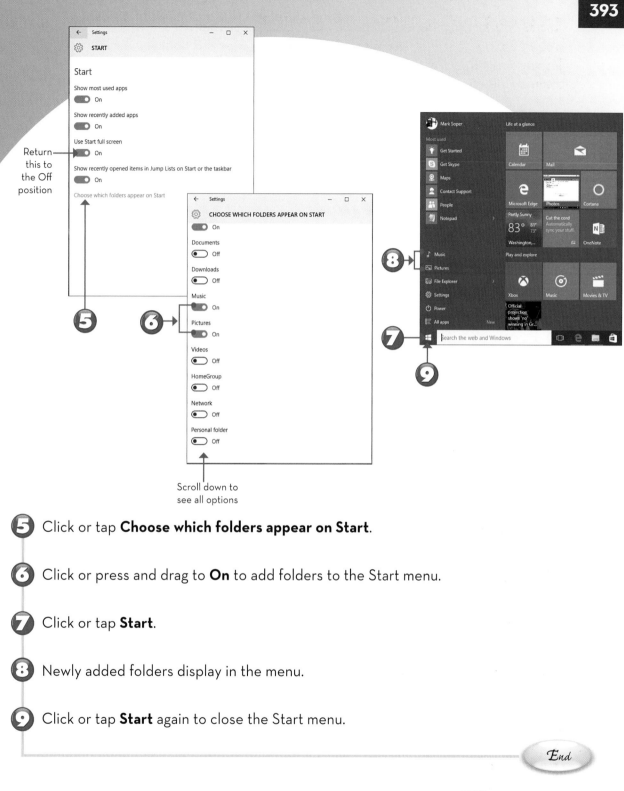

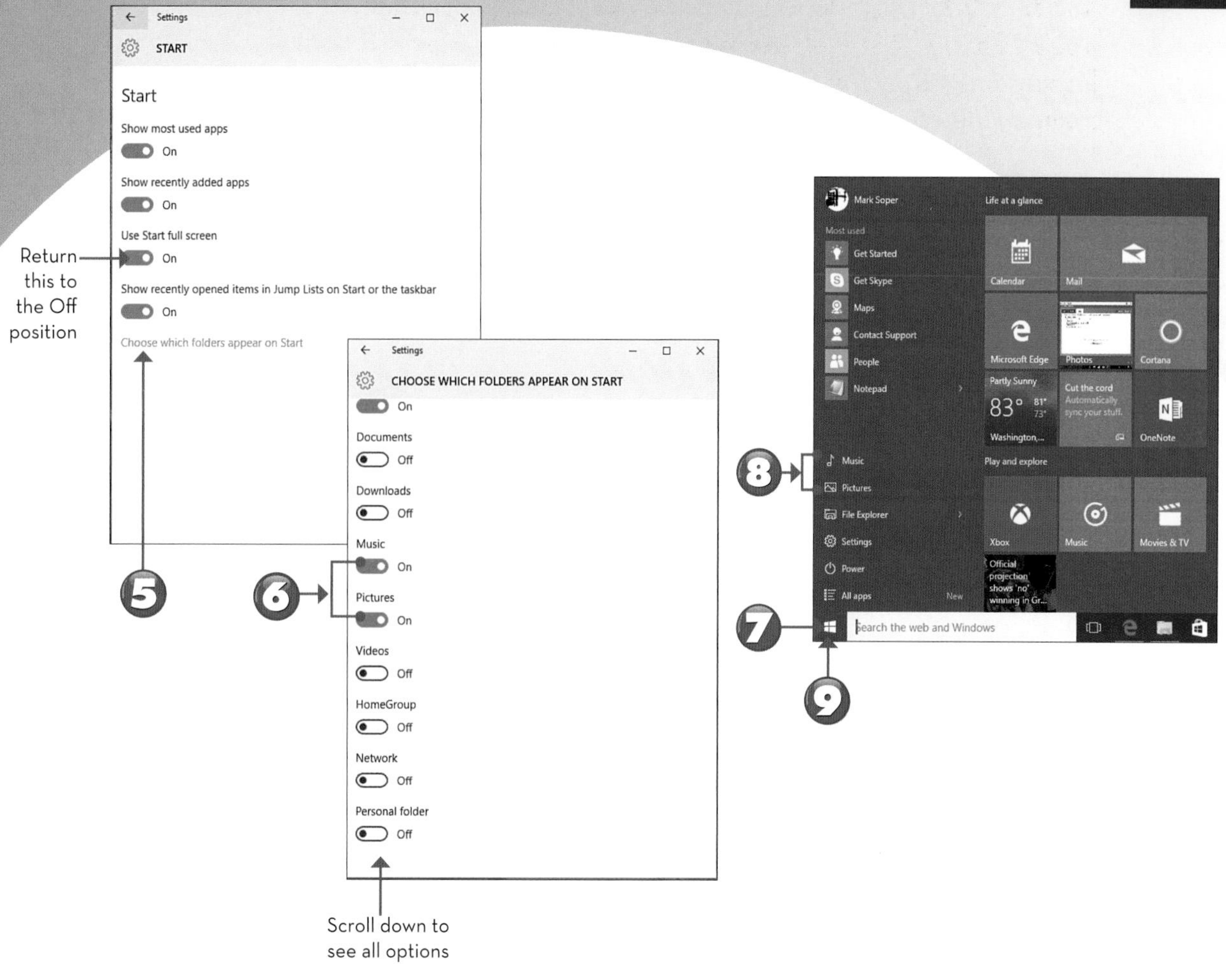

Return this to the Off position

Scroll down to see all options

5. Click or tap **Choose which folders appear on Start**.

6. Click or press and drag to **On** to add folders to the Start menu.

7. Click or tap **Start**.

8. Newly added folders display in the menu.

9. Click or tap **Start** again to close the Start menu.

End

SELECTING A SCREEN SAVER

The Windows 10 screen saver function helps to protect the privacy of your display when you're away from your computer. This feature also helps to prevent an image being permanently burned into your screen—still a concern if you use a plasma HDTV with your computer. This tutorial shows you how to select and customize your favorite screen saver from the Lock screen dialog box.

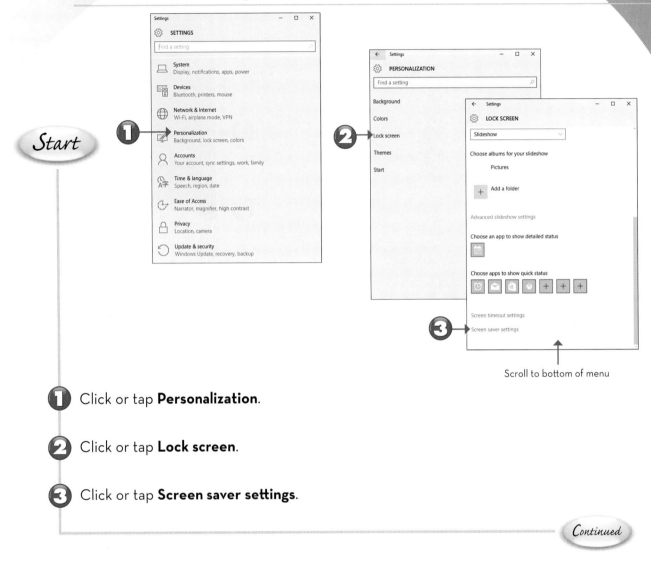

Start

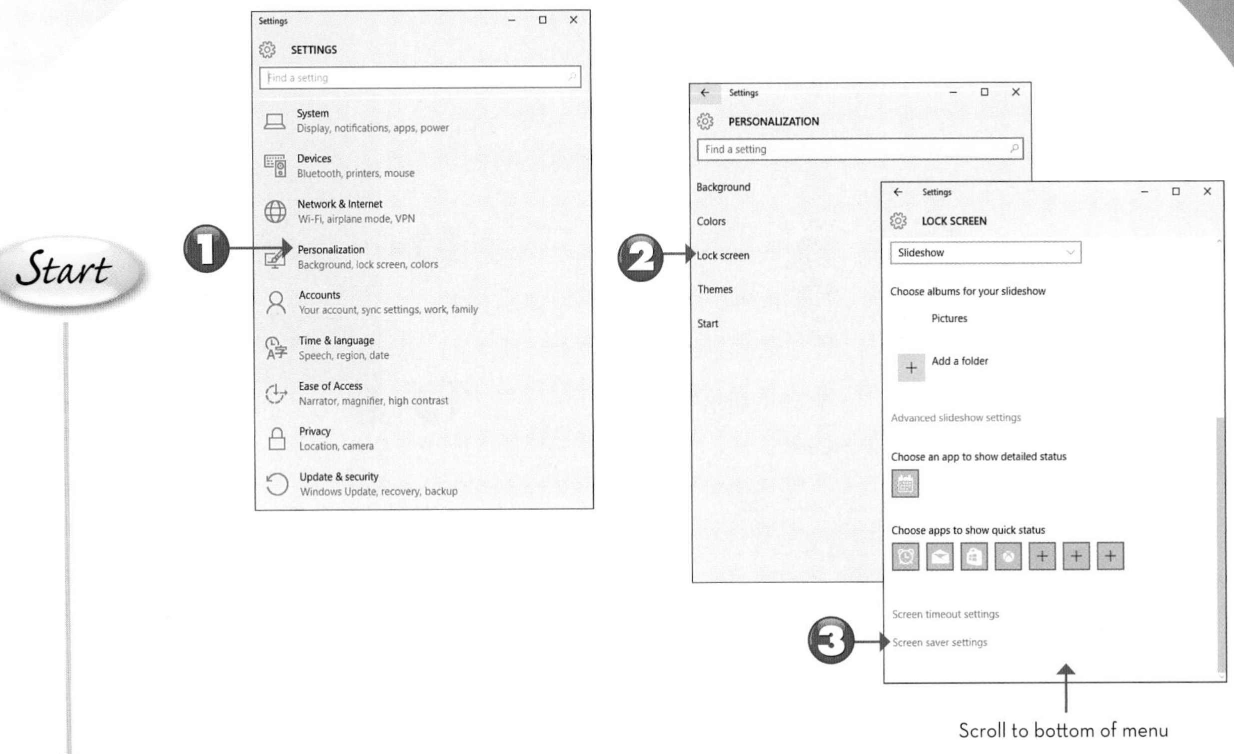

1. Click or tap **Personalization**.

2. Click or tap **Lock screen**.

3. Click or tap **Screen saver settings**.

Continued

NOTE

Screen Saver and Screen Timeout Settings If your screen blanks out before the screen saver starts, open the **Screen timeout settings** link shown in step 3 and adjust how long the screen stays on. ■

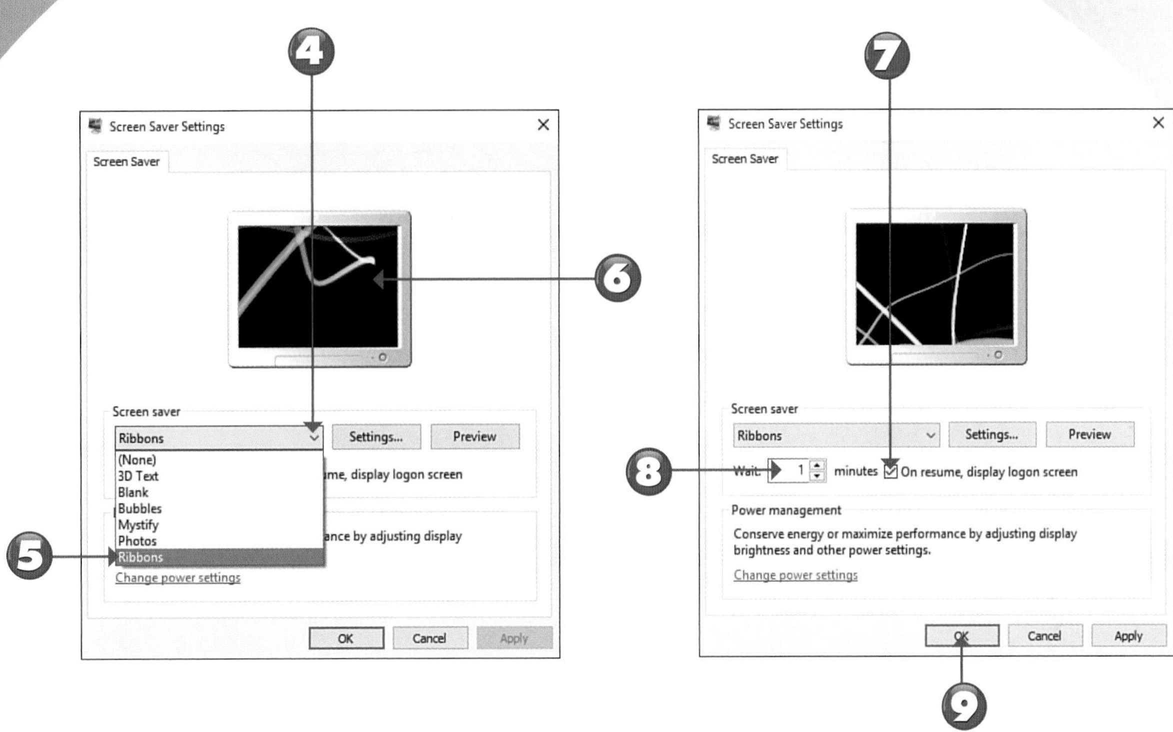

4. Open the **Screen saver** menu.
5. Select a screen saver.
6. A preview of the screen saver appears.
7. Click or tap the empty check box to require login after the screen saver starts.
8. Adjust the wait time as desired.
9. Click or tap **OK** to use the screen saver.

End

CONFIGURING A TIME ZONE

New computers and tablets are often set to the wrong time zone for your area when you first receive them. Fixing the problem is easy with the Settings Time & language dialog box.

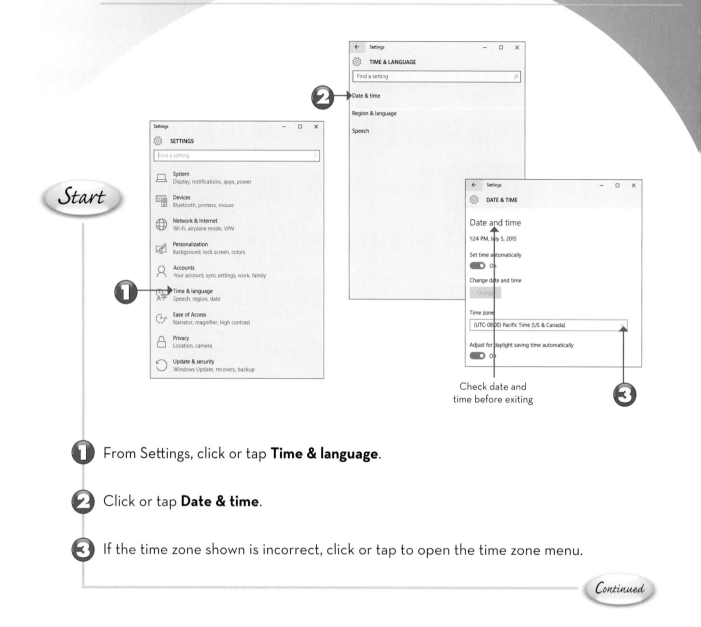

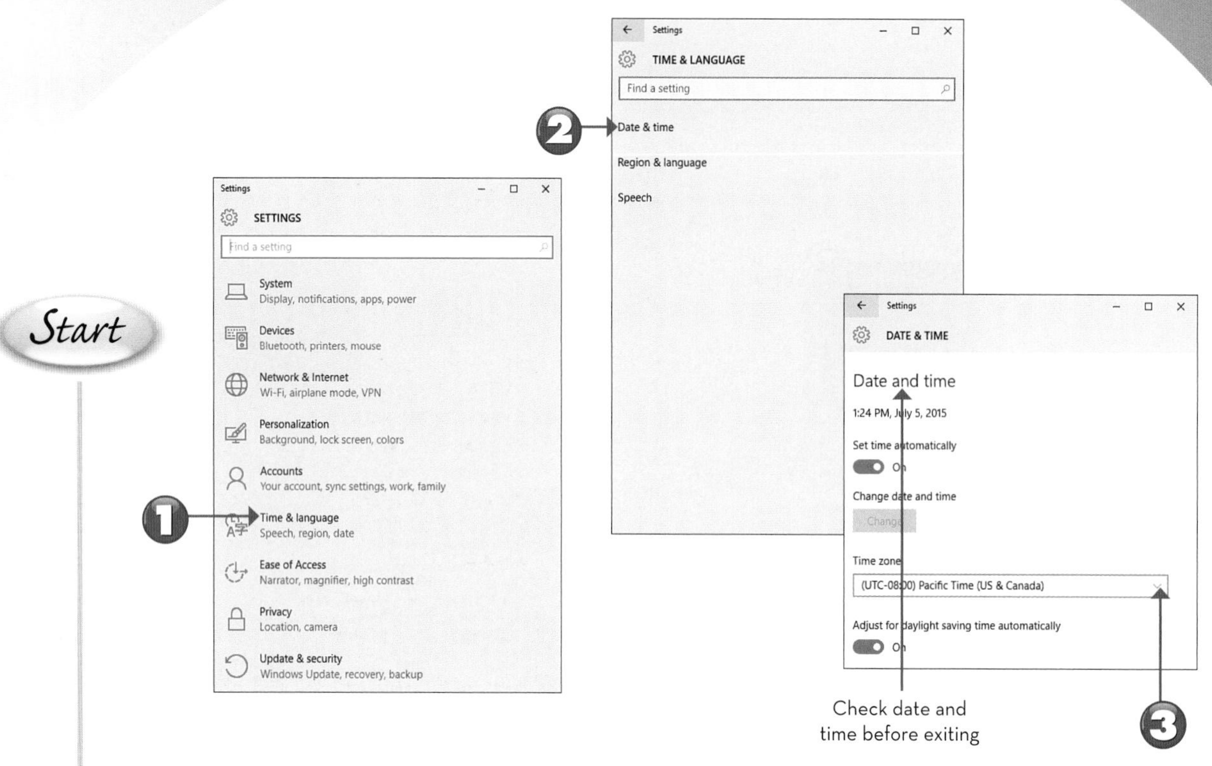

1. From Settings, click or tap **Time & language**.
2. Click or tap **Date & time**.
3. If the time zone shown is incorrect, click or tap to open the time zone menu.

Continued

NOTE

When to Change the Date and Time Although the time zone is listed after the date and time, you should make sure the time zone is checked (and, if necessary, changed) *before* you make any changes to the date and time. If you need to change the date and time, turn off **Set time automatically** and use the **Change** button shown in step 3. ■

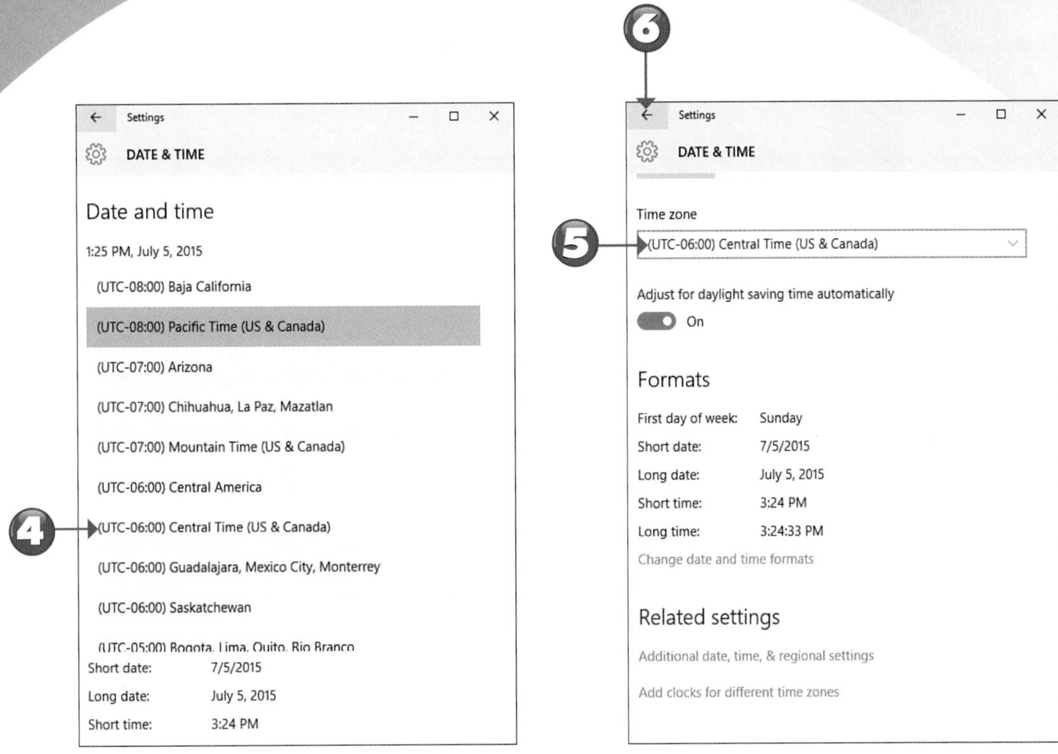

4. Select the correct time zone.
5. The correct time zone is now listed.
6. Click or tap to return to Settings.

End

NOTE

Changing Date and Time Formats If you prefer different date and time formats to the ones shown in step 5, click or tap **Change date and time formats.** ■

CUSTOMIZING THE TASKBAR

Use the taskbar customization options in Windows 10 to change the appearance of the taskbar. Here's how to change taskbar button label settings.

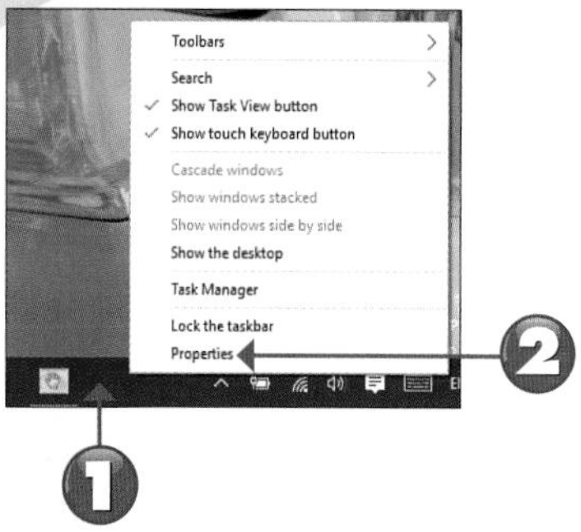

Start

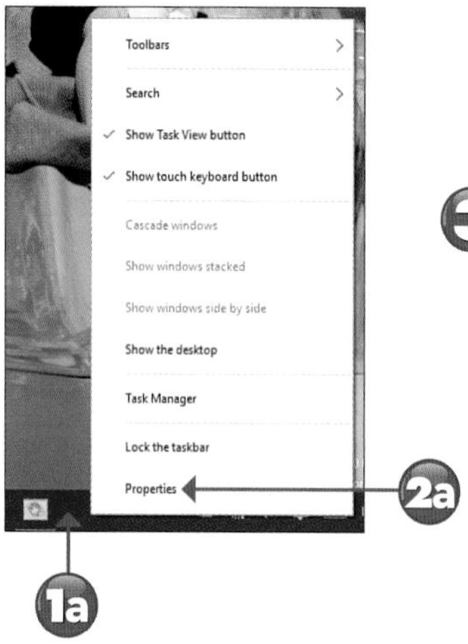

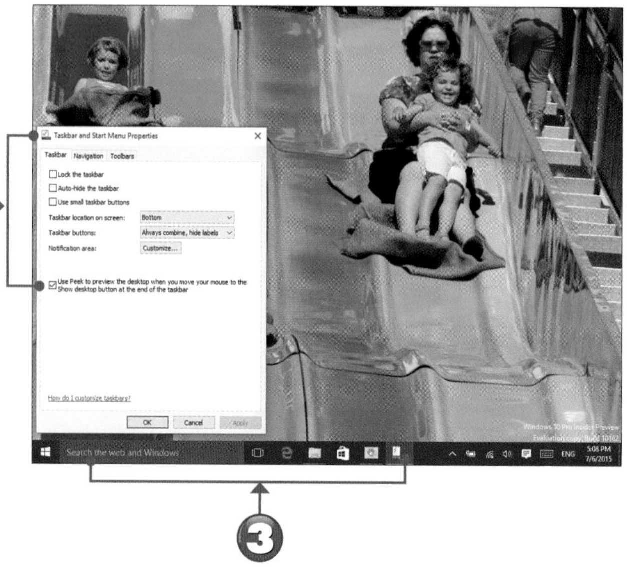

1. Right-click an empty area of the taskbar or the **Start** button.
2. Click **Properties**.

1a. Press and hold on a touch screen for a touch-friendly version.

2a. Click or tap **Properties**.

3. These are the default taskbar appearance and settings.

Continued

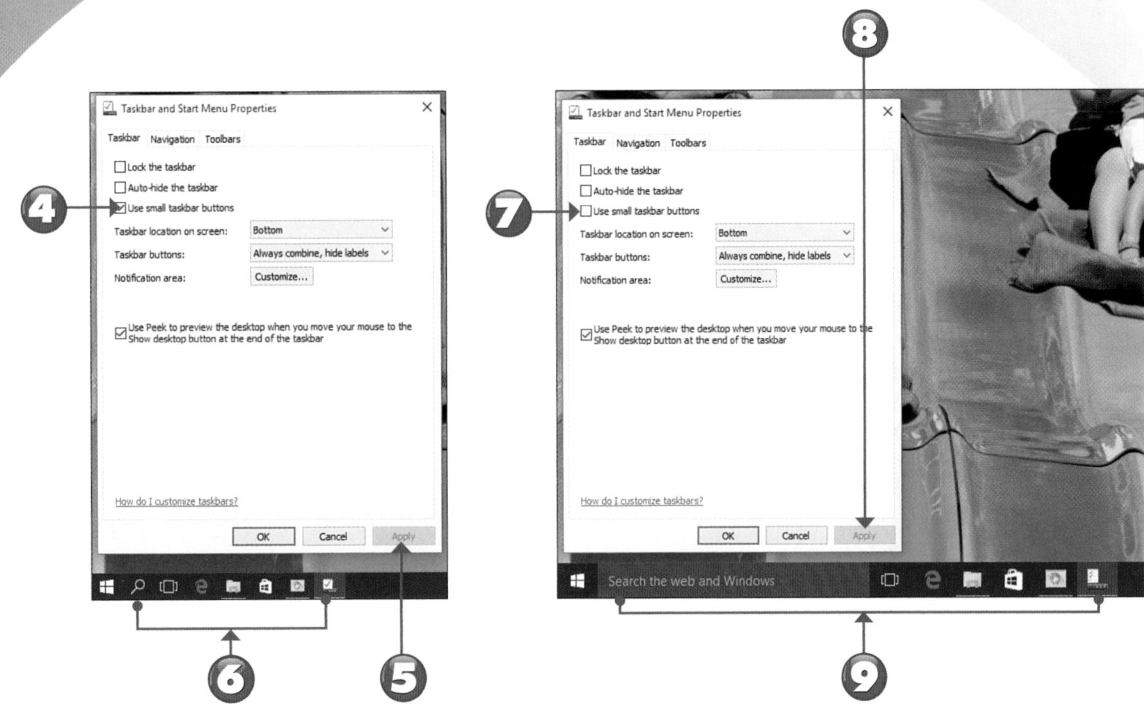

4. Select **Use small taskbar buttons**.
5. Click or tap **Apply** to use this setting.
6. The taskbar buttons change to the small setting.
7. Clear the check box for **Use small taskbar buttons**.
8. Click or tap **Apply**.
9. Default taskbar appearance returns.

End

NOTE

Locking and Auto-Hiding the Taskbar Lock the taskbar so it can't be changed until it's unlocked. Use Auto-hide to maximize screen space; the taskbar is visible only when you move your mouse or finger to the bottom edge of the display. ■

ADDING AND MANAGING USERS

Windows 10 provides new and improved ways to log in to your system and keep it secure, whether you are the only user of a device or you share it with others. Windows 10 also supports Microsoft Family, which permits you to set up child accounts that can be monitored and controlled.

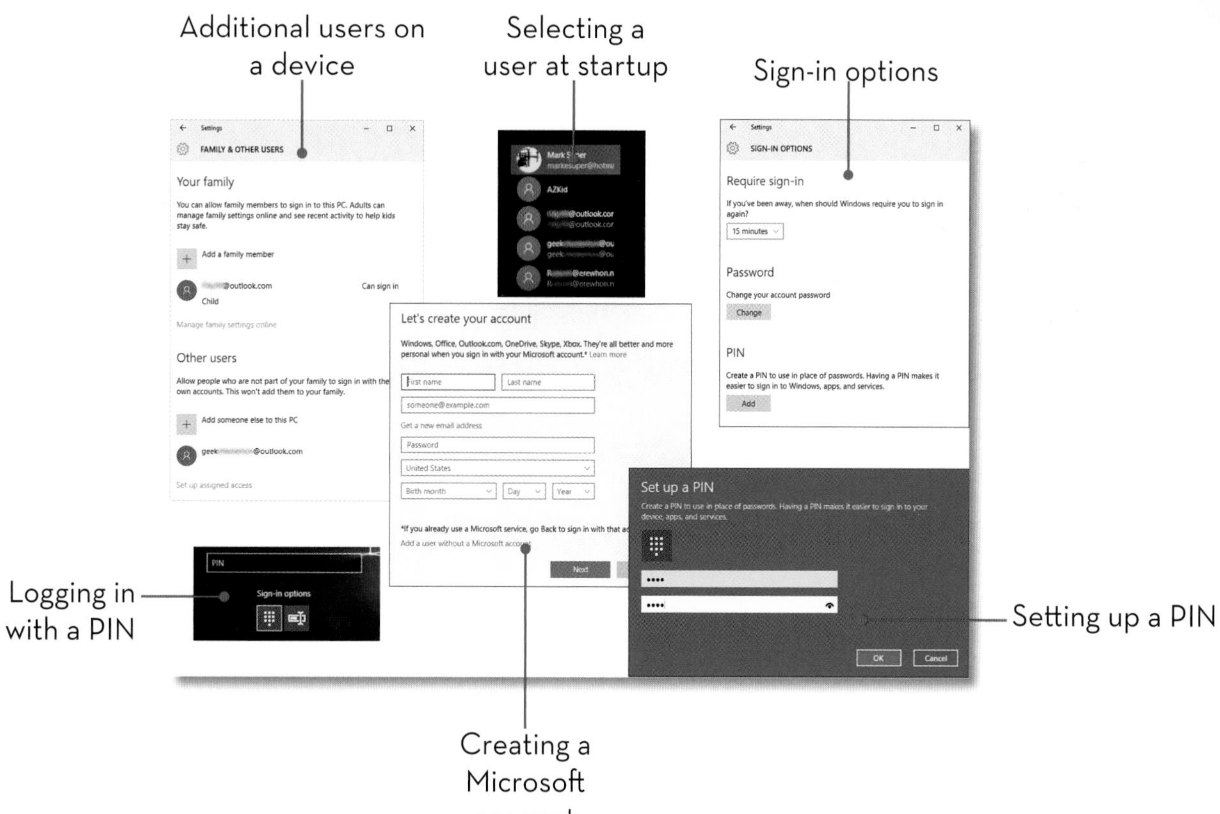

Additional users on a device
Selecting a user at startup
Sign-in options
Logging in with a PIN
Setting up a PIN
Creating a Microsoft account

PREPARING TO ADD A USER

A Windows 10 computer always has at least one user account. However, if you share your computer with other users at home or work, each user should have his or her own account. By using this feature, Windows 10 can provide customized settings for each user, and each user's information can be stored in a separate folder. In this section, you learn how to access the menu where you can select the type of user to add from the Settings menu. In later sections, you learn what happens next.

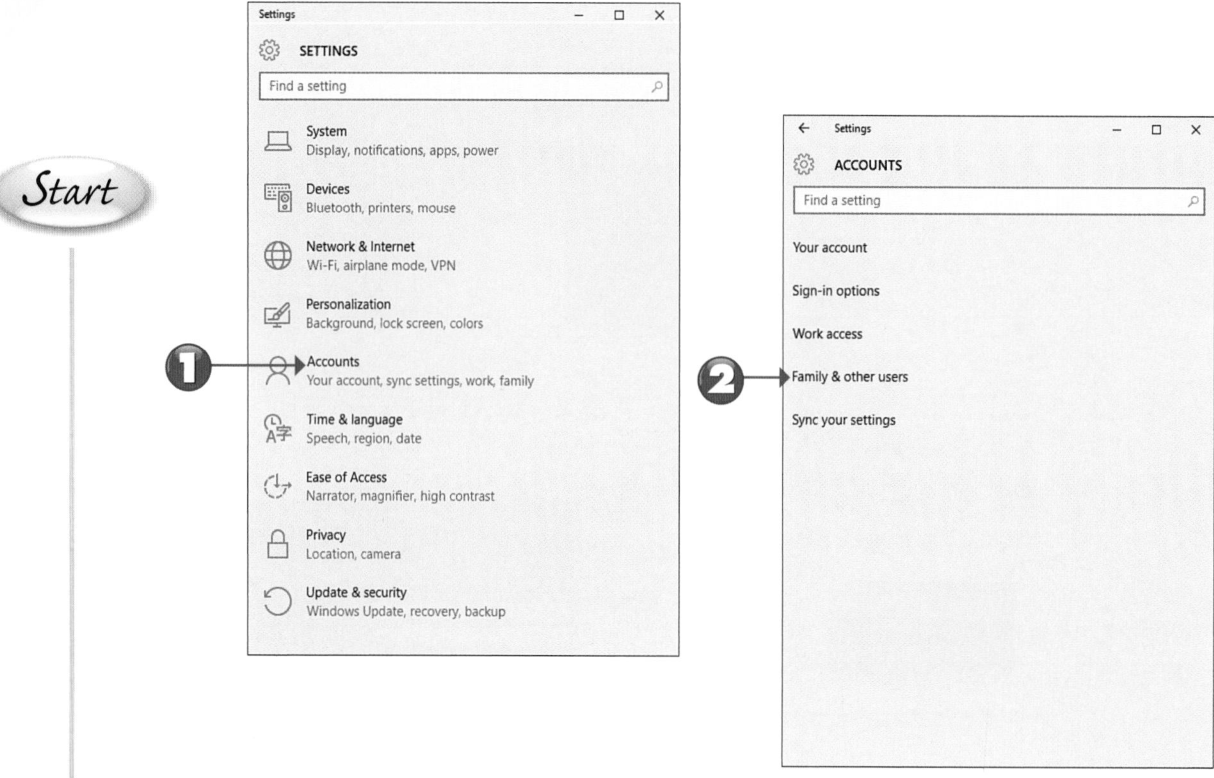

1. From the Settings menu, click or tap **Accounts**.

2. Click or tap **Family & other users**.

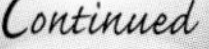

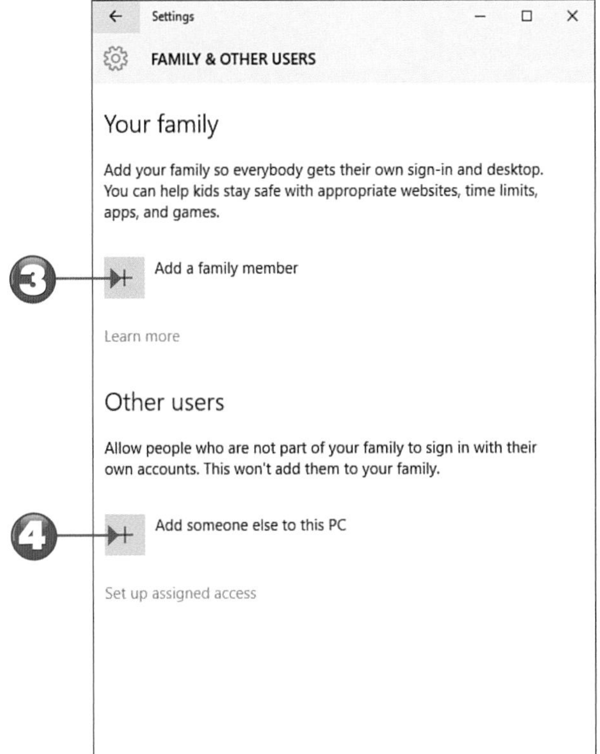
Settings
FAMILY & OTHER USERS
Your family
Add your family so everybody gets their own sign-in and desktop. You can help kids stay safe with appropriate websites, time limits, apps, and games.
3
Add a family member
Learn more
Other users
Allow people who are not part of your family to sign in with their own accounts. This won't add them to your family.
4
Add someone else to this PC
Set up assigned access

3. Click or tap **Add a family member** to add an account for a member of your family.

4. Click or tap **Add someone else to this PC** to add an account for a co-worker or a friend.

End

NOTE

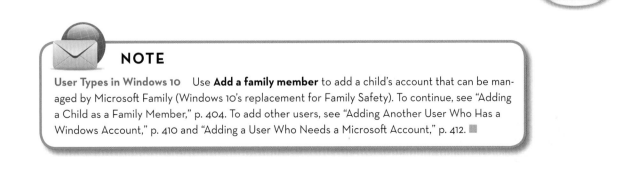

User Types in Windows 10 Use **Add a family member** to add a child's account that can be managed by Microsoft Family (Windows 10's replacement for Family Safety). To continue, see "Adding a Child as a Family Member," p. 404. To add other users, see "Adding Another User Who Has a Windows Account," p. 410 and "Adding a User Who Needs a Microsoft Account," p. 412.

ADDING A CHILD AS A FAMILY MEMBER

You can add children or adults as users to your Windows 10 device. In this example, we'll add a child in your household. When you add a child, you can manage their computer and Internet activity with Microsoft Family (formerly Family Safety).

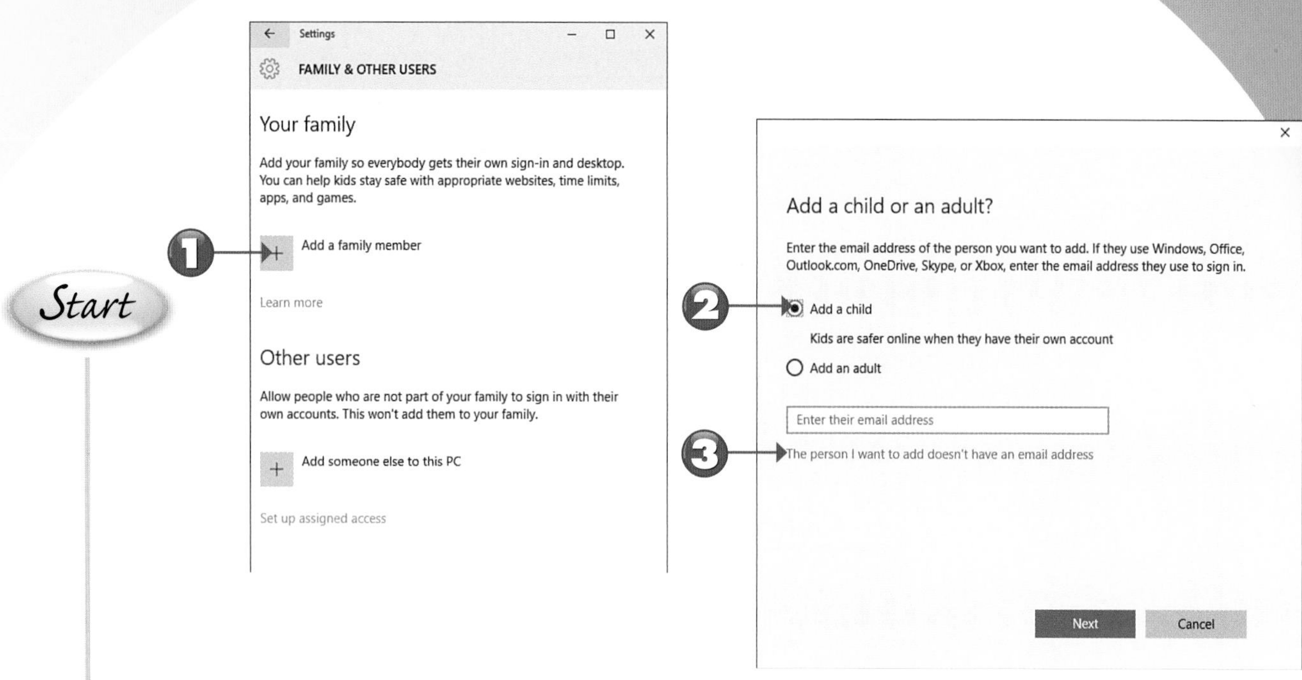
Start
Settings
FAMILY & OTHER USERS
Your family
Add your family so everybody gets their own sign-in and desktop. You can help kids stay safe with appropriate websites, time limits, apps, and games.
Add a family member
Learn more
Other users
Allow people who are not part of your family to sign in with their own accounts. This won't add them to your family.
Add someone else to this PC
Set up assigned access
Add a child or an adult?
Enter the email address of the person you want to add. If they use Windows, Office, Outlook.com, OneDrive, Skype, or Xbox, enter the email address they use to sign in.
Add a child
Kids are safer online when they have their own account
Add an adult
Enter their email address
The person I want to add doesn't have an email address
Next
Cancel

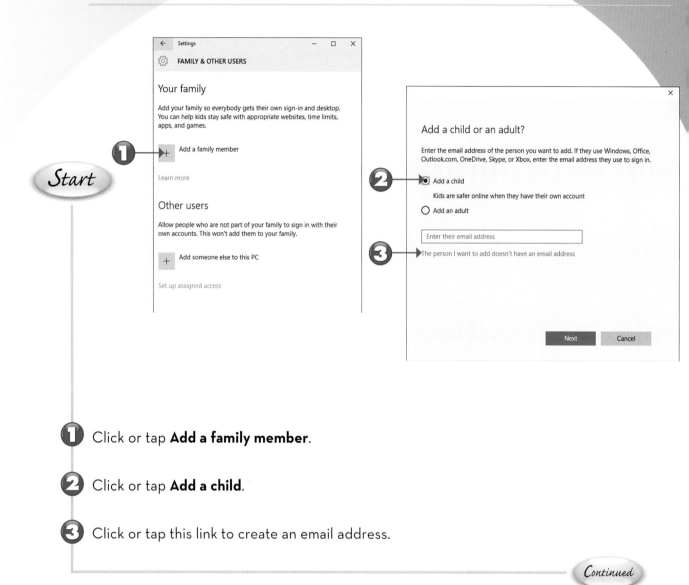

1. Click or tap **Add a family member**.
2. Click or tap **Add a child**.
3. Click or tap this link to create an email address.

Continued

TIP

Adding a Child Who Already Has a Microsoft Account Add the child's email in the blank provided (after step 2), click **Next**, and click **Confirm**. An invitation is sent to the email address, and after the child confirms the invitation, that account is added to your family members and can be managed by Microsoft Family.

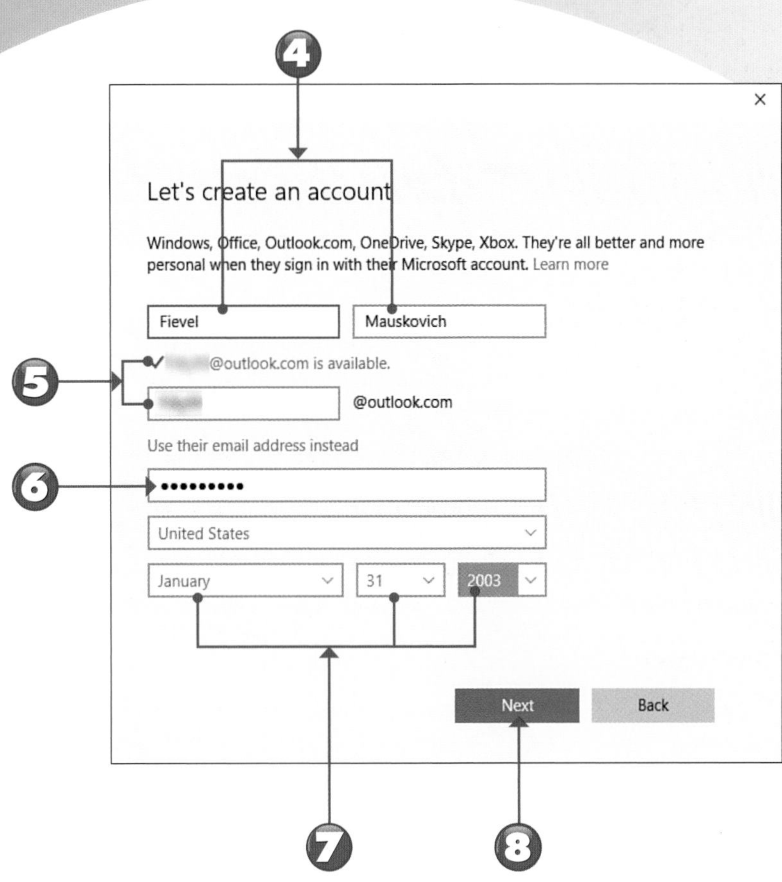

4. Enter the child's first and last name.

5. Enter an email address. If this address is available, continue; otherwise, try a different address until you find one that works.

6. Create a password.

7. Enter the child's birth date.

8. Click or tap **Next**.

Continued

NOTE

Email Addresses and Child Accounts Microsoft Family now requires that each account it manages has an email address. In this example, we'll create a Microsoft email address for use by the child account. ■

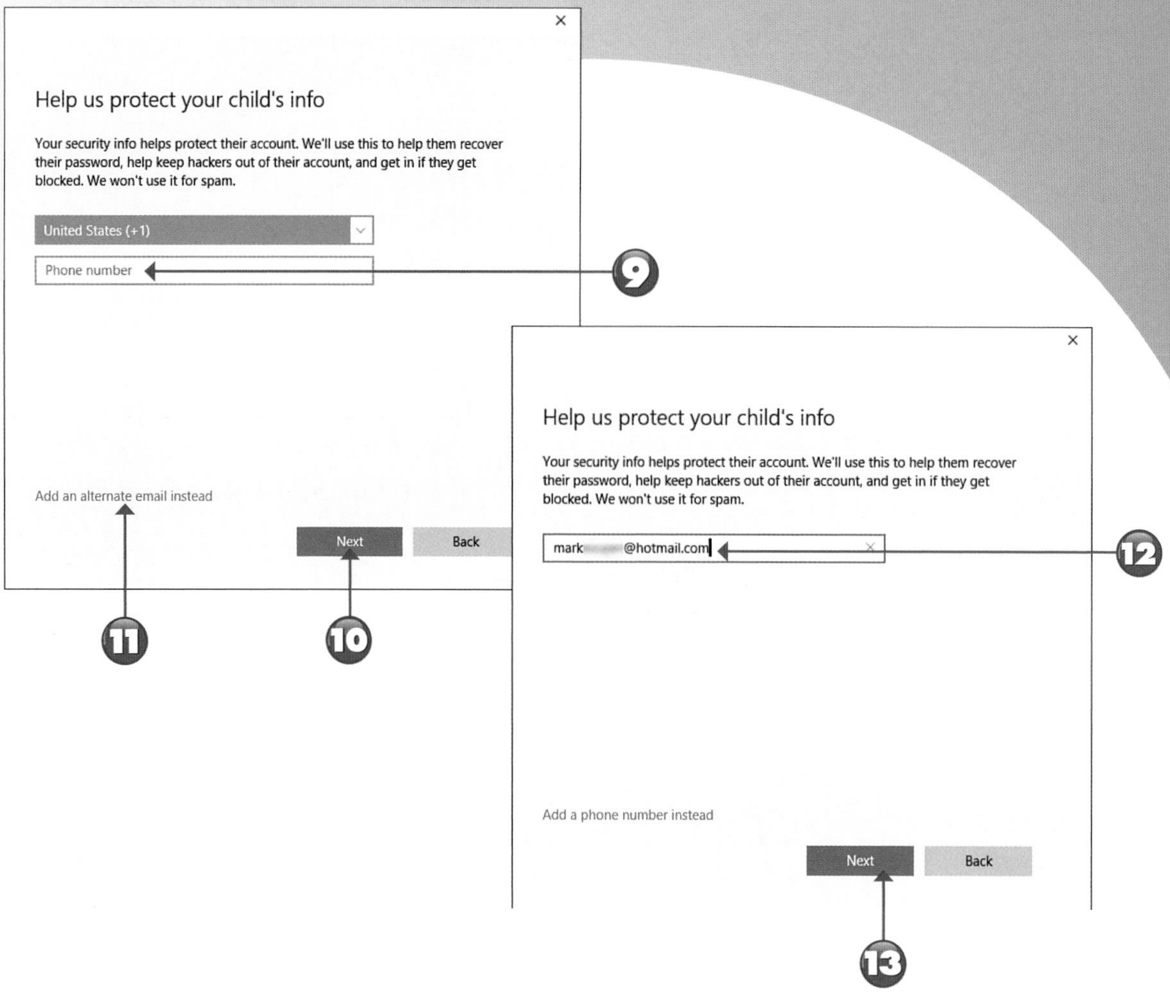

Help us protect your child's info

Your security info helps protect their account. We'll use this to help them recover their password, help keep hackers out of their account, and get in if they get blocked. We won't use it for spam.

United States (+1)

Phone number

Add an alternate email instead

Next Back

Help us protect your child's info

Your security info helps protect their account. We'll use this to help them recover their password, help keep hackers out of their account, and get in if they get blocked. We won't use it for spam.

mark @hotmail.com

Add a phone number instead

Next Back

9. To add a phone number for security, click or tap here and enter it.
10. Click or tap **Next** to continue and skip to step 14.
11. To use an alternative email instead, click or tap here.
12. To add an email address for security, click or tap here and enter it.
13. Click or tap **Next** to continue.

Continued

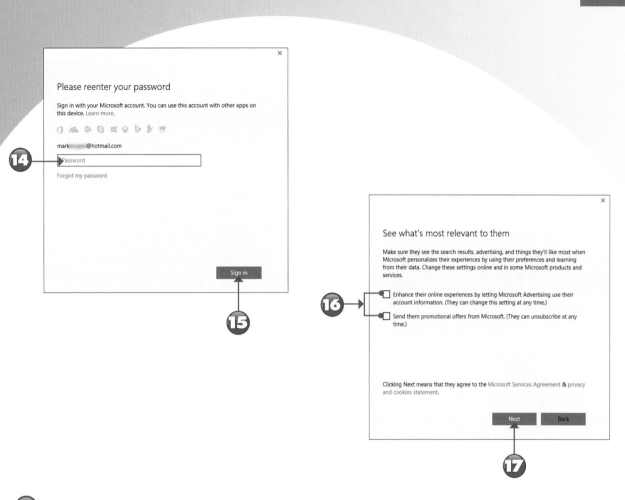

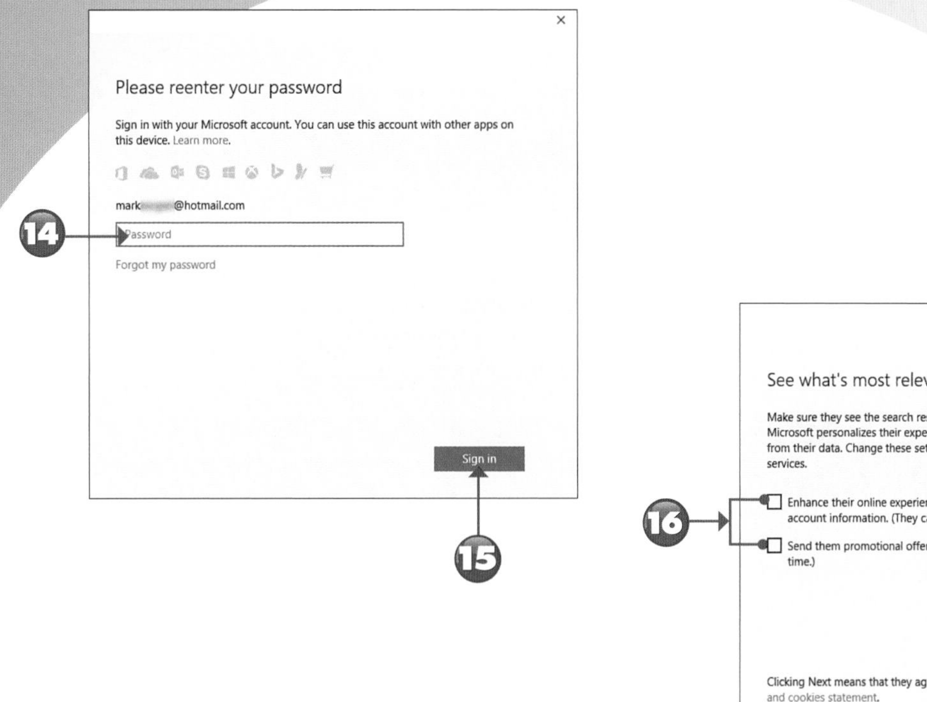

14. Enter the password to your Microsoft account.

15. Click or tap **Sign in**.

16. These options are enabled (checked) by default. Click the check boxes to clear them if you don't want your child to receive advertising.

17. Click or tap **Next**.

Continued

CAUTION

Extra Protection for Your Child In this example, we used a made-up name and birth date for the child we added. If you are concerned about revealing your child's actual identity online, consider a similar strategy. Be sure to record this information in a safe place!

Let your child use their Microsoft account online?

Your child wants to create a Microsoft account to use with Microsoft websites, apps, app stores, online services and products like Outlook.com, OneDrive, Xbox Live, Bing, Skype, and Windows.

To create a Microsoft account, we need certain information from your child, like your child's name, birth date, and an email address or phone number. We may also collect additional info from your child as described in our privacy statement.

Once you consent below, your child's account generally will be treated like any other Microsoft account. Your child might share info when using or communicating with others through the online features of Microsoft online services, products and apps. For example, Xbox Live displays your child's online presence and gamertag to others using the service and shares gamertag, usage info, and other info with third party game and app publishers on Xbox Live when users interact with those games or apps.

You can change the available settings on your child's Microsoft account or delete the account at any time by signing into your own Microsoft account. Go to https://account.microsoft.com/family and set parental settings for activity

Yes No

Charge a card to verify you're an adult

To verify that an adult is granting this permission, we will charge your credit or debit card 50 cents because federal law allows a card to verify parental consent only if charged. This charge doesn't allow your child to make purchases on that card.

After you select Confirm, you won't be able to cancel this transaction.

Payment

$0.50

Credit Card

Confirm Cancel

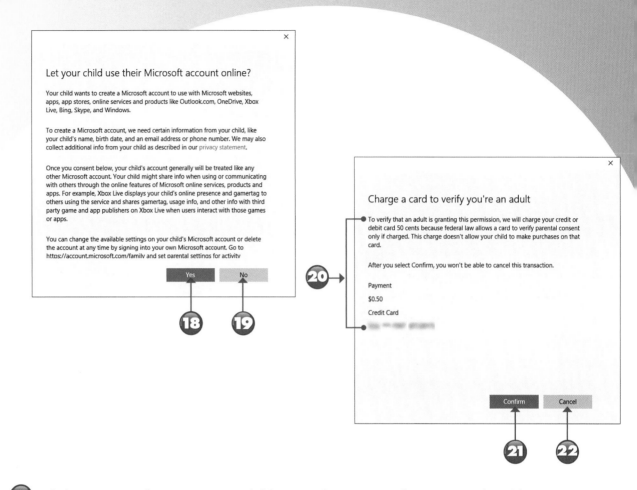

18. Click or tap **Yes** if you want your child to use their Microsoft account online (skip to step 20).

19. Click or tap **No** if you don't want them to (skip to step 23).

20. If you selected **Yes** in step 18, you are asked to pay $.50 to verify that you are granting permission for your child to go online.

21. Click or tap **Confirm** to charge your card.

22. Click or tap **Cancel** and your child cannot use the account to go online.

Continued

TIP

Setting Up Microsoft Family Click or tap the **Manage family settings online** link shown in step 24 to open Microsoft Family. Use it to set up usage, web browsing, and other controls for each child account. ■

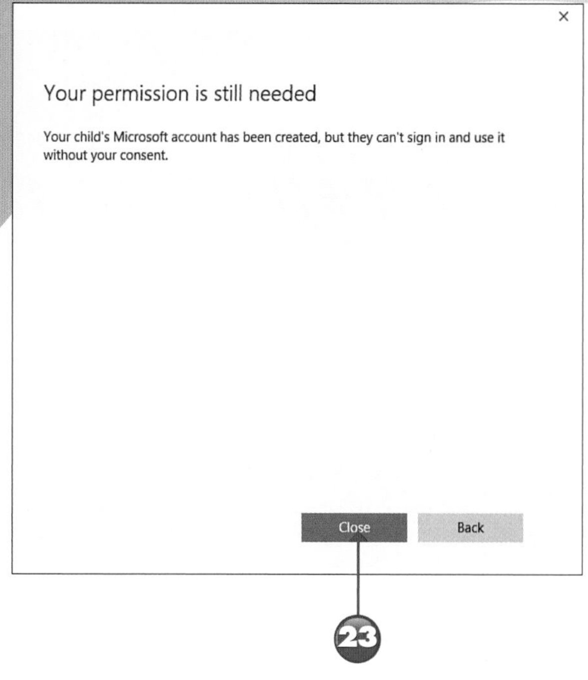
Your permission is still needed
Your child's Microsoft account has been created, but they can't sign in and use it without your consent.
Close
Back
23

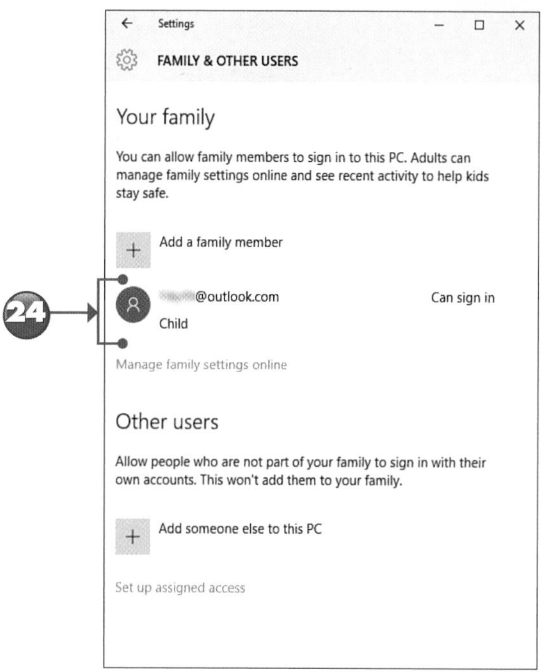
Settings
FAMILY & OTHER USERS
Your family
You can allow family members to sign in to this PC. Adults can manage family settings online and see recent activity to help kids stay safe.
Add a family member
@outlook.com
Can sign in
Child
Manage family settings online
Other users
Allow people who are not part of your family to sign in with their own accounts. This won't add them to your family.
Add someone else to this PC
Set up assigned access
24

23 Click **Close**.

24 The new account appears in the Your family dialog box.

End

TIP

Blocking a Child's Account After you add a child's account to a device, you can block the account from using that device: Click or tap the account name, and click or tap **Block**. You can unblock the account at any time.

ADDING ANOTHER USER WHO HAS A WINDOWS ACCOUNT

Need to share your Windows 10 device with a co-worker or want to set up an account for a roommate? Here's how to provide other adults with their own accounts on your system if they already have Windows accounts.

Start

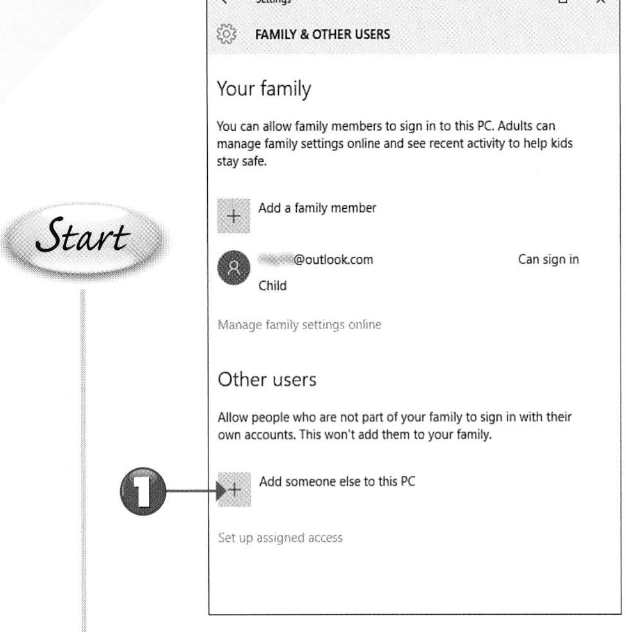

Settings
FAMILY & OTHER USERS
Your family
You can allow family members to sign in to this PC. Adults can manage family settings online and see recent activity to help kids stay safe.
Add a family member
@outlook.com
Can sign in
Child
Manage family settings online
Other users
Allow people who are not part of your family to sign in with their own accounts. This won't add them to your family.
Add someone else to this PC
Set up assigned access

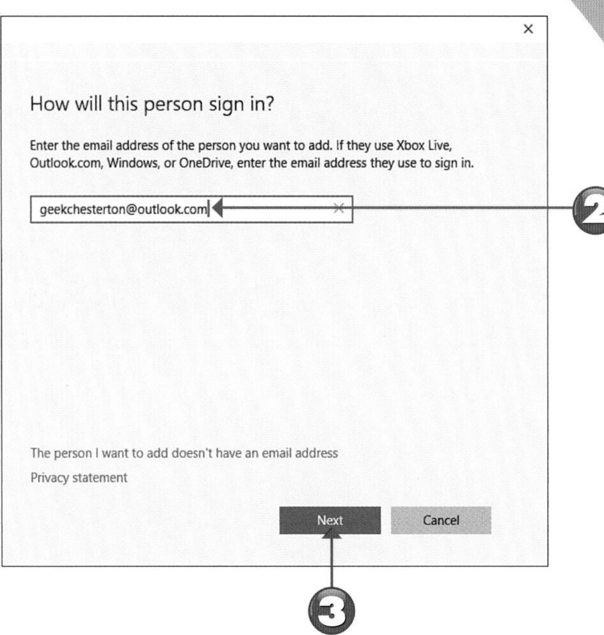

How will this person sign in?
Enter the email address of the person you want to add. If they use Xbox Live, Outlook.com, Windows, or OneDrive, enter the email address they use to sign in.
geekchesterton@outlook.com
The person I want to add doesn't have an email address
Privacy statement
Next
Cancel

1. Click or tap **Add someone else to this PC**.
2. Enter the email address from the user's Microsoft account.
3. Click or tap **Next**.

Continued

NOTE

Benefits of a Microsoft Account With a Microsoft account, all of a user's online email, photos, files, and settings (favorites, browser history, and so on) are available on any Windows 10 device that person signs in to. A Microsoft account can also be used to purchase or rent apps, music, TV shows, and movies from the Windows Store.

Good to go!

To log in the first time, geek@outlook.com will need to be connected to the internet.

Finish

Settings

FAMILY & OTHER USERS

Your family

You can allow family members to sign in to this PC. Adults can manage family settings online and see recent activity to help kids stay safe.

Add a family member

@outlook.com Can sign in

Child

Manage family settings online

Other users

Allow people who are not part of your family to sign in with their own accounts. This won't add them to your family.

Add someone else to this PC

geek@outlook.com

Set up assigned access

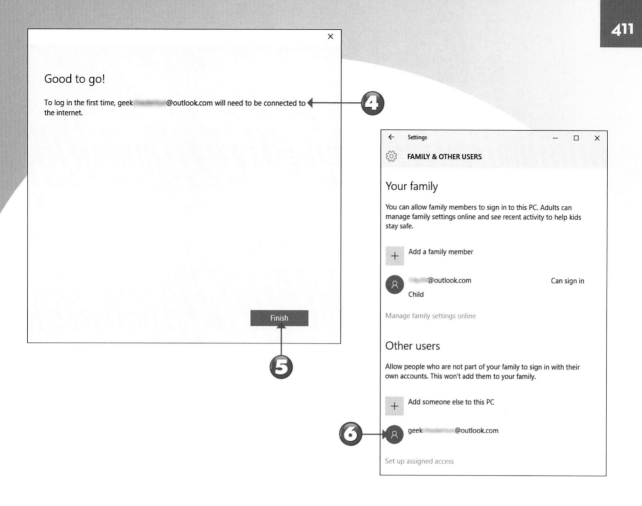

4 Remind the new user to be connected to the Internet when they sign in on this device.

5 Click or tap **Finish**.

6 The new user is listed on the Family and Other Users page.

End

ADDING A USER WHO NEEDS A MICROSOFT ACCOUNT

As you saw in the previous exercise, there are a lot of good reasons for a user to have a Microsoft account. Here's how to create one using an existing non-Microsoft email address.

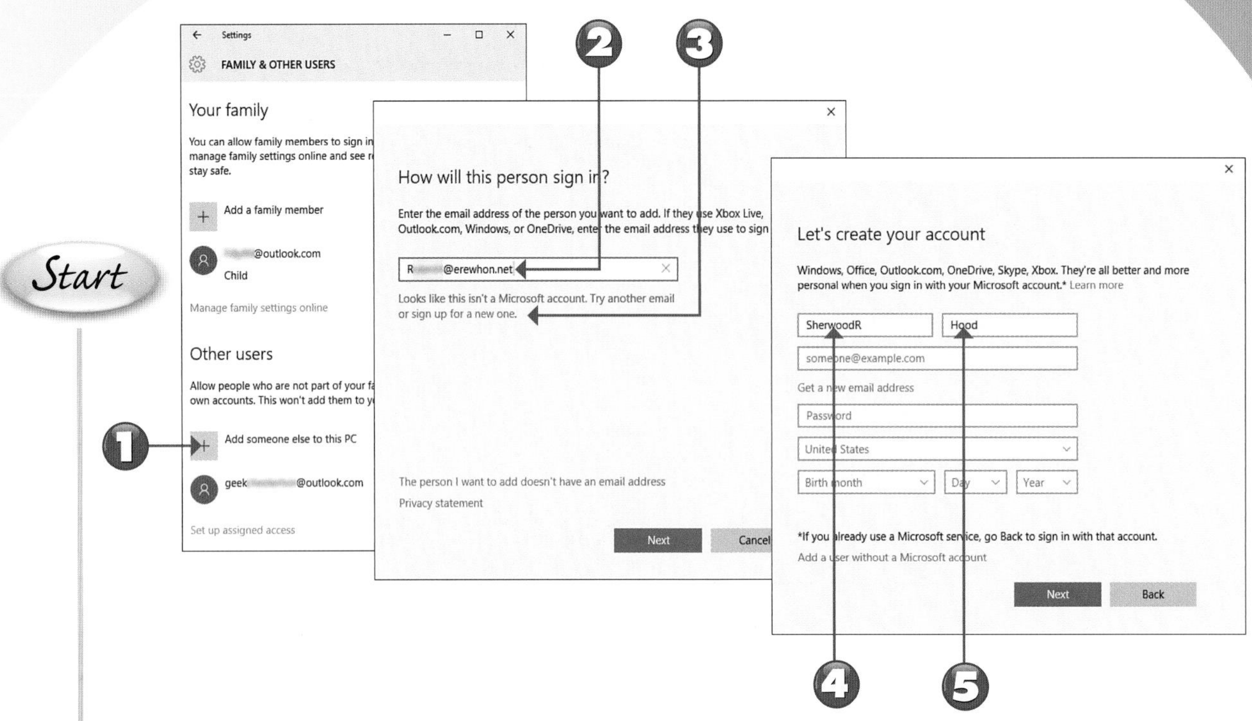

Start
Settings
FAMILY & OTHER USERS
Your family
Add a family member
Child
Manage family settings online
Other users
Add someone else to this PC
Set up assigned access
How will this person sign in?
Enter the email address of the person you want to add. If they use Xbox Live, Outlook.com, Windows, or OneDrive, enter the email address they use to sign
Looks like this isn't a Microsoft account. Try another email or sign up for a new one.
The person I want to add doesn't have an email address
Privacy statement
Next
Let's create your account
Windows, Office, Outlook.com, OneDrive, Skype, Xbox. They're all better and more personal when you sign in with your Microsoft account.* Learn more
SherwoodR
Hood
someone@example.com
Get a new email address
Password
United States
Birth month
Day
Year
*If you already use a Microsoft service, go Back to sign in with that account.
Add a user without a Microsoft account
Next
Back

1. Click or tap **Add someone else to this PC**.
2. Enter the user's preferred email address.
3. Click or tap **sign up for a new one**.
4. Enter the new user's first name.
5. Enter the new user's last name.

Continued

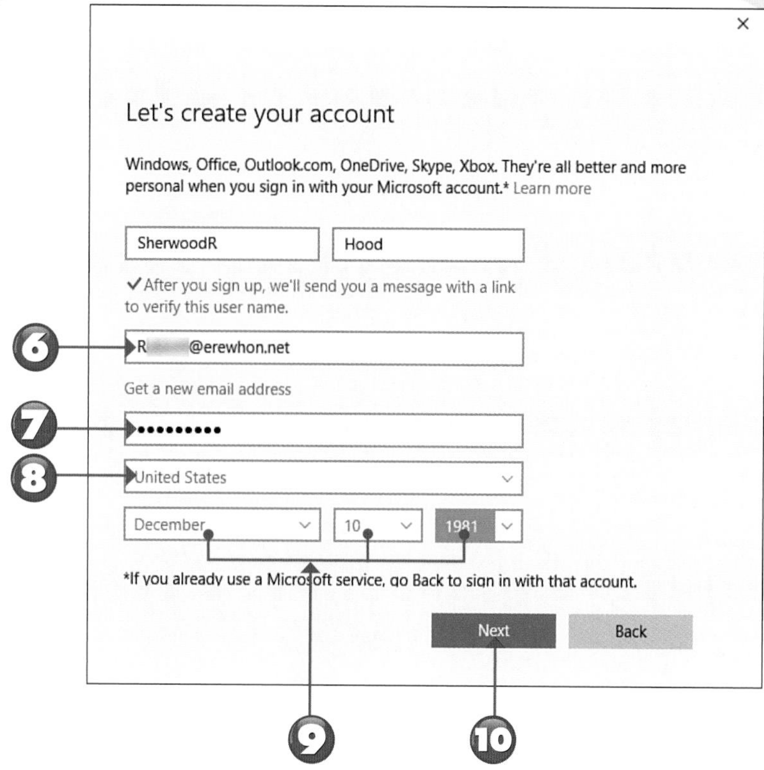

Let's create your account
Windows, Office, Outlook.com, OneDrive, Skype, Xbox. They're all better and more personal when you sign in with your Microsoft account.* Learn more
SherwoodR
Hood
After you sign up, we'll send you a message with a link to verify this user name.
@erewhon.net
Get a new email address
United States
December
10
1981
*If you already use a Microsoft service, go Back to sign in with that account.
Next
Back
6
7
8
9
10

6. Enter the email address you entered in step 2.

7. Enter the password you want to use to log in to your system.

8. Verify or change the country where this user lives.

9. Select the user's birth date.

10. Click or tap **Next**.

Continued

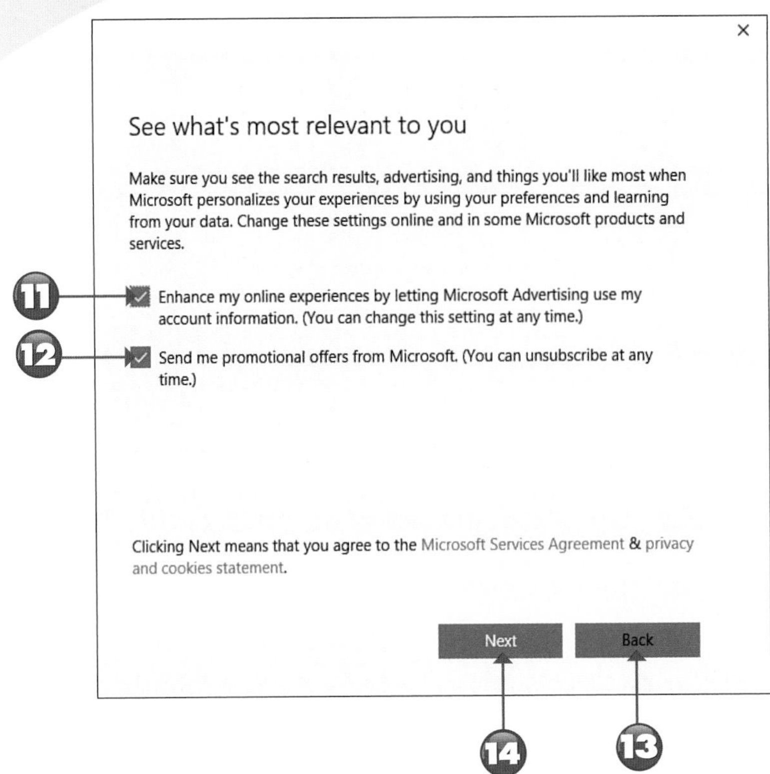

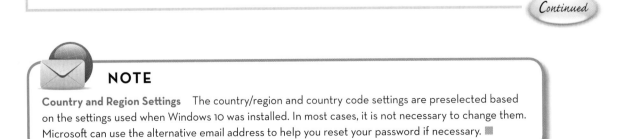

11. To opt out of letting Microsoft Advertising use your account information, clear this check box.
12. To opt out of receiving promotional offers from Microsoft, clear this check box.
13. To go back to the previous screen, click or tap **Back**.
14. Click or tap **Next**.

Continued

NOTE

Country and Region Settings The country/region and country code settings are preselected based on the settings used when Windows 10 was installed. In most cases, it is not necessary to change them. Microsoft can use the alternative email address to help you reset your password if necessary.

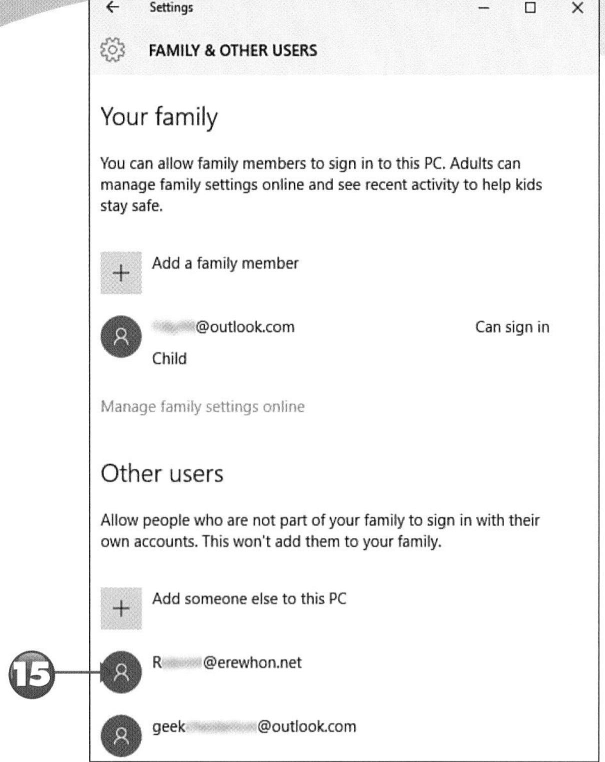

Settings
FAMILY & OTHER USERS
Your family
You can allow family members to sign in to this PC. Adults can manage family settings online and see recent activity to help kids stay safe.
Add a family member
@outlook.com
Can sign in
Child
Manage family settings online
Other users
Allow people who are not part of your family to sign in with their own accounts. This won't add them to your family.
Add someone else to this PC
R @erewhon.net
geek @outlook.com
15

15 The new user is listed on the Family & Other Users dialog box.

End

ADDING A LOCAL USER

Windows 10 is more powerful and easier to use on multiple devices if you have a Microsoft account. However, if you don't want a user to have a Microsoft account, you can set up that person as a local user. Here's how, starting from the **Family & other users** dialog.

Start

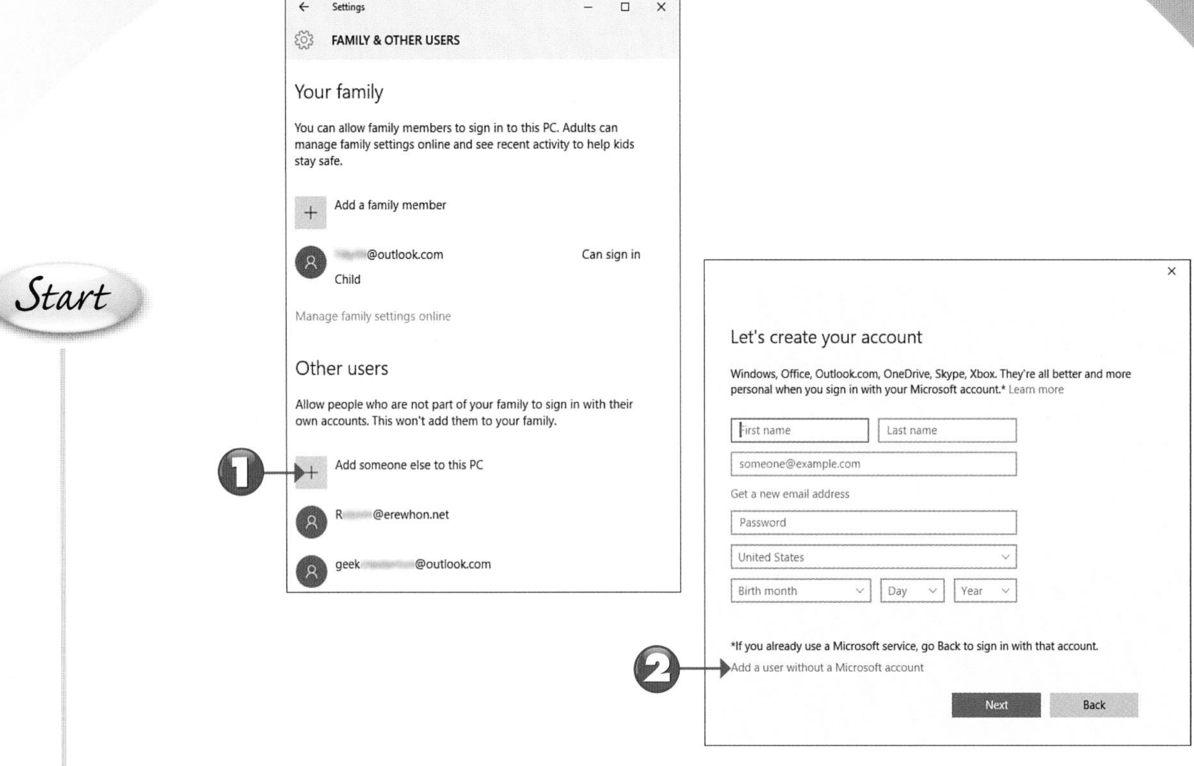

Settings
FAMILY & OTHER USERS
Your family
You can allow family members to sign in to this PC. Adults can manage family settings online and see recent activity to help kids stay safe.
Add a family member
@outlook.com
Can sign in
Child
Manage family settings online
Other users
Allow people who are not part of your family to sign in with their own accounts. This won't add them to your family.
Add someone else to this PC
R @erewhon.net
geek @outlook.com
Let's create your account
Windows, Office, Outlook.com, OneDrive, Skype, Xbox. They're all better and more personal when you sign in with your Microsoft account.* Learn more
First name
Last name
someone@example.com
Get a new email address
Password
United States
Birth month
Day
Year
*If you already use a Microsoft service, go Back to sign in with that account.
Add a user without a Microsoft account
Next
Back

1. Click or tap **Add someone else to this PC**.

2. Click or tap **Add a user without a Microsoft account**.

Continued

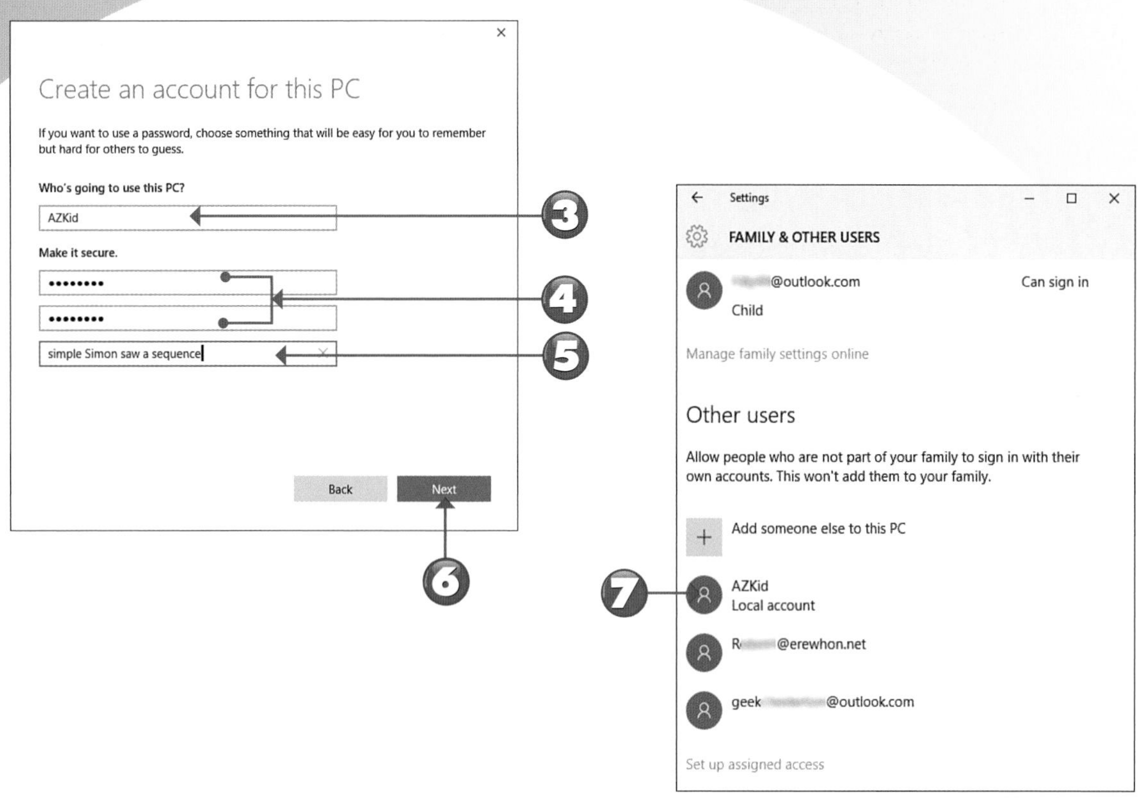

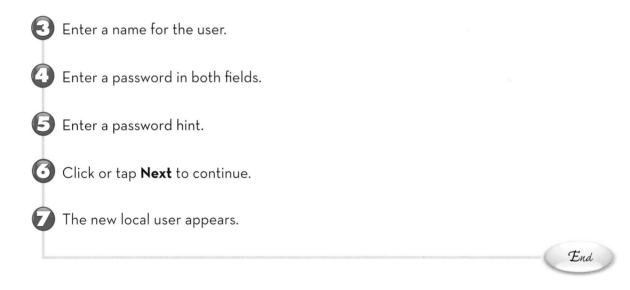

3. Enter a name for the user.
4. Enter a password in both fields.
5. Enter a password hint.
6. Click or tap **Next** to continue.
7. The new local user appears.

End

SELECTING AN ACCOUNT TO LOG IN TO

After you add one or more additional users, Windows 10 offers you a choice of accounts at startup or whenever the computer is locked. Here's how to choose the account you want.

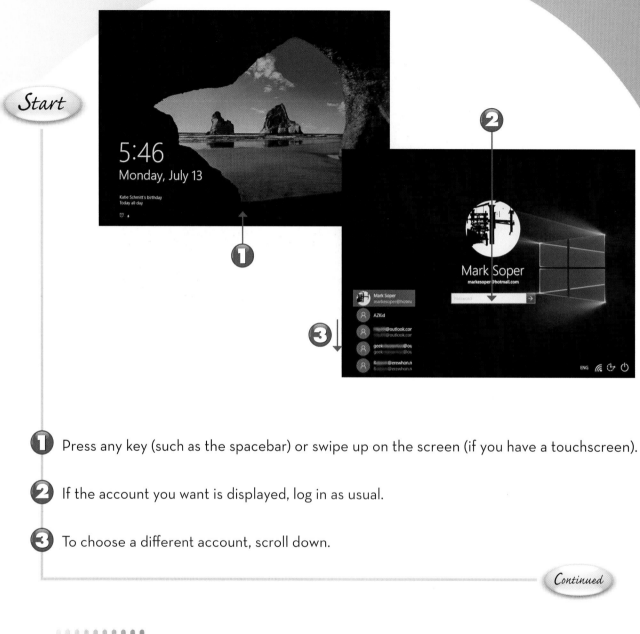

Start

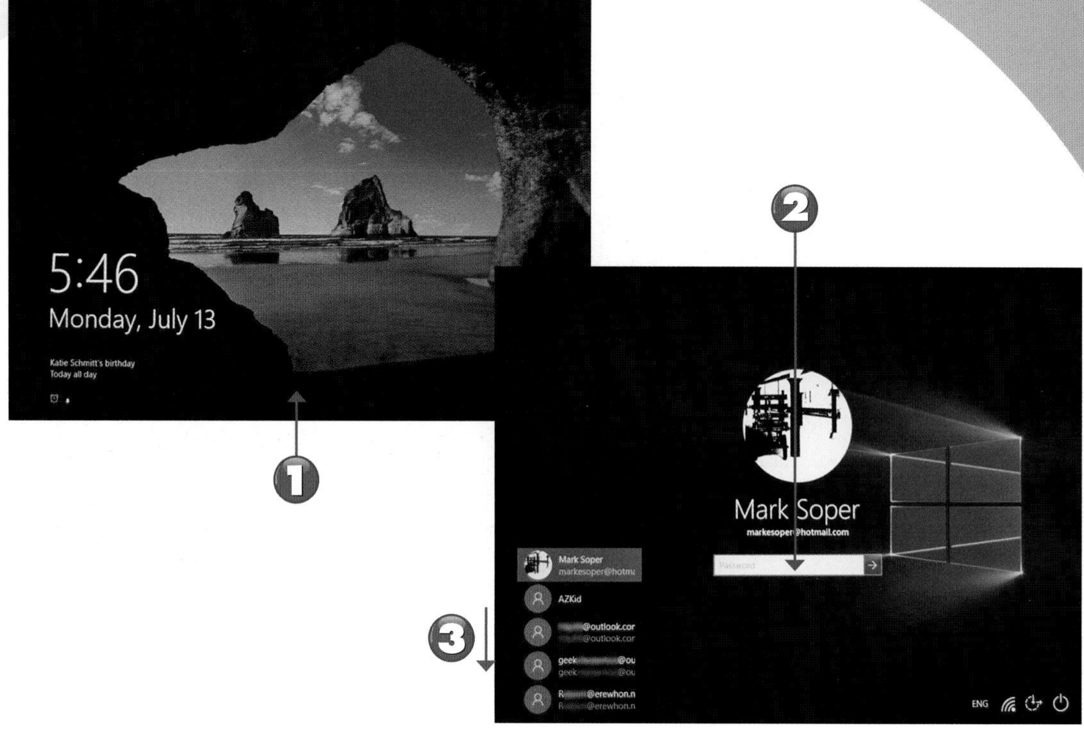

1. Press any key (such as the spacebar) or swipe up on the screen (if you have a touchscreen).
2. If the account you want is displayed, log in as usual.
3. To choose a different account, scroll down.

Continued

4. Click or tap the account you want to log in to.
5. Log in to the selected account.

End

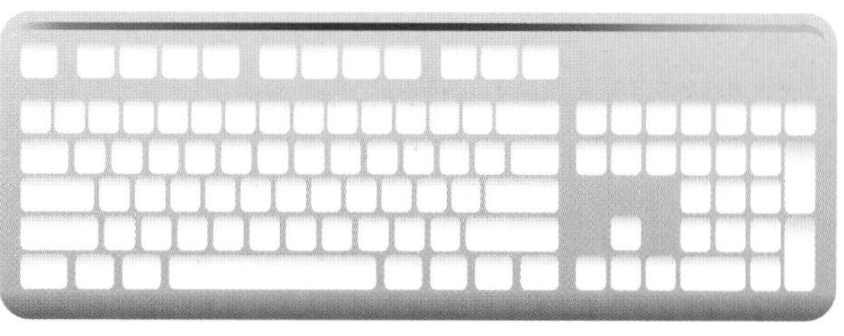

CHANGING AN ACCOUNT TYPE

The first account on a Windows 10 computer is an administrator account. The administrator can add, change, or remove accounts, and can install apps and make other changes that affect all users. When you create an additional user account in Windows 10, it's a standard account. If you want another user's account to be set as administrator of the computer, use the following steps.

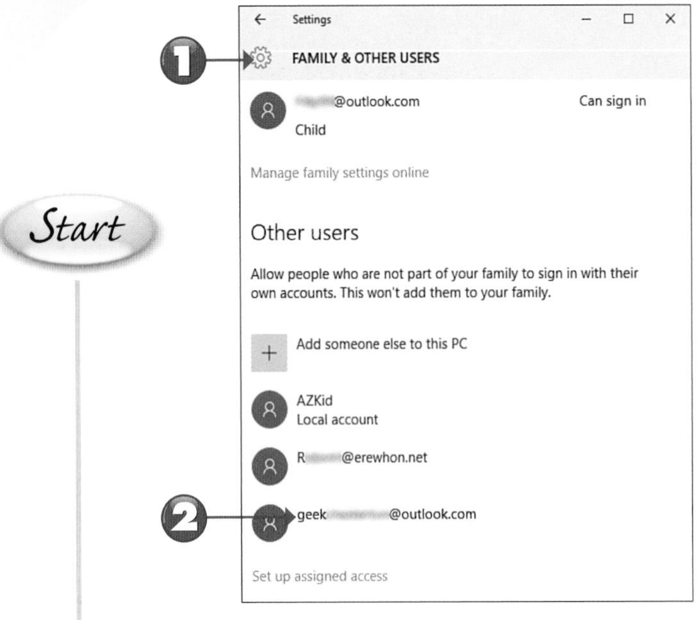

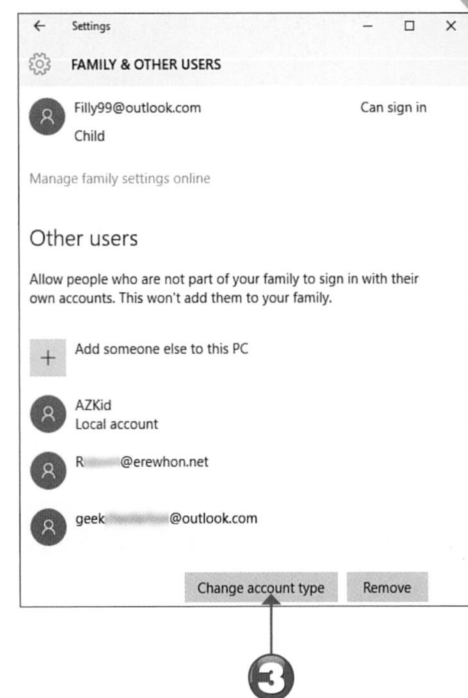

Start

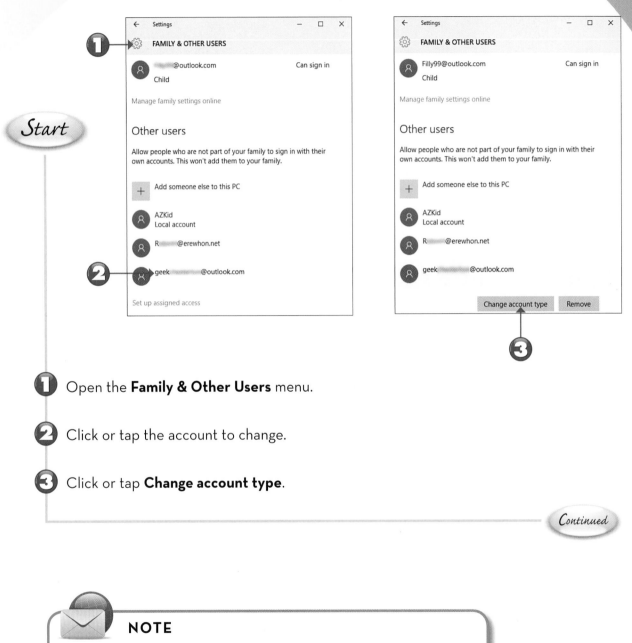

1. Open the **Family & Other Users** menu.
2. Click or tap the account to change.
3. Click or tap **Change account type**.

Continued

NOTE

Standard, Administrator, and Child Accounts A standard account needs administrator permission (given through User Account Control) to complete tasks that could change the computer. An administrator account can perform all tasks. A child account is similar to a standard account but can also be monitored by Microsoft Family. ■

Change account type

Change account type

geek @outlook.com

Account type

Standard User

OK Cancel

4

Change account type

Change account type

geek @outlook.com

Account type

Administrator

OK Cancel

5 6

Settings

FAMILY & OTHER USERS

Child

Manage family settings online

Other users

Allow people who are not part of your family to sign in with their own accounts. This won't add them to your family.

Add someone else to this PC

AZKid
Local account

R @erewhon.net

7 geek @outlook.com
Administrator

Set up assigned access

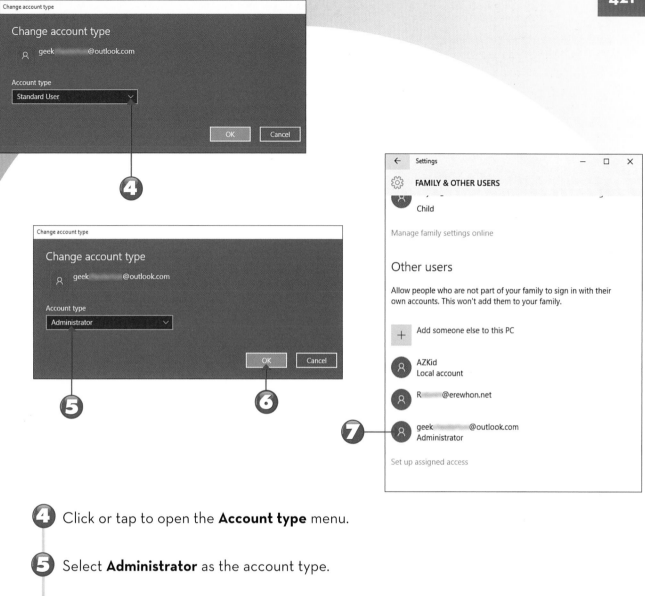

4. Click or tap to open the **Account type** menu.
5. Select **Administrator** as the account type.
6. Click or tap **OK**.
7. The new administrator account is added.

End

NOTE

Using Assigned Access Use the **Set up assigned access** link shown in step 7 if you want an account to be limited to a single task, such as running a presentation. ■

NOTE

Why You Might Need Two Administrators When would you want to create more than one administrator account for a computer? There might be times when the original administrator is not available while the computer is in use and system-wide changes need to be made—such as new programs or hardware installations. Be sure that the user you select is trustworthy and not likely to mess around with the computer just for fun. ■

SETTING UP PIN ACCESS

Windows 10 enables users with Microsoft accounts to set up a PIN as an alternative to a regular password. You must set a regular password before you can set up PIN access. Using a PIN for login can be easier for tablet users or users with limited typing ability. Here's how to do it.

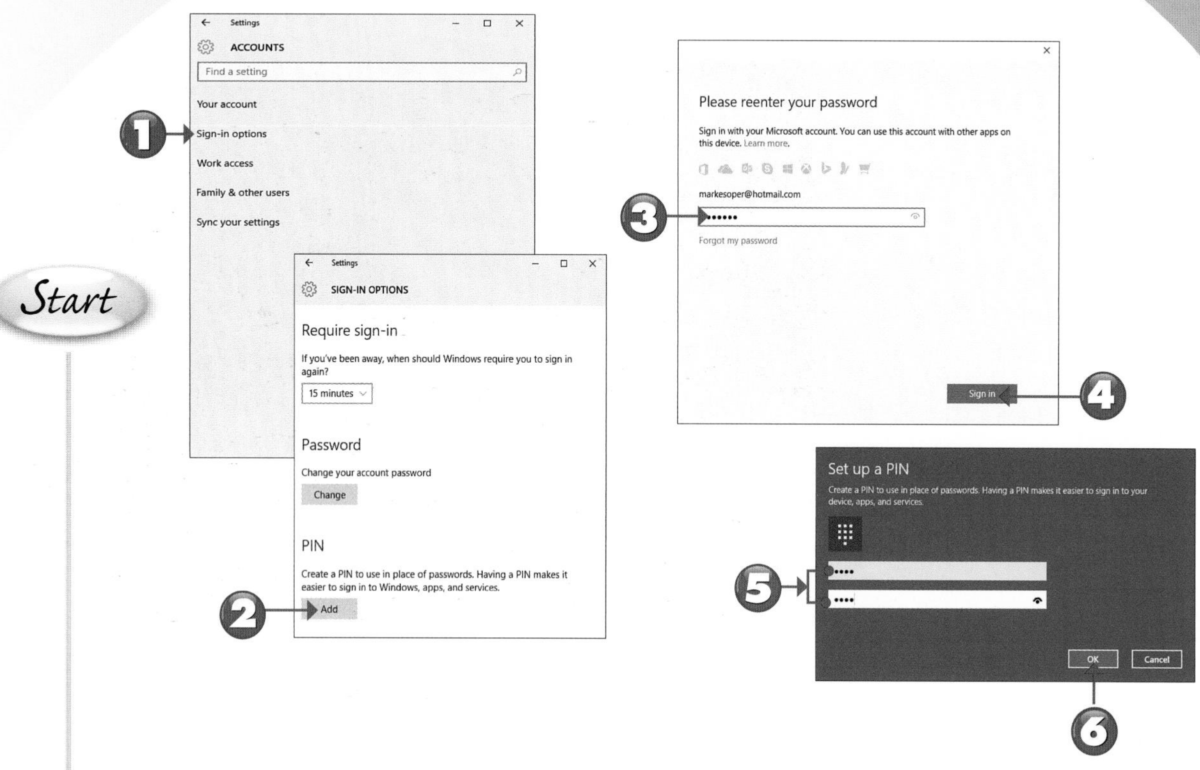

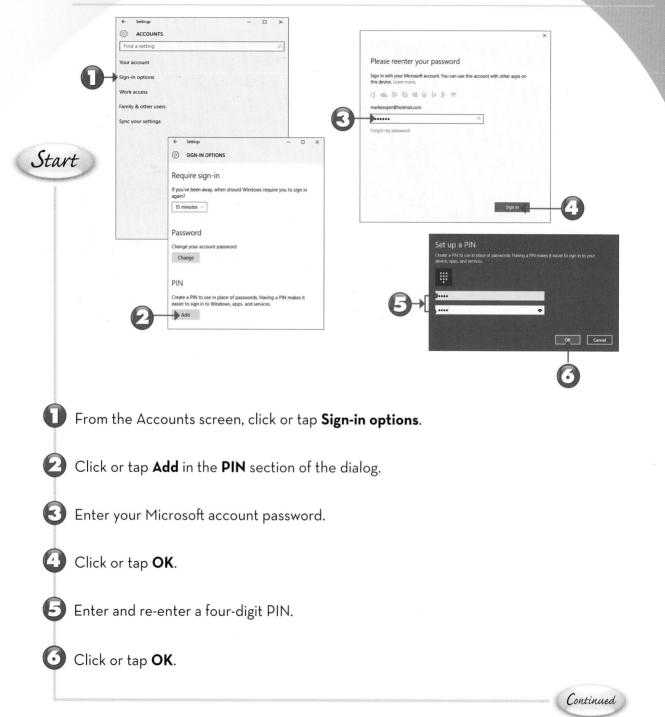

1. From the Accounts screen, click or tap **Sign-in options**.
2. Click or tap **Add** in the **PIN** section of the dialog.
3. Enter your Microsoft account password.
4. Click or tap **OK**.
5. Enter and re-enter a four-digit PIN.
6. Click or tap **OK**.

Continued

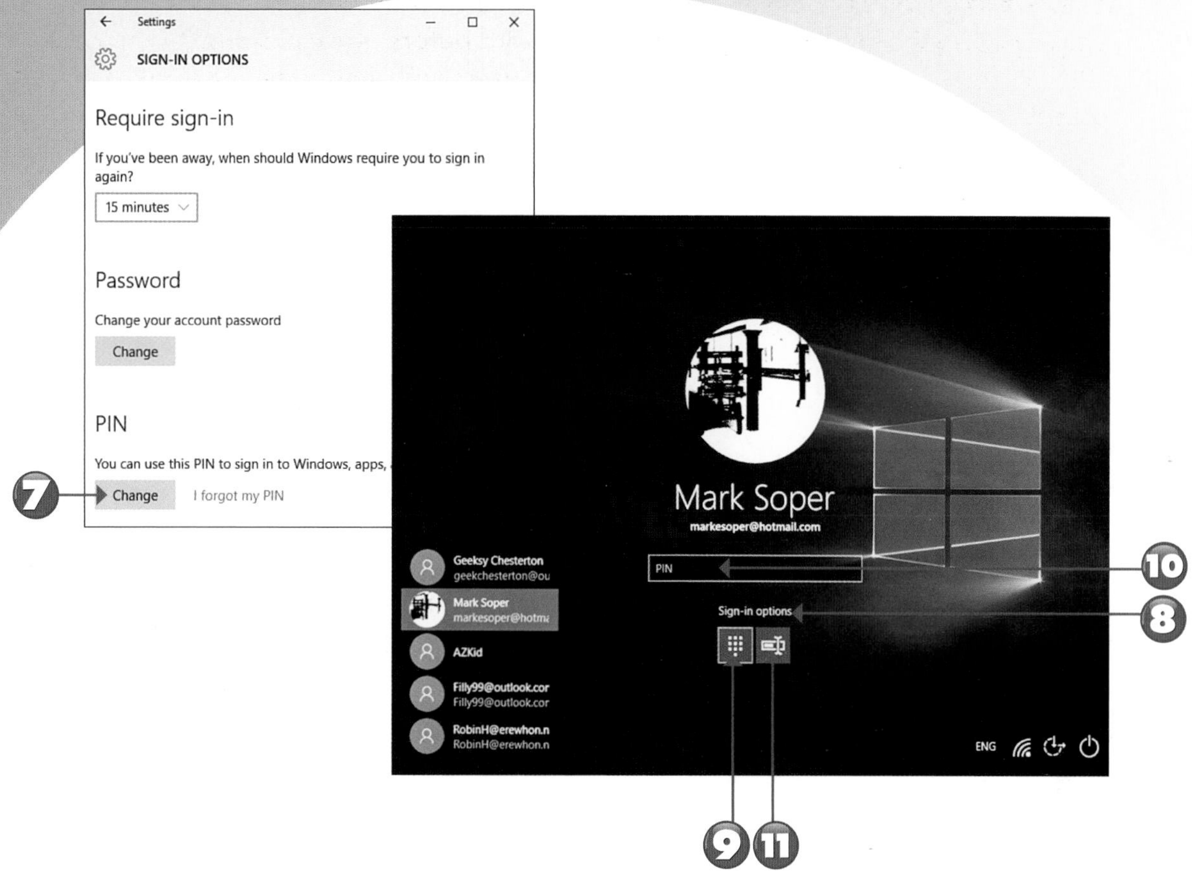

7. The Sign-in Options dialog now provides the option to change your PIN.

8. Click or tap to display sign-in options.

9. Click or tap to use a PIN for login.

10. Type your PIN in the login screen.

11. Click or tap to use a password for login.

End

NOTE

Adding a Photo to Your Account To make changes to your account, including adding a photo, click or tap **Your Account**. You can take your picture with your device's camera or browse for a photo.

PROTECTING YOUR SYSTEM

Today's computers and storage devices don't cost much to buy or replace, but the information you store on them—from documents to photos, video, and music—is priceless. In this chapter, you learn about a variety of easy-to-use features in Windows 10 that are designed to help you protect your computer's contents.

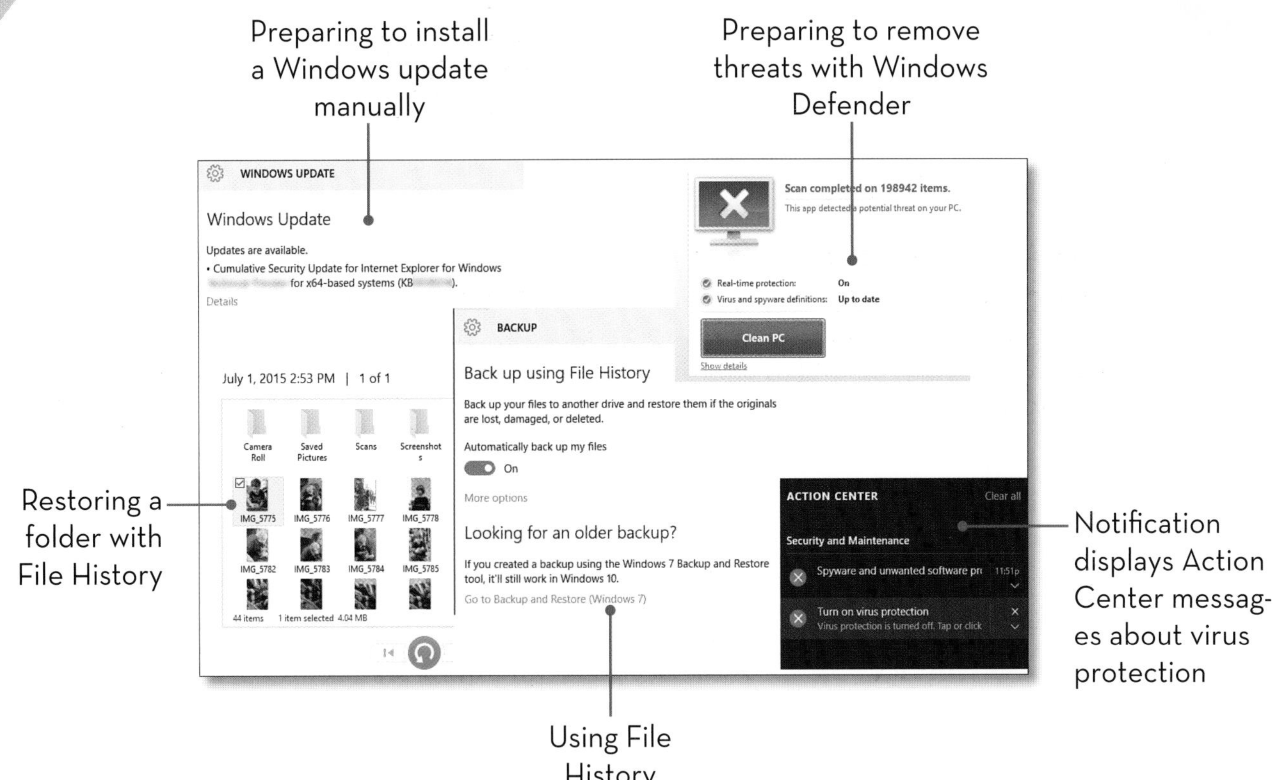

Preparing to install a Windows update manually
Preparing to remove threats with Windows Defender
Restoring a folder with File History
Notification displays Action Center messages about virus protection
Using File History
WINDOWS UPDATE
Windows Update
Updates are available.
• Cumulative Security Update for Internet Explorer for Windows
for x64-based systems (KB).
Details
Scan completed on 198942 items.
This app detected a potential threat on your PC.
Real-time protection: On
Virus and spyware definitions: Up to date
Clean PC
Show details
BACKUP
Back up using File History
Back up your files to another drive and restore them if the originals are lost, damaged, or deleted.
Automatically back up my files
On
More options
Looking for an older backup?
If you created a backup using the Windows 7 Backup and Restore tool, it'll still work in Windows 10.
Go to Backup and Restore (Windows 7)
July 1, 2015 2:53 PM | 1 of 1
Camera Roll
Saved Pictures
Scans
Screenshots
IMG_5775
IMG_5776
IMG_5777
IMG_5778
IMG_5782
IMG_5783
IMG_5784
IMG_5785
44 items 1 item selected 4.04 MB
ACTION CENTER
Clear all
Security and Maintenance
Spyware and unwanted software pr
11:51p
Turn on virus protection
Virus protection is turned off. Tap or click

CHECKING FOR WINDOWS UPDATES

Windows Update is normally set to automatically download and install updates to Microsoft Windows 10 and to other Microsoft apps such as Office. However, you can check for updates whenever you want. This is a good idea if you hear about a security problem.

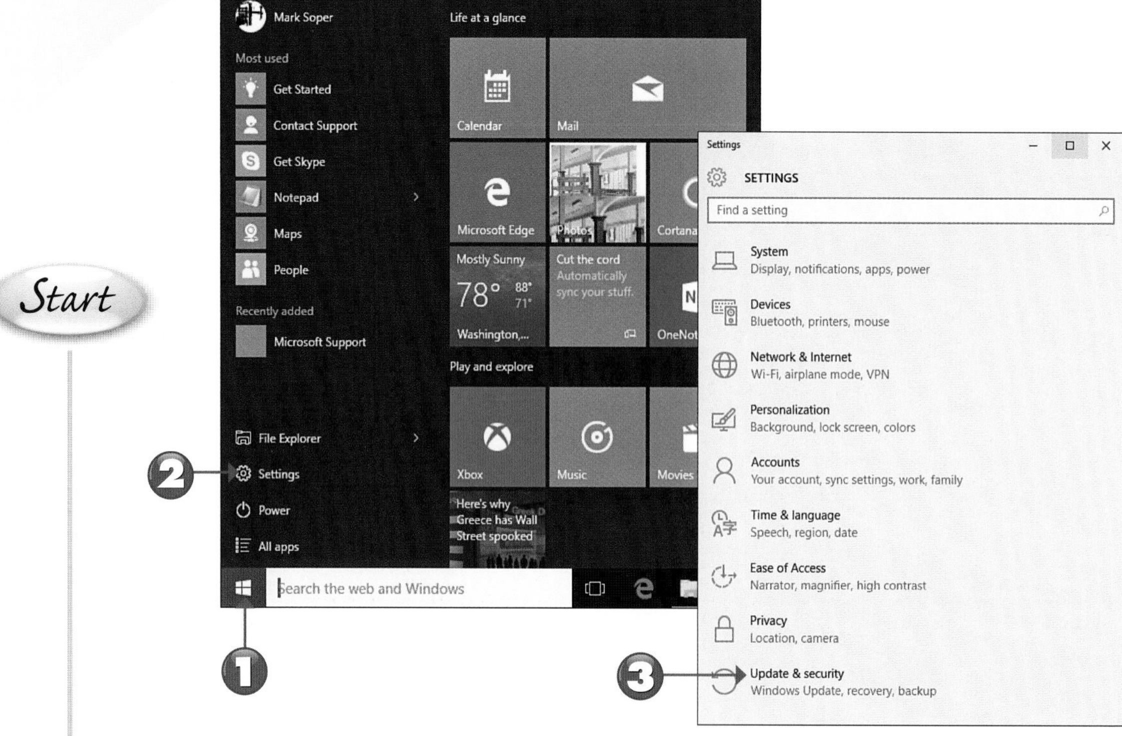

1. Click or tap the **Start** button.
2. Click or tap **Settings**.
3. Click or tap **Update & security**.

Continued

TIP

Opening Settings in Tablet Mode If you use Tablet Mode, follow these steps instead: Step 1, tap the **Notifications/Quick Actions** button. Step 2, tap **All settings**. To learn more about using Tablet Mode, see Chapter 3, "Logging In, Starting Up, and Shutting Down Windows 10 with a Touchscreen."

NOTE

Install Now or Later? If the update is a security update, I recommend you install it now. For other updates, you can wait for Windows 10 to install them for you.

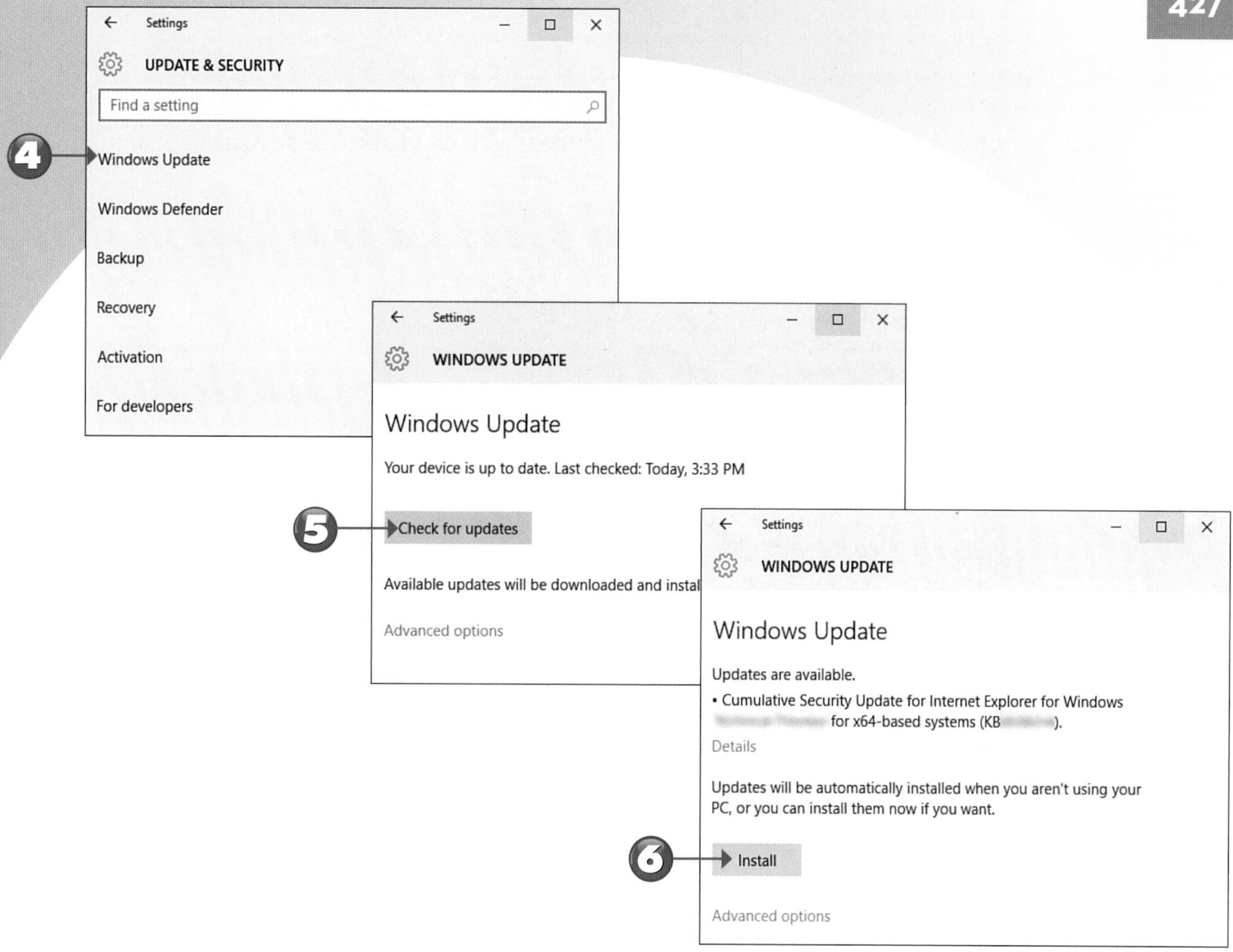

4. Click or tap **Windows Update**.

5. Click or tap **Check for updates**.

6. If there are any updates, they are listed. Click or tap **Install** to install them now.

End

NOTE

What Does the Update Do? Want to know more about an update? Click the **Details** link, and click **Details** again to learn more.

PROTECTING YOUR FILES WITH FILE HISTORY

If your computer or tablet is lost or stolen or it stops working, the information on your device is the one thing you can't replace—*unless* you make backup copies on a separate drive. File History is designed to do just that. Before starting this task, make sure you have connected a USB hard disk to your computer.

Start

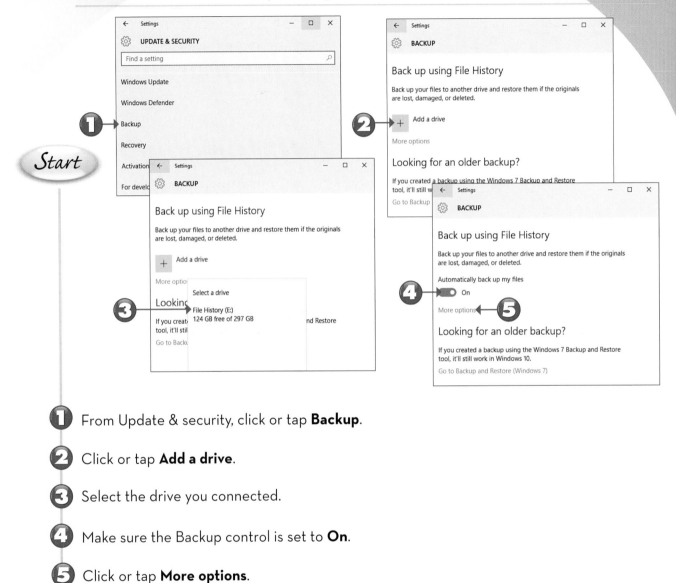

1. From Update & security, click or tap **Backup**.
2. Click or tap **Add a drive**.
3. Select the drive you connected.
4. Make sure the Backup control is set to **On**.
5. Click or tap **More options**.

Continued

NOTE

Retrieving Backups Made with Windows 7 Windows 10 includes the Windows 7 Backup and Restore app, so you can retrieve files from a backup you made with this tool. To learn more about using this tool, see this author's articles "Windows 7 Backup and Restore, Part 1" http://www.quepublishing.com/articles/article.aspx?p=1396503 and "Windows 7 Backup and Restore, Part 2," http://www.quepublishing.com/articles/article.aspx?p=1400869.

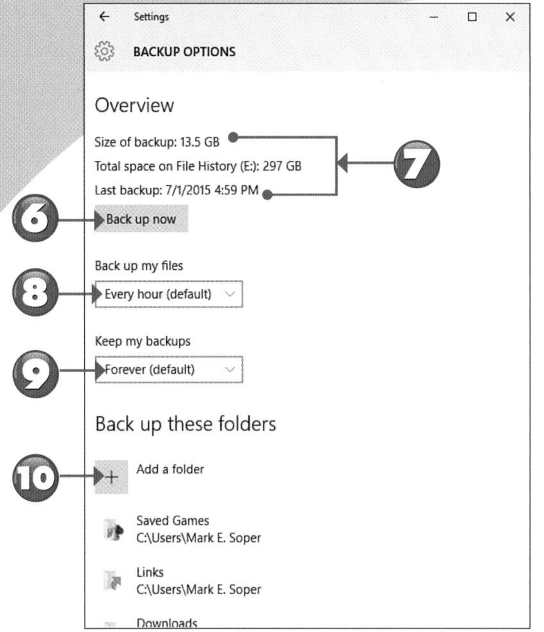

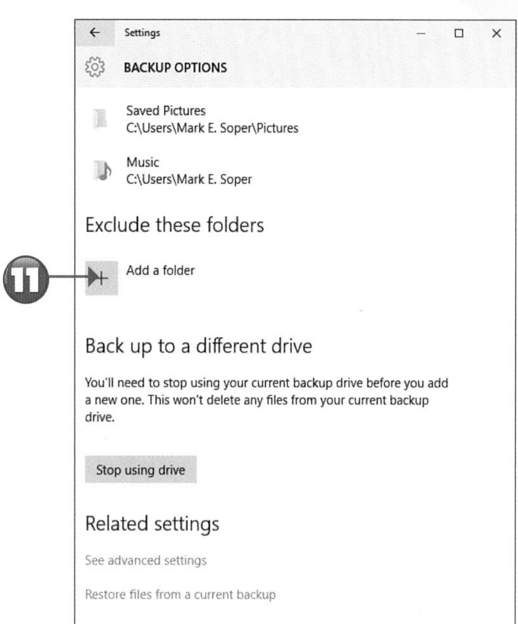

6. Click or tap **Back up now**.
7. Review the information about your backup.
8. Click or tap to change how often File History is run.
9. Click or tap to change how long to keep File History backups.
10. Click or tap to add a folder to the backup.
11. Click or tap to exclude a folder.

End

CAUTION

Backing Up the AppData Folder Although File History backs up all of your visible folders, hidden folders such as AppData (used for mail by Microsoft email apps) is not backed up by default. To add it to your backup, you must first open File Explorer, open the View tab, and make sure the **Hidden items** check box is checked. You can then use **Add a folder** to select AppData for backup. For more information about using File Explorer, see “Using the View Tab,” in Chapter 14, “Storing and Finding Your Files.”

RECOVERING FILES WITH FILE HISTORY

File History creates backups of your files so if a file is erased or damaged, you can get it back. If you haven't yet enabled File History in Windows 10 and run a backup, refer to "Protecting Your Files with File History," earlier in this chapter. Here's how to retrieve a lost file or folder after it's deleted.

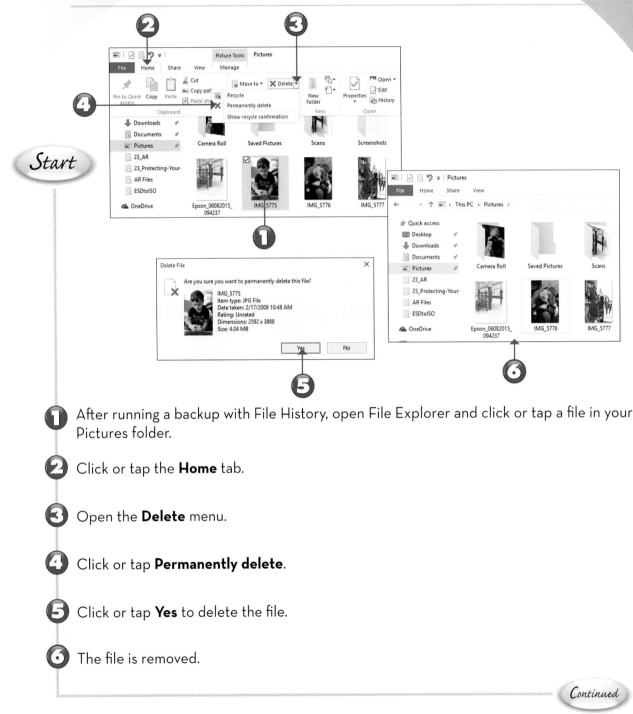

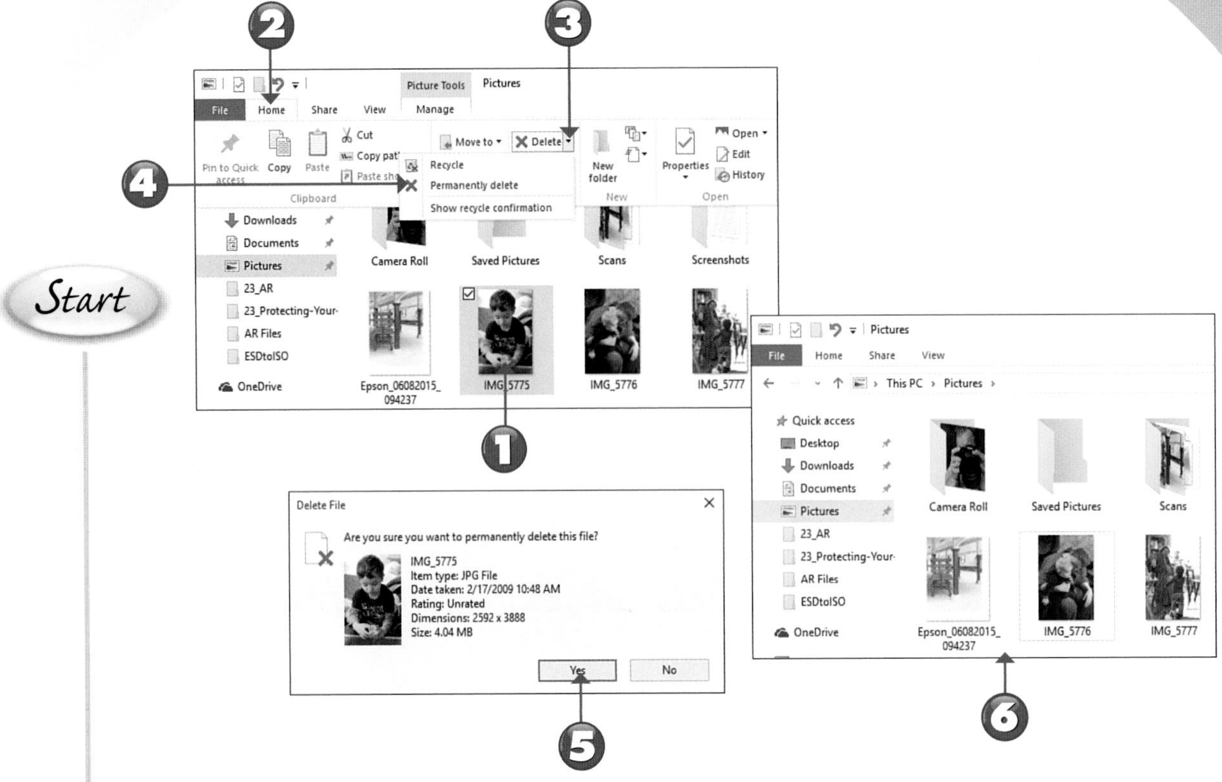

1. After running a backup with File History, open File Explorer and click or tap a file in your Pictures folder.
2. Click or tap the **Home** tab.
3. Open the **Delete** menu.
4. Click or tap **Permanently delete**.
5. Click or tap **Yes** to delete the file.
6. The file is removed.

Continued

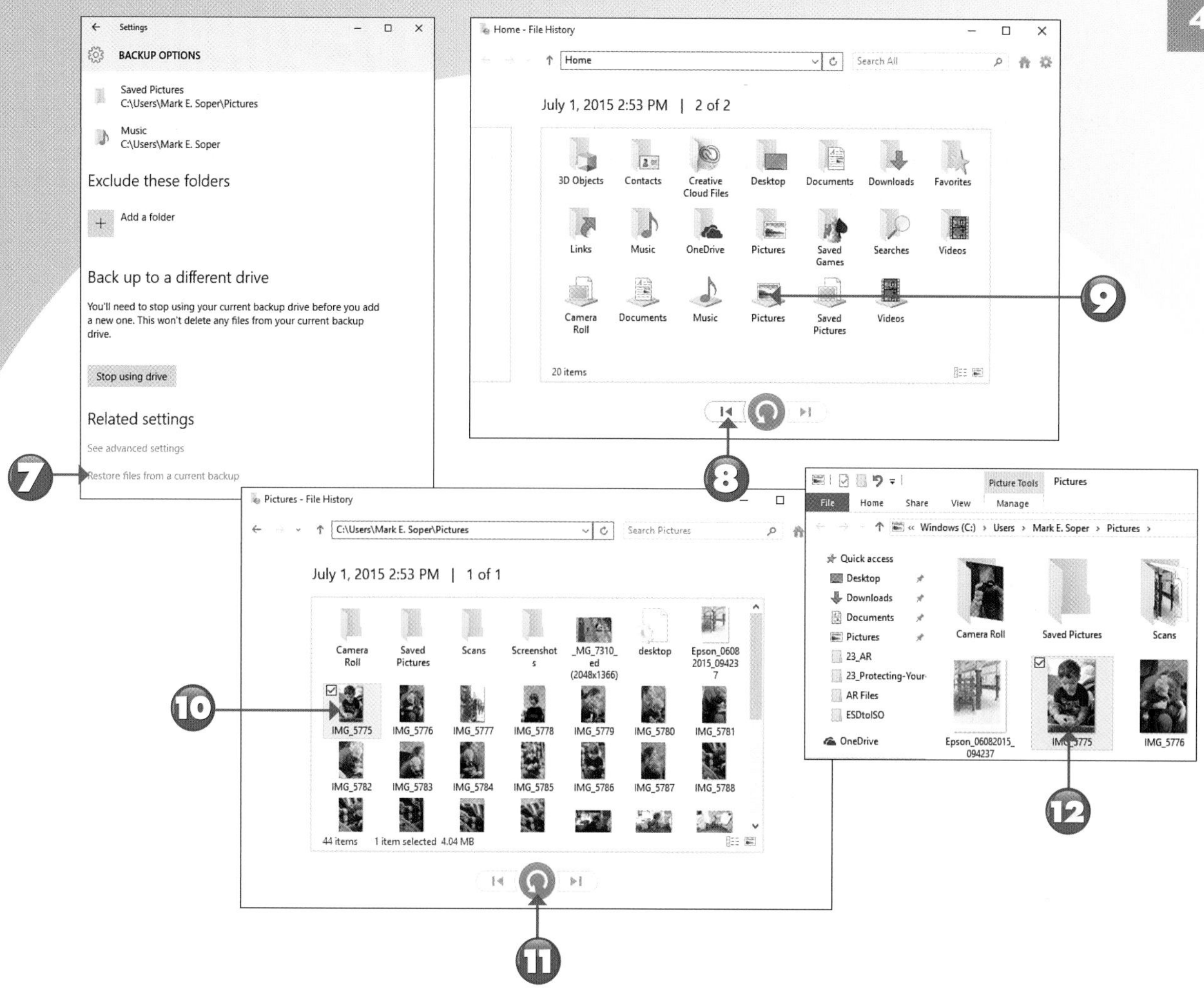

7. From the Backup options dialog, click or tap **Restore files from a current backup**.
8. Click or tap left or right arrows if necessary to locate the backup from which to restore.
9. Click or tap the folder from which to restore.
10. Click or tap the file (or folder) to restore.
11. Click or tap the green **Restore** button.
12. File Explorer opens. The folder and its contents are returned to their original location.

End

NOTE

Selecting a Version If the left and/or right arrows at the bottom of the File History dialog box can be clicked or tapped, you can select a different version of the folder or file. The most recent version is shown first.

TIP

Restoring Multiple Files from a Folder To restore only selected files, click the first file you want to restore, and then use Ctrl+click to select additional files. Click or tap the **Restore** button—only the files you selected will be restored.

USING WINDOWS NOTIFICATIONS

Windows 10 includes the brand-new Notifications feature, which makes it easy to see information about problems with your system or events taking place in your system. In this example, you learn how Notifications informs you of a problem with Windows 10's built-in Windows Defender anti-malware program.

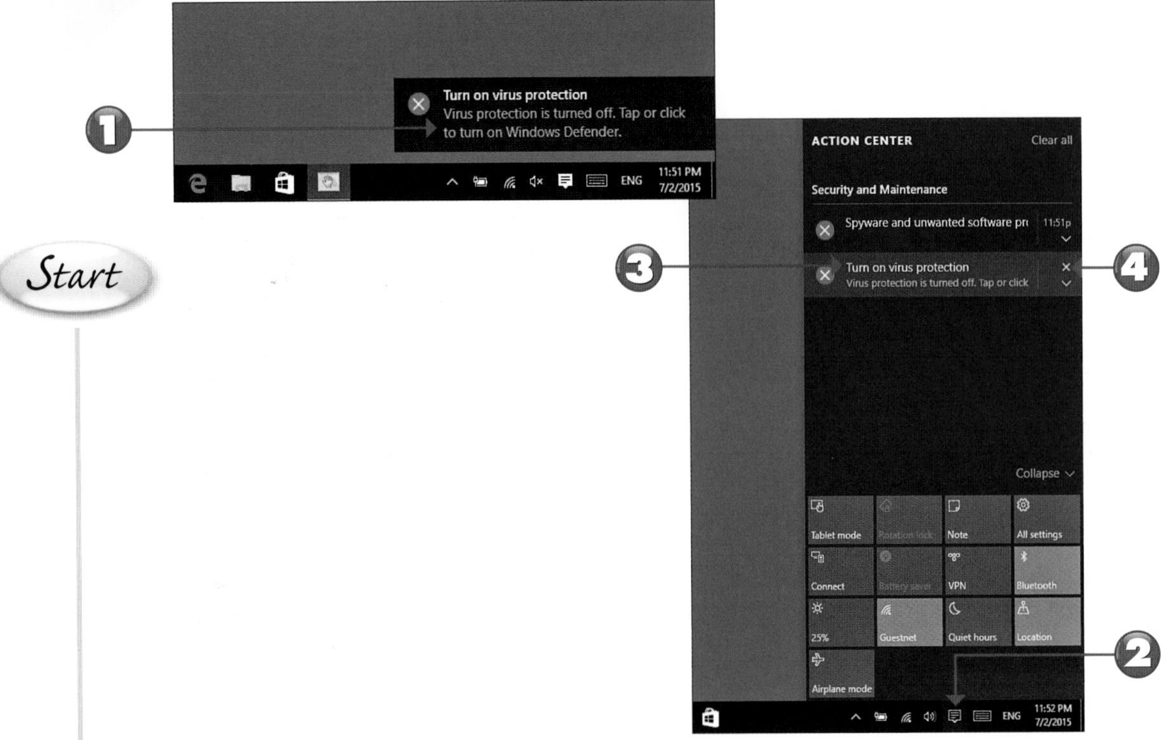

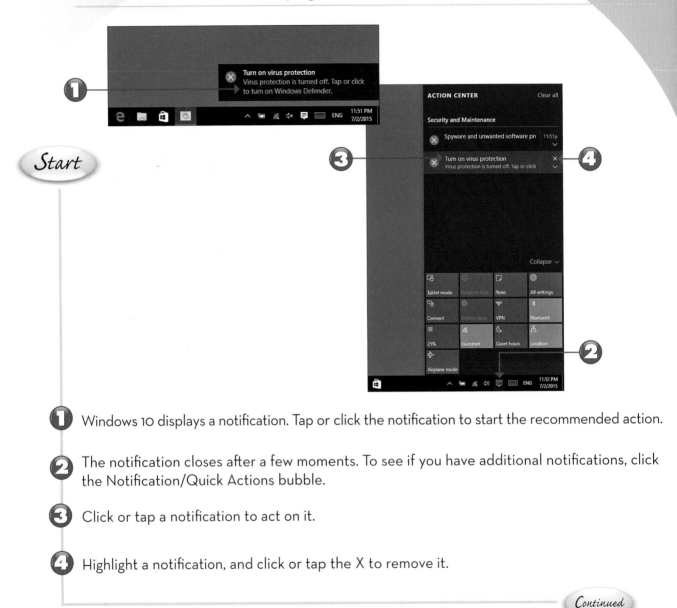

1. Windows 10 displays a notification. Tap or click the notification to start the recommended action.

2. The notification closes after a few moments. To see if you have additional notifications, click the Notification/Quick Actions bubble.

3. Click or tap a notification to act on it.

4. Highlight a notification, and click or tap the X to remove it.

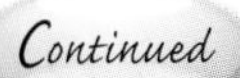

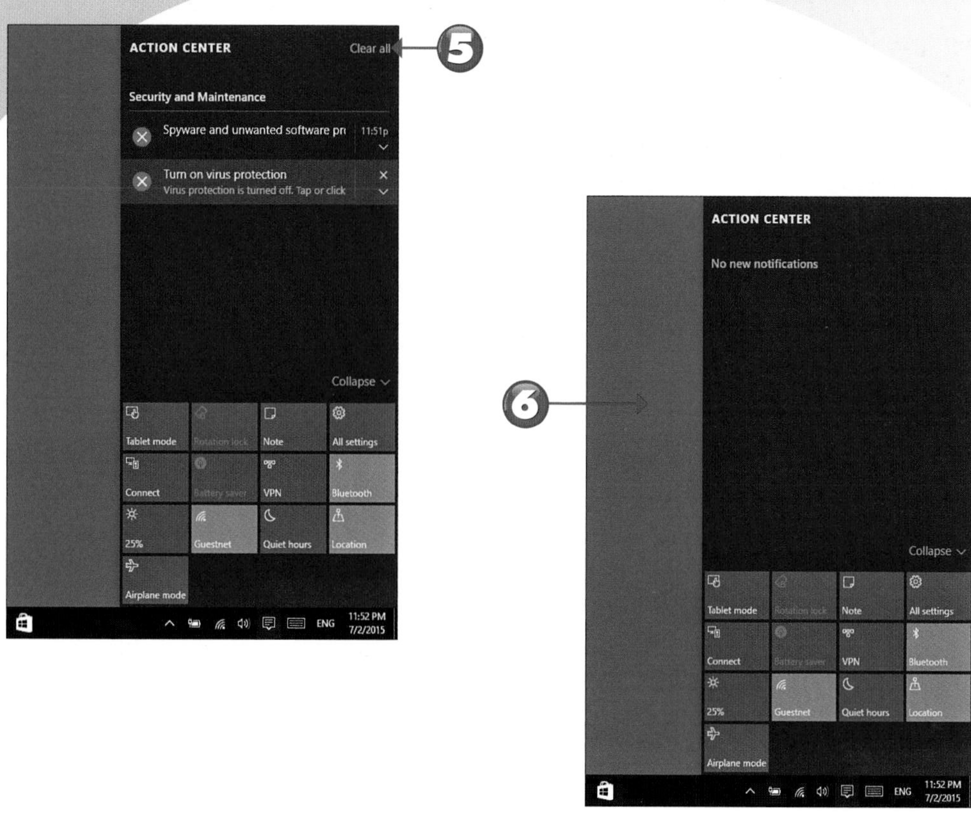

5 Click or tap **Clear all** to remove all notifications.

6 Click or tap an empty space on the desktop to close Notifications.

End

NOTE

Windows Notification and Your Apps Windows 10 might be able to fix the problem that is responsible for the issue that Notifications displayed. In this example, when you click or tap **Turn on virus protection**, the real-time protection in the anti-malware program in use, Windows Defender, is turned on. Otherwise, Notifications opens the app so you can take action yourself.

TIP

What to Do Next If Your Antivirus Is Turned Off Malware running on your system can turn off an anti-malware program's real-time protection, or you might be required to turn it off to install some apps. After turning on real-time protection, scan your system, as shown later in the "Checking for Malware with Windows Defender" task.

CONFIGURING AND STARTING WINDOWS DEFENDER

The Windows Defender program included with Windows 10 provides protection against spyware, malware, and viruses. In this task, you learn how to configure it and how to start it manually from the Settings menu.

Start

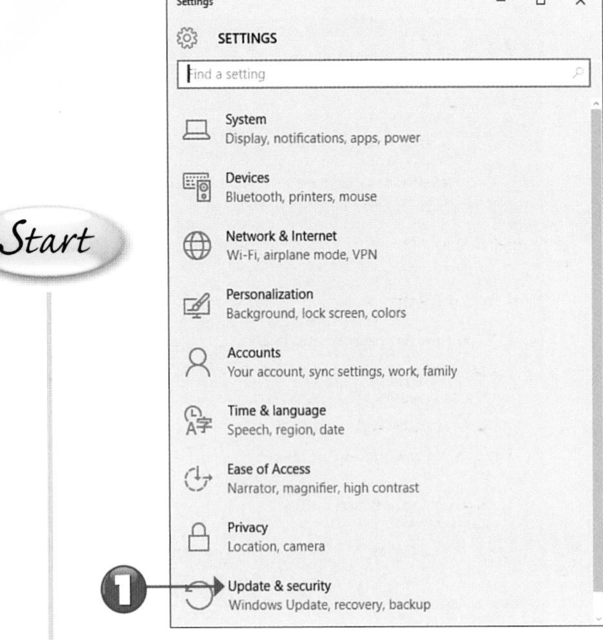

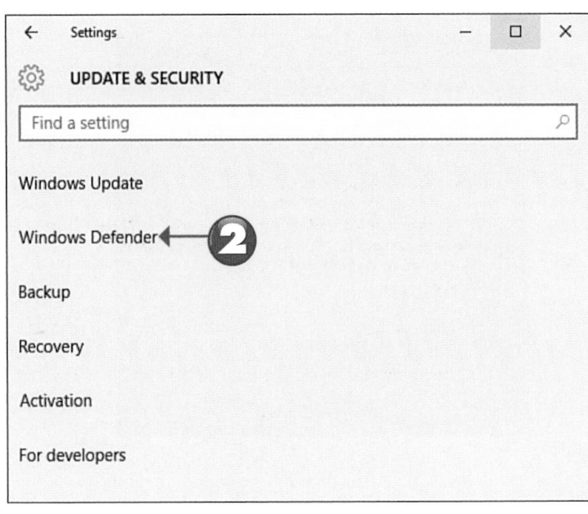

1. Click or tap **Update & security**.

2. Click or tap **Windows Defender**.

Continued

NOTE

Opening Windows Defender To open Windows Defender from the Taskbar, click the wall icon (you might need to click the up-arrow button to see additional icons). To open Windows Defender in Tablet Mode, search for `defender` and tap the Windows Defender desktop app icon. In either mode, you can also go to All apps, open the Windows System folder, and click or tap **Windows Defender**.

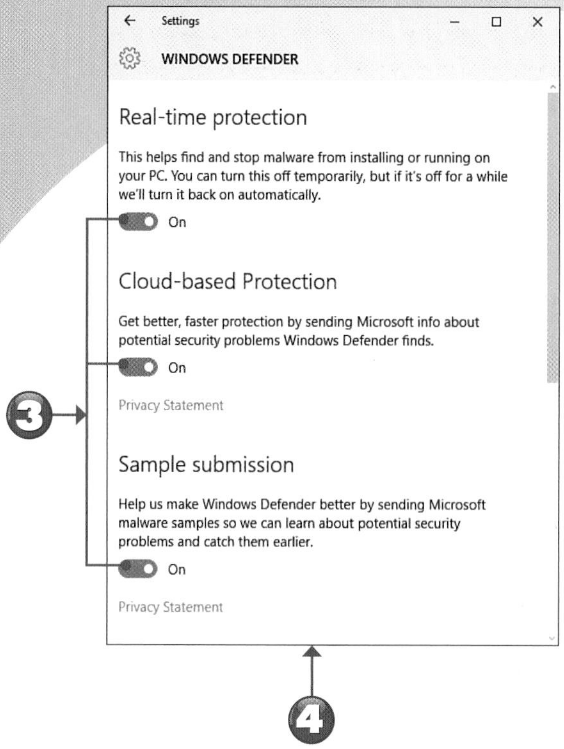

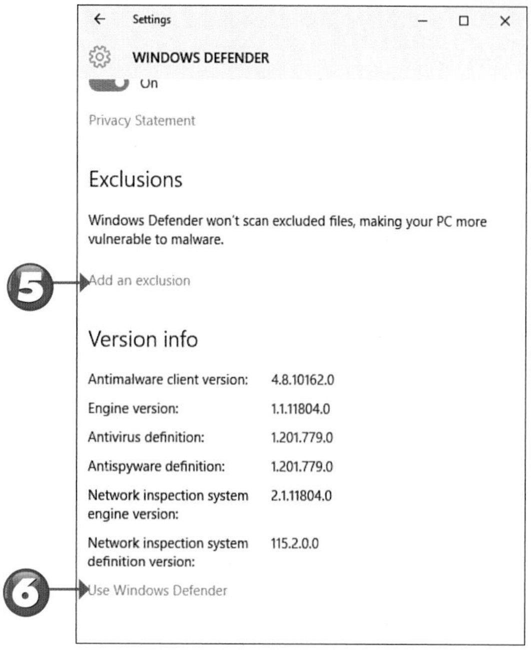

Settings

WINDOWS DEFENDER

Real-time protection

This helps find and stop malware from installing or running on your PC. You can turn this off temporarily, but if it's off for a while we'll turn it back on automatically.

On

Cloud-based Protection

Get better, faster protection by sending Microsoft info about potential security problems Windows Defender finds.

On

Privacy Statement

Sample submission

Help us make Windows Defender better by sending Microsoft malware samples so we can learn about potential security problems and catch them earlier.

On

Privacy Statement

Settings

WINDOWS DEFENDER

On

Privacy Statement

Exclusions

Windows Defender won't scan excluded files, making your PC more vulnerable to malware.

Add an exclusion

Version info

Antimalware client version:	4.8.10162.0
Engine version:	1.1.11804.0
Antivirus definition:	1.201.779.0
Antispyware definition:	1.201.779.0
Network inspection system engine version:	2.1.11804.0
Network inspection system definition version:	115.2.0.0

Use Windows Defender

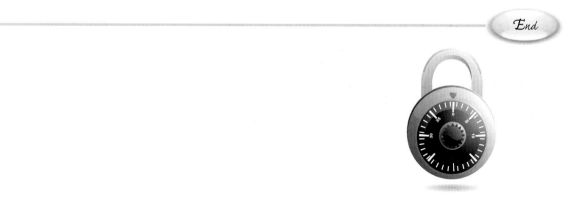

3. Having all settings turned on provides maximum protection; click and drag (or hold and drag) to the left to disable a setting; click and drag (or hold and drag) to the right to enable a setting.
4. Scroll down or flick up for additional information.
5. To skip scanning some files, click or tap **Add an exclusion** and specify what to skip (not recommended).
6. Click or tap **Use Windows Defender** to open Windows Defender to scan for malware or view history.

End

CHECKING FOR MALWARE WITH WINDOWS DEFENDER

The Windows Defender program included with Windows 10 provides protection against spyware, malware, and viruses. In addition to real-time protection, Defender can scan your system for malware. In this exercise, you learn how to run a scan and what to do with malware after it is discovered.

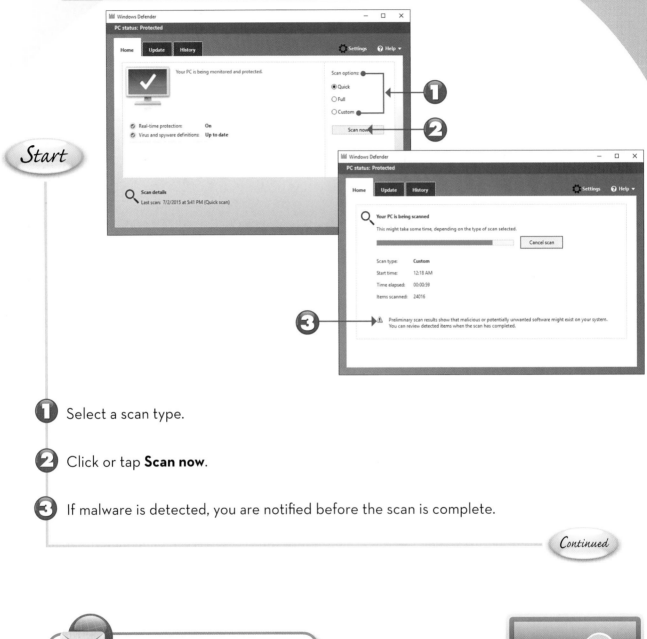

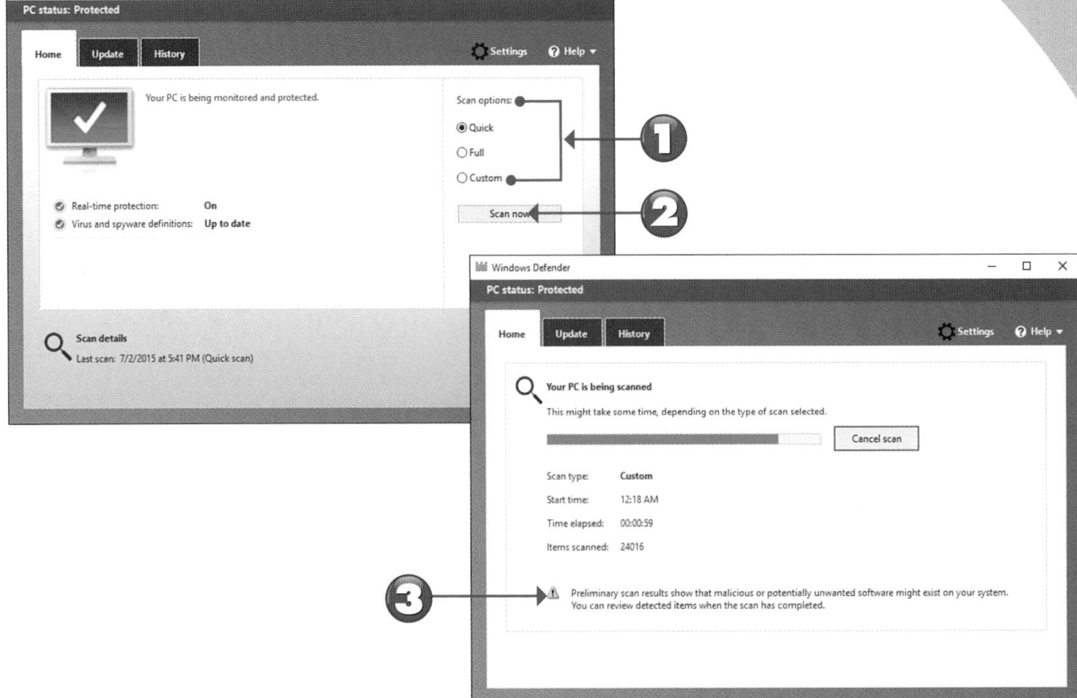

1. Select a scan type.
2. Click or tap **Scan now**.
3. If malware is detected, you are notified before the scan is complete.

Continued

NOTE

Using Custom Scan Use Custom Scan if you want to scan a particular drive or folder. When you select this option, you are prompted to select the drive(s) or folder(s) you want to scan.

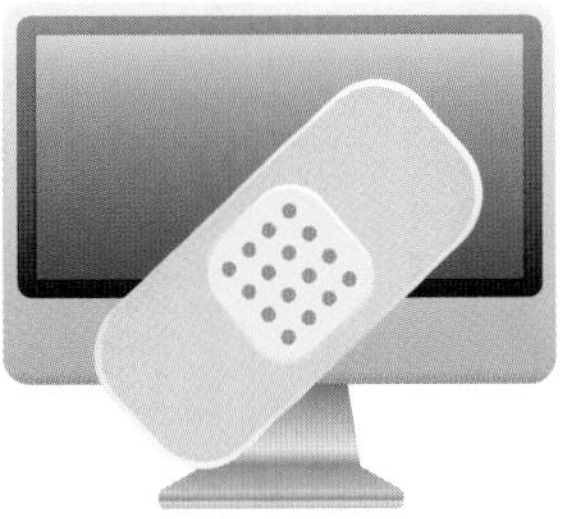

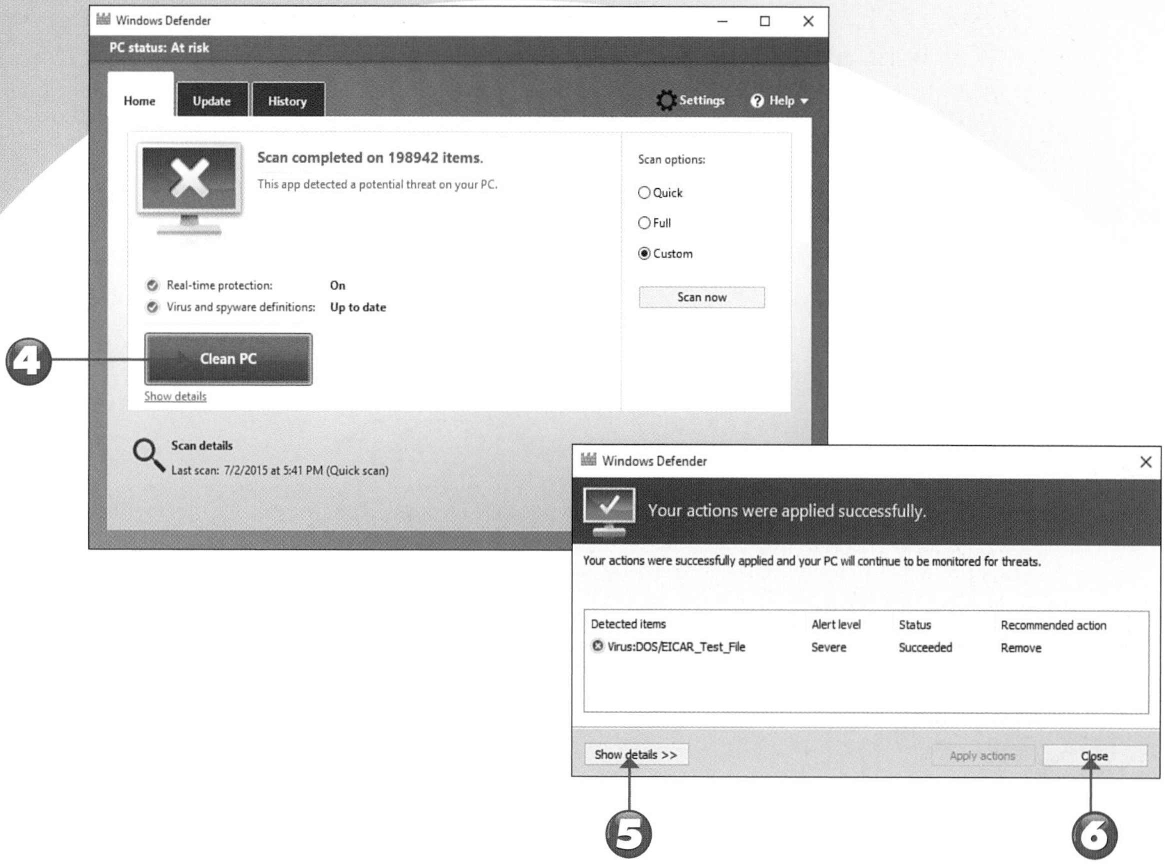

4 Click or tap **Clean PC** to remove all threats.

5 Click **Show details** if you want to learn more about the malware removed.

6 Click **Close** to return to the main menu.

End

NOTE

Using the Update and History Tabs Click or tap the **Update** tab to update Windows Defender manually (note that updates are normally delivered via Windows Update). Click or tap the **History** tab to see the malware files that have been detected and to learn more about each threat.

SYSTEM MAINTENANCE AND PERFORMANCE

Windows 10 includes a variety of tools that help solve problems, automate tasks to save time, and keep Windows working at peak efficiency. In this chapter, you learn how to use drive error-checking, check battery charge settings, create tasks, use troubleshooters, view open apps with Task Manager, and fix Windows problems with Refresh.

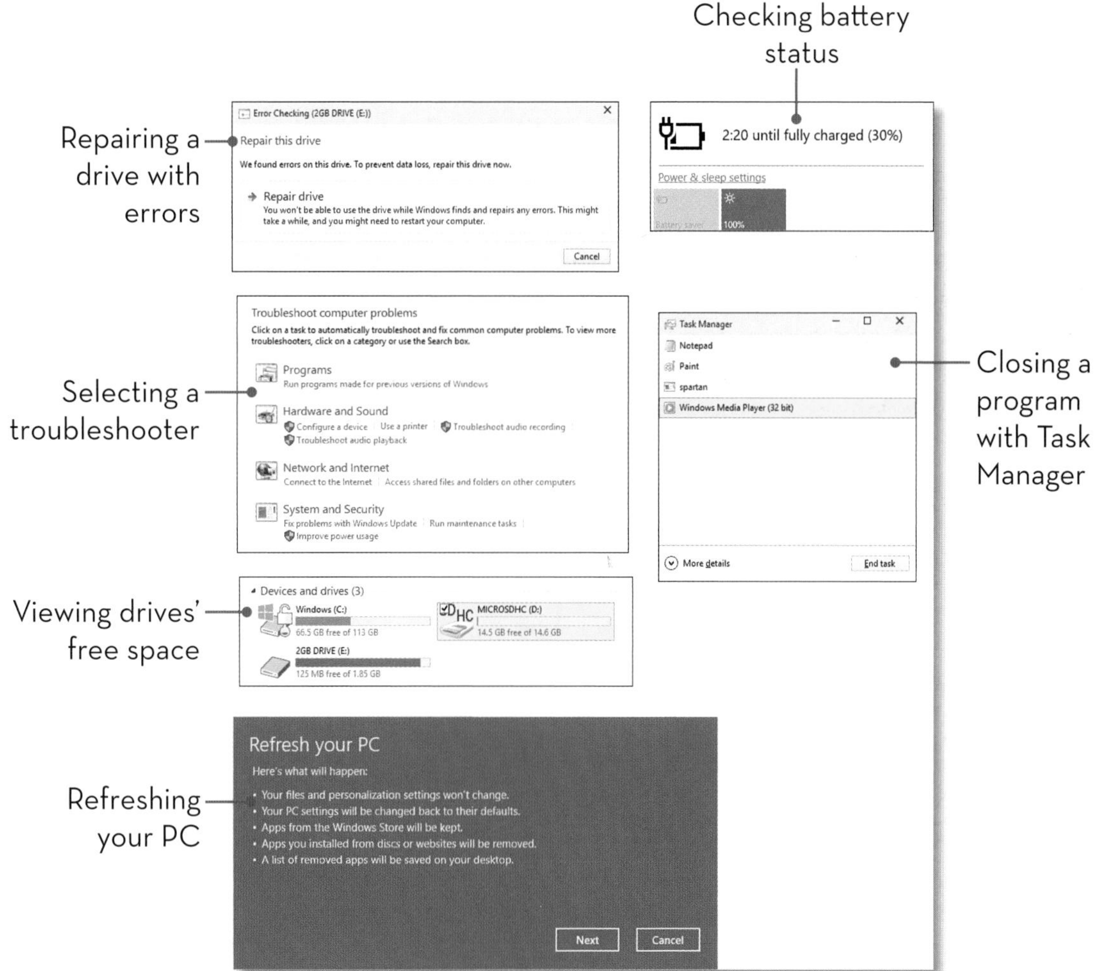

Checking battery status
Repairing a drive with errors
Error Checking (2GB DRIVE (E:))
Repair this drive
We found errors on this drive. To prevent data loss, repair this drive now.
Repair drive
You won't be able to use the drive while Windows finds and repairs any errors. This might take a while, and you might need to restart your computer.
Cancel
2:20 until fully charged (30%)
Power & sleep settings
100%
Troubleshoot computer problems
Click on a task to automatically troubleshoot and fix common computer problems. To view more troubleshooters, click on a category or use the Search box.
Programs
Run programs made for previous versions of Windows
Hardware and Sound
Configure a device
Use a printer
Troubleshoot audio recording
Troubleshoot audio playback
Network and Internet
Connect to the Internet
Access shared files and folders on other computers
System and Security
Fix problems with Windows Update
Run maintenance tasks
Improve power usage
Selecting a troubleshooter
Task Manager
Notepad
Paint
spartan
Windows Media Player (32 bit)
More details
End task
Closing a program with Task Manager
Devices and drives (3)
Windows (C:)
66.5 GB free of 113 GB
MICROSDHC (D:)
14.5 GB free of 14.6 GB
2GB DRIVE (E:)
125 MB free of 1.85 GB
Viewing drives' free space
Refresh your PC
Here's what will happen:
Your files and personalization settings won't change.
Your PC settings will be changed back to their defaults.
Apps from the Windows Store will be kept.
Apps you installed from discs or websites will be removed.
A list of removed apps will be saved on your desktop.
Next
Cancel
Refreshing your PC

CHECKING CHARGE LEVEL

If you use a device that runs on battery power, you can quickly check its charge level from the Windows taskbar. Here's how.

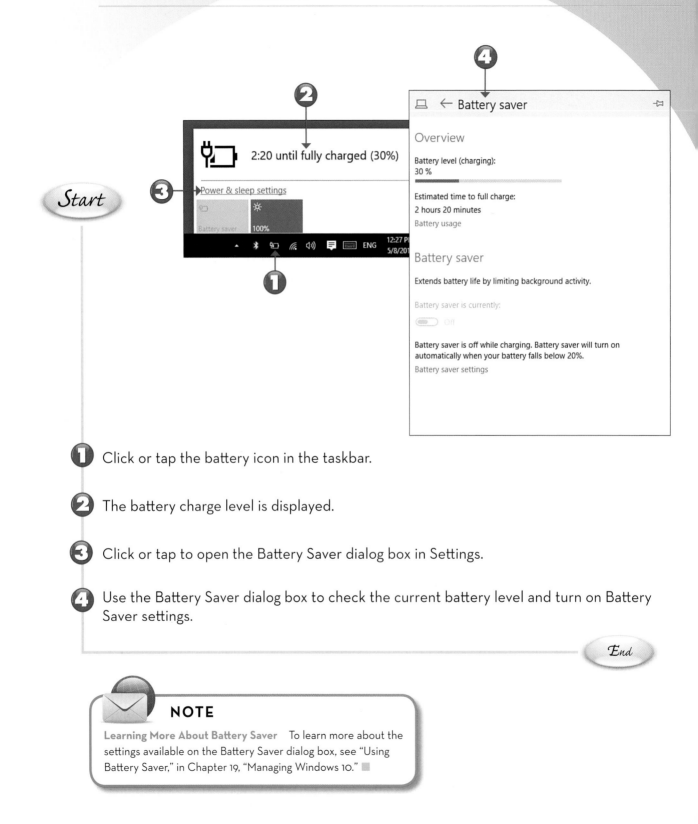

2:20 until fully charged (30%)

Power & sleep settings

Battery saver

100%

ENG

Battery saver

Overview

Battery level (charging):
30 %

Estimated time to full charge:
2 hours 20 minutes

Battery usage

Battery saver

Extends battery life by limiting background activity.

Battery saver is currently:

Off

Battery saver is off while charging. Battery saver will turn on automatically when your battery falls below 20%.

Battery saver settings

Start

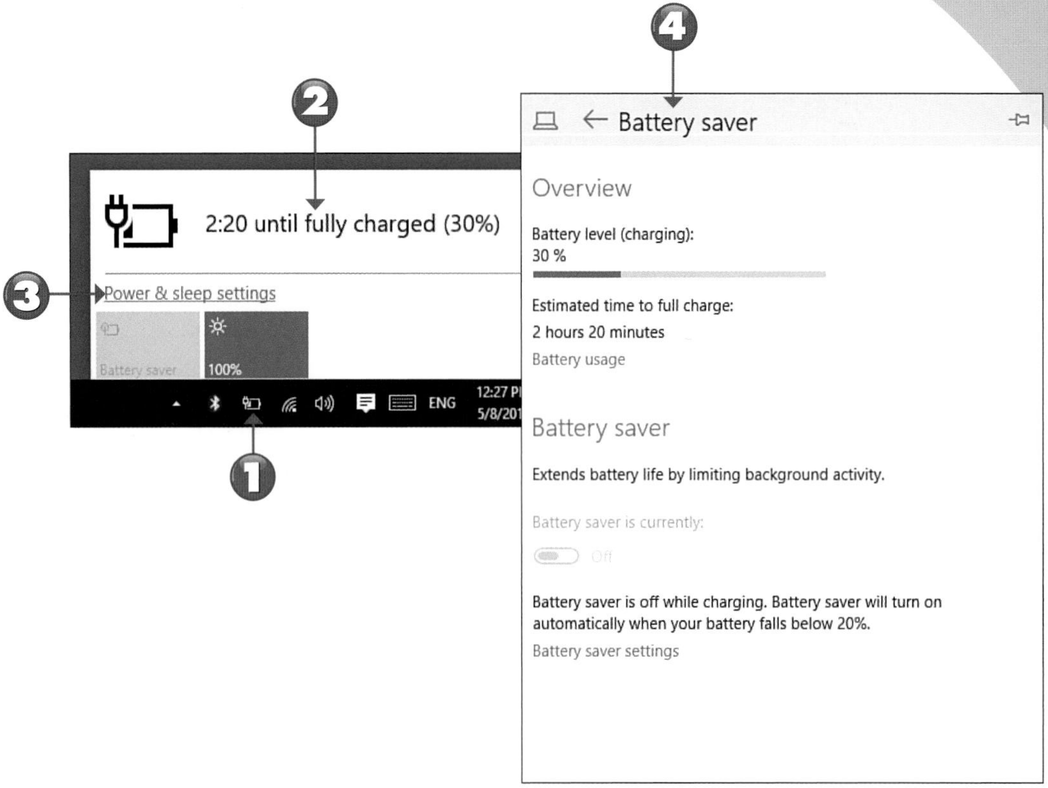

1. Click or tap the battery icon in the taskbar.
2. The battery charge level is displayed.
3. Click or tap to open the Battery Saver dialog box in Settings.
4. Use the Battery Saver dialog box to check the current battery level and turn on Battery Saver settings.

NOTE

Learning More About Battery Saver To learn more about the settings available on the Battery Saver dialog box, see "Using Battery Saver," in Chapter 19, "Managing Windows 10."

SELECTING A POWER SCHEME

With laptops, desktops, and all-in-one devices, you can select a power scheme in Windows that will stretch battery life as far as possible or keep your system running at top speed all the time. Here's how to select the power scheme you want from the Windows taskbar.

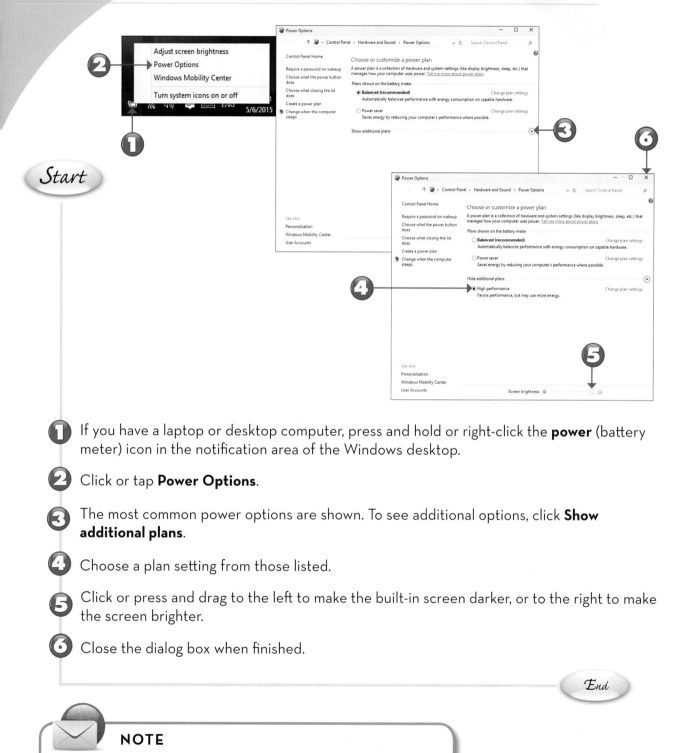

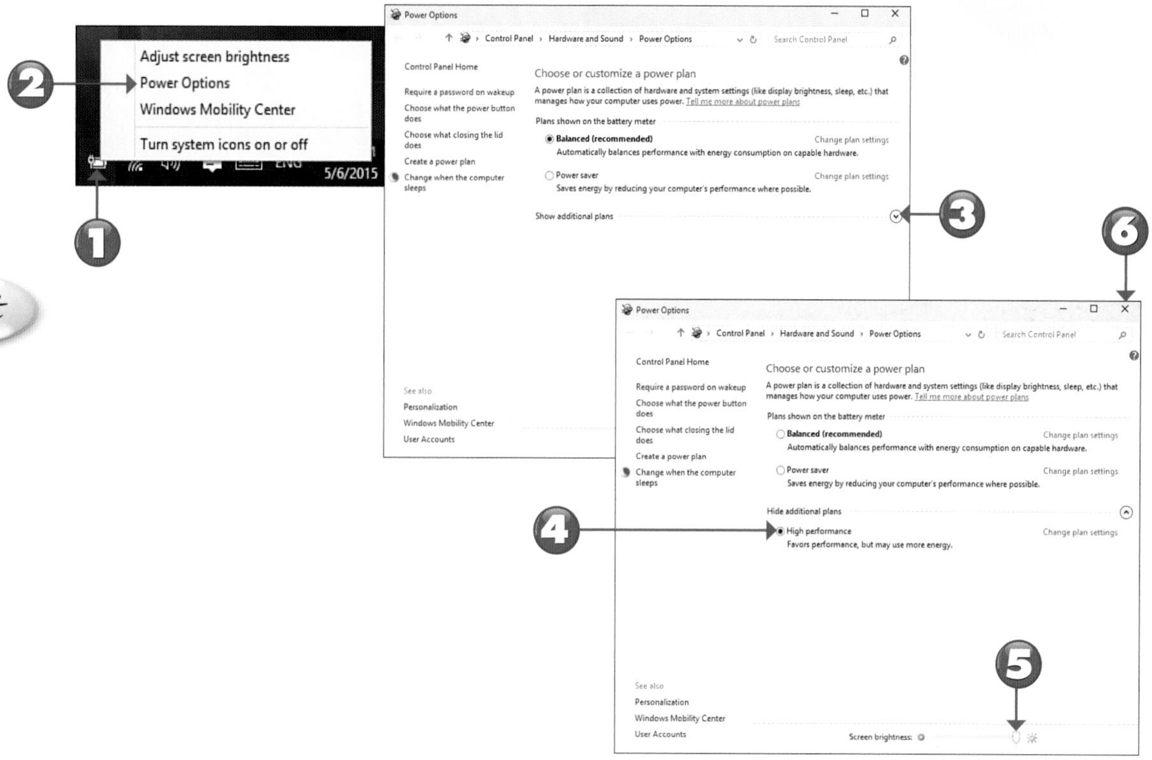

Start

1. If you have a laptop or desktop computer, press and hold or right-click the **power** (battery meter) icon in the notification area of the Windows desktop.
2. Click or tap **Power Options**.
3. The most common power options are shown. To see additional options, click **Show additional plans**.
4. Choose a plan setting from those listed.
5. Click or press and drag to the left to make the built-in screen darker, or to the right to make the screen brighter.
6. Close the dialog box when finished.

End

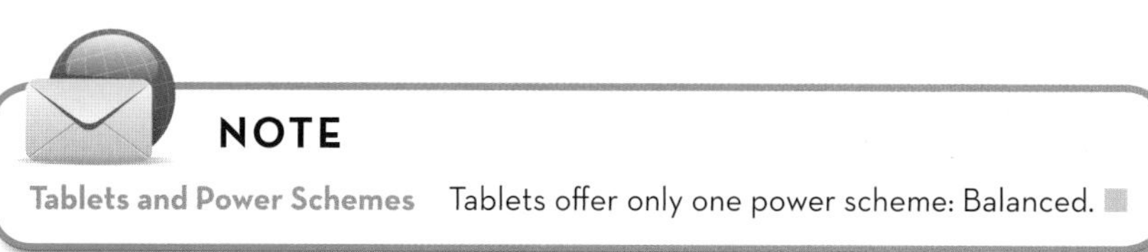

NOTE

Tablets and Power Schemes Tablets offer only one power scheme: Balanced.

VIEWING DISK INFORMATION

How much space is left on your drive? What drive letter does your external hard disk use? Use the This PC view in File Explorer for answers to these and other questions about the drives built in to and connected to your computer.

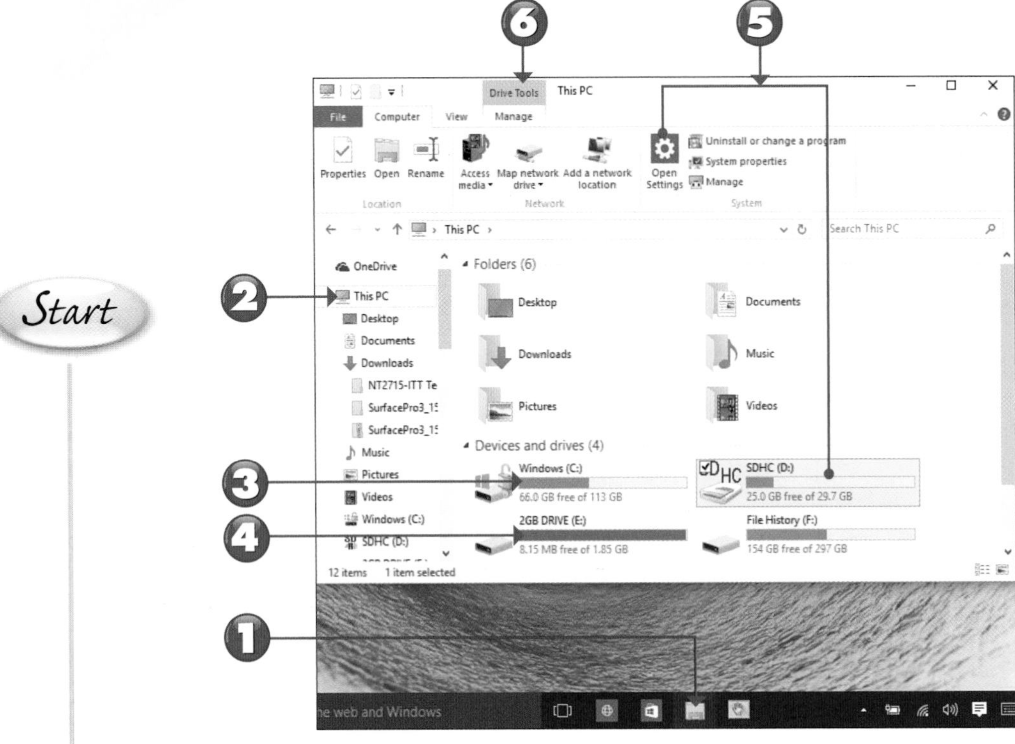

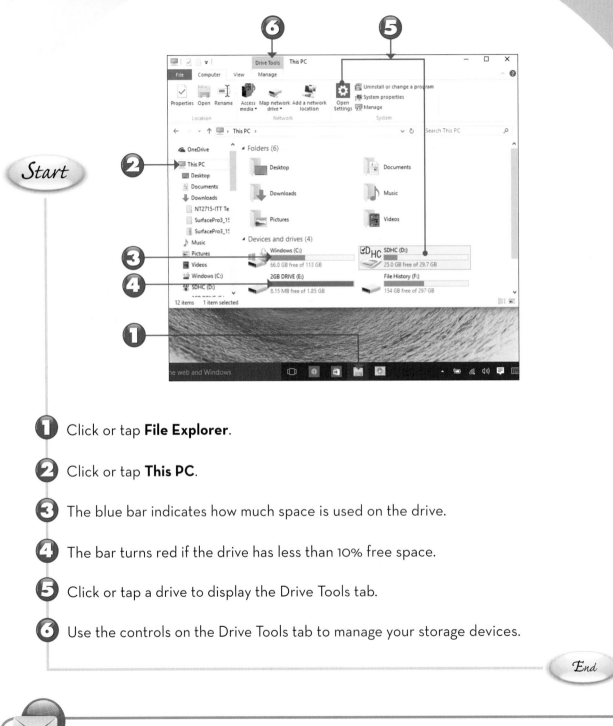

1. Click or tap **File Explorer**.
2. Click or tap **This PC**.
3. The blue bar indicates how much space is used on the drive.
4. The bar turns red if the drive has less than 10% free space.
5. Click or tap a drive to display the Drive Tools tab.
6. Use the controls on the Drive Tools tab to manage your storage devices.

End

NOTE

Using the View Tab If you do not see bars listing drive capacity, click or tap the View tab and select Tiles from the Layout menu.

CHECKING DRIVES FOR ERRORS WHEN CONNECTED

As drives are connected to your system, Windows watches for errors. If an error is detected, Notifications displays a message. Here's what to do next.

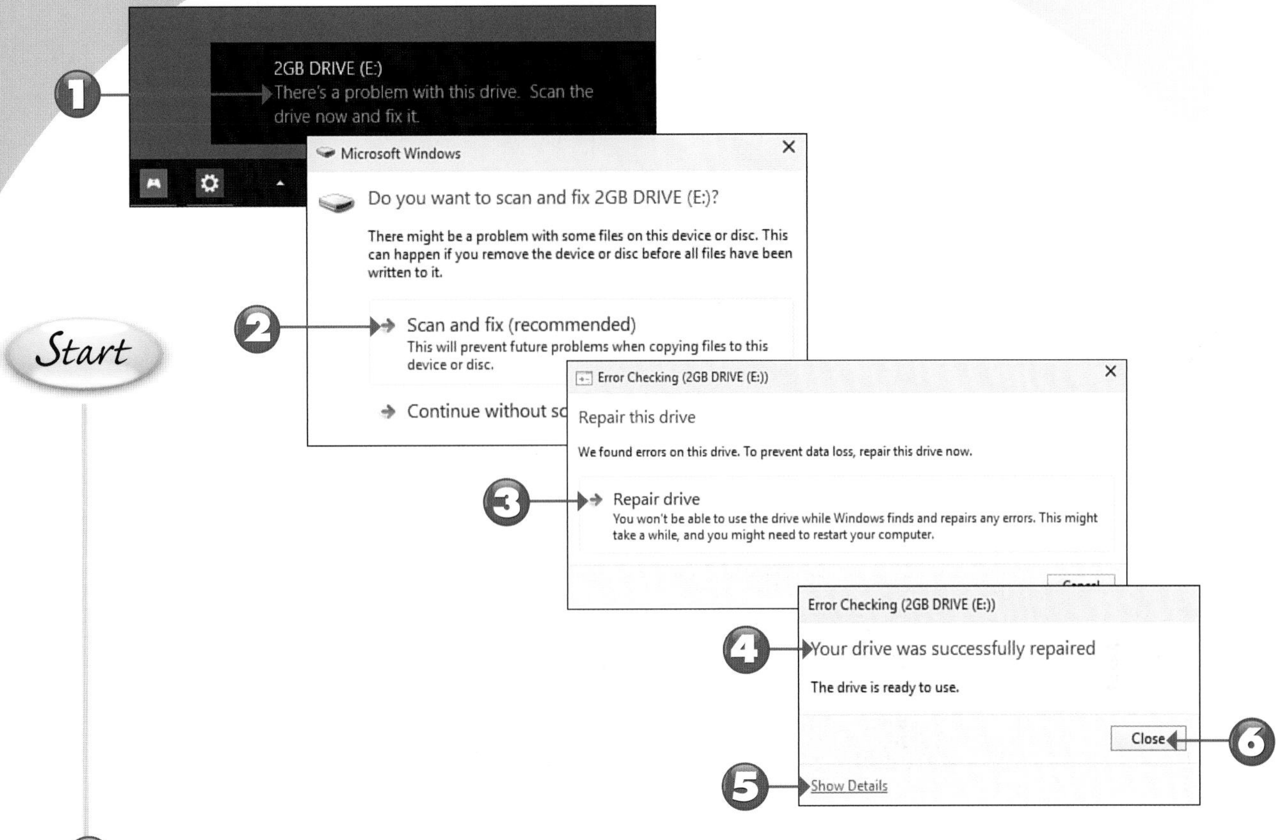

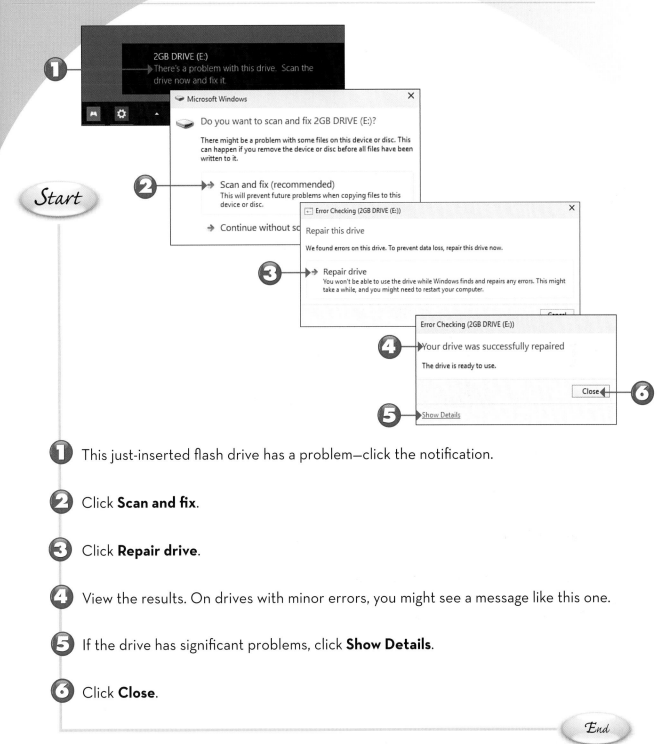

1. This just-inserted flash drive has a problem—click the notification.
2. Click **Scan and fix**.
3. Click **Repair drive**.
4. View the results. On drives with minor errors, you might see a message like this one.
5. If the drive has significant problems, click **Show Details**.
6. Click **Close**.

End

CHECKING DRIVES FOR ERRORS WITH THIS PC

You can check a drive for errors at any time using This PC. Here's how.

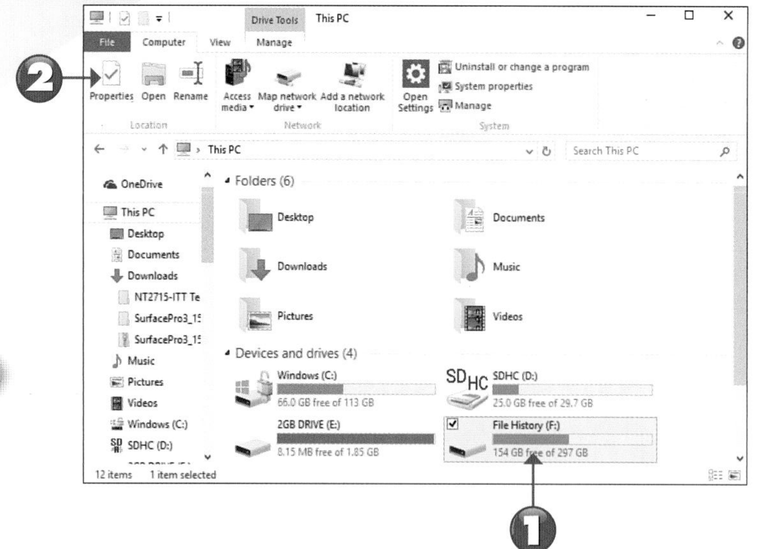

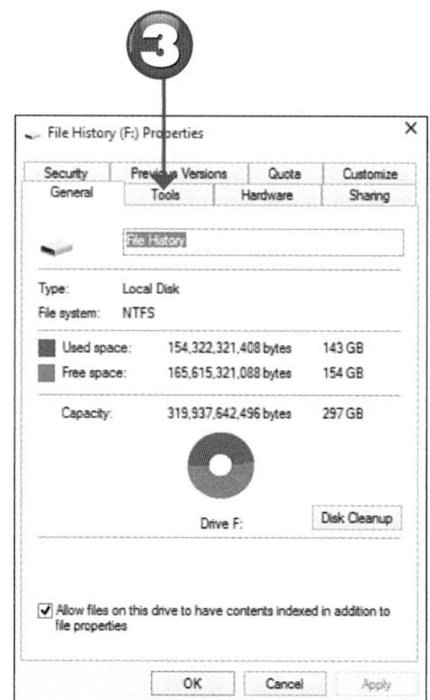

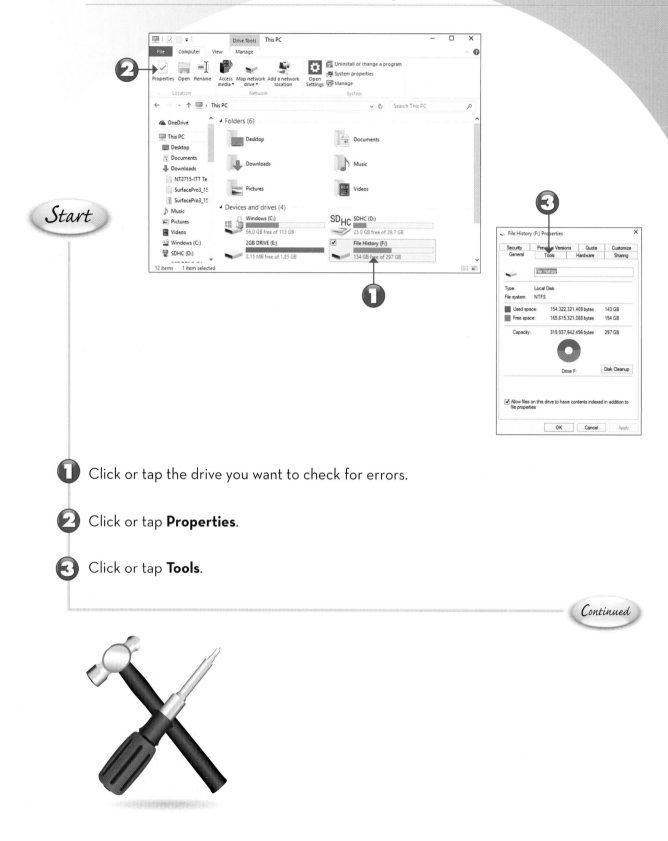

Start

1. Click or tap the drive you want to check for errors.
2. Click or tap **Properties**.
3. Click or tap **Tools**.

Continued

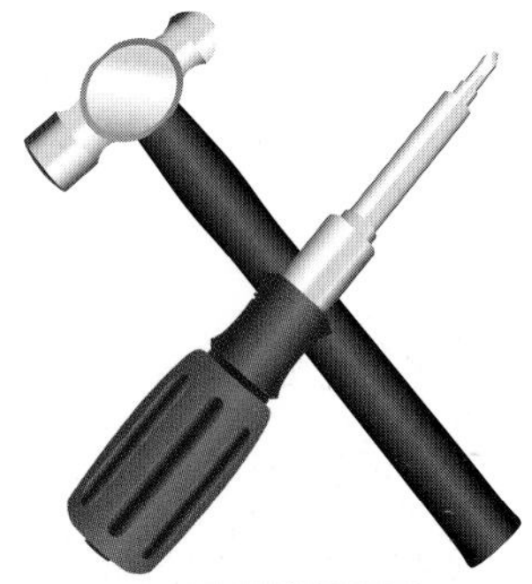

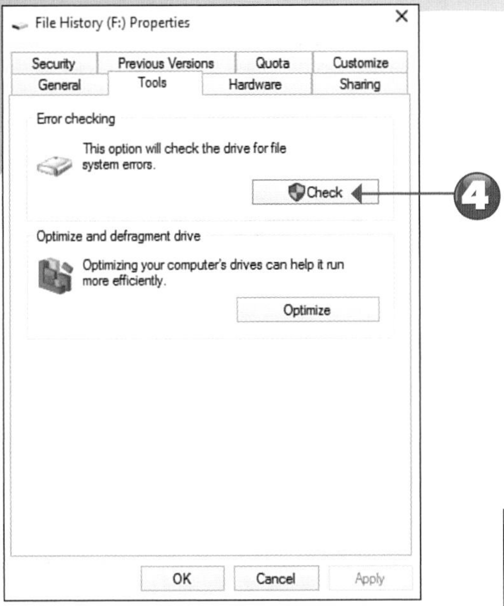

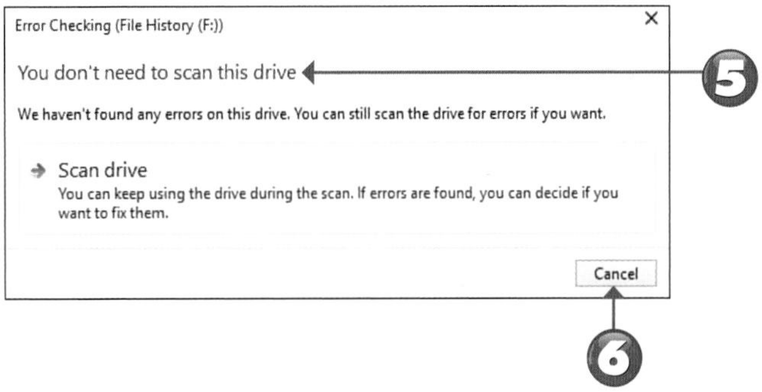

4. Click or tap **Check**.

5. This drive does not need to be scanned for errors.

6. Click or tap **Cancel**.

End

USING WINDOWS TROUBLESHOOTERS

Windows includes a number of troubleshooters to help solve problems with your system. Here's how to use a troubleshooter to fix an audio playback problem. In this example, the speakers were muted.

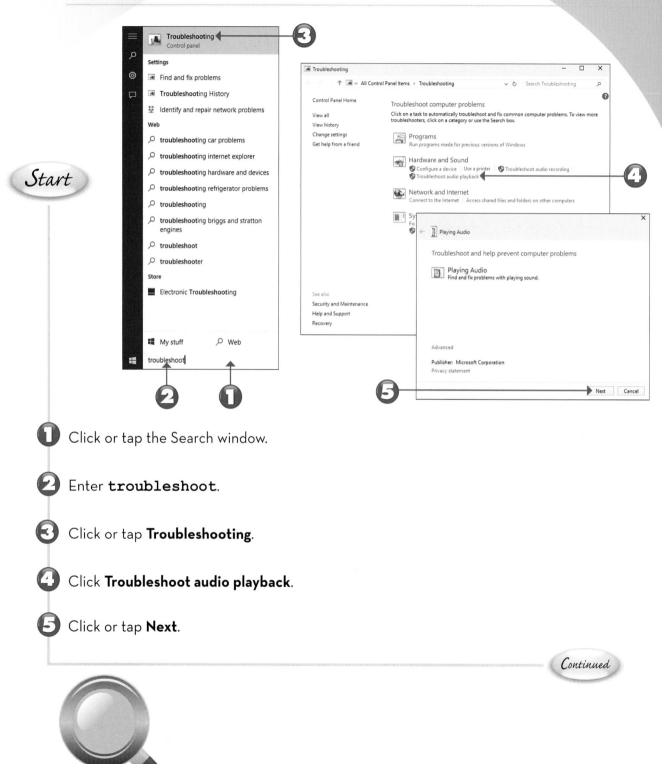

Start

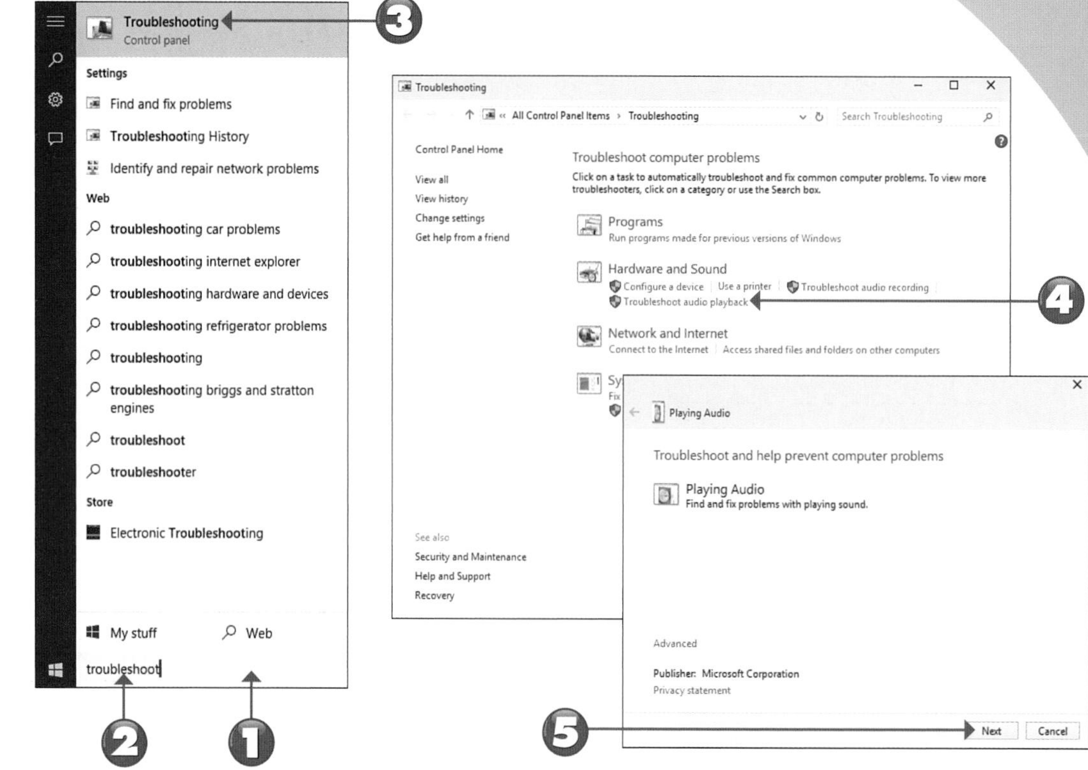

1. Click or tap the Search window.
2. Enter **`troubleshoot`**.
3. Click or tap **Troubleshooting**.
4. Click **Troubleshoot audio playback**.
5. Click or tap **Next**.

Continued

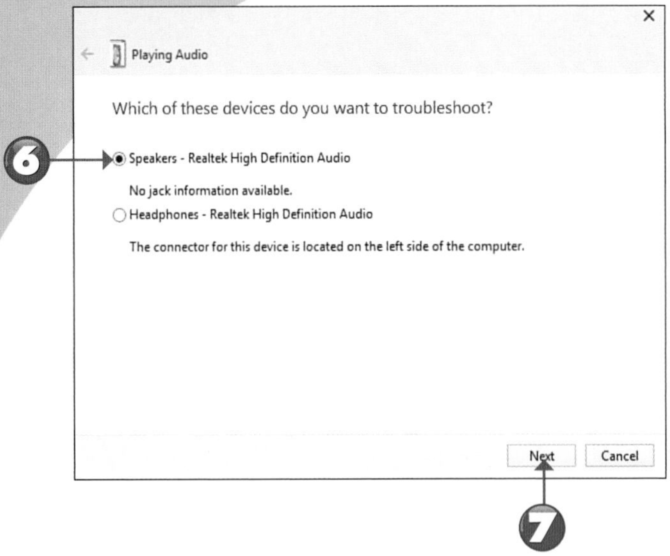

Playing Audio

Which of these devices do you want to troubleshoot?

6 Speakers - Realtek High Definition Audio

No jack information available.

Headphones - Realtek High Definition Audio

The connector for this device is located on the left side of the computer.

Next Cancel

7

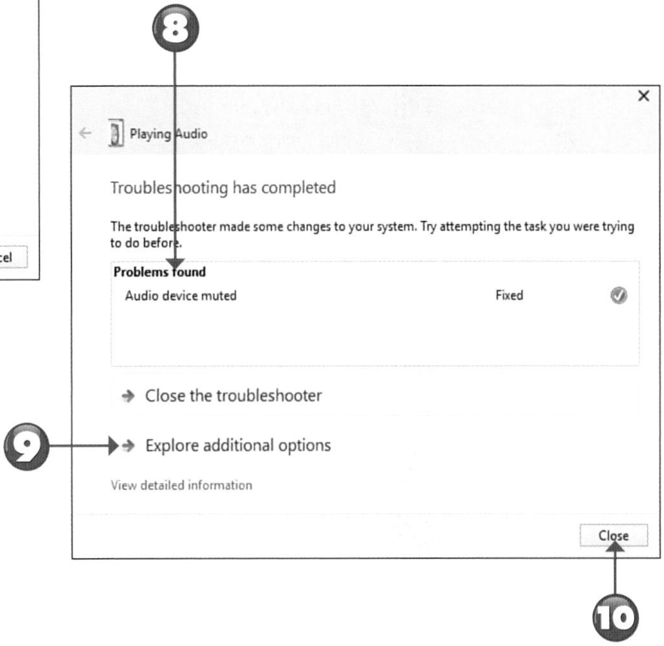

8

Playing Audio

Troubleshooting has completed

The troubleshooter made some changes to your system. Try attempting the task you were trying to do before.

Problems found		
Audio device muted	Fixed	

Close the troubleshooter

9 Explore additional options

View detailed information

Close

10

6 Choose your playback device.

7 Click or tap **Next**.

8 Review the results.

9 If the troubleshooter could not solve the problem, click or tap for more options.

10 Click or tap **Close** to close the window.

End

NOTE

Helping the Repair Process If you need to turn on a device, plug in a cable, or make other changes to your system, you are prompted to do so during the process.

USING RESET

If you're not sure why Windows isn't running correctly, or your system has gradually been running more slowly, the problem could be apps and programs that didn't come from the Windows Store. Reset, available from the Settings menu, reinstalls Windows 10 for you and can retain your personal files. To reinstall the apps from the Windows Store, revisit the Windows Store. Use the original discs or download files to reinstall apps from other sources. In this tutorial, you learn how to run Reset with these options.

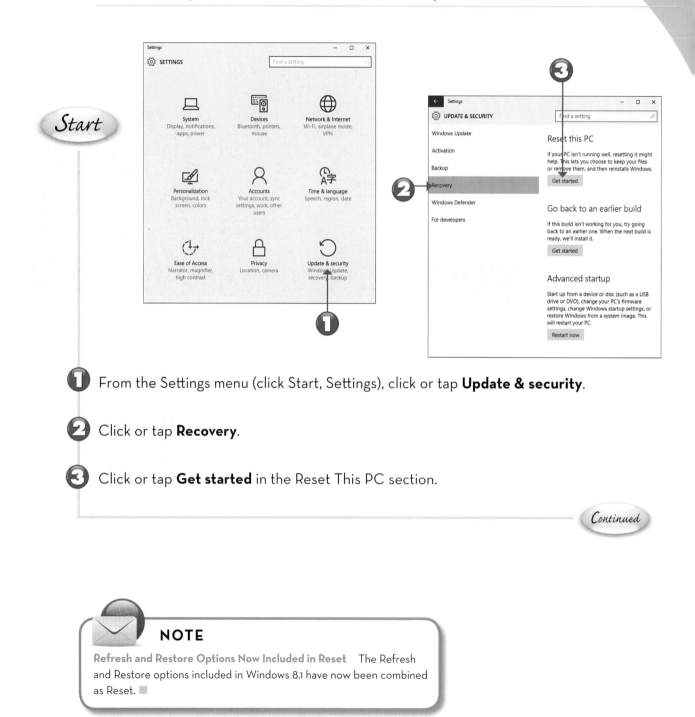

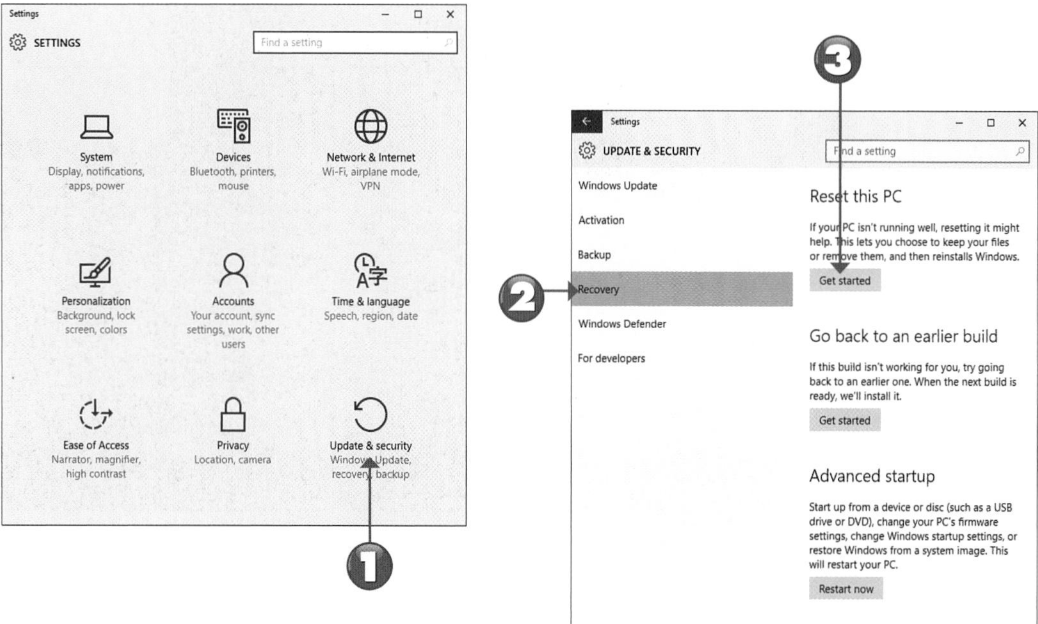

1. From the Settings menu (click Start, Settings), click or tap **Update & security**.
2. Click or tap **Recovery**.
3. Click or tap **Get started** in the Reset This PC section.

Continued

NOTE

Refresh and Restore Options Now Included in Reset The Refresh and Restore options included in Windows 8.1 have now been combined as Reset.

Choose an option

Keep my files
Removes apps and settings, but keeps your personal files.

Remove everything
Removes all of your personal files, apps, and settings.

Restore factory settings
Removes your personal files, apps, and settings, and reinstalls the version of Windows that came on this PC.

Cancel

Your apps will be removed

Many apps can be reinstalled from the Store, but the following apps will need to be reinstalled from the web or installation discs. This list will be saved to the desktop after you reset this PC.

BB FlashBack Express 5
Epson Event Manager
EPSON Scan
EPSON WorkForce 600 Series Printer Uninstall
EpsonNet Print
Ezvid

Next
Cancel

4. Click or tap **Keep my files**.
5. These apps will be removed; if you want to use them again, you must reinstall them after Reset is finished.
6. Click or tap **Next**.

Continued

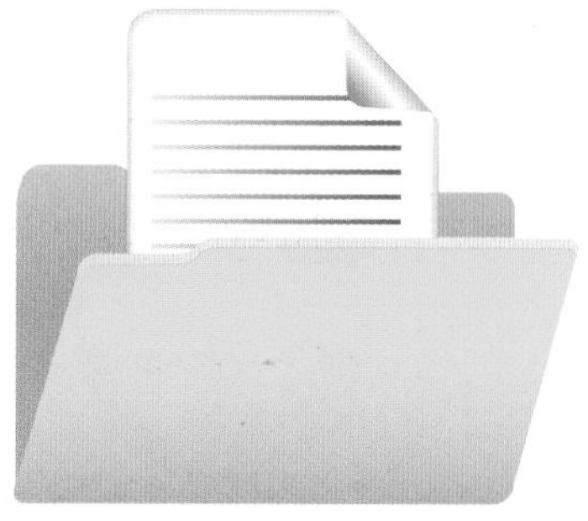

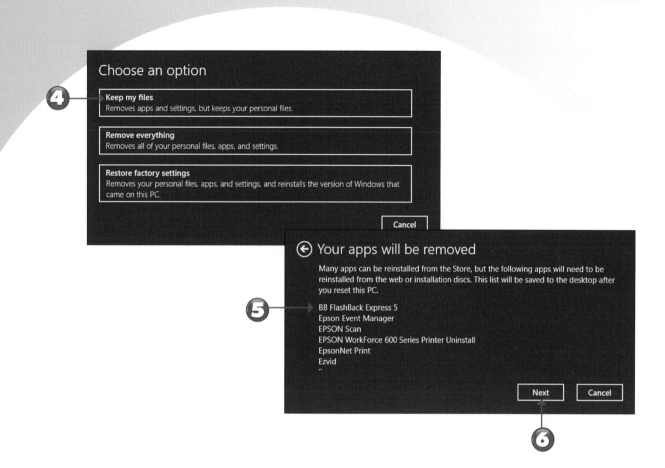

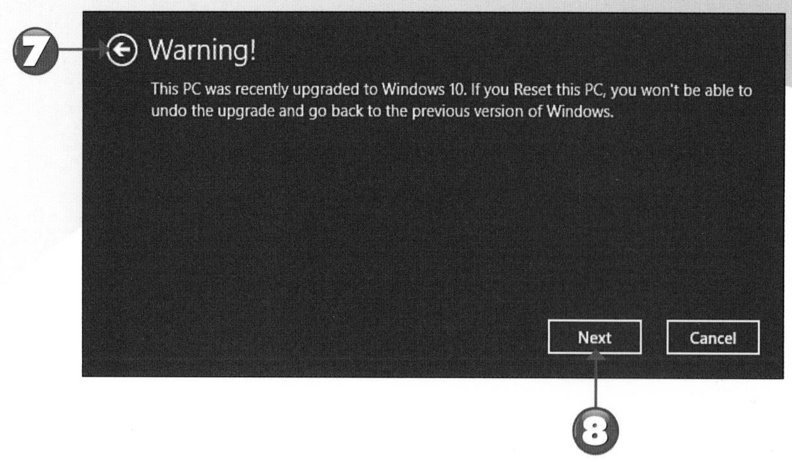

7 This warning appears if you recently upgraded to Windows 10. If you decide not to run Reset, click or tap **Cancel** in step 8 to stop the process.

8 Click or tap **Next** to continue with Reset.

9 Review what the Reset process does.

10 Click or tap **Reset**. Windows restarts and runs the Reset process.

Continued

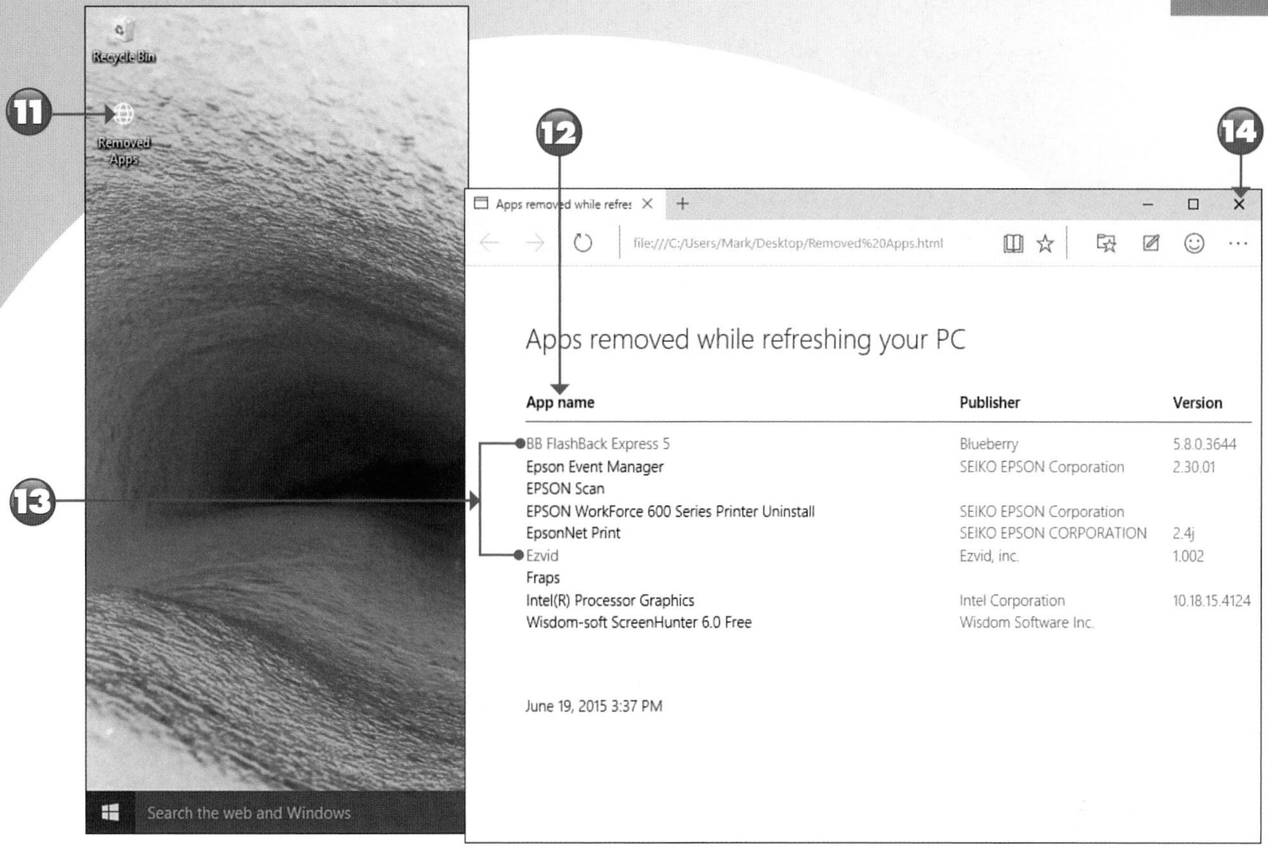

Recycle Bin

Removed Apps

Apps removed while refreshing your PC

file:///C:/Users/Mark/Desktop/Removed%20Apps.html

Apps removed while refreshing your PC

App name	Publisher	Version
BB FlashBack Express 5	Blueberry	5.8.0.3644
Epson Event Manager	SEIKO EPSON Corporation	2.30.01
EPSON Scan		
EPSON WorkForce 600 Series Printer Uninstall	SEIKO EPSON Corporation	
EpsonNet Print	SEIKO EPSON CORPORATION	2.4j
Ezvid	Ezvid, inc.	1.002
Fraps		
Intel(R) Processor Graphics	Intel Corporation	10.18.15.4124
Wisdom-soft ScreenHunter 6.0 Free	Wisdom Software Inc.	

June 19, 2015 3:37 PM

Search the web and Windows

11. After Windows restarts and you log in to your system, double-click or double-tap **Removed Apps**.
12. The apps removed during the Reset process.
13. Click or tap a link to open the app's website.
14. Click or tap to close.

End

NOTE

Finding "Hidden" Desktop Icons If you don't see any desktop icons, you must make them visible before continuing with step 12. Right-click or press and hold an empty part of your desktop and select **View**, **Show Desktop Icons**.

STARTING TASK MANAGER WITH A MOUSE OR A TOUCHSCREEN

You can have many programs running at the same time with Windows 10, even if you see only one program window visible and your taskbar is not displayed. To find out what programs and apps are running at a given moment, you can open the Windows Task Manager. In this exercise, you learn how to open Task Manager with a touchscreen or your mouse.

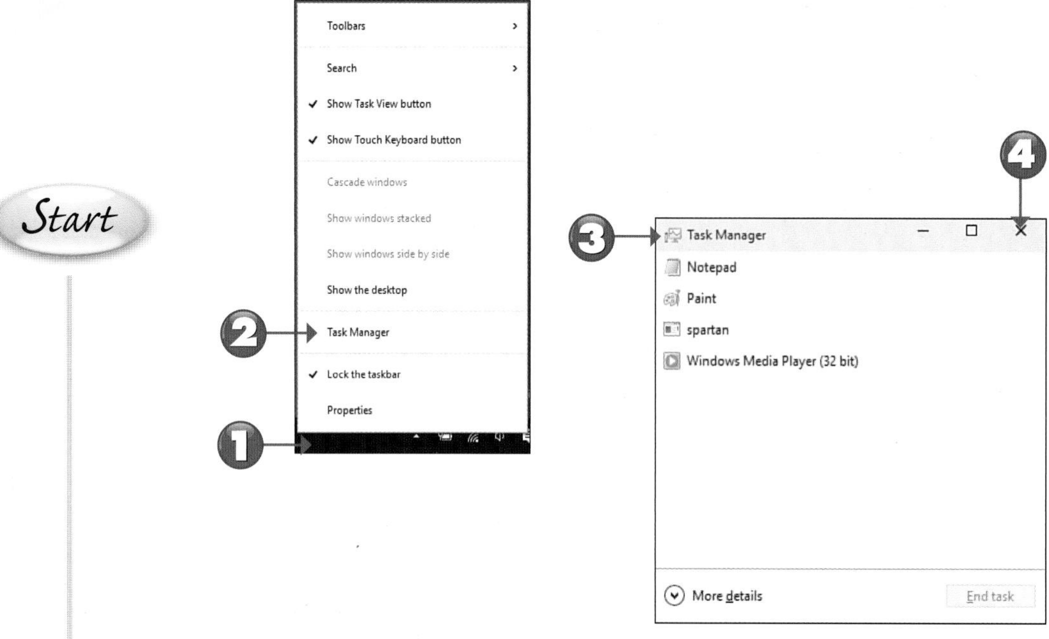

1. Press and hold or right-click an empty portion of the taskbar.
2. Select **Task Manager**.
3. Task Manager opens, displaying the currently open apps.
4. Close the window.

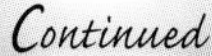

STARTING TASK MANAGER FROM THE KEYBOARD

You can also start Task Manager without taking your hands off the keyboard.

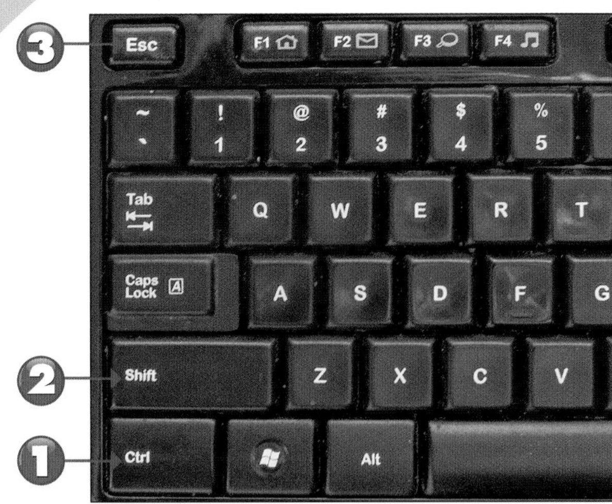

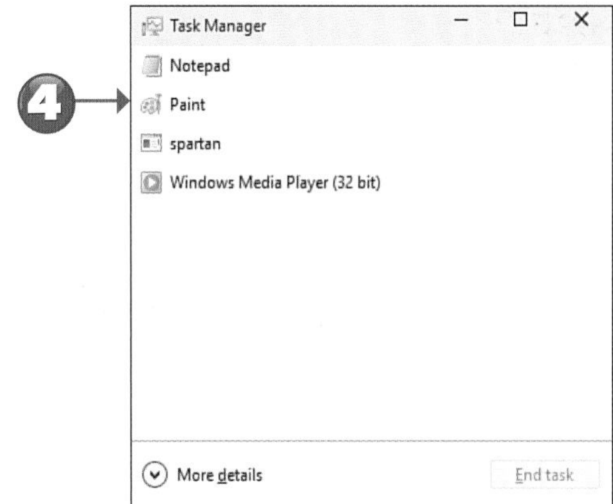

1. Press and hold the **Ctrl** key on your keyboard.
2. Press and hold the **Shift** key.
3. Press the **Esc** key.
4. Task Manager (simple view shown) displays the list of running programs and apps.

End

NOTE

More Ways to Start Task Manager The Task Manager app is known as Task Manager. You can use Search to locate and run it, or start it from the All Apps menu. Task Manager's executable (program) file is called taskmgr.exe, and you can also start it by using the **Run** command.

NOTE

Simple and Detailed Views Task Manager might open in detailed view (see next task) instead of simple view. You can switch views by clicking or tapping the **More details/Fewer details** arrow at the bottom of the Task Manager window.

VIEWING AND CLOSING RUNNING APPS WITH TASK MANAGER

Task Manager displays active (running) apps. It can also provide a detailed view of services and other activities that are running. In this task, you learn how to change views and how to close a running app.

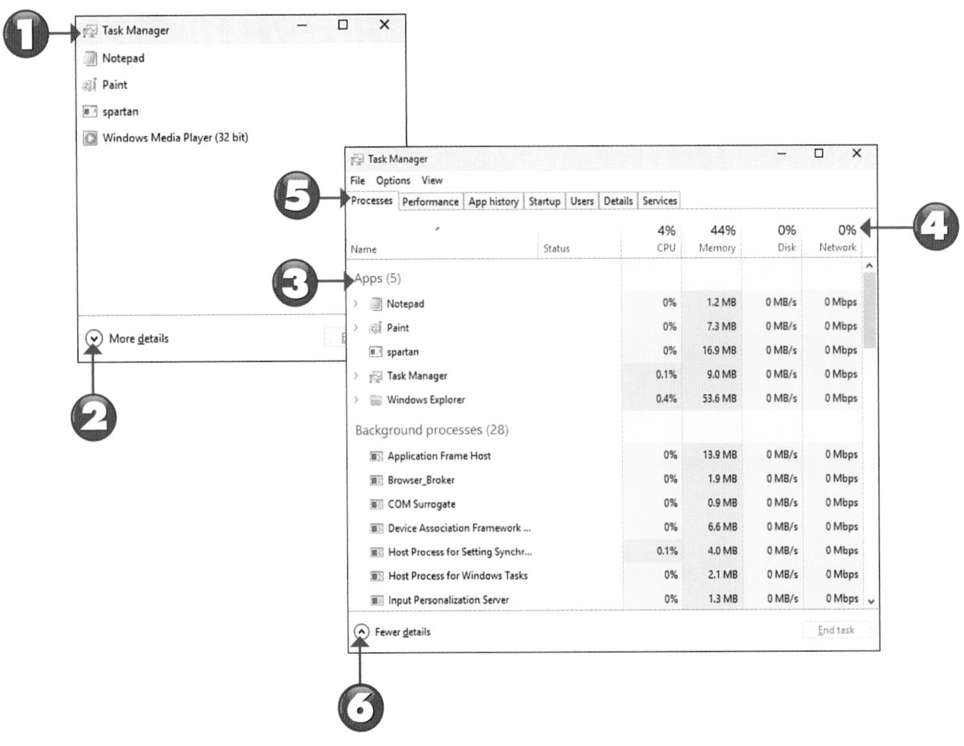

1. Task Manager shows the list of currently running apps.

2. Click or tap **More details** to switch to detailed view.

3. The Apps section lists actively running programs.

4. Amount of CPU, memory, disk activity, and network activity (real time) in use.

5. Click or tap a tab to learn more.

6. Click or tap **Fewer details** to return to simple view.

Continued

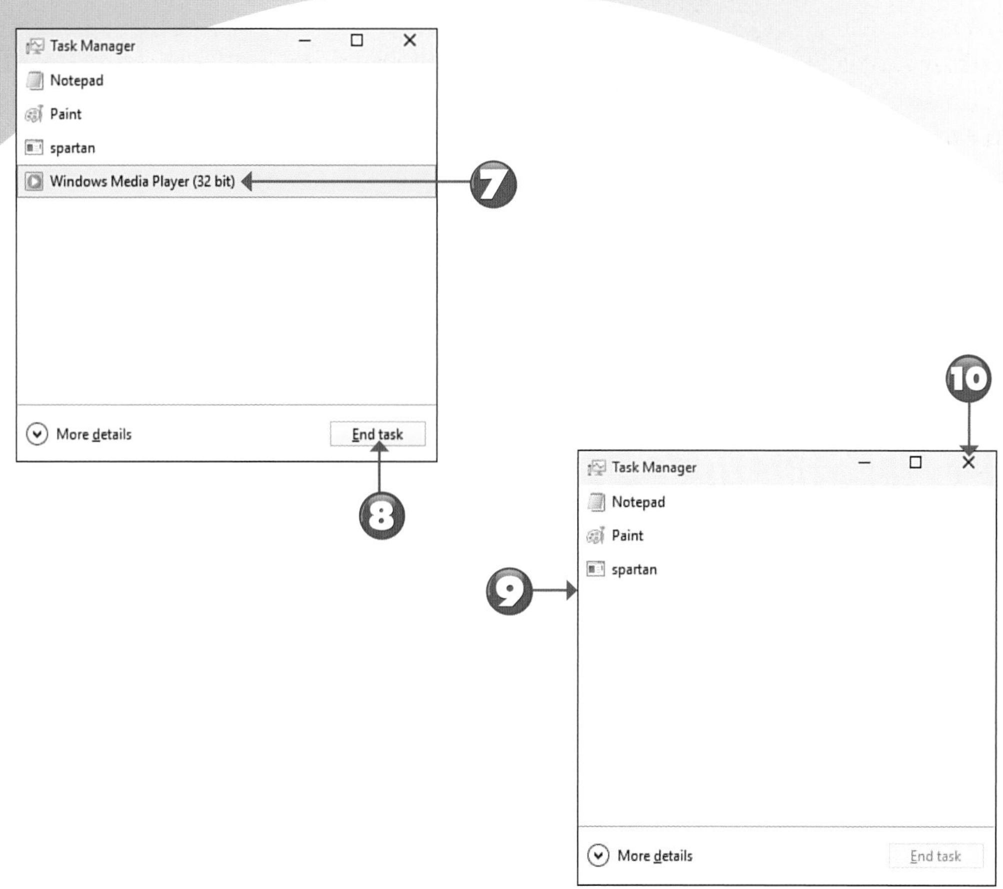

7. Click or tap an app you want to close.

8. Click or tap **End task**.

9. The app is removed from the list of open apps.

10. Click or tap to close.

End

Glossary

Use this section to bring yourself up to speed on important concepts and terms relating to Windows and to your computer. *Italic* terms within definitions are also listed in the glossary.

A

access point Device on a Wi-Fi network that provides a connection between computers on the network. Can be combined with a router and a switch.

administrator Windows term for the manager of a given computer or network; only users in the administrator's group can perform some management tasks. Other users must provide an administrator's name and password for tasks marked with the Windows security shield icon.

apps Program that runs on Windows. Might refer to a program designed for use with touchscreens (but can also be used with a keyboard and mouse), but can also refer to programs that work with Windows 7 and earlier versions. Some apps are preinstalled, whereas others are available from the Windows Store. See also *Universal apps*.

application program Program used to create, modify, and store information you create. Microsoft Word, Adobe Photoshop, and CorelDRAW are all application programs. See also *apps*.

B

backup A copy of a file made for safekeeping, especially using a special program that must be used to restore the backup when needed; backups can be compressed to save space. A full backup backs up the entire contents of the specified drive or system; a differential backup backs up only the files that have changed since the last full backup. Windows 10 includes the *Backup and Restore (Windows 7)* and *File History* backup apps.

Backup and Restore (Windows 7) This file and system *image backup* app was originally included in Windows 7 but is also included in Windows 10. It is primarily intended to let Windows 10 users retrieve backup files originally created in Windows 7 but can also be used to make a backup of the Windows 10 installation that can be used to restore a device to operation.

BitLocker A full-drive encryption technology used in Windows 10 Pro. Before you can use special boot options (such as Safe Mode), you must provide your BitLocker encryption key. Log in to https://onedrive.live.com/recovery key with your Microsoft account to obtain your recovery key.

Bluetooth A short-range wireless networking standard that supports non-PC devices such as mobile phones and PDAs, as well as PCs. Bluetooth uses frequencies ranging from 2.402GHz to 2.485GHz, with a range up to about 30 feet. Data transmission runs at 1Mbps, 2Mbps, or 25Mbps, depending on the version of the technology supported by the devices. Windows 10 includes Bluetooth support.

boot Starting the computer. A *warm boot* involves restarting the computer without a reset or shutdown. A *cold boot* involves a shutdown or reset before startup.

boot disk A disk with operating system files needed to start the computer. Windows 10 DVDs are bootable, as is the Recovery Drive you can create with Windows.

broadband Internet Internet connections with rated download speeds in excess of 25Mbps download and 3Mbps upload as announced by the Federal Communications Commission in January 2015. Most common types include cable modem and fiber optic (FiOS and others).

browser A program that interprets HTML documents and allows hyperlinking to websites. Windows 10 includes Microsoft Edge (originally known as *Project Spartan*) as its standard (default) web browser. Windows 10 also includes Internet Explorer 11, mainly for corporate users.

BSOD Blue Screen of Death. This is a fatal system error in Windows that stops the system from functioning; it is also called a "stop error," and is named after the blue background and the white text error message.

C

CD Compact Disc.

CD-R Recordable CD. Contents of a CD-R can be added to but not changed.

CD-ROM Compact Disc-Read-Only Memory. Standard optical drive. Most drives can read CD-R media but require MultiRead capability and a UDF reader program to read CD-RW media.

CD-RW Compact Disc-Rewritable. Rewritable CD. The contents can be changed. A CD-RW drive can also use CD-R media.

Compact Flash A popular flash-memory storage standard used by digital cameras. It can be attached to desktop and portable PCs by means of a card reader or PC Card adapter.

Continuum A new Windows 10 feature that enables easy switching between touchscreen and traditional Start menus and back when the user attaches or removes a keyboard on a convertible tablet. Tablet functionality is known as *Tablet Mode*. See also *Tablet Mode*.

Control Panel A Windows 10 feature that sets Windows options. See also *Settings*.

convertible tablet A tablet that converts into a laptop by attaching a keyboard with integrated touchpad. See also *Continuum*.

Cortana Microsoft's voice-enabled, integrated search and personal assistant app. Also known as Microsoft Cortana.

D

DAE Digital Audio Extraction. The process of converting tracks from a music CD to a digital format, such as MP3 or WMA, at faster than normal 1x analog speeds. Windows 10's Windows Media Player uses DAE to rip (convert) audio into digital form.

defragment Reorganizing the files on a drive to occupy contiguous sectors to improve retrieval speed; a defragmenting utility is included in Windows 10.

desktop Windows 10 uses the desktop for the Start menu, program shortcuts, access to components such as the Recycle Bin, and for program windows.

device driver A program used to enable an operating system to support new devices.

Device Manager The Windows portion of the system properties sheet used to view and control device configuration. This includes drivers and other configuration options.

Devices and Printers A Windows 10 feature that displays all devices and printers in a single window for quick access to the management features for each device.

drag and drop Windows term for clicking and holding on an object (such as a file or a tile on the Start screen), dragging it to another location, and releasing it.

DVD Digital Video Disc. Also known as Digital Versatile Disc. High-capacity replacement for CD-ROM.

DVD-R Digital Video Disc-Recordable.

DVD+R DVD+Recordable.

DVD-RAM Digital Versatile Disc-Random Access Memory. A rewritable *DVD* standard developed by Panasonic and supported by the DVD Forum. A few of these drives also support DVD-R write-once media.

DVD-ROM Digital Video Disc-Read Only Memory. Retail and upgrade editions of Windows 10 are distributed on DVD-ROM media, as are many other application and utility programs from major publishers.

DVD-RW Digital Video Disc-Rewritable. A rewritable *DVD* standard developed by Pioneer Electronics and supported by the DVD Forum. These drives also support *DVD-R* write-once media.

DVD±RW Refers to drives that support both *DVD-R*/RW and *DVD+R*/RW media.

DVD+RW A rewritable *DVD* standard supported by the DVD+RW Alliance and sold by HP, Philips, Sony, and other vendors. Most of these drives also support *DVD+R* write-once media.

E

email Electronic mail. The contents of email can include text, HTML, and binary files (such as photos or compressed archives). Email can be sent between computers via an internal computer network, a proprietary online service such as AOL, or via the Internet.

F

FAT File Allocation Table. The part of the hard disk or floppy disk that contains pointers to the actual location of files on the disk.

FAT16 16-bit file allocation table. FAT method used by Windows 10 and earlier versions for flash drives used for data. It allows 65,535 (2^{16}) files per drive and drive sizes up to 2GB in Windows 10.

FAT32 32-bit file allocation table. The FAT method optionally available with Windows 10 and earlier versions. It allows about four million (2^{32}) files maximum per drive and drive sizes up to 2TB (terabytes). Windows 10 supports FAT32 for data drives only.

file attributes Control how files are used and viewed and can be reset by the user. Typical file attributes include hidden, system, read-only, and archive; Windows 10 also supports compressed and encrypted file attributes on drives that use *NTFS*.

File Explorer Windows 10 file manager. Provides access to most-used folders and files (Quick access), *OneDrive* cloud storage, *This PC* local storage, Network, and *HomeGroup*.

file extension Alphanumeric identifier after the dot in a filename; indicates file type, such as .html, .exe, .docx, and so on. Windows 10 does not display file extensions by default, but you can make them visible through the Control Panel's Folder Options utility.

File History The Windows 10 backup feature that automatically backs up different versions of personal file folders (photos, videos, documents, music, downloads, and optionally other folders) to a specified drive.

file system How files are organized on a drive; *FAT16*, *FAT32*, and *NTFS* are popular file systems supported by various versions of Windows.

firewall A network device or software that blocks unauthorized access to a network from other users. Software firewalls such as Zone Alarm or Norton Internet Security are sometimes referred to as *personal firewalls*. Routers can also function as firewalls. Windows 10 includes a software firewall.

font A particular size, shape, and weight of a *typeface*. For example, 12-point Times Roman Italic is a font; Times Roman is the typeface.

Windows 10 includes a number of different typefaces, and you can select the desired font with programs such as WordPad, Paint, and others.

FORMAT A Windows program to prepare a drive for use; hard disks must be partitioned first.

G

GB Gigabyte. One billion bytes.

GHz Gigahertz.

GUI Graphical user interface. The user interface with features such as icons, fonts, and point-and-click commands; Windows and Mac OS are popular GUIs.

H

hard drive A storage device with rigid, nonremovable platters inside a case; also called hard disk or rigid disk.

hardware Physical computing devices.

HDD Hard disk drive. Windows 10 is typically installed to an HDD. See also *SSD*.

Hi-Speed USB Another term for USB 2.0.

high-speed Internet Internet connection with a download speed of at least 256Kbps. Sometimes used interchangeably with broadband Internet, but broadband Internet runs at much higher speeds. Most commonly provided by cable or DSL connections, but ISDN, fixed wireless, Fiber optic (FIOS and others), and satellite Internet services are also high-speed Internet services. See also *broadband Internet*.

HomeGroup A Windows network feature that enables two or more devices running Windows 7 or newer versions to belong to a secure, easy-to-manage *network*.

home page The web page that is first displayed when you open a web browser; it can be customized to view any web page available online or stored on your hard disk.

I

icon An onscreen symbol used in Windows to link you to a program, file, or routine.

image backup A backup that can be used to restore a working Windows installation in the event of system drive failure or corruption. Windows 10 includes *Backup and Restore (Windows 7)*, which can be used to create image or file backups. See also *File History*.

install The process of making a computer program usable on a system, including expanding and copying program files to the correct locations, changing Windows configuration files, and registering *file extensions* used by the program.

Internet The worldwide "network of networks" that can be accessed through the World Wide Web and by Telnet, FTP, and other utilities.

J

jump list A Windows 10 feature that enables programs and documents to offer commonly used shortcuts from the program's taskbar icon.

L

LAN Local area network. A *network* in which the components are connected through network cables or wirelessly; a LAN can connect to other LANs via a router.

landscape mode A print mode that prints across the wider side of the paper; from the usual proportions of a landscape painting.

Live Tile A Windows 10 feature that uses some tiles on the Start screen or Start menu to display information being fed from local storage (Pictures) or from websites (Weather, People, News, and other tiles).

lock screen This screen appears when Windows 10 is started or locked. The user must press the spacebar, click a mouse, or press the touch interface to see the login screen. This screen displays the date, time, and a full-screen image.

logging Recording events during a process. Windows 10 creates logs for many types of events; they can be viewed through the Computer Management Console.

mastering Creating a *CD* or *DVD* by adding all the files to the media at once. This method is recommended when creating a music CD or a video DVD. Windows 10's built-in CD- and DVD-creation feature supports mastering.

Microsoft account Account setup option supported by Windows 10. Log in with a Microsoft account (for example, somebody@outlook.com), and your settings are synchronized between systems. This was previously known as a Windows Live ID.

Microsoft Knowledge Base The online collection of Microsoft technical articles used by Microsoft support personnel to diagnose system problems. The Microsoft Knowledge Base can also be searched by end users via the http://support.microsoft.com website.

MMC Microsoft Management Console. The Windows utility used to view and control the computer and its components. Disk Management and *Device Manager* are components of MMC.

monitor A TV-like device that uses either a cathode ray tube (CRT) or a liquid crystal display (LCD) screen to display activity inside the computer. The monitor attaches to the video card or video port on the system. Windows 10 supports multiple monitors.

mouse A pointing device that is moved across a flat surface; older models use a removable ball to track movement, but most recent models use optical or laser sensors.

MP3 Moving Picture Experts Group Layer 3 Audio. A compressed digitized music file format widely used for storage of music; quality varies with the sampling rate used to create the file. MP3 files can be stored on recordable or rewritable CD or DVD media for playback and are frequently exchanged online. The process of creating MP3 files from CD is called "ripping." Windows Media Player and Windows Media Center can create and play back MP3 files.

MPEG Motion Picture Experts Group. MPEG creates standards for compression of video (such as MPEG 2) and audio (such as the popular MP3 file format).

multitouch A Windows feature that enables icons and windows on touch-sensitive displays to be dragged, resized, and adjusted with two or more fingers.

N

netbook A mobile computing device that is smaller than a laptop and has a folding keyboard and screen (usually no more than about 10 inches diagonal measurement). Netbooks have lower-performance processors, less RAM, and smaller hard disks (or solid state drives) than laptop or notebook computers. Windows 10 runs on netbooks as well as more powerful types of computers.

network Two or more computers that are connected and share a resource, such as folders or printers.

network drive A drive or folder available through the *network*; usually refers to a network resource that has been mapped to a local drive letter.

Network and Sharing Center The Windows control center for wired and wireless networking functions.

Notifications A Windows 10 feature that displays security and maintenance messages and provides quick access to the most common settings.

NTFS New Technology File System. The native *file system* used by Windows 10 and some earlier versions of Windows. All NTFS versions feature smaller allocation unit sizes and superior security when compared to *FAT16* or *FAT32*.

O

objects Items that can be viewed or configured with File Explorer, including drives, folders, computers, and so on.

OneDrive A Windows online file and photo storage and sharing site formerly known as SkyDrive. Requires a free Microsoft account (formerly known as a Windows Live ID). Windows 10 provides access to OneDrive from the All Apps menu and File Explorer.

OS Operating system. Software that configures and manages hardware and connects hardware and applications. Windows 10, Linux, and Mac OS X are examples of operating systems.

P

password A word or combination of letters and numbers that is matched to a *username* or resource name to enable the user to access a computer or network resources or accounts.

path A series of drives and folders (subdirectories) that are checked for executable programs when a command-prompt command is issued or a drive/network server and folders are used to access a given file.

personal firewall Software that blocks unauthorized access to a computer with an Internet connection. Can also be configured to prevent unauthorized programs from connecting to the Internet. Windows 10 includes a personal (software) firewall.

PIN Personal identification number. Windows 10 supports PIN codes as an optional login method.

pinning The act of locking a program or document to the Windows *taskbar* or *Start menu*. You can use this feature along with *jump lists* to create shortcuts to your most commonly used programs in either location.

POP3 Post Office Protocol 3, a popular protocol for receiving *email*. The Mail app in Windows supports POP3 email services.

portrait mode The default print option that prints across the short side of the paper; it gets its name from the usual orientation of portrait paintings and photographs.

power management BIOS or OS techniques for reducing power usage by dropping CPU clock speed, turning off the monitor or hard disk, and so on during periods of inactivity.

PowerShell A Windows utility that runs from the command prompt and enables experienced users and system administrators to write scripts (series of commands) to perform tasks. Included in most editions of Windows 10 as an optionally installed feature.

properties sheet A Windows method for modifying and viewing object properties. Accessible by right-clicking the object and selecting Properties or by using Control Panel. On a tablet or touchscreen-based device, press and hold the object until the properties sheet appears. It is located on the bottom of the screen when run from the *Start screen* or Apps menu.

Q

QWERTY The standard arrangement of typewriter keys is also used by most English or Latin-alphabet computer keyboards; the name was derived from the first six letter keys under the left hand.

R

Recycle Bin The Windows holding area for deleted files, allowing them to be restored to their original locations. The Recycle Bin can be overridden to free up disk space.

Reset A Windows 10 system recovery feature that resets Windows to its as-installed state. All user changes (new programs, files, and settings) are also wiped out.

resolution The number of dots per inch (dpi) supported by a display, scanner, or printer. Typical displays support resolutions of about 96dpi, whereas printers have resolutions of 600dpi to 2,400dpi (laser printers). Inkjet printers might have even higher resolutions.

Ribbon toolbar The program interface used by many Windows 10 components. Click a tab on the Ribbon to display related commands.

ripping The process of converting CD audio tracks into a digital music format, such as *MP3* or *WMA*.

router The device that routes data from one network to another. Often integrated with wireless access points and switches.

S

safe mode Windows troubleshooting startup mode; runs the system using BIOS routines only. To restart in Safe Mode, select Advanced Startup Options in the Settings menu, Restart Now, Troubleshoot, Advanced Options, Startup Settings, Restart, and select 4 (Safe Mode), 5 (Safe Mode with Networking), or 6 (Safe Mode with Command Prompt). If your device uses BitLocker encryption, you will also need to enter your BitLocker encryption key. See also *BitLocker*.

SD card Secure Digital card. Popular flash memory card format for digital cameras and other electronic devices with a capacity up to 2GB. See also *SDHC card*.

SDHC card Secure Digital High Capacity card. Popular flash memory card format for digital cameras and other electronic devices with a capacity ranging from 4GB to 32GB. Devices that use SDHC cards can also use *SD cards*; however, devices made only for SD cards cannot use SDHC cards.

SDXC card—Secure Digital eXtended Capacity card. Popular flash memory card format for high-performance digital cameras and devices. Capacities range from 64GB up to 2TB. Devices that use SDXC cards can also use *SD card* and *SDHC card*; however, devices made only for SD or SDHC cards cannot use SDXC cards.

shared resource A drive, printer, or other resource available to more than one PC over a *network*.

shortcut A Windows *icon* stored on the desktop or in a Windows folder with an .lnk extension; double-click the icon to run the program or open the file.

SMTP Simple Mail Transport Protocol. The most common method used to send *email*.

Snap A Windows 10 feature that enables a program or app to be snapped to the top, bottom, left, or right of the display where it is running, adjusting the window size so other programs or apps are also visible. To use Snap, hold down the Windows key and then press the up arrow, down arrow, left arrow, or right arrow.

software Instructions that create or modify information and control *hardware*; must be read into RAM before use. Also known as program or app.

SOHO Small office/home office.

SP Service pack. A service pack is used to add features or fix problems with an OS or application program. Windows 10's Windows Update feature installs service packs for Windows and for Microsoft apps such as Microsoft Office automatically when standard settings are used.

spam Unsolicited *email*. Named after (but not endorsed by) the famous Hormel lunchmeat. Many email clients and utilities can be configured to help filter, sort, and block spam.

SSD Solid state drive. A storage device that uses high-speed flash memory and can be used in place of a hard disk drive (HDD). SSDs are several times faster than HDDs, but are more expensive at a given capacity than HDDs. Tablets and many Ultrabook laptops use SSDs. See *HDD*.

SSID Service Set Identifier. The name for a wireless *network*. When you buy a wireless router, the vendor has assigned it a standard SSID, but you should change it to a different name as part of setting up a secure network.

standby The power-saving mode in which the CPU drops to a reduced clock speed and other components wait for activity.

Start menu The Windows 10 user interface that pops up from the lower-left corner of the screen when you press the Windows key or click the Windows button. The Start menu includes both desktop and Universal apps, and can be customized. The Start menu works differently in *Tablet Mode* than in normal mode. See also *Tablet Mode*.

storage Any device that holds programs or data for use, including HDDs, SSDs, flash memory cards, USB drives, DVD drives, and so on.

suspend The power-saving mode that shuts down the monitor and other devices; it saves more power than standby. Windows 10 calls suspend mode "sleep mode."

System Restore A feature built in to Windows 10 that enables the user to revert the system back to a previous state in case of a crash or other system problem. System Restore points can be created by the user and are created automatically by Windows when new hardware and software is installed or on a predefined schedule.

T

taskbar A Windows feature that displays icons for running programs, generally at the bottom of the primary display. In Windows 10, the taskbar also contains *jump list* shortcuts to frequently used programs.

Task Manager Displays running programs, apps, and services, and enables you to disable unnecessary startup features.

Task View Switches between running apps and sets up virtual desktops. Task View replaces App Switcher. To use Task View, tap the Task View key on the Windows taskbar, use the Windows key+Tab keys (for use with virtual desktops) or use Alt+Tab keys (for app switching only).

TB Terabyte. One trillion bytes.

TCP/IP Transmission Control Protocol/ Internet Protocol. The Internet's standard network protocol that is also the standard for most networks.

This PC Displays local drives, network locations, and user folders in File Explorer. Replaces My Computer or Computer views in Windows Explorer or File Explorer in earlier versions of Windows.

tile The Windows 10 term for the Universal app icons on the right side of the *Start menu*. Tiles can be moved to different places on the Start menu by using drag and drop.

touchpad A pressure-sensitive pad that is used as a mouse replacement in some portable computers and keyboards.

touchscreen A touch-sensitive screen built in to tablets, many laptops, and some desktop computers.

Trojan horse A program that attaches itself secretly to other programs and usually has a harmful action when triggered. It is similar to a computer *virus* but cannot spread itself to other computers, although some Trojan horses can be used to install a remote control program that allows an unauthorized user to take over your computer. Antivirus programs can block Trojan horses as well as true viruses.

typeface A set of *fonts* in different sizes (or a single scalable outline) and weights; Times New Roman Bold, Bold Italic, Regular, and Italic are all part of the Times New Roman scalable typeface.

U

UDF Universal Disk Format. A standard for *CD* and *DVD* media to drag and drop files to compatible media using a method called "packet writing." Windows 10 supports various UDF versions.

uninstall The process of removing Windows programs from the system.

Universal apps Mobile touch-oriented apps that can run on Windows phones, laptop and desktop PCs, and tablets.

URL Uniform Resource Locator. The full path to any given web page or graphic on the Internet. A full URL contains the server type (such as http://, ftp://, or other), the site name (such as www.markesoper.com), and the name of the folder and the page or graphic you want to view (such as /blog/?page_id=38). Thus, the URL http://www.markesoper.com/blog/?page_id=38 displays the "About Mark" page on the author's website.

USB Universal Serial Bus. High-speed replacement for older I/O ports; USB 1.1 has a peak speed of 12Mbps. USB 2.0 has a peak speed of 480Mbps, and USB 3.0 has a top speed of 5Gbps. USB 3.1 has a top speed of 10Gbps. USB 2.0 ports also support USB 1.1 devices. USB 2.0 devices can be plugged in to USB 1.1 devices but run at only USB 1.1 speeds. USB 3.0 ports support USB 2.0 and 1.1 devices, which run at their original speeds. USB 3.1 ports support USB 3.0, USB 2.0, and USB 1.1 devices, which run at their original speeds.

username Used with a *password* to gain access to network resources.

V

virtual desktop A *desktop* that includes your choice of running apps. You can switch between virtual desktops by clicking the Task View button or by pressing the Windows key plus Ctrl and left or right arrow key. See also *Task View*.

virus A computer program that resembles a *Trojan horse* but can also replicate itself to other computers.

VoIP Voice over Internet Protocol. Enables telephone calls to be transmitted or received over an IP network. Windows 10 can use Skype for Desktop (available from the Windows Store), and Skype technology is also available in other apps.

W-Z

WAV A noncompressed standard for digital audio. Some recording programs for Windows can create and play back WAV files. However, WAV files are very large and are usually converted into other formats for use online or for creating digital music archives.

web note A feature in the Microsoft Edge web browser that enables the user to add handwritten or typed notes and callouts to a web page. The page can be saved to local storage or OneDrive cloud storage.

WEP Wired Equivalent Privacy. A now-obsolete standard for wireless security. Replaced by *WPA*.

Wi-Fi The name for IEEE-802.11a, IEEE-802.11b, IEEE-802.11g, IEEE-802.11n, or 802.11ac wireless Ethernet devices that meet the standards set forth by the Wi-Fi Alliance.

Windows Hello A Windows 10 feature that enables users to log in to their systems using facial recognition.

wireless network The general term for any radio-frequency network, including *Wi-Fi*. Most wireless networks can be interconnected to conventional networks.

WLAN Wireless local area network. Instead of wires, stations on a WLAN connect to each other through radio waves. The IEEE 802.11 family of standards guide the development of WLANs.

WMA Windows Media Audio. This is the native compressed audio format created by Windows Media Player. Unlike *MP3*, WMA files support digital rights management.

WPA Wireless Protected Access. Replaced *WEP* as the standard for secure wireless networks. Original WPA uses TKIP encryption. An improved version known as WPA2 uses the even more secure AES encryption standard.

WWW World Wide Web. The portion of the Internet that uses the Hypertext Transfer Protocol (http://) and can thus be accessed via a web browser such as Microsoft Internet Explorer, Google Chrome, or Mozilla Firefox.

Zip The archive type (originally known as PKZIP) created when you use Send To Compressed (Zipped) Folder. A Zip file can contain one or more files and can be created, viewed, and opened in File Explorer. Formerly also referred to the Iomega Zip removable-media drive.

Symbols

M

Q-R

S

T

U

V

X-Y

Z